ISBN 978-0-243-26050-8
PIBN 10760525

This book is a reproduction of an important historical work. Forgotten Books uses
state-of-the-art technology to digitally reconstruct the work, preserving the original format
whilst repairing imperfections present in the aged copy. In rare cases, an imperfection in
the original, such as a blemish or missing page, may be replicated in our edition. We do,
however, repair the vast majority of imperfections successfully; any imperfections that
remain are intentionally left to preserve the state of such historical works.

English
Français
Deutsche
Italiano
Español
Português

www.forgottenbooks.com

Mythology Photography **Fiction**
Fishing Christianity **Art** Cooking
Essays Buddhism Freemasonry
Medicine **Biology** Music **Ancient
Egypt** Evolution Carpentry Physics
Dance Geology **Mathematics** Fitness
Shakespeare **Folklore** Yoga Marketing
Confidence Immortality Biographies
Poetry **Psychology** Witchcraft
Electronics Chemistry History **Law**
Accounting **Philosophy** Anthropology
Alchemy Drama Quantum Mechanics
Atheism Sexual Health **Ancient History**
Entrepreneurship Languages Sport
Paleontology Needlework Islam
Metaphysics Investment Archaeology
Parenting Statistics Criminology
Motivational

ILLUSTRATIONS

NOT THINGS, BUT MEN.

President, CHARLES C. BONNEY.   Treasurer, LYMAN J. GAGE.
Vice-President, THOMAS B. BRYAN.   Secretary, BENJ. BUTTERWORTH.

THE WORLD'S CONGRESS AUXILIARY

OF THE WORLD'S COLUMBIAN EXPOSITION.

NOT MATTER, BUT MIND.

THE WOMAN'S BRANCH OF THE AUXILIARY,

FOR THE WORLD'S CONGRESSES OF 1893.

Mrs. Potter Palmer, *President.*   Mrs. Chas. Henrotin, *Vice-President.*

DEPARTMENT OF LITERATURE.

PRELIMINARY ADDRESS OF THE COMMITTEES ON A FOLK-LORE CONGRESS.

The World's Columbian Exposition, which will be held in Chicago in 1893, will be eminently a gathering of the people. It will be, therefore, a most appropriate time to study the lore and literature of the people. An opportunity to assemble for this purpose is now offered to those interested in the study of Folk-Lore, under the auspices of the World's Congress Auxiliary, formed for such purposes, with the support of the Exposition Authorities and the recognition and approval of the Government of the United States.

To this end, the Local Committees below named, and an Advisory Council, chosen from persons eminent in Folk-Lore Studies, both in the American States and abroad, have been appointed to organize a Folk-Lore Congress, to meet in Chi ago during the summer of 1893.

8   c

It is desirable that this Congress shall be so organized and managed as to result in the greatest possible good to the Science of Folk-Lore.

The work will therefore be divided into appropriate chapters, as indicated below, and separate days will be assigned for their respective sessions. The Chapters of the Congress will also be subdivided into convenient sections to facilitate the work, and rooms will be provided for the meetings of the several sections, apart from the main audience room.

It is deemed advisable that where Folk-Lore Societies are organized, an appeal be made to them to assist in this work, and such societies are therefore invited to appoint " Committees of Co-operation," with whom the General Committee may consult, so that, through such appeals to the Societies, their members may be reached and interested in the Congress.

This will not preclude personal appeals to all persons in and out of such societies, and kindred organizations, who may be interested in such studies. It is intended, therefore, that such societies as those below named shall be included in the invitation to participate in this Congress for the Study of Popular Traditions, namely : Oriental and Linguistic Societies, Ethnographical and Anthropological Societies, Indian, Egyptian, and Synologue Societies, and the Gypsy Society.

It is earnestly hoped that all these associations, and all persons interested, will give us their hearty co-operation and assistance, so that full advantage may be taken of this auspicious time, when scientific and literary men from all parts of the world will be assembled here.

It is not perhaps advisable in this Preliminary Address to do more than to indicate the general lines on which such a Congress will be formed, and the divisions into which the subjects to be considered may fall. The Committee will welcome suggestions in this matter, while believing that the arrangement proposed may be satisfactory in the main.

The subjects to be considered may find appropriate place in the following chapters :

    I. Myths and Traditional Beliefs.
    II. Oral Literature and Folk-Music.
    III. Customs, Institutions, and Ritual.
    IV. Artistic, Emblematic, and Economic Folk-Lore.

In the first may properly come the consideration of such subjects as these :

The Survival of Ancient Myths in Folk-Lore, and their influence on modern beliefs ; Theories of the Origin of Myths ; Survival of Myths in History ; Nature Myths, and their Bearing on Scientific

Belief ; The Philosophy of Myth-Making ; The Myth-Making Faculty ; Native American Myths and their relative place in Folk-Lore ; Myths of the Forces of Nature ; Hero Myths ; Animal Myths and Beast Epics ; The Relation of Traditional Beliefs of our Negroes to African Native Myths ; Traditional Beliefs and their Effect on Religious Ideas ; Theories of Spirits ; Metempsychosis in Folk-Lore.

Under the second head, the following and kindred subjects may be presented :

Definition of Oral or Traditional Literature ; the Formation, Composition and Classification of Stories and Legends ; Types of Stories ; the Relation of Indian, Negro, Mexican and Other Native American Stories and Tales to European Stories ; Dialects, Popular Slang and Argot, and their Effect on Language ; Bibliography of Folk-Lore ; Rhymed Literature ; Relation of Imaginative Poetry to Folk-Song ; the Historical Value of Popular Songs ; Their Influence on Patriotism ; Improvisation ; Labor Songs ; Song as Applied to Ceremonies ; the Influence of Instruments upon the Songs ; Variants of Popular Songs ; Folk Rhymes, Jingles, etc. ; the Philosophy of Proverbial Literature.

In the third division will properly belong Customs, Rituals and Institutions. This is an important department of Folk-Lore, since in these customs and institutions are embodied popular beliefs. A few of the subjects to be considered under this head are these :

A History of Customs and Institutions ; the Effect of Ritual upon Religion, and *vice versa ;* Ceremonial Customs and their Meaning ; The Effect of Particular Customs upon National Character ; the Influence of Climate and Locality upon Customs ; Juridical Customs and their Relation to Law ; Civil Customs and their Effect on Popular Games and Pastimes ; Superstitious Ceremonies in their Relation to Medicine and Hygiene ; the Philosophy of a Belief in Sorcerers and Witches ; Ceremonial Agents and their Influence ; Indian Ceremonies ; Voodoo Rites ; Folk-Lore Survival in Modern Ceremonies ; Survivals of Popular Beliefs in Games ; Totemism, Castes, Clan Organization and Tribal Relations ; Popular Notions as to the Status of Woman ; Marriage Customs and their Influence upon Society ; Ceremonies at Birth and at Death ; Social Customs and their Effect upon Civilization : the Identity of Customs and Institutions in Different Lands.

The fourth division embraces all in the Graphic, Plastic and Industrial Arts, bearing upon the questions considered pertinent to Folk-Lore. The subjects to be considered in this division, illustrated by the material exhibits in Ethnography and Archæology, are divided into four general classes : 1. Those which relate to ritual ; *a,* Divinities ; *b,* Cults ; *c,* Fetiches and amulets ; *d,* miscellaneous small objects. 2. Those relating to political or legal affairs ; *a,* emblems of command ; *b,* emblems of servitude ; *c,* society emblems ; *d,* emblems of peace or war : *e,* Juridic emblems. 3. Those relating to civil life; *a*, clothing; *b*, ornaments and decorations; *c*, badges and medals; *d*, popular imagery; *e*, playthings and toys; *f*, furniture. 4. Those relating to particular superstitions and beliefs, such as witch-pins, instruments of torture, iconographic representations of popular superstitions, popular and magical remedies, etc.

The questions to be considered will include Folk-Lore in Art, Mythology in Art, The Effect of Popular Beliefs on the Drama, The History of the Popular Drama, etc.

This incomplete sketch of the questions to be considered barely outlines the work. Suggestions in reference to it will be welcomed, and modifications of the scheme made, after consultation with the Advisory Council.

The exact date of the Congress is not yet fixed, but will occur in July, 1893, this month having been set aside for the Congresses of Science, Literature and Education.

Inquiries and suggestions in reference to the Congress of Folk-Lore may be addressed to the Chairmen or the Committees.

FLETCHER S. BASSETT, Lieut. U. S. N., *Chairman*,
5208 Kimbark Avenue, Chicago,

ELWYN A. BARRON, *Vice-Chairman*,

CAPT. ELI L. HUGGINS, U. S. A.,   DR. EMIL G. HIRSCH,
JOSEPH KIRKLAND,

—

MRS. POTTER PALMER, *Chairman*,
MRS. FLETCHER S. BASSETT, *Vice-Chairman*,

MISS ELIZABETH HEAD,   MRS. NELSON A. MILES,
DR. S. H. STEVENSON,

*Committees of the World's Congress Auxiliary
on a Folk-Lore Congress.*

WORLD'S CONGRESS HEADQUARTERS,
CHICAGO, *June 28, 1892.*

Advisory Council of the World's Congress Auxiliary on a Folk-Lore Congress.

G. Laurence Gomme, F. S. A., President Folk-Lore Society, London, Eng.

M. Charles Ploix, President de la Société des Traditions Populaires, Paris, France.

Dr. Eugene Monseur, President de la Société de Folk-Lore Wallon ; Professor of Sanscrit, University, Brussels, Belgium.

Herr H. Molandr, President of Finno-Ugrien Folk-Lore Society ; Senator and Finance Minister, Helsingfors, Finland.

Aug. Gittée, Professor at University, Athenée Royal, Belgium.

M. Dragomanov, Professor, University, Sofia, Bulgaria.

Prof. P. D. C. Saussaye, Amsterdam, Holland.

Michel de Zmigrodzaki, Galicia, Austria.

Dr. Guiseppe Pitré, editor L'Archivio dei Tradizioni Popolari, Palermo, Sicily.

Rev. H. F. Feilberg, Denmark.

Dr. John Karlowicz, Warsaw, Poland.

Petrecelca Bogdano Hasdeu, Membre de l'Academie, Archives Royales, Bucharest, Roumania.

Vid Vuletic Vukasovic, Dalmatia.

T. Benihelos, Syra, Cyclades Is., Turkey.

John Bachelor, Japan.

Rev. Dr. W. Gill, LL. D., Sydney, N. S. W., Australia.

J. Cornu, Professor University, Prague, Austria.

René Basset, Professor, L'Agha, Algiers, Africa.

E. Jacottet, Thaba Mission, Basutoland, Africa.

Maj. R. C. Temple, The Palace, Mandalay, Upper Burmah.

John Reade, Montreal, Canada.

J. S. Udal, Esq., Attorney-General, Fiji Islands.

D. F. A. Hervey, Esq., The Residency, Malacca, East Indies.

Francis J. Child, Ph. D., LL. D., Professor of English, Harvard University, Cambridge, Mass.

Kaarle Krohn, Professor of Folk-Lore at the University, Helsingfors, Finland.

Alessandro d' Ancona, Professor at the University, Pisa, Italy.

Machado y Alvarez, Madrid, Spain.

N. Politis, Editor of L'Estia, Athens, Greece.

Henri Zimcien Wissendorff, St. Petersburgh, Russia.

Leité de Vasconcellos, Biblioteca Nationao, Lisbon, Portugal.

Hjalmar Petterson, University Library, Christiania, Norway.

J. P. Lewis, Esq., Ceylon Civil Service, Negombo, Ceylon.

Gilmore McCorkell, C. S., Goojerat, Bombay, India.

A. Landes, Administrateur des Affaires Indigènes, China.

Judge J. Loyzon, Tunis, Africa.

Dr. Teoflo Rodriguez, Venezuela.

Prof. Otis T. Mason, National Museum, Washington, D. C.

D'Arbois du Jubainville, Member of the Institute, Paris, France.

Prof. Theodore Braga, University, Lisbon, Portugal.

Prof. Domenico Comparetti, University, Florence, Italy.

Dr. Friedrich S. Krauss, Editor of Am Urquel, Vienna.

Senor Maspons y Labros, Barcelona, Spain.

Prof. Moltke Möe, University, Christiania, Norway.

Mons. Pol de Mont, Professor at Athenée Royal, Antwerp, Belgium.

Kristoffer Nyrop, Professor University, Copenhagen.

Paul Sebillot, Secretaire General de la Société des Traditiones Populaires, Paris, France.

Prof. A. C. Haddon, M. A., M. R. I. A., F. L. S., Dublin.

Rev. Walter Gregor, Scotland.

Prof. A. H. Sayce, Queen's College, Oxford.

Prof. John Rhys, Jesus College, Oxford.

Joseph Jacobs, Kilburn, London.

Prof. Steinthal, Director Zeitschift des Vereins für Völkskunde, Berlin.

Gen. Tcheng Ki-Tchong, Chinese Chargé d'Affaires at Paris.

Prof. C. P. Tiele, University, Leyden, Holland.

Prof. Alexander Wesselofsky, University, St. Peterburg.

Prof. E. Windisch, University, Leipsic.

J. B. Vervliet, Director of Ons Volksleven, Antwerp, Belgium.

J. B. Andrews, Le Pigautier, Mentone, Italy.

Hon. John Abercromby, Edinburgh, Scotland.

Emile Blémont, Paris.

Dr. Karl Blind, London, Eng.

Prince Roland Bonaparte, Paris, France.

E. W. Brabrook, F. S. A., Balham, London, Eng.

Dr. D. G. Brinton, Philadelphia, Pa.

Loys Bruyére, Paris, France.

T. Canizzaro, Messina, Sicily.

Doctor Paulus Cassel, Berlin, Germany.

E. Clodd, Esq., London, Eng.

Compte de Charency, St. Maurice les Charency, France.

Prof. T. F. Crane, Cornell University, Ithaca, N. Y.

President W. R. Harper, The University of Chicago.

Prof. W. D. Whitney, Yale College, New Haven, Conn.

Maj. J. W. Powell, Bureau of Ethnology, Washington, D. C.

Thomas Davidson, Edinburgh, Scotland.

Prof. Jean Fleury, St. Petersburg

Henri Gaidoz, Editor *Mélusine*, Paris.

Hon. J. J. Forster, London.

Rev. Dr. Gaster, London, Eng.

W. A. Clouston, Glasgow. Scotland.

Dr. M. Bartels, Berlin, Germany.

Mons. Louis Leger, Paris.

Mons. Emile Legrand, Paris.

Rev. W. S. Lach-Szyrma, M. A., Barkenside Vicarage, Ilford, Eng.

Andrew Lang, Esq., M. A., London.

Charles Godfrey Leland, Florence, Italy.

Right Hon. Sir J. Lubbock, Bart., M. P., F. R. S., Beckenham, Eng.

F. M. Luzel, Quimperlé, Finisterre, France.

Sir Edgar MacCulloch, F. S. A., Guernsey I.

David MacRitchie, Edinburgh,Scotland.

E. S. Hartland, F. S. A., Gloucester, Eng.

Gen Pitt-Rivers, Salisbury, Eng.

J. H. Rivett-Carnac, C. I. E., F. S. A., M. R. A. S., F. G. S., Ghazipur, India.

Prof. E. B. Tylor, F. R. S., The Museum House, Oxford, Eng.

Vicomte Hersault de Villemarqué, Membre de l'Institut, Keransker, Finisterre, France.

Wentworth Webster, Maison Bechuena, Sara, Basses Pyrenees, France.

Braulio Vigon, Colunga, Spain.

Raoul Roslères, Meudon, France.

Compte de Puymaigre, Paris.

Doctor Stanislas Prato, Professor of Italian Literature in the Royal Lycée Agostino Niso, Sessa-Auranca, Italy.

Mons. Emanuel Cosquin, Vitry-le-Francois, France.

G. Maspero, Membre de l'Institut. Paris.

Senor Emilio Pardo Bazan, Madrid.

Jos. Cornelisen, Editor *Volksleven*, Brecht, Belgium.

H. B. Hulbert, Zanesville, Ohio.

Mr. Anton Hermann, Director Ethnologische Mittheilungen, Buda-Pesth, Austro-Hungary.

Louis Frechette, LL. D., Montreal, Canada.

Commandeur Constantine Nigra, Italian Ambassador to Austria, Vienna.

Professor Athanasios Sakellarios, Athens.

Wilhelm Schwartz, Berlin.

Ignaz Zingerle, Professor University, Innspruck, Tyrol, Germany.

Angelo de Gubernatis, Professor of Sanscrit, University of Rome, Rome.

Prof. Gaston Paris, Membre de l'Institut, College de France, Paris.

Alejandro Gulchot y Sierra, Seville.

Luigi Molino del Chiaro, Editor *Giambattista Basile*, Naples.

E. H. Meyer, Professor University, Freiburg, Germany.

Dr. Sylvio Romeiro, Professor at Lycée Dom Pedro II., Rio de Janeiro, Brazil.

Prof.Otto Donner,DirectorFinnish Folk-Lore Society, Helsingfors, Finland.

Dr. Ludwig Frankel, Leipsig, Germany.

Basil H. Chamberlain, University, Tokio, Japan.

Salvatore Salomino- Marino, Professor University, Messina, Sicily.

Rev.Wm. E. Griffis, LL.D., Boston,Mass.

Dr. Maurice Wilmotte, University, Liège, Belgium.

Dr. N. B. Emerson, Honolulu, Hawaii Islands.

Louis Katona, Fünfkirchen, Hungary.

Dr. Ernest Hamy, Musée d'Ethnographie, Paris.

James J. Frazer, Trinity College, Cambridge, England.

H. H. Bancroft, San Francisco, Cal.

Prof. Rasmus B. Anderson, Madison, Wisconsin.

Frank H. Cushing, Arizona Territory.

C. G. Jones, Augusta, Ga.

George W. Cable, Northampton, Mass.

Prof. John Fiske, Cambridge, Mass.

M. D. Conway, Boston, Mass.

T. M. Crawford, U. S. Consul, St. Petersburg.

Dr. Franz Boas, Clark University, Worcester. Mass.

J. Walter Fewkes, Boston, Mass.

Prof. Alicée Fortier, Tulane University, New Orleans, La.

Prof. W. P. Johnson, New Orleans, La.

H. Carnoy, Editor *La Tradition*, Paris.

C. F. Lummis, Bandelier Exploring Expedition, South America.

Washington Matthews, Surgeon, U. S. A., Fort Wingate, New Mexico

Eugene Field, Chicago.

Eugene Rolland, Paris.

Dr. Teofilo M. Escobar, Professor University, Havana, Cuba.

Jean Urban Zarnick, Professor University, Prague, Bohemia.

C. Chabaneau, Professor University, Montpelier, France.

Arthuro Graf, Professor University, Turin, Italy.

Joseph Défrecheux, University, Liége, Belgium.

Joachim Costa, Director Boletino de la Libra Ensenada, Madrid.

Eliel Aspelin, Professor University, Helsingfors, Finland.

Luigi Bruzzano, Director *La Calabria*, Monteleone, Italy.

Dr. Paul Meyer, Director of *Romania*, Paris.

Benjamin Wolf Segel, Lemberg, Galicia, Austria.

Prof. K. E. Haase, New Ruppin, Mecklenberg, Germany.

Prof. Dr. A. Wiedemann, Bonn, Germaay.

Dr. Marcus Landau, Vienna.

Herr Heinrich Carstens, Lunden, Holstein, Austria.

Rev. W. M. Beauchamp, Baldwinsville, N. Y.

Henri Cordier, Paris.

A. Certeux, Paris.

P. Ristelhuber, Strasburg, Germany.

W. G. Black, Edinburgh, Scotland.

Dr. Robert Brown, London, Eng.

G. L. Apperson, Esq., London.

W. F. Kirby, Esq., London.

T. F. Ordish, F. S. A., Ellison Road, Barnes, London.

J. Stewart Lockhardt, Hong Kong, China.

H. B. Wheatley, F. S. A., London.

G. H. Kinahan, Esq., London.

A. Granger Hutt, F. S. A., London.

Dr. C. Zirbt, Editor *Cesky Lid*, Prague, Bohemia.

Walter Besant, M. A., London.

Gloger Sigismond, par Varsovic, par Tycocin, à Yesewo. Poland.

M. Antonowicz, University, Kief, Russia.

Prof. Frederick Starr, The University of Chicago.

Prof. O. Knoop, Rogasen, Posen, Germany.

Dr. A. Haas, Stettin, Germany.

Prof. Wm. I. Knapp, Ph.D., LL. D., The University of Chicago.

THE ADVISORY COUNCIL OF THE WOMAN'S BRANCH OF THE WORLD'S CONGRESS AUXILIARY ON FOLK-LORE.

Lady Camilla Gurdon, Suffolk, Eng.

Miss Mary A. Owen, St. Joseph, Mo.

Miss Laura Alexandrine Smith, Newcastle-on-Tyne, Eng.

Miss Roalfe Cox, London.

Mrs. Annah Robinson Watson, Memphis, Tenn.

Miss Burne, Pyebirch, England.

Countess E. Caetani Lovatelli, Rome.

Miss Lucy M. J. Garnett, London, Eng.

Countess Evelyn Martinesco-Cesaresco, Italy.

Mrs. Mary Hemenway, Boston, Mass.

Mrs. Eva Wigstrom, Helsingborg, Sweden.

Miss Rachel H. Busk, London, Eng.

Mrs. Gutch Holgate, York, Eng.

Miss Hawkins-Dempster, London.

THE INTERNATIONAL FOLK-LORE CONGRESS
OF THE WORLD'S COLUMBIAN EXPOSITION.

The Folk-Lore Congress at Chicago in 1893 was one of the series of World's Congresses held in connection with the World's Columbian Exposition. As a matter of convenience it was held during the week of the Literary Congresses. The Local Committee appointed from the Chicago Folk-Lore Society was assisted by an Advisory Committee, composed of two hundred of the most prominent folk-lorists of the world.

The Congress held twelve formal sessions extending over eight days—July 10 to July 17. Contributions were read coming from many countries. Much interest and enthusiasm were shown.

The programme as carried out follows:

TUESDAY, JULY 11, 10 A. M.

Introductory Address—The Folk-Lore Congress—Lieutenant F. S. Bassett, Chairman Folk-Lore Committee.

Address of Welcome, on behalf of the Chicago Folk-Lore Society—Professor Wm. I. Knapp, The University of Chicago, President Chicago Folk-Lore Society, and active presiding officer throughout the Congress.

Unspoken—Rev. Walter Gregor, Pitsligo, Aberdeenshire, Scotland.

Notes on Cinderella—E. S. Hartland, Gloucester, England.

The Legendary Lore of the Northwestern Coast Tribes—James Deans, Assistant of Department of Anthropology, World's Fair, Chicago.

The Fatality of Certain Places to Certain Persons—Miss C. S. Hawkins-Dempster, London, England.

The Rise of Empiricism—Prof. Otis T. Mason, National Museum, Washington.

TUESDAY, JULY 11, 2 P. M.

The Northern Trolls—David McRitchie, Edinburgh, Scotland.

Myths, Symbols and Magic of East Africans, Illustrated by Objects Personally Collected—Mrs. M. French-Sheldon, London, England.

The Cliff Dwellers of Southwestern America—Mrs. Palmer Henderson, Minneapolis, Minn.

The Development of Art in Pottery, and the Relation of Woman to it—Monsieur T. Bilbaut, Special Commissioner for French Colonies.

The Worship of the Hop in Poland—Erasmus Majewski, Warsaw.

TUESDAY, JULY 11, 8 P. M.

Honorary American President, Eugene Field.
Honorary Foreign President, Hon. J. Abercromby, Vice-President English Folk-Lore Society, Edinburgh.

Some Sacred Objects of Navajo Rites, Illustrated by Paraphernalia —Washington Matthews, Surgeon U. S. Army, Vice-President Chicago Folk-Lore Society.

Comparative Afro-American Folk-Lore—Mrs. Annah R. Watson, President Tennessee Branch Chicago Folk-Lore Society, Memphis.

Telling the Bees—Eugene Field.

Sepulchres and Funeral Rites among the Ancient and Modern South Slavs, Illustrated by Sketches and Engravings. Cav. Vid Vulletic Vucasovic, Curzola, Dalmatia.

Creole Folk Songs—Geo. W. Cable, Vice-President Chicago Folk-Lore Society, Northampton, Mass.

WEDNESDAY, JULY 12, 10 A. M.

The Symbolism of the Vase in Mythology, Ideography, Language, Hagiography, Literature and Folk-Lore—Dr. Stanislas Prato, Professor Royal Lycée Agostino Nisso, Sessa, Aurunca, Italy.

Sioux Mythology—Dr. Chas. A. Eastman, President Minnesota Branch Chicago Folk-Lore Society, St. Paul.

Modern Greek Mythology—Miss Lucy M J. Garnett, London, England.

The Antiquity of the Folk-Lore of the American Indians—Miss Katherine S. Stanbery, Zanesville, O.

Buried Alive—Rev. H. F. Feilberg, Axov, Denmark.

WEDNESDAY, JULY 12, 8 P. M.

Honorary President, Major-General Nelson A. Miles, U. S. A.

The Magic Poetry of the Finns, and its Application in Practice— Hon. John Abercromby, Vice-President English Folk-Lore Society, Edinburgh, Scotland.

The Sign Language of the Plains Indians—Captain H. L. Scott, U. S. Army. Demonstrated by Sioux Indians, Flat Iron, Horse-Come-Last, Standing Bear and Painted Horse.

Voodooism—Miss Mary A. Owen, St. Joseph, Mo.

Bulgarian Wedding Ceremonies, with Costumed Figures — Prof. Vulko I. Shopoff, Commissioner General from Bulgaria, Sofia, Bulgaria.

THURSDAY, JULY 13, 10 A. M.

Korean Folk-Lore—Prof. Homer B. Hulbert, Zanesville, Ohio.

Maui, the Prometheus of Polynesia—Dr. N. B. Emerson, Honolulu, H. I.

Japanese Folk-Lore—Rev. Wm. E. Griffis, Ithaca, N. Y,

Græco-Roman and Japanese Folk-Lore — Prof. E. W. Clement, Chicago.

Tamaro-the-Terrible, a Myth from Manihiki — Rev. W. Wyatt Gill, Sydney, New South Wales.

Scraps of Liberian Folk-Lore and Customs—Rev. J. Martis, Owen's Grove, Liberia.

Discussion—Hon. A. R. King, Commissioner from Liberia.

THURSDAY, JULY 13, 2 P. M.

Venezuelan Folk-Lore—Dr. Teofilo Rodriguez, Caracas, Venezuela.

Some Superstitions of South American Indians—Lieutenant Roger Welles, U. S. Navy.

Musical Instruments of British Guiana—Hon. J. J. Quelch, Commissioner General from British Guiana, Georgetown, B. G.

Diurnal Birds of Prey and Mexican Symbolism—Count H. de Charency, Paris, France.

Discussion—Capt. John G. Bourke, U. S. Army.

Pigments in Ceremonials of the Hopi—A. M. Stephen, Keams, Arizona.

FRIDAY, 10 A. M.

How San Geronimo Came to Taos—Mrs. Virginia McClurg, Denver.

Navajo Songs and Prayers, as Recorded by the Edison Phonograph, with Sacred, Agricultural, Building, War, Gambling and Love Songs—Washington Matthews, Surgeon U. S. A., Fort Wingate, N. M.

Bosnic-Herzogovinian Folk Songs—Described by Vid Vulletic Vucasovic and Sung by Vukan Ceho Mihic in native costume.

Polish Folk Songs—Sung by Michel Zmigrodzki, Suchu, Poland.

FRIDAY, JULY 14, 2 P. M.

Honorary Foreign President, Hon. Anton Leffler, Commissioner for Sweden.

Marriage Customs in Roumania—Arthur Gorovei, Director of the Folk-Lore Review—"Sezatorea," Falticena, Roumania.

1. General Sketch of the Latavian People. 2. Niedrischu Widewuts —A Heroic Latavian Epic—Henry Wissendorff de Wissakuok, St. Petersburg, Russia.

A Sort of Cult of Ancestors in Finland—Prof. Kaarle Krohn, Professor of Folk-Lore in the University of Helsingfors.

National Latavian Costume, Illustrated by Costumed Female Figure —M. Skruzit, Mitan, Courland, Russia.

Why Popular Epics are Written, a Study of Bosnic-Herzogovinian Guslar Songs—Dr. Friedrich S. Krauss, Director "Am Urquell," Vienna.

The Antiquities of Cyprus—Dr. Richter, Berlin.

The Primitive Horde, A Study of Circumcision—Ludwig Krzyuroki, Poland.

FRIDAY, 8 P. M.

Popular Concert of Folk-Lore Songs, under the direction of Frederic W. Root.

SATURDAY, 10 A. M.

Some Popular Beliefs of Egypt—Prof. Gaston Maspero, Paris, France.

1. Popular Tradition in France from 1889 to 1893. 2. Oral Literature of the French Creoles—Paul Sébillot, General Sec'y Société des Traditions Populaires, Paris.

Discussion by Marquis de Chasseloup, Laubat, Paris.

Taming of the Shrew in Ukraine Folk-Lore—M. Dragomonov, Sofia, Bulgaria.

Discussion by Franklin H. Head, Chicago.

The Customs, Beliefs and Popular Songs of the Argentine Gauchos —Paul Groussac, Librarian National Library, Buenos Ayres.

Concerning a Loup Garou—Mrs. Mary H. Catherwood, Hoopeston, Illinois.

SATURDAY, 2 P. M.

The following papers were read by title only :

Bibliography of Irish Folk-Lore—John Canon O'Hanlon, Irishtown, Ireland.

German Beliefs and Customs in Longfellow's Golden Legend—Dr. Robert Sprenger, Northeim, Germany.

Death and Burial Ideas and Customs in Pomerania—Dr. A. Haas, Stettin, Germany.

House Ghosts in Pomerania—Prof. O. Knoop, Rogasen, Prussia.

Contributions to Spring and Tree Worship on the Lower Rhine— Prof. O. Schell, Elberfeld, Germany.

The Present State of Inquiry into Lithuanian-Latavian Mythology —Herr E. Wolter, St. Petersburg.

Notes on Carnival Customs—C. Rademacher, Cologne, Germany.

What Have we to Eat ? — A. Weichel, Hochspalesohen, East Prussia.

Constitutional Royal Customs from an Ethnographical Standpoint —Dr. Th. Achelis, Bremen, Germany.

An Old Egyptian Creation Myth—Prof. A. Wiedemann, Bonn, Germany.

SUNDAY, JULY 16, 10 A. M.

Honorary President, Rev. J. Vila Blake, Chicago.

History of the Swastika, Illustrated by Tabulated Designs—Michel de Zmigrodzki, Sucha, Poland,

Studies of the Ligotnes ; Songs of St. John's Eve—André Jurjan, Charkow, Russia, with illustrations on the piano by Frederic W. Root.

German Christmas Eve Ceremonies and Beliefs in Schleswig-Holstein—Dr. Heinrich Carstens, Darenswurth, Germany.

Discussion by Henry E. O. Heinemann, Chicago, Ill.

In addition to these stated meetings the Congress enjoyed several informal or social conferences. On the evening of July 10 the members attended the reception given at the Art Institute to all the Literary Congresses ; on the afternoon of July 12 they were guests of Col. W. F. Cody at his *Wild West Show*. July 15 they were invited by Dr. Ulrich Jahn and Herr Miller to inspect the remarkable ethnographic collection at the *German Village ;* and in the evening of the same day they visited the *Cliff Dwellers Exhibit*, by invitation of the manager, H. Jay Smith.

Mr. Frederic W. Root was invited to take charge of the Folk-Song Concert. This was a remarkable success. So great was the demand for tickets that the concert had to be presented in two halls at the same time—the Hall of Columbus and the Hall of Washington. Very hearty and kind was the response made by the Commissioners of the various nations to the appeal of the Chairmen of the Congress for assistance. They promptly allowed the people under their charge to participate in the concert, upon understanding the scientific interest of the performance and the fact that no admission fee was to be demanded. The singers were dressed in national costume and played on original instruments taken from the exhibits at the Exposition.

The phonographic records illustrating Navajo music and collected by Dr. Washington Matthews were secured through the kindness of Mr. Lombard, general manager of the Northwestern Phonograph Company, who loaned an instrument for their collection at the request of the Chicago Folk-Lore Society.

The interesting demonstration of Indian Sign Language connected with Captain Scott's paper was made possible through the polite assistance of Col. W. F. Cody (Buffalo Bill), who sent four of his Sioux Indians—Flat Iron, Standing Bear, Painted Horse and Horse-Comes-Last, for the purpose.

During the Congress the following valuable donations were made to the Chicago Folk-Lore Society's Collection : Japanese Placque, Antique Cloisonne, Miss Mary A. Owen ; Chart, giving 1360 illustrations of the use and development of the Swastika, Michel de Zmigrodzki ; Navajo Cult Objects, Washington Matthews ; Latavian Peasant Costume and Collection of Latavian Portraits, Henry Wissendorff.

The long delay in publishing the Proceedings of the Congress is regretted, but was unavoidable.

Papers read at the Congress but published since that time elsewhere are omitted.

The selection of portraits of essayists for publication in this volume has been made upon two bases—personal presence at the Congress and publication of their essays herein.

THE EDITORS.

Charles Carroll Bonney

LIEUTENANT FLETCHER S. BASSETT.

The organization and conduct of the World's Folk-Lore Congress of 1893 was so largely the work of the late Lieutenant Fletcher S. Bassett that any publication of the proceedings of that Congress would be deemed incomplete without some biographical notice of him. The following brief sketch is therefore given, with the belief that it will be read with interest by all the participants in the Congress.

Mr. Bassett was born in Adams County, in the State of Kentucky, of the United States of America, on December 21st, 1847. He entered Monmouth College, in the State of Illinois, early in the year 1863. The great American Civil War was then in progress, and in May, 1864, Mr. Bassett left college and enlisted as a volunteer in Company A of the 138th Regiment of the Illinois Volunteers. On September 21, 1865, he left the military service and entered the United States Naval Academy at Annapolis, in the State of Maryland, as a midshipman. He graduated from this institution in June, 1869, and was promoted to the position of ensign in July, 1870. In this capacity he served on the staff of Admiral John Rodgers, on the Asiatic Station, and commanded a section of howitzers in the attacks on the forts of the Kaughra Islands below Seoul, the capital of Corea. In 1871 Mr. Bassett served in the American squadron in the North Atlantic Ocean, and later during the same year in the South Pacific Ocean squadron, and was promoted to the office of Lieutenant in June, 1875. He was placed on the Naval Retired List in 1882.

Lieut. Bassett began his literary work while in college, and was constantly employed on it, in some form, to the date of his death. He did a great deal of newspaper correspondence and wrote numerous magazine articles, both of a technical and literary character, and did a considerable amount of professional writing for naval and military journals. He also assisted in the preparation of Hammersly's Naval Encyclopedia. His first book was published in 1885, and was entitled "Legends and Superstitions of the Sea." It was simultaneously issued in London and Chicago. This work opened a new and fascinating field of research and was highly appreciated in the literary and scholastic world. It directed many other minds to the same lines of investigation, and has been acknowledged as an original and authentic treatise of the subject to which it relates. It has already passed through two editions.

In 1892, Lieut. Bassett published "The Folk-Lore Manual;" or Questionnaire of the Folk-Lore Society. Lieut. Bassett, through an incessant correspondence and the publications to which reference has already been made, did probably as much as any other student in this department of research to arouse the popular interest in Folk-Lore studies, and stimulate the formation of Folk-Lore societies. He was secretary of the International Folk-Lore Association and an honorary member of the French Society of Popular Traditions. His wide knowledge, his practical familiarity with modern languages, and his official experience in the American Navy led to his appointment as Chief Interpreter and Translator of the World's Columbian Exposition of 1898.

As chairman of the Folk-Lore Congress, he conducted an extensive correspondence with the leaders of Folk-Lore in all parts of the world; solicited their co-operation and participation in the work; and made engagements for the papers and addresses more especially desired. Without entering into the details of this important work, suffice it in this connection to say, that his efforts resulted in the completion and successful execution of a well-ordered plan for the largest and most representative Folk-Lore Congress ever convened.

The exhausting responsibility and toil involved in this great work, as well as in his labors as general interpreter and translator of the World's Columbian Exposition, proved to be burdens greater than his health and strength could bear, and resulted in his death on October 19, 1898, a few days before the close of the Exposition. The ability, fidelity and zeal with which Lieutenant Bassett discharged the duties which came to him in the course of his career well deserve a more extended account and higher tributes of praise than the present occasion will permit, but this much is due to his memory in connection with the publication of the proceedings of the World's Folk-Lore Congress of 1898.

CHARLES C. BONNEY,
General President of the World's Congresses
of the World's Columbian Exposition.

FLETCHER S BASSETT

THE FOLK-LORE CONGRESS.

ADDRESS BY LIEUT. F. S. BASSETT, U. S. N.

IT is with feelings of pleasure peculiarly great that, in the name of the local and advisory committees of the World's Fair Auxiliary, I perform my agreeable task of welcoming you to the Third International Folk-Lore Congress. You will pardon me if I insist, with some pertinacity, upon calling attention to some matters concerning it.

I have called it the Third International Congress, and I think that the justice of this name can be fully established. It is a matter of regret that the official International Council, organized for the purpose, should not have fully participated in this Congress, and that the council of the oldest American society should, from local feelings of jealousy, hold aloof from it.

Such disadvantages as these, however, have in no wise discouraged the committee. Imbued with a sense of the greatness of the event and of the fitness of the occasion, it has steadily gone on with its preparations, with the result that must be apparent to you, upon an examination of the programme. That this is truly an International Congress, is shown by the wide geographical range embraced therein. Further than this, it derives its origin from authority higher than a self-appointed, or elected committee.

The World's Columbian Auxiliary regularly constituted as a part of the local corporation, and recognized by formal decree and official prescription, on the part of the Government, is its source of authority. The official participation of three-fourths of the societies forming the International Alliance, as well as of some not of that body, the adherence of individual members of all the societies, and the presence here of officers from all, and their participation in our proceedings, consoles us for the non-adherence of the official bodies. It is, then, the first American International Folk-Lore Congress. Furthermore, we insist that it is the first really broad World's Congress, in an unrestricted sense.

At the first Folk-Lore Congress, in Paris, in 1889, the following countries were not represented : Germany, Norway, Russia, Austria, Spain, Portugal. At the second, held at London, in 1891, the great German nation was not represented, nor were several other European nations. Now, for the first time, the co-operation of all has been asked, and representatives from all parts of the world have contributed papers. and some have travelled great distances, to be with us. We think these facts fully show that this is the first great International Folk-Lore Congress.

Folk-Lore is one of the youngest of the scientific branches. It has accomplished much within the short time devoted to its study. We all remember the silly guesses at mythological interpretation of sixty years ago, the wild imaginings of our brothers, the philologists, in attempting to unlock mysteries of the mind of man with their skeleton keys, warranted to open any lock, the erroneous dicta of our friends, the anthropologists, who count all men as varieties of the simple savage.

Into this chaos of widely-differing conclusions about the habits of action, thought, and feelings of man, came the new science, Folk-Lore, to correct, by the data of experimental comparison, these erroneous ideas. Nor was it useless to the sciences inaccurately yclept exact. Says President Gomme of the London society : " No science dealing with man is quite perfect without the aid of Folk-Lore." Geological facts are sustained by traditional accounts, historical statements shown to be illusions, botanical knowledge has been forwarded, mythology entirely reconstructed ; and literature, always drawing its inspiration from the people, owes much to Folk-Lore. In short, every study, whose end is that proper study of Mankind to which the great poet alluded, is assisted by this most universal, wide-embracing science.

Folk-Lore is not merely a study of the survival of decay,

it is the demonstrator of the possible and probable in history, the repository of historical truths otherwise lost, the pre-server of the literature of the people and the touchstone of many of the sciences. History may lie, tradition never does ; literature may claim to have found the new thing under the sun, but comparative Folk-Lore detects the analogies to other creations,

After the categories of modern science had been drawn up, and knowledge was parcelled out among them, savants be-came aware that a certain wide range of facts would not fit into the official pigeon-holes designed for them, and so, a bright precursor of modern Folk-Lorists, Mr. Thoms, suggested the name, Folk-Lore ; the study of Folk-wont, Folk-thought, and Folk-speech, the beginnings of history, of laws of religion, of language, and of song. So apt has the term been found, that it has passed bodily into Spanish, French, Italian, Rus-sian, and other languages, the Traditions Populaires and Volk-skunde of European nations being national protests against the English name, Folk-Lore. The range of subjects con-sidered is remarkable. The imaginings of man from all time, about the physical world, its history, origin, and destiny, about the animal, mineral, or vegetable kingdom, the air, fog, mist, fire and water, have a place in this study. His views of the supernatural world, the historical legends of places and things, the study of human life, of birth, of death, and of marriage, of customs and ceremonies, of the habits of men of all trades and callings, are appropriately a part of Folk-lore. Folk-medicine, the comparative study of the literature of the people—the tale, the myth, the legend, the ballad, the song, even the nursery-rhyme, the proverb, the riddle, and the nickname, are to be carefully collected, analyzed, and studied. No scrap of information concerning the habits, thoughts, or customs of man, is to be neglected." " It is an extremely dangerous proceeding to suggest that folk-lore possesses any worthless items," says highest authority.

To these studies, there are devoted many hundreds of people, organized into societies, which have their headquar-ters in the cities of Chicago, St. Paul, Memphis, Boston, New-York, Philadelphia, New-Orleans, Montreal, London, Paris, Liege, Antwerp, Helsingfors, Berlin, Vienna, Buda-

Pesth, Florence, Bombay and Sydney, besides numerous Anthropological societies, Literary, Asiatic, American, Sinico, African, Archæological, Gypsy, and other societies, whose objects are correlative to those enumerated.

Publications, annual, quarterly, monthly, and weekly, appear in your own city, in Boston, in London, in Ghent, in Antwerp, in Liege, in Helsingfors, in Copenhagen, in Berlin, in Leipsig, in Leyden, in Paris, in Palermo, in Vienna, in Warsaw, in Bombay, and in other cities, devoted to this study, besides others whose columns are largely devoted to Folk-Lore.

America is doing a part of her share in this work of arranging, classifying, collecting, and studying this Lore of her people. Much can, and is, done by the intelligent students of the Smithsonian Institution, and of the bureau of ethnology. Mrs. Hemenway's munificent expedition, the important Bandelier expedition, the various United States Exploring Expeditions, Mr. Lorillard's valuable aid in sending a party into Central America, and the work of the officers sent out by the World's Columbian Exposition, have been of the greatest assistance in developing Folk-Lore, as well as Archæology and Ethnology. The labors of the eminent scholars of America in this direction, demonstrate that Folk-Lore study is far advanced in our midst, in spite of the youth of our existence. Our Chicago society, now in its third year, is in a prosperous condition, and new branches of it are coming into existence. Folk-Lore has become a subject of the day, and many of our prominent journals and periodicals contain valuable and attractive materials, contributing to its study.

May we not hope that colleges and universities, which foster other branches of Science and literature, will not neglect this, and that the example of Helsingfors, the solitary instance of the appointment of a professor of Folk-Lore, may be followed by Harvard, Yale, and by Chicago, and that Prof. Krohn may only be one of a learned body of professors of this science, who shall direct the congresses of the future.

Who shall say that the founders and the masters in this new science have not builded well? When Prof. Pitrè may point to the beautiful bibliography of Italian Folk-Lore, the work of twelve years' labor, and show, with becoming pride, his own half-hundred volumes upon the subject, shall we say that there is no place for this work ? When Lönnrot, Aspelin, Krohn, and the faithful Finnish societaires rescue hundreds of thousands of the most pregnant popular riddles, songs, charms, etc, from the oblivion into which all traditions, lost in the irresistible march of modern civilization, shall not our highest praise be given to them for their work ? And here, in our midst, one race is being ruthlessly swept out of existence, and its lore fast perishing, another has just passed from a condition favorable to the development of legend and popular literature, and another stratum of our population is evanescent, and with Americanization of the emigrant, passes away his rich fund of inherited customs, superstitions, and literature. Folk-Lore societies encourage the collection, publication, and study of this important and beneficent information and serve an important purpose in our civilization.

What, then, shall be said to those zealous scholars who claim that Folk-Lore is but a part of some other science—as only a proper dependency of some other kingdom of thought ? Not indeed to any new nomenclature or arrangement of science, but to some branch of it which was in existence when Folk-Lore, less than fifty years old as a science, was imagined. What say some of the masters upon this subject ? Monsieur Gaidoz, of the highest authority as a scholar and savant, defines it as "that ensemble of traditions and popular literature, which, to abridge, is called to-day, ordinarily, by the English name of Folk-Lore. True it is, that closely allied to Folk-Lore are other sciences, which in turn assist it, and derive aid from it." "It is true," says Professor Sayce, "that it is often difficult to draw the line between Folk-Lore and Mythology, to define exactly where one begins, and the other ends, and there are many instances in which the two terms overlap each other." "Folk-Lore," says Machado y Alvarez, "has close relations with Sociology." It falls within certain limits, within the limits of Sociology. Again, "It follows, from what has been said, that though Folk-Lore, in my opinion, has something in common with Psychological biology, something in common with Sociology, and, of course, something in common with Anthropology also, it cannot be confounded with any of these sciences, nor even form a mere chapter of them." But if Folk-Lore, in its extent, embraces the matter of the sciences, by the quality and the degree of knowledge which it expresses, it differs from them all. One of the greatest authorities has said in advocating a Folk-lore section of the British Association : " I think the time has come for this. Anthropology has long since been recognized there ; Folk-lore should also, now be recognized, and independently."

The records of the survivals that go to make up this new science are, for the most part, to be preserved by the antiquarian scholar, and by the student collector, and published and studied by societies organized for the purpose. They form a part of the literature of the people, and must be separated and kept separate from other written records. The story, the song, the riddle, the rhyme of the nursery, illustrate this class of folk-literature. As literature itself is a science correllated to the others, Folk-Lore is at once a part of literature and of science, but ought to be preserved apart from any other study, and not merged into or made a portion of any other science.

I come now to what we have to offer you. The programme is before you, and its very length forbids my enumerating categorically the constituent essays therein. It will not, however, be out of place to call your attention to the wide range in time, in geography, and in variety of topic embraced by it, from the border lands of the most remote historical times, from Egypt and Greece, from the east of Europe, from the most advanced as well as the most primitive European states, from the oldest kingdom to the newest state, from heathen Africa, from distant India, from progressive Japan and stereotyped China, from placid South Sea isles and turbulent Hawaii, and from Alaska to Paraguay, on our continent, we bring you legends, myths, ceremonies, songs, and even natives. Many distinguished scholars from these lands have sent us papers, and some come to read their contributions. No department of the study of Folk-Lore is left untouched. It is a matter of congratulation that we have upon our programme a representative from every Folk-Lore society, and that officers and members of these societies are with us. Cel-

ebrated travellers and distinguished commissioners to the
World's fair assist us in the most valuable and agreeable way.

The committee and the Auxiliary owe the heartiest thanks
to the scholars who have so kindly consented to assist us in
this undertaking.   The authors of these papers have all expressed a desire for their publication, and the promise has
been made that this shall be done.   The Congress should,
before adjourning, make sure that the steps necessary to insure this will be taken.

With these few remarks, the chairman has the pleasure of
inviting you to the sessions of the Third International Folk-
Lore Congress with the hope that you may be amply benefitted
by them, and that Folk-Lore, Literature and Science may be
the gainers from the labors of the many workers who have
contributed to its successful accomplishment.

ADDRESS OF WELCOME ON BEHALF OF THE CHICAGO FOLK-LORE SOCIETY.

BY ITS PRESIDENT, WM. I. KNAPP. PH. D., LL. D.
THE UNIVERSITY OF CHICAGO.

Brothers and sisters in the hope and confidence of our immense racial affection.

The crowning principle of the 19th century is the recognition of the brotherhood of man. For forty years the peaceful procession has moved on from the remotest corners of the earth to a few common centres. Quaint faces, strange costumes, unintelligible tongues, have blended with the dominant civilizations of Western Europe and the New World beyond, while venerable races have made obeisance to the material prosperity of younger and novel institutions. London, Paris, Vienna, Philadelphia, Madrid, and Chicago, have vied with each other in hospitality toward the distant members of their long-estranged kindred. It is a sublime spectacle, and what does it portend? A profound mystery underlies this unconscious recognition of the solidarity of the nations. It is messianic in its deepest philosophic import, and reminds one of that beautiful passage in the Hebrew prayer-book : *M'shîhénu yishlakh méhérâ,* " He shall send us our Anointed in haste." Conceal it as we may from our consciousness, old things have passed away and all things, with their joys and dangers, are becoming new. New ideas, new intellectual disfranchisement, new aspirations, new yearnings, new life. We have sailed away from the moorings of our fathers into an atmosphere surcharged with the pyrotechnics of exultant individualism, and though our balloon-cable still holds us captive to the old planet, a wide-spread moral revolution is driving us out of sight of landmarks and ushering us into a climate of storms and adventure.

So all this gathering of human races and faces from the

MRS. FLETCHER S. (HELEN WHEELER) BASSETT.

four winds of heaven, contains a lesson that will soon be in-carnated into a purpose. We are transforming, almost trans-formed. The oriental gazes into the face of the occidental, and both cry, "Behold, my brother!" The human family stand before their Joseph, opposing to his "Doth my father yet live?" that cry of conviction and resolve: "It is enough, Joseph my son is yet alive; I will go and see him before I die!" This is the voice of the forerunner, the import of so-called Expositions Universal. They are forces, and Chicago is to-day the centripetal maelstrom toward which the tidal wave is rolling and from which the centrifugal reaction will be world-wide.

Love shall yet be the universal religion. The weapons of war shall be transformed into the innocent implements of joyful harmony, and the recognition of the old God of the ages shall convert hatred and ambition into a vague tradition, only known to the annals of a long-past history.

Brethren, members of an estranged household, we welcome you to the table of a common Father in the hearty affection and sympathy of a happy family. And as we talk over the extravagant vagaries of ancient religions, now become super-stitions, let us thank the All-Father for the light and liberty He has vouchsafed us and strive to make ourselves worthy of the trust.

Här tricka vi brorskål.

THE MAGIC-POETRY OF THE FINNS AND ITS APPLICATION IN PRACTICE.

BY HON. JOHN ABERCROMBY.

THE word magic is of very wide significance. But according to the purpose for which it is used it may be classed as beneficent or injurious. Here I only propose to deal with the beneficent class, and further to limit myself to its special development among the Finns. By beneficent magic I understand the many various methods, verbal or ceremonial, by which weak, helpless mortals thought to defend themselves against the attacks of evil spirits or the machinations of their human enemies. How and when the notion of spirits, ghosts and supernatural beings first sprung up in the human mind is an open, probably an insoluble, question, though it is safe to assume that it has existed for a very long period. But however the idea arose, we find in the earliest Egyptian and Babylonian records, and amongst all people all over the world, that spirits were, and are, conceived of as made in man's own image, as duplicates of his incorporeal self. Hence, it was perfectly natural, as we shall find further on, for evil spirits to be abused, scolded, insulted, implored, bribed or consigned to the infernal regions by the wizard, just as if he were addressing another man. Sometimes they are naïvely treated as naughty little boys, whose mischief the wizard threatens to report to their mothers. Indeed, the main difference between a spirit and a mortal is that the former is invisible, or at least generally so, while the other is not.

The original home of the Finns was somewhere in Siberia, though there is no historical or traditional record as to when they crossed the Ural Mountains. When they reached eastern Europe they still lived mainly by hunting, trapping and fishing, so that their civilization must have been of an elementary kind. If they are the Fenni or Phinnoi, mentioned by Tacitus

26

JOHN ABERCROMBY.

and Ptolemy, this would bring the first historical notice of them to the first century of the Christian era and place them east of the Vistula, somewhere in Poland, a long way to the south and considerably to the west of their present geographical position. Tacitus expressly mentions that their immediate neighbors were Germans. However that may be, the investigations of philologists like Ahlqvist and Thomsen have made it quite certain that a large body of words indicating ideas relating to social progress and material civilization have come from two sources : from Gothic or from Scandinavian on the one hand, or from Lithuanian, Lett or Russian on the other ; in other words, from Teutonic or Slav sources. The oldest stratum of the seloan-words is referable to Gothic, and as some of these words exhibit older forms than the Gothic of Ulphilas they must have been borrowed considerably before the fifth century. The Lithuanian loan-words are not much later than the Gothic ones. Hence, we may conclude that about the beginning of the present era, the Finns were in contact with Goths and Lithuanians and had not yet entered Finland. In order to account for the close relationship between the Finnish and Mordvin languages it is believed by G. Koskinen that, at that period, the Finns occupied a position about half way down the Volga on its western bank.

From Asia the Finns brought with them the belief that every tree, plant, rock, river and living being was inhabited by an indwelling spirit or *haltia*. They also had gods—a thunder-god, a god of the forest, a water-god, etc. To these they made sacrifices either to appease their wrath or to propitiate them beforehand. But, as Prof. D. Comparetti has well remarked, partly owing to the undeveloped state of society among the Finns and their isolated mode of life, the gods never became frankly anthropomorphic. They were conceived of in human shape certainly, but they remained cold and passionless, taking no interest in the affairs of men unless specially invoked by prayer or sacrifice. They had no social intercourse, no place of meeting, every god had a wife, but gods and goddesses never make love, are never moved by jealousy and are little more than a spectral host. In this world of gods and spirits must also be included the evil spirits of disease and sickness, for it is with them the magic songs

chiefly deal and to exorcise them away was the principal function of the wizard or wise man.

The book of Finnish magic poetry, edited by Lönnrot
(Loitsurunoja, 1880), is an interesting phenomenon and
unique of its kind if compared with the bald prose incantations of European folk-lore. It is true that Mr. Charles
Leland has recently unearthed in Tuscany some specimens of
magic-song, but the resemblances between the northern and
southern varieties are very slight. The Finnish magic lays
are all couched in the same trochaic measure of four feet, enriched by alliteration and parallelism by which each thought
expressed in a single line is re-echoed in the following line in
different words. The mere fact that the vehicle of these songs
is metrical and not prose is a proof that we do not possess the
magic formula in their original shape. None of the Finno-
ugrian people east of the Ural Mountains have developed
a regular metre; they have not got beyond an irregular
rhythmic prose. It is therefore believed that the Finns only
invented a national metre after long contact with a people
possessed of bards and poets like the Scandinavians, at a
period approximately fixed at about a thousand years ago.
But though the form of these songs, like all traditional poetry
handed down by word of mouth from generation to generation, is in a constant state of flux; the spirit that animates
them, the conception of nature that underlies them is much
the same as in very ancient times. And if in individual songs
mention is made of the Lord God, and of Christ or of Christian
saints there is nothing astonishing in the fact. Such palpably
modern insertions can readily be discounted and appreciated
at their proper worth, for nothing is easier or more common
than the substitution of one proper name for another. As
the whole collection has been taken down by collectors within
the last hundred years, it is distinctly modern in language,
and of course has been subject to perpetual small changes
and modifications to bring it into harmony with the fancy of
the singers, though partly owing to the imperfection of their
memories. In its printed form, as edited by Lönnrot, it has
undergone a further change. For in order to give complete-
ness, as he thought, he fused sometimes as many as twenty
variants into one whole, just as he did in constructing the

Kalevala. Hence the songs, in the shape we have them, are not exactly what were sung by any one wizard. But too great stress need not be laid on this defect, for all the thoughts expressed are the genuine, unadulterated outcome of the popular mind finding utterance through the mouth of the wise men or wizards. Lönnrot felt perfectly justified in doing what he did, as a Finn will never surrender to another man the whole of a magic song ; he always keeps back a few words to prevent the formula losing its force, as it would do, if he gave it in its entirety, when he again has occasion to use it. As the object of this paper is to show the practical application of the magic songs, the liberty taken with them by the editor does not seem to me to affect their value to any material extent. He has arranged the collection under no less than 233 different headings, not including variants, a statement which gives an idea of the manifoldness and comprehensive nature of the subjects swept into the magical net. There is hardly a conceivable eventuality in the simple peasant life of the Finns that is not provided for. The very few specimens that I have time to place before you on this occasion must serve as samples of the whole, and for the same reason I have had to select the shorter ones, which are not always the best.

The chief function of the wizard or wise man was healing the sick or removing pain, and was best performed in the vapor bath-house. This was heated as secretly as possible, so that no malevolent person should know of it and therefore attempt to counteract the good result anticipated. For firewood, trees that had been shattered by lightning; or else driftwood, were preferred. But if the object was to excite love in a certain person's bosom, then the wood of two trees that had got twisted together like hops round a pole, was most suitable for the purpose. The water was drawn from a stream running north, or from the bubbly water below rapids. But water from a natural source was equally good if it had been "bought" by scraping a little gold or silver into the place it was drawn from. The bath switch, for belaboring the patient, was made of three-branched sprigs of birch taken from three or from nine rent-paying properties, and was termed an exorcising bath-switch. When everything had been prepared as secretly as possible, the wizard was ready to perform his office. After entering the bath-house, he wiped the couch, the walls and roof with his bath-switch and forcibly adjured all malevolent persons to depart from the neighborhood. To harden himself he bit a knife three times, and then was ready to proceed with his recitations. First he repeated in a low tone the "fire," "water" and "vapor" formulas, then he began to switch, stroke and rub down the patient, but all the time working himself up more and more into a frenzy by grinding his teeth, by jumping and stamping about, by making contortions and yelling "hoh, hoh, let a fellow breathe." The wizard was bound to excite himself to the utmost pitch and to fall into an ecstasy, which could be done, if other means failed, by repeating the proper formula, and he did it in such a way as to frighten the sick person. In fact, the wizard made a point of startling and alarming his patients, considering this nearly as helpful towards the success of the treatment as the patient's confidence in his skill and power (*Loitsur.* p. ix.).

It is not known in what order the magic songs were sung, though, no doubt, it was not everywhere the same, and much would depend upon circumstances. For instance, if the patient had an open sore on his body, the "vapor formula" was always recited to prevent the vapor entering it and causing pain. Then, before or after this, the "foundation," "protective" and "jealousy" formulas. If the ailment or injury was known to have resulted from fire, frost, colic, cancer, a snake bite, a stone, a knife, etc., then the "origin" of the offending object was rehearsed.[1] If the cause of the ailment was not apparent the wizard recited a special formula "to ascertain the cause." He then sang, in no particular order, but as the occasion seemed to demand, the "reparation," "expulsion," "boasting," "exorcising," "making fast," "falling into an ecstasy" formulas, etc. Diseases and bodily injuries of all sorts were classified in two divisions, according to their supposed cause. They were either natural and sent by God, or unnatural and the result of spells. The first kind attacked, for the most part, only old people. The other class was attributed, either to the machinations of

---

[1] I have translated these "origins" in *Folk-Lore*, vol. I, 1890 ; vol. II, 1891 ; vol. III, 1892 ; vol. IV, 1893.

human enemies and jealous persons acting through the
medium of a witch or sorcerer, or else to the malevolent
spirits that haunt fens, forests and places of burial, or reside
in water, wind and air. In addition to magic songs, use was
made of physical remedies, such as herbs, butter, honey, salt,
tar, fish-fat, water, etc., which were made into potions for internal use, or into ointments for external application. But
these concoctions were rendered more potent if a magic ditty
were recited over them (*Loitsur.* p. x.).

The small selection of examples that I can give here will be
taken in the following order, the "vapor," "foundation,"
"ascertaining the cause," "divining," "protective," "jealousy," "boasting," "reparation," "expulsion," "exorcising," "making fast," "falling into an ecstasy," and "for a
surgical operation" formulas. These thirteen all concern the
treatment of the sick. The last seven are to meet various
contingencies in the daily life of the peasant, the fisherman
and the hunter. These are the formulas "against wasps,"
"against spiders," "against grubs," "to make yeast rise,"
"to spell-bind a judge," "for luck in fishing," and "for
catching hares."

A VAPOR FORMULA (*Loitsur.* p. 136.)

O Steam, be kind, be moderate, Heat,
Fall, Noxious Vapor, to the ground,
O Evil Vapor flee away
Out through the keyhole of the door,
Or into the stones of the stove, inside
The moss that stops the crevices,
Or into the yard through a pipe, or through
The door, thou Vapor reeking of the bath.

A FOUNDATION OR PRELIMINARY FORMULA (*Loitsur.* p. 39.)

If I'm not man enough,
If Ukko's son is not the man
To bring about deliverance,
To cast this evil spirit out,
Let Louhi, mistress of Pohjola, come
To bring about deliverance,
To cast these evil spirits out.
If I'm not man enough,
If Ukko's son is not the man,
Let the strong maiden daughter of the Sun
Come to effect deliverance and remove
These injuries, these troubles wrought by spells.

      *   *   *   *

If I'm not man enough,
If Ukko's son is not the man,

> Let Hiisi come from Hiitola,
> The humpback from the home of gods,
> To cast out that which needs must be
> Cast out and cause this monster's death.

Here it will be noticed that the wizard identifies himself with the son of the thunder-god, Ukko. Hiisi is an evil spirit, who in later times became almost synonymous with the Devil of the New Testament, and Hiitola is his home.

FORMULA TO ASCERTAIN THE CAUSE (*Loitsur.* p. 14.)

> From what, Destroyer, came you here,
> Whence, needless Sickness, did you slip
> Into these pine-constructed nests,
> Into these dwellings built of fir ?
> From winds, or from the sky, or is
> It from deep water-springs that you
> This room have entered as a wind,
> As smoke have penetrated here ?
> From fire, from tar, from molten iron,
> Or is it from an ancient site,
> From stone-heaps grown with raspberries ?
> From farmyards or from fields,
> From tree-stumps or from stones,
> Or were you hatched from boughs of pine,
> Pressed out of willow-shoots or come
> From sandy heaths of burial,
> From six churchyards,
> From circuits made around a church,
> Gyrations round a holy place,
> Where an offering may cause a spell,
> A wish may be expressed in prayer ?

The last four lines refer to the possibility that a rival wizard or some evil wisher of the sick man had made circuits round a church or churchyard, and had made an offering there with a view to increasing the potence of the spell he wished to cast. As no answer is given to the interrogatories of the wizard, I imagine that, exactly as in the "divining" formula, which comes next, some instrument of divination, a magic drum with figures on it, or a sieve, or lots, or something of that sort was used simultaneously with the recitation of the song, and that from the movements of the apparatus an answer was obtained.

The way in which a sieve was used to divine the cause of a disease, or of any other matter, was this. It was placed mouth downwards on the ground ; two bits of charcoal and two of clay were arranged so as to form a cross round the sieve in such a way that the charcoal was opposite the charcoal and one piece of clay opposite the other piece. In some places salt, bread, clay and charcoal were placed at the four corners. To the centre of the bottom of the sieve a brush— one that had four times brushed the head of a corpse was pre- ferred—was suspended by a string attached to the handle, while the other end of the string was in the diviner's hand. The brush was then asked the origin of the disease in this sort of way : " If the disease has come from the earth, move towards the charcoal, if from water go towards the clay." The brush, which hitherto had been steady, now began to swing more and more violently along the clay or the charcoal line, according to the nature of the ailment. Divination of this sort was much in vogue in the middle ages in some parts of Europe (J. Grimm, *Teut. Myth.*, Eng. ed., p. 1108) and no doubt was borrowed by the Finns from their Scandinavian neighbors. In the formula which follows, the exact nature of the divining gear is not expressly stated.

A DIVINING FORMULA (*Loitsur.* p. 111.)

I crave of the Creator leave,
Assistance from the Lord I beg,
I desire it from heaven's Governor,
Who breaks the surface of the earth.
O God, inform the Divining gear,
Divining gear ! declare to me
Whence this calamity arrived.
Begin, divining gear, to move.
If from a burial place the harm has come,
Move with the sun, Divining gear.
If it proceed from village spells,
Then move thyself against the sun.
If from the water comes the hurt,
Then seawards quickly turn thyself.
If from the earth the fellow rose,
Then northwards veer without delay.
If thou give true intelligence,
Trustworthy and from falsehood free,
Then steady as a wall stand still,
Firm as a fence, Divining gear !

By repeating a " protective " formula the wizard metaphor- ically armed himself for the fray.

A PROTECTIVE FORMULA (*Loitsur.* p. 6.)

May the fiery fur coat of my sire
To serve as a fiery covering,
May my mother's fiery shirt
To serve me as a fiery shirt,

Be brought from the house of Death
And put on me, so that
No sorcerer's arrows penetrate,
Nor an archer's shooting implements.
If that should insufficient prove,
Let the might of Ukko from the sky,
The might of the Earth-mother from the earth,
And old Väinämöinen's strength come forth
To help and favor me,
To strengthen me and give me might,
Lest a Devil's arrows penetrate,
The arrows of a sorcerer.

The use of the "envy" formula was to drive away or counteract the evil influence of jealous or envious persons, while the operations of the wizard were going on.

AN ENVY FORMULA (*Loitsur.* p. 9.)

Whoever looks with envious glance,
Peers eagerly with perverse eye,
Or keeps bewitching with his mouth
And imprecates by means of words,
May his eyes be filled with Hiisi's filth,
His face be smeared with Hiisi's soot,
May his mouth be plugged with a fiery bung,
His jaws be locked with Lempo's lock,
May his mouth get overgrown with moss,
The root of his tongue be broken off,
May one eye flow like honey and
The other one like butter drip,
Into the raging fire,
Into the Devil's place for coals.
May his head dry into stone
And a skin grow on the stone.

A BOASTING FORMULA (*Loitsur.* p. 27.)

No sorcerer bewitches me,
No Lapp can place me under spells,
For my bewitcher I bewitch,
My would-be conqueror I subdue.
I gouge the eye of a jealous man,
I tweak the nose of a sorcerer,
Let him be any man alive,
A dark-complexioned country lout,
Or any woman now alive,
A reddish-brown-complexioned witch,
Or a woman of complexion blonde,
Of any complexion—'tis the same.
When I begin to sing a charm,
Myself commence to chatter words,
I split their shoulders with my song,
Bisect their jawbones with my lay,
I rend the collar of their shirts,
From the breast-bone I tear it off.
Then on their heads by song I bring
A cap, and underneath the cap

> A sheaf of Viborg worms,
> Of hair worms, quite a heap.
> Him that would eat me up I feed with these,
> And make them bite whoever would bite me.
> I feed the best divining men,
> The sorcerers, the jealous ones,
> On toads with all their feet,
> On lizards with their wings, on snakes,
> Black snakes with their venom, paws and all.

The object of a "reparation" formula is to induce the evil spirit of sickness, pain, rheumatic twinges, or what not, to repair or undo the harm he has committed.

A REPARATION FORMULA (*Loitsur.* p. 15.)

> If thou art one that eateth heart,
> Or twisteth lungs, or whiningly
> For liver begs, or one
> That dodgeth up and down the ribs,
> Or in the temples causeth smart,
> Or ruineth the teeth,
> Or causeth gaping of the jaws,
> Or shooteth along the shoulder blades,
> Come hither now to feel ashamed
> And to repair what thou hast done,
> Or to thy mother I shall tell
> It and thy father I'll inform.
> A mother hath enormous work
> In treading where her son has trod,
> Removing traces he has left,
> Anointing sores that he has caused.

By an "expulsion" formula, the spirit of disease was ordered off without ceremony, especially if it was believed to have been sent by the spells of an envious neighbor.

AN EXPULSION FORMULA (*Loitsur.* p. 18.)

> At once begin to take thy leave,
> O Needless Sickness, sent by spells,
> Thou evil eater of the flesh,
> Remove and thy departure take,
> From the body of the wretched man,
> From the body racked with pain,
> As I with mine eyes have seen,
> While mine eyelids oped and shut.
> Now is the Mischief's time to move,
> The turn of the earth's Fiend to flee,
> Now is the Scamp's dismissal hour,
> The Monster's time to slink away
> From the belly and the heart of one
> That's innocent, devoid of guilt.
> Ere now, a real fiend, that had
> A mother too, decamped, ran off
> The while this wizard exorcised,
> And while this child was utt'ring words.

So why dost thou, an unbegotten
Heathen wretch, not now depart,
Thou dog without a master, cur
Without a mother, not decamp ?

The exorcising formulas are very numerous, and by them
the spirit of disease was consigned to hell, to Hiisi, to a
churchyard, to foaming rapids, back to the person who had
laid the spell, to its own home, to the forest, to Pohjola, to a
battle-field, to the sky, to a mountain or a stone, to the fire,
to a foreign land or to the water.

AN EXORCISING FORMULA (*Loitsur.* p. 41.)

I order smarting pain away,
I cause the sufferings to sink
At the side of an awful cataract,
At the whirlpool of an awful stream,
Which by their roots drags trees along,
That causes branching headed firs to fall,
O'erwhelms heather with its flowers,
Sweeps grass with all its husks away.
In the cataract is a fiery reef,
On the reef is a fiery bull
Whose mouth is all aglow with fire,
Whose throat is hot with flames.
To Mana it will take the pain,
The sufferings to the home of Death,
Whence in their life they won't escape,
Nor in their time be fetched away.

If the injury or sickness was believed to result from a spell,
the evil spirit could be exorcised by reciting the following :
(*Loitsur.* p. 46.)

If thou art the result of art,
An evil caused by any one,
A harm produced by another man,
An evil raised by a sorcerer,
Or by a scheming woman wrought,
By a strong woman shaken out,
Return to the man that cast the spell,
To the jaws of him that sang the charm,
To the throat of her that pronounced the curse,
To the heart of her that incited thee,
To the breast of the witchcraft-using man,
To the chest of him that conjured thee,
Before the rising of the sun,
The uprising of the orb of day,
The dawning of the god of dawn,
Ere the cock's crow is audible.

After an evil spirit had been banished to a certain spot, it was chained up, as it were, by reciting a formula "for making fast."

A MAKING FAST FORMULA (*Loitsur.* p. 56.)

Begone whither I ordered thee,
Commanded thee, exhorted thee,
Whence—unless loosed—thou'lt ne'er get loose,
Unless set free wilt ne'er be free
While this world lasts, while the Lord's moon shines.
No liberator liberates
Thee, no releaser sets thee free
Unless I come to liberate,
Myself shall go to set thee free
In company with my three dogs,
With five or six of my woolly tails,
With seven white collared dogs,
With my eight hounds,
And accompanied by stallions nine
Foaled of a single mare.

FOR FALLING INTO AN ECSTASY (*Loitsur.* p. 25.)

I cause my Nature to uprise,
I summon forth my Genius (*haltia*)
My Nature ! from thy hole arise,
From under a fallen tree, my Genius,
From under a stone, my Helper, and
From under the moss, my Guide.
Come dread-inspiring Death,
Since I am in dreadful agony,
As my protection and support,
To give me help, to strengthen me
For the work that must be done,
For the sores that must be searched.

In another formula for the same purpose, the guardian spirit, genius or *haltia* of the wizard is described not only as living under a stone or a fallen tree, but also as having brilliant eyes and spotted cheeks. So possibly the *haltia* was thought of as a snake, like the guardian spirit of the house, the *domovoi* of the Russian peasant.

The mere recitation of a charm was not sufficient for a surgical operation, such as removing a tumor or cutting off a warty growth. A knife had to be used, though the wizard might pretend it was of miraculous origin.

FOR A SURGICAL OPERATION (*Loitsur.* p. 74.)

A knife fell from the clouds,
A knife rolled from the sky,
Forged by the sky most cleverly,
With a silver blade, with a haft of gold.

It fell upon my knees
And into my right hand.
The haft remainèd in my hand,
The blade in the Creator's hand.
With it I cut excrescences
Away and shall uproot their roots.
Pray do not be the least alarmed,
The treatment will not last a month,
I shall not fumble for a year,
One moment will the treatment last
And all is over in a trice.
I shall not touch with heavy hand,
I shall not prune to cause thee pain,
With river-horsetail (*equisetum arv.*) I shall touch,
I'll stroke it with a water sedge (*cares aquat.*),
I'll push it with a rush's edge,
I term it "blown away by wind,"
"Removal by a chilly blast,"
"A snatching by a raging storm."
Where I make incision with the knife,
Where with the iron blade I rasp,
Upon that spot let honey stream,
Let virgin honey trickle down,
Pure virgin honey into the wound,
Honey where iron has made a gash.
And if the iron acts amiss,
If Lempo cause the knife to slip,
The flesh of Lempo shall be sliced,
The evil one be cut in twain,
Even upon his mother's knee,
Though shielded by his parent dear,
With a blade that he himself has made,
With iron forgèd by himself.

Before passing on to subjects other than disease and bodily sickness, I must give one very short charm against heartburn to illustrate the observation already made that an evil spirit might be cajoled with flattering words and also threatened.

FOR HEARTBURN (*Loitsur.* p. 74.)

Kindly heartburn, lovely heartburn,
Heartburn sweet of the Virgin Mary,
Get thee gone, return elsewhither.
Ukko, god of thunder, struck fire
On a hard and tinny surface,
Into a heap of alder shavings,
Into which I blow the heartburn
From this wretched human body.

The following could be used as a charm against wasp-stings, and illustrates the quaint humor of the people.

AGAINST WASP-STINGS (*Loitsur.* p. 56.)

O wasp that dwells in meadow sweet (*spiræa ulm.*),
Who bade you do this evil deed,

Incited you to a sneaking act,
What fool made such a dolt of you,
What madman made you so insane,
That you with your sharp pike should sting
That human being's skin ?
Don't shoot, O wasp,
Don't sting, O stinging bird.
Perhaps you think you are no bird
At all, unless you use your pike.
Then sting a pile of wood, or thrust
Into a juniper your spur,
Or hurl your arrows at a stone,
Making them rattle on a rock.
Confine the feathers of your wings,
Into a hook twist up your snout,
Or shoot yourself, to one
Of your companions give a prod.
To pass the time shoot stones or stumps
Of trees, and each of them six times.
For my part I've a sandy skin,
An iron-colored cuticle.

AGAINST SPIDERS (*Loitsur.* p. 113.)

Shrivelled, wizen, shaggy spider,
Jesus' ball of reddish worsted,
The Creator's golden flower,
If thou evil hast committed,
Come to recognize thine action,
Else I'll flay thee with my fingers,
With my thumbs shall make incisions.
I shall take thy hide to Viborg,
To the German town convey it,
Where I'll get a hundred shillings,
Shall receive in piles a thousand,
Five at a time in Viborg money,
Six at a time in golden pennies.

AGAINST GRUBS AND PALMERWORMS (*Loitsur.* p. 115.)

O Field, thy gadfly larvæ hide,
O Earth, conceal thy little grubs,
So that they shall not eat my crops,
The result of all my heavy toil,
Of the many times I turned the plough.
Now, Grub, depart from my growing corn,
Thou Good-for-nothing from my crops,
Away, O Snail, from my sprouting seed,
Avaunt from my food-producing plants,
From these life-giving herbs of mine.
Away, away, a war's at hand,
Thy life's departure draweth nigh,
I'll fetch an awe-inspiring lad,
With iron mouth, with iron head.
To destroy thy jaw, to disperse thy teeth,
I'll bring destruction on thy head,
With a pestle I shall crush thy pate,
In a mortar I shall pound thy lips,
And with a millstone grind thy teeth.

TO MAKE YEAST RISE (Loitsur. p. 127.)

Rise, Yeast, when you are raised,
Ferment when you are let ferment,
Before your raiser rise,
Ferment in your fermenter's hand.
Rise without being raised by ropes,
Without being hauled by tarry cords.
The sun and moon have risen both,
Yet you have not begun to rise.

TO SPELL-BIND A JUDGE (Loitsur. p. 128.)

May the barristers be smothered, and
May the jurymen be mollified,
May the judge be suffocated, may
The law fall prostrate to the ground,
And the law books tumble on the floor.
Let Justice stand before the door
Upon my entering the room,
While I am standing by the wall,
While I remain behind the door,
While I am walking to the court.
May the magistrate become a child,
The jurymen become as sheep,
But myself become a ravening wolf
Or a destructive bear.
Though bitter is the gall of bears,
Yet mine is twofold bitterer.
May any word that I shall speak
Have the effect of a hundred words,
So that I shan't incur a fine
Nor find myself compelled by force.

The fisherman's address to the fish to take the hook is infinitely naïve and humorous.

FOR CATCHING FISH (Loitsur. p. 116.)

O Perch, beloved little fish,
And you, O Pike, with scanty teeth
Come here to take the hook,
To twist the barbèd iron,
To bend the crooked hook,
To tug the line, to jerk the rod.
Now is the time to take the hook.
The time for bending crooked hooks,
The time for twisting barbèd iron,
The time for tugging fishing lines.
Approach with a wider open mouth,
With jaws to their utmost stretch distent,
With teeth as few as possible.
Come hither and come quicker too
Right past the hooks of other men,
Avoiding other people's lines,
Straight to this hook of mine.
Then take the hook, gulp down the nail,
At the bent iron make a snatch.

Tug straight my line and bend
With a sudden jerk the rod.
Of virgin honey are my lines,
My hooks of honey, my bait is sweet,
The lines of other people are
Of dung, their hooks are barbed,
The bait of others is of tar.

FOR CATCHING HARES (*Loitsur.* p. 167.)

O forest matron, Elina,
Woman with body undefiled,
Bring now thy game from far away,
From Forest Castle's furthest edge,
From the honey-dripping forest wilds,
From behind the " copper " mountains there.
Permit a bandy-legs to run,
A skew-eyed hare to lob along,
To come this way without alarm,
Bobbing along without a thought.
Let a big one come or a little one,
Or one of only medium size,
Towards my trap, towards my snare,
With its feet to tread upon my gin,
Standing in front of its two paws,
Avoiding other people's snares,
Shunning the traps of other men.

With this I must conclude, and can only hope that I have succeeded in making clearer to you than before how the Finns employed their magic songs. There has evidently been a continuous development and adaptation of them to meet new circumstances. They are naïve and often whimsical, certainly, but there is nothing savage, barbarous or nonsensical in them, and their intention is good. To this latter circumstance must be attributed their persistence to the present day, in spite of the strong hold that Christianity has upon the people at large. The collection of magic poetry of the Finns is one of the most interesting survivals in the whole of Europe, and is worthy of a closer study.

THE NORTHERN TROLLS.

BY DAVID MAC RITCHIE.

In the traditional and semi-historical literature of Scandinavia, there are many references to a race of beings known as "Trolls," who are described as in frequent contact with the ancestors and contemporaries of the saga-writers. That they originally constituted a distinct race, wholly different from the Scandinavian colonists, is indicated by Professor Nilsson, when he states that—"The name *Troll* is never given to any man or woman of the Saga, relating to the Asa race ; it was given out to the foreign (*i.e.* aboriginal) tribes who were looked upon as conquered, for *troll* or *tröll*, seems to be the same as *thrall*,[1] and signifies "serf."[1] But he points to an amalgamation of the two peoples when he says, on another page [2] that a certain Scandinavian Chief, was the son of Stalbjörn, surnamed *Half-troll*, which shows that his mother was descended from a Troll race." That such an amalgamation was apparently general is also indicated by Mr. Du Chaillu in his *Viking Age*, "At the time of the arrival of the Asar on the Baltic Shores," says this writer, "they found the large Scandinavian Peninsula and that of Jutland, and the islands and shores of the Baltic, populated by a seafaring people whose tribes had constant intercourse with each other. . . . These people intermarried with the Asar . . . and hence arose tribes called half-Risar and half-Troll."[3] It will be seen from an extract which Mr. Du Chaillu makes [4] from the Hervarar Saga (ch. i.) that the term "Risar" has no reference to the invading people, for it is there stated that "*before* the Tyrkjar [5] and Asia-men (or

[1] *The Primitive Inhabitants* of *Scandinavia*, by Sven Nilsson, 3d edit., London, 1868, p. 239. *Note.* In Larsen's Dansk-Norsk *Engelsk Ordbog*, *troll* is a "thrall," "serf," etc., *trælle-flok* is a "crowd of slaves ; " and *trællo-hær* is an "army of serfs." [2] Op. cit., p. 221.
[3] *Viking Age*, Vol. 1. p. 51. [4] Ibid.
[5] This word may be translated "Turks" or "Saracens" or "Indians."

42

Asar) came to the Northern lands, Risar and half-Risar lived there." It is unnecessary to enter into a consideration at this point of the precise significance of the word "Rise" (pl. Risar) and it is enough to observe that this is the Northern form of the German *Riese*, signifying a "giant." On the other hand the *Trolls* or *Trows*, as they are called in Orkney and Shetland are identified by Sir Walter Scott with the genuine Northern Dwarf.[1] Round both of these names an atmosphere of mystery and unreality has gathered; and the conclusion arrived at by so judicial an observer as Dr. E. B. Tylor is, "That the evidence brought forward by Grimm, Nilsson and Hanusch has "settled beyond question" that some, at least, of the tales relating to both classes are connected with the traditions of real indigenous or hostile tribes."[2]

So much, however, has been said and written from the opposite point of view that it may be necessary here to give a brief summary of Professor Nilsson's "Proofs that the Dwarfs and Pigmies of the Sagas were Human Beings (and) that they belonged to the same Race as the Laplanders of the present day." Professor Nilsson remarks as follows :—

"It has often been asserted that the dwarfs mentioned in the ancient Sagas were not real men, but mythical and allegorical beings, meant to typify certain powers and conditions of nature. . . . But in the description of dwarfs, as given by the Sagas, we find too many and too distinct ethnological characters to admit of any such theory."[3]

The chief points brought out by Professor Nilsson are these :—The dwarfs are said to have lived in caves, in underground structures, and in chambered mounds. The Lapps formerly occupied such dwellings, and even yet, the winter dwelling of the Lapp is practically only a modification of the "hollow-hill" of the dwarf. The Lapp is in stature dwarfish, if not actually a dwarf. Both the traditional dwarf and the actual Lapp are distinguished further by the characteristics: ugliness of feature, cowardice and cunning, a love of hoarding up glittering metals, a knowledge of witchcraft,

---

[1] *Letters on Demonology and Witchcraft*; Letter IV.
[2] *Primitive Culture.* Vol. i. p. 385.—3d edition.
[3] Op. cit., p. 207. et seq.

skill as craftsmen ; both of them speak the language of their conquerors imperfectly, both are regarded as of inferior race and both are described as wearing blue or red caps, and gray kirtles of reindeer skin.

" It has often been asserted that the dwarfs, mentioned in the ancient Sagas, were not real men, but mythical and allegorical beings, meant to typify certain powers and conditions of nature. . . But in the description of dwarfs as given by the Sagas, we find too many and too distinct ethnological characters to admit of any such theory. The reason for supposing that the dwarfs have no historical reality is probably, in the first instance, that they are said to have performed several supernatural and impossible feats, or, in other words, that they practised sorcery. But this does not fully entitle us to deny their historical existence. In that case, not only the Laplanders in Europe, but, also, the whole Esquimaux race in America, ought, for the same reason, to be regarded as mythical and allegorical, because it is not long since that people living in their neighborhood believed, and probably still believe, the former to be sorcerers ; and the Indian tribes in America think, even to this day, that the latter are still acquainted with the black art."

As a proof that the Eskimos were so regarded by Europeans, as well as by Red Indians, I may here interpolate Sir John Lubbock's observation that " when Frobisher's crew, in 1576, captured an old Esquimau woman, they took her for a witch, and pulled off her boots to see if she had cloven feet." [1] And I shall also show that the term *troll,* which signifies " witch" and " wizard " as well as " dwarf," was applied to the natives of Greenland by the Scandinavians as recently as the fifteenth century.

It is impossible to repeat here all the various matter-of-fact incidents cited by Nilsson as showing that the dwarfs of Northern tradition " were corporeal and human beings, and considered as such by the narrators themselves, although of another race." [1] But one passage specially deserves quotation. Referring to the numerous instances in which the dwarfs are spoken of as inhabiting caves, underground dwellings and

---

[1] Note by Sir John Lubbock, p. 264 of Prof. Nilsson's Book.
[2] Op. cit., p. 210.

chambered mounds, Nilsson states that formerly this was also, a Lapp custom. Then he goes on to say :—

" The Laplanders, however, now live almost generally in huts, called " gammar " (which themselves are only modifications of the chambered mound). It is, therefore, very elucidative of our subject—continues Professor Nilsson—that at least, in *one* of our ancient Sagas it is expressly mentioned that a dwarf was living in a *gamm*. In Didrik of Bern's Saga (Chap. xvi) we are told how one day Didrik was out hunting on horseback in a forest, and that while chasing a stag, he saw a *dwarf* running at some distance from him. He hastened after him and seized hold of him before he had time to reach his *gamm*. The name of this dwarf was Alfrik ; he was a famous thief and a great artificer. He had forged the sword *Nageling*, which was owned by Grim, whom he (the dwarf) advised Didrik to challenge." [1]

Now although Nilsson cites this as an exceptional instance, he omits to see that it is far from being so. It is merely a question of translation. The writer he quotes has employed the word still used to denote a Lapland mound-dwelling, whereas other writers make use of more archaic and descriptive terms. The name of the dwarf inhabiting this *gamm* was " Alfrik," and he appears in the *Heldenbuch*, the *Vilkina saga* and the *Nibelungen Lied* under various forms of the same name.[2] But the *gamm* inhabited by " Albric, the wild dwarf" of the *Nibelungen Lied* is styled a " hollow hill." This is a perfectly correct description of the chambered mound, which is the prototype of the Lapp *gamm*. For the latter is obviously a modification of the former, " having the appearance of a large rounded hillock, which indeed it may be termed," to quote the words of a traveller of seventy years ago.[3]

If, therefore, the word *gamm* were to be substituted for the numerous terms which seem in old sagas and folk-tales (of which " pigmies," " hillock " and " elf hillock " are examples), Professor Nilsson's parallel would be still more clearly drawn.

---

[1] Op. cit., pp. 212-3.

[2] Grimm refers to him as " Alpris," more correctly Alfrikr," and again as Alfrigg, Elperich, Alerich, Alberon, Auberon, and Oberon (these three last being derived through the French, in the 13th century). However, as the name seems only to signify Elf King, it may have been applied to various dwarfs.

[3] SirArthur de Chapell Brooke, *A Winter in Lapland*, London, 1827, p.318.

Nilsson briefly "sketches the outline of his parallel" as follows :—

(1) "The Laplanders are ugly and short, just as the dwarfs of the Sagas are represented to be." (He might have added that the Lapps and the dwarfs are each described as having disproportionately long arms.) [1]

(2) "The Laplanders are clothed in a gray reindeer kirtle, and they wear a blue or a red cap. The pigmies are also so identified in the Sagas."

(3) "The Laplanders, for instance,—in Norway,—speak the language of the country very badly. When the Norwegians imitate the Laplanders it is done nearly in the same way as when the Danish peasant imitates the pigmy."

(4 & 5) Lapps and Dwarfs, alike, are represented as cowardly, cunning and deceitful.

(6) Lapps and Dwarfs are skilful craftsmen.

(7) Lapps and Dwarfs delight to hoard up glittering metals, especially silver. (Both are, also, noted for burying their hoards).

(8) "It was thought that the Dwarfs were skilled in sorcery, the same was believed of the Laplanders."

(9 &10) "The Lapland race is considered inferior . . . The Laplanders, therefore, marry and hold feasts only amongst themselves as was the case with the mountain-pigmies. (As regards intermarriage, however, there are many exceptions to this rule, both in the case of the modern Lapps and of traditional Dwarfs.)

These, then, are the chief points of Professor Nilsson's argument; which receives scant justice when set forth in this very condensed form. And it appears to me, as it has

---

[1] See a paper read by Dr. J. G. Garson at a meeting of the Anthropological Institute of Great Britain and Ireland, June 9th, 1885.

appeared to others, that he is very successful in proving his case. To believe this, does not, of course, imply a belief in his infallibility.

Crossing the Atlantic, we find similar evidence in North America. According to the "Algonquin Legends of New England," as these have been collected by Mr. C. G. Leland,[1] the region which embraces Maine, Nova Scotia, and Eastern Canada was inhabited by "little men," "dwellers in rocks," at a time when there were, as yet, no red Indians in that territory—"only wild Indians very far to the West." The date of arrival of the Beothuks in Newfoundland, and of the Algonquins in the St. Lawrence region, is only of minor importance in the present question. And yet it can be approximately fixed by means of these same "little men, dwellers in rocks," who preceded them. Because, when the Norsemen first landed on the northeastern coast of North America, in the beginning of the eleventh century, the red Indians had not, as yet, appeared upon the scene. The chief Norse accounts of those landings are so well known, having been before the world ever since the publication of Rafn's *Antiquitates Americanæ* in 1837, that it is unnecessary to do more than to refer very briefly to the description there given of the people whom the explorers encountered. They seem to have been most frequently styled "Skroelings," a word which "Rafn" renders by *Homunculi, i. e.*, "little men."

An equivalent translation is that given by Claus Magnus in the 16th century, at which period his map shows that the eastern part of Greenland was inhabited by "pigmies" commonly called "Skroelings." Rafn's remark that the descriptions of the 11th century "Skroelings" of the New England coast coincide with the accounts given of modern Greenlanders or Lokimoes,[2] is not only fully justified by those descriptions, but it is still further corroborated by the statement of Claus Magnus that the people of Eastern Greenland in the 16th century were "Skroelings." And this word he also regards as a synonym for a "dwarf." For all these reasons, then, we find that the Norse records fully bear out the traditions of the Algonquins that their precur-

---

[1] London ; Sampson Low. 1884. [2] Antiq. Amer., p. 45, n.

sors in the territory stretching on both sides of the Gulf of St. Lawrence were " little men." With regard to the dwellings of those " little men," the Algonquin tradition is also justified by the Norse records. One reads in the *Saga of Thorfinn Karlsefne* that when that leader and his followers were in the territory now known as New Brunswick, in the year 1011, they encountered five Skroelings, of whom two were boys. They captured the boys, but the adult Skroelings disappeared "beneath the ground." From the boys, whom the Norsemen carried away with them to Iceland, they learned that the Skroelings possessed no houses, but dwelt in caves and dens. Thus the Indian tradition that they were preceded by "little men, dwellers in rocks," is wholly verified by European Chronicle.[1]

In connection with these references, especially with that of Claus Magnus as to the " pigmies" or "Skroelings" of Eastern Greenland, the account of the Italian voyager, Antonio Zeno, was also fitly cited. According to this traveller the natives of Eastern Greenland seen by him in the latter part of the fourteenth century, were " half-wild" people of small stature, *di picciola statura,* and very timorous, who, as soon as they were seen, hid themselves in caverns.[2]

The eleventh century cave-dwellers of Maine and the St. Lawrence region were not, however, only styled " Skroelings" by the Norse writers. Arnas Magnusson, a native of Iceland, writing about seven centuries after the first encounter with the Skroelings, observes : "These people are called ' Lapps ' in some books."[3] This reference is very suggestive. To what extent modern Lapps and modern Eskimos resemble one another is not a question that needs to be considered here.

[1] Antiq. Amer, p. 149, n.

Dr. A. S. Packard ("The Labrador Coast." New York, N. D. C. Hodges, 1891, chap. xiii.) gives many interesting references which show that the Eskimos were still pretty numerous in the Gulf of St. Lawrence in the eighteenth century. At that time they frequently visited Newfoundland, spending the summer months there, and in 1771 one of them was seen in his " kayak" hunting the great auk, off the east coast of Newfoundland, south of the 5th parallel. Assuming that they had retreated from more southern regions at a similar rate, it is easy to accept the first quarter of the 15th century, (the date given by M. Beauvois, *Les Skroelings,* p. 48), as the period when they were finally expelled by the Algonquins from Maine and the adjoining territories.)

[2] *Les Skroelings.* par E. Beauvois (extracted from the *Revue Orientale et Americaine.* Paris, 1879, p. 45.

[3] *Antiq. Amer.,* p. 196.

The important fact is, that the Norsemen applied the term "Lapp" to a dwarfish people, inhabiting caves and underground retreats on the northwestern shores of the Atlantic, just as they did to a people of similar characteristics, living on its northeastern shores. In short, they regarded the words "Lapp" and "Skroeling," otherwise "pigmy," as synonyms. And this is what Professor Nilsson contends.

But the identification may be made still more complete. Not only were those North Americans of the eleventh century referred to as "Lapps" and "pigmies"; they were also styled "trolls." This will be seen from the following extracts from the monograph of Monsieur E. Beauvois, entitled "*Les Skroelings, Ancêtres des Esquimaux dans les temps precolombiens,*"[1] to which I am indebted for much information upon that subject.

M. Beauvois points out that when Ari Frodi, writing in the twelfth century, described Eric the Red's first visit to Greenland (in 985), he mentions that Eric observed, both on the eastern and western coasts, various relics which showed that these places had been visited by men of the race inhabiting Vinland (understood to be the modern New England) whom the Greenlanders (that is the twelfth century Norsemen in Greenland), call Skroelings."[2] As M. Beauvois remarks, the home of the Eskimos was still on the American continent at this period, and although they had paid several visits to Greenland, they had not yet begun to *settle* there in sufficient numbers to displace the Norsemen. Thirteen years after Eric the Red's visit, his fellow-countryman, Thorgils, (the step-son of Orrabeen), was shipwrecked on the eastern coast of Greenland. He and his companions were without food, until Thorgils happened to find a stranded whale beside which were two "troll" women. They had cut off a quantity of the meat, and one of them was stooping to pick up her bundle, when Thorgils made a slash at her with his sword and cut off her hand. The "troll" woman, thereupon, let the bundle fall, and fled with her friend.[3] That

---

[1] *Paris,* 1879 ; extracts from the *Révue Orientale et Americaine.*

[2] Quoted by M. Beauvois (op., cit. p. 29) from the *Islendingalok.* 5.

[3] Quoted by M. Beauvois (op. cit. p. 30) from *Greenlands Historske, Mindesmaerber,* Copenhagen, 1838-1845. Vol. iii. p. 108. See, also, pp. 96-98 of *Thorgils' Historie* (the Floamanna Saga), Copenhagen, 1809,

4

these two "troll" women were female Skroelings is taken
for granted by M. Beauvois, and as no other race is mentioned
as then inhabiting or visiting Greenland, it is difficult to
avoid arriving at this conclusion. "These trolls," says Beauvois, referring to an incident of later date, "could be no
other than Eskimos, travellers not having reported any other
natives of Greenland than the Kalalis, called Skroelings by
some writers and 'trolls' by others." The special incident
which called forth his remark occurred in the latter part of
the fourteenth century. In, or about the year 1385, an Ice-
lander named Bjoern Einarsson was wrecked along with his
followers, on the Greenland coast. During his stay there,
he happened to rescue two young trolls, a brother and a
sister who had taken refuge on a reef which the flowing tide
would soon have submerged. They swore allegiance to him,
and from that moment he never lacked food, for, by their
skill in hunting and fishing, they were able to procure him
everything he required. The young girl esteemed it a great
favor when her mistress, Solveig, allowed her to carry and
caress her infant. She also wished to have a head-dress like
the lady's and made one for herself from whale-gut. The
brother and sister killed themselves by leaping into the sea
from the crags in endeavoring to follow the ship of their
dear master, Bjoern, who had not wished to carry them with
him to Iceland." [1]

Contemporaneous with this episode is the visit of the Italian voyagers, Nicolo and Antonio Zeno to Greenland. Those
whom the former saw in the northeast of Greenland are,
as M. Beauvois says, obviously Eskimos, or Skroelings.
Apparently, Zeno does not apply any special name to them,
merely styling them "natives." But their skin canoes, as
described by him,[2] are the Eskimo kayaks.

Those seen by his brother, at Cape Farewell, the "half-
wild people, of small stature and very timorous, who took
refuge in caverns at the sight of man," "correspond well
with the Skroelings of the Sagas"—to quote again the words
of M. Beauvois.[3]

Those Italian voyagers do not, of course, use the Norse

[1] *Les Skroelings*, p. 41 ; quoted from *Groenl. Hist. Mind*, vol. iii. pp. 436-439.
[2] See pp. 43-44 of *Les Skroelings*.   [3] Op. cit., p. 45.

word "troll," but the author from whom so many of these references are obtained gives us an instance of its application, in the same locality, so recently as the middle of the fifteenth century. The Danish Governor of Iceland, at that period, was one Bjoern Thorleifsson, and he and his wife were on one occasion wrecked on the coast of Greenland, being the sole survivors of the ship's company. "Two old trolls, a man and a woman," then arrived on the scene and befriended the castaways. These trolls carried large hampers on their shoulders, and the male troll, placing Thorleifsson in his basket, while the female carried the governor's lady in hers, the party made their way to the residence of the Danish Bishop at Gardhs, where the two refugees passed the winter.[1]

From these various references, therefore, we see that the Norsemen, during a period of several centuries, applied the three terms—"Lapp," "troll" and "pigmy"[2] to one people on the western shores of the Atlantic, and it is the contention of Professor Nilsson and others that they applied the same three terms to one people on the eastern side of the Atlantic. It is obvious that they regard the three words as synonymous, when used in America; and this being so, one can hardly avoid the inference that they had previously regarded them as synonyms when used in Scandinavia.

Of several customs uniting the Scandinavian Lapps to the so-called Lapps of North America, perhaps the most striking is the use of semi-subterranean and wholly underground dwellings. Of this, there is ample evidence on both sides.

Yet, in spite of many strong reasons for regarding the Lapps and Eskimos as the representatives of the legendary dwarfs or trolls, there are other considerations which would lead one to believe that they are so only in a modified degree. Both races have traditions of underground folk of still smaller stature with whom, in the case of the Lapps, at any rate, their forefathers intermarried. This tradition quite accords with the statements referred to by Paulus Jovius, a writer of of the first half of the sixteenth century, who says that the territory lying between the Varanger Fiord, on the east, and Tromsö on the west (the territory known as Scrid-scrit, or

---

[1] *Les Skroelings*, p. 42 (quoted from *Groenl. Hist Mind*, vol. iii. p. 469).
[2] " *Pygmei onigo Screlinger dicti.*" (*Claus Magnus.*)

Scric Finnia), was reported to be inhabited by veritable pigmies. "Several trustworthy witnesses have reported," he says, "that beyond the country of the Lapps in the twilight region between the Northwest and the North (of Scandinavia) pigmies are to be met with." He adds that their adults are scarcely taller than Italian boys of ten ; and refers to the timorousness and general inferiority of the race. These [1] statements would not have much weight if they depended solely upon the assertions of Jovius, himself a very unreliable author. Jovius, however, is now only repeating here the accounts of earlier writers, but very similar evidence is given in the following century by the Dutch scholar, Vossius, who is cited in this connection by his contemporary, Professor Scheffer of Upsala—"It is almost peculiar to this people to be all of them of low stature," says the writer last named, speaking of the Lapps, "which is attested by the general suffrage of those writers who have described this country. Hence the learned Isaac Vossius observes that Pygmies are said to inhabit here." [2] These two scholars, therefore, Vossius and Scheffer, both residents of seventeenth-century Sweden, had no doubt as to the identity of the Northern Pygmies and the Lapps, or a race occupying the same territory that is now Lapland. But it is to be observed that Jovius and other early writers tend to corroborate the Lapp traditional belief, that they are partly descended from a race of smaller stature, now quite lost in the great Lapp population. [3]

This appears to me all the more probable because, while the Eskimoid tribes that stretch half way round the Arctic Circle declare themselves to be the kinsmen of those Skroelings, Lapps or Trolls whom the early Norsemen encountered in America, yet there is another race [4] which, in several re-

---

[1] Jovius is quoted by Dr. Edward Tyson, in his " Essay Concerning the Pygmies of the Ancients," London, 1699, p. 361.

[2] The History of Lapland, by John Scheffer, Oxford, 1676, p. 12.

[3] Of a family of Lapps exhibited at a meeting of the Anthropological Institute of Great Britain and Ireland on June 9th, 1885, the men averaged 5 feet 1 1-2 inches, and the women 4 feet 11 1-2 inches. These were regarded as typical Lapps. But this stature is considerably above that of the Italian boy of ten years, the height of the ultra-Lapponian pygmies, according to Jovius.

[4] Professor Romyn Hitchcock, *The Ancient Pit-Dwellers of Yezo and the Ai'nos of Yezo*, Smithsonian Report of 1890, gives much information on the subject. See also my monograph, " The Ai'nos (Supplement to Vol. IV. of *Internationales Archiv für Ethnographie*, Leiden, 1892.)

spects, answers more fully to the trolls of tradition. As one goes westward from Alaska into Asia, *via* Kamchatka and the Kurile Islands, the Eskimo type becomes gradually blended with the Ai'no. The Eskimo "kayak" is found in the Kuriles, the sledges of the Ai'nos are drawn by teams of curly-haired "Eskimo" dogs, and there are other links of custom, and even of *physique*, uniting the Eskimo to the natives of the Kuriles, of Yesso and of Saghalien. Now, the people have scarcely yet relinquished the custom of living in half-underground houses, during winter,—a custom which was formerly more general.[1] And, in these islands, the people living in such habitations and in caves were, according to history and tradition, dwarfs. Chinese records of very early date speak of an island, understood to be Saghalien, in which there was a nation of dwarfs, living in grottoes, and having no covering but their own shaggy skins. Japanese and Ai'no tradition further states that those earth-dwelling dwarfs "were only about three or four feet in height," and that "their arms were very long in proportion to their bodies."[2]

As recently as 1613, an English traveller reports a remnant of the dwarfs then living in the north of Yesso ;[3] and indeed the Ai'nos of to day are regarded by some as their modified descendants. Be this as it may, those dwarfs of northeastern Asia resemble the trolls of Scandinavian tradition more closely than do the Lapps and Eskimos, not because of their pit-dwellings and their cave-dwellings (for that does not distinguish them from the others) nor even because of their disproportionately long arms (for that, too, is a Lapp characteristic) but because of their shaggy skins. It is true that the male "Skroeling" who escaped from Karlsefne's party was described as "bearded"; but that only seems to denote that he was a man, as distinguished from the females. In this respect, therefore, the earth-dwelling dwarfs of Yesso more nearly represent the hairy trolls of Scandinavia than any modern race. But the Picts of British tradition, although extinct for many centuries (as a separate race) show us the

---

[1] Professor Schlegel of Leiden has established the identity, *Toung Pao*, Leiden, May, 1892.   [2] See page 47 of my *Ai'nos*.

[3] "Purchas his Pilgrimes," London, 1625, p. 884.

European wing of the same army. For they are described as possessing all the desired qualities,—low stature, hirsute bodies, alleged "supernatural" qualities, and the residence in underground galleries and chambered mounds which is so characteristic of the traditional dwarfs. The Picts, therefore, in Europe, and the Ai'no or semi-Ai'no dwarfs of Asia seem to represent the ancient type which preceded the Lapps themselves.

These conclusions, too briefly stated to be as lucid as I could wish, are nearly or quite the same as those arrived at by Mr. Charles H. Chambers in 1864. Writing to the *Anthropological Review* in that year, Mr. Chambers says :—"I believe the race which inhabited the northern shores of Europe to have been akin to the Lapps, Finns and Esquimaux and the Pickts or Pechts of Scotland, and to have given rise to many of the dwarf, troll and fairy stories extant among the Sagas and elsewhere."

In this paper I have adhered to Sir Walter Scott's acceptation of the trolls as "the genuine northern dwarfs"; a definition endorsed by many others. But various other meanings are attached to the word. Some of these, such as "magician," "serf," and "wicked person,"—do not in any way contradict the assumption that the trolls were dwarfs. But there is one interpretation sometimes given to the word that, at first sight, seems quite inconsistent with this belief. This is the term "giant." Nevertheless, there is much evidence tending to show that the "giants" of many popular tales were merely *savages*,—of no greater height than their foes. Indeed, there are instances where "giant" and "dwarf" are applied to the same people. It thus appears that the word "giant" was often employed without conveying the meaning of unusual height; and even with an opposite signification. In short, just as one may speak of "a *little* wonder," without denoting anything of great size, so a "giant" of tradition was obviously in some cases not *gigantic* (paradoxical though that sounds). When the Norsemen applied the name "troll" to these North American natives whom they also called "Lapps" and "puny people" or pigmies" (Skroelings), it is

---

[1] See Dr. J. G. Garson's remarks at meeting of Anthropological Institute of Great Britain and Ireland, June 9th, 1885.

evident that they did not understand the word "troll" to imply a person of even so great stature as their own. Mr. Benjamin Thorpe has also recognized this apparently contradictory state of things when he identifies the *jotuns* with the fates, who, he says, were not Danes, but seem to have been "a still earlier (Finnish) race, out of whom the Gothic conquerors made their *trolls* and *giants.*" [1]

With this last reference I must bring these remarks to a conclusion. I have purposely ignored many considerations which naturally present themselves to one; but my object has been, not to deal with the magical and unreal qualities often attributed to the trolls, but to demonstrate that the people so designated by the Norsemen were actual flesh-and-blood. Nobody who reads the references to the "trolls" on the western side of the Atlantic can assert that those were anything but real people, and it can hardly be assumed that the word "troll," when used by the same Norsemen on the eastern side of the Atlantic, a month sooner or a month later, bore a perfectly different meaning.

[1] Thorpe's *Beowulf*; London, 1875; Pp. 76—77 and 390.

UNSPOKEN.

BY REV WALTER GREGOR.

In performing certain ceremonies, the performer had to keep complete silence, to make the ceremony effective. The ceremonies were generally performed at stated times, mostly after sunset in the twilight "atween the sin (sun) and the sky." When the ceremony had to be performed with water, the water was commonly drawn from a ford, or from below a bridge, a spot, where "the dead an' the livin' cross," and up the stream. The ceremonies, so far as my knowledge goes, were employed but for two purposes—Divination, and the cure of disease. The water, drawn in silence, was usually designated "unspoken water." The word "unspoken" was employed at times to designate other substances gathered in silence, and used in the cure of disease, as, e. g., "unspoken nettles."

Examples of silence in ceremonies of Divination are first given, and then of the cure of disease. Evidence of the same custom is adduced from other countries, and then reference is made to the custom among the Greeks and Romans, among whom it was very prevalent, as their literature shows.

DIVINATION BY THE BIBLE.

The girl who was desirous to see her future husband had to read, after supper, the third verse of the seventeenth chapter of Job : " Lay down now, put me in a surety with thee ; who is he that will strike hands with me ; " wash the supper dishes, place below her pillow the Bible open at the passage read, with a pin stuck into the verse, and go to bed without uttering a single word, after reading the verse. The future husband appeared in a dream.

"THE SANTIE BANNOCK."

On "Shrove Tuesday," or "Fastereven," "Fastrenseven," "Brose-day," "Bannock-nicht," a cake was baked, called, in some districts, "the santie bannock." It was baked after all the pancakes were baked, and of the same ingredients, but of a much thicker consistency. The baker had to do the work in silence, and every sort of means was used to make her break the silence. If in an unwary moment, her tongue was loosed, another took her place. A ring was put into the cake. When baked it was cut into as many pieces as there were unmarried persons present. Each chose a piece. The one who got the ring was the first to enter into married life. I have taken a hand in this ceremony.

DIVINATION BY THE PLANT "YARROW."

A young girl, if she wished to know who was to be her lover, adopted the following plan—She went, on the first evening of May, O. S. (12th), "atween the sin an' the sky" and, without speaking to any one, gathered some of the flower Yarrow, or "the thousant-leaft flower" (thousand-leaved), (*Achillea-millefolium*), repeating the words :—

> "Good-morrow, Good-morrow
> To thee, brave Yarrow,
> And thrice good-morrow to thee,
> I pray you tell me, or to-morrow
> Who is my true lover to be."

She carried it home, put it below her pillow, went to bed without speaking a word. Neither must she speak till morning. During the night she saw her lover in a dream. My informant's mother did this.

(Corgarff, Aberdeenshire.)

CURES FOR WITCHCRAFT OF THE "ILL EE" IN ANIMALS.

A silver coin with a cross on it—a florin at the present day —is taken and laid at the bottom of a milking cog, "atween the sin and the sky," in the evening. The one who does this sets out with the cog to a place in a stream of water where

" the dead and the livin' cross," and draw water up the stream, and fetch it back without uttering a word. A little of the water was given to the animal that was ill, to drink from the cog with the silver coin still on its bottom. A little of the water was dropped into each ear, and the sign of the cross was made on its back and the remainder of it poured over it in the name of the Father, Son, and Holy Ghost. If it was a human being that was to be cured, the same course was followed with the exception of dropping the water into the ears.

(Corgarff, Aberdeenshire.)

TO TAKE OFF WITCHCRAFT.

A woman had to spin without speaking, a hank of lint on Sunday during the time of divine service. The thread was twisted round the neck of the one on whom the spell had been cast.

(Told by a woman 80 years of age, who saw the ceremony performed. Portsoy, Banffshire.)

When a cow or any other animal fell ill, and the "ill ee," (evil eye) or witchcraft was suspected as the cause, "Unspoken Water" was administered as a cure. The water was taken from a part of the stream where "the dead and the livin' cross," *i. e.*, a ford. The usual time chosen for drawing the water was after sunset, "atween the sin (sun) and the sky," but sometimes in the "silence o' the nicht," *i. e.*, about midnight. It was, usually, one that fetched the water, but at times, two went. They must not speak to each other, and if they chanced to meet anyone that saluted them, they must pass on without speaking. Not a word must be uttered, till the draught of water had been administered to the ailing animal. A shilling was put into the cog, on setting out to draw the water. On returning, the water was given to the animal, and the cog was turned upside down. If the shilling stuck to the bottom of the cog, the animal was under the spell of a witch, but the unspoken water had taken effect, and a cure would follow.

My informant has been sent on an errand of this kind.

(Strathdon, Aberdeenshire.)

A CURE FOR HEART DISEASE.

The one that was to perform the cure, before setting out on the journey, repeated the words :—" In the name of the Father, Son, and Holy Ghost, I am going to do this for so and so ; and O God ! remove his (her) disease." The operator took an iron pail and tied it round with three threads as hoops and set out to draw water from a stream at a point where " the dead and the livin' cross." From this spot, three small stones were lifted, one for the head, one for the heart, and one for the body, and water was drawn up the stream in the pail, or other iron vessel. These were carried to the house of the patient, and the stones were placed on the hearth, among the ashes over night, and the vessel with the water was laid in a safe place, commonly in the milk-house below the lowest shelf. Next morning the hot stones were dropped into the water. The water and stones were kept till next morning, when they were carried back to the spot from which they were taken and thrown down the stream. The three threads were removed from the vessel and each thread was cut into three pieces and burned while the following words were repeated :—" In the Name of the Father, Son, and Holy Ghost, remove so and so's trouble." During the fetching of the stones and the water, not a word must be uttered by the one doing so. Sometimes, a companion went along to speak to anyone met.

(Corgarff, Aberdeenshire.)

CURE FOR FEVER OR ANY LINGERING DISEASE.

The one that was to carry out the cure had to set out in the morning "atween the sin (sun) an' the sky " or during the twilight, to a stream that formed the boundary between two lairds' lands and draw water from it in a " tree luggit cap," *i. e.* in a wooden basin with three " lugs " or ears formed on the turning-lathe out of a block of wood. On the journey back the operator had to turn round according to the course of the sun at three separate spots, three times at each spot. On reaching the door of the house in which the patient was, the operator had to stand at the door till the moment the

disk of the sun appeared above the horizon when the water
was blessed in the name of the Father, the Son, and the Holy
Ghost.   The operator then entered the house and presented
the "capful" of water to the patient in God's name.   The
patient drank three draughts or "hawps" of the water, the
first in the name of the Father, the second in the name of
the Son, and the third in the name of the Holy Ghost.   A
cure was effected.

(Corgarff, Aberdeenshire.)

UNSPOKEN WATER.

Two brothers lived on a small farm in Strathdon, Aberdeenshire, along with their sister.   It was harvest, and the two
brothers were busy all day in the harvest-field.   They had an
ox grazing in a field at a little distance from the dwelling-
house.   After the day's labor was over, and after supper,
the two set out in the "gloamin'" to fetch home the animal,
and carried a halter to lead him.   They soon secured the
animal, as they thought, and set out on their homeward journey.   The two jogged quietly along shoulder to shoulder,
with the animal following quite gently.   After walking for a
time they halted to look behind them, and the animal they
had in the halter all of a sudden bolted with a loud bellow,
and escaped.   The two in their surprise at what had taken
place, fancied they saw a large animal with huge horns running from them.   In their fear they took to their heels, and
never halted till they reached home.   When they entered the
house, they were in a state of great excitement, and told
their sister what had taken place.   Said the good woman, in
afterwards telling what had befallen her brothers :—" Bonnie
kent I faht (what) ailt them (was the matter with them).   I
rins (run) t' the wall (well) for oonspoken wattir, an geed
(gave) them a sup o't, and that made them a' richt.   Taht
wiz't (was it) it they hed (had) hailtert bit (but) water vielpie."
The ox was found next day.

The same custom is met with in different parts of Europe.
"In der Osternacht—gerade um die zwölfte Stunde (vor
Sonnen aufgang) soll man aus einem fleissenden Kreuzwasser
gegen den Strom Osterwasser schöpfen, aber kein Wort spre-

chen. Das hält sich das ganze Jahr, und ist gut gegen allerlei Uebel vornehmlich gegen Schreck und wehe Augen."

W. von Schulenburgh, *Wendische Volkssagen und Geb-rauche aus dem Spreewald.*

Here is another example, but with a variation as to the mode of drawing the water :—"In den Osternacht gehen junge Mädchen an einem Bach und schöpfen dort still—schweigend das Osterwasser. Es muss immermit und nicht gegen den Strom geschöpft werden. Dasselbe ist heilsam, vertreibt die Sommersprossen und macht das Gesicht schön und Glanzend." Witchel, *Sagen, Sitten, und Gebrauche,* aus Thuringen, p. 197.

Another example of a cure for a cow when " der Nutzen genommen ist" is recorded in *Zeitschrift für Volkskunde,* p. 360 (11). "Des Abends nach Sonnen-untergang wird er (a certain decoction) stillschweigend in das fliessende Wasser Getragen."

The same custom is found in Sweden, in Aland :—"Man far ikke tala, när ett fynd ur jorden skall upgräfvas ty da draken bort det." *Kyare Bidrag till kannedom om de Svenska Landsmalen ock Svenskt Folklif, vol. 11, Smärre Wedelanden,* p. 1.

CURES FOR TOOTHACHE.

The patient takes a little oatmeal, puts it into the palm of the hand, and, in front of the fire, allows the saliva to drop on it. The meal is then kneaded, baked, and carried to a point where two roads cross, and buried. The whole ceremony must be performed without a word being spoken. The cake gets the name of the " Dumb Cake."— (Corgarff, Aberdeenshire.)

Let the patient go to a stream where three lairds' lands meet, and take three draughts or " howps " of water from the stream, with the mouth. Three stones are then lifted from the bed of the stream, one of which is placed in the mouth and one in each hand. In this fashion the patient walks home, goes to bed, and lies all night without uttering a word.

My informant saw this done in Corgarff, Aberdeenshire, about sixty years ago.

Here is a cure for toothache :—

"Nar man har tandpine, skall man en tarsdag aften efter solnedgang ga hen till en hyldebusk i et markskjoel og af hylden skoere en pind. Med denne pind skall man prikke den tand till blods, som man har ondt i, og derpa soette den pa sin plods in hylden og ga stiltiende hyem, sa bliver man fri for sin tandpine.

Ibid. Fjerde Halvergang Iuli. Dram ber p. 137, n. 391.

Two examples may be given from Belgium ; and both relate to the cure of toothache :—

"Aller, sans saluer les personnes que l'on rencontre, dire cinq paters et cinq avés devant une croix ou une personne a été tuée et placer sur la crois une piece d'un sou."—*Bulletin de Folklore* 11, p. 7, n. 12.

"Aller à une eau courante sans parler à personne et y boire un verre d'eau fraiche. *Ibid.* 11, p. 8, n. 27.

The same custom of keeping silence on certain religious ceremonies prevailed among the Greeks and Romans. Among the Greeks the technical expressions used regarding this sacred silence were : εὐφημειν to keep silence, hold the tongue ; εὐφημία, silence during religious rites, and ἔυφημος, religously silent. A common expression was εὐφήμει, or ευφημειτε silence ! hush ! be still ! So ευφημειν χρή, Arist. : Nul. l. 263 εὐφημος κὰς ἐσεαλδώς, Στομα συγκλεισας, Arist. Thesmoph. l. 39 Another example may be given from Eschenes, εὐφημον κοίμησου σεόμα, Ag. : l. 1247.

Among the Romans there was the "sacrum silentium."

"Utrumque sacro digna silentio mirantur umbrae dicere" Horatii Carm : II. 13. ll 29, 30,

Seneca refers to the same : "Imperatur silentium, ut rite peragi possit sacrum nulla voce mala obstrepente."—*De Vita beata*, 26.

The formula used by the Præcones in enjoining this silence was "Favete linguis." See Horatii Carm. III, 1, l. 2.

Propertuis says :—

Sacra facit vates : sint ora faventia sacris, Ut cadat ante meos icta juvenca focos" v. 6,

Tibullus says :—

" Quisquis adest faveat, fruges lustramus et agros, Ritus ut a prisco traditus exstat avo."

II. 2, ll. 1, 2. See *Ibid.*, II. 2, ll. 1. 2.

One reason of this silence may be found in the words of Horace (although there is some doubt about the correct reading)—

" Male ominatis
Parcere verbis."

iii. 14, ll. 11, 12.

Silence was kept lest any word might be uttered to offend the spirit or deity.

Another reason may be the following :—In the thought of primitive man, disease was attributed to spirits of evil. When a cure for any disease was attempted, every means had to be used to conceal the attempt from the spirit. No words, then, were to be spoken, lest the attention of the spirit might be drawn to what was to be done.

A KIND OF WORSHIP OF THE DEAD IN FINLAND.

BY PROF. KAARLE KROHN.

(From the Researches in Finnish Mythology by the late Prof. Julius Krohn.)

THE Finns in Finland are divided into two tribes, the Tavasts and the Carels. The former, who had settled in the west part of the country, came under the influence of the Swedish rule, and the occidental division of the latter again became dependents of the Russian empire, and of the Oriental church. Only three of their westmost countries were separated from the rest of Carelia and surrendered to Sweden in 1323. Of these countries two were situated at the seaboard, but the third one, called Savo, lay in the interior of the country by the lake Saimac, the outflow of which is through the cataract of Matra, the second Niagara in the world. This population in Savo became the proper colonists of the interior of Finland. The Tavasts, as well as the Carels, certainly made long shooting and fishing expeditions into the wilderness, but they always returned to their native places, where they lived in large village communities. The Savolax people again appreciated more individual liberty and independent ' household. As soon as the native place had become unable to satisfy this want, they moved farther into the country. Their own hunting-grounds soon were inhabited, and they did not find any other expedient than to occupy the wildernesses in Tavastia and Carelia.

This could naturally not be done in a friendly manner, but the Savolax people often had to endure bloody attacks from both sides. Nevertheless their colony made great progress in the 16th and 17th centuries, so that besides their original territory by the lake Saimaa at present almost all of Finland north of the 62d and 63d degrees of latitude is inhabited by a population from Savolax. But this is not

enough. When the Swedish realm during the Thirty
Years War was enlarged, a great many of these settlers were
sent to the conquered provinces, as, for instance, to Livonia
and Pomerania and particularly to Ingria, where, up to this
day, the population around St. Petersburg is of Finnish and
for the most part of Savolaxian extraction. They were also
called by the Swedish Government to settle in the woody
border-land between Sweden and Norway and the descendants
of these Savolax people are still living in Vermland. Not
even here was their disposition for colonization satisfied,
but the Finns in Vermland took a very active part in the
attempts at colonization made by the Swedish Government
in the 17th century, on the banks of the River Delaware in
America.

Concerning the Savolax people in the 16th century we
know that, although they had long ago been converted to
Christianity, they kept up many of their heathen customs
and put up many of their carved idols in places where they
intended to settle. Of another heathen custom, which was
attended to immediately at the founding of a colony, there
are still some memorials left. As they throw light upon the
important question of the worship of the dead, and at the
same time show how a religious cult can degenerate into a
mere conventional custom, I take the liberty to call your attention to them for a few *moments*, ladies and gentlemen.

When one or several members of a tribe or family had
moved to a new place of abode, the first care of the settlers
was to select for the farm a place for " karsikko," that is to
say, they left a grove of trees in a suitable place in the vicinity
of the house. In this grove a tree was lopped when some-
one in the house died, and this was repeated for every one
who died at the farm, for grown up people as well as for
children, for members of the family as well as for servants.
From the moment the first tree was lopped they began to
sacrifice there to the dead. These sacrifices which were not
performed separately for each of the dead persons, but for all
of them together, were of many kinds. When a bullock
was killed at the farm the first dish of cooked food was
carried to the grove. When in spring the first fish was
caught the dead person's share of the food must be set apart,

5

before any one was allowed to taste it.   In autumn, at harvest
time, a birch-bark basket of every kind of corn was taken to
the place of sacrifice ; in the same manner they did with the
crust of rye-bread.   If at any time they had received a comparatively large sum of money, a small copper was taken to
the place of sacrifice before they could use this money to
some other purpose.

The earliest change concerning the " karsikko," that
took place was when they ceased to look upon the menials
and servants as belonging to the family.   They were not
thought capable of doing harm in any way to the persons
living at the farm.   Another change in this custom took
place, when they, by and by, ceased to snag a special tree for
the children, and then later on they did it for no other grown
up people than for the host and hostess, and generally also
for the oldest son.   In the course of time the grove of sacrifice was reduced to a single tree, which retained the name
of "karsikko."   In a suitable place in the vicinity of the
farm, generally either by the road or at the sea-shore, a
sturdy fir was chosen—hard-wood trees were never used—and
the dry branches were snagged off from below, but the sound
ones were left.   When then at the farm an esteemed person
died, for whom it was considered necessary to make a sacrifice,
the lowest sound branch was lopped from the tree, and the
sacrificing at the foot of the tree commenced.   In the same
manner a branch from the "karsikko" tree was lopped at
the death of every one of the more esteemed members of the
family, and thus that tree became the common "karsikko"
of the dead.   Such a tree has been found in the parish of
Vütasaari in central Finland.   It was an old fir, so thick
that two men could barely measure its periphery with their
arms.   The tradition tells that it had been planted at the
foundation of the farm, that always before some one in the
family died, a branch fell down, and that when the last
member of the family, an old woman died, the fir itself
broke down.

When they now a days make a " karsikko," the tree is
lopped along part of the stem from the lower end upwards,
and from some place the bark is excorticated—sometimes the
side is carved quite even—and in the bark the dead persons

initials, the year of his birth and that of his death, and some-times, also, the dates are cut. But not all the "karsikkos," are made of growing trees. The end of a board, in which they have carved the above-mentioned marks and then fastened it on to the wall of a cold house, is also called "karsikko." In the same manner, they cut the defunct's initials, the year of his birth and that of his death, in a large stone that happens to be near the court-yard, or also in a slab of stone that is put against the wall of a house, and this is then also called "karsikko."

To the worship of the dead belongs also "karsikko," which the persons who follow the dead to his grave, make on the way. They lop a tree, cut in it the usual marks, and take a dram to the memory of the dead. In the "karsikko" thus made they leave one branch like an arm, generally pointing towards the church. During a passage by boat, the "karsikko" is made at some place where they stop, the oars-men relieving each other. If in that case there should not be found any fir trees, but only birches, they carve the end of a board, which then is nailed to a tree. Sometimes the "karsikko" is made in a rock. In the parish of Kristine, at the shore of Louhivesi, there is a steep mountain, called the Graphic Mountain. On the side of it, which is five fathoms high and two fathoms wide, the dead persons, in-itials are cut, which their followers have done. Beneath some of them are also the year of their death and a cross.

Still another kind of "karsikko" there is, viz.: those erected to the memory of some misfortune or some remarkable event. They are made by lopping a tree and carving in it the year, or by erecting a stone with similar marks on the spot. Between the parishes of Nurmes and Sotkamo at the eastern frontier of Finland, a traveller saw, in 1892, by the road, a fir, in which they had with an axe cut through the bark the image of a man, and beneath it some marks, prob-ably the year. From the post-boy he learned that near the place, on the other side of the road, a mad woman had a few years ago hung herself. In the parish of Kijanta in northern Finland the "karsikko" was made on account of a suc-cessful fishing; such a one was also to be found on the shore of the parish-clerk! Along the torrents of Kijanta and below them, there were several "karsikkos," especially in the place where they had found precious pearl-mussels.

When somebody for the first time visited a farm, it was thought proper to make him a "karsikko." For this purpose they chose a fir tree which was lopped so that only the top, and in some cases also the lower branches were left. In the middle part of the tree, however, two branches were left, if the "karsikko" was made for a married person, and only one branch if it was for an unmarried one.[1] The branch of the tree dedicated to the guest pointed sometimes in the direction from whence the visitor had come.

In the same way they acted when, on a long journey, a person came to the border of regions unknown to him. When they reached the last stretch of wood close to a town, the whole party stopped, and he who travelled here for the first time made himself a "karsikko." He lopped a tree all the way up to the top; an unmarried person left the top; a married one cut it so that there arose two tops; a widower spared not even the top. The lopped branches were put into a heap in a row on each side of the path leading to the tree. These trees were also called "brandy-trees," because he who had made the "karsikko" was obliged to offer a dram, which was taken on the heap of the lopped branches. Such "karsikkos" were also made for school-boys near the school town. Probably the servant did the cutting, but the boy was obliged to stand the treat.

Two miles up the country from the town of Fredrikshamn on the shore of the Gulf of Finland, there were by the road some lopped fir trees. The middle branches were cut out for middle-aged persons and the lowest for aged ones. When a tree was in a suitable place it was lopped for persons of different ages. Quite close to the town, there was such a fir in the village of Husula, behind the new cemetery of the town. It was mostly the Savolax people who made these "karsikkos," but it is not at all impossible that some of them were made by the part of the people from Tavastia, who lived in

---

[1] Also in the tree, lopped for a dead person on the way to the cemetery two branches towards the wood were left, if he had been married, but only one branch toward the road if he had been unmarried. In the same manner the trees were lopped, which at the burial were put up on each side of the door of the house. These trees were also called "karsikkoo."

the nearest neighborhood of the Savolax people. At least they used in the parishes of Hollola and Nastola to make "karsikkos" for them who saw the town for the first time. In the parish of Titti there was a custom in near connection with the worship of the dead. On their way to town they made "karsikko" not only for him who travelled here for the first time, but for the old people too, whom they thought to make such a journey for the last time.

From the preceding we have found three different kinds of worship of the dead, represented by a sacrifice-grove, a special sacrifice-tree, and a memorial without any religious signification. The oldest form must have existed already at the time when the Savolax people emigrated from Vermland to Delaware. That they had not forgotten their Finnish magic in their long journey, is shown by a notice from the year 1653, when two Delaware-Finns, a man and a woman, were sentenced for sorcery.

Ladies and gentlemen! These first Finns in America have long ago changed their nationality. Towards the end of the 17th century they had fused with the Swedish colonists. Together with these they had in the 18th century accepted first the Dutch, and afterwards the English language. Their descendants are at present entirely Americans, whose Finnish extraction an historian would have difficulty in finding. Perhaps there are some of these honored folk-lorists, assembled at the Congress in Chicago, the ancestors of whom at the banks of the Delaware, have in the aforesaid manner honored their forefathers from the remote Finland. It may be!

FUNERAL CUSTOMS AND RITES AMONG THE SOUTHERN SLAVS IN ANCIENT AND MODERN TIMES.

BY VID VULETIC VUCASOVIC.

Honorable Congress,—The Southern Slavs (Süd Slaven) have popular traditions of a very glorious kind, and these traditions, even now, especially among the Servians (a generous and heroic people) are repeated by the *guslar* (bards) and by the *pripovjedač* (story-tellers) in songs and in recitals,[2] which Vok Stefanovic Koradzic, Servian savant, first gave to the scientific and lettered world.

The Slavs of the south occupy the Balkans ; at the east the Bulgars, the Servians from the east to the south, and the Croats and the Slovenians to the west. These groups combine with each other, especially the Servians and Croatians, who have almost similar customs, into a principal group, that is the South Slavic group.

There are in these later days political factions, and a kind of religious fanaticism, which have brought out certain differences between these various branches, and especially between the Servian and the Croatian ; Servia belongs chiefly to the Orthodox Greek Church, and Croatia to the Western, or Roman Catholic Church. A judicious ethnographer sees in the South Slavs a single Slavic stock, under various names, which has had a single common source.

The Southern Slavs above all honor the departed, and therefore, upon the Balkans, there are thousands and thousands of colossal monuments called *stecci* (standing stones). Under these historical monuments repose the Slavic heroes. These monuments are most numerous in Bosnia and in Herzogovina, land now occupied by Austria-Hungary, and they form hundreds of necropoli. These same *stecci* com-

[1] Translated from the Italian by Lieut. F. S. Bassett.
[2] See episode upon the battle of Korovo in 1389, sung by the Servian Bard (Guslar).

mence as early as the 4th century of the Christian era ; they
are numerous from the 12th. to the 14th., in the epoch of
national independence in Bosnia, and already begin to decline
in the 18th., since from that time simple sepulchres with
medium and small crosses are seen.

These monuments were erected over their dead, and so are
called followers of the National Bosniac church, which was
known to the world, especially in the west, under the title of
the Bogomila or Patarena church, etc., while the followers
called themselves simply *Brothers* or *Christians*. The church
spoken of was certainly not Manichean, but Rome and Byzan-
tium accused her of it, because the priests of the Bosnian
church would not learn the Greek or Roman language, nor
the cumbrous rites, because they wished to adore God in spirit
and in truth. Many Christian people, in the middle ages, had
clothed the religious dogmas in superstition, a thing then not
done by the followers of the Bosnian church, investing the
pure faith with superstitions of an invisible world, divining
certain occult or mysterious powers, and combating against
these with fasts and prayers, wherefore the soul, after death,
passes into the light. They respected the dead, saying of
them that their souls had already passed into light, and they
raised monuments to them, separating them, leaving them
detached under their own designation, by groups, under
families, and in common necropoli.

These monoliths are enormous ; sometimes they weigh as
much as a hundred tons, and are for the most part of a calcareous stone. In the beginning, the Slavs found in Bosnia
and Herzogovina, Roman sarcophagi (such as are found yet
to-day), and which they imitated, but, as is shown by the
sketches accompanying this, only in their forms.

The most interesting to the folk-lorist is the fact, that all
four sides of the monuments are covered with sketches of
funeral rites and customs, that is to say, there are graven
there *Carmine*, or the rites, which lasted seven days, also
called *Sedmine*. Here it is to be remembered that for the
most part is sculptured the funeral dance, which they danced
backwards. They are composed of women and men, for the
most part in odd numbers, as for example, *three, seven*, etc.
Besides the rites there are sculptured also some episodes of

the life of the defunct, whom they represent either as a great hero, or as a hunter fond of the chase, which was the chosen occupation in the middle ages of feudal lords and free men. The defunct is on horseback with falcon in hand ; in others, with the lance in rest, engaged in a duel with a rival ; in others he mounts his horse, with his faithful dogs at his side, after a sta 's horns, a wild boar, etc. The monument is varied in its sculptures ; there are seen stags, does, boars, falcons, hounds, etc. At the feet or at the head of the defunct is sculptured the target or shield, with the dagger or sword behind it, as arms of the defunct, or signs of trophy, such as they used in the times of Frederick Barbarossa, the Emperor, great master of tournaments.

The patricians and all the nobility, that is to say, the feudal seignors (*vlastela, vlastelicici, plemici*) erected these monuments, and the people buried their dead around the sanctuary, and possibly carved on the *kami* (stones) or *bilig* (signs) the instruments of their calling, or a rose, a bee, etc.

The followers of the Bosnian church erected in the beginning, as I have said, like monuments, called to-day by the people *stecci, groke-place*, (Greek-stones), *kami* (stones), *bilizi* (signs), *maseti* (big stones), etc.

We should not also exclude the followers of the Romish church, the Byzantine, and, lastly, the Slav servants of the same place, because they erected almost similar monoliths, but at a posterior epoch, and they are for the most part crosses, prostrate stones, or rather headstones like a small obelisk.

Unfortunately, the monuments with inscriptions are few in number ; in one necropolis of two or three hundred, but forty are found.

The inscriptions are in Slav, with ancient Bosniac letters (civitica bosancica) like the fac-similes : *" This is the sepulchre of Ivan Pas'lovic."*

The inscriptions are laconic, and in them is shown *love towards God, towards the nation*, and *for heroism.*

From some specimens (from two hundred inscriptions which I have copied in Bosnia, in Herzogovina, etc.), one may judge of the original epigrammatic style. Here are the specimens :

This sign rests over Signora Vukava, with my good (wishes), for while she lived she served me faithfully, now dead, she has served me.

(*a.*) I preferred her living, I buried her when dead.

In that time I was the best man in *Dubrave* (his native land.)

I pray you, brothers and gentlemen, not to disturb my bones.

(*a.*) And I pray you, not to tread upon me ; I was as you are, you will be as I am.

(*b.*) This is the sepulchre of the good Serv, Miotinic ; approach, brothers, and mourn.

Thrice accursed be he who shall disturb me.

(*a.*) Accursed whatsoever stranger who shall dare to intrude his progeny here.

(*b.*) Whoever shall annihilate this monument (bilig), God will kill him.

(*c.*) Whoever shall destroy this writing, accursed by God.

(*d.*) Whoever shall remove this, accursed be he by Father, Son, and Holy Ghost.

Who steals these bones ——.

Oh God, have pity, in thy mercy, upon me !

Upon other monuments it is said, also in praise of the defunct :

(*a.*) The good hero ; (*b.*) The celebrated hero ; (*c.*) The good hero and man ; (*d.*) The good cavalier.

The inscriptions about other heroes end :

Who does not beseech (does not humble himself to) any man, not even the most powerful.

Elsewhere it is simply recorded :

Here lies Ivians Komlinovic (name and lineage of the hero).

Here lies the good Radal, son of the leader Stipan (Stephen).

(*a.*) In the name of God. Here lies the servant of God, Prince Radoslav Sirinic.

Give men, O God, the Christian grace.

This house is that of Milutin Marojevic and of his wife Vladisava, and of their sons.

To the Southern Slav, even though dead, the natal soil is sacred, the noble soil of his grandfathers, as is shown by a few examples :

Here lies upon his own *noble land.*

(*a.*) Here lies Vittso upon his own noble possessions.

(*b.*) The good cavalier on his own inheritance.

For the most part, at the end of the inscription is recorded who placed the monument, as in the examples :

This is the sign of Prince Radoja, of the great Bosniac prince, and his son, Prince Radic, places it with the aid of God, of his faithfulness and of his son, nor with any other company whatsoever as assistance, but alone he placed it.

In the name of the good God ! This Mihal erects to his lord, to Prince Vuk.

Here lies Radve Prigoevic Obradovic, and his mother Tradisava puts the monument here.

Here lies Mihal Veselinovic, and the three brothers put the stone over him.

His seven sons put here the monumental stone.

The donor of the monument employs for the most part the formula *siece i pisa,* meaning *sculptured and written,* as,

And over him carves the stone his chieftain, Miotos of *Luzice,* with the aid of God, and by the grace of Prince Paul, which entombs Ventko, thanking God.

Often these sentences and national epigrams are recorded, with the title of *Kovac* (faber) which they add to the man's name as an epithet, for example :

Radoc Kovac (*a*). Ogost Kovac made me (*b*). Grubac Kovac (*c*). Semoradid wrote this form : Bolasnia Bogacic (*a*). Vukadin wrote it (near the Bosnian clerks). Upon the monument of a renegade of the family of the Servian despot. Vuk Brankovic, the Christian epigrammatist writes and carves upon the theme in this way :

And he perished in the battle of the despot. This (is the) monument of Mamut Brarkovic, at his own cost, at Petrovo-polje (field). Blessed be the hand that carves and writes.

To the end that the honorable Congress may have a clear idea of the Bosnian inscriptions, I repeat three of them entire, two of them with fac-similes :

Here lies Radivoj Ilic, of Rama (region in Bosnia), of Kovacevo Polje (field). (Fig. 1.)

In the name of the Father, and of the Son, and of the Holy Ghost. Amen.

FIG. 1. ANCIENT BOSNIAN INSCRIPTION IN CUKLICI.

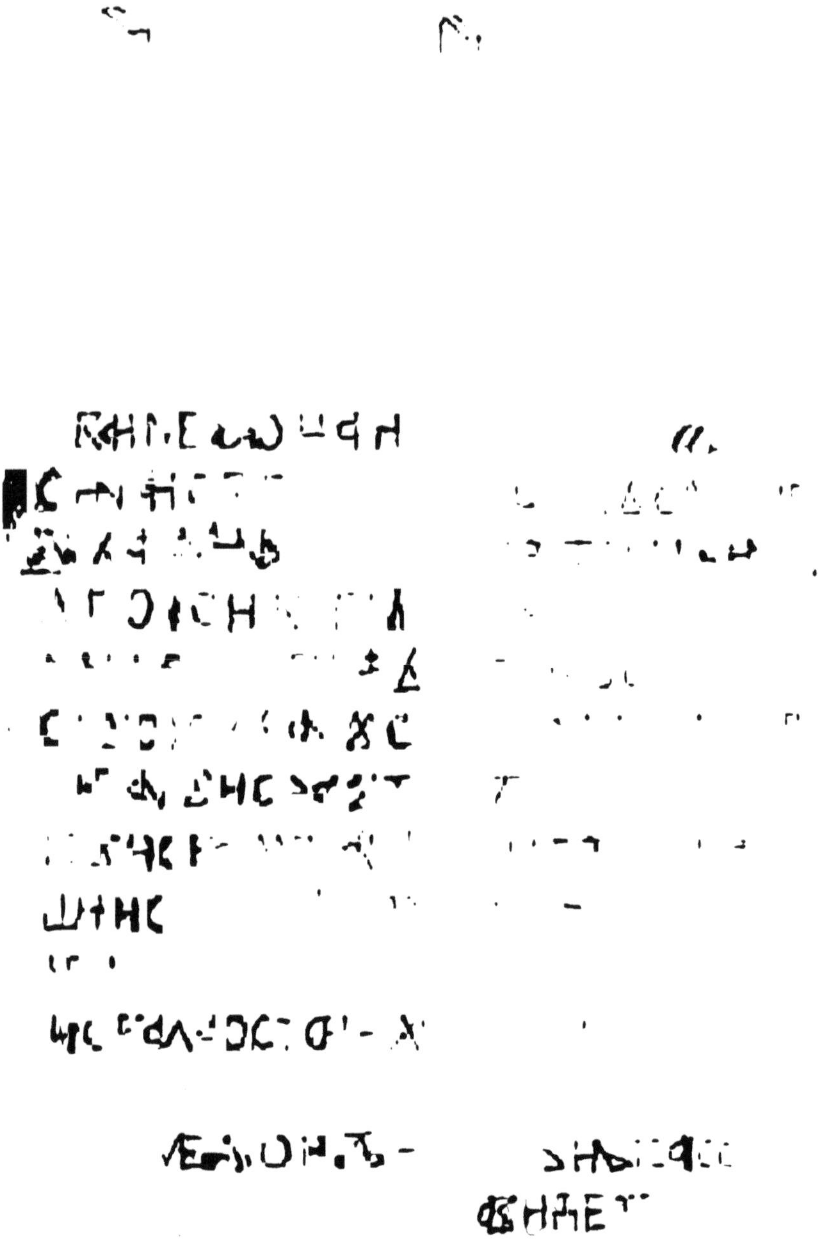

FIG. 2—ANCIENT BOSNIAN INSCRIPTION OF THE XV. CENTURY, A

N

Here lies Vigarj Milosevic. (Fig. 2.) He served the Ban, Stipan, and the King Tursko, and the King Pobisa, and the Queen Gruba, and the King Ostoja. In that time King Ostoja came and quarrelled with the Duke (Stefano Kosaca, duke of San Saba), and with Bosnia and against the Hungarians Ostoja went out. In which distant time came the end of sight to me. Vigarj is already here on his own noble meadow under Kocevin. And I pray you, do not tread on me; I was as you are; you will be as I am.

In the name of the Father, and of the Son, and of the Holy Ghost. Amen. Here lies Prince Balic on his own land, upon noble territory, by the grace of God, and of the glorious King Tursko, Bosnian Prince over Visoko (Bosnian territory). I was ill here in Duboko (a locality in Bosnia), the (fatal) day reached me. Signora Vukam places this sign with my *goods,* so that, when living, she served me faithfully, and dead she has served me.

There are monuments without any symbolical sign and ornament, but they are only found, and rarely, of a curved (kuke) form, in the manner of a spiral, and simply banded (pruge).

Some of these stecci are placed on prehistoric tumuli of earth, particularly the primitive ones, because the first Slavs were already contemporaneous on the Balkans with the aborigines; wherefore it is important to know that the aborigines are interred under tumuli of earth and stone; and the later Slavs under the stecak or sarcophagi. The difference between the stecak and the sarcophagus is, the sarcophagus is hollowed out to contain the body, while the stecak is simply a standing stone, under which reposes the defunct in a ditch in the earth, in such a way as to make it solidly walled up, but for the most part without lime.

The stecak is in the manner of a sarcophagus, but varied in form and proportion, also assuming the shape of a tomb. It is embellished, for the most part, with crosses, which vary: trefoils, anchors, Teutonic crosses, etc.

The ornaments come then, and they are of various friezes and palms of Slavic fashion, and which are yet to-day used on cloth, upon wood, upon stone, etc., in the manner of trifoliate vines, of twisted cord, of zigzags, etc. Finally come the architectural features and the basso-relievo, like ordinary Roman, Moorish, etc. The figured part is the most interesting, after the inscriptions, since the hero, on horseback as I have said, is ordinarily turned to the left.

The hero is seen in the hunt, with dogs, etc., and near him, on foot, is the faithful shield-bearer. The cavalier is also with a falcon, and under him various animals, for instance, stags and roes. The most interesting, as I have said, is the dance backwards, that is to say, from left to right, seven, thirteen persons, etc., and the leader conducts the dance, as is read in a heroic song of the Southern Slavs :

" When I will see the decorated mourners turn backwards in the dance ; they commence to sing the mournful song, and in this they praise the hero."

The leading dancer has frequently the shield in hand, and the dancers (men and women) appear with a bunch of flowers in hand, more confusedly, stretched out like a chain. They dance as a sign of mourning, with uncovered head. Still to this day, as will be seen hereafter, they lament the defunct with lugubrious songs.

Many times the hero stretches his bow to kill a wild boar, the chamois and the golden-winged duck, as we read in the popular Servian songs.

Rarely the cavalier is sculptured trotting his horse with crusading banner, but he is often seen where the faithful bride or wife, or the old mother awaits him, and the con fratello (pobratim), and from him they receive the valiant war-horse. His son, his brother, his companion await him, and they rejoice that he has returned from the chase, or from some assembly of heroes, etc. This is also well represented in popular songs : " They stretch out the hands, they kiss the gloves ; they ask for the heroic salute."

" May he be happy whom thou hast procreated, and whom thou hast taught to govern with the knife (sword) : may thy hand be sanctified to the shoulder."

The heroes pray God that He may be merciful and propitious to them :

" He dances on foot ; he raises the hands towards heaven ; thanks be to God and to this morning."

FIG. 4. BOSNIAN STECAK. FOOTSTONE.

FIG. 6. BOSNIAN STECAK. HEADSTONE.

Sometimes the hero is shown leaning on the hilt of his sword, and his faithful wife has laid her hands on his breast. Sometimes the horse is shown on the *stecak* without a master, and according to the songs, behind the same, through his grief.

"Throw away the saddle, pull the rein."

Sometimes, also, the wife receives the horse without his rider, and holds up a garland of glory.

One sees on the monument, a child standing with folded hands, and, nearby, a dove or a cuckoo, as in the songs, "Shoot the russet cuckoo."

Otherwheres, near the cross, are two peacocks, according to the antique Christian custom, two doves opposite to two tapers, as was the Slav custom towards the dying.

The defunct is accustomed to hold the cross in his right hand, above him, and the demi-lune with the star (which is the dearest symbol to the South Slav, and which signifies fortune. It was then taken as a coat of arms by Bosnia). In the left he has a sword and defends himself against a mystic monster (azdajaidra) which would devour him.

Sometimes the champion walks, holding in his right hand a garland, and the left supported at his side. Of this latter I only make mention, through want of time, adding the description of one of the most antique stecci (it is a prison) in Dalmatia (fanali), near Ragusa, and may it be ab uno disce omnes. (Figs. 3, 4, 5, 6.)

The anterior part of the said *stecak* is divided into three fields.

1. In the upper part, towards the left, something like a dragon, with two feet. He opens his fangs towards a mythical animal with a double tail. This animal with curved legs, after the manner of a goat, strikes to the left. ?

Under this is a bird (a dove ?) with outspread wings, and in the third row a wolf, assaulted by a dog. Towards the left, a roe butts at a serpent, which is in flight.

2. The dance of ten (?) women, towards the left.

3. Two roes behind a stag, turned to the left. ?

At the foot of this *stecak* the growing half moon; under it the encircled star with a garland; under the star a woman who holds with both hands a basket on her head in sign of abundance as of endowment. At the bottom is a cavalier with shield, on horseback, who is playing at hurling the javelin (dzilit), or the stick (buzdovan).

On the posterior portion,

1. The dance of nine men towards the left.

2. Six birds of different sizes fly towards the left, and are apparently doves.

3. The dance of nine women towards the left.

4. Two roes behind a stag going to the left.

At the head of the stecak is a trefoil cross with two wax tapers attached to it, as symbols, which burn for the defunct at the point of death. (Svijece samstnice.) Under the cross is an inscription, very simple ; then underneath a cavalier on horseback, turned towards the left, who holds in the left hand the reins, and a falcon in the right. He has no helmet on his head (which is ordinarily made like a beretta). The inscription runs :

This Anko (John) writes, the nephew (son's son) of Utjesen, and companion now of Ljuboevic, the nephew (on the side of the brother, to the brother of his father) Pasitjen Ljuboevic.

Ordinarily, the stecci are placed extending east and west. Thus, as soon as the defunct is placed in the ditch, which is tolerably well made, as I have said, and covered with slabs of stone, on this is placed much earth, then comes the monument as an external sign.

The monuments, being transported from a distance, avoid being of great height, as in distant countries, although they are sufficiently so, perhaps, and very bulky.

For the most part, the trench contains one or two bodies, and rarely more. Seldom are any objects found near the defunct, and it seems that, as he came upon earth naked, so he would descend into the earth.

Often the defunct has perished in a foreign country, and the relatives raise a cenotaph for him upon the noble manor, without the body under the monument.

Stecci are found in Dalmatia, in Herzegovina, Bosnia, Old Servia, Albania, as far as Macedonia, but most frequently the most numerous and interesting are those of Bosnia and of Herzegovina, and therefore in studying them I have called

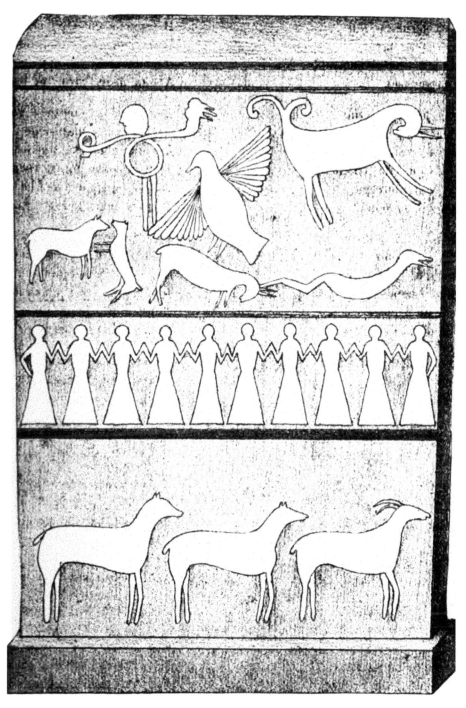

FIG. 5. BOSNIAN STEĆAK. FRONT VIEW.

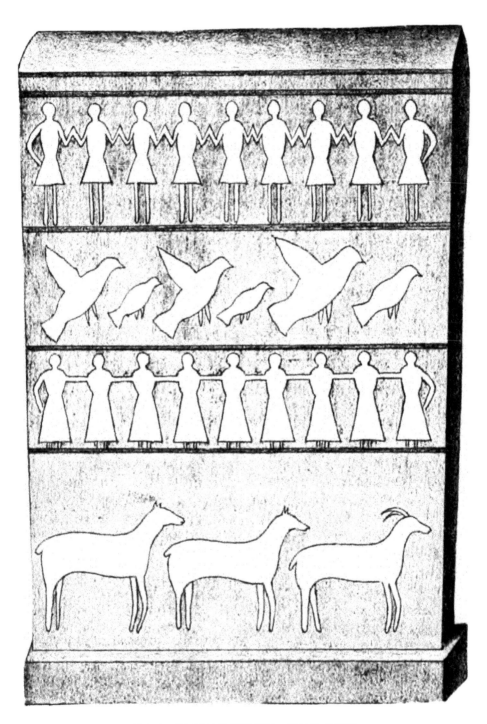

FIG. 3. BOSNIAN STEĆAK. REAR VIEW.

them *Ancient Bosnian Monuments,*[1] and I for the first proposed to the scientific world that there be undertaken a "Corpus inscriptionum Slavorum Meridonialium," with illustrations of the said monuments, but this is still in embryo, since the museum in Sarajevo (in Bosnia) is intrusted to the care of a profane man, and this idea of mine remains in obscurity; but if put into effect, it would enlighten us greatly, as well for popular tradition, as for the history of the middle ages.

Many foreigners have undertaken the study of these monuments, but they were ignorant of the Slavic language and of the usages and customs, and should give over this idea; among these Signor Arthur J. Evans makes an exception, and has rendered the greatest service to science.[2]

II.

I have been somewhat diffuse upon the rites and customs of the South Slavs in ancient times, and I will be brief upon the modern usages, because these are a survival of the ancient customs. I intend here to allude to those of our country, where foreign customs, principally the western ones, have not come into use. Certainly in Dalmatia, along the coast, and in part of Croatia, the said popular customs are very corrupt and are daily disappearing.

Here are some funeral customs, which are used in the Military confines (Lika and Grbava), in Bosnia, in Herzegovina, in Montenegro, etc.

[1] *Revue Archéologique* (A. Bertrand-Perot) 1869-415—*Nouvelles Archéologiques et correspondance.* "The trimestrial review of the Croatian Archæological Society has just entered into its eleventh year. Since the occupation of Bosnia by Austria, this Review has published a great number of Slavic inscriptions, of interest to the history of that province."

[2] "Through Bosnia and the Herzegovina on Foot during the Insurrection, August and September, 1875." With an historical review of Bosnia, revised and enlarged, and a glimpse at the Croats, Slavonians, and the ancient Republic of Ragusa, by Arthur J. Evans, B. A., F. S. A., with a map and fifty-eight illustrations from photographs and sketches by the author. 2nd ed., London: Longmans, Green & Co., 1877.

"Illyrian Letters," a revised selection of correspondence from the Illyrian provinces of Bosnia, Herzegovina, Montenegro, Albania, Dalmatia, Croatia, and Slavonia, addressed to the *Manchester Guardian,* during the year 1877, by Arthur J. Evans, B. A., F. S. A., Author of Through Bosnia and Herzogovina on Foot. London, Longmans, Green Co., 1878.

The person is hardly dead, when the body is washed, is clothed, and is put on a table, and covered with a white cloth. They put at its head a lighted taper, the one which the person held in his or her right hand when in the last agony, since it is bad for the salvation of the soul to die without the said candle.

When the defunct has expired, the people of the family ascertain it, and commence to lament and weep bitterly, and the women commence a kind of lugubrious song (naricauje, bugarenje) about the bier, and seem inclined to commence a funeral dance. The mother expresses herself in one way, the daughter in another, etc., and each wishes in her own way to lament, and to praise the defunct. The males commence to make the death known, the parish priest arrives with head bared (he remains uncovered at least until the burial is over, and even then he goes bareheaded for eight days wherever he goes). The mixed songs continue in the house of the defunct, and the head of the family looks out to provide all that is necessary for the funeral feast (*podusje, karmine or sedmine*). The relatives, the friends and the neighbors are invited to this banquet. The relatives are bound to bring to this meeting in the home of the defunct, wine and food. Ordinarily the banquet is held as soon as the defunct is interred. The burial then occurs on the second day, although formerly it took place after a few hours. The body, beyond the military frontier, is put into a wooden chest after the setting of the sun. The chest is not fastened up until the moment of burial. If the defunct had been an usurer or a blasphemer, etc., and was born under a fatal star (zla zviezda), they are accustomed privately to make a great cut under the knee, so that the evil spirit (hudoba, grijeh, hudic) shall not fill it with its breath ; they introduce into the mouth a tube, because otherwise he might become a vampire (vukodlak). Woe to the country if they unite together a male and a female (vukodlacica). This custom is almost extinct, as is that of going to hunt the vampire on Good Friday, by the sound of bells taken from the altars into the sepulcher, and to perforate the body with a stake of white thorn (truov Kolac) through a bull's hide, because, if the blood moistens any one of them present, so he after death will become a vampire.

The defunct is placed on a bier, which is composed of two sticks, ordinarily of cornel-tree wood (drenovina), called outside of the military border *vrljike*, in Herzegovina and also in Montenegro, *nosila*. These biers are interlaced with a cord (uze), or with a band of fagots or wythes. During the preparation of this, the women keep up the funeral chant, and there are such professional women called *bugarilje*, who know how to move the hardest hearts by making apparent by their lamentations the virtue (and the valor in Montenegro) of the defunct. This custom flourishes in Montenegro, and is also preserved in certain parts of Dalmatia. The relatives in Herzegovina turn the beretta (in Ragusa they dye it black) and the clothing inside out, and keep it so for various periods of time as a sign of sorrow and of mourning. In certain parts also of Bosnia, the sister cuts the caps and puts them on a pall on the sepulcher of the brother, in sign of the greatest abandonment and sadness, as also in Montenegro. The defunct is ordinarily put in the ground with his head turned towards the setting sun. When he is already lowered into the ditch, then the women commence with vigor to sing groaningly, then performing a species of funeral dance before the entombment ; they remain side by side holding hands, and advancing forward, and moving the head from right to left, they mention their own love, as if wishing to go down, I would say as if, through vivid grief, into the sepulcher. In Herzegovina, upon the tomb of a young girl is placed a richly embroidered handkerchief on a pole, and on that of a young man, an apple pierced by a stick. There, they also have a little refreshment in the cemetery, that is, they drink brandy, wine, etc., and they eat the *koljivo* (boiled wheat), which was used anciently.

When the funeral cortége returns to the house of the deceased, a woman waits at the threshold of the house, with a vase full of water and with a large spoon, and pours from it on the hands of the guests who enter into the house.

Infrequently all those invited to the banquet may be there in the house, but they can improvise tables also out of doors, in the court, etc.

First the poor are placed, and abundantly provided for ; they drink and eat abundantly. Healths are also drunk.

6

"Happiness to the soul which passed into the other life!"
"To the health of the living and to the repose of the dead!"
"God give health to the living and repose to the dead!"
When some rich person dies, the poor carry the remains of
the banquet to their homes, and some one, turning towards
the house gayly, sets to work singing on the way, "He lives
no longer, he eats not the bread, and God brings joy and
health to us, his brothers."

These are the principal points of the funeral customs,
usages and rites among the Southern Slavs. They are varied
and interesting, therefore, to the folklorist, while the epi-
graphist will find an extended field for investigating the
culture of the said Slavs (in particular, of the Serbs and
Croats), of a culture which existed but which is until now,
little known.

VID VULETIC VUCASOVIC AND VUKAN CEHO MIHIC

A FEW NOTES ON THE SONGS OF THE SOUTHERN SLAVS.

VID VULETIC-VUKASOVIC.[1]

PERHAPS no nation has so many folk-songs as have the Southern Slavs. Some of these songs contain five thousand or more verses. The first person who made a good collection of them was the great Servian Scholar, Vuk Stefanovic-Karazdic; and now the Literary Society, " Matica Hevatska," of Agram, in Croatia, is making a great collection, as are also various scholars, among whom are Dr. Fr. S. Krauss, Marjanovic, the writer of these lines, and others.

Heroic songs are sung by the Southern Slavs in a lugubrious tone, and the subject is a continual lament, because the whole group of poems is in commemoration of the terrible defeat of Kosovo in 1389, when the Sultan Murat I. shook the throne of the Servian emperors. The heroic song is accompanied by the " gusle " (an instrument of one string) and the lyric by the " tamburica," a kind of lute.

The lyric has different and varied themes and many lyrics have been set to music by the Croatian Kuhač and the Servian Pacu ; but only a small proportion, for the harvest is abundant, even in this field of the Southern Slavs.

The songs are divided into (a) mythical; (b) heroic; (c) love songs, that is those sung by young girls; and (d) ballads, which are for the most part love songs. This is a general division according to groups, but these groups also have many variations and subdivisions. The dirge certainly does not belong either to the first or the second group, although on account of the rhythm it might be connected with the second. The heroic verse, with few exceptions, is decasyllabic, while the erotic is multiform in syllables and accents. In heroic verse is sung chiefly the defeat at Kosovo and, after

---

[1] Translated by Susan Rhoda Cutler.

the defeat, the various avengers of the national glory, who are exiled for the holy cross and golden liberty.

The Mohammedan of Slavic origin also sings, but his is the song of the conqueror, which is quite different. A collection of these songs has been made by Dr. Fr. S. Krauss and Mr. Hermann in Sarajevo (Bosnia).

The love songs and ballads treat of love or other themes of a merry or light nature.

Here are examples of the four groups.

I.

Selection from the Song of the Battle of Kosovo.

The Empress Nilizza sets forth with majesty from the magnificent city of Krusevac. With her go only two dear daughters, Vukosava and the charming Mara. Toward them rides the captain Vladeta, on a horse of pomegranate color, a noble steed. Vladete rode hard, and his horse was covered with white foam :

The Empress Nilizza asks him :

"In God's name, I entreat thee, O Captain of the prince, why hast thou ridden so hard ? Dost thou not come perchance from the field of Kosovo ? Hast thou not seen the happy prince, my lord and thine ? Hast thou not seen the aged Jug Bogdan and his nine sons ? Hast thou not seen my two sons-in-law, Brankovic and Milo's Obilic, and all the other lords according to their rank ? "

Vladeta, the captain, makes answer ;

"I swear in God's name, Empress Nilizza, that I come this day from the field of Kosovo. I did not see the happy prince, but I saw his iron-gray horse. The Turks at full speed were pursuing it over the field of Kosovo, and I think that the prince has perished ; the nine sons of Jug also perished, and last of all, the aged Jug Bogdan ; and as for thy two sons-in-law, Brankovic and Milo's Obilic,——Milo's is dead, my lady ; he slew the Turkish emperor, Murat, and, as for the accursed Vuk, cursed be the one who begat him, cursed be his race and offspring ; he betrayed the happy prince, my lord and thine ! "

II.

A LOVE SONG.

The little bell is tinkling, the Shepherd is driving his sheep. . . " Listen, Shepherd, I will steal your lamb ! May it be my fortune to wed you ! "

" We two, a single cloak, a cloak of four breadths. I embrace thee, O my beloved doe ! " " O mamma, give me to my choice, and then may I also have my house in a garden of plum trees ! "

III.

A BALLAD.

A fountain of living water was gushing forth, was flowing in the midst of a little garden where Niljana plants her flowers ; at the fountain she cools her feet.

Oh, how beautiful she is ! How the world would fix its gaze upon her ! Well may the white day envy her ! Oh what pangs for a young hero, when he sees her thus barefooted, and yet again when he goes to a greater depth !

IV.

A MYTHOLOGICAL SELECTION.

The Moon chides the Morning Star :

" Where hast thou been ? Where hast thou been wasting thy time ? For three white days thou hast been wasting it."

The Morning Star replies :

" I have been above Belgrade, where the Jaksic were dividing the treasure : Jaksic Mitar and Jaksic Stjepan (Demetrius and Stephen) ; the brothers divided it between them magnificently, but again they fell into a fierce dispute. Would that there had been, at least, a reason for it ! It was about a mere trifle, about a black horse and a falcon."

I.

Posetala carica Milica
Ispred grada bijela Krusevca,
Snjome secu do dv'je mile koeri :
Vukosava i lijepa Mara,

K njima jezdi Vladeta vojvoda
Na doratu, na konju dobrame ;
Vladeta je konja oznojio
I u bijelu pjenu obukao.
Pita njega carica Milica :
—" Oj bogati, knezeva vojvodo,
Što si tako konja' oznojio ;
Neideali sa polja Kosova,
Nevigjeli cestitoga Kneza,
Gospodara i moga i tvoga,
Nevigjeli starog' Jug-Bogdana
I njegovo devet Jugovica ;
Nevigjeli do dva zeta moja,
Brankovica, Milos-Obilica,
I ostalu svu gospodu redom ? "—
Progovara Vladeta vojvoda :
—" Oj bogami, carice Milice,
Ja sam jvtros sa polja Kosova,
Ja nevigjeli cestitoga Kneza,
Al' ja vigjeh Knezeva zelenka :
Vijaju ga po kosovu turci,
A knez mislim da je poginuo ;
Pogibe ti devet Jugovica
I deseti Jug-Bogdane stari ;
A sto pitas za dva zeta tvoja :
Brankovica, Milos-Obilica,
Milos' ti je gospo, poginuo,
On raspori turskog' car-Murata ;
A sto pitas za prokletog' Vuka,
Proklet bio ko ga je rodio,
Prokleto mu pleme i Koljeno,
On izdade cestitoga Kneza,
Gospodara i moga i tvoga ! "—

II.

Zvonce zvoni, coban cera ovce.
—" Oj cobane, ukrascu ti janje,
Makar s tobom posla na vjencanje ! "—
—" Nas dvojica, jedna kabanica,
Kabanica od cetiri pole,
Zagrlim te slatko lane moje ! "—
—" Mila mati, podaj me za doku,
Ma mu bila kuca u sljivljiku ! "—

III.

Izvir voda *izvirala*,
Kroz basciou *proticala*
Gdje Miljana *cv'jece sadi*,
Na izvor u *noge hladi*.
Ja, kakva je *sv'jet je gleo*,
Dan joj beo *zavideo !*
Ja kakvo je *mlad'-junaku*,
Kad je onak'vu *bosu spasi*,
Pa jos dublje *kad zagasi !* . . .

IV.

Mjesec Kara svijezdu Danicu:
—" Gdje si bila, gdje si dangubila,
Dangubila tri bijela dana ? "—
Progavara svijezda Danica:
—" Ja sam bila vise Biograda,
Gdje Jaksici blago dijelise:
Jaksic Mitar i Jaksic Stjepane;
Lijepo se braca podjelise,
Al' se opet Guto zavadise,
Da je oko sta, vece ni oko sta,
Oko vrana konja i sokola." . . . .

THREE POLISH FOLK-SONGS.

BY MICHEL DE ZMIGRODZKI.

I WILL sing for you three of the folk-songs of Poland.   I am not a musician, do not even know the notes, but these songs which I shall sing you I learned by heart from the people themselves.   This is certainly folk lore par excellence.

The first songs come from the country along the banks of the Dnieper, a country of great prairies where the sound of a song fading into the distance, never re-echoes, but loses itself in infinity.

Picture to yourselves a regiment of horse riding over these vast prairies singing :

> Là-bas travaillent les faucheurs,
> Et par la prairie, par la verte prairie,
> Passent les chevaliers—hey ! hey ! les Koraks passent.
>
> Hey ! qui se trouve dans la prairie,
> Qu'il se rejoigne à vous, qu'il chante avec vous,
> Nous briquetons de feu, nous allumons les pipes,
> Que diable emporte la tristesse.

A few years ago the government of Austria was not so liberal as it is now.   Military service began at fifteen years, and was always in a district far removed from the home, so that the soldier should lose his attachment to his country and become a blind machine in the hands of the state.

The mountaineers of the Carpathians deserted in a body, and taking refuge in their mountains became brigands.   This trade being regarded by the lowlanders as a protest against the despotism of the government, did not dishonor them in their eyes, but was looked upon as heroism, and often lauded in popular song.

I will sing you a song somewhat modified by the arranger, but still truly a folk-song.   Imagine in an ancient forest a dozen brigands (who perhaps to-morrow will have disap-

peared) seated about a fire singing songs in which are mingled
spirit, boundless courage, and despair. You will note this
mixture of sentiment in the second part of the song, which
is always accompanied by a dance and orgies.

> Hé ! mes frères! versez dans mon vers,
> Ajoutez du bois à notre feu,
> Je vous chanterai une chanson joyeuse,
>   Chantons, rions mes frères, Cha ! cha ! cha !
>   Dansons, dansons, cha ! cha ! cha !
>
> On nous attrapera, on nous conduira
> Dans les pays étrangers.—Les cloches
> De notre village natale ne nous sonneront plus,
>   Hey ! dunaj, dunaj, da !
>   Hey . . . . dunaj, dunaj, da !
>
> Soyons joyeux, tant que nous pouvons,
> On ne nous laissera pas vivre longtemps,
> On nous attrapera, nous mourons pendus,
>   Alors nous ne chanterons plus, nous ne buverons plus.
>   Chantons, rions, mes frères, cha ! cha ! cha !

There is also a song of the Carpathian mountaineers in
whose melody you will catch that echo that reverberates and
loses itself among the mountains.

> Hey, Vistule! Vistule ! notre rivière bien aimé,
> Elle prend la source dans nos montagnes
> Et court vers la mer, hey, hey, hey.
>
> Joue moi ! joue une belle chanson,
> Que Dieu rend la liberté à notre pays, hey, hey, hey.

THE PREHISTORIC WORSHIP OF THE HOP AMONG THE SLAVS, AND ITS RELATION TO SOMA.

BY ERASMUS MAJEWSKI. .

The origin of the hop remains for the present an unsolved riddle in botany.[1] The origin of the name of the plant is likewise unknown. The majority of botanists, indeed, with Alphonse de Candolle at their head, reckon it to the European and American flora, but this opinion is not so much based upon ascertained facts as on the absence of proof to the contrary. The conclusion rests chiefly on the circumstance that hop is found *wild* everywhere in Europe, and grows even in countries where it never has been cultivated ; whereas, it is altogether absent in the East of the Old World. This fact, nevertheless, does not settle the question. If we consider the *wild* hop in any country as *degenerated*, the presence of the uncultivated form cannot prove the hypothesis of de Candolle. Then we have no answer to the question, where in its present geographical extent, to find the primordial origin of the plant.

The ancient Babylonian, Assyrian, Semitic, Egyptian, and even Greek and Latin monuments prove that the southern and south-eastern ancient peoples did not know the plant, the blossom itrobil of which could be used as an agreeable ingredient of beer. In the earlier middle ages of Europe, silence reigns on the subject of hop. The first traces appear in Central Europe about the 9th and 10th centuries.

In the documents of that period and the following we find *humularia*, as well as other Latin names in a curiously undetermined condition : *humulus, humols, humele, omulo, umlo, fumlo*, and even *hoppa*, and mention is made of particular *duties* being levied on hops. Entire silence is, however, kept by contemporary writers as to the beginnings of hop ; we are not told if the indigenous plant was cultivated, or if it was in-

---

[1] " Der Ursprung der Culturpflanzen," von A. de Candolle, Leipzig, 1884, p. 201.

troduced from foreign parts. Inquirers in search of a surer footing were led to seek for the key of the riddle in linguistic disquisitions. It is a remarkable circumstance, that at the very first sight all the European names of hop show a close etymological affinity, and that the names of *humulus, chmiel, horblon, hop, hoppe, hoppen,* derive from a common source. The question, which appellations are older, and where their origin might be found, was solved in various ways.

A. R. Perger takes the word *humulus* (mediæval Latin *humela*), for a latinized German name. Others derived it from *humlis.*

De Candolle, on the other hand, seems not to recognize the affinity of the German with the French, Italian and Slav names.

Weigand considers the Low German *hopps, hopp,* the primitive form, and derives it from the Latin *hupa.* The latter may be traced to Dutch and English.

The reason, however, given for the derivation of *hoppe* from hoppen, *hüppen* (to skip, to jump), to wit, that the hop climbs up poles, is decidedly weak, as creeping up with the help of tendrils cannot well be called jumping, inasmuch as that action has a distinct name : Ranke (tendril), ranken (climb, creep up).

Nevertheless, it must be acknowledged that the appellation of *hoppe* is very ancient, as it is met with in the 9th century, and is etymologically related to the barbaric *hubalus,* which latter evidently is the father of the French *houblon, horbelon* and *hubillon.* The supporters of the hypothesis that Germany is the cradle of the European names of the hop, have derived the Latin *humlo, humelo, humulo, humolo, humela, homelus,* as well as the Finnish *humala, hummal,* and the Slav *chmiel,* from *hoppe* or *hupa.*

Others maintain with Du Cange that *hupa, hoppe* have been produced by Pliny's form of *lupus* with the loss of the *l ;* whence the more modern forms are said to be derived.

Yet others compare the names of hops with the Greek κύπτω (to bend, to stoop) ; Grimm puts them in relation with the Latin *cubare* (to lie) ; de Candolle in his Geography of Botany calls our attention to the affinity of the Slav names with the Greek κλῆμα (sprig, graft, vine).

In general there is no agreement among linguists on this head.

In all disquisitions hitherto, the Slav names have been but slightly and superficially noted. They either were not taken account of, or were considered as younger and even as the youngest. Even the distinguished Miklosich derives them from the Latin *humulus*. Other linguists are more circumspect. Matzenauer and Buditovich abstain from giving an opinion in the matter, Fick gives no explanation at all, and Victor Hehn, profoundest in this question, makes the reflection that the Slav forms may be as well derived from the Central European ones as the latter from the former.

It is therefore clear that western science does not furnish evidence sufficient to settle the question, and I shall try to sift the matter independently.

As there is no mention of hop in the West before the 9th century, as the admixture thereof to beer begins on the sudden, and soon spreads so widely that governments consider it expedient to levy duties upon the article, we may conclude that the plant became known very recently. Of this we find undoubted mention made in mediæval writers. Bishop John of Liege, for instance, complains to Charles IV. of his income from the malt-tax being lessened by the introduction of hops. " In consequence of *a new plant*," says he, " *called humulus or hoppa*, being mixed with beer, the same quantity of malt is no longer used." The complaint had a good result, and the Emperor, in the year 1364, permitted one grossus to be levied per barrel of beer with hops. Pope Gregory confirmed this privilege later on to Bishop Arnold of Trèves. Some countries, the Netherlands for instance, begin to add hops to beer only in the 14th and 15th centuries; it is introduced into England and Sweden only in the 16th, while the Dukes of Bohemia levy a duty on hops in the 11th century, and many localities in Poland and Podalia even before the 11th century take their names from the hop gardens. Why should people have waited several centuries in the more enlightened countries without using a plant for admixture to beer if they knew it? Why did the wise bishop of the 14th century call it a *new* plant? This is evidently a riddle, and if we look for the native country beyond the frontiers of central and southern

Europe, the question arises, which country could furnish it to the Germans ? Evidently only the east.[1]

Consequently, we must investigate first of all, the age of the Slav names of the hop. Their great similarity strikes us at once. Common to them all is one and the same root, consisting of the consonants *h., m., l. ; m* remains invariable. We find in Polish, Russian, Ruthenian, Bulgarian, Old Slavonic, Bohemian,. Serbian : *chmiel* or *chmil ;* in Lusatian : *khmjel ;* the other Southern Slav forms are : *hmeiji, hmel, hmelina, melji, melika.* The occurrence of the same word with very slight changes in the whole Slav family may prove one of two things : either the great age of the word, dating from a time when the whole people spoke one language, or that the word was borrowed in late times from another race. In order to arrive at the conclusion which of the two cases is true, we shall turn to the Polish linguistic documents. Our herbariums and dictionaries of the 16th century have the word. It is not wanting in much older manuscripts. Written documents, quoting geographical names owing their origin to our plant, take us yet a step farther back. For instance : *Chmielno, chmielnik, chmielniki, chmielow, chmielowice, chmielowka, chmilno, chmiel. Chmielno,* a village in Kassoubia, is mentioned in documents of 1235. *Chmielnik,* in the district of Hopnica, is memorable by a battle with the Tartars, 1241. *Chmielnik,* on the Boh, is said to be one of the oldest towns in Podolia. *Chmielnik, chmielrko* (Bohemian *chmel nice,* Lausatian *Khmelnieza*) means a garden or field where hops is reared. And the aforesaid appellations of localities either owe their names to hop gardens or to the names of their proprietors : *Chmiekwski, Chmielnicki, Chmiel,* who evidently derived them from the hops. In both cases the source of the names, belonging to the beginning of the 13th century, remounts to the end of the 11th.

It will not be amiss also to mention that *Alberki,* an Arabian writer of the 10th century, relates that the Slavs used hops to make their hydromel.

Considering the scarcity of ancient Slav documents it

---

[1] The Egyptians did not use hops to their barley wine called *hag* and *zythos* (Columetta, Strabo) ; nor did the Israelites to their barley beer, *chithun* and *carian;* nor did either the Chinese or many other peoples of the far east and south.

might easily have happened that we could not find even a
slight proof of the hop being known to the Slavs at a yet
earlier age.   Happily we possess weighty testimony in the
Chronicle of Nestor.   Under the year 985 we find the following : "In the year 6493 Volodimer marched against the Bulgarians, and Volodimer made peace with the Bulgarians.
And the Bulgarians took an oath and said : ' Peace shall no
longer be between us, when the stone begins to swim, and the
hop to sink.'   And Volodimer came to Kiev."

The picturesque connection of the heavy stone and the
light hop is of great moment to us.   In a solemn oath the
half-savage chief would not use the name of a foreign or a
recently introduced plant ; he would not employ it in a rhe-
torical phrase intended to convince the prince of the im-
probability of breaking the peace.   To heighten the contrast,
he chooses an object of which the qualities are generally well
known.   If the stone is the symbol of heaviness, and water
the scale, we must acknowledge that the hop was very well
chosen as a symbol of lightness.   We shall not be far from
the truth in asserting that the saying was a kind of proverb,
or a form of oath.   In Polish prehistoric time we had an
oath : "by the stone in the water," and the expression remains to this day : "lost as a stone in the water."

Knowing that in the 10th century the hop was a
plant known and used by a people recently come from the
banks of the Volga (the strobils being called hops, as is
generally the case at present) we may conclude, appealing to
our manuscript document, that this knowledge was *at least*
several centuries old.   Even if the literal accuracy of the
speech recorded by Nestor would be questioned, the fact that
he used the expression would be sufficient proof that the
object, crystallized in a common form of speech, was known
to his contemporaries since ages.

Consequently, if the hop at that time was not an indigenous
plant in Southern Russia, its introduction would have to be
put back to the 7th century at least.

Nobody will contend that at the time when the hop only
became known in western Europe, it at once was introduced
into a country which for many years following was deprived
of the blessings of mediæval civilization.   This would be

altogether improbable. It is much easier to conceive the contrary to be the case.

If thus we have arrived at the conviction that the Slavs have not borrowed the plant or its name from the Germans, and that the former possessed it independently, it is now our duty to investigate some tracks which may lead us to the decision of a question, seemingly unimportant, but interesting as a page in the history of culture.

We will begin with a group of very easy words. In the Slav languages a state of ebriety, besides being denoted by the words *upic sie, pijany, pyanstvovati* (to drink, drunk,), and is also commonly expressed by words derived from *chmiel* (hops), comprising not only drunkenness arising from hops, but having the same general meaning as the former. *Podchmiclie sobie, pod chimelony* means not only to be drunk with ale, but with any other liquid. The same in Bohemian: *chmeliti nachmeliti, ochmelitise,* means to get drunk; *ochmela,* drunkard. In Russian the words: *pod, chmelkom, chmelem chmelek,* and the old Slavian *ochmelie* have the same meaning. There exist more derivates of the same kind.

The hop must have been known a long time to the Slavs in order that words could be formed describing its peculiar action, and that these words could represent their idea so well as to supplant others already existing. We meet no such derivates in the German languages, although the hop is used on a large scale since the 9th century.

We have no means of proving the age of these expressions, but such proofs, perhaps, will be found in directing our investigations to the east. In the mean time in order to study the Polish documents, we must turn to folk-lore.

The hop must be a plant known well and long ago to our ancestors, if no wedding even now can take place among us without the song of the hop. No doubt it was sung beside the cradle of our nation. But not only with us, with all Slavs, we may say, the hop is the most ancient symbol of happiness, pleasure and joy, the ally of love and the patron of marriages.

In all the provinces of Poland the typical song of the hop is heard with innumerable variations. The principal parts remain the same everywhere. The following, for instance, is

sung during the ceremony of putting the cap on the bride's
head.   It begins thus :

> Oh hop ! oh hop ! thou fertile herb,
> Without thee there is no joy.
> Oh hop ! oh dear one !
> Thou climbest low, and climbest high,
>   Dear hop ! "

> " If, hop, thou didst not climb upon the poles,
> Maidens could not become wives,
> But thou climbest upon the poles
> And takest the wreath of many a maiden.

The song is strikingly characteristic, and undoubtedly very
ancient.

If we take into consideration that at the present day the
whole people of Poland sing the song of the hop while putting
on the bride's cap, if we remember further that the hop has a
symbolical signification in the wedding ceremonies of almost
all other Slavs, and even of the Lithuanians, and if we read in
old Russian chronicles the description of such a ceremony of
" capping," we cannot but arrive at the conclusion that the
hop is an ancient Slav plant.   When Helen, daughter of
John III. of Moscow, was married to the Grand Duke Alexander, in Wilno, her companions undid her tresses in the
church before the altar of the Virgin, and having placed on
her head an ornament in the form of a magpie, strewed hops
on her hair.

The strewing of hops on the hair is no longer in use among
our rural classes, it is oftener done now with grain, but it
must have been the custom generations ago, as it still persists
in Polesie and some other parts under the form of spilling a
quantity of hops over the married couple.   In the Volhynian
Polesie the mother comes out with bread and salt in her
hands, strews hops and corn over the young couple, and introduces them into the cottage ; in other places before the
bride and bridegroom go to church the elder guests throw
hops, oats, and little geese, made of bread, among the company, and the children present.   A handful of hops is also
thrown on the floor.   In Lithuania the heads of the married
couple are strewed with barley.

I will not analyze our poetical monuments any more, as I
am obliged to enter into other details.   In the Ruthenian

songs our plant is also called a fertile herb ; the Russian songs say : " There is no joy without the hop." In the Bohemian the same elements prevail, but few of them have been handed down to us. It is remarkable that neither the German nor the Latin peoples have such songs and such customs. I do not affirm this absolutely, as not much has been done in this particular question, but, as far as I know the literature of the subject, only indistinct traces are to be found.

We rather turn to Lithuania. The ceremonial significa- ' tion of the hop is the same with the Lithuanians as with us, and their poetry as rich as ours in wedding hop-songs. There are details in these songs which it would be worth while to submit to the judgment of ethnologists, as they prove the old age of the verses, but I cannot occupy too much attention in this place. I will only say that many songs, although very different as to their character, begin in the same way as the Slav ones.

| O tu apoynèli | *i. e.* | Oh thou hop ! |
| Zalias puronèli | | Green puronèli ! |

or,

| Apoynèli puronèli | *i. e.* | Oh hop puroneli ! |
| Apoynèli Zaliusis | | Green hop ! |

The constant epithet of the hop *puronèli,* used as a noun, is interesting, as it cannot be accurately translated, and in song it is only coupled with the hop and the poppy. (Both intoxicating.) Perhaps this epithet is not accidental, as well as the Polish "nieboze" (dear one), which to-day is alto-gether out of keeping. But we will leave the songs.

We must take a view of the horizon our investigations have opened. We find that we have to deal with *a mythological survival, with a trace, a fraction, perhaps only a particle of some religious ceremony of worship that has survived princi-pally in the Lithuanio-Slav family.*

If our guess holds good, if we find the connection of the hop with a worship, we may perhaps arrive at the origin of the plant. Our imagination catches at the Greek worship of Bacchus, the worship of wine ; frenzy, revel and drunken exultation. His attributes are the vine and the ivy, both creepers and symbolic plants.

The worship of Bacchus in Europe has its historical origin in Thrace, and on the soil of Greece has developed into a thousand ramifications, which did not belong to it at first; but its oldest form corresponds best with our modern symbolization of the hop. If we bear in mind that many authors consider the Thracians a Slav people, that Thrace, once the frontier of the Lithuanio-Slav race, is that enigmatical knot, where the great historic moments of various Aryan peoples meet, the hypothesis of a certain mythological community of the hop and the vine will become stronger. I even venture to rest this hypothesis on the affinity of the name of our plant with the Greek names of various creepers, as e. g., Phaseolus vulg., Smilax aspera, Convolvulus sepium, and even Auercus, which Theophrastus and Dioscorides call *smilax*.

The source of the Bacchian worship is well known. The god of wine is in mythological relationship with the old Hindoo god *Soma*. Soma by his principal qualities strongly reminds us of the primitive, uncorrupted character of Bacchus. I believe that in the mythology of the hop there are to be found many elements and traces of the Aryan worship of Soma.

Soma is at the same time a beverage, a plant and a god. He is the god of pleasure, often sensually conceived; he bestows strength, delight and immortality on men and gods by the liquid soma. As a beverage he heals, inspires courage, enlightens, rouses the spirits, makes happy and intoxicates. It is a sweet and intoxicating liquid, something like beer or hydromel. The just on the other side of the grave drink and enjoy it in the company of the gods. This divine drink is mythologically akin to the *amrita* of the Mahabhârata, and to the *ambrosia* of the Greeks. The ninth book of the Rig-Veda is nearly entirely filled with hymns addressed to *soma*. We find numerous details as to the preparation of the beverage from a holy plant. Cow's milk or whey was added, sometimes honey, very often a fermented liquid extracted from barley or any other corn. Soma, as we see, was sometimes a beer, sometimes a genuine Polish hydromel. Grit was added:

roasted grains, wheat, etc. These latter items were only mixed with soma, destined for ritual uses; they did not enter into the common fermented beverage.

We do not know as yet what plant soma was; that it was a creeper is proved by its name *somalatá.* The modern Hindoos take for soma (somalatá) the plant Sarcostemma viminale. But somalatá is not a plant of the primitive Aryans, nor of the Hindoos. The importance of the worship rests in the fact that it is found in the Iranian documents. In the Avesta we have *Haoma* for Soma. The worship is the same but the plant is another. It was a creeper like the vine, with leaves like those of jessamine. *Haoma* also is a god, an intoxicating drink and a plant.

It was the same ancient worship which was brought away from their common country by both peoples. What plant soma or haoma was in its first home is not known to us. This circumstance, however, is of no account; we follow the wanderings of the religious worship, of the idea, not of the thing. This pre-Aryan worship must have been deeply rooted, as it obtained in so many countries, and maintained itself in great purity, considering change of soil and time. We see how the Aryans carry it with them over the northern Caucasus, across the Black Sea, through the modern Balkan countries to Greece. The proper Aryan plant failing, the vine becomes the object of worship. The climbing Thracian plant gives a beverage which strengthens, heals, intoxicates, excites, breeds merriment, and creates a comfortable repose. Such had been the effects of Soma or of the Iranian Haoma. The same worship was brought by the Aryans to the countries of Central Europe. No vines were met with on the road, and the worship could not cling to them as it did in Greece.

We remarked that a ferment of corn or honey was an ingredient of the ritual liquid and of the beverage of the ancient Aryans. And consequently the latter contained the elements of hydromel and beer. A holy plant being required for ritual purposes, a new one had to be chosen, as already had been the case in India and Iran. And so it happened that attention was drawn to a plant growing on the confines of Asia and Europe, a creeper, and containing an intoxicating element. As the plant probably had all the required qualities, it was made an object of worship and called *haoma*. In a wine-growing country the typical Aryan beverage gave way before the nobler juice of the grape, here it kept nearer to the primitive ideal of the priests, it scarcely changed, and has held its own with the Slavs in all its forms : beer, hydromel, and even *krupnik.*

The Lithuanio-Slav race in its march to the west carried with it the worship of Haoma, and the knowledge, the appliances and the name of our plant. I do not think I go too far in my hypotheses if I take the hop in that remote age to have had the primitive threefold signification of a god, a beverage and a plant. Later on the godhead was divided among a certain number of gods with other names, and the first name remained to the drink and the plant. We cannot admit that the Slavs, mixing the plant with the drink for the god, would have refused themselves the benefit. On the contrary, the admixture was approved of, and became the rule.

I now may venture to express my opinion that the intoxicating beverage of the ritual, known in modern times under the names of beer, hydromel and krupnik was called *chmiel.* The classic as well as the modern Armenian language throws a peculiar light upon this somewhat novel opinion. The Armenian language is the link between the Lithuanio-Slav and the Indo-Iranian group ; it contains some of the characteristics of both groups. If soma or haoma is related to chmiel, there ought to be traces of this relationship in Armenian. To be able to compare the Old-Persian *haoma* with the Slav *chmiel,* we should find in Armenian a word linking them as to meaning and as to sound. And we actually find in various Armenian dialects the words : *hrmelu, hrmol, hrmadz.* They signify *to drink, drunkard* and *drunk.* The language of the Ossetes, nearest to Old-Persian on one hand, and to Armenian on the other, has the word *hmallak* for chmiel—hops—(in the Iranian dialect), and the New Persian equivalent is *hymel* or *himel.*

Zonaras, the Greek historian of the 11th century, mentions a foreign beverage *humeli* which intoxicates, although it is not wine. It evidently was similar to the Slav hydromel or beer, the strength and taste of which were the admiration of the ancient classic authors.

We can no longer derive the Slav words and expressions, mentioned above from the *plant chmiel*, but from the beverage; the plant and the drink entered Europe at the same time surrounded by the glory of religious worship. We now understand the song of the hop better which begins with the apostrophe "Oh hop! oh hop!" exactly like a Vedic hymn, "O Soma, Soma!" And we understand at the same time its symbolic meaning, corresponding with the character of soma.

But scant are the remains of the worship of the hop among the Slavs in the form of songs, half-religious customs and the hop-dance. To the German race, even these are wanting; long wanderings in the far-off North were not favorable to the preservation of ancient traditions. Like the Hindoos, the Iranians, the Slavs, there can be no doubt the Germans also linked their tradition with some northern plant, and after that with another on the continent, if they did not lose the worship altogether. Neither the one nor the other was the hop; the proof lies in the near relation of the Teuton and Slav names for our plant, and at the same time in the absence of all traces of the worship on one side and of abundance thereof on the other.

It is easy now to understand why till about the 8th century no mention is made of hops in Western Europe, and that the acquaintance with the plant only spreads when by conquest, and gradual but steady assimilation the warlike German race penetrated ever deeper into the lands inhabited since centuries by the Slavs. Just about that time the German element took possession of the western Slav territories, and received the hop brought thither from the East. But the Germans did not accept the worship, which already had become faded in the memory of the Slavs. I shall quote only one instance in support of the view stated above.

In a document of 716, we still find in the Saalgau in Turingia, a castle (gród) the "*castrum Hamulo,*" vel *Homols.* Sixty years later, in 777, the Germans changed the name to *Hamalumburg.* I believe this to have been a Slav castle named from the hop. It might be objected to that there is no proof of the castle being Slav, and that the name could as well be German. I answer with William Bogustawski that till the 12th century the Germans had neither castles on the

Slav model nor cities of the Roman type. The consequence is that wherever we find a castle in Germany before the 12th century, we must conclude the lands to have been formerly Slav. As the Germans as early as the 6th century had conquered a great many castles, they gradually introduced their own ways and manners, and time and circumstances soon wiped out the traces of Slavism.

I will say no more about the vestiges I have found of Polish hops; it is time to conclude.

That the hop was not an European plant, that it was introduced into central Europe by the Lithuanio-Slavs is also sufficiently proved by its Finnish names. Before the waves of the Aryan emigration reached the shores of Europe, this continent was inhabited by Turanian tribes. Then, if the plant had existed in Europe, if only in the present Southern Russia (not to speak of the far West), it would have its indigenous Turanian name, in no way connected with the Aryan appellation. But we know no such name. All those we have, seem to be Aryan and have a common root. Hungarian, *kumló;* Estonian, *hummel, ummal, hummaled;* Finnish, *humala;* Tchouvas, *humlá,* etc., all of these signify hops.

It is impossible to suppose that the Slav names could be derived from the Turanian, because we should have to believe that the Hindoo Soma and Iranian Haoma have a Turanian origin. Such a supposition would shake all Ethnology and all Comparative Linguistics to pieces.

If the Turanians had no proper word for hops, and accepted the Slav appellation, they evidently did not know the plant before the Aryans came. So much the less could the Teutonic people have such a word before they came into contact with the Slavs. If they had a special word of their own, it could not have been like the Slav word, and what is more, it would have persisted most certainly. We see nothing of the kind. On the contrary, the linguists connect the Turanian, Slav, German and Latin names of the hop, and derive one from the other.

I hope that future inquirers investigating the survivals of the people's tradition, together with the connecting links, will add much to the handful of facts I have given.

The subject of my research being far from exhausted, I conclude my arguments by declaring that I do not at all think them the last word in this matter. It may be that I am mistaken in some points ; my excuse will be found in the fact that many details, necessary to create full conviction are not thoroughly investigated hitherto. I should be very glad indeed if my hypothesis could incite somebody to subvert it. I am only anxious for truth. But on the other hand, I cannot but feel gratified if my suppositions were strengthened by new and convincing arguments.

In recapitulation of what has been said, I venture to affirm as follows :

1. The hop is not an original plant in Europe.

2. Its cradle may have been the regions encircling the Caspian, more or less distant from the shores.

3. The time of its spreading in south-western Europe was the epoch of the migrations of the Aryan race towards the west.

4. It was brought to Europe by the Slavs several centuries at least before Christ. The Germans received it from them by conquering their lands in the 7th and 8th centuries.

5. Later on the hop was introduced in the whole of Europe, in some parts of Asia and in America.

6. The hop is called among the Slavs by the name of a liquid used for ritual purposes in worshipping an ancient deity of the same name.

7. This worship probably resembled to a certain degree the Hindoo worship of *Soma,* the Old-Persian worship of *Haoma,* and the ancient Greek worship of the vine, or *Bacchus.*

8. The origin of these nearly related religions is to be sought for in the unknown land inhabited by the primitive Aryans.

9. The Slav names of the hop-plant with the sound *hm* are the oldest for it in Europe. They are derived from the Aryan root *su,* and may be regarded as parallel to the Old-Persian name of Haoma.

10. The German, Turanian and Latin (the youngest) names of the hop are derived from the Slav.

BURIED ALIVE.

BY REV. H. F. FEILBERG.

Ladies and gentlemen : As a foreigner and a somewhat poor scholar of English, I am obliged to begin my paper asking your kind forbearance. I am only able to express my thoughts with difficulty in your tongue, and may perhaps give offence by more or less objectionable expressions. Will you kindly take the will instead of the power ?

Wherever I look I discover survivals. If one in a company sneezes, it was some years ago always a gentleman's social duty most politely to say : " God bless you ! " But who may tell why such a wish is uttered to a sneezing person and not for instance to a lady who coughs or gets an attack of hiccough ? Why am I to sign my mouth with a cross, when I am yawning ? Why am I wont to say, when I am happy and praise something in my house, among my cattle : " I want to say all this in a good hour ? " A married lady of my acquaintance would never pick up a pin on a Monday. If she discovered one on the floor on that fatal day, she pushed it carefully beneath the threshold, from whence she took it as soon as she rose from her bed Tuesday morning. In West Jutland, where I have lived for many years as clergyman, there is still to be seen in the eastern or western gable wall of some old farmhouses, a low arch filled out with bricks ; it is called the " corpse-door" (ligporten) by the old, and in former times, fifty years ago, the coffin with the dead body was placed in the large room inside that wall. On the day of the burial the bricks filling the " corpse-door " were thrust out, the coffin put out through the opening, which again must be walled up till the funeral procession returned from the service in the church. I don't doubt for a moment, that this is a survival from the widely-spread belief, widely-spread as regards time and countries, that if the opening through which the corpse is borne is again bricked up, the ghost of the deceased will not be able to find the entrance to his old home to frighten or to disturb the survivors. Among the "sagas," or legends of my fatherland is an often-recurring tale of immured men and women. There is hardly a castle in Denmark or in Sweden lacking those tales of immured ladies or swains. As far as I am able to see, these tales may mostly depend on a popular interpretation of an old Danish phrase, where to "immure" simply signifies to imprison, and the tales may be due to a kind of popular etymology. Quite another thing is it, when I notice the custom which I suppose may be found in vigor in some far-off nooks of my country till this very day, of burying living animals beneath the walls of a building, the threshold of a stable, or the gate of a farm. Before I try an explanation, I may be allowed to give some instances.

If the cows of a farmer cast their calves, he will bury a living viper, inclosed in a new earthen pot, and to this very day traces of this custom may be found. Some years ago an old building in a village, Kragelund, was demolished, and beneath the entrance of the cattle-house, a bottle containing the skeleton of the common viper was found. If a living mouse is buried beneath the hearthstone in a new pot, it is impossible for sorcerers to spoil the beer. Beer is still commonly brewed in the farms all over our country. If a number of mice or any other living creature is buried within small interstices in the boundary of a farmer's field, it will be impossible for sorcerers or bad people to cross the boundary, in order to make mischief. If the boundary, the gate, or the door is sufficiently watched, everything being within is left in peace. In Fyn, a ghost had its walk every night through the gate, but as soon as a dog was buried alive in the very entrance, the ghost was obliged to stay outside. In a farm on Laaland, a new stable was built, but in vain were the horses brought to their stalls in the evening, every morning they were found trembling, as if they had been working beyond their power. A "wise man," at last counselled the people to bury a dog alive in the stable, and all would be right, but the farmer did not like to bury his own dog, and thereby matters were left for a time, but as it came out, that an old woman some day had been looking at the work, the "wise man," said, "Never mind, you must only dig a deep hole in the stable, and you shall get a dog, when you want one." Well, the laborers dug a hole, and just as they were leaving their work a strange hairy dog came along sniffing around the place. As it approached the opening, one of the men kicked it down into the hole, and in spite of its howling, it was buried in a moment. Afterwards the ghost ceased to walk, and some favored the opinion that the witch, who had caused the mischief was herself buried in dog's shape.

In Kongsted near Soro, the townsmen in their turn yearly supplied a heifer. The finest calf was chosen, and when the day arrived a large trench was dug in the gateway or in the middle of the yard of that farm from which the heifer was to be supplied. In the trench was put some hay and straw, the heifer was led down, afterwards rafters and boards were placed over the opening, the space left was filled up with earth in the form of a small mound, afterwards each head of cattle belonging to the parish was led over the place, and it was deemed a favorable sign if the heifer were heard bellowing underneath, for that was considered as a good omen for the coming year. Later in the day, a feast was arranged, the guests danced till late in the night, and the more noise, the better luck to come. The heifer must die as it stood, and nobody was allowed to dig on the place. As late as 1875, a farmer in Mariestad in Sweden buried a cow alive, to cause the cattle-plague to cease in his stable. It would be very easy to bring forward instances of the same custom from Germany or from Scotland (cf. Black, Folk Medicine p. 74.) but what I have alleged from Denmark and Sweden, I suppose, will suffice to show the custom and point out how it was used as a kind of sacrifice to bury an animal alive, thereby to drive disease or evil powers away.

But the "sagas" have instances of another kind of sacrifice. Every year, the North Sea washes land away during the heavy winter gales, sometimes the fields of a whole parish have been destroyed. Now it has been told from former times, that a child was put in a barrel with a small coin, marked with a cross, in its hand, and buried alive on the very place where the attacks of the sea are most violent. This is in our days omitted, thencefrom the great loss of ar-able land near the outlet of the Limfjord. Those who have seen the violence of the sea during a southwestern gale, will easily understand that a barbarous or half-civilized people may look upon that power as one, which, if possible, must be propitiated. A similar power was the plague or, as we would say, the Black Death, during the middle ages. It was thought by the popular belief to be represented by two aged persons, a man carrying a rake accompanied by a " carling " with a broom in her hand. Where the man used his rake some few of the inhabitants escaped death, but where the woman swept the ground with her broom, every life was taken. Now the " sagas " tell of a small village, Gaderis, the plague there took every living soul away. The inhabitants of the neighboring parish, Ejsing, bought a gypsy's child, and buried it alive on the boundaries of the village, and the plague was obliged to leave its inhabitants alone. It is also told from the small island, Fur, that a living child is buried in the eastern part of the churchyard to stop the progress of the plague. In Dalsland in Sweden, people died by thousands, many fled to the woods, others travelled to far-off countries, the churches stood empty, and at last the survivors were too few to bury the dead. At last an old man from Finland arrived, the Finlanders are deemed wise men, strong in witchcraft. He said that no change would take place until something living was buried. First a cock was taken and put alive beneath the ground,—in vain ; afterwards a live goat, also in vain, and people were at their wits' end. At last they were counselled to take a child and try a human life. A poor beggar boy was induced to step down into a deep pit, dug on a hill, where the Daleborg river falls into the lake of Wennern. They gave him a large piece of bread and butter in his hand and began speedily to fill up the trench. The child, who understood nothing of it all, asked them pitifully not to throw sand on his bread. A few moments later he was suffocated beneath the earth. I remember another instance. It is told from France, that the ignorant people said during the plague in a certain city of France : " We cannot think of averting the disease, till we have buried a man alive ; let us throw our priest into the ditch !" When the priest afterwards went to an open grave to throw earth on a dead body, he was pushed into the ditch by his own parishioners and buried alive together with the corpse.[1] From Alt-Paleschken in Prussia a remembrance may still be found of a poor, old, idiotic woman being buried alive during a plague.

I may perhaps still in this connection name the tale of Quintus Curtius, the Roman knight, who, sitting on his horse, precipitated himself into the crevice that had sprung up on forum Romanum, as a sacrifice for his people.

No doubt but there might be many more instances advanced as to how people in former times have tried to guard themselves against the dark powers of Fate, revealing themselves through sea or sickness, by a kind of sacrifice. I take this word as it has been used, not to lay stress on its signification. And there is still another large group of "sagas" in which the same thought seems to prevail, that a living animal or a human life must be sacrificed to insure that a wall, a castle, a church, a bridge, may stand "for ever." In preference I take northern instances. Everywhere in my country tales are common of a kind of church-ghost, mostly called the "church-lamb" (Kirkelammte). Wherever it is seen, it forebodes death. A young mother sat weeping beside the cradle of her sick child; at once, hearing a faint noise, she looked up and discovered at the window a little white lamb standing on its hind legs and looking in through a pane. She understood instantly what the vision meant, gently pushed back the cover from the head of her child, its soul had departed, the "church-lamb" came for it. Another ghostly animal is the so called "death-horse" (helhesten), that at midnight slowly wanders from the churchyard through the lanes of the village on three legs with rattling shoes, and where it is seen stopping and looking through the window of a house, a person will die within. And there are other animals still, stags, cows, bulls, goats, geese that seem to have quite a similar function to perform, always to forebode illness or death.

Now the question arises : from whence have these superstitions arisen, and why are even these, mostly domestic, animals foreboders of death ? Still to this day "sagas" are told, how the builders of a church, when they were to begin their work

_____
[1] Crane, Jaques de Vitry, p 112, 268.

or perhaps when they were going to finish it, took the first
animal they saw on their way tó the place of work and bricked
it up in the wall, or below the foundations of the building.
This animal was looked upon as the guardian spirit of the
church, and as it was thought to live in or about the church,
it is no far off idea to let it bear messages from the kingdom
of death and fetch those who are "fey." Beneath the foundation stone of Tise church a lamb is buried, that the church
may stand to the end of the world. In the choir of the cathe-
dral of Roskilde a horse is buried. In the church of Dalby
in Denmark a goose or a gander is buried, in Mesinge a bull,
in Gūdme a sow, in Viby a black sheep, in Stubberup two red
bullocks, Tyregod church in Jutland is founded upon two
greyhounds, and so on. From South Sweden is told that no
church has been built there without either a bull or a cock
having been buried alive beneath its foundation.

The guardian spirit of the church, "kyrkogrimmen," is
supposed in Sweden to watch the church, taking care to prevent any disturbance or profanation of the holy place. As a
farmer's daughter late one night tried to look through the
keyhole into the church, she got her leg broken by the
"church guardian." He chooses his seat on the roof of the
church, when a funeral takes place in the churchyard, therefore the clergyman always will be seen looking at the church
roof, when he throws the three spadefuls of earth on the
coffin. The fact is, that he may see by the behavior of the
"guardian," whether the deceased is lost or saved. And in
Sweden it is a common popular belief, that if the old custom
of burying a living aninal beneath the foundation-stone of
the church is dispensed with, the first person buried in the
churchyard will be appointed as "guardian," and the first
child baptized in the church will be a poor deformed one,
and so it really happened in Vierstad, when the first baptized
child became a poor wretch for life. In some churches, a
human being instead of an animal is buried, that is said to be
the case in Hvidbjœrg church, Thy, where a boy was placed
alive beneath the foundation stone of the entrance to keep
ghosts and witches away. A similar tale is related from
Asarum church, Sweden. A human life is costlier than anything else, when a sacrifice is to be offered. Touching tales

are narrated of innocent children of whom the legends tell, that they have been buried alive beneath the foundations of large buildings. Many, many years ago Copenhagen was to to be surrounded by a wall, that its inhabitants might be shel- tered from assaults of foes. But in spite of every device, and of incessant working, no wall could be raised ; what was built up during daytime was destroyed in the night. At last the builders took a little innocent girl, placing her on a chair at a table, they put sweets and playthings before her and while she sat smiling and playing, twelve masons hastily formed a vault over her, closed it while drums were beaten and trum- pets sounded ; the child was buried alive, and from that day the workmen were able to raise the walls. You will perhaps allow me to quote another tale. In the year 1689 a heavy breach was made in the sea dike near Brunsbüttel during a heavy western gale, the country was flooded far and near, and ruin was impending for the inhabitants. The people were told that any endeavor to close the breach would be in vain, if a child was not put as foundation. Men were instantly chosen, the legend tells, who were to go out, and, if possible, buy a child. In one of the streets of Herzhorn they met a poor woman, called Talcxe Holms, carrying a child in her arms, a boy one and a half years of age. The men pressed her hard to sell her child, and at last she answered jokingly : yes, she might be willing to give up her boy, if they would pay handsomely for him, and she demanded, to get rid of the men at once, 3000 marks. After some haggling one of the messengers exclaimed : " Well, it is a fine boy, he may be worth the money, I take him," and instantly he pulls out his purse and pays down the money, to the indescribable dismay of the mother who, crying and wringing her hands, walked through the village. Fortunately she discovers Heinrich Knee, to whom she tells the sad occurrence, asking his counsel and help. He instantly sought the messengers out and compelled them with a bludgeon in his hand, to return the child to its mother. I proceed to give a variant of the tale. The child of a gypsy at last was bought for 1000 marks, but the case was still very difficult, as nobody wanted to take the child's life. At last a plank was put as a see-saw over the deep hole, and on the farthest end of the plank a wheaten loaf.

Being hungry, the child instantly ran out along the plank, tried to catch the loaf, bobbed down and fell into the pit. Three times it returned to the surface of the water, the first time saying : "Nothing is softer than the bosom of my mother !" Thereafter : "nothing is sweeter than the love of a mother." And the third time : but *my* mother's heart is harder than flint," and was seen no more. But afterwards the breach was easily filled.

Other sagas tell us how large castles were built. I only take one single instance, many might be adduced, from Germany. The castle of Liebenstein has never been taken by any conqueror, and the cause is, that a child has been buried alive among the foundation stones. A hard-hearted mother sold her child to be walled up, and while the masons began their work a cake was given to the child to keep it quiet. It looked out from the hollow wall : "I can see mammy still !" and when only a small opening was left : "I am still able to see mammy." And when the last stone closed the opening, the child's voice still was heard plaintively crying : "Mammy, I can't see you any more." It is to be understood that a mother like this cannot rest in her tomb, but must wander as a restless ghost till doomsday. It is to be understood, what a Low-German farmer said, speaking of those "sagas" : "I certainly have heard tell of a little child being bricked up in a wall, where they have put it into a wooden barrel, and given it a bun in its hand. The child has, with a happy smile, thrust out its small hands to get the cake, but I don't think that I should have been able to stand that smile."

You may find traces of this so-called "building-sacrifice" in many countries besides Denmark and Germany. In Cornwall is found a strong bridge near Rosporden. Many times the construction of a bridge there had been tried in vain ; as soon as a rainstorm swelled the river, it was destroyed. At last a messenger was sent to a witch asking her counsel. "Had you come sooner, you might sooner have been advised. If the bridge is to stand, a child of four years must be buried alive beneath its foundations. He must be put naked into a barrel and be given a consecrated light in one hand and a bit of bread in the other." A child of course was procured, a feast celebrated, and the poor child immured alive in the

barrel. After that day, the work advanced without hin-
drance, till the bridge was finished, where it now stands and
will stand in all eternity. But often during still nights a
young child is heard wailing. There may be many instances
besides. So is the holy Oran buried alive beneath the foundation stone of his own cloister. Especially among the Slavs
"sagas" of this kind are common. -I have been told that
hardly one of the large bridges may be found without either
a child or a grown up person having been buried there.
Among those "sagas" one is especially touching, the tale of
Manoli, the master-builder's young wife. He together with
other masters was to build the cloister Arges, but, every
night, the work of the foregoing day was destroyed in a
mysterious manner. At last he dreamt, that any attempt to
raise a building would be in vain if a woman were not immured. He told his fellow-masters the dream and the appointment was made, that whoever of the wives of the masons
came first the next morning, to bring her husband his breakfast was to be bricked up in the wall of the cloister; but a
solemn oath was sworn, that none of them might betray their
decision. Next morning Manoli's young, loving wife was the
first. Vainly he prayed God to let the rain-storm and afterwards the tempest keep her back; she advanced through
floods of rain, through the howling tempest, for she loved
her husband. When she came, she was asked as a joke to let
the masons wall her up. At first she allowed it smilingly,
but soon discovering the grim earnest, she entreated her husband to save her and her unborn child. All in vain, the vow was
given, the decree of fate unalterable, the cloister must be built,
and her last sigh was stifled behind the merciless bricks.

Only one tale more and I have done. In the year 1884,
Dr. F. Krauss tells us that a technical school was established
in Brod by the Sava river; twelve young girls were invited to
come there to learn weaving, pupils had come, everything
went happily on, when, unfortunately, the rumor was spread
that the Austrian government wanted to buy these girls to
immure them in, the new ramparts that were to be erected.
The girls fled instantly and were only with the greatest difficulty again induced to return to their work.[1]

[1] Krauss, Bauopfer, p. 18

When I now am looking back on these examples that legends have retained the remembrance of, how life, animal or human, has been given away to guard against the powers of the sea, of plague, to make castles unconquerable and bridges to stand in spite of storm and flood, the question arises : What may the original aim have been of these sacrifices of life ? I take it for granted that these tales are not wholly imaginary. The sacrifice has perhaps not been offered when this or that bridge, this or that castle or cloister has been built, but still a reality may be hidden behind those touching legends. Things of that kind have in former times happened. As to animals that have been buried alive, I am convinced, that here or there in the nooks of my own country, at least kittens and puppies have lost their lives in that way within man's memory. I shall not deny that the thought of a sacrifice to some mysterious power may have been working in the minds of those who have buried the poor animals alive. More than one of the sagas, as far at least as I am able to see, give evidence of a train of ideas like this. There is, for instance, a very characteristic saga told by Mr. Krauss among his "Südslavische Märchen." A Servian peasant was fortunate enough to save the child of a river nixie from an imminent danger. Shortly afterwards the nixie appeared before the man as a richly-dressed, venerable old man, asking him what he wanted as reward for his kindness. The peasant, being a well-to-do man, was content with his circumstances and answered that he wanted nothing at all. "Well," the water-sprite replied, "your house has a bad situation, let us search for a better ; come, I'll help you !" Arrived outside the nixie struck the earth with his golden rod, saying : "Proprietor, what do you want in lease when I am going to build my house here ?" A dim voice from the ground answered : "I want every life that is in the house !" "So much I will not give !" nixie replied ; he walked farther, again and again striking the ground in different places, repeating the same question. In one place the lives of husband and wife were demanded, in another those of the children, until at last the underground voice answered : "*I* demand nothing, am willing to make you prosper in every way, if you place your house here." "Build up your house here," nixie

8

said, "and you will be a happy man !" The idea is evident, the man who builds a house somewhere must pay a lease, a ransom, offer a sacrifice to be allowed to do so, at least as a rule.

With all that, a long course of customs, as far as I can see, point in another direction, which to me seems the primitive idea. Life is given away, sacrificed, to create one or more "guardian-spirits," that are to watch the place and keep away from it every foe, every disturbance or danger. An instance or two may throw light on this. From Farther India (Bangkok) missionaries have told that whenever a gate was to be built among the ramparts of the town, some persons were caught in the streets to be buried beneath the foundations. On the appointed day, the victims are in procession led out to the fatal spot, where a beam is hung in ropes over a deep trench. King and court are present, and the king, taking leave of them, enjoins them to watch the place, which he entrusts to their care, faithfully ; he has the hope that they will give warning instantly if enemies or rebels attack. As soon as he has spoken his last word, the beam hanging over their heads is cut loose and they are killed by its fall. Upon their bodies the gate is constructed, and the Siamese believe that these victims become "guardian-spirits." It is no uncommon thing, that a rich man, who wants to conceal his treasures in the earth, buries with them one or more slaves, that are to watch the hidden money.[1] I pass by, that customs of a similar kind are mentioned from Japan, from Tenasserim (British Burma), from Galam in Senegambia, from Australia, from the Chipkas of America, and shall only mention what has been told from India. A certain man having by the tribunal been deprived of a field belonging to him, led his wife out there and burned her alive, that her spirit after her death might haunt the place and make the sojourn there unbearable for everybody. When the arrival of the tax-gatherers was announced, or of another magistrate who was to undertake something against the Brahmins, these would erect a kind of enclosure, in which they piled a great deal of wood up, where they at last burned an old woman alive, believing that she after her death would return as ghost and harass those who had caused her death. And it is

[1] Mélusine IV., 14. (From 1831–32.)

told, that Brahmins have ordered their wives and children to lie down on the ground, threatening to kill them if their wishes were not complied with and often they are said to have fulfilled their menaces. From 1795, the English Government took very severe measures against this superstition, which in our century has been quite abolished.[1]

It seems to be a common idea that the ghost of a deceased person is more powerful, as well in every good as in every evil work, than a living person. I only name the custom of "fasting upon" an adversary, known as well in Aryan Ireland, as in Aryan India. Still it is not necessary to search among far-off countries or among barbarous or semi-barbarous nations for beliefs in relation to the commemorated customs. In Iceland is found more than one "saga" speaking of persons, who, after their death, walk about to do mischief. Having been unable during lifetime to call down revenge on their adversary, they harass and persecute him to death as ghosts; they even will commit suicide to get their vengeance sooner.[1] I must also lay stress on this, that the victim, man or animal, is buried in or under the gateway, the threshold, the boundaries of a parish, in the place where the sea is most dangerous. Originally the idea seems to me to have been this: we create a guardian-spirit to watch the exposed place, the house, the castle, the bridge, the boundaries of the parish, the beach; a spirit being more powerful than any living man, we want ghosts for mounting guard, they alone are capable of defending the place, and body and soul will in a certain manner keep together after death; where the body lies buried, the ghost keeps watch. I see this corroborated when I look to the saga literature of Scandinavia. Ivar, son of the Danish king Regnar Lodbrok, died king of a part of England. On his deathbed he ordered his men to bury him where the kingdom was most exposed to onsets of Vikings, for he hoped that those who landed near his tomb would get no victory. So it was done. When years later William the Bastard arrived at the shores of England, he, as his first work, opened the mound in which Ivar lay buried, and seeing his dead body uncorrupted, a large fire was lighted, in which Ivar's corpse

---

[1] Mélus. IV., 15, quoting Calcutta Review, January, 1877, p. 166.
[1] Arnason Thjodsögur, I. 222.

was burned to ashes. Afterwards he landed his army and
came off victor. The same is further illustrated by a Celtic
saga from Ireland. The Connaught men buried their king,
Eoghan Bell, according to his orders, with his red javelin in
his hand, his face towards the north on the side of the hill,
by which the Northerners passed when flying before the host
of Connaught. This was done, and ever after the invading
Northerners were routed panic-stricken, until at last they
made a great hosting and raised the body of Eoghan and carried it northward and buried it with the mouth down, so that
it might not be the means of causing them to fly before the
Connaught men.[1]

This seems clear enough. As long as the ghost of the deceased chieftain, together with his dead body, keeps the attacking or defensive position, spear in hand, in the mound,
no enemy can proceed beyond ; when the body is removed or
burned, the soul is incapable of watching the post. I may
quote one instance still. Bendigeid Vran commanded them
that they should cut off his head. "And take you my head,"
said he, "and bear it even unto the White Mount, in London, and bury it there, with the face towards France." And
they buried the head in the White Mount . . . . it was the
third ill-fated disclosure when it was disinterred, inasmuch as
no invasion from across the sea came to the island while the
head was in that concealment.[1]

But this is so very, very long ago and forgotten, who
knows, how long ago ? Well, but in superstitious beliefs now-
a-days, this or that curiously reminds of these sagas, it may
perhaps only be necessary to replace man by animal, a mighty
Celtic chieftain by a black cat. A couple of years ago I was
told from the northern part of our country, that it, within
the memory of man, had been customary to bury a living
black cat, sitting upright, beneath the threshold of the byre,
with her claws out. Just in that way the animal is to be
placed, and its posture is in a certain way the same as that of
the ancient Celtic king, it watches, defending the entrance
against any approaching foe whatever. I can't withhold the
observation with which I began this short paper : wherever I
look, I discover survivals.

[1] Folk-Lore, I. 243.   [1] Lak Ch. Guest Mabinogion (1877), p. 381, 383.

THE RISE OF EMPIRICISM.

BY OTIS TUFTON MASON.

By the phrase " the rise of empiricism " is meant the beginning of invention among mankind. There was a time when men commenced to experiment and to make observations upon phenomena, originally. According to some, Lord Bacon was the original experimentalist ; according to others, it was Aristotle. Perchance a few would allow Solomon a place in the list, because he said that man had sought out many inventions. But there never was a time when men did not invent, when they were not empiricists. The relation of such an inquiry to folk-lore should be made apparent in order to give it a standing in this congress.

The student of folk-lore is supposed to deal rather with survivals, with customs, with common beliefs and common practices. He deals chiefly with those who follow suit. He does not frequent patent offices, but places of assembly, and listens to the repetition of things that do not seem to have had an origin, or watches the doing of things that have been done often and often before.

It is not here denied that the mass of humanity are travelling together the broad road of custom, that each man goes on by a kind of automatism walking the same gait, that thousands tread in one another's footsteps, and that whole tribes and races get a trend and a set in everything they think, or do, or say. This is not denied ; it is rather affirmed and emphasized beforehand, lest some one might conceive the notion that the writer does not believe in custom at all.

It is with equal ardor maintained that there are delightful exceptions to this rule, and that these very exceptions constitute the genius of historic progress in all ages.

One man invents a machine in our day and thousands use it. One man writes a book and many read it. One man

plants a grove and the multitude bask under its shade.   One
man composes a song and millions of patriotic or devout
voices sing it.   One man devises an institution and nations
are blessed thereby.   So has it been since the origin of man.
This is the distinctly human characteristic.

If there ever existed a man who in his life never departed
from beaten tracks to do or think originally, he was an im-
becile.   Should there be found living in the suburbs of a city
or of the world a family or a tribe not contributing in the
least to that change for the better which constitutes the progress of mankind, that group of human beings have done this
favor, at least, of keeping alive the memories and practices of
the past, and have preserved the history of lower stages of
culture.

Invention has experienced a fivefold evolution or elabora-
tion,—1, in the needs or wants out of which all empiricism
springs ; 2, in the mental act, the process in the mind of the
experimenter ; 3, in the processes and products of the work, in
the manner of operation and in the thing effected ; 4, in the
rewards of the effort, public and private ; 5, in the tribal or
national genius and idiosyncrasies engendered.   From the
very first man worthy of the name to the latest decade of the
nineteenth century this empiricism has never ceased.

At the very first, as at the very last, invention springs from
two causes, needs and resources.   The wants, the appetites of
men, on the one hand, and the possible means of gratifying
them in each area on the other, constitute the stimulus to experiment.   As the wants of men are quite uniform in each
grade of culture, the resources of the earth, the total environment, varying in character and amount from place to place,
has been the uncertain quantity for each race or people.

The evolution of wants is seen in the creation of new desires with progress and the greater complexity of each want
as it became more exacting.   The hungry stomach of a savage, for instance, craves not more than two or three articles
of diet prepared after the crudest methods.   But the same
organ in the higher races will not be satisfied with less than
half a dozen viands at least, served in as many fashions.

The same is true of the desires for shelter, dress, sensuous
pleasures, social pleasures, intellectual gratification, religious

enjoyment. The progress of men in all these had been marked first by a more numerous and delicate body of wants and by a more widely diffused area of selection among the things desired.

The fact is that the most favored races and the most diversified areas seem to have found one another. Mutually they have aided each other, blessing and being blessed. The people exalted the land, the land exalted the people, the former stimulating empiricism, the latter exercising it.

The evolution of resources or of the sources of supplying wants has been a progress from naturalism to artificialism. The three kingdoms of nature supplied at first the raw materials upon which ingenuity was exercised. Men helped themselves, ate the fruits of the fields, perchance devoured meat raw, made weapons of stone, knew not the myriad uses of fire. This was the age of naturalism. There are a few favored spots on earth now where it would be possible for men to exist in savagery indefinitely with little artificial exertion.

But the wonderful fact in the study of ethnology is that in every quarter of the globe where savages have been found they had already mastered the book of nature for their wants. Every edible plant and animal had been discovered. The best wood for bows and arrows aud basketry, the best plants for textiles, many of the most potent drugs were familiar. The stone worker could tell you the finest material for each implement, where and under what conditions to obtain it, and the best method of its treatment.

Still more wonderful is the fact that the history of all our domestic animals, and of our staple foods and textiles, and plants of delight, is lost in the dim past. Before a page of history had been written, savage and unlettered peoples had searched the whole earth, tried every plant and animal, and picked out those that were capable of domestication, those that would yield the greatest amount of comfort and service willingly to man. It may be thought that men stumbled on all these. To admit this absurd proposition would not rob men of their honor. Those who have eyes and see not, do not observe. All the original grains and fruits and flowers had been for millenniums waving their resources in the very faces of the whole animal world without stimulating a desire to cultivate them.   But the rapidity of the evolutionary process since the advent of this inventive race is in no way better attested than in the ransacking of the earth for material by savages, and the enlistment of so many useful species before historic time began.

The second empiric evolution is that of the mental change involved in the act of invention.   The earliest experiments were not made in laboratories, they were of the simplest character.   The first of these was the power of apperception, which animals possess in a dormant condition only.   By apperception in this connection is meant the ability to take notice, to pay attention to.   The natural furniture of man seems most excellently fitted to stimulate him in this direction.

Nature having deprived him of hair, and nails, and cutting-teeth, and fleet limbs, and wings, and fins, she has left him little more than the power of taking notice,   He apperceived that his animal associates were rich while he was poor, but his necessities stimulated him to notice a little further that he could provide himself from his mother's bountiful storehouse with all these things that he lacked.   He does not seem to have been slow in noticing that these very creatures that surpassed him could be made to yield their excellences to him. Following the guidance of the folk nowadays, and the savage tribes with which we are acquainted, we do not require long to notice that most departures from the beaten track of industrial custom are not so much those "happy thoughts" which come to the peaceful mind.   The normal mind is not ever in the mood of apperceiving, nor are the brightest minds given to constant invention.   Men have always had "happy thoughts" it is true.

But nowadays men must get into a "tight place" before their empirical faculties are awakened.   A countryman with his wagon broken down three miles from home when night is coming on, or the hunter strayed from his camp with meagre resources, is not altogether a modern picture.

Men and women have been hard pressed always by the elements, by hunger, by danger, by fatigue, by the restless and inexplicable longing for better comforts.

The cerebral changes, the mental operations involved in

the invention of a way out of the humble savage's difficulties are the beginning of an evolution which ends in the great co-operative laboratories of invention, where not one man, but perhaps a hundred men, are required to conceive a slight change in an electric light, an air-brake, a chemical product, or a destructive weapon. The savage man inventing his rude stone axe by slightly changing the form of a natural object is the same absolutely in every particular as the experimental inventor in the laboratory of Edison, or Bell, or Krupp. No new faculty has been added to the mind of the latter. He merely occupies the last position in a series of mental activities that have grown more and more complicated from the beginning. Perhaps, after all, Watt is not the greatest of inventors. The devisor of marriage in groups, of the bow and arrow, of pottery, of the decimal system, may have been greater than he.

The third evolution mentioned in the progress of empiricism is the change and improvement in the implements and materials and products of invention.

The cave-dwelling is no more the ancestor of the palace than the stone hammer is of the trip-hammer; the carrying-strap across the forehead of the savage man or woman, of the freight trains and passenger trains; the stone mortar, or the Mexican metate, of the rotary mill or of the roller mill; the torchlight of the electric light. From one to the other end of these series there have been relays of human thought, adding fresh impetus to the progress from age to age. The evolution that has taken place in the tools and processes of empiricism resemble those that have taken place in nature. There has been a ceaseless change from homogeneous to heterogeneous structure, accompanied by a change from extension to intention of function. Processes and tools were exceedingly simple in structure at first, growing to more complex machines. In their working they satisfied many wants at first and only few at the last.

The definition of a savage invention, however, would not be in the slightest particular different from that of the latest patentee. It would be in either case a change in some pre-existing process or thing, for the purpose of arriving at some end more expeditiously or with greater economy. The thing in which the savage made his "improvement" was a natural object. He ground off the end of a conch to make a trumpet, or scraped out a cave to create a shelter. These two were the starting-points of other "improvements," so called. And so on each experimenter laid his superstructure upon the results of his predecessor's work. But when some skilled examiner goes to work on all these machines and methods of procedure and new substances, he works by elimination backward to the first man, the primitive patentee, and finds his device to be an intentional modification of some natural object or process for the first time by him devised to effect a beneficent end.

The exception to this concatenation of efforts and results might be the starting of new series from time to time. Benjamin Franklin and his co-workers would furnish an example in modern times, and the real Prometheus in primitive ages. Is it not curious to see, however, that the moment these new forces are developed they fall into the old traces and go to work doing the same drudgery that once was done with men's hands alone.

In this same connection we must not fail to notice the change from naturalism to artificialism in the laboratory of the inventor. The first empiricists had only hands and feet and bodily senses. Their workshop was under the open canopy of heaven. The tools were forged by nature. The processes were simply the ways of the animal world, the experiences of tyros, extremely minute departures from the methods of nature. But how changed in modern laboratories! The hand, the feet, the senses can no longer be trusted in the smallest particular. Instruments of precision are demanded, measuring inches and seconds by tens of thousandths, thermometers so delicate as to gauge the temperature of moonbeams, rolling mills making transparent sheets of gold, sensitive wires belting the earth so that the antipodes may converse. Extreme delicacy and accuracy and complexity characterize all our best efforts. The experimenter is hampered for want of better apparatus. The thought is more refined than the thing, and yet has been refined by the things it has created. It will go on refining and being refined indefinitely.

The fourth evolution of empiricism is the gradual change in the public and private rewards to the inventor. The first man who made a stone or a stick sharper to effect a definite object was both inventor and manufacturer and patentee and consumer of the product. In plainer words, his chipped axe or ground-digging stick (for this was before the age of fire) brought him more food, quicker, surer and with less effort. The consumption of this made him stronger and intellectually brighter and more joyous. He took to himself or attracted to himself more and choicer wives. His children were better fed and cared for. That was his self-bestowed patent.

Around him were men less favored, who wondered at him, respected, and feared, and obeyed him. He is now the chief, founder of a royal family, having on his shield two stone axes, or two pointed digging sticks crossed, for his escutcheon. Society has granted him a patent of nobility, and, on the principle that to him that hath shall be given, his vassals, as a reward for his being already able to get more food than he needs, give him a portion of their meagre supply in the shape of tithes and offerings. This was the first patent office. The right did not run out in seventeen years always.

The long series of public and private honors and endowments conferred upon inventors down to our day constitute the evolution, of which this is the starting-point.

The last evolution of which it is necessary to speak here is the unfolding of that national, or tribal, or family genius which constitutes the mark by which they have become known. The folk-lorist is thoroughly acquainted with this feature of my subject. In any community some families seem to have been predestined to certain forms of work, to develop particular ideas. That was their mission.

Should one of them move away, he would in some other sphere of action develop a fresh nucleus of that pursuit. Much more than families have great consanguineous groups, called tribes, repeated the same experiences. The folk-lorists of England discover groups of customs, groups of beliefs, that are peculiar. They cannot believe that a homogeneous people, now called the English, have passed through these clusters of experiences one by one. But they look upon these as the arrested developments of tribes, each of which was for itself laboring in the line of its own hereditary genius. The study of the four phases of empiric evolution leads us at last to the evolution of folk. Each folk becomes a unit when it has been isolated in the same peculiar region or craft until it begins to think and speak and act as one. When the traits become traditional and hereditary among its members, they retain them though they be carried away into captivity or overwhelmed by contest. They communicate their inventions sparingly to others by a kind of acculturation, making contributions to a common fund. But the *ensemble* of traits and intellectual products belong to them.

Each family of mankind in its native home, has invented a series of arts, the relics of which lie buried in their tombs and places of business. The history of their industries is written in these things. At the same time, by frequent trials and failures, they have invented languages and social structures, philosophies and mythologies, the history of which is written in the sayings and doings of the folk.

The evolution of thought in the world is to be studied in these immaterial relics of the past.

NOTES ON CINDERELLA.

BY E. SIDNEY HARTLAND, F. S. A.

THE volume of six hundred pages, recently issued by the Folk-Lore Society and entitled *Cinderella*, is the largest and most important contribution ever made to the study of a single folk-tale. It consists entirely of abstracts of variants, with a few useful notes on special points. Miss Marian Roalfe Cox, to whom we owe it, has been unwearied in her industry; and her judgment, skill and wide knowledge of folk-tales have enabled her to produce a collection simply indispensable to every student. We may differ, perhaps, on certain points of arrangement—for instance, on twofold tabulation; but we are quite sure that neither this nor any other detail of method has been adopted without due consideration, and at least it has been followed logically to the end.

I feel, however, that, to those students who know the volume, praise is superfluous. The book has become as much a part of the apparatus of their study as the blow-pipe is of an analytical chemist's. The following notes, therefore, aim at stating (rather than fully discussing) a few of the many questions raised by the variants brought together.

In view of recent controversies the most important of the problems connected with a folk-tale relates to the possibility of tracing its origin to any definite locality or race of men. Of such a problem a collection of three hundred and forty-five variants ought to offer some hopes of solution. Miss Cox finds in the stories three well-marked types, which she has named after the stories best known to English-speaking students: Cinderella, Catskin, and Cap o' Rushes. Beside these three, there is a number of variants sometimes approximating to one, sometimes to another, of the types, but not properly to be comprised under either of them, and consequently classed together as indeterminate.   The stories occur in the following proportions :

Cinderella	137
Catskin	79
Cap o' Rushes..................................	26
Indeterminate..................................	80
	322

To these must be added twenty-three hero-tales, that is, tales wherein the hero is a masculine Cinderella.

Discarding the last class, we may take the smallest of the other classes for the sake of convenience, and inquire whether it reveals anything as to its place of origin.   All the stories of the Cap o' Rushes type open with an incident familiar to us as the starting point of King Lear's misfortunes.   A king asks his daughters how much they love him.   The elder ones give answers which are satisfactory.   The youngest merely says she loves him like salt.   At this he is so indignant, that he either casts her off, or, in some cases, goes the length of ordering her to be put to death and her blood or some of her organs brought to him in proof of compliance.   We may, I think, safely assume that this order is the most archaic form of the incident; for with the softening of manners which accompanies progress in civilization, such an order would become more and more repulsive and more and more useless for the purposes of the story; and it would be, therefore, dropped out.   Here we have accordingly taken one step in our search.   The next is to examine the form and consequences of the order to kill.   The order appears in two forms: first, a simple order to kill; and second, an order accompanied by the requirement of proof, and followed by the king's deception with the blood, etc., of some brute slain for the purpose.   Here, again, the simpler form is undoubtedly the less archaic; and we may, therefore, discard it.   This is a second step in our search.   We have left nine stories containing the deception of the king with a possible tenth, No. 317, only given by Dr. Pitré, who reports it in outline.   They are as follows :

No.	Locality or People.	Proof of Death.
313	Avellins, Southern Italy.	Sheep's blood and heroine's finger.
208	Parma...................	Sheep's heart.
209	Venice..................	Dog's eyes and heart.
312	Abruzzi	Heroine's clothes soaked in dog's blood.
315	Sicily..................	Dog's tongue and heroine's garment, rent.
316	"	Dog's blood.
211	Gascony................	Dog's tongue.
226	Basque	Horse's heart.
210	Ovideo, Spain..........	Bitch's eyes.

But the order to kill, and the subsequent deception, occur in some other stories recorded in the volume.

CINDERELLA TYPE.

58	Poland..................	Dog's heart and finger of corpse with heroine's ring on it.

CATSKIN TYPE.

204	Poland	Hare's heart. (A dog is the messenger.)

INDETERMINATE (QUEBY, CATSKIN ?) TYPE.

304	Basque..................	Ass's heart.

INDETERMINATE (LITTLE SNOWWHITE ?) TYPE.

286	Tuscany................	Lamb's heart and eyes, and blood-stained dress.

MASCULINE TYPE.

330	Poland..................	Some portion of dog.

Let us note, before proceeding, the geographical distribution of these proofs of obedience. They occur in Italy, France, Spain, and Poland. In Italy, on the western side of the Apennines, a sheep's blood or heart and a lamb's heart and eyes are found.   On the other side of Italy (Venice and Abruzzi), and in Sicily, we get a dog's eyes and heart, clothes soaked in dog's blood, a dog's tongue and a dog's blood.   In Gascony, France, we find a dog's tongue ; in the province of Oviedo, Spain, a bitch's eyes ; and in Poland a dog's heart, and some portion of a dog.   Elsewhere in Poland, we come upon a hare's heart, but a dog is sent by the heroine's father to kill her.   Among the Basques, the trophy is either a horse's or an ass's heart.   Further, in Italy, a part of the heroine's dress is brought, in stories from the Abruzzi, from Tuscany, and from Sicily ; in a story from Southern Italy, the heroine's finger, and in a Polish tale, a corpse's finger, wearing the heroine's ring.   There appears at first sight to be some trace of local or racial influence in the selection of these proofs. The incident, however, occurs in other tales not belonging to the Cinderella Cycle, and, therefore, not included in Miss Cox's selection.   We will examine some of these.

Group to which the Story belongs.	Locality or People.	Proof of Death.	Authority.
Persecuted wife...	Tuscany....	Heroine's eyes..	De Gubernatis, Sante Stephano, p. 35.
Outcast child (language of beasts).	Monfratto....	Dog's heart.....	Comparetti, vol. i., p. 242.
Persecuted wife...	Pistoja.....	Dog's tongue....	Nerucci, p. 421.
Outcast child (language of beasts).	Mantua.....	Dog's heart......	Visentini, p. 121.
Persecuted wife...	Sicily.......	Two kid's hearts and tongues. (Two children)	Gonzenbach, vol. i., p. 15.
Outcast child — Joseph.	Abruzzi	Sheep's eyes....	De Nino, vol. iii., p. 172.
Persecuted wife...	Italy........	Shift dipped in wild beast's blood.	D'Ancona, Sacré Rappresentazioni, vol. iii.; p. 200 citing M.S. Italian poem of the 16th century.
" " ...	Italian Tyrol	Dog's heart.....	Schneller, p. 137.
" " ...	German Tyrol.	Dog's tongue...	Zingerle, vol. ii., p. 124.
Outcast child (language of beasts).	Upper Valais, Switzerland.	Deer's eyes and tongue.	Grimm's tales, transl. by Wm. Hurst, vol. i., p. 136.
Persecuted wife...	Hesse	Hind's eyes and tongue.	do. p. 127.

Group to which the Story belongs.	Locality or People.	Proof of Death.	Authority.
Outcast child (language of beasts).	Alsace......	Roebuck's heart and heroine's hands and feet.	Stoeber, vol. i., p. 78.
" "	Normandy..	Bitch's heart....	Fleury, p. 123.
" "	Brittany....	Dog's heart.....	Mélusine, vol. i., col. 300.
Little Snowwhite ?	Lorraine....	"	Cosquin, vol. ii., p. 323.
Persecuted wife...	France......	H e r o i n e ' s clothes.	Chaucer Analogues, p. 397, citing poem in Latin of the 12th century.
Little Snowwhite..	Iceland.....	Dog's t o n g u e, blood, and lock of h e r o i n e's hair.	Powell and Magnussen, vol. ii., p. 402., from Arnason.
O u t c a s t c h i l d (value of salt).	Catal o n i a, Spain.	Cup of blood and heroine's big toe.	Maspons y Labros, vol. i., p. 55.
Persecuted wife...	Spain.......	Eyes and heart of another person.	D'Ancona, vol. iii., p. 203, citing poem by Juan Miguel del Fuego of 18th century.
Little Snowwhite..	Portugal....	Bitch's tongue..	Pedroso, p. 8.
O u t c a s t c h i l d (Joseph type).	Brazil.......	Heroine's finger.	Romero, p. 12.
" "	Basque.....	Dog's heart.....	Webster, p. 187.
" "	Transy l v a-nian gypsy	Dog's blood.....	Von Wilslocki, Volksdichtungen, p. 289.
" "	" ..	He-goat's blood.	do p. 294.
" (?) "	" ..	Dog's heart.....	do p. 269.
" "	Astypalala, Greece.	Blood s t a i n e d shirt and finger	Geldart, p. 154.

This list contains stories from countries as far apart as Iceland and Japan; and an inspection and comparison with the previous list will dissipate any hopes of being able to trace either local or racial influence in the form assumed by the incident.

If there be direct connection between stories containing the same form of the incident, it must be by oral transmission over vast spaces, and independently of race; a difficult matter to prove or disprove without a much larger collection of examples, and which would lead us far outside the subject of Cinderella. At present, all we can say is that the dog appears to be the favorite animal, whose blood or organs supply

9

the place of the hero's.   This is but natural, seeing how universally he is the companion of man.

There is another point to which we may turn for information.   In a small number of variants the heroine in disguise becomes a menial having charge of the poultry ; and the creatures under her care, seeing her when she dons the gorgeous dresses, betray her by their admiration expressed in human language.   Now it need hardly be said that talking birds, like other talking animals, are found all the world over.   But the special incident here referred to is found in a very small area, namely, only in Italy (Nos. 139, 140, 141, 183, 217 and 285), and in Brittany (No. 251).   In two Spanish tales (Nos. 178 and 210), the geese forget to feed in their admiration, and die, and in a Wallachian story (No. 298), the heroine is seen by reapers when she secretly changes her dress, and they tell of her.   These three stories may perhaps be considered as modernized variants.   The incident also occurs in a Spanish tale (Masponse y Labros, vol. i., page 55), mentioned in the list given on a preceding page.   It could, of course, only be related in places where poultry (hens, geese, or turkeys) were an important part of the domestic *ménage*.   It seems, in fact, to be a form of the animal witness, an important personage in a large number of Cinderella variants. But there is nothing to show whence this particular form was derived, unless we may conclude from the greater number of instances which have been collected in Italy, that it is Italian in origin.   This, at best, would be a doubtful inference.

Passing for a while from the consideration of single incidents, can we gather by any examination of the story as a whole, whence it has come ?   It would be impossible to make any such examination exhaustively in a short paper.   The most we could do is to test the claims of one country as an example of the method which may be adopted with all.   And as India has had more advocates for her copyright of fairy tales than any other land, we may as well deal with her claims to the invention of Cinderella.   Miss Cox gives three Indian variants : one (No. 25), originally published in the Bombay Gazette, in 1864 ; one (No. 235), told to Miss Frere by an ayah who had heard it from her grandmother, a Christian convert with much heathenism still lingering about her ; and the third (No. 307), from Salsette, near Bombay.

We may dispose of the second of these tales at once. It is often difficult to decide whether a tale comes within the definition of a given group, so infinitely do the plots shade off into one another. The story of Sodewa Bai has no connection with the Cinderella group, save the lost slipper. The rajah, who is the heroine's father, causes the lost slipper to be cried and reward offered for its restoration. A prince, find-it by his mother's advice, asks for her lady's hand in recompense and obtains it. The heroine, however, was born with a golden necklace, which contains her soul, and the greater part of the tale is concerned with the necklace and the consequences of its loss. It is obvious that if this tale was rightly included in the tabulation, the Egyptian fable of Rhodopis had still better claim.

In the third tale, the heroine is born of a blister on a beggar's thumb. She and her six sisters (born in the ordinary way) are abandoned by their father and find a palace, where they live. The heroine's room is the best, though her sisters do not know it. The six elder sisters go to church ; the heroine follows them in gorgeous array, including golden slippers. At church the king's son falls in love with her. She loses a slipper in hurrying home, and is ultimately identified by it and married to the prince. The tale then falls into the persecuted wife type. Her sisters accuse her of giving birth to a stone and brooms, but the three babes who are really born are providentially preserved from death, and at length the heroine, through them, triumphs over her accusers. Here the heroine's birth and her sisters' envy contain many details which appear to be native. On the other hand, all the Cinderella incidents bear decidedly the impress of Europe. The people who tell the tale are Roman Catholics, and the tale, whatever its primitive form, has become so inextricably mingled with European elements, that no argument can be drawn from it in favor of an Indian source.

There remains the first story. Unfortunately we have it only at second or third hand, and only in an abstract. It is said to run as follows :—"Heroine is ill-treated by stepmother, who, finding that cow nourishes her with its milk, resolves to kill it. Cow bids heroine be comforted, and to take care to collect its bones, horns, skin and every part that is thrown away ; above all, to avoid eating its flesh. Cow is killed, and heroine does as bidden. Prince is making choice of bride ; heroine is left at home to cook supper whilst step-sister goes to palace. Cow returns to life, gives dresses and gold clogs to heroine. She drops one of these when prince is pursuing her, and when he comes to seek her she is hidden in granary. Cock betrays her presence. Prince marries her. Step-mother and step-sister are punished." This is a very important story for the advocates of the Indian origin of fairy tales ; but we have so little information about it that it is not easy to build any structure of argument upon it. The cow certainly does not seem Hindoo. In a variant, we learn it is a fish that befriends the heroine. In Annam, there is a tale of which Mr. Landes has collected two variants (No. 68 and 69). In both of these the helpful animal is a fish beloved of the heroine ; when the fish is killed and cooked, its bones collected by her pious hands turn into shoes, and (in the one case) to dresses. A crow carries off one of the shoes to the prince's palace. A proclamation is issued by him, offering marriage to the owner. The heroine, of course, is successful, in spite of the difficulties thrown in her way by her step-mother. Then follows the step-mother's scheme for substituting her own daughter. The heroine is put to death, and undergoes a series of transformations which end in her re-appearance out of a fruit more beautiful than ever. She persuades her rival to jump into boiling water, in order to become equally lovely, and pickling her flesh, sends it to her mother as a delicacy. Notwithstanding Buddhism prevails in Annam, there is little evidence of it in this tale. The chief incidents disclose ideas as savage as can well be desired, though many of the externals have been adapted to the comparatively advanced style of civilization enjoyed by the Annamites and Tjannes. We may assume, therefore, that if the story entered Annam from Hindostan, as to which there is at present no evidence, it was not by a Buddhist channel.

Still more archaic are the Santal variants not given by Miss Cox, but found in Mr. Campbell's collection of *Santal Folk*

Tales, recently issued from the Mission Press at Pokhuria,
India. The Santals are non-Aryan aborigines of Bengal,
interesting to students of folk-lore from their curious rites as
well as their oral traditions. They have a masculine, as well
as feminine, Cinderella. The former undergoes the following
adventures : He has charge of a cow that gives him food
when his step-mother starves him. The step-mother feigns
illness, in order to have the cow killed, but the cow and boy
escape. From the cow descends a whole herd, which the boy
tends in the jungle. Bathing one day he drops a hair in the
river. A princess lower down the stream finds it and deter-
mines to marry the owner. A tame parrot helps her father's
servants to find the boy, by stealing his flute and drawing him
after it in pursuit. In one variant he is unfortunate, and
the princess refuses to marry him after all. In the other, he
has three flutes, with magical properties, uttering articulate
sounds which twice balk the messenger's efforts to capture
him, and ultimately, after his marriage, obtain for him a
herd, from whence are descended all the tame buffaloes in
India.

The feminine Cinderella is first drowned by her seven
brothers' wives. She then reappears as a bamboo, out of
which a fiddle is made. The fiddle is acquired by a village
chief. The maiden comes out of it, in the absence of the
household, and prepares the family meal. The chief's son
watches, discovers and marries her. In a variant, she is first
eaten by a monkey. The monkey dies. From his dead body
a gourd grows, out of which a banjo is made, wherein the
heroine hides. She is at length found and married to the
rajah, who is already her sister's husband. Another variant
relates that she was given by her brothers to a water spirit,
in return for water. She reappears as a flower, and is married to the bridegroom, to whom she had been previously
betrothed. Her brothers having become poor, come to her
village offering firewood for sale ; she recognizes and *fêtes*
them, treating her youngest brother as Benjamin was treated
by Joseph. The brothers, at her reproaches, cleave open the
earth and plunge in. She catches the youngest—who had
been no party to her ill-treatment—by the hair to save him,
but in vain. The hair comes off in her hand. She plants it

in the earth, and it becomes the blackthorn grass that now grows in the jungles.

The conclusion suggested by these tales is that the European tales were derived from at least two primitive forms, one approximating to the Cinderella type, the other to the Catskin type, and growing out of incidents of which our oldest example is, in the one case, in the Egyptian tale of the Two Brothers, where the lady's perfumed hair falls into the river and is found by the king, and in the other case in Ragnar Lodbrok's saga, where Aslang, Sigurd's daughter, is concealed in Heime's harp. But, if so, there is probably no direct connection between the Indian and European stories. This is confirmed, as to stories of the Cinderella type, by a Gaelic tale from Inverness-shire, which, amid much of a more modern cast, has preserved two very antique traits. A king, we are told, has a wife and children, and also a daughter by a sheep. The wife causes the sheep to be put to death. Its bones are preserved by its daughter; and the sheep, after a time, revives as a beautiful princess. On the return of the king's son there is to be a three days' feast, but the other children only beat the sheep's daughter when she asks about it. Her mother, however, clothes her in finery, and sends her to the feast, where the king's son falls in love with her. She disappears each day, but on the third day leaves one of her golden slippers behind. A proclamation is issued offering marriage to its owner. A woman, in order to wear it, cuts her big toe off, but the heroine is pointed out by a bird and married to the king's son.[1] In other tales of this type, where the heroine's mother and the helpful animal are identified, the mother has originally had human form and has suffered a magical transformation. In many cases, as in the Indian tale reported from the *Calcutta Review*, the identity has been completely forgotten. We cannot doubt that the Gaelic tale, just cited, comes nearer to the original, in this particular, than when the mother is afterwards transformed, or where her identity with the helpful animal has been forgotten. It is obvious, at least, that the tale could only have arisen among a people so low in civilization that they had not yet attained to the repugnance against sexual union in

[1] Cinderella, p. 534.

stories between man and beast, and in actual fact between children of one sire but different mothers. The Santals have passed beyond this stage. Still more certainly have the Aryan Hindus, to whom the invention and dispersion of fairy tales is attributed by Mr. Cosquin and others; and they had passed beyond it ages before the Buddhist propaganda, from which the dispersion is usually dated.

With regard to the Indian origin of stories of the Catskin type, another test may be applied. They usually open with an attempt by a widowed father to marry his daughter, the heroine. All these stories are European, with one exception (No. 189), which comes from Kurdistan. The incident, needlessly repulsive to the feelings of every European nation, could hardly have been imagined at a period when the marriage of father and daughter was a thing quite unheard of. More likely it was transferred from real life, at a stage in civilization when the sentiment of the community was against such a marriage, though it may not have been, or may only recently have become contrary to the tribal customs. Certain obscure references in the classics may, perhaps, imply that such marriages were not unknown to some of the barbarians with whom the Romans were brought into contact; but, with this possible exception, they have never been known during the historic period. They are reported, however, as practised in modern times among the Wanyoro, of Central Africa,[1] and among the Caribs;[2] while we are assured that it is the rule of the Piojes, of Ecuador, that "a widow shall take her son, a widower his daughter, to replace the deceased consort."[3] The ancient Persians are also asserted to have followed the same custom, though this is contested by the Parsees of the present day,[4] the kings of Siam, who are compelled to marry only into their own family, are said to be sometimes reduced to wedding their own sisters or daughters.[5]

---

[1] Featherman, *Social History of the Races of Mankind.* Nigritians, p. 110.

[2] Ibid. *Chiopa and Guarawo.* Maranonians, p. 268.

[3] Brinton, *The American Race,* p. 274. Arthur Simpson, *Travels in the Wilds of Ecuador.* (London, 1886), p. 196.

[4] See *Next of Kin Marriages in Old Iran,* by Darab Dasher Reshotan Aunjana, B. A. (London, 1888), where the question is fully discussed by a Zoroastrian priest, anxious to remove the stigma fastened upon his religion.

[5] Col. James Low, in *Journal of the Indian Archipelago,* vol. i., p. 350, citing De Lombre.

The practice is foreign to the universal sentiment of India, nor has the incident yet been discovered, so far as I am aware, in any Indian tale. The existing state of our knowledge, therefore, seems to preclude our attributing either the Cinderella or the Catskin type to an Indian origin.

I regret that the limits of human endurance, even at a Folk-Lore congress, do not permit of carrying these inquiries further, and the more so because I have felt hitherto compelled to draw wholly negative inferences. The subject opens so many vistas that it seems inexhaustible. I have merely attempted to put one or two tests to examine the bearing of a small portion of the material gathered in Miss Cox's learned volume on the question of origin. That the attempt has hardly penetrated beneath the surface of the problem, I should be the first to acknowledge. But it may serve to lead a valuable discussion by some who have studied the question more profoundly.

THE FATALITY OF CERTAIN PLACES TO CERTAIN PERSONS.

BY MISS C. S. HAWKINS DEMPSTER.

THE DEATH OF SIVENO.

ONCE upon a time there was a king in Sweden, and his son sailed on the seas. On a certain day he took ship, with many men on board, and red gold in heaps. And when he went away his stepmother bid him beware of *Cape Wrath* (Poraft), and *Poldhu* (the black pool), and *Poltarrach gawn* (the pool of the dun steer).

It fell out that as he sailed he came to the place called Phorsten Stivanaigh (port of Siveno or Sweno), and did not know what land it was that he had made. And the men of the isles armed themselves, and blackened their faces with soot from the pots, and went out in boats. They told him this creek was called *Poltarrach gawn*. Then cried the king's son, " God forbid that I should bide in these waters, and the Lord have mercy on my soul if this be *Poltarrach gawn.*" He weighed anchor and made to stand out again to sea, but the men of Assqut (west coast of Sutherland), and the isles (summer islands off Ullapool) were too many for him. They came on board his ship and cried to Siveno that he should yield himself. The Swedes and their prince being stout men fought on deck and below. When the king's son was wounded they put him below, and went on fighting till a man of Glendhu (the black glen), looking through a hole in the deck, saw the king's son, and shot him. Then the Swedes lost heart. They yielded up the gold and all that was in the ship, and only asked to get away with the vessel and their lives. The islesmen began to work with the gold, and to take it out in their plaids ; one man holding the plaid on the ship's side and another making it fast in the boat. But the gold was so heavy that the plaid tore, and only a few pieces slid into the boat and the rest of the treasure still lies in Glendhu. A year later the man who had shot the king's son said : "I go a fishing, and in the port of Siveno."

While he fished he saw a small boat coming over the water towards him, and in the boat was a man with gold sewed all over his clothes, and a sword. The little boat came alongside, and then the man, who had the face of Siveno the king's son, shot the fisherman of Glendhu. He cried, "I gave it before, and I get it now," and he died.

The harbor is called the port of Siveno, or Sweno, to this day.

"GETTING A RESPONSE."

Sir James Stewart, the favorite of the Scottish king, was murdered in 1596, at Cotstark, in the parish of Symington, Lanarkshire. He had defied the Douglas clan, but Douglas of Torthorwald, overtook and slew him in that glen. Says Archbishop Spotteswoode in his history (III. 40) : "Captain Stewart had asked the name of the piece of ground on which they were, and, on learning the name of it, commanded his company to ride more quickly *as having gotten a response* to beware of "such a place." Query ? What did an Archbishop mean by a "*response*" ?

THE JERUSALEM CHAMBER.

King Henry IV., having a holy purpose to go to Jerusalem, was dissuaded by a prophecy that he must die in Jerusalem. Falling mortally sick at Westminster he learnt that the room where he lay was named "*the Jerusalem Chamber.*" "*In that Jerusalem shall Harry die,*" said the king, and kept his word, passing away in that same room and bed in Westminster.

KING CAMBYSES.

The oracle of Buto in Egypt warned Cambyses that he should die in Eckbatana, so he determined never to go there. One day in the chase the king was wounded. He asked the name of the place in which they laid him down to have his wound dressed. He was told that it was Eckbatana, and soon afterwards expired

THE DEVIL IN ROME.

Twardvoski, the Faust, or Michael Scott, or D. D. McKay, of Lithuanian legends, sold his soul to the devil, but the fiend could only lay claim to it if they met in Rome. At a hamlet of his native country which chanced to be called *Rome*, the devil accosted him, and claimed his own, but Twardvoski by some subterfuge baffled him.[1]

THE SIEGE OF LAON.

The seigneur de Givry, lover of Mlle. de Guise, was killed at that siege. "On lui avait prédit depuis peu qu'il mourrait *devant l'an*, et celà pouvait entendre devant l'année ou devant la ville de Laon. Le chevalier de Cheverney, son beau-père, dit qu'il fut tué devant Laon."[2]

TICONDEROGA.

Captain Campbell, of Lochawe, while at home in the Highlands, had a vivid dream, in which a long-ago murdered ancestor of his own appeared to him. Believing that the apparition might forbode his death, he asked of his spectral visitor if he was soon to die. "No," replied the ghost, "not soon, but at Ticonderoga." Captain Campbell awoke repeating to himself this strange name, which to his memory and to his knowledge conveyed no idea whatever. He thought of it only as a place in dreamland.

Some years later, and during the war of American independence, his regiment was engaged in an action under the walls of Fort Edward. Captain Campbell was wounded and carried to the rear. After the battle a brother officer mentioned to him that the real, the Indian name, of the place was a curious one, "Ticonderoga."

Captain Campbell died two days later of his wound.

[1] Ostrovsby's Notes.   [2] Tallemant des Reaux, I. 125.

QUERIES.

What is the origin of this idea? Is it the shadow side of the once prevalent idea that certain spots were holy, and advantageous as fraught with supernatural gifts? Jerusalem was so to the Jews. Pilgrims used to go to Canope, in Egypt, pray and sleep on the spot, believing that in dreams they would obtain the blessing or the guidance they desired. The oracle had to be consulted at Delphi. Christ treated this notion with contempt. Is the fatality of places twin with the sanctity of places? Does the notion arise in the belief that Fate or Destiny, *Ananké*, is always sitting waiting to catch us. Grim as the stories are they contain a grim jest : for sometimes as a *Laon* a life is lost in pursuing, and sometimes, as in the tale of the "devil at Rome," the human being turns the pun to his advantage, and foils the Fiend. Is the notion of fatality in spots an enlargement of the notion "the hour is come ; *and* the man," adding, "and the *place !*"

EUGENE FIELD.

TELLING THE BEES.

BY EUGENE FIELD.

OUT of the house where the slumberer lay
Grandfather came one summer day;
And under the pleasant orchard trees
He spake this-wise to the murmuring bees;
"The clover-bloom that kissed her feet
And the posie-bed where she used to play
Have honey store, but none so sweet
As ere our little one went away,
O bees, sing soft, and, bees, sing low;
For she is gone who loved you so."

A wonder fell on the listening bees
Under those pleasant orchard trees,
And in their toil that summer day
Ever their murmuring seemed to say;
"Child, O child, the grass is cool,
And the posies are waking to hear the song
Of the bird that swings by the shaded pool,
Waiting for one that tarrieth long."
'Twas so they called to the little one then,
As if to call her back again.

O gentle bees, I have come to say
That grandfather fell to sleep to-day,
And we know by the smile on grandfather's face,
He has found his dear one's biding place.
So, bees, sing soft, and, bees, sing low,
As over the honey-fields you sweep,—
To the trees a-bloom and the flowers a-blow
Sing of grandfather fast asleep;
And ever beneath these orchard trees
Find cheer and shelter, gentle bees.

Ladies and Gentlemen :

Some of the most charming literature we have in the line of folk-lore has been done by women. Speaking for myself, I am very proud to acknowledge on this occasion, that it was a woman who first interested me in folk-lore, or, more accurately speaking, in folk song, for it was not until I had read the delightful work of Madame the Countess Martinengo-Cesaresco, that I became aware of the vastness and the beauty and fascination of the study to which that charming lady introduced me. It is to a woman that we are indebted for the only compilation of West Indian folk tales; to a woman for several delightful volumes on the ancient charms and the old legends of the Irish; to a woman for our acquaintance with "Myths, Symbols and Magic of the East Africans;" to a woman for the learned and delightful treatise upon "Old Rabbit, the Voodoo,"—in short, it is to women that we are indebted for a very large share of the curious, entertaining and instructive literature, in which all people as intelligent and enterprising as we are delight.

It is largely owing to the perseverance, and patience, and discretion of a woman that there exists and flourishes in Chicago to-day a Folk-Lore Society, and but for the fear of offending the solemnity of this occasion, I should call for three cheers for Mrs. Helen W. Bassett.

THE SYMBOL OF THE VASE, IN MYTH, IDEOGRAPHY, LANGUAGE, HAGIOGRAPHY, LITERATURE AND FOLK-LORE.[1]

BY DR. STANISLAS PRATO.

GENTLEMEN,—The signal indulgence, by which my very modest merits have been judged sufficient to influence my nomination as a foreign member, a representative of Italy upon the Advisory Council of this International Congress of Folk-Lore, gives me the courage to send this communication, to submit for your very intelligent judgment the development of a subject which, I allow myself to believe, will, by its novelty, merit your sagacious attention; of which your delicate courtesy is a very certain assurance. And I the more willingly enter upon this theme, which in giving me the occasion of studying it in its ideography, language, hagiography, literature and folk-lore, presents also the opportunity to show the intimate bond which unites them, the affinity which Cicero has already recognized among the various human relations, and to verify the very common Latin proverb, *vis verita fortior.*

Closely observing the children of to-day and primitive people, we can very readily perceive the imagination predominating among the various faculties of the mind, and reflection not existing at all, or being very feeble with them; this proves to us that the human mind passes from synthesis to analysis, from the fact to the rule, from art and ·poetry to science. On this account we find that at first sentiment and fantasy are everything; ideas are but poetical images, reality is absorbed by the ideality, while the truth is enshrined in the fiction of myth, and the supernatural element imposes itself on nature, which is soon filled with deities, which will

---

[1] Translated from the French, by Lieut. F. S. Bassett.

be the personification of its powers, and being accredited with the production of its phenomena, suffice it to give an explanation of them, a thing which men of these times could never have done. Now, I intend to indicate to you how the vase, or any other recipient,[1] has inspired in the fantasy of ancient people many facts belonging to the sensible, intelligible and moral order; nevertheless, before commencing, allow me to appeal to your indulgence, with regard to my weakness in the use of the French, as a universal language, by which I must make myself understood by all learned men of different nations. Beginning with myth, to apply the ancient Latin proverb, *Ab Jove principium Musæ*, we may recall the seductive woman Pandora, created by the other divinities, who were jealous of Jupiter, the creator of men, and endowed with all the perfections of beauty; with wisdom, with great talents, with music, with eloquence, by Venus, Minerva, Apollo, Mercury; in a word, the advantage of every gift, and for this reason named Pandora (every gift), the Tillottama of the Vedas, and well did Jupiter avenge himself; he caused the beautiful Pandora to be brought before his throne, so as to make her a present also on his part; this was a box, which he ordered to be carried to Prometheus. Epimetheus, the brother of the latter, curious to know what this mysterious box contained, opened it, and all the evils escaped at once, to spread over the earth; this was the commencement of the

---

[1] *Vase*, according to some, from the Gallo-Celtic and Irish *fas*, concave, hollow, empty: in German, *fass*, cask; in Dutch, *vat*, vase, tun; in Arab, *vi-a* and *vu-a*, place in which something is contained, and *basan*, bound with bronze; in Hebrew, *buth*, measure of capacity of 18 litres. Vase, generic name for all the utensils made to receive or hold something in them, particularly liquids, and ascending to the different materials, called *cup*, *vial*, *box*, *urn*. We cannot follow the etymology which Bopp gives to vase, deriving it from the Sanscrit verb *vas*, to live, to dwell, to lodge; there would be another reason for seeing the appropriateness of the vase, the symbolic image of the soul, of which it would also be the ideographic word, and it would signify vase taken in the acceptation of soul—that which resides, which dwells, which lodges in the body. Compare also the Latin *testa*, which, from the signification of earthen pot, passes to the other metaphoric meaning of skull, box for the brain, and the Sanscrit words, *kapala*, and the Latin *caput*, in the two acceptations, one proper, the other metaphorical, of cup, vase, head; in any case, *caput*, Latin, connected its common theme with the Latin verb *capere*, that which takes, which receives (confer the same metaphors, capire, capace, capacita) is the ideographic periphrasis of vase, which receives in itself, takes that which is placed therein, or what is poured in it, and by the belief of many that the soul might be in the head. Here then is another reason for which the soul, the mind, may be a vase which receives, which takes within it, the reflections, the knowledge placed there.

Iron Age. Hope alone remained at the bottom of the box, as the last consolation of unfortunate mortals.[1]

A myth of Brazilian Indians, according to Mr. Conto do Magalhaeus, in his work *O Selvagem*, thus presents to us the imagined creation and the apparition of Night sleeping at the bottom of the waters, just as in the Iliad of Homer (xiv. 289-97) under the form of Cymandis, the bronzed bird, dyed by the foliage, sleeps among the branches of a pine. Here is the Indian legend : "At the commencement there was no night, there was only day all the time. The night was sleeping at the bottom of the water. There were no animals. Everything could speak."

The daughter of Cobra-Grande (the great serpent), it is said, was married to a young man who had three faithful servants ; one day he engaged them to go out and take a walk, for his wife would not sleep with him ; afterwards he called his wife, but she would not fulfil his wish for her to go to bed because it was not yet night ; the husband said to her that there was no night, and there was indeed only day. The young woman then answered him that her father had the night, and that if he wanted her to sleep with him, it was necessary to hunt for him across the great river. The young man called his three servitors, and the young woman sent them to her father's abode, so that they might bring back a tucuman kernel.[2] The servitors went away, and coming to the house of Cobra-Grande, he restored to them the tucuman kernel closed tightly, with the absolute prohibition to open it unless everything should have been lost. The servitors went away, and they heard a noise in the middle of the kernel of the tucuman, a noise sounding thus : "*Tin! tin! tin!*—chu!" This was

---

[1] Spes ultima Dea—Latin proverb, La Speme ultima Dea (Ugo Foscolo) Canne di Sepoleri (v. 16-17) and Pierre Metastasio says :

" Speranza lusinghiera	Flattering hope,
Dolce dell'uom conforto	Sweet consolation of man,
Forti la prima a nascere	You were the first to be born,
Sei l'ultima à morir."	And you are the last to die.

Cf. also the Tuscan proverb, "La speranza 6 l'ultimo a perdersi " (Hope is the last thing to lose).

[2] Tucuman kernel (Astroceergum tucuma Martin). The tucuman is a handsome thorny palm tree which grows in the valley of the Amazon and that of the Plata. The fruit of this palm tree, which serves as food for the Indians, is round, and of a beautiful orange color when ripe. It is composed of a tough envelope, a fleshy, fibrous interior, surrounding a kernel, shaped like a cocoanut.

the noise of the crickets and of little frogs, who were singing about the night. Pursuing their way as long as they continued to hear the same noise at the interior of the kernel of the tucuman, they did not know what noise it was, as it was already quite distant, so they assembled in the middle of their boat, lighting a fire, melted the resin which sealed up the kernel, and opened it. Suddenly, all became dark.[1]

Then all things scattered throughout the woods were transformed into birds and fish. The ounce was created from the basket;[2] the fisher and his vessel were transformed into a duck; the body of the duck from the boat, and the oars became the legs of the duck. The young wife, as soon as day commenced to break, having, with a thread, separated the night from the day, seeing that through the fault of the servitors, trying the night, all was lost, transformed them into monkeys as a punishment.[3]

In the popular tradition it is not rarely that we encounter a box, or something else, confided to some one with the same prohibition against opening or uncovering it; thus, in a story from Great Britain, the son of the King of Tethertown, as a reward for saving its life, received a package from the hands of a duck, which became a handsome boy, with a prohibition against opening it. Finding the package become very heavy, he was tempted to see what it contained, but what was his astonishment on opening it! In the twinkling of an eye there appeared in the midst of an immense space a large château surrounded by an orchard, where all sorts of plants and fruits flourished. The prince remained struck with

---

[1] The tucuman kernel, of the cosmic legend of Brazil, recalls the stem of the Greek ferule (the Indian *Pramantha*) in which Prometheus, after having removed it from the solar wheel, concealed within it, and kept there, to carry upon earth, from heaven, the ray of light which he afterwards scattered over the surface of the earth, symbol of the light of civilization, of which he was the author, the propagator, and the martyr among men. The myth of Prometheus is cosmogonic, or to say it better, palingenesic; the only difference which distinguishes it from the Indo-Brazilian, refers to the diversity between the tucuman kernel and the stem of the ferule of the myth, the diverse, or rather opponent, nature of the obscurity which the kernel of the tucuman, and the ray of light contained in the stem of the ferule, offers.

[2] It is for this reason that the ounce is spotted, the marks of the basket becoming its spots.

[3] F. T. de Santa Anna Very, *Folk-Lore Brésilien*, préface du Prince Roland Bonaparte, Paris, Didier, etc., 1889, ch. iv., pp. 55–57, Contes Indiens du Brésil, collected by General Conto de Magolhaes, and translated into French by E. Allaire, Rio de Janeiro, Faro & Lind, 1883, p. 5.

astonishment and regret because he had made so many pretty things come out in a wood, instead of the little green valley opposite his father's house. But a giant whom he met put the garden, orchard and château back in the box, on condition of receiving in exchange the first son of the Prince as soon as he should attain seven years of age.[1] In a popular Comarca tale from Carallasca published by me in No. 6 (June, 1891), of La Tradition of Paris, with the title, "Le roi et les deux malcontents," a mysterious plate uncovered in spite of the prohibition of the King by a man and a woman (settled in his palace and treated very generously by him), in order to rid them of the duty of working the land, imposed upon them by the son of Adam and Eve, allows a little bird to fly out through the open window. This gave the King, who, concealed, had seen all, the opportunity of approving of the punishment of Adam and Eve for their sin by God, and just as they had been chased from the terrestrial Paradise, he banished the two discontented guests from his palace. In the article cited, I compared with this popular tale the story in verse of Grecourt, *La linotte de Jean XXII,* in which a little bird also flies out of the window, coming out of a closed box which Pope John XXII. had given to two nuns to watch over, with a prohibition against opening it, and which they opened through curiosity.[2] This story is also found in the *Matinées* of Seigneur de Cholières, in the *Sirées* of Guillaume Bouchet, and in the *Moyen de Parvenir* of Bervalde de Verville, and also in the *Pantagruel* of Rabelais.

Apropos of the tucuman kernel, enclosing night, one may recall popular stories, particularly in those belonging to the theme of *Psyche* and the *Serpent King,* where are found walnuts, hazel-nuts, almonds and other fruits containing precious things, received from the hands of a fairy or other marvellous person, and given by the woman who is seeking her lost husband, from her who keeps him in her palace so as to see him once more.

[1] Contes Populaires de la Grande Bretagne par Loys Bruyère, Paris—Hachette, 1875—Première partie contes d'origine aryenne No. 13—La Bataille des Oiseaux—Campbell, Popular Tales of the West Highlands, 4 vol., 12 mo.

[2] The curiosity of women in general and particularly of nuns recalls to my mind the very common and metrical French proverb : " Désir de femme est feu qui dévore, Désir de nonne est pis encor."

To resume our subject, according to Felix Liebrecht, a cosmogonic legend is found among the Ashantees which may be referred to the myth of Pandora by the episode of the vase. Here it is : "From the beginning of the world, God created three white men and three black men, with an equal number of women, and so that these creatures might have nothing to complain of to him afterwards, he gave them the choice of good and evil. A great box or calabash was put down in the ground with a scrap of sealed paper upon one side of it. God gave first choice to the blacks ; they took the box, expecting to find something good in it, but on opening it there came out only a piece of gold, a piece of iron, and several other pieces of metal, the use of which they did not know ; the whites having next opened the paper, learned everything from it. God, therefore, left the black men in the forest, but he conducted the white men to the edge of the water, communicated with them every night, and showed them how to build a little vessel which carried them away to another country (for all this happened in Africa), and they returned from it a long time afterwards." See for this cosmogonic legend Albert Montemont *Bibliothèque Universelle des Voyages*, etc., vol. xxviii., page 407, and *Jahrbuch für Romanische und Englische Litteratur 1–5 Miscellen ;* Felix Liebrecht *Zum Kaufmann von Venedig* (Oben Jahrbuch, vol. ii., § 330.[1]

But if in Mythology there is a trace of the vase, or of some other recipient, one also sees vestiges of it in language, and also in writing, in the ideography of Egypt and of China, and especially in that of Egypt ; among them the letter B is represented by a lapwing, or heron, by the scent-box or incense-pan, with or without flames and perfumes—compare the corresponding Chinese character Hi representing a box, that which contains ; it should also be noted that this same letter B, by means of the sparrow-hawk or the crane (sound Bai), indicating the symbol of the soul, the spirit, and also the man versed in sublime things, will justify the symbolic representation of the soul in the image of the vase, which we will hereafter recall. The letter H (heth) is represented by a sieve, a fan (ventilabrum), sound, hai, and in Memphitic

[1] One may also recall to memory the cosmographic story told in the account of the Ark of Noah in the Bible.

chai, and with the images of the lotus plantation or of the papyrus, the anterior parts of a lion, and the human face, symbolizes human life, by means of the particularization of the ideas of life (plantation of lotus), of force (anterior parts of the lion) and of man (human faces) ; this ideographic sign confirms the image of the vase, symbol of the soul, the more so as also among the Egyptians, and an enclosure represents the letter Heth, and an enclosure represents a field among the Chinese (sound Thian), and the source of life (the earth, the grand mother, is the first principle of life) ; which is very natural because the letter E (sound sang) vowel, of which the η in Greek is the equivalent, has the signification of existence and of life.   The letter *Caph* among the Egyptians is represented by a basket or a vase (sound Kabi), and also by a field of reeds, symbols of life, by its generative principle, the earth. The letter *M* is indicated by a basin or reservoir full of water (we may recall the generative and regenerative character of the waters, called mothers in the Vedas, and the generation of all things by water according to Talete Milesius) sound, *Mesan ;* the root of a tree, sound *Motdg,* virgulte, propago (symbol of life) ; as also among the Chinese, the tree, productive being, indicates the letter *M* (sound *Thras*) ; the idea of life in this letter *M* is represented also by the following homophonic sounds : Vulture, the symbol of maternity, sound *Mut* (mother) ; a landscape, *Mo, Memau, Memo,* place, country, land ; a sort of plough, *Mahro,* seminatis, cultura agri, sati.   The letter *N* is represented by two vases (Noun) without bulge with water or with bowls, symbol of Egypt, of the country, where water plays a remarkable role ; by a shuttle (Nath), emblem of the goddess Neith, inventress of the art of weaving ; perhaps the regular coming and going of the shuttle in the hands of the workmen recalls with the continual movement of the water, the genetic principle of cosmic life, motion, the indication of the life of the body and of the spirit (whence the well-known proverb).   Another sign of the letter *N* is a kind of cresset, or vase, carefully wrought in metal) and also a sort of basin filled with water, a round vase carried on two legs, etc.   M. Paravey notes among the cycle of ten days called *Ty,* or *Kans* by the Chinese, that the first, pronounced *Kid,* corresponding to number 1, and to the *M* of

all people, seems to show a valve, symbol of the sources, from
the beginning, and of the waters and the shells seen there which
recalls the *Mim* (water in Ethiopic), and also the breasts of a
mother, and in a complex form, or a large vase, surmounted
by a cover and containing the symbol of felicity, happiness,
which itself offers the character of wisdom, virtue, for God
was in fact like the great and Supreme Unity in the antique
style of the vase of wisdom *par excellence*, the mysterious
source of happiness. Bnt the great and true ideas were so
well designated, in symbolic numbers, that a vase exactly
similar to the preceding, but containing the character, misfortune, is the symbol of the earth, that is to say of matter,
the source of the misfortunes of the spirit ; compare the vase
containing all the evils of the world given by Jupiter to Pandora, in its myth, or above.   Another vase represents also
the 10th hour. So, one of the antique and complex forms of
its number 2, which the syllable *ami* explains, interpreted in
a manner rather too subtle, shows besides, a bivalve shell,
natural symbol of purity, has also led here the ideas of *pearls*
and *union*, in fact Horace in the 3d Ode of Book I., says of
Virgil his friend : *Animæ dimidium meæ*, which recalls the
expression of popular Tuscan usage concerning friends,
called—*Due animæ in un nócciolo* (two souls in one kernel),
and the biblical expression concerning spouses, of whom it is
said, *Erunt duo in carne una*. The idea of containing, of
capacity (the union of two souls represented as two vases), is
affixed to the number two, represented by ten bars upright or
laid down, and has produced the Hebrew B, a letter expressing among the Egyptians in its figurative representation, as
has been seen, the idea of containing, of capacity ; but the
Beth, showing also the image of the hands, and *Caph*, being
translated by hands, a letter also signifying the idea of taking,
containing, we are not to be astonished at the same signification annexed to the number two, and to the letters
Beth and *Caph*, their analogues. The 5th hour also sets
forth a vase, perhaps a clepsydra, of which it is a sort
of abridgment, measures the time and the hours, the
number 5 being *par excellence* the number of these, because the clepsydras at the 5th hour, stop going and the
sun, rising sufficiently above the horizon, commences to

measure the hours upon the meridians or the dials ;[1] further, the antique form of the 5 is that of an hour-glass, with rounded angles, which the ancient chemists, even in Europe, employed as a sign of the word hour in their prescriptions ; just as our chemists did at a very late period (see for this the ancient formulæ). So, under this acceptation, the 5th hour is confounded with the sign of the letter H, of the Chaldean alphabet. One sees this sound, *He,* sounded in the word hour (heure) ; in the *hezards* of the Parsees, that is their hours, and the letter *E,* forming the number 5 of the ancient financiers, in place of the Roman V, while, by a very natural change, the pronunciation *Chin* or *Cin*[2] (from whence the epithet of *Chine,* the empire of the middle) as the five is the middle one in the series of tens, indicates stars, planets, times, which is the name of the planet Mercury, to which *epsilon* responds among the vowels. We should not be astonished that the 5th hour should be represented by a vase, because the very sound given to this number 5 in the hieroglyphic language, is that of the *U* or *V* of Latium (which presents exactly the form of an elongated vase, and the cipher 5 figuring among the Romans, and in the antique forms of the Chinese 5, one finds ten U's joined back to back by their convex parts, or ten V's put end to end, or even in the commercial figures, our U scarcely modified, which is also the figure 5 among the Arabs and Indians. Sound and figure are then found here, as the poet Hager has

---

[1] A vase, rounded and enclosed by a cover ♂ is also the symbol of the 10th hour, in which the day ceases, or the clepsydras commence to be used, and to empty themselves, in such a way, that in putting this vase with hieroglyphics on its side, that is to say, sloping this vase—emptying it—one obtains the figures 1—0 (the empty vase is the image of the zero put near unity in ten. Compare the etymology of *zero*, empty, nothing, empty circle, the *ovδèv* of the Greeks; the number 10, in its antique forms, and also among certain slave peoples, is marked as a black ball, traversed by a line, like the l of several Gothic manuscripts.

[2] The name of China, or rather of Sin, as the Orientals write it (compare the word *Sinus*, of the Latins) designates the heart, the middle, the centre ; while the Chinese themselves call their country *Chine*, that is to say, the middle of the heart, the reason of which has been traced to the false idea of the Chinese that their country had been the centre of the inhabited earth. From these the symbol of Egypt in the Hieroglyphic writing (Hor. Apoll., Bk. 1, emb. xxii.) consisting of a heart, placed over a censer, and the idea, that this country was at the middle of the earth (Do., Bk. 1, emb xxi.) According to De Guignes' Dictionaries, Nos. 298 and 5787, Chin, with the key of Chien, signifies monkey, cynocephalus (animal figured in the clepsydras, according to Horapollon) emblem of Mercury, of letters, of the hours.

already observed (explanation, p. xiv.) not only for unity,
but also for the number 5, and in China, as well as among
the ancient Romans, and this ancient analogy between two
peoples so distant the one from the other, as well as that
which results from the sound *Chin* or *Cin*, of the 5th hour;
that of the &, which was already used in place of the Roman
V, demonstrates really a common centre and a continual
fusion of the figures and the letters.[1]   *Chin*, as we have seen,
is the name of a star in Upper Asia, classing the sun and the
moon by themselves, for the Egyptians and the Chinese
admitted, in fact, but five planets, of which the Heon, or
week of five days, demi-decades, carrying names; it was
natural, then, that after the Indian fashion *Veda* should
signify four, because the Indians only admitted four Vedas,
one star, or rather one of five planets measuring the time,
signified 5.   Among the hieroglyphs the number 5 is found
expressed by a figure analogous to the figure 8, or to that of
a clepsydra, when it is drawn upright, but it is also made
lying on its side (∞) and then it represents, without doubt,
that mystical knot (confer the strand or two-threaded cord
indicating, in the Egyptian hieroglyphics, H, more or less
aspirated,[2] a long vowel, derived from the &, representing 5,
as has been seen) which the Pythagoreans saw in the number
5; for the modern explanation, more or less subtle and false,
which the Chinese have given in their figures, they say concerning the X of the number, that it is the number of the
middle.   (See the word *Chin* or *Cin* from which we have derived the epithet Chine, the empire of the middle, as the 5 is
the middle of the tens) or of the *Earth*, and that it represents
the *Yu*, or female principle, combining itself with the *Yang*,
or male principle, between two lines, figures of heaven and
the earth (Dictionnaire *Tsen-Goey*, at the number 5), and
we find among the Pythagoreans the same ideas, since they
made also of the number 5 (confer *Histoire Critique de la*

---

[1] The symbolic vase of ten can also be explained with the Roman ten, represented by the capital X in printing, which presents to us two capital V's reversed
(that is, two triangular vases, and united by their points, which form the middle
of the figure X—X. One should also note that the 5 in its hieroglyphic figure is
analogous to the figure 8, and thus presents two round vases joined together, con-
forming the vase ideogram of 5, already noted.

[2] Dictionnaire Egyptologique d'Horapollon, p. 367.

Philosophie) [1] the symbol of the fertile earth, the number of *Juno,* goddess of marriages, the symbolic sign of themselves also, being formed, as they said, of *two,* first, an even number and female, and of *three,* odd number *par excellence* and male. We do not repeat these absurdities, although resembling each other on two sides, except to prove the common origin of all these ideas of a degenerated philosophy, very far from attributing them to their creators, enlightened by hieroglyphic writing, but also to assemble these ideas of the Chinese, unreasonable but cosmogonic, of the number 5 (of which the vase is the ideographic expression, with the cosmogonic myths and the legends already reported concerning the vase.

Passing on to linguistics, we find the idea of the vase in metaphors, and the image of the soul regarded as a measure ; in fact, the Sanscrit *ma,*[2] signifying to measure, and then *to think,* has given rise to the Sanscrit word *manas,* to the Greek μένος, to the Latin *mens ;* from the Sanscrit forms *mas* and *madh,* signifying also measure, are derived the Sanscrit *mali,* the Doric ματυς, the Attic μητίς, the Gothic *madhs,*[3] and the German *muth.* From the same root *ma* are also derived *matron,* μεαρυν, *metrum,* metre[4] or measure, and *masas,* the moon, the star which measures the time (English moon, German *mond*) and also μήν, and *mensis, mois,* the measure of time, *man* (whence the Sanscrit words mann, manava, manushya, the Greek *minos,* the German *munnus,* name of the son of Tuisco, ancient parent of the Germanic people, and also the other German words *mann, mensch,* (high German, Mennisch) signifying all the men ; coming from the same root *man,* to measure, to think, from which one may see that this has been the most noble and perhaps the most superb name that man could have given to himself ;

[1] Deslandes, Histoire Critique de la Philosophie, t. 2, pag. 77, and t. 40, of the Mémoires de l'Academie des Inscriptions et Belles Lettres, Desguignes, p. 174.

[2] To this word is closely united the Latin *mos, moris* (whence the plural substantive of the French, *moeurs,* from *mores,* and the derivatives *morale,* moralité, moralizer, measure, rule, precept.

[3] To this word is united the Hibernic *meadaighim,* to measure, and the Latin *meditari,* that is, to measure things with the mind.

[4] Confer the metaphorical signification in which V. Monti, in his poem La Basoitliana, c. 1, p. 55, takes the word *metro,* in Italian, saying *Di vitroso fanciul seguendo il metro.*

that is to say, that of measurer, thinker, and by this Mann, Minos, Mannus, proper names must signify, the Measurer, the Thinker, or the sage *par excellence.* This is why Horace of Archite, the illustrious Pythagorean philosopher and geometrician, in the first book of his odes—ode 28—has also said :

Te maris et cœli numeroque carentis arenæ
Mensorum cohibent. . . . . .

But since the measure is also of capacity (the more evasive Italian *capire,* from the Latin *capere,* to take, to contain, passes on to be comprehended by the mind, to contain, or to be contained in it, whence the two other words, *capare, capable,* admit in seizing, in understanding, and *capacité,* address in understanding, experience, etc.), as the bushel, the measure, the litre, the sack, etc. Here is how the mind has been represented as a species of vase. The Greek ἀγγεῖον, vase, indicates the body, and Cicero—Quæst. Tuscul. 1, 22—upon the end of the word vase, in Latin, says also : *Corpus quasi vas est aut aliquid animi receptaculum.*

Without doubt, to come now to study the idea of the vase by the means of specimens from writers, from the idea of the spirit—of the soul regarded as a measure of capacity—one may deduce the extreme suitability of the symbols which Dante and other writers have made use of ; the first, in fact in chapter II. of the Inferno—says of Saint Paul (called in the Bible *vas electionis,* Acts ix. 15) in v. 28 : "Andovvi poi lo vas d'elezione."—Go there[1] after the vase of election.

In Paradiso, 1. v. 13-15 :

O good Apollo, for a final test,
Make me,[2] by thy valor, such a vase,
As you should wish to give the laurel loved by you !

In the VII. Purgatory, v. 115-117.
And if after him had remained king
The young man, who sat behind him,
Well had valor gone from vase to vase.[3]

Inferno, ch. xxii. v. 81-82.

FRATE GOMITA.	BROTHER GOMITA.
Quel di Gallura, vasel d'ogni froda.	He of Gallura, vase[4] full of all guile.

[1] Here it is intended to say that St. Paul went to hell.
[2] Make me, that is to say, my soul, which by this indicates the sensible, intelligible and moral personality.   [4] This means Peter III. of Aragon.
[3] That is to say, " From soul to soul, valor, or rather virtue, passes.

Nevertheless Dante has not only seen in the soul a vase, but also a purse, and even a basket, as is here seen :

Inferno, ch. xi. v. 52-4.
Fraud, with which every conscience is dead,
Never may use towards him who trusts in it
And towards him whom confidence goes not, pocket.[1]

Inferno, ch. xxiv. v. 7-12.
The young villain, who lacks in goods,
Arises, and watches, and sees the fields,
All whiter, whose breadth he beats,
Returns home, and mourns both here and there,
How the unfortunate scarce know to do,
Afterwards, he goes anew and replaces hope in the basket (i. e. recovers it),
Seeing the world change[2] its face
Within an hour.

We also find it in several other poets and Italian and foreign prose writers, of which the following is a specimen :

F. BERNI, *Rime*, 1, 12.
I will fill you to the rim of the vase
With intellect.

L. PULCI, *Morgante Maggiore*, xvii. 6.
What say'st thou, Jan de Mayeuse,
Who art vase of every science and virtue.

P. SEGNERI, *Christiano istruito*, 1, 22, 16.
And now you will hasten like a vase of election all full of such fine hatred (towards sin), when you are a vase of rage, so full of wickedness that you overflow from every side.

The womb is called also *vase, natural box*, and so is the human body with reference to the soul which is lodged therein. Saint Gregory calls it *little vase*, or *little mortal vase; small vase*, for the body is found in G. B. Alberti, *Trattato del governo della famiglia*, 64 ; St. Paul, *Epistle to the Thessalonians*, i, 4 ; A. M. Salvini, *Sacred prose*, 306.

[1] I translate this *vase*, and not *little vase*, because afterwards the poet says of it, v. 89, *Barattier fu non picciol, ma sovrano*, which shows that the diminutive of the word is only in appearance, not in reality.
[2] That is to say, does not receive in the soul as a purse.
[3] Recovers it in the basket ; here imagining the soul.

G. B. ALBERTI.
God does not will to place his treasures most precious in fragile vases, nor cast pearls before filthy swine.

Treatise on the Government of the Family.

That each may know to possess himself his little vase in sanctification and honor, not in the passion of desire, like the heathen.

Salvini, Sacred Prose, 306.

These very holy bodies which were little vases for such great souls.

St. Paul Epist. ad Tess. iv. 4.

That each one should know how to possess his little vase in purity and honor.

Mor. Saint Gregoire.

So that he cannot presume in this mortal vase to investigate beyond what is agreed upon.

Jeremiah—Prophesies, vi-viii. 11.

Moab was fertile from his youth, and reposed in his bed, nor is changed from vase to vase.

Purgatorio, xxv. v. 44-45.

Wept.

Upon the blood of others in a little natural vase.

A. M. Cecchi, Dote, iv., 5.

If I had not this thing to give Frederick to think about, I had other than cries from him. In such fashion had Frederick blown into the box (that is, in the troubled soul, excited one against another).

Horace, Epistles, 1-2, 69.

The vase long preserves the perfumes of the fresh liquor with which it is filled.[1]

Michel Aignan at *Psalm* 118, v. 9, with very laconic efficiency, says : Quod nova testa capit inveterata sapit.

And St. Jerome, *Epist. ad Lætam :* Recens testa diu et saporem retinet, et odorem, quo primum imbutu est.

From the above line of Horace, Pierre the Venerable, *Epist.* 24—Hunc saporem, quocum ad huc testa rudis essem imbutus, et diu per gratiam Dei etiam hoc usque servavi.

The Church of the Virgin, in its Litanies, says : *Vas spirituale, vas honorabile, vas insigne devotionis. Vase d'iniquité, de misericorde, de pureté, d'élection,* is said of the soul, according to its virtues and vices.

Belonino.

Woman is a vase of election, in whom God has enclosed treasures of love and of faith.

Mme. de Sevigné.

I regard Mlle. de Gignan as a vase of election.

---

[1] In fact the soul was compared to a vase of pottery, having as text the verse of Horace, to indicate that a sentiment once received into the spirit, was preserved there eternally.

NICOLE.

"Our heart is a vase which may corrupt all it receives."

ALFRED DE MUSSET.

A pure man's heart is a deep vase,
When the first water put in is impure.
The sea might wash it without cleansing the stain.

BOURDALOUE, *Annonciation de la Vierge*, Myst. t. ii. p. 64.

It is humility which renders us capable of possessing God, of being vases of election, fit to contain the gifts of God.

MASSILLON, *Panegyric of Saint Bernard.*

"These were the first benedictions, by which heaven. foretells our vase of election."

J. B. ROUSSEAU.

God can, with his holy light,
Enlighten the eyes of the unjust,
Render holy a heart of sin,
Transform the bush into the tall cedar,
And make an elect vase from a rejected vase.

Vase de colère is the soul of him upon whom presses the rage of God.

Sacy Bible, St. Paul—Epistle to Romans ix. 23, who can complain of God (compared to a potter) of wishing to show his anger and make known his power, he supports with a supreme patience the vases of anger, destined to perish, in order to show forth the riches of his glory over the vases of mercy which he has prepared for glory?

In Portuguese *vaso terreno* is the human body; it is also said, *vaso dé barro;* that is to say, vase of mud. *Encher e vas das iniquidades.* Fill the soul with vices. Camoens Od. 5, *O meu peito, he para tanto bem pequeno vaso.*

Idem—Os Lusiados viii., 65, *Homo, vaso d'iniquicia.*

Idem—Ar corrupto, que n'este meu terreno vaso tinha, mes fez manjar de peixes em ti, bruto mar.

Páua-Paiva, Deus fez huns vasos de honra para mostrar sua bondade e mi misericordia; e outros de ignominia para mostrar sua justiça (Justos e peccadores). In Swedish, *Udvalgt Redskab* (vas electionis). In Hollandish, *Uitrerkoren Vat* (vase of purity). In Polish, *Naczynie Czystosci; Naczynie Wybrane* (vase of election for a sainted spirit). In German, *Ein gefass zu Ehren zu Unehren* (vase of honor, of dishonor). *Gefass des Zorns* (vase of rage).

We further find the vase represented in symbolic science very often, and always in relation with the soul; it was com-

pared to the pot of earth placed over the potter's wheel, while
he attends with his hands to giving it the last perfection
with the words *Ductu perficior*, the honest soul, supple and
polished with the sage precepts of others.   See Jeremiah,
Prophesies xviii. 3–4.   "I descended into the house of a
potter, and lo, he performed his work seated on his bench—
and the vase which he was making from clay, which was in
his hand, was spoiled, and he made of it yet another vase, as
it seemed good to him to do.   Saint Jérome—"I am fallen
almost in another matter, and propelling the wheel, when I
think to make a bottle, my hand turns out a flask ; which
recalls the more pleasing and original image of Horace, *Ars
Poetica* (of which this is an imitation rather unsuccessful),
v. 21–22.

| Amphora cœpit | You start an amphora, |
| Institui, currente rota, cur urceus exit ? | Why from the turning wheel does it become a cup ? |

A little brass cup, enclosing delicate perfumes, with the
words *calore odor*, indicated already the soul of Mary Mag-
dalen, her warm charity and her precious spiritual odor, so
St. Peter Gregory in his Homilies says of the same, *Amando
fortiter ardebat, et domus repleta est ex odore unguenti.*

The same Pope, in order to indicate the soul afflicted with
misfortunes, but entirely exhaling an odor of pity and devotion, says of the same, "Et ascendit fumus aromatum in
conspectu domini."   St. Cyril, the Alexandrian, writes of
book x. of Genesis : "Ut optimum quoque thus, cum igni
inhæserit, tum odoris suis suavitatem emittit sic anima
sancta cum laboribus, periculisque velut igne exanimata est,
tum clariorem, perfectioremque suam virtutem certissime
reddit.

A full vase, overturned with its mouth downward, which
goes on dropping out its liquors little by little, serves to indicate a spirit which does not know how to find expressions
suitable to render others the necessary thanks, with the
words, *ex copia inops.*   Justus Lipsius *Centur. sing ad Germ.*
"Ut in angusto canali aut tubo, ubi aqua aquam trudit, sis-
titur,   nec invenit egressum, itahoc ipso, quoad   interdum
multa simul dicere volumus, et debemus dicimus paula."

The souls of the justified, or of the saints, tormented and harassed, are sometimes symbolized under the image of vases of clay moistened in water, and afterwards hardened in the sun, with the sentence on them, *Transivimus per aquam et ignem*, so Abraham was removed from this "Chaldean life" (Gen. i. 5), that is to say, from the fire; and Moses (Ex. ii.) was drawn forth from the bosom of the water, and all the Jews passed both through the fire of the Egyptian furnaces and through the water of the Red Sea. Further, the souls of the just pass without scath through the surrounding flames of misfortunes, as well as through the refreshing waters of goodness.

The name acquired through sin is indicated by broken vases, which allow the water to escape from them, with which they were filled, with the sentence "*Quassatis diffluet.*"

To a broken vase pouring out liquid with the words, "At odorem diu," was compared the soul of the martyrs, who shed their blood in a moment, but the odor of their merits nevertheless was preserved, lasting eternally; the motto is read in the line cited from Horace—*Epistles*, Bk. 1, 2—and recalls to mind the other verse of Peter the Venerable.

As the vase, when it is full, looks equally well, whether it is whole and sound, or broken and defective, so the soul of man, as soon as he has acquired honors, charges and dignities, shows forth its qualities, whence the Greek proverb: Ἀρχή ἄνδρα δείχνυσι and the Latin, "Magistratus virum indicat," which recalls the sentence of Sophocles, in his tragedy *Antigone*, Ἀμήχανον δὲ παντὸς ἀνδρὸς ἐχμαδεῖν ψυχὴν τε χαὶ φρόνημα χαίγνώμην πρίνᾶν ἀρχαῖσ τε χαι νόμοίσιν ἐντριβής φανῇ.

The Church which, receiving within its communion proud and uncultured men, succeeds in making them pliable and pure; and the virgin who, receiving in her bosom a God, who seemed severe, made him peaceable and loving, are both symbolized: the one with the image of a vase of virgin wax plunged into the sea, and which, filling up with the waters of the same, takes away from them entirely their saltness and bitterness, and renders them sweet and purified, with this motto on them, *Haustam purificat;* and the other below the image of the same vase, also submerged, with the motto, "*Dulcorat haustam.*"

The vase of chalk, mended with wax, also with the motto, *Reficitur ex eadem,* is the ideogram of the resurrection.

To the chalk vase, placed upon the wheel by the potter, is compared the soul created differently by God, with the motto : *Usus a figulo,* taking its subject from the *Epistle of St. Paul to the Romans,* iv. 21, "At non habet potestatem figulus luti facere aliud quidem vas in honorem, aliud vero in contumeliam ?"

A vase, containing wine and water, with a piece of cloth over its mouth, by means of which the water is separated from the wine, clearly sets out with the motto, "Se cernit et disperdit impurum," indicating the last judgment, in which the good will be separated from the bad.

The device on a large vase, which is pouring forth its liquor into other vases of different capacity and size, has a motto, "Aquam non æque ;" showing us that in the republics and religions there must necessarily exist justice, by the means of which the grade and honor suitable to their capacity is given to each subject.

The vase of potter's clay and also a little empty vase, if it is struck hard with the finger, resounds, and has a motto, "Sonat inane," indicating the man when most defective in virtue and good qualities, the more so because he is of all others a great talker ; on this point Plutarch says : "Vascula inania maxime hinniunt ita quibus minus inest mentis, hi sunt loquacissimi." And Cornelius à Lapide, in *Proverb,* cap. 17, num. 28, after the citation of a Hebrew prophet, says : "Lagena plena nummis non sonabit ; unicus et alter si in ea nummus fuerit sonum edet, et tinniet." Adds also, "Sic sane quo quis doctior, eo est et modestior, et taciturnior, quo indoctior, eo audacior et loquacior." Jacques Bruck, in *Les Emblemes,* 30 :

    "Vasa velut nullos edunt impleta sonores
       Aut exhausta levi pollice tacta sonant,
       Sic doctus vanis se nunquam laudibus effert
       Arte rudis laudes detonat ore suas."

A great vase which is shedding its liquor into another smaller and narrower one, both in the neck and in the mouth, dropping it slowly, so as not to spill it on the ground unnecessarily, has the motto : "Sensim ne diffluat," or with

another "Non totum sum," indicating the spirit of the
master and of the tender pupil, and shows that precepts
ought to be given little by little, so that the tender spirit of
the latter, less receptive, can yet receive them all, and the
work of the first shall not be in vain; as to this Cornelius
à Lapide says, *Proverbs* 22, 6: "Mens pueri est velut vas,
habens os angustum, cui liquor sensim instillandus; alioqui
si totum simul infundas, ad latera diffluet et perdetur." A
vase which sheds by its cracks the liquid, which is poured
into it, with the motto: "Combien, recueille répand," is
the soul of the spendthrift and of the ungrateful man, who
receives benefits and throws them aside, completely losing
remembrance of them. On this point Guido Casomi, *Emblems*, 18:

> Unfortunate pains, neglected work,
> Vain industries, and useless studies
> Are theirs, who cast their good deeds
> As if in a deep gulf, in a heart.
> Ingrates, who grasp them with avidity
> And waste them through the apertures of neglect.

And Paul Mascio, emblem 6:

> Ingratus plenum est vas rimis, omnia frustra
> Injicias haurit, fundit et illa brevi.

Cornelius à Lapide, in a reticulated vase, pictures the unhap-
piness of women, who, with the traffic of their honor, make
many conquests, nevertheless they cannot enjoy any of their
riches, always remaining poor and abandoned. Here is the
verse of *Proverbs*, cap. xxiii. 27: "Meretrix est dolium per-
foratum, in quo etiam, si Croesi opes injicias affluunt, et prod-
igantur, ipsaque semper eget, remanetque inops et pauper."
This device particularly indicates the person incapable of
keeping secrets to himself, which have been confided to
him.

Terence, in his comedy, *Eunucus*, act 1, sc. 2:

Quæ vera audivi, taceo, et contineo optime
Sin falsum, aut vanum, aut fictum est, continuo palam est;
Plenus rimarum sum; hoc atque illæ perfluu.

The vases of chalk placed in the furnace to bake were
marked with the motto: *Solidamur in usus;* symbol also of
souls in purgatory and of men skilled in the exercise of

II

arms and in works, so that they may, at the opportune time,
afterwards serve at any time of need. The motto serves
also for the apostles, for the descent of the Holy Spirit in
the form of fire marvellously hardened to be courageously
held rigid against the ferocity of pagans and to prevail against
them ; the device also serves well for the just tormented by
divine will ; in order to make them constant in virtue and
increase their merit ; in fact, in *Ecclesiasticus* xxvii. 6, we
read : "Vasa figuli probat fornax, et homines justos tentatio
tribulationis." And the benefit of the fire goes on increasing
until the just succeed not only in pushing on to the acquisi-
tion of new and more durable vigor, or of unexpected victories,
but still incorruptible ones, as Saint Gregory affirms apropos
of the words of *Psalm* xxi. 16, "Aruit tanquam testa virtus
mea," he says, "Quid est testa ante ignum, nisi molle tutum ?
Sed ei ex igne agitur ut solidaretur. Virtus ergo humanitatis
ejus (that is to say, King David and allegorically the Saviour)
velut testa exaruit, quia ab igne passionis ad virtutem incor-
ruptionis crevit."

As several vases of different sizes near a fountain are filled
with water one at a time, according to their capacity, so in
the same way the gifts of divine grace are shed abroad according to the capacity of those who receive them, as Saint
Jerome, lib. ii., *Epistola ad Ephesias*, cap. 24, says, "Gratia
justa mensuram credentibus datur, non quod ad mensuram,
spiritum et gratiam tribuat Deus ; magnificentia enim ejus
non est finis, sed quod juxta mensuram vasculorum infundat
liquorem, tantum largiens, quantum potest ille, cui donatur,
accipere."

A vase, when seen plunging into a fountain with the
motto : "Mergitur, dum impletur," is the symbol of the libid-
inous person who, while he tries to satisfy his wicked
appetites, remains pitiably submerged in them.

The device on certain vases glazed in the furnace, with the
motto, "Non Sine Fabri Spiritu," indicates St. Ignatius de
Loyola, who, by means of Pierre Fabre, one of his disciples
and companions, had drawn to him I know not what faithful
ones, to have them acquire sanctity and true perfection.
Each man became a vase of grace by the influence of the
Holy Spirit, whence comes all sanctity.

According to Saint Isidore (*origins*), "Vas aureum indicat praeclarum, subtilioremque Dei intelligentiam."

Should any one seek what interpretation to make of the two casks, anciently placed in a Roman chapel, in the street, near the Cloaca Maxima, which leads to the Carènes,[1] place in which it was forbidden to spit; as to this Plutarch advises us that this chapel was called "The Chapel of the Casks (Sacellum Doliola)." Without doubt, as some affirm, of these two casks, one was that in which were already placed things sacred to Numa, and the other empty, but in which at the time of the invasion of the Senonian Gauls, some relics had been hidden by the Vestal Virgins; when they, seized with fear, abandoned the city, saving themselves by flight. These same writers also relate that in the above-named spot were formerly found ten statues in military garb, which were seated, holding in their hands darts, with the inscription placed below, *Di Penates*, signifying that they are fatigued with having established the seat of the empire, the darts indicating that they had driven the enemy from it, and the other arms symbolizing of themselves virtue and the restoration of the power of the Roman people.[2]

Let us now see how vases enter into the cycle of literary tales and of popular stories; in the place of vases, coffers are found, or caskets, or boxes, or, even loaves, or pies, but that makes no difference, because from the commencement of our work we have said we would take the idea of the vase in an acceptation much more generic, and this is how we keep the promise.

Before all, it is necessary to recall *The History of Barlaam and Josaphat*, in which the legend appropriate to our subject is thus given : "A rich king, desirous of giving to the officers of his court a lesson upon the foolishness of judging by appearances, caused four little chests to be made, of which two were filled with the decaying bones of human corpses, but covered with gold and closed with gold bars; the other

---

[1] Carinæ-arum formed the part of ancient Rome in the 4th quarter where was the temple of the Goddess Telluria (earth), that of Juno (Sororia), the palaces of Cicero, Pompey, and other great lords.

[2] These Hagiographic notices upon the vase have been thought out for us by Filippo-Picinelli; *Mondo simbolico*, lxv. c. 26—Venezia Combi, 1670, and *Hiero-glyphica* of Pierre Valeriana.

two, covered with pitch and bound with heavy cords, but full of precious stones, of the most exquisite jewels, and of very odorous perfumes. The courtiers, invited to indicate among them which might have the greatest value, they pointed out the two first; then the king, to show how the senses could be deceived, and how the spirit alone could safely see, penetrating into the midst of things,[1] having opened the two chests of gold, caused them to see the bones of human corpses which they contained, at which the spectators were overwhelmed with horror."

In the *Açoka Avadâna,* the same vase is found full of fresh milk, and another full of sour, which recalls the milk-pot in the well-known *fable* of La Fontaine " La Laitière et le pot au lait," (*Liv. vii., No. 10*), so well studied by Mr. Muller ; the pot of flour in the *Pantschatantra* (Liv. v. No. 9) ; the jar of oil in the artistic and popular literature of Portugal (O pote de azeite; A bilha de azeite), for which see Adolpho Coelho, *Contos nacionaes para creanças,* Porto, Magalhaes No. 8 (extract from the works of Gil Vincente), and Theophile Braga *Contos tradiciones do pavo portuguez,* t. ii, Porto Magalhaes e Moniz, No 150.

In *Labitavis tara* there is a legend of Buddha, who waits seven days meditating under the tree Bodhi, without taking any nourishment, and when the celestial minister descended there to bring some, he only wished to have some put in a very poor vase, which he had chosen from among several others of great value, presented to him previously.

The *Legend of the Book of Barlaam and Josaphat,* a little disguised, is found in the *Gesta Romanorum,* Latin text, c 109 (see Grässe, i. 216, p. 246–46) ; in it the four little chests became three pies, the first full of dirt, the second of bones, and the third of silver, found by an innkeeper, who wished to see if it was the will of God that the smith should lodge with him, and he who sought must choose. But, having engaged him to eat them, the smith first took that full of dirt, then the other full of bones, and left the third to the inn-keeper ; the latter, having seen that God had not wished,

---

[1] Dante in his Paradiso c. ii. v. 52.57, S'egli erra, L'opinion—de mortali Dove chiave di senso non dissera, certo non ti dovrien punger gli strati D'ammirazione omai por dietro ai sensi Vedi che la ragione ha corte l'ali ; then reason, following sense, ought always to be decided.

and that he might take back his money, and, having called
in the poor, he divided it with them.

One of the *Cento Novello Antiche*, which is founded really
upon the proverb, *L'homme propose et Dieu dispose*, No. 65
(Borghini Text), which, with some modifications, is the
No. 14 (Papanti Text), contains also the same episode ; only
the three pies become two loaves ; here is the abstract of
them, by Professor A. D'Ancona.[1] "During the war of the
King of France with the Count of Flanders two blind men,
quarrelling together to solve the question as to who would
conquer ; the one sustained the part of the King, the other
said, "What God wills, will be." The King, advised of this,
caused two loaves to be cooked, in one of which he had two
golden besants put, and had them given to him who had
chosen for him. The two blind men returned to the house,
and he who said, "What God wills, will be," ate his bread
with his wife, while the other proceeded to sell the bread
received from the King, and to eat another purchased one.
The companion, to whom the loaf of the King seemed very
good, proposed to buy his bread, and found the silver in it.
The morning after, he related this to his companion, who
was obliged to agree himself that things in this world are in
the hands of God, and the King himself, as soon as he learned
this, must also agree to it. According to Robert, *Fables
Inedites* (1–149), this story is also found in *Renart le contre-
fait*. Something like this recital is found in Dunlop *Geschichte der Prosadichtung übersetzt von Liebrecht*, Berlin,
Müller, 1851, p. 250, and Simroch, *Quellen des Shakespeare*,
1–246 ; the first account, without mention of a war, contains
the question, which would be more profitable, the favor of
God or of Cæsar ; it is, perhaps, the story which is found in
the *Latin Stories of Wright*, London, 1842, No. 104, and in
Pauli, *Schimpf und Ernst* edition, Œsterley, Stuttgart, 1866,
No. 326, where his notes are seen, and also those of the same
on page 729, of chap. 109 of the *Gesta Romanorum ;* see also
Simroch's *Novellenschatz der Italiener*, Berlin, 1832, page 24
pf. ; and *Franz Pfeiffer, Altdeutsche Uebungs buch zum Geb-

---

[1] Studi di critica e storia litteraria, Bologna, Lanichetti 1880, page 345 ; Le fonti
del Novellino. This story, with the title, "Qui conta di due ciechi che conten-
deano insieme," a very important work, first appeared in Romania of Paris
in 1873.

rauch der Hochschulen, Wien, 1866; but in this story the
bread of one of the two blind men contains a golden sword
(sic), and the other a chapon (sic); a closer resemblance
with the story of the Novellino and the legend of Giovanni
Damasceno is a version in prose of the story of the two blind
men, for which, see Pauli, Schimpf und Ernst (Œsterley,
c. 326), where, in one of the loaves, there is some gold; in
the other, some bones of human corpses. The story is also
again altered in *Rudlieb,* in which there is no question of
choice nor of exchange, because both the loaves are full of
gold and precious stones, and the entire story may show
finally that wisdom and knowledge may be the best treasures
of the world, so that the man who possesses these things is
provided with true riches.

But there are other oriental and Western writings containing the episode of the vases of the *Book of Barlaam and
Josaphat* more definitely; three of them are found in *The
Benfey, Pantschatantra Einleit,* 1-407. Here is a resumé of
the first : " A rich merchant, dying, leaves, to his four sons,
four vases with their names, which have the portion of their
estate allotted to them ; as soon as they have opened them,
they find in the first, dirt ; in the second, coal ; in the third,
some bones, and in the fourth, some straw, as an indication
that they shall merit lands (fields and farms) ; metals, gold
and silver (symbolized by the coal) ; elephants, horses, buffaloes, goats, slaves (the bones being allegorical of these living
creatures) ; sheaves and products of the soil (indicated by the
straw). The second story relates that a king of Pandya,
who, in order to justify himself to his wife, for the bestowal
of a thousand pieces of gold upon his minister of state,
although he was only able to serve him with words, while
to others who had attended day and night to minister to him,
he gave but two or three pieces of gold each month, having
taken two little boxes for jewels, he filled each of them with
ashes and hair, and put on the lid ; afterwards, by means of
his minister, he sent one to the King of Sera, and the other,
by means of a soldier, to the King of Saren ; the minister
made the King of Sera believe that the cinders and the hair
were given to the King of Pandya by a genius ; that, in
knowing of their salutary virtue, he really begrudged send-

ing him a little, and so succeeded in calming the rage of the King of Sera, who thought himself derided ; the soldier, on the contrary, not knowing what to say to the King of Saren when he found the box full of cinders and hair, only succeeded in doubling his ire, and was chased out and whipped ignominiously. The third story is like it, with the sole difference, that instead of two boxes, there is but one, filled with cinders, and sent to the King of Augo by the King Somita from the City Sancravati by the hands of Vishun, son of his minister Suçila ; with the same ruse as to the nature of the cinders contained in the box, the young man obtains a success similar to the minister in the other story.

In the *Gesta Romanorum*, Latin text of Œsterly (Appendix, 251), Honorius, Emperor of Rome, in order to prove if the young woman, saved by a nobleman, were worthy of his son, had three chests made, the first full of the bones of dead men, covered with pure gold and precious stones, with the motto : "Whoever opens me, will find in me that of which he is worthy ;" the second, full of dirt, although covered with very pure silver and enriched with jewels, with the motto : "Whoso makes choice of me, will find in me that which nature designs for him ;" the third, full of precious rings, although covered with lead, with the motto : "I would rather be here and stay here than to rest among the treasures of the king." The young girl makes choice of the leaden casket, and all ends well.

John Gower, in his English poem, *Confessio Amantis*, relates that a king, in order to prove to some of his officers and courtiers (they complaining to him of not being recompensed in equal measure, according to their merits) that this depended solely on chance, had two boxes made, exactly alike, so that one might be easily exchanged for another ; he had one of them filled with gold and precious stones, and the other with straw and rags, and the courtiers and officers having preferred the second to the first, he took the argument from this to confirm what he had formerly said.

In the *Decameron of Boccaccio*, first novel of the tenth day, although an Italian gentleman chooses the second of the two chests (the one containing the royal crown, the sceptre, and several rings and jewels, and the other dirt, given him to choose from by Alphonso, King of Spain) the king, in order to mollify the adverse fortune of the gentleman, gives him the other one, of which fortune had wished to deprive him.

In the drama of Shakespeare, "*The Merchant of Venice*," whose subject is taken from Giovanni Fiorentino *Le Pecorone*, (No. 1, 4th day) with the necessity of knowing how to choose from three chests, the one in which is the portrait of the woman, in place of having to fulfill the office of husband without being such, was to obtain both the right and the name ; the same as in Jean Fiorentino : The three coffers are : one of gold, with the motto, "He who chooses me will gain what many men desire ;" and the two other, of silver and of lead, with the mottoes, "Whosoever chooses me ought to give and risk all he possesses." Bassanio makes choice of this chest and obtains his Portia as a wife.[1]

In a story of Jérôme Morlino, *Fabuleè, Novelle*, No. 5, *of the Sovereign Pontiff Sixtus, who with a word enriched his servant* (Jérôme Riario) and in the imitation, or rather the translation, made by Straparola, in his *Plaisants Nuits* (5th of the 12th No.) the pontiff, Sixtus IV., two covered urns are presented, of which one is filled with carbuncles, precious stones, and antique jewels, the other full of metal. The servitor makes choice of the second, and from this fact the pope, who did not, on the contrary, give him the first, took the argument to reprimand him for his sins which brought contrary fortune to him, and besought him to do penance for them, having for this very reason shown him the precious things of the other urn, which he had lost.[2] This recital of the vases to be chosen is found in Vincentius Bellovacensis, *Speculum Historiale*, liv. xiv. In the *History of Ali Cogia, Merchant of Bagdad*, of the 1001 Nights, a vase of a certain capacity is found, containing a thousand pieces of gold cov-

---

[1] These citations upon vases and chests in several works have been taken from Simrock's *Quellen des Shakespeare*, from Th. Benfey *Pantschatantra*, and an important study by the illustrious Italian Giuseppe Chiarini, Le due leggende del Mercante di Venezia, in Nuova Antologia, liv 1, Apr., 1892.

[2] Dante, in ch. vii. of Inferno, making of Fortune a celestial Intelligence, who governs for God the possessions of the earth, says of her (578-77-81) : "*Colui, lo cui saver tutto transcende * * * Similemente agli splendor mondani, Ordino general ministra e duce, Che permutasse a tempo il ben vani, di gente in gente e d'uno in altro sangue oltre la difension di senni umani.*"

ered over with olives, confided by him to another merchant, his friend, who, having seen them, by a certain chance, stole them ; but Cogia, by means of a ruse, succeeded in recovering them. This story, under the title of the Unfaithful Guardian, is found, on the contrary, in the 1001 Days, edition of Loiseleur Deslongchamps, p. 652. It is also contained in the Mélanges de Littérature Orientale of Cardonne, t. 1, p. 62. It is also found in the *Disciplina Clericalis* of Pierre Alphonse, c. 161, t. 1, p. 16, of the Paris edition ; see also the notes of Schmidt (p. 137), in the Fabliaux, gathered by Barbazan (t. ii. p. 107), and Le Grand d'Aussy (t. iii. p. 248), in the *Cento Novello Antiche*, No. 74, p. 48, edition 1802, in the Decameron of Boccaccio, t. viii. n. 10. Here one may also recall the 10th novel of the sixth day of Frère Cipalla and his wallet, holding a box containing a parrot's plume, which the Friar proposed to make the superstitious people believe to be a feather of the Archangel Gabriel ; this box is filled with charcoal by two young wags ; as soon as the friar sees the substitution of coal for the plume, he made his auditors believe that he had exchanged the box containing the feather of the Archangel Gabriel for another of the charcoal on which St. Lawrence was roasted.

Before concluding, I may be permitted to note how in Folk-Lore there is the episode above-noted of *Barlaam and Josaphat ;* in fact, in the remarks to No. 48 of his *Contes Populaires de la Lorraine*, the author gives an indication of several popular stories where it is found ; really in a Tyrolean story of Zingerlé, *Tiroler Kinder und Hausmärchen*, t. 1, Innsbruch, 1852, No. 1, a little girl goes out to gather strawberries with her brother ; she responds politely to the questions of a beautiful lady, who is the Holy Virgin, while the little boy responds falsely ; for this she receives a box of gold, from whence come two angels, who carry her to the sky, and he receives a black one, from which two serpents emerge, who carry him away. In a German story of Kuhn and Schwartz, *Nord-deutsche Sagen Märchen und Gebräuche*, Leipzig, 1848, p. 335, a little boy having refused to give some of his breakfast to a dwarf, the devil comes out of a box given to him by the dwarf, to twist his neck. In a Swabian story of Meier, *Deutsche Volksmärchen aus Schwaben*, Stuttgart,

1852, No. 77, a young girl having been courteous to an angel encountered while she was out promenading, to whom she gave at once her breakfast, received from him a box filled with precious stones and pieces of gold; on the contrary, another girl, who did not wish to give anything to the angel she met in the same road, and to whom she spoke rudely, received from her a box full of little black devils. The two boxes became two balls, one black and one white, which rolling along led one to a black gate, from whence came forth the devil to carry to hell the little girl who spoke evilly to the Holy Virgin and Jesus; the other, to the white gate, whence came forth angels to lead to heaven the little girl who acted well towards them; this, with Wolf Deutsche Märchen und Sagen, Leipzig, 1845, No. 38.

In Vouk Karadschich, *Volksmärchen der Serben,* in *Deutsche übersetzt von dessen Tochter Wilhelmine,* Berlin, 1854, No. 36, two girls, one good and the other bad, asked by a dragon to choose among several chests, the first modestly takes the lightest, and opening it at her home finds it full of ducats; the second does precisely the contrary, and having brought the heaviest one to the house, as soon as she has opened it, two serpents come out, who tear out her eyes as well as her mother's. The choice among three coffrets, of gold, of silver and of lead, proposed to two young girls ends with the choice of the last, made by the good one, which, as in all the literary stories yet seen, contains precious treasures; and the choice by the wicked girl of the first, full of toads and of serpents, which being opened, they come out and fill the whole house. See for this a popular Irish story of Kennedy II.—The Fireside Stories of Ireland, Dublin, 1875, p. 33. In a story of the extreme Orient, gathered among the Kairens of Burmah, for the analysis of which see M. F. Mason, *Journal of the Asiatic Society of Bengal,* t. 34, 1865, 2d part, p. 228, the choice falls between two baskets, one older than the other—the first filled with gold and with silver, the other with human skulls (very like the legend in Jean Dumarceaux) the one is obtained by a young girl, although she has behaved badly towards an old giant (because the story, which M. Cosquin well notes, has been changed) and the other by a young man.

In a Japanese story translated by A. B. Mitford, *Tales of Old Japan,* London, whom he visits 1871, p. 249, is found the choice between two willow baskets proposed by a sparrow to a good man who chooses the lightest, full of gold, of silver, and of precious objects; his wicked wife, going to the sparrow's home, obtained nothing at all.

Finally, in a popular Annamite story by Mons. A. Landes, *Contes et Légendes Annamites* (appearing at Saïgon in the collection *Cochinchine Française Excursions et Reconnaissances*), 5 parts, published from Nov., 1884, to Jan., 1886, ii. p. 121–23, No. 72, a beloved rich sister and a poor younger one went to gather in a field of potatoes, each one with a basket; a serpent entered into the two baskets, but that of the basket of the younger, carried to the house and baked, changed into a bar of gold; on the contrary, the serpent of the basket of the elder, brought to the house, multiplies into a nest of others, which fill the whole house, and kill the wicked woman with their bites.[1]

Here I recall a verse of the *Carmi dei Sepolcri d'Ugo Foscolo,* which are to our purpose (v. 114–118); here they are :

> " Cipressi e cedri
> Di puri effluvi i zefiri impregnando
> Peranne verde protendean sull 'urna
> Per memoria perenne e preziosi
> Vasi accoglican ie lagrime votive."

Ugo Foscolo makes this remark—(The lachrymatory vases, the lamps and the funeral rites of the ancients) : " Although these precious vases, according to the best authorities, were destined to receive perfumes and unguents to put in the tombs of the dead, as objects which had been dear in life, and not lachrymatories to receive the tears of the mourners and the *prefiche,* nevertheless I believe it best to follow the beautiful image of the sublime poet, and compare these precious poetical vases with the tombs of the dead destined to receive the votive tears with the urn, placed with the marble bier, where sleeps the enchanted prince, in filling which with tears thus so completely, that in making it run

---

[1] The resumé of this story, instead of being among the remarks in the Lorraine story, is found in the Supplement aux Remarques, p. 362 of t. ii. of *Contes Populaire de la Lorraine.*

over, they will succeed in reanimating the prince, who is as
one dead;" further, I believe in the verse of Foscolo to be
outlined a reminiscence of popular tradition; in fact, in the
different versions of the popular story of the *Serpent King*,
the woman, who has lost her husband, in order to find him
again, must fill seven flasks with her tears; to have lost him
was to be death to her, one and the same.   Finally, the *Vase
of Tears* is the subject of a very pretty popular German
legend, for which see Grimm's *Kinder und Hausmärchen*,
t. ii. p. 118; [1] here is the resumé of it: A good widow, who
had lost a very gracious daughter, and a very dear one, wept
ceaselessly day and night, not being at any time able to take
any nourishment; one evening, being overwhelmed by her
profound and unconsollable grief, before the little bed, where
her dear daughter was lying dead, she saw the door mysteri-
ously open, and her dear child appear, resplendent with celestial beauty.   She carried in her hands a vase, full of tears to
the brim, and said to the mother, "Good mother, do not
weep so; see, the angel of grief has caught your tears in this
vase, which will run over if you continue to weep.   Your
tears flow over me and trouble my sleep in the tomb, and my
sanctification in Paradise."   Having said these words, the
young girl disappeared.   The mother checked her tears so as
not to disturb her repose in Heaven.

Before taking leave of you, very honored gentlemen and
dear confrères, with the most humble excuses for the great
length of my memoir, and the fatigue which it has doubtless
produced in you, permit me to note that in several legends of
the middle age is found the superstition, according to which,
the most bitter tears may be a cause of suffering to the dead,
so for example we read in a Swedish ballad *Sorgens Magt* in
Svenska Folk Visor of Geiger och Afzelius t. i. p. 29.

> St. xiv.   "Each tear shed from thine eye
>   Wets with blood my funeral pyre
>
> St. xv.   "Each pleasure felt by thee on earth
>   Fills my tomb with roses sweet."

[1] See the Italian translation which I have made with the title, Il vaso di *lagrime*, *Leggende popolare tedesca, tradatta per la pinna volta in Italiano*, in the bro-chure, Stanislas Prato, *Tre conti inediti originali et una Leggenda Germanica tradatta per la pinna volta* in *Italiano*. Como, F. Solinelli Dec., 1882 (Extract

The same image is also found, indicated in the same way, in a Danish ballad, *Aage og Else*, St. xi. and xii., in Danske Viser fra Middelalderen, edition of Nyerup, t. i. p. 212.

from the sole copy—*Charitas*, in aid of the flood-stricken), I have there proposed as a dedicula the following beautiful verse of Ugo Fosculo, Como de Sepolcri, v. 29-35. Celeste e'questa corrispondenza d'amorosi sensi, Celeste ·doti i negli umania sperso, Per lei si vive con l'amico estinto, e l'estimo con noi."

SOME POPULAR BELIEFS OF EGYPT.

BY G. MASPERO.

IN the month of February, 1884, one of the employés of the Museum of Boulaq, Khourshid-Effendi, who usually accompanied me in my journeys to Upper Egypt, was seized with severe lumbago at Luxor. The remedies which I had at my disposal, and the treatment under which I attempted to place him, not having effected any alleviation of his sufferings, one of my sailors, Hamdan-el-Gousî, informed him that the Sheikh interred at the village of Qournah, had been a great saint, and had cured many maladies, among others gout, and the various kinds of rheumatism. Kourshid-Effendi had himself carried to the spot indicated to him, accomplished the required ceremonies, and returned greatly benefited by his pilgrimage. Some days later he had a relapse, while we were at anchor in the harbor of Assouan ; he found a new cure for his malady, and received benefit therefrom, in the environs of the city. I never succeeded in persuading him to reveal to me the precise spot where the remains of the saint of Assouan reposed, or the name given to him : he had promised not to tell it to infidels. He did not preserve the same discretion at all as to the saint of Qournah, who rested in ground attached to the space under excavation, and which he accordingly believed to be placed under my jurisdiction.

He pointed out to me the place consecrated to the cures, only begging me not to approach it, except as by chance, and when I did go there, not to say or do anything which could cause any one to suppose that I knew the virtues of it ; the fellahs of the neighborhood would not have pardoned this petty treason on his part. It was a tolerably large grotto, the chapel of an ancient tomb, whose walls showed no traces of painting or of ornament ; its anterior wall had been partially thrown down, and allowed the light to penetrate fully. The manner of proceeding of the Saint is peculiar. The invalid who seeks his aid, must prostrate himself at the entrance of the grotto, and recite several rekahs, with his face turned towards the bottom of the grotto. When his prayer is ended, he stretches out at full length on the ground, and waits. If the Sheikh resolves to hear him, he falls into a sort of swoon, during which an invisible force seizes him and rolls him from one end of the grotto to the other. Arriving at the spot where the passage opens out, he arouses, still dazed by the treatment, but already helped by it. The devotees renew the operation many times in succession, so long as the saint continues to roll them. The process is about the same at Assouan, and upon the hill of Sheikh Abd-el-Qournah. Khourshid-Effendi assured me that he felt much afraid on coming out of his mysterious trance, and that he had not dared to repeat the experiment; he attributed his imperfect cure to his want of faith.

I only stopped once in the grotto, and cannot indicate its precise situation. It is excavated in the rock, near the modern chapel of Sheikh Abd-el-Qournah, not very far from the tomb numbered 19 on the map of Wilkinson. The people who have visited this corner of the Theban Necropolis know how difficult it is to find one's whereabouts here; the rubbish thrown out each instant from the excavations, and the shifting of the sand by the wind, changes its appearance from month to month, and it often happens that the reis of antiquities, living in the neighborhood, do not recognize the locality from week to week. Furthermore, the fellahs do not love to show the place to strangers; all those to whom I spoke of it during that year and the following, began by denying that there was a healing saint, then ended by acknowledging that they knew him, but that this was a tale of *long ago, long ago* (*min zamân zamân*), that stories were still told about it, but that no one had ever seen the pretended miracles The sailor, Hamadan, to whom I applied, at first promised to lead me there, as Khourshid-Effendi had already done, then the next day he confided to me hesitatingly that he had feared that he could not find the site, and finally he acknowledged that he had been threatened with rough treat-

ment, if he should persist in serving me as guide. He informed me that, according to the people of the country, the
Sheikh had been formerly interred at the very foot of the
mountain, in a brick building now almost destroyed and
whose ruins are seen to the north of the Ramesseum. He
had been transported later into his present tomb on the hill
of Qournah. The cult of the Sheikh Abd-el-Qournah, whose
name has been given to the hill, has, then, three locations :
the one in the grotto, which is the scene of the miraculous
cures, the second in a ruined edifice built in the style of the
Pharaohs, and the third in a modern chapel.

I had never been troubled with rheumatism at that time.
The curiosity which impelled me to become acquainted with
the Sheikh was not then an interested one. It had, however,
its *raison d'être*. A prolonged visit to the Museum of Turin
had led me, in 1880, to study a whole collection of monuments dedicated to one of the least-known goddesses of the
Egyptian Parthenon. She who possesses the significant
name of Miritsakro (*She who loves silence*). They came from
Thebes. The goddess there has sometimes the face of a
woman ; oftener, she is a woman with the head of a serpent,
crowned with two plumes. Miritsakro was, then, one of
those serpent divinities which are found in such great numbers among the Egyptians. She seems to have been the
goddess of the dead in the Theban religion, anterior to the
XVIIIth Dynasty, the veritable companion of Amon before
the artificial hatching out of the goddess. She resided on
the Brow of Thebes (*ta tehnit*), that is to say, upon the spur
of mountains which faces the city of the living, in the hills of
El Assasif and of Sheikh Abd-el-Qournah. A stele in the
museum of Turin (No. 296) represents her domain, and shows
us that it was identified with her, so far as to call her *ta
Tehnit uirit rite Amentit, the great summit* (litt. *the great
brow of the west*, or simply *ta Tehnit, the summit*, like the
mountain itself. Her principal chapel stands to the north of
the Ramesseum, near the chapel of Ouazmosou, disinterred by
M. Grébaut and reached, if it did not comprise, the present
ruined edifice where the testimony of the sailor Hamdan per-
mits us to place one of the sanctuaries of the healing Saint.
It is there, or in the immediate neighborhood, that I have

brought to light a certain number of fragments representing the goddess, or carrying the remains of inscriptions in her honor; it is from there that all those of the Steles consecrated to Miritsakro come, the origin of which I have been able to establish.

Like the greater portion of the gods of the dead, Miritsakro was also a medical divinity. She took care of the devotees who applied to her, and they manifested their recognition of this by depositing, in her sanctuary, a proscynema which took the place of a sacrifice. The greater part of these *ex-votos* contained nothing more than a customary formula, applicable to all the other gods, and did not provide us any information concerning the motives which had impelled the donor to an act of piety. One of them which is at the Museum of Turin very happily passes out of this common category. The goddess is there represented under the form of a serpent, with three heads,—of a woman, a viper, and a vulture. The *servant of the Necropolis,* Nofiráboui, has before her the following discourse: "Adoration *to the Summit of the West,* proscynema to his double. I make my adorations, listen! I, at the time when I walked upon the earth, and when I was a *servant* of *Necropolis,* Nofiráboui, an ignorant individual, a fool, who knew not how to discern good from evil, I committed a number of sins against *the summit.* She chastised me, I was in her hand day and night; I remained on the brick-bed like a pregnant woman, and I cried to get fresh air, but the air did not come to me. I addressed myself to *the summit,* the most powerful of the gods, the goddess of the town, and behold, I will say to any one great or miserable who is found among the people of the necropolis: Beware of *the summit,* for there is a lion within *the summit,* and she strikes as a fascinating lion strikes, and she is always on the track of those who sin against her! I cried out then to my lady, and finding means to come towards me like a soft breeze she united herself with me, which showed to me her hand. She came back to me pacified, and caused me to forget my sufferings, and to have fresh air; for the *summit of the West* is pacified, when one cries out to her. Nofiraboui has said, saying, 'Hear, then, all ears which are on earth: Beware of the *Summit of the West.*'" Nofiraboui does not specify the kind of malady which was tormenting him. The oppressions of which he complains, the want of air or the absence of respiration, seem to indicate asthma or angina pectoris.   The malady must in fact be of the number of those which are frequently fatal, since they attribute their cure to a miracle.

The hill of Sheikh *Abd-el-Qournah* was inhabited in antiquity by a medical Goddess; it is inhabited in our day by a Sheikh, who works his cures there.   The chapel of the Goddess was built at the foot of the hill, at the place where we have located the oldest sanctuary of the Sheikh. Is this a chance coincidence, or must the pagan goddess and the Mussulman saint be connected with each other? I have no doubt at all on my part, that the Sheikh was but the goddess, disfigured and transformed in the course of ages.

The good uraeus of former days could not survive in her first state at the fall of paganism.   She has only been tolerated by the new doctors, upon the condition of concealing herself in the person of a saint known to the religion of the day.   I think that a Christian saint must have been introduced between her and her Mussulman incarnation, the one perhaps whose church I found not far from the Mussulman grotto; the native Christians share, in fact, the confidence of the Muslims in the curative powers of the Sheikh.   The same phenomenon has taken place upon the hill of Sheikh Abd-el-Qournah, which has been accomplished at Athmîm, at Bibéh, at Assouan, at Kouft; the being which produces the miracle has changed religions according to the times, and has become Christian, then Mussulman, but his power has remained, and the belief in the miracles which he operated has persisted to our days.

II.

Besides the ordinary serpents, which crawl under the sand or remain hidden in the fields of maize and sugar cane, modern Egypt knows other serpents of a more rare species, and whose genealogy can still be traced back to Pharaonic times.   They are rarely seen, but their presence is felt at each instant, and there are but few old fellahs who have not one or two stories to tell about them.

I do not wish to speak here of the immortal serpent who lives on the Gebel Sheikh-Haridi, and who receives a cult there; he is as old as Egypt itself, since he had given his name to the mountain and to the nome which it traverses, *Dou Hfo, the Serpent Mountain,* as Dûmichen was the first to discover. The Nile is inhabited, to this day, by an immense serpent, who hides at the bottom of the river, and seldom issues thence. His presence is manifested at long intervals by pretty serious accidents, which the Europeans attribute to various causes, because they do not know the single veritable cause of them. A dahabeyeh, on board of which were some English travelers, which sank towards 1878 abreast of *Gebel-Abou-Fedah,* was not upset, as it was said, by a sudden squall. She sailed by night, contrary to usage, and it is by night that the serpent ordinarily shows himself; it had the misfortune to find itself over the serpent at the moment when it rose to the surface, and was overturned by a blow from its tail. If the bodies were not all found, it was because the monster had swallowed several of the wrecked persons. This version is evidently authentic, for it was furnished me near Akhmîm, in 1882, by one of the sailors who escaped shipwreck, who saw distinctly the long undulating body at the surface of the river. In 1883, an English officer, then garrisoned at Qénéh, took a bath imprudently in the Nile, a little to the south of the landing of the steamboats, and disappeared. One might well have believed that the current, which attains there at certain moments an irresistible strength, had dragged him down. The Ghafir of the temple of Denderah, who was on the spot at the time of the accident, knew better than to believe that, and and clearly saw that the unfortunate man had been swallowed by the serpent of the Nile. And it is not only men whom the monster attacks, it is the soil of Egypt itself. At the time when the Nile is falling, it often happens that the earth of the cliffs, which are no longer maintained by the water, split apart for long distances, then detach themselves and fall into the river, carrying all they support at the time. The fellahs give to these movements of the earth the name of *bat-bit* (plural *batabît*), and attribute the formation of those batabît to the avidity of the great serpent, or to his anger; he can only be appeased by offering him some kind of sacrifice.

In 1884 or 1885,—I do not precisely recall the date,—a batbît partly carried away the garden of the Hotel Karnak, then recently built at Luxor, and seriously endangered the solidity of the dwellings. The servants and the Greek manager of the hotel believed that the serpent had a grudge against them, for what reason I do not know, and hastened to pay it a heavy ransom, so that it should spare the house. They cast into the river at night, with some ceremonies, and words which they refused to reveal to me, a sheep, some chickens, a turkey, some eggs, some fruit and some vegetables, then the hotel was no longer threatened.

I give these stories for what they are worth; they have been told to me, and I relate them. The serpent is very old; he was called Apopi in the Celestial Nile of the Ancient Egyptians, and issued occasionally from the water to fight the sun, and overset his boat.

A bas-relief of Philae, reproduced often since the commencement of our century, shows him coiled up between Elephantis and Bégéh, around the shrine of the god Hapi. It was not the only one of its species, but the two sources which are assigned to the river at the first cataract, possessed each its own, which disgorged itself at the moment of the inundation; and contributed to the rise of the waters. Each nome adored, besides, under the form of a serpent or Agathodemon, the portion of the Nile which waters and renders fertile its territory. I had the opportunity to become acquainted, eight years ago, with the serpent of the Theban nome. He lodged in one of the chambers of the temple of Amenhatpou III, which was situated then under the *House of France*. It descended regularly to the river, and the people of the neighborhood pretended to see it enter, and come out from time to time along the slope which led to the Ptolemaic quay. It was very long, and big in proportion. When I commenced the excavation, the workmen refused for a long time to dig in this place, so great was their fear of meeting the beast face to face. I had to bring from Médamout and from Bayadîyeh some people who were ignorant of

. the local tradition, or did not care for it. An accident which happened several days later, and in which three men lost their lives, was considered as a revengeful act of the monster ; his injury avenged, he probably re-entered the river, for I never heard anything more of him.

MODERN GREEK FOLK-MYTHOLOGY.

BY LUCY M. J. GARNETT.

THE identity of many of the popular beliefs current among the Greeks of the present day with the myths of classic Greece has not escaped the notice either of foreign students of Greek folk-life, or, more recently, of cultured Greeks themselves. This survival of paganism has been more especially dwelt upon by Mr. Stuart-Glennie, in his elaborate essay on the subject, published some years ago ; and a serious study of the folk-beliefs and folk-ceremonies of the modern Greeks cannot, I think, but lead to the conclusion at which he has arrived, namely, that notwithstanding the charming Plutarchian legend and Milton's beautiful lines in the "Ode on the Nativity," Pan is not dead. The genius still haunts

> . . . . "Spring and dale,
> Edged with poplar pale ;
> And the Nymphs with flower-inwoven tresses "

still inhabit the localities assigned to them in classic myth. Even the greater Olympian gods are only slightly transformed, and are still worshipped under names substituted from the Christian deology.

The ancient home of the gods, the Thessalian Mount Olympus—Olympus of the "two and forty peaks and two and sixty fountains," as it is described in folk-song—is itself worshipped as divine by the Klephts, who find refuge in its fastnesses. By them it is addressed as a living being, "Old Olympus," and extolled in song with every kind of poetic fantasy. Of the cult of the greater gods who had their abode on its summit, we still find survivals in popular customs, in invocations, and in oaths. The peaks and promontories, sacred of old to the sky-god, almighty Zeus, are now dedicated to the omnipotent ($Παντοκράτωρ$); the Virgin Ashená

(Παρθένος) has been, like many other female deities, replaced by the Virgin Mary (Παναγία); and in the localities once sacred to the Sun-god, Helios (Ἥλιος), or Apollo, "Saint Elias" (Ἅγιος Ἐλιας) is now propitiated. There is, in fact, in Greece and Turkey, hardly a mountain summit which is not crowned by a chapel bearing the name of this divinity, and the annual feast in his honor is still held at the time of harvest, the 20th of July (old style). This modern cult of Saint Elias in a locality formerly sacred to Apollo is perhaps best illustrated on Mount Taygetus, in Laconia, which Pausanius describes as having been consecrated to this deity, and which is now locally known as "Mount Saint Elias." Hither on the saint's feast day flock the peasants in great numbers, bringing with them branches of incense-wood, which they pile into a huge bonfire and then distribute into smaller fires, a survival evidently of the ancient method of sun-worship. Power over rain is also attributed to this saint; and in time of drought the people flock to his churches and monasteries to supplicate the sun-deity in his other character of the "Rainy-God."

In folk-speech, however, as well as in folk-song and folk-tale, the Sun is directly personified. He has a mother, and a daughter who, like himself, is the highest type of human beauty. "As beautiful as the Sun," or "as beautiful as the Sun's Daughter," are common forms of speech. His setting is designated by a word which signifies "reigning as a king" (βασιλεύω). He is represented as pityingly addressing a sad and lonely deer; as stealing away a twelve-year-old maiden from her mother, to whom he had given her in answer to her prayers; and as "angry with the Moon and Stars." He "sleeps on the mountain;" stops on his way home to listen to the spinning-song of a woman, and is consequently late in setting, for which the woman is cursed by his mother, who, however, changes the curse into a blessing when she learns the cause of the woman's gayety—the expected return of her husband, long absent from his home.

As to the other gods, Póseidon may still be found under the name of Saint Nicholas (Ἅγιος Νικόλας); an Epirote folk-tale describes the drowning of his children by Chronos; and legend still connects Diónysos, as of old, with the island of

Naxos.   A portion of a colossal statue of Demeter, removed
to England at the beginning of the present century, was,
while it remained at Eleusis, an object of worship by the
country people.   Garlands of flowers were offered at this
shrine of Saint Demetra, as the ancient Goddess of Plenty
was locally named, and the fertility of the fields of Eleusis
was attributed to her blessing.   In a local legend concerning
Saint Demetra, which was related to Monsieur Lenormant by
an old priest, can still be traced the main outlines of
the classic myth of the Sorrow of Demeter—though Proser-
pinë is carried off, not by the lord of Hades, but by a
Turkish Agha, who is at the same time a wicked magician
and rides a fire-breathing black horse ; a compassionate stork
aids the mother in her search for her daughter ; and the
usual marvellous elements of folk-tale have become blended
with the story.

The Fates (*Μοῖραι*), who have still their abode on the highest
peaks of Olympus, closely resemble their classic prototypes
and are assigned, as of old, a place above and behind all
gods.   They are represented as presiding more particularly
over the three great events of man's existence : birth, marriage, and death—the "Three Evils of Destiny (*Τᾶ τρία κακά
τῆς Μοιρᾶς*)—a very significantly pessimistic phrase.   According to popular belief, the Three Fates visit every child when
three days old, and assign to it its destiny, which no power
can alter, nor precaution avert.   The anxious mother will
often seek to propitiate these dreaded Powers, by placing
under the baby's pillow on this eventful night gold and silver
coins, bread and weapons, if it be a boy, or a spindle and
bundle of flax, if a girl.   Two of the Fates suggest a destiny
for the infant, but the dictum of the third is final.   She becomes thenceforward the *Moira* (*Μοῖρα*), or Fate, of that individual, and takes upon herself to see that her predictions,
good or bad, are fulfilled.   In folk-tale the Fate often acts
the part assigned in the West to "fairy godmothers," and
appears at critical moments to help the hero or heroine out
of their difficulties.   Though generally represented as per-
petually wandering about the world for the fulfillment of
their arduous labors, the peaks of Olympus are, as I have
already mentioned, their special place of abode ; and it is to

this mountain that those who desire their assistance turn to utter this invocation :

> "Oh, from the summits of Olympus high,
> From the three corners of the sky,
> Oh may my own Fate hear me,
> And, hearing, hover near me ! "

The Power who ranks next to the Fates in Greek popular belief is the pitiless and inexorable Charon. The Earth, which is sometimes spoken of as the " mother " of Charon, is also identified with him ; and hence, in the dialect of Epirus they say for " he died," " The earth has eaten him " (Τὸν ἔφαγεν ὁ γῆς), or " Charon has eaten him " (Τὸν ἔφαγεν ὁ χάρος). This ruthless Power goes out hunting on his black horse, and returns laden with human spoil of both sexes and of all ages :

> " The young men he before him drives,
> And drags the old behind him ;
> While ranged upon the saddle sit
> With him the young and lovely."

In many folk-songs Charon is represented as challenged by Heroes to a wrestling match before they follow him to the under-world ; but rarely indeed do they succeed in throwing their fell adversary. The abode to which Charon bears away his prey when he does not " eat " them, is generally pictured as an underground region, to which there is a descent by stairs, or as a tent, green or red outside, but always black within. Sometimes, as in a Cappadocian song, he possesses fields which he sends his victim to cultivate. But in neither of these abodes is there any possibility of escaping the vigilance of their lord. Though attempts are described as being made by various heroes.

Next in importance to the god-saints and superior powers just described are the *Stoicheia* (Στοιχεῖα) or genii, which, however, would appear to be but personifications of the Powers of Nature. These are, according to their place of habitation, stoicheia of seas or rivers, of fountains or wells, of mountains or rocks, and of trees. They are evidently the modern survivors of the beings referred to by St. Paul as " The weak and beggarly elements[1] whereunto ye desire

---

[1] Τὰ ἀσθενῆ καὶ πτωχὰ στοιχεῖα,—*Gal.* iv. 9.

again to be in bondage;" the "rulers of the darkness of this world;"[1] the "rudiments of the world,"[2] etc. For the translation of the word *stoicheia* as "rudiments" or elements, also followed in the Revised Version, completely obscures what appears to be the far more probable meaning of these passages. In the Apostle's use of the phrase *Tà Stoicheia tou Kosmon* (*Tà Στοιχεῖα τοῦ κόσμου*), he evidently attributes to these genii, or Powers of the Universe, a distinct personality. A folk-song belonging to Salonica similarly mentions the "Three Powers of the Universe" (*Οἱ Τρεῖς Στοιχειά τοῦ Κόσμου*), which Mr. Stuart-Glennie thinks may be identified with the Kabeirian Trinity of Samothrace, for the worship of which this city was, in ancient times, famous.

The Stoicheia of Mountains, Rocks, and Waters are, at the present day, generally conceived as man-devouring monsters of horrible shape, who lie in wait for travellers, and can only be slain by that popular hero of Greek folk-poesy, the Widow's Son, or by the youngest of the three brothers. The Stoicheia of the Sea are said to be addicted to wrecking ships, if the sailors fail to salute them when passing their haunts. These dreaded beings occasionally appear also under the designation of *Therion* (*θηρίον*), a wild beast or monster, as in the ballad in which one is described as slain by St. George. In some songs they are represented as taking the form of lovely women, and luring youths on some pretext or other to descend the wells which constitute their abode, and in this character they are often confounded with the Lámia. The Stoicheia appear also to have replaced the Dryads of old, for we find a Stoicheion of the Plane, Walnut and Olive trees, endowed with the same propensities as their brethren inhabiting the mountains, rocks and waters. A strange legend current in Roumelia relates that the Stoicheion of the Sea was at war for a thousand years with the Stoicheion of the Plane Tree, and every time a struggle took place between them and one was worsted, there was great mortality among human beings in the neighborhood.

In folk-tales the Stoicheia of a well occasionally appears as a gigantic negro, who has a magnificent palace at the bottom.

---

[1] Τοὺς κοσμοκράτορας τοῦ σκότους τούτου,—*Ephes.* vi. 12.
[2] Κατὰ τὰ στοιχεῖα τοῦ κόσμου,—*Col.* ii. 8, 20.

Professor Politis suggests[1] that this is probably a souvenir of the terror inspired by the negro guards of Sultan Mahmoud II. But I venture to think that it is merely a feature borrowed from Arabian story, as the negro is often represented in Greek folk-tale as an amiable and benevolent character. Other Stoicheia, those of springs, wells and rivers more particularly, are also often represented as harmless if propitiated with a gift by those who have occasion to approach their places of abode. Hence, before drawing water from a well or fountain, especially for the first time, the women and girls throw into the water some small object as a peace-offering to its inmate, and a peasant bride performs this act with great ceremony.

Famous springs of water, both hot and cold, are, when not appropriated by Stoicheia, under the nominal patronage of the *Panaghia*, or Virgin Mary, who has, indeed, for the most usurped the functions once attributed to the Nymphs. In the plural name of "The Holy Virgins" (°*Αι 'Αγίαι παρθένοι*), still connected with a celebrated fountain in Crete, we have, perhaps, still a reminiscence of these deities; and a "Virgin of the Grotto" (*παναγία Σπηλαιότισσα*), may often be found who receives from the Greek peasant women honors similar to those paid in ancient times to the Nymphs of whose temples she has usurped possession. Several fountains, or *Agiasma* ('*Αγίασμα*), as they are generally called, may often be found situated in private houses as well as in Christian churches, Turkish mosques, and each has its annual festival to which people of all creeds flock for the cure of their diseases. And even into the church wells little offerings are dropped by the pilgrims who drink or bathe themselves in its waters. In the Greek church at Belgrade, a village near Constantinople, which is much resorted to for the cure of ophthalmia, it is customary for the devotees to drop into the well seed pearls which have never been strung, before bathing their eyes with water from it.

There, is, however, another class of Stoicheia not less curious and interesting than the foregoing, that known as "Sacrifice Stoicheia" (*Στοιχεία τοῦ θυσιοῦ*), which have their abode in houses, bridges, churches and other edifices. Numerous

---

[1] *Νεοστηρικά Μυθογογία.*

ballads relate how a bridge in course of construction over some famous river, such as the Danube or Euphrates, fell down every night until the master-mason, instructed by a dream, buried his wife alive under the foundations; and thus provided with a Stoicheion, or *life*, the bridge became secure. In more than one of these ballads the victim laments that her two sisters have also become Stoicheia, one to build a church, and the other a monastery. Considered in connection with the traces of this practice found in other countries, and especially with a discovery made some years ago in Devonshire of the skeleton of a person apparently buried alive within the masonry, these Eastern ballads—for they exist among all the Christian peoples of the East—seem to point to a very wide distribution of the customs of "foundation sacrifices." But this is a subject into which I need not here enter further, as it has already been ably and fully discussed by Dr. Robertson Smith. It is, however, at the present day believed in the East that the man or beast whose shadow first falls on the first laid stone of a house or other edifice will die within the year, and his shadow, remaining in the building, will become its Stoicheion. The existence of such a belief helps to explain modern practices connected with laying foundation stones. For, in order to avert this calamity from those engaged in the work of building, or from passers by, a lamb, or fowl is sacrificed on the stone, coins being also at the same time placed upon it in order to ensure prosperity to the edifice. Care is, however, taken not to touch the blood of the sacrificed animal, as this would have fatal results. Sir Paul Picaut, writing in the last century, says that a Greek having a quarrel with another, and wishing him ill, would measure the length and breadth of his body with a thread or stick, and bribe a mason about to begin building a house to bury this in the foundations, in the belief that, as the thread or stick decayed, the person whose measure they represented would also pine away and die.

Next to the Stoicheia, the Nereids appear to occupy the most important place in the popular imagination of the Greeks. Like our fairies, they are proverbial for their beauty, but they differ from "the good people" in being always of the full stature of mortals, for in the East no traditions exist regarding diminutive races. Like the stoicheia, they haunt lonely places, and popular belief divides them into two classes, nereids of the sea" (Θαλασσιναῖς) and "nereids of the mountain" (Βουνήσιαις), between whom a deadly feud is continually maintained. Every Saturday evening the nereids of the mountain leave their heights to fight against their sisters of the sea, who issue from their caves to defend themselves. When the mountain nereids return victorious they load with benefits any mortal they may chance to meet; but if they are worsted, they vent their malice upon the unlucky wight. As a rule, the nereids are solitary in their habits; but they may occasionally be seen, dressed in white, dancing in companies, in moonlit glades, or on the glistening sands of lonely isles and promontories. It is fatal to see them when crossing a river, unless a priest be at hand to read passages of scripture, and so counteract the spells of the "devil's daughters," as they are sometimes called. It is usual, however, to propitiate them by some complimentary epithet, such as "the beautiful" or "the good ladies," in the same way as the Furies were formerly termed the Eumenides, and as the owl is, at the present day, called the "bird of joy." They are said to have the power of banefully affecting women of whose beauty they are jealous, and to be in the habit of carrying off unbaptized infants. A mother and her new-born child are carefully watched over and never left alone, as the nereids are sure to be hovering near a house in which a birth has recently taken place, on the lookout for an opportunity of exchanging one of their own fractious offspring for a mortal babe. For the manners and customs of "the strangers" (Τὰ Ξοτιχά)—the general term for all such uncanny visitants—strongly resemble those of our northern fairies, as described by Ben Jonson:

> When larks 'gin sing,
> Away we fling,
> And babes new-born steal as we go;
> An elf in bed
> We leave instead,
> And wind out laughing Ho! ho! ho!

In Rhodes, no stranger, save the nurse, is on any account allowed to enter the house until the baby has been blessed by

the priest; and for forty days after its birth the house door
is shut at sunset, and not opened again until sunrise for fear
of the Nereids. All kinds of maladies, too, are attributed
to the malevolence of the "Beautiful Ladies," and the
women and children thus afflicted are termed "nymph-pos-
sessed" (νυμφολήπτης), and can only be cured by going to
reside for a time in a church or convent, or by pilgrimage to
some special shrine.

As a rule, the Nereids marry male beings of their own
kind, called *Neraidhi* (Νεραΐδοι), but they also occasionally
fall in love with men who, if they return their affection and
prove faithful to them, they reward with great prosperity;
but if the mortal they deign to favor with their notice vent-
ures to slight their advances, the Nereids revenge themselves
by inflicting upon him some dire calamity. They manifest
this power chiefly at the noontide hour, when they rest under
the shade of the trees, usually planes and poplars, and near
springs and streams—a practice which has earned for them
the name of "Noontiders" (Μεσημερgιάταις) from the inhabitants of Milo; and the wary peasant, fearful of the consequences of annoying these capricious beings, will carefully
avoid disturbing their siesta. At midnight they bathe in
the streams, which are then believed to be warm, and any one
venturing to enter the water at that hour becomes "nymph-
possessed." Phenomena of nature, such as whirlwinds and
storms, are popularly ascribed to the Nereids, and it is
customary to crouch down while they are supposed to be
passing overhead. If this precaution is not taken, the Nereids
may seize the irreverent individual, and carry him off to
the mountains. Offerings of milk, honey, and cakes are made
to them, placed in certain spots which they are believed to
frequent; and the countrywomen, when they see the wind-
driven cloud scudding overhead mutter "milk and honey"
(γάλα καί μέλι) to avert all evil from themselves. Storms are,
indeed, in the East, invariably connected with demons, whose
wild flights from place to place cause these elemental disturb-
ances; and tempestuous weather is also sometimes attributed
to the festivities attendant upon a wedding among the Nereids.
Some folk-tales, however, describe a Nereid as living in a
beautiful palace of her own, and playing the part of a good

fairy to the hero, whom she eventually marries. The "Queen of the Gorgons" also appears in the same character in an Albanian story.

The little waterspouts formed of gathered wreaths of spray, so often seen in the Ægean Sea, are regarded with great awe by the dwellers in the islands and on the sea-board. "The Lamia of the Sea is abroad," say the peasants and fisher-folk, when they see the wind-driven spray-wreaths ; and having recourse to Christian aid when frightened by pagan super-stition, and *vice versa*, they cross themselves repeatedly, and mutter prayers to the *Panaghia* for protection against these Powers of the Air and Water. The Lamiæ are generally represented as ill-favored and evilly-disposed beings of the female sex, who haunt desert places and lonely seashores. The popular beliefs respecting them are similar to those of the ancient Greeks, and they are, at the present day, no less than in classic times, as recorded by Strabo, made use of by mothers and nurses to terrify naughty children into obedience. Sometimes, however, they take the form of lovely women who, like the Sirens, now called *Tragondistria* (Τραγυνδίστρια or "Songstresses," lure men to destruction by their sweet voices and graceful dancing, or, as is recorded in a Salonica folksong, lay wagers with them in which the mortal is sure to be the loser. Occasionally, too, they, like the Stoicheia, entice youths into their abodes in wells, under the semblance of distressed damsels who have let a ring fall into the water.

There are stories of Lamiæ who, under the form of beauti-ful maidens, have wedded mortals and borne children to them. But unlucky is the man who has such a helpmate ! For she can neither spin, weave, knit, nor sew, and is equally incapable of sweeping, cooking, baking, or taking care of the domestic animals. So firm a hold has this belief on the popular mind that the expression—"a Lamia's sweepings" [1] exists as a domestic proverb, generally applied by indignant housewives to a careless use of the broom.

The satyrs and fauns of antiquity appear to have survived in the *kali-kántzaroi* (Καλικάντσαροι), who are represented as having the legs of donkeys, or stags, and ugly human faces ; and in the stories respecting them traces may be found of

[1] "Τὰ φρουκάλιά τῆς Λαμίας."

the cult of Bacchic divinities. Another connecting link pointed out by Professor Politis is the word *kalòs* (χαλὸς),[1] which
is often found on ancient sculptures, under the grimacing
figures of satyrs. The kalikántzaroi are generally represented as mere tricksy sprites who live, as a rule, underground, appearing to men only on the nights of the year
between the 25th of December and the 6th of January.
They pass the days during this period in dark caverns, where
they subsist on serpents and lizards, and come forth to dance
in the moonlight, either alone or in company with the nereids
or other "strangers," and also with mortal women, if they
can lure any to join them. They play mischievous pranks on
belated travellers, and frequent the mills, where they make
great havoc among the miller's stores of flour and grain.
They also haunt the abodes of men, and the house-wife, while
cooking over the fire the doughnuts which it is customary to
eat at this season, fancies she hears them asking for the remains of these dainties left in the frying-pan. They disappear underground "ere the first cock his matin rings;" and
on Epiphany day when, according to the custom of the
Greek Church, the priest goes round the parish to bless each
house with prayers and holy water, the kalikántzaroi finally
depart, crying:

> " Let us flee and fly away,
>   For the big Papas is coming,
>   With his holy-water sprinkler,
>   With his crutched stick he is coming;
>   And sprinkle us will he,
>   And we defiled shall be!"

and they return to their underground abode, where they are
occupied during the rest of the year in trying to saw through
the tree which supports the world.

Similar beliefs in the activity of magical beings during

---

[1] Under the slightly different name of *karakandjalos*, the same sprites terrify
the Turks, Armenians and Albanians during the dark nights of mid-winter. Professor Tebéraz, who mentions this superstition in a paper on Armenian mythology, read before the Congress of Orientalists (London, 1892) appears to ignore
its Greek form, and attempts to derive the name—which, he says, has nothing
Armenian in it—from the Sanscrit *kancukālus*, a serpent. I venture to think that
a derivation from Greek through Turkish—in which language the prefix *Kara*
signifies, besides " black," anything calculated to inspire terror—is much more
probable. Professor Politis derives *Kalikántzari* from Καλὸς Κάνθαρος, " the good
beetle." Νεοελληνικὰ Μθολογία.

winter, though for a longer period, may be found among other peoples. In a series of articles on the "Legends of the Lincolnshire Cars," published in *Folk-Lore*, we are told, in the words of a peasant narrator : that people "Thought "the earth was sleeping all the winter, and that the bogles— call them what you will—had nothing to do but mis- chief, for they had naught to see to in the fields ; so they were afraid on the long, dark winter days and nights, in the midst of all sorts of unseen fearsome things, ready and "waiting for a chance to play them evil tricks."[1]

It is popularly believed that all children born on the 25th of December inevitably become kalikántzaroi, and between this date and Epiphany day escape at night from their swaddling-clothes and roam about the streets, annoying all whom they may chance to find abroad, and regaining their cradles before cock-crow. Professor Politis suggests[2] that the barbarous old custom recorded by Leon Allatius and others of placing in the fire the feet of infants born on this day, is probably connected with this curious belief.

The *Gello* of antiquity is still to be found under this name in some districts, though its modern representative is more frequently met with under that of *Stringla* (*Στρίγγλα*), also called in Epirus the *Choursoúsa,* and in the Cyclades, the *Grousoúza*. This creature, who in some stories bears many points of resemblance with the mœnads, is, unlike the fore- going, "strangers," of mortal origin—a horrible kind of witch-hag, with cannibalistic propensities. Some people are believed to be born stringlæ, as in the Athenian story of the "stringla-princess," a translation of which I hope to publish shortly ; others develop in later years their gruesome propen- sities ; while among the Albanians a belief exists that when men or women live to be more than a hundred years old they become stringlæ, their very breath is poisonous, and kills healthy people. The stringlæ are said to be fond of the

---

[1] "Tha' thout as th' yarth wor sleepin' ahl th' winter ; an' 'at th' bogles—ca'all um what 'ee wull—'d nobbut mischief to do, fur they'd nowt to see to i' tha fields ; so they wor feared an' th' long da'ark winter da'ays an' noights i' tha' mid' o' ahl so'ts o' unseen fearsome things, ready an' waitin' fur a chance to play un evil tricks."—*Folk-Lore*, Sept. 1894, p. 260.

[2] *Loc. Cit.*

13

flesh of little children, and a child which has died in infancy is said in some districts to have been "eaten by the gello" (Τελλό-βρωτοι) or witch-hag. The professional witch, or *may-issa*, however, comes under a different category, and she and her magical powers are, in the East, held in great respect by persons of all creeds.

The drakos (Δράχος or Δράκοντας), a very popular character both in folk-song and folk-tale, would seem to be a descendant of Polyphemus or the Cyclops. He is sometimes represented as having but one eye, but is always of gigantic stature . and superhuman strength—"as strong as a drakos" is, indeed, a common expression. Though he resembles the stoicheion in his characteristics of inhabiting mountainous and lonely places, and being at enmity with mortals, he in other respects more closely resembles the *Rakshása* of Indian, the *Troll* of Scandinavian and the giant of our own nursery tales. He has a wife called the *Drákissa, Drákaina*, or *Dra-kóntissa*, and sons and daughters, is of cannibalistic habits, but is exceedingly fond of cheese, which, if he has no flocks of his own, he steals from the nomad shepherds. He carries off princesses and marries them, and possesses magical objects, such as "enchanted wands" and "flying horses." Like the Cyclops, he generally lives in a cave, or tower, pastures his own sheep and tills his fields, or engages mortals to perform some of this labor for him, though he is sometimes represented as inhabiting a magnificent palace, above or underground. This palace contains untold treasure, is furnished with every luxury, and its owner is occasionally so highly civilized as to go to Mass. But though of great stature and possessing extraordinary strength, the drákos, like our own giants, is not remarkable for intelligence, and is easily outwitted by a crafty and courageous hero. These heroes are, like the slayers of stoicheia, usually widows' sons, or the youngest of three brothers, though a beardless man also plays a prominent part in such adventures.

Traditions also of other beings of unusual strength and gigantic stature are preserved in folk-song, or are still related by the peasants of the remoter parts of Asia Minor and of the islands. Round about Mount Ida, in Crete, the belief still lingers that this island was in early times peopled by a race of giants whom they designate *sarandapichoi* (Σαραντατίχοι) or "Forty-ells," and to whom they attribute the erection of the Cyclopean buildings, the ruins of which lie around. According to one legend, this race was driven by a cataclysm which submerged the lower parts of the island, to take refuge on the summit of Mount Ida. Finally the flood reached the summit, but the sarandapichoi, by reason of their immense stature, were able for many days to keep their heads above water. The worms, however, began to gnaw the soles of their feet, and when they stooped to remove these insects, they lost their balance and were drowned. Most of these legendary sarandapichoi are anonymous. But one, said to be the most powerful, is called Digenes by the people of Mesara. The isolated boulders which are to be seen lying in the valleys are said to have been thrown by this giant when playing at the game of astrágalos, or "knuckle-bones;" and near the village of Kamára is pointed out his "saddle," namely, a hill, the crest of which is divided by a hollow, caused, according to the natives, by the weight of Digenes sitting astride upon it. On the slope of the same hill is shown his "footprint," a depression in the earth shaped like a gigantic foot. Legend says that, being one day thirsty, Digenes placed one of his feet there, and the other on an opposite hill while he stooped to drink from the river Letheos, the waters of which becoming dammed by his beard, inundated the plains of Mesara. An elevation on the plain is known as the "tomb of Digenes," and in various other places in the island, the graves of other sarandapichoi are pointed out.

This particular giant is evidently a reminiscence of Digenes Akrítas, a famous hero of the Byzantine period, to whom superhuman strength is generally attributed in the many ballads to be found describing his exploits, or his death. Of another famous personage belonging to the same cycle, Porphyrós, are related many of the characteristics of Herakles. According to one story, he ate seven ovensful of bread before he was seven months old, and strangled a three-headed snake while yet in the cradle. When seven years old, there was not a single famous man in the inhabited world who did not fear to stand up against him. And when

there finally came the invincible Charon to wrestle with
him :

> " Full seven times upon the earth
> The youth did throw down Charon ;
> But after that he chanced to slip,
> For so his Fate would have it ;
> And Charon, the black spider, then
> His soul did take from out him."

I ought not, perhaps, to omit to add here a few words on
the notions of the Greek peasants with regard to the ruins of
ancient cities and buildings, among and in the neighborhood
of which so many of them live.   It is popularly believed that
these edifices were erected by a race whom they call Hellenes
('Ελλήνοι), but who were vastly superior, not only in bodily
strength, but also in wisdom, skill and industry, to the people
now known by that name.   "He works like a Hellene," is
the highest praise that can be given to an unusually laborious
artisan ; and an exceptionally well constructed edifice is said
to be "built as by the Hellenes."   The peasant mind has,
however, no conception of time, and the date of these people
whose work they so much admire, is put back only a few generations.   According to one story, the last survivor of this race
died at Constantinople about a century ago.*   Though an old
woman, and blind, when visited by the grandfather of the
narrator, he thought it prudent as she offered him her hand,
to place in it, instead of his own, a bar of iron, which she
immediately squeezed out of shape.   "You are pretty
strong," was her remark, "but not so strong as my people
used to be."

In conclusion, I will attempt a brief description of that
most ghastly of all Greek superstitions—the vampire, generally known in the Balkan peninsula by the Slavonic name
of *vrykólahas* (Βρυκόλακας).   This circumstance, and the fact
of the widespread belief in this spectre among Slavonic
nations, have been by some folk-lorists considered sufficient
to justify their assigning it an origin purely Slavonic.
This opinion can, however, I venture to think, hardly be
sustained.   For not only does this ghoul bear in Crete and
in Rhodes the thoroughly Hellenic designation of *katakhnás*
(χαταχνᾶς) "the render "; in Cyprus that of *Sarkoménos* (σαρ-
χωμένος) "the fleshy one "; and, in Tinos, of *Anaikathoú-*

menos ('Αναιχαθυύμενος), "the restless one"; but there appears
to be distinct evidence that, like so many other superstitions,
it is of Chaldean origin.[1] One of the curious customs connected with Greek burials is the disinterment of the body
after it has been three years in the grave, in order to ascertain if it is properly decomposed. Should this not be the
case, the dead man—the *vrykólahas* is generally of the masculine sex—the dead man is believed to be in the habit of
leaving his grave and roaming about, revelling in blood, and
tearing out the livers of his victims. The causes of vampirism are various, and among them are the following: The
fact either of having perpetrated, or of having been the victim of a crime; having wronged some person who has died
resenting the wrong; or of a curse, pronounced either in ex-
communicatory form by the priest, or by a person to whom
an injury has been done. "May the earth not eat you!"
is a common expression in the mouth of an angry Greek.
Vampirism is also believed to be hereditary in certain families, the members of which are regarded with aversion by
their neighbors, and shunned as much as possible. Their
services are, however, called into requisition when there is a
vampire to be laid, as they have the reputation of possessing
special powers in that direction. It is generally believed that
the vampire retires to his grave at cock-crow; but some
maintain that he visits it only once a week, on the Saturday.
When it is discovered that such a vrykolahas is about, the
people go on that day and open his tomb, where they always
find the body just as it was buried, and entirely undecom-
posed. The priest who accompanies the party reads certain
parts of the ritual believed to be of peculiar efficacy in putting a stop to the restless wanderings of vampires, and sometimes this course suffices to restore the neighborhood to peace
and quiet. But cases happen in which the priest does not
prove a sufficiently powerful exorcist; and when all his en-
deavors are found to be of no avail, the people of the neighborhood again open the tomb, and either drive a stake through
the heart of the undissolving corpse, or take out the body
and consume it with fire. Occasionally when a vampire-
haunted community have not cared to proceed to the

[1] Compare, for instance, Lenormant, *Chaldean Magic*, pp. 87 and 100.

extremity of burning the corpse suspected of troubling them, they have, if practicable, removed it to one of the small uninhabited islands in the Ægean, and thus secured themselves from its visitations, for a vampire, like other uncanny beings, cannot cross salt water.

SOME NOTES ON THE PRIMITIVE HORDE.

BY LUDWIG KRZYURCKI.

McLENNAN has introduced the term " Primitive Horde " into science. It has the right of citizenship therein, as a word which means the social organization of the human tribe in the remotest time, when our ancestors were living in the very low stage of culture. The term exists, but nothing more is added to it. Only the biologists tried to throw a light upon this question, when studying the animal societies. Among the folk-lorists, I know but one note on the Primitive Horde, that of Mr. Gomme in the Journal of Anthr. Institute of Great Britain. Notwithstanding, I believe, the question can be explained and resolved only by the folk-lorist on the basis of ethnographical data. By the help of the statistical method, inaugurated by Mr. Tylor in his essay upon the primitive family, I have compared many rites of the most savage tribes. I am endeavoring to give here some con-clusions, to which I am conducted by my studies.

Among the islanders of the Pacific and in other neighbor-ing countries, we find this peculiar custom, that the sexes live in the utmost separation, and the men possess a special organization of club-houses. " Idolatry " so narrates W. Ellis [1] " had exerted all its withering and deadly influence, not only over every moment of their earthly existence, but every department of life, destroying, by its debasing and un-social dictates, every tender feeling and all the enjoyments of domestic intercourse. The father and the mother, with their children, never, as one social happy band, surrounded the domestic hearth, or, assembling under the grateful shade of the verdant grove, partook together, as a family, of the boun-ties of Providence. . . . The institutes of *Oro* and *Tane* in-exorably required not only that the wife should not eat those

[1] W Ellis : *Polynesian Researches*, Lond. 1830.

199

kinds of food of which the husband partook, but that she should not eat in the same place and prepare her food at the same fire. This restriction applied not only to the wife with regard to her husband, but to all the individuals of the female sex from their birth to the day of their death. In sickness or pain, or whatever other circumstances the mother, the wife, the sister or the daughter might be brought into, it was never relaxed. . . . The fires at which the men's food was cooked were also sacred, and were forbidden to be used by the females. The baskets in which their provision was kept, and the house in which the men ate, were also sacred and prohibited to the females under a cruel penalty." Yet another example : " At S. Cruz (Melanesia) the separation of the sexes in daily life is carried far, the men and the women never work together promiscuously or assemble in one group. . . . In Nutilile the separation is complete, men and women are never out together "[1] Even the mother is separated from her son, the sisters from their brothers. In the N. Hebrides, "the boy puts on his *malo* dress, when his parents think him big enough. Before this he had lived at home, but now he eats and sleeps in the *gamali* club-house, and now begins his strange and strict reserve of intercourse with his sisters and mother. He must not use as a common noun the word which is the name or makes part of the name of his sisters. . . . He may go to his father's house to ask for food, but if his sister is within, he has to go away before he eats. If by chance brother and sister meet in the path she runs away or hides. . . . The reserve between son and mother increases as the boy grows up. If they talk together she sits at a little distance and turns away, for she is shy of her grown-up son."[2] These examples are sufficient to illustrate the separation of the sexes in the primitive life of Polynesians. The men are organized into club-houses, where they eat, lodge, sleep, etc. We find the elements of such separation also in other countries, the only difference being in the intensity of the custom : the woman is forbidden to do men's work, to touch their weapons, to enter in their council-rooms, etc.

The pictured separation begins when the first signs of the

male instincts appear in the boy. There are certain rites connected with this moment of his life and known as the ceremonies of the initiation into manhood. The initiation changes its character during the evolution of the human society. The culture is higher, the rite is less savage and bloody. In the highest stage the initiation has nothing but religious purposes : it is a covenant with the tribal god and has lost its sanguinary features. But the aspect is a very different one in the lowest degree of culture, i. e., among the Australian blacks. The ceremony of manhood is here partially a sort of school : the candidates are carefully instructed by the old men in their traditions, in the very exact laws of consanguinity. But the character of the rites which accompany the ceremony is terribly cruel. The severity passes all limits. In all parts of the continent those to be initiated endure most rough treatment. "During the celebration of the rites the youth suffered severely, and he had sympathy from none. When the youth has been led to a suitable place, his hair is cut off with sharp chips of quartzite, the head is then daubed with clay. . . . To complete the picture he is immediately invested with a garment of strips of opossum skins, strings of opossum fur, and the like, which serves to cover his middle only, and his body is daubed with clay, mud, charcoal and filth of every kind. Though this ceremony is performed generally in the winter season, when the weather is very cold, the youth is not permitted to cover himself with a rug. He carries a basket under his arm, containing moist clay, charcoal powder and filth. In this state he wanders through the encampments, day and night. He gathers filth as he goes. No one speaks to him, no one molests him, all seem to fear him. When he sees anyone come out of a *miam* he casts filth at him, but he may not intrude himself into any *miam*. The women and children scream when they see him and rush to their *miams* for shelter."[1] But in the case of that narration, the initiation, I believe, is a little changed, under the influence of the conditions which have been created in Australia with the white man. In most cases the ceremony is more cruel, and the separation of the youth from the community is more com-

[1] Brough Smyth, *Aborigines of Victoria*, I. 60.

plete. The initiated boy is from seven to eight months under
strict rule, eating only certain prescribed food and secluded
from social intercourse, except of the old men. The long
course of alternate fasting and suffering is a very severe
ordeal. It has often been observed that young men come out
of it exhausted and sometimes half dead.

I have said that the purposes of the initiation change during the social evolution, but the rites are the more conservative part of the ceremony. When, in time, the character of
the initiation becomes very different, the rites remain the
same or vary slowly, and contradict the new aims of the
ceremony. If we compare the ritual sides of the ceremony
among Australians, we find therein some absurdities, i. e.,
rites which are without real and rational meaning, or are
quite useless, or even contradict the essence of the ceremony.
We have a right to look at them as survivals of the more
remote stage of culture, when the initiation had other desti-
nations and they were in consent with its purpose ; intelligent,
rational and useful at one time, they become to-day more or
less absurd in their connection with the ceremony. These
primitive features consist in the following : (1) The youth
does not know the time of his initiation. Among the tribes
of the Darling river a dance is arranged at sunrise, a sham
fight is got up to attract the youth's attention, and then he
is caught and carried off into the bush. In Central Australia
the boys run away when the camp cry aloud, and wander alone in woods ; while a sham-fight takes place, the
old men practise most horrible customs during the whole
night ; the women and children are ordered off to a distance
from the camp, where they remain beating a kind of wooden
trough with their hands, the men replying to the noise in
like manner. When the youth is captured, the women of
the tribe pretend always a sorrow and set up a lamentation,
resist the seizure by throwing firebrands to his captors, until
they are driven to their *miams* and compelled to stop there.
(2) The youths are very strictly separated from their tribe,
i. e., from the women and uninitiated boys. No woman is
permitted to see either the ceremony or the youth. So strong
is this feeling against the women knowing anything of the
secret rites, that one of the Kurnai head men said to Mr.

Novitt : "If a woman were to see these things or hear what we tell the boys, I would kill her." I think we know in Europe more about it than any Australian woman. Everything which the initiated possess, becomes sacred from the touch of women ; even the bird hit by their *waddies*, or the kangaroo speared by their spear, even when these instruments are used by other hands than their own, is forbidden to all females. When admitted by the old men into the community, the young man no longer lives in the same camp with his parents and sisters, but in special encampment. (3) The youth is placed in a position of actual scarcity and isolation, stays away for months seeking for them, and goes through much fasting and privations. This is yet rational from the standpoint of the aims of the initiation. But there are many absurdities. The hairs, especially those of approaching puberty, are pulled out ; the stages of the ceremony are named in a corresponding manner, *i. e.*, plucked cheek. After all the boy is submitted to certain operations ; fingers are cut off, teeth spat out, the circumcision is practised. The circumcision has a severe character. Yet one absurdity more : among Dieri tribes the youth, after the terrible rite of the Australian circumcision is permitted to appear before women without wearing anything to hide his person. (4) Only old male people direct the ceremony. There are remarkable peculiarities. In the Lincoln port tribe, during the performance of the rite of circumcision, the old people grow angry against the youth, stamp, throw the dust into the air, bite their beards, swing the youth with such fury as if they intend to dash it, but in the same time they assure the boy all the while, that they mean no harm. Among the tribes of Parkunji and Burgyarlee, some old men visit the youth's camp, where they meet some younger men, who arrange themselves in a row in front of the youth ; they ridicule and insult them, until the old men get into a rage and throw sand in their own faces and then throw fighting sticks or boomerangs at the young men. The old men then rush forward at the young men, who seize and throw them on the ground, after which the old men retire to the camp, but return later and dance with the youth and his companions, repeating their friendly visits until the end of the ceremony.

Such are the facts. The conclusions are evident. Why these lamentations of the other sex, these secrets and mysteries ? The ceremony of the initiation into manhood would have its actual meaning and would reach its aims without all those doings. Let us go further. Are these sham fights— now in a contradiction with the purposes of the ceremony— between the old people and the youth—not a survival of the real ones ? Are these circumcisions, scars, cutting off fingers and other bloody customs not a survival of more serious wounds ? The body of data I have collected and compared compels to answer positively, Yes, there, in some remote and obscure past, there was a stage in the evolution of the human society, when old men tolerated only little ones of their own sex in the horde. As the children were grown up and the sign of puberty appeared together with the male instincts, old people persecuted their future rivals and expelled them. Some tribal signs, now in use among the lower tribes, are probably of such an origin, and exist in the present as survivals of a half-animal past, *i. e.*, the circumcision. The last operation possess very bloody forms in many cases ; it is connected with loss of one *testiculum* in South Africa ; the terrible rite in Central Australia is a horrible custom, the warriors who are present shed tears, and some authors (Mikhicho-Maclag) affirm that those subjected to it are probably often incapable of begetting children. We find the like spectacle and the same expulsion of the youth, as we contemplate the life of social *mammalia*. In the herds of guanacos, the mules persecute all young rivals and expel them out of the herd, when they begin to approach females. Such was the practice also in the primitive human horde. The rites of the initiation arose in later time, as a compromise between fighting males of different ages ; male camps and club-houses appeared as an institution which permitted the youth to live in the community, but regulates their intercourse with the other sex in a manner more agreeable to the old people.

In my notes I have given only the general account of my studies on some absurd rites of the to-day savages. But there are other features connected with the seclusion of the youth. Young females of *guanacos* follow the expelled young males.

The like custom must have existed partially in the life of the primitive mankind. The survivals of such a stage are in great enough quantities. Among Narrinyeri tribes the initiated youth is allowed the abominable privilege of promiscuous intercourse with the younger portion of the other sex that visit the camp of the young men. The armenegols of Pelew Islanders had arisen from the same custom. Further we can demonstrate, that monotheism, at its beginning, was the property of the males, no woman knowing anything about it. In the like way I hope to be in possibility of explaining many other features of the savage society and of throwing a light on some institutions, *i. e.*, on the totemism. But, not wishing to go beyond the limits of my essay, I put these questions aside.

THE SIGN LANGUAGE OF THE PLAINS INDIAN.

BY H. L. SCOTT, CAPTAIN 7TH CAVALRY, U. S. ARMY.

THE origin of the Plains Indian is lost in the night of ages : whence he came, and when, will, in all probability, never be discovered.

There has been no copper-colored Macaulay or Gibbon to record his history ; no moccasined Homer or Virgil to sing of his deeds of prowess, and the following generation has witnessed the oblivion of his proudest exploits.

He has left but little material evidence of his early sojourns; here a rude picture graven upon a sandstone rock, or a pile made from the boulders obstructing his pathway through a rocky pass ; there a stone mallet, with which some old woman cracked the thigh-bones of the buffalo, to extract the marrow for her younger rival ; or a flint arrow-head, common to the primitive stages of all mankind ; but to attempt to follow his migrations by such means is like endeavoring to trace the flight of a bird by a feather dropped from its wing.

The traditions of his later descendants are mingled with absurdity and fable, and going back to impossible beginnings are unreliable in the extreme.   In them the mother of all the Kiowas is seen sliding down from heaven upon a rope, twisted from the back sinews of the buffalo ; and the primal ancestors of the Gros Ventres escaping from an under-world by climbing up a tree, or perhaps others who originated as did Topsy, who "just growed."

His only monument which has so far endured has been unconsciously builded from his many languages ; these bear internal evidence of relationship between those families having a common origin, and carry within themselves a part of the history of the travels and vicissitudes, the culture and environment of the tribes and nations who speak them, and if rescued before they fade away may yet be the means of

H. L. SCOTT.

extending the light of history further back into this otherwise impenetrable past.

Co-existent with his many vocal languages for at least a considerable period, has been a language of gesture signs, about whose origin we are but little more enlightened than we are concerning that of the Indian himself. We can surely trace it back to the beginning of this century by our own historical records, and inferentially farther, and by comparison with what it now is, we can see that it is by no means of recent growth, but whether it is part of the primitive utterance of mankind on this continent, elaborated and enriched by time and environment, or whether it has been entirely of later origin we may never know.

If we were to consider the question of the age of this manner of expressing thought, we would find that philologists have long discussed as to whether the gesture or vocal language of primitive man is entitled to precedence in priority of origin, and the accepted conclusions, as stated by Professor Whitney, are that "it is altogether probable that gesture at first performed the principal part, even to such an extent that the earliest human language may be said to have been a language of gesture signs: indeed, there exist at the present day such gesture languages as those in use between roving tribes of different speech (the most noted example is that of the gesture language of a very considerable degree of development, of the prairie tribes of American Indians) or such signs as are the natural resort of those who by deafness are cut off from ordinary intercourse with their fellows." And again, "It is past all reasonable question that in the earliest communications between reasonable beings, gesture long played a considerable part, and that our race learned only by degrees the superior capacities of spoken signs, and by degrees worked them out to a sufficiency for the ordinary needs of expression," and Professor Sayce of Oxford has said that : "Man is man in virtue of language, and it was gesture that first made language possible."

Dr. E. B. Tylor in his researches into the early history of mankind, has told us that "the mother tongue of the deaf mute is a language of signs, which he is capable of originating by an independent process in his own mind, and which

develops, as his knowledge and power of reasoning expand,"
and, after mentioning the various sign languages, such as
those of ancient Greece and Rome, of the later Neapolitans
and Cistercian monks, leads us to believe that while it may
be but little cultivated by civilized peoples, the art of com-
municating by signs is common to all mankind.

It has been asserted, and denied, that such a thing exists
as "the sign language of the Indians," but it is thought
that this issue would have been avoided by limiting the
statement, as it is the purpose of this paper to so limit it,
as to apply only to the nomadic tribes of the great plains.

Colonel Mallery voices the opposition as follows : " But Colonel Dodge's conclusion that there is but one true Indian sign-
language, just as there is but one true English language, is
not proved unless it can be shown that a much larger proportion of the Indians who use signs at all, than present
researches show to be the case, used identically the same
signs to express the same ideas : it would also seem necessary
to the parallel, that the signs so used should be absolute,
if not arbitrary, as the words of all oral language, and not
independent of preconcert and self-interpreting at the instant
of their invention or first exhibition, as all true signs must
have been originally and still measurably remain."

The principal points of difference here seem to be that
Colonel Dodge treats of the sign language of the prairie
tribes, while the author quoted refers to the Indians of North
America at large.   While there are many variants, the greater
part of the signs used by the former people *are* almost identically the same to express the same ideas, and while it is
believed that most of them were self-interpreting in the beginning, yet many of them have now become so conventionalized that the reason for their origin has become entirely
lost to the great majority of their users.

As to the unity of the sign language used by the prairie
tribes, it will be instructive to compare Professor Whitney's
answer to the question,"What then is the English language ?"
"We answer that it is the immense aggregate of the articulate
signs for thought, accepted by and current among a certain
vast community which we call the English-speaking people.

" It is a mighty region of speech, of somewhat fluctuating

Rain In The Face

Standing Bear

and uncertain boundaries, whereof each speaker occupies a portion, and central tract is included in the portion of all. There they meet on common ground, etc. The one fact that gives it unity is that all who speak it may to a considerable extent, and on subjects of the most general and pressing interest, talk so as to understand one another."

Having seen then that "mutual intelligibility is the only test of unity," and having had the good fortune, upon one occasion, to see Joseph, the chief of the Nez Percés, relate, in the sign language, his experiences from the departure from Washington Territory to his capture by General Miles, at the Bear Paw, to an audience of several hundred people, composed of Arickarees, Mandans, Gros Ventres, Nez Percés, Cheyennes and Sioux, the representatives of six different spoken languages, and noted their perfect comprehension of the narrative, without a spoken word from the narrator; and having been present and taken part in the talks without number, using practically the same signs, in mixed assemblages of prairie Indians of almost every tribe, from British America to the Texas border, I must give my unqualified adherence to the belief that the sign language of the Plains Indians does exist, and that it has reached a high degree of development.

Conceding, then, its existence, if we were to examine into its more recent past we would probably find that we cannot trace it with absolute certainty, by our own historical records, prior to the beginning of the present century; although a number of the earlier explorers have mentioned their having conversed with the aborigines of this country by means of gesture signs, they have left us no description of these signs, and we cannot, therefore, surely determine whether these belonged to an organized conventional language, or were but the evanescent pantomime which suggested itself to the mind of the individual explorers at the moment; and it is not until we consult the papers of William Dunbar, 1800; the works of Brackenridge and Bradbury, who ascended the Missouri river about 1811, the former with Manuel Lisa, the fur-trader, and the latter with Hunt and Crooks, who were on their way to found Astoria; and the report of Colonel Long's expedition to the Rocky Mountains, in 1819—that we find

14

signs described, many of which we can recognize as those in use at the present day.

Various writers since that time have incidentally touched upon this subject notably, Prince Max Van Neuweid, about 1832; George F. Ruxton, about 1848; Captain W. B. Marcy, 1854, and others, but it is not until after 1880, when the works of the late Captain Philo Clark, 2nd Cavalry, U. S. A., Colonel R. I. Dodge, 11th Infantry, U. S. A., and the comparison of the sign language of foreigners, deaf mutes, and American Indians, by Colonel Garrick Mallery, of the Smithsonian Institution, made their appearance that the subject can be said to have been seriously treated and discussed.

Notwithstanding the fact that our earlier records cast such a feeble light upon this subject—if we were to compare what is known of the sign language during the past ninety years with what it now is—noting the permanence of many of the signs and remembering also that savages are the most conservative of all peoples, we could not fail to be convinced that a very considerable period of time would be necessary to render this language conventional over such a vast extent of country and among so many wandering tribes, most of whom were at war with each other.

In endeavoring to ascertain the Indian traditions concerning this language, members of nearly every tribe on the Plains have been interrogated; they all unite in saying that it is of vast antiquity, that it was handed down to them in the same manner as were their spoken languages.

The Cheyennes and Arapahoes and some other tribes assert that their ancestors received it first from the Kiowas who invented it; while on the other hand the Kiowas state that it was originally obtained from the Cheyennes, but from what we know concerning the growth of language in general—that it is not invented, but is gradually evolved in the course of years, if not ages, we can readily perceive that to neither the Cheyennes alone, nor to the Kiowas, can the honor of being the originators of the sign language be justly accorded—that each of these tribes had a potent influence, together with all other prairie peoples in the evolution of this language, it is not possible to doubt, but the most that we can say now concerning it is, that it has arisen from their necessities of inter-communication, or that it existed before in its germs, and was perfected by them.

If we were to compare the ability with which this mode of expression is made use of by the various tribes we would find that a great diversity exists not only among the tribes themselves, but also among the individuals who compose them.

Those who do the most travelling and meet the greatest number of people of a different tongue, have the greatest necessity for its use, and when this need dies away for any cause, the sign language falls at once into decay, and is soon forgotten, surviving only in tradition and inherited gesture.

Such is the condition of some of the Eastern bands of Sioux the Cut Heads and Sissitonwans of Fort Totten, who formerly used the sign language, but who have been separated from all other Indians, and associated only with white people for so many years, that it is only the very oldest among them who are aware of its existence.

This partial decay typifies the end, when another generation or so of Indians will have passed away, their languages, vocal and gesture, will have disappeared with them, and the sole remainder of these will be their mummies, embalmed among our records in the characters of the language which has displaced them.

There are still, however, many men among the Crows, Blackfeet, Kiowas, Cheyennes and Arapahoes, who are very skilful in its use, but experience leads to the belief that there are more exceptionally graceful and fluent talkers among the Northern Cheyennes than in any other tribe thus far encountered.

That the Comanches are less versed in it than any other prairie people is easily accounted for by the fact that the Comanche is the court language of the Southern Plains, and is understood by many individuals among all the uncivilized tribes of the Indian Territory, and the need of any other method of communication by the Comanches, was consequently but little felt.

Having seen, then, that the sign language not only does exist, but is one of the natural and fundamental languages of the human race ; in order to properly consider it we must search for its analogies among those languages which have already been analyzed, and it has been well said (Whitney) that "Etymology, the historical study of individual words is the foundation and substructure of all investigation of language," so must the sign language be studied from the individual signs as we now find them, from their recorded history, by searching among the spoken languages for the words used to express the same ideas, from the standpoint of tradition, and by the light shed by their ancient customs many of which we may find embalmed therein.

We shall then see that while many of the signs are immediately suggestive of the concrete object, or of the idea they are intended to represent, others are greatly abbreviated and conventionalized beyond recognition—that most of them are made with graceful and flowing gestures, but with none of the swiftness observed in the intercourse of deaf mutes, for the Indian being seldom pushed for time, or, as he expresses it, "having all the time there is," he prefers grace of motion to rapidity of execution—the more expert talkers making their signs rather slowly, not allowing a halt, but causing each sign without hesitation to flow into another, just as the words of the softer languages of Europe glide into each other by the elision of harsh sounds—and often for the sake of elegance they cause the hand at the end of many signs to make a slight rebound.

We shall see that but few postures or facial movements are necessary—that many of the conceptions which suggested the original pantomime, can by the light shed by their ancient customs, be traced to their sources with great probability, or a clue pointed out by a word or a name in some spoken language, long after the memory of their origins have faded completely away.

We shall see also that the sign language is a living language, finding new expressions for new thoughts as they arise —choosing the most enduring and conspicuous quality of the object to be represented which usually differentiates it from all others of the same class—and finally, that it is sufficiently copious to express the thoughts and satisfy the needs of the primitive people whose instrument it is.

And now we will consider some of the more important individual signs, tracing, when possible, the conceptions from

which they have sprung, glancing briefly at the order or sequence in which they follow one another in practical use,
and, if time will permit, closing with representation and interpretation of the Kiowa legend concerning the coming of
the buffalo, and first the signs for the different divisions of
time—for the day when all is clear light and open—for the
night when all is covered over by darkness as with a blanket.
Yesterday is the "day before", and to-morrow for the
Indian will commence when the sun rises in the East, early
dawn when it is a little below the horizon, noonday when it
is overhead, evening when it disappears in the West, and
midnight is literally translated into the middle of the night.

The end of a month is represented by the death or wiping
out of the moon, the years are counted by the number of
winters, the spring is shown by the coming of the grass, the
summer by the heat or bearing down of the rays of the sun,
the autumn by the redness of the trees, and winter begins
when it is a little cold, and generally future time is that which
comes hereafter, and past time that which has gone before.

Water is symbolized by the act of drinking out of the hand,
a lake or pond would be a round body of water ; the water
sign with the direction of its course would be a stream, or with
a name would represent a river—as the Arkansas or Flint
River, as it is called by the Prairie Indians, the Yellowstone
or Elk River, the Tongue, Big Horn, Powder, the Platte
or Shell or the Neck River, the Lodge Pole or Washita
River, or the Muscleshell River of Montana.

There are but two specific signs for colors ; *i. e.* that for red
and black,—as the Canadian River is called Red River by all
the Southern Indians.

The abstract sign for color is made by rubbing the back of
left hand between roots of forefinger and thumb with the
palmar surface of fingers of the right hand ; when any object
is pointed out in connection with this sign, it is always understood that is referred to and not the object itself.

The animals are generally described by their most prominent characteristics as the elk by its large and branching ant-
lers, the mountain sheep by its horns curving to the rear, the
antelope by its pronged, and the buffalo by its in-curving,
horns.

The mule is portrayed by his large ears, the wolf by his manner of carrying his ears erect, and by derivation comes the sign for wisdom analogous to our word "foxy." Hence an idiom " to consider " is to have one's wisdom look over an object or proposition, and to have one's wisdom miss the mark is to make a mistake.

The beaver is represented by his habit when disturbed or frightened of striking his broad tail on the water in order to facilitate his diving, the spider by his many legs crawling rapidly away, the fish by his course under water, the cactus, by its many sharp spines : hence, the porcupine is the one with "prickly hair ; " the rabbit when started from its form first ambles off to a safe distance, then sits up with its ears erect to observe its enemy ; the turtle moves in a slow and tortuous course ; and the rattlesnake is recognized at once by the vibration of its tail when accompanied by its peculiar sound.

The sun dance is shown by a representation of the whistle made from the wing bone of an eagle, which is always used by the dancers ; the Omaha or Grass dance, by the hopping motion made to keep time to the drum ; the calumet, by the swaying of the calumet feathers in the dance, and the Messiah or Ghost dance, by the circular motion made by rings of dancers in close proximity.

The rain is typified by the sprinkling of drops from above, the lightning by its downward zigzag course, the thunder by its noise, like the discharge of a gun that occurs during a rain.

To tell the truth is to tell a straight story, to lie is to speak with a forked tongue, this sign is often used without the offensive meaning in the sense of a mistake, to abuse is derived from the idea of throwing lies at one.

To remember is to hold fast to a thing, to forget is to have it slip away and be lost.

To be hungry is to feel a sawing in the abdominal region, to be thirsty is to be water hungry, to have enough of any thing is to be full of it up to one's eyes.

To try anything is to push or strive at it, to die a natural death is to leave the erect position of the living and lie underground, to kill is thus made often with both hands—this is said to have originated from the idea of killing by striking, but it institutes no manner of striking, either with a club, a knife or with the fist. It can be accounted for, however, in a satisfactory manner by referring it to the idea of a death in agony as it imitates the action of the fore-legs of a deer or buffalo in its death-struggles.

The Indian considers that his heart is the seat of most of his emotions ; when he is sorrowful he says that his heart is on the ground or else that his heart is weeping.

When he is glad his heart is open; when bold it is stung ; when discouraged it is wiped out ; when doubtful he has two or more hearts which are alternately up and down; when disturbed his heart flutters up into his throat ; when brooding over an injury it feels as if it is being stabbed ; when he is homesick it goes out in search of home ; when he is angry, however, his mind is twisted ; and when he feels astonishment he puts his hand over his mouth to indicate that he has no word adequate to describe it.

As we have stated before, there are a number of signs that have become purely conventional, and indeed the great majority of them have long been so to the Indian ; for when asked concerning the reasons for the origin of all but the most obvious, he usually has but one answer, viz., that the old men from whom he learned it talked in that way and that that is all he knows about it. But the inference as to the original pantomime can be drawn by the intelligent white man in many cases, and as our knowledge of this language expands, the number of signs to which no conception can be assigned becomes less and less and it is possible that some day we may be able to trace the origin of all ; of this class are the signs for " assent," to " want," for " good," and " strong," for which no satisfactory conceptions have so far been met with.

Some other signs are purely derivative, as the sign " to know " or understand often made, particularly in the North with both hands ; no connection could be discovered between this sign and its meaning for many years, but it is highly probable that it has been derived from the sign to " wake up " or open one's eyes—as we say in English that a person is wide awake or has his eyes open to a situation to indicate that he fully understands it.

The tribal sign for the Cheyennes has usually been accounted for by saying that it came from their habit of slashing their arms—but they are no more addicted to this practice than are any of their neighbors, and the Cheyennes themselves cannot account for it. They did have a peculiar practice of using turkey feathers on their arrows, the sign for the turkey is the striped winged bird from the broad band of gray on their wings; this connection was discovered through the name for the Cheyennes in the Comanche tongue, "Tsee nabo" or "striped feather people."

One of their peculiar idioms is shown in the "prairie gift." This is first described in George F. Ruxton's Book on "Life in the Far West," 1848, and it means a free gift or one from which no return is expected. Another is "to hold the pipe," which signifies that the person who "holds the pipe" is a leader; the conception underlying this sign and that for the "war-path" is from their ancient custom of recruiting a war-party somewhat after the manner of the old crusaders, but instead of a flag the leader carried before him a pipe; in the sign for "war-path" the thumb represents the bowl and the forefinger the stem, and the movement is made in the direction of the location of the tribe against whom they intended going to war.

Still another idiom is the sign to "kill" in certain connections where it has no reference to actual killing, but to the destruction of opposition—as to overcome; to kill a woman is to gain her affections, or to beat a game, or to win at a horse race.

If a white man were asked for a sign for "digging" he would in all probability imitate the digging with a spade because that is the method most familiar to him—but the Indian sign embalms their custom of digging in ancient times with hoes made from the shoulder blade of the buffalo; their sign for dog also contains the idea of the uses to which he was put before the coming of the horse, viz., the dragging of the travois poles when the village was on the march.

That it is a living language is shown by the sign for the "trap"; for coffee, which the Indian associates with the mill by which it is ground; for the Cheyenne and Arapahoe agent, because the first one they received had false teeth; for telegraph, and by other modern signs which have arisen since the coming of the white man.

SYNTAX.

These gestures will probably be sufficient to give an idea of the nature of the individual signs, or the etymology of the sign language ; and before examining the syntax, it will be well to warn the student versed in the grammars of the spoken tongues, not to look for grammatical signs analogous to those words by which the relations of the different parts of a sentence are pointed out, for conjugations of verbs, for declensions of nouns—these relations must be indicated by position, by pointing with the hand, or by extraneous and independent signs.

The sign language resembles the Chinese in its want of inflections, and its consisting largely in what one might call roots ; but while one sign may be a noun (as dog), or an adjective (as good), or a verb (as to know) the next may comprise a whole English sentence in a single motion, as " I tell you," in which the subjective and objective relations are expressed by direction alone.

A conversation in the sign language has been likened to a series of moving pictures, and as the relations between object's actions in such pictures are represented by the relative positions and sequence, and are evident to the eye, so also are those expressed in the sign pictures when viewed by a person trained to see with the eye of the natural man ; for this sequence is not that in which the English-speaking person arranges his expressions for thought, but is analogous to that used by the deaf mute.

Dr. Tyler has told us that the syntax of speaking man differs according to the language he may learn, as " equus niger," a " black horse "; or " hominem amo," or " j'aime l'homme "; but the deaf mute strings together the signs for the various ideas he wishes to connect in the natural order in which they follow one another in his mind, for it is the same in different countries, and is wholly independent of the syntax that may happen to belong to the language of his speaking friends.

The English phrase, a fast horse, would be inverted by Indian and deaf mute alike, and expressed by signs which would be literally translated into " horse fast " ; a good heart into " heart good," and it may be said generally that the attribute follows the object, the adverb precedes the verb, and the subject is often placed last of all ; and that there are but few dependent sentences used ; for instance, " I shot with an arrow, last night, an eagle which was sitting upon the limb of a tree, and it fell to the ground," it would be necessary to make the signs in the following order : " night ; before trees, looking, I saw, bird, curved beak, trees, standing, arrow, bow, aim, shoot transfix, whirl downward, strike on the ground ; " this would be very nearly the sequence of the steps of the actual occurrence, and the order also of the series of sign pictures used to describe it.

The various tenses of the verb are expressed by some one of the different signs for the divisions of time, such as yesterday, to-morrow, or last summer. This is almost invariably placed at the beginning, in order to put the minds of speaker and spoken to in accord at once, as in the last example—when the sign for last night was made—it was at once understood that the action about to be described took place in the past.

Continued and expressive action is often expressed by a species of reduplication as the sign to increase one's knowledge comes from using the sign to know in a more extended sense.

Comparison is indicated by some of the signs for comparative adjectives—big or little—by the sign of equality, sometimes by a special sign ; as to long for anything is to want it exceedingly, a thing that does not come up to one's expectation is said to be behind or to fall short, or it may be ahead.

The superlative is signified by the adjective " strong." This sign is one that occurs very frequently and may be used to intensify every action or quality.

Gender is signified by the signs for male and female, used as adjectives, except in a few cases where there is a special sign, as in that of the buffalo bull, which is shown by the long hair of his mane, which is wanting in the female.

The ownership of any article is shown by the sign for possession, as that horse is mine.

The pronouns are indicated by pointing either towards oneself for the first person, toward the person spoken to for the second, to a third person present or to a suppositious person who has before been spoken of. This amounts to an abstract sign for he or him; there is also an abstract sign for the demonstrative pronoun "that."

The sign for interrogation has various meanings according to the connection in which it is used—if it was made to a personal acquaintance riding by at a distance, it would mean "Where are you going?" if to a person sitting near without any previous conversation, it would be intended simply to draw his attention; if made to a stranger when meeting him at some distance on the prairie, it would mean "Who are you?" If used during a conversation it would be intended either to ask a question, or "What did you say?" according to the person who used it, and it is often used also to signify doubt or probability; it was probably derived originally from the sign to doubt, or to have many hearts struggling for the mastery.

The grammatical part of the sign language is the portion least understood by the white man, partly because of the inverted order of sequence so opposed to the genius of the English tongue, and partly because his attention at first, and for a long period is directed solely to the acquirement of the individual signs, the proper way to learn it is to study it directly from the Indians themselves—to go with them upon their migrations and hunting excursions—upon expeditions, travelling with the scouts by day, or seated around their camp-fires at night.

But you ask if the sign language cannot be acquired from the study of the elaborate works written with such care upon this subject. It has not been the experience of many persons coming from the East, struck with the picturesque novelty of the Indians as a people, who endeavored to learn from books to speak the sign language in order to converse with them, for we have seen that it is primarily a language of motions and not of positions, and the rates of these motions often vary in the different parts of the same sign, and cannot be accurately recorded by a description or by a stationary picture; and while many other signs can be properly described, no book can give an idea of the graceful and flowing sequence with which signs are used by a master of the art, and the books have soon been laid aside, to be taken up later as a means of comparison.

If you could have witnessed the scenes enacted in many of their lodges during the long nights of the winter, in some isolated village upon the buffalo range, or sheltered from the wind in a mountain park, when some one of their older and more skilful men, fired with enthusiasm by the memories of his youth, was relating his stories of the warpath and adventure, the ancient customs of his people, or the ceremonies of their religion, to a silent band of dusky warriors,—then only could you realize the great force, the intense meaning, and the exceeding gracefulness and beauty of the sign language of the Plains Indian.

SIOUX MYTHOLOGY.

BY DR. CHARLES A. EASTMAN.

THE tendency of the uncivilized and untutored mind is to recognize the Deity through some definite *medium*. The mind has an inborn recognition of the *highest good* or *God*. The aborigines of this country illustrate this truth. But the province of this paper is to deal, in the brief time allowed, with the mythology of the Sioux Nation, and more especially that portion of the tribe with which I am very familiar, although the others are not distinctively different in their religious customs.

The human mind, equipped with all its faculties, is capable, even in its uncultured state, of a distinct process of reasoning. Free from the burdensome theories of science and of theology it is impressed powerfully by God's omnipresence, omniscience, and omnipotence.

Alexander Pope's worn-out lines :

> " Lo, the poor Indian ! Whose untutored mind
> Sees God in clouds, or hears Him in the wind,"

is true as far as that the Indian recognized the power behind every natural force. His thought instantly goes back to the God who made the wind to blow, the sun to shine, the fire to burn, and so forth. Thus he not only sees God in the sky, but in every creation. All nature sings his praises : birds, waterfalls, tree-tops, everything whispers the name of the mysterious God.

The Indian does not trouble himself concerning the nature of creation. He is satisfied that there is a Supreme God, to whom all nature bows her head ; whose laws all must obey. Beyond this he does not dare to go. He looks to Him for help.

The relation between *God* and *man* he conceived from the

221

analogy of nature, that God is a gracious and exacting friend.
He both punishes the disobedient and evil-doers, and forgives
and helps the good. He hears prayers. He is called *Wakantanka* or Great Mystery. The first half of the word, viz.,
wakan, means mystery or holy; and *tanka* means great,
mighty or supreme. Neither of the two words which compose the *Wakantanka* signifies *spirit,* however it may imply
that. The *wakán* may also mean *reverenced* or *sacred.*

Before the coming of the missionaries the Sioux never
prayed or gave any offering direct to the Great Mystery. It
was then believed he was too great to be approached directly.
But a prayer or gift through his attributes will reach him.
The legend is that God occasionally visits the earth, in the
shape of some animal, or envelopes himself in a great wind.
If any person sees the Great Mystery's face he dies instantly,
although the same person may be born again as a child and
become a great "medicine man."

Before the advent of the white man these people believed
that the earth was round and flat, and was suspended in a
dark space, and sheltered by the heaven or sky, in the shape
of a hollowed hemisphere. The sun was made by the Great
Mystery, the father, and the earth, the mother, of all the
things that live and grow. But they have been married
long, and had become the parents of many generations of races,
therefore they were called *Tunkan'sida* and *Uncida,* or *great
grandfather* and *grandmother.* As far as I can make out the
moon seems to be their *servant,* or at least she is required to
watch, together with the stars, the sleeping world below;
while the *Sun* comes down to sleep with his wife, Earth, and
his children. The moon is considered a man and the stars
are his brothers. In the sense that the *Sun* and *Earth* constitute the parents of the world, they believed that the Great
Mystery holds them responsible. Therefore it was natural
for them to appeal to these two, who will in turn appeal to
the Supreme Being.

In the thunder they believed that God has a warrior who
presided over the more powerful elements, such as the storms,
rains, etc. Also he was appointed to act as soldier (in the
sense of police) keeping order here below. He is held as a
large bird, and is called the *thunder-bird,* and depicted as the

impatient and wrathy god of war, at whose presence even the ever-smiling and kind *great grandfather,* the *Sun,* hides his face. In the sea dwells a great chief, too, whom they called *Unktehé.* The whale is called by this name now, but it is my belief that the name had applied to an imaginary one at first. The latter has many sub-chiefs in each of the great *lakes* and *rivers.*

Yet all these cannot possess the power of speech. The *Great Mystery* had shown them some great truths, which he denied to man, but he could not trust them, for some reason or other, so he made them dumb. Even then they often show to man by sign some supernatural power.

Thus the savages hold that the *key* of heaven is vested in the visible phenomena of the universe. Each animal, each thing has just so much purity and holiness, and it is dumb and helpless. The rocks, the trees, etc., are all imprisoned for life ; yet they hold some of the *mysteries* of their maker. The mighty river and the little brook, in proportion to their strength and wonderfulness, show the power of the god.

The root-eating animals were considered the leading medicine-givers, such as the *bear,* the *badger,* the *beaver* and the like. The *sun* and the thunder-bird both have some claims on the medical profession, and none of the animals are entirely exempted from it.

The *spirits* of the departed having once left this sinful world are immediately admitted into the mysteries of the *Great Mystery,* except the very wicked, who are transformed into some lower animal and are returned to earth and allowed to know only one or two things of the mysteries of the Great God. This was their punishment. Yet such a spirit may retrieve its misfortunes by good behavior. Then it is promoted to a higher grade of animal life, until it is returned to man again. But if it grows opposite of this it is changed to a lower and lower grade successively from animal to the vegetable and finally to the inorganic kingdom. This is his last punishment.

In man there are believed to be *three spirits.* After death one of these at once travels through the *Milky Way,* escorted by the heavenly servants, the stars, who were crowded on the spirit-path, and it is at once received into the mysteries of the

Great God. The second remains as guardian over the grave, and it is usually called the *ghost.* The third travels about with his relatives. All three become supernatural and are capable of doing anything with the consent of the Great Mystery. Therefore prayers are offered through them. I do not know just how this trinity of soul was originally conceived.

There is a strong implication that the Great Mystery has made man after himself ; therefore, whatever the latter enjoys he also appreciates. He is in form like man, with a few exceptions or modifications. He has horns, and his eyes are like the sun ; in fact all his senses are unlimited in their sphere of usefulness. A model of dignity, honor, sacredness, power and mystery—all these together create the atmosphere of awfulness to their mind.

Inasmuch as they conceived that there is *good* and *bad*—the opposites—they seem to think that the Great Mystery created everything in pairs, with a few exceptions. Therefore there is an evil spirit, as well as the good spirit.

Their strong belief was that the trees, rocks, etc., hear what they say, in other words the Great Mystery is " all ears," " all eyes," etc. Every one of his creation is his ears, eyes, etc., except man, but he, too, becomes as such, as soon as his spirit enters the spirit-land. It is my belief that on this account the natives had no word for swearing and never blasphemed, for the spirit of the Great Mystery is everywhere.

In the old régime the Indian's idea of nobility and strength of character was based on bravery and success in warfare, in hunting, in feast-making, etc., but these are not possible unless the Great Mystery is obeyed and first considered in everything. Therefore all well brought up and ambitious youths usually sought for God's good-will in *solitary seasons* of *prayer* and *fasting,* and gave feasts to the more experienced " medicine-men " for advice. As one of these savage sages once remarked to an ambitious youth, " Without the help of the Great Mystery you need not expect to be a great warrior or a great hunter, and you never could be a feast-maker unless you are a hunter."

And so the Indian youth seeks some manifestation of

the blessing of his God through some one of his attributes. He usually selects a most impressive and conspicuous yet lonely spot for his hope for a communion with one of the Great Mystery's mediators. Here he pours out from his simple heart the most devout prayer, then sings, and finally weeps that his God may hear that one of *his* children is seeking him in tears. Thus he sojourns for two or three days, until all his physical forces are exhausted, for he fasts all the time, then when he is delirious he imagines that he had heard his voice. While there have been remarkable coincidences in regard to what such a young man predicts and prophecies after one of these fastings, I am inclined to believe that in most cases a delusion resulted from exhaustion of the body and mind. Much faith is wasted in dreams.

Occasionally an Indian without seeking hears a *voice*, either disclosed to him some mysteries of life, by means of which he becomes a great "medicine-man" or a great "war-chief," or a great prophet. But human nature is so prone to deceive that it was hard to believe all such claims, unless they were verified.

There are certain implements of war and the "medicine-man's" pouch, rattles, etc., which may be considered as *idols*. Yet they are not purely so. For they are only considered as the gift of the Great Mystery effected through one of his attributes, therefore they must be respected and reverenced in the remembrance of the giver. It is in fear of him that the *implement* is kept and observed as *sacred*.

The savage belief is that the more powerful elements often contended for the exhibition of strength. The thunder-bird, the war-chief, is supposed to have often waged war against the "people of the deep," or the "water demons"— more definitely the fishes, in which, of course, their chief, the *Unktehé,* leads them. Very often the thunder-bird punishes some animal here on earth. The more peaceful *Sun,* the great father, even occasionally displays his wrath by sending down from heaven a fiery missile—such as a falling star or a comet.

These few hurriedly collected facts concerning the mythology of the Sioux Nation will tend to show that the American Indian, before the coming of the whites, had a great faith in

15

his "unknown God," whose colossal power, physical, moral, and mental, was so impressed upon his untutored mind and made him so conscious of his own sinful life, that he felt he was not warranted to approach Him direct, but through some mediator, who will intercede for him with his Great Mystery.

WASHINGTON MATTHEWS

SOME SACRED OBJECTS OF THE NAVAJO RITES.

BY WASHINGTON MATTHEWS, SURGEON, U. S. ARMY.

SOME one has said that a first-class museum would consist of a series of satisfactory labels with specimens attached. This saying might be rendered : "The label is more important than the specimen." When I have finished reading this paper, you may admit that this is true in the case of the little museum which I have here to show : a basket, a fascicle of plant fibres, a few rudely painted sticks, some beads and feathers put together as if by children in their meaningless play, form the total of the collection. You would scarcely pick these trifles up if you saw them lying in the gutter, yet when I have told all I have to tell about them, I trust they may seem of greater importance, and that some among you would be as glad to possess them as I am. I might have added largely to this collection had I time to discourse about them, for I possess many more of their kind. It is not a question of things, but of time. I shall do scant justice to this little pile within an hour. An hour it will be to you, and a tiresome hour, no doubt ; but you may pass it with greater patience when you learn that this hour's monologue represents to me twelve years of hard and oft-baffled investigation. Such dry facts as I have to relate are not to be obtained by rushing up to the first Indian you meet, notebook in hand. But I have no time for further preliminary remarks, and must proceed at once to my descriptions.

THE BASKET DRUM.

The first thing that I present to you is a basket. Wordsworth tells us of Peter Bell that :

"A primrose by a river's brim,
A yellow primrose was to him,
And it was nothing more."

227

To most observers this may seem a yellow basket, but it is much more to many an untutored savage. The art of basket-making is to-day little cultivated among the Navajos. In developing their blanket-making to the highest point of Indian art, the women of this tribe have neglected other labors. The much ruder, but cognate Apaches, who know how to weave woollen fabrics, make more baskets than the Navajos and make them in greater variety of form, color, and quality. The basket I show you is, however, of Navajo make, and it is skillfully fabricated; yet it is with one exception almost the only form and pattern of basket now made in the tribe. They buy most of their baskets from other tribes. But, having generally let the art of basketry fall into disuse, they still continue to make this form, for the reason that it is essential to their sacred rites, and must be supplied by women of the tribe who know what is required. It is made of twigs of aromatic sumac—a shrub which has many sacred uses—wound in the form of a helix. The fabricator must always put the butt-end of the twig toward the centre of the basket and the tip toward the periphery. A band of red and black, with zigzag edges, is the sole decoration. This band, it will be observed, is not continuous, but is intersected at one point by a narrow line of yellow, or, more properly speaking, of uncolored wood.

When I first observed this, years ago, I fancied that it had some relation to the "line of life" observed in the ancient and modern Pueblo pottery, and that its existence might be explained by reasons as metaphysical as those which the Pueblos give for their "line of life." But the Navajo has at least one reason of a more practical character. The line is put there to assist in the orientation of the basket, at night, in the medicine-lodge when the fire has burned low and the light is dim. In an article published in the *American Anthropologist* (October, 1892), I explained the law of butts and tips in Navajo ceremonies and shall not now repeat the explanation. It must suffice to say that throughout their ceremonies careful discrimination is made between the butt and the tip, the central and the peripheral ends, and that the butt has precedence over the tip. This law applies to the basket before you as well as to other sacred things. The

BASKET DRUM.

butt of the first twig, placed in the centre, and the tip of the last twig, in the edge, must lie in the same radial line, and this line is marked by the hiatus in the ornamental band. The rim of the basket is often so neatly finished that the medicine-man could not easily tell where the helix ended were not the pale line there to guide him. This line must lie east and west when the basket is employed in the ceremonies.

The most important use of the basket is as a drum. In none of the ancient Navajo rites is a regular drum or tom-tom employed. The inverted basket serves the purpose of one, and the way in which it is used for this simple object is rendered devious and difficult by ceremonious observances. To illustrate, let me describe a *few* of these observances belonging to the ceremony of the Night-Chant. This ceremony lasts nine nights and nine days. During the first four nights song is accompanied only by the rattle. During the last five nights, noises are elicited from the basket-drum by means of the yucca drumstick. The drum is beaten only in the western side of the lodge. For four of these five nights, the following methods are pursued : A small Navajo blanket is laid on the ground, its longer dimension extending east and west. An incomplete circle of meal, open in the west, of the diameter of the basket, is traced on the blanket near its eastern end. A cross in meal, its ends touching the circle near the cardinal points, is then described within the circle. In making this cross a line is first drawn from east to west, and then a line is drawn from south to north. Meal is then applied sunwise to the rim of the upturned basket so as to form an incomplete circle with its opening in the east. A cross, similar to that on the blanket, is drawn in meal on the concavity of the basket, the east and west line of which cross must pass directly through the hiatus in the ornamental band. The basket is then inverted on the blanket in such a manner that the figures in meal on the one shall correspond in position to those on the other. The western half of the blanket is then folded over the convexity of the basket and the musicians are ready to begin. But before they begin to beat time to a song, they tap the basket with the drumstick at the four cardinal points in the order of east, south, west

and north. The Navajos say, "We turn down the basket,"
when they refer to the commencement of songs in which the
basket-drum is used, and, "We turn up the basket," when
they refer to the ending of the songs for the night. On the
last night the basket is turned down with much the same observances as on the previous nights; but the openings in the
ornamental band and in the circles of meal are turned to the
east instead of to the west, and the eastern half of the blanket
is folded over the convexity of the basket. There are songs
for turning up and for turning down the basket, and there
are certain words in these songs at which the shaman prepares
to turn up the basket by putting his hand under its eastern
rim, and other words at which he does the turning. For
four nights when the basket is turned down, the eastern part
is laid on the outstretched blanket first, and it is inverted
towards the west; on the fifth night, it is inverted in
the opposite direction. When it is turned up, it is always
lifted first at the eastern edge. As it is raised, an imaginary
something is blown toward the east, in the direction of the
smoke-hole of the lodge, and when it is completely turned
up, hands are waved in the same direction, to drive out the
evil influences which the sacred songs have collected and imprisoned under the basket.

The border of this, as of other Navajo baskets, is finished
in a diagonally-woven or plaited pattern. These Indians say
that the Apaches and other neighboring tribes, finish the
margins of their baskets with simple circular turns of the investing fibre, like that in the rest of the basket. The Navajo basket, they believe may always be known by the peculiar finish described, and they say that if among other tribes
a woman is found who makes Navajo finish she is of Navajo
descent or has learned her art of a Navajo. They account
for this by a legend which is perhaps not all mythical. In
the ancient days a Navajo woman was seated under a juniper
tree finishing a basket in the style of the other tribes as was
then the Navajo custom, and while so engaged she was in-
tently thinking if some stronger and more beautiful margin
could not be devised. As she thus sat in thought, the good
Qastceyelci tore from the overhanging juniper-tree a small
spray and cast it into her basket. It immediately occurred

to her to imitate in her work the peculiar folds of the juniper leaves and she soon devised a way of doing so. If this margin is worn through, or torn in any way the basket is unfit for sacred use. The basket is given to the shaman when the rites are done, he must not give it away, and he must be careful never to eat out of it, for, notwithstanding its sacred use it is no desecration to serve food in it.

THE DRUM-STICK.

The next thing to be examined is the drum-stick with which this drum is beaten. I show you now only the stick used in one rite—that of the night chant. The task of making this stick does not necessarily belong to the shaman, any assistant may make it; but so intricate are the rules pertaining to its construction, that one shaman has told me he never found any one who could form it merely from verbal instructions. Practical instructions are necessary. The drum-stick is made anew for each ceremony and destroyed in a manner to be described when the ceremony is over. It is formed from the stout leaves of *Yucca baccata*, a species of Spanish bayonet. But not every plant of this kind is worthy to furnish the material. I have seen an hour spent in search for the proper plant on a hillside bristling with *Yucca baccata*. Four leaves only can be used, and they must all come from the same plant—one from each of the cardinal points of the stem. All must be of the proper length and absolutely free from wound, stain, withered point, or blemish of any kind. These conditions are not fulfilled on every yucca. The leaves may not be cut off but must be torn off downwards, at their articulations. The collector first pulls the selected leaf from the east side of the plant, making a mark with the thumb nail on the east or dorsal side of the leaf near its root, in order that he may know this leaf thereafter. He walks sunwise around the plant to the west side, marks the selected leaf near the tip on its palmar surface and culls it. He then retreats to the south side of the plant and collects his leaf there but does not mark it. Lastly he proceeds sunwise to the north and culls his last leaf,—also without marking it. When the leaves are all obtained the sharp flinty points and

the curling marginal cilia are torn off and struck, point upward, in among the remaining leaves of the plant from which
they were culled.   The four leaves are then taken to the medicine lodge to be made up.   The leaves from the east and west
are used for the centre or core of the stick and are left whole.
The leaves from the north and south are torn into long shreds
and used for the wrapper.   But since the shaman cannot ade-
quately explain in words, to the devotees who assist him,
how the stick is made I shall not attempt the task for you to-
night.   I have learned how to make it ; but I have, now, no
fresh yucca leaves on hand to illustrate the process of making.
So I shall say nothing more of the process.   Any one who is
not satisfied with this decision may come with me to the
yucca-covered deserts of Arizona and there I may show him
how to make a drum-stick.   In figure 2, which represents
the drum-stick, you will observe that the core of the stick is
divided, by a suture of yucca-shred into five compartments,
one for each night during which the stick is used.   Into each
of these sections are usually put one or more grains of corn,
which, during the five nights that the implement is in use,
are supposed to imbibe some sacred properties.   When the
ceremony is all over these grains are divided among the visiting medicine men, to be ground up and put in their medicine
bags.   On the last morning of the ceremony, at dawn, when
the last song of sequence has been sung and the basket turned
up, this drum-stick is pulled to pieces in an order the reverse
of that in which it was put together.   This work may only be
done by the shaman who conducted the rites, and, as he proceeds with his work, he sings the song of the unravelling.
As each piece is unwrapped it is straightened out and laid
down with its point to the east.   The debris which accumu-
lated in the manufacture of the drum-stick and which has
been carefully laid away for five days is now brought forth,
and one fascicle is made of all.   This is taken out of the lodge
by an assistant, carried in an easterly direction and laid in
the forks of a cedar tree (or in the branches of some other
large plant, if a cedar tree is not at hand) where it will be
safe from the trampling feet of cattle.   There it is left until
destroyed or scattered by the forces of nature.   The man who
sacrifices these fragments takes out with him in the hollow

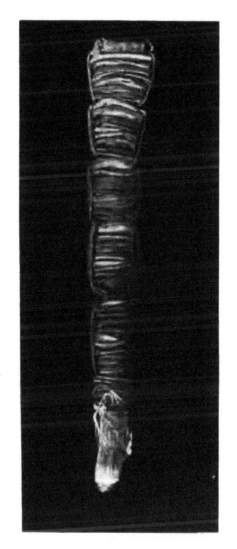

DRUMSTICK OF YUCCA LEAVES.

of his left hand some corn meal which he sprinkles with the same hand on the shreds from butt to tip. He takes out also in a bag some pollen, which he sprinkles on them in the same direction with his right hand. As he does this he repeats in a low voice the following prayer or benediction :

" Qojolel koçe

Qojogo năcaɬo koçe cıtsoi "

" Thus will it be beautiful

Thus walk in beauty my grandchild."

·The drum-stick which I hold in my hand is withered, shrivelled and loose. It has long ago lost its freshness ; a few taps of this on the basket would knock it all to pieces. Even during the short time that the stick is in use for its sacred purpose it would shrivel and become worthless were it not buried in moist earth all day and only taken forth from its hiding-place when needed for the ceremonies of the night.

THE PLUMED WANDS.

THE next objects to be described are the Incia of the night chant. These are eight plumed wands which are set up as guardians around the sacred pictures and the sudatories of the rite. They represent ancestral Navajos of the mythic days when the people dwelt in the fourth world, before they came up to the surface of this world. They are made of willow, which should be cut only on the banks of the San Juan River—the sacred stream of the Navajos. In cutting them, the shaman begins on the south bank of the stream. He faces west and cuts the first stick ; his next stick he cuts at a point west of the first and so he proceeds westward, cutting, until he has procured four sticks. These he wraps up in a bundle by themselves and observes something in their appearance by which he shall know afterwards that they are the sticks of the south. When four suitable sticks have been obtained on the south bank, the shaman scatters pollen before him in the way that he must go, and crosses the river to the north bank. Here he cuts four more sticks proceeding from west to east or in an opposite direction to that which he took on the south side, observing in his whole course the sunwise ceremonial circuit. These four sticks are wrapped in another fasces. As each willow is cut it is trimmed off to the proper length and the discarded top is placed, upright, among the growing willows, as close as possible to the stump from which it was cut. The stump is then rubbed with pollen and pollen is scattered in the air by the ascending hand, upwards from the stump in the place where the shrub grew, as if in sacrifice to the spirit of the shrub. The proper length for the wand is the natural cubit, measured from the inner condyle of the humerus to the tip of the middle finger and throughout this distance, the stick must be free from branch, knot, cicatrix or blemish. One stick measured on the arm is taken as a standard for the other sticks. The sticks are then denuded of their bark and each whittled to a point at the butt end, in order that it may be stuck in the ground. Each of the four sticks cut south of the river has then a facet cut at its tip end to represent the square domino or mask worn by the female dancer in the rites. The sticks cut on the north side of the river have no such facet, their round ends sufficiently represent the round or cap-like masks worn by the male dancers. In numerous other articles made of sticks for the Navajo rites, this distinction is made between male and female. I have observed among the Moquis a similar feature in their sacrificial sticks or bahos ; but I am not aware if a similar explanation is given by the latter people. The sticks are now painted—those of the south, blue, those of the north, black. Blue in all Navajo symbolism is the color of the south and of the female ; black is the color of the north and of the male. The sticks that come from the south of the San Juan represent females ; those from the north, males. I might read you a separate lecture on this particular symbolism ; but I can now only take time to mention a few instructive points. From various analogies in Navajo myth and language, I am led to believe that the male is assigned to the north for the reason that the north is a land of rigor and fierceness to these people. Not only do inclement and violent winds, typical of the male character, proceed from the north ; but the country north of the Navajo land is very rugged and mountainous—within it lie the great peaks of Colorado. And the female is assigned to the south because thence come gentle and warm breezes and the landscape of the south is tame

compared with that of the north. However this may be, all
through Navajo myth and ceremony the south and all its
symbolism is associated with the female; the north and all
its symbolism with the male. There is a special portion of
the Creation and Migration Myth of the tribe which has relation to these sticks. It is told that when the Navajos lived
in the nether world, a great river, the exact counterpart of
the San Juan, flowed from east to west through their land.
The two sexes of the tribe quarrelled and separated; the
women took the south side of the river, the men the north.
It is a long story, how they fared during their separation and
how they were at last reconciled and came together again,
and it need not now be told. But the shamans connect the
custom of cutting these sticks on the San Juan—the female
sticks on the south and the male sticks on the north bank
with this ancient myth.

The black sticks are painted white at their upper extremities in accordance with a fixed law of Navajo hieratic art to
which I shall again refer. The facet on each blue stick is
daubed with small black spots to represent the eyes and mouth
of the female mask, and at its bottom is the yellow horizontal
streak seen on the female mask which symbolizes the Naqot-
soi or land of yellow horizontal light, *i. e.* the last streak of
departing daylight. The upper extremity of each blue stick
is painted black to represent the hair of the female characters in the dance, which flows out freely, not being confined by the domino; while the hair of the male dancer is
hidden by the cap-like mask. When the painting is done
the sticks are decked with two whorls of turkey and eagle-
feathers—each whorl secured by one continuous cotton string
which terminates in a downy eagle-feather. The string must
be twilled from raw cotton on an old fashioned spindle, the
material manufactured by the whites would never do. It
must be remembered that this use of cotton shows no degen-
eracy of the rite, since cotton was grown and spun in New
Mexico and Arizona from a remote prehistoric period and
cotton fabrics are to-day found among the ruins of the cliff-
houses. When the sticks are finished the debris of manufacture is carried to the north and thrown away among a
cluster of willows on the north bank of a stream. As I have

said, these sticks are, afterwards, stuck up around the sacred
dry paintings and the sudatories, and when in this position
the black are always erected in the north and the blue in the
south. These sticks are permanent property of the shaman.

The feathers used in these plumed wands and in other more
important implements of the rites must be taken from live
birds. The smaller birds, whose feathers are used are captured
on their nests at night. The eagles are caught in earth traps
such as I have seen and described among tribes of the north
a quarter of a century ago, and the Navajo eagle-hunt is accompanied by rites, prayers, and songs much like those of the
same northern races. Each eagle plume must be provided
with a well-developed hyporachis; otherwise, it must not be
used.

KETHAWNS.

But I must reserve a large share of my time for a description of the kethawns—the sacrifices and messages to the gods.
These are perhaps the most interesting of all the sacred objects of the Navajo rites, for they are almost endless in variety
and each one embodies concepts usually easy of explanation.
Sacrifices of a character analogous to these are widely diffused.
All the tribes of the southwest, to and beyond the Mexican
line, use them or have used them, and I have found them employed by Indians residing within sixty miles of the British-
American boundary. The inahos of the Ainos of Japan seem
closely allied to the kethawns.

Navajo kethawns are of two principal kinds, viz.: Cigarettes made of hollow cane, and sticks made of various exogenous woods. Many of them are sacrificed with feathers, either
attached or enclosed in the same bundle with them, and such
are, no doubt, to be classed with the plume stick of the
Zuñis. Much as these sacrifices differ from one another in
size, material, painting, and modes of sacrifice, there are certain rules which apply to all, and these I shall describe at
length when speaking of special kethawns.

CIRCLE KETHAWNS.

I shall first show you a set of kethawns made of exogenous
wood and of unusual shape—circular. I present these now

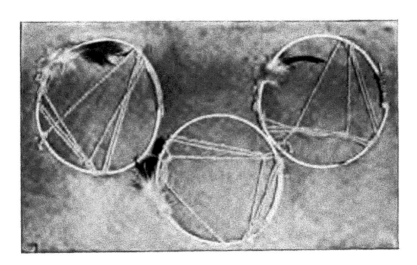

CIRCLE KETHAWNS.

for an illustration only, but I shall not attempt to describe them, because I have already spoken of them at some length, in an article entitled, "A Study in Butts and Tips," already alluded to, and to this paper I refer you, although it tells by no means all that is to be told about the sacrifices.

SACRIFICIAL CIGARETTES.

I shall speak next of the sacrificial cigarettes. These are usually made of the common reed or *phragmites communis,* which grows all over the United States, by the shores of Lake Michigan as well as on the banks of the San Juan. The reed designed for sacrifices is first rubbed well with a piece of sandstone—this is done, no doubt, for the very practical purpose of removing the glossy silicious surface of the reed, in order to make the paint stick. It is next rubbed with a composite plant which grows abundantly in the Navajo country, *Gutierrezia euthamiæ,* the tcililgizi or scare-weed of the Navajos—this is done chiefly for metaphysical reasons. The reed must be cut up with a stone knife or arrow-point, and it must be a perfect knife. If the point has been broken off, or if it has been otherwise mutilated, it is dead, "Just the same as a dead man," the shamans have told me—and must not be used in ceremonies which are intended to cure disease and prolong life. In cutting a reed to form a series of cigarettes the operator holds the butt-end toward his body, the tip-end toward the east, and cuts off first that section which comes next to the root ; for the butt, as I have told you, has precedence over the tip. This section he marks near its base, and on what he calls its front, with a single transverse notch made also with the stone knife. The severed section he lays on a clean stone, buckskin or cloth (for it must never touch the earth, at least until it is sacrificed) and proceeds to cut off another section from the remaining part of the cane which is next the root. If it is the same length as the preceding piece he marks it with two horizontal notches, in the manner described. A third section he would mark with three, and a fourth with four notches. These notches are put on in order that, throughout all subsequent manipulations—particularly if they are sacrificed in the dark—the butt may be distinguished from the tip, the front from the back, and the order in which they were cut may not be disregarded. But in making the notches, the sacred number four must never be exceeded. If there are to be more than four cigarettes of the same size in one set, the fifth must form the beginning of a new series to be marked with one notch, and the operator must depend on his memory and his care in handling to keep the sets separate. The nodal part of the stem or culm must not be used; it is carefully excluded and split into fragments with the point of the stone knife before being thrown away, lest the gods, coming for their sacrifices, might mistake empty segments for cigarettes and, meeting with disappointment, leave in anger. The god, it is said, examines and smells the cigarette to see if it is made for him; if he is pleased with it he takes it away and rewards the giver.

The second section cut off is laid south of the first and parallel to it. The last section is placed furthest to the south; the order of precedence being from north to south when sacrifices are laid out in a straight line. If there is an order of precedence among the gods to whom they are given, the higher god owns the more northern sacrifice.

The cut ends of the section are next ground smooth on a stone and a splinter of yucca leaf is inserted into each, to serve as a handle while the cigarette is being painted. A thin slice of yucca leaf is also used as a brush, and curved sections of the leaf are used as saucers to hold the paints. The decorations in paint are in great variety, a very few only will be, at present, described and exhibited.

When the painting is completed, a small pledget of feathers is inserted into the hollow of each section at the tip end and shoved down toward the opposite extremity; this is to keep the tobacco from falling out. The feathers used here are commonly those of blue-bird and yellow bird, and an owl-quill is in most cases the implement with which the wad is shoved home. The sections are then filled with tobacco, not the tobacco of commerce, *nicotiana tabacum;*— this does well enough for men, the gods despise it—but some of the species of native tobacco of the southwest. *Nicotiana attenuata,* the dsil-naco, or mountain tobacco of the Navajos, is the kind used in all the rites I have witnessed;

but the Navajos tell me that *nicotiana palmeri* is used in some ceremonies, and it is not improbable that other species are used. Pollen (usually of corn) is sprinkled on the open end of the cigarette, after the tobacco is inserted, the pollen is moistened with a drop of water and thus the cigarette is sealed. There are very particular rules as to how this water is to be collected, used and disposed of, to which I must now only allude. After the cigarette is sealed, it is symbolically lighted. To do this a piece of rock crystal is held up in the direction of the smoke-hole, or in the beams of the sun, should they enter the lodge; it is then swept down from on high and touched to the tip of the cigarette. On one occasion when I saw cigarettes prepared early in the morning, the sun rose just as they were to be lighted, and shot its ruddy beams in through the doorway of the lodge over the ragged blanket which hung there as a portière. The shaman caught these first beams on his crystal and then touched the crystal to the cigarette.

I have spoken of the front or face of the cigarette, this corresponds with the side of the internode on which the alternate leaf grows, and is marked at the base of the internode in winter by the axillary pit or scar which the Navajos call the eye, this is the side which is notched and which lies next to the ground when the cigarette is sacrificed or planted.

Throughout the work on the kethawns, songs appropriate to different occasions are sung. There are songs for the painting; songs for the filling, when the tobacco is put in; songs for the lighting; songs for the application of the sacrifices to the body of the patient; songs for the application of the pollen, and songs for the sacrifice when the kethawns are taken out to their hiding-places. Some of these I have secured on the cylinder of the Edison phonograph, and I hope, ere we part, to give you a sample.

I present to you now a set of sacrifices which are all cigarettes. They belong to the morning of the third day of the ceremony of kledji-qaçal. This ceremony, or a portion of it at least, the myth tells us, originated in the Cañon de Chelly, in Arizona; hence, the reeds of which these cigarettes are made should be culled only in the Cañon de Chelly. The cigarettes may be either six, eight, ten or twelve in number. The shaman who is master of the ceremonies never prepares the same number at two successive ceremonies. He changes the number constantly, and so, too, he makes changes in the songs that accompany the manufacture. In the set which I show you, and which is illustrated in fig. 5, there are but six cigarettes.

In the Cañon de Chelly, Arizona, there still stands, in an excellent state of preservation, a remarkable ruined cliff-house, built of yellow sandstone. Its upper portion is painted white, horizontally. As it lies in a deep rock shelter, well overshadowed by the towering cliff above, the coating of white paint has been protected from rain and snow, and looks almost as fresh and white now as when first applied, many centuries ago. The Navajos call the edifice "Keninaekai," which signifies a stone house with a white horizontal streak. Freely translating this name the Americans call it the White House. Here, acccording to the myth, certain divine beings once dwelt, who practised these rites and taught them to the Navajos. It is to this house, or more properly speaking, to the old divinities of this house, as the accompanying prayers indicate, that these sacrifices are offered :

"Kininaekaigi.
"Qayolkal bilnàhacinàhi.
"Qayolkal bilnaciçàha.
"Qastceyalçi.
"Nigel icla'.
"Naci hila'."

In the House of Horizontal White,
He who rises with the morning light,
He who moves with the morning light.
Oh Talking God !
I have made your sacrifice,
I have prepared a smoke for you.

Thus does the first part of the prayer begin and then the devotee, following the dictation of the priest, mentions what blessings he expects to obtain in return for the present of a cigarette—restoration of all parts of his body, of his mind and voice, prosperity for all his people, increase of his flocks, long life and happiness. All these things and many more : but never one word of vengeance on his enemies or of evil to any one. Qastceyalçi, or the Talking God, is the chief in many groups of Navajo local divinities.

In the set here presented, there are two long and four short cigarettes. Like all other things made in the course of Navajo rites, they have a definite, if not a very accurate or scientific measure. The length of the small kethawns equals the width of three finger-tips : first, second, and third, pressed closely together. This measurement is much used and I shall call it three finger-widths ; on my own right hand it measures about 1¾ inches. The longer kethawns, which are twice this length, are painted half yellow and half white, to symbolize this White House, as I have described it. The first kethawn is made white at its eastern extremity ; the second is made white at its western extremity, for reasons that cannot be briefly explained. A cotton string is attached to each, at its centre, by means of a very peculiar knot in whose circles are included three feathers of the blue-bird (*sialia*), and three feathers of the Yellow Warbler, or of *Pipilo chlorurus*— caçoinogáli, "he who shakes the dew," the Navajos call it. One of each kind of feather is taken from a different wing of the bird and one from the tail. Five beads are strung along each string : one of white shell for the east, one of turquoise for the south, one of haliotis shell for the west, one of cannel coal for the north, and one more of white for the east. Beyond these a bunch of three feathers is secured, by means of the peculiar knot already referred to. One of these is a downy eagle feather, the second is the breast feather of a turkey, the third is a "hair" from the "beard" of a turkey-cock. The position of the five attachments on the string are determined by stretching out, on the latter, the digits of one hand—an attachment is made where the centre of each digit falls. The string is originally two spans long, but when it is tied to the kethawn and all objects are attached, the end is cut off, three finger-widths beyond the last attachment.

The four smaller kethawns are called Naakqaigi kethawn or cigarettes sacred to the original dancers of the last night of the ceremony. But as the original dancers all lived once in the Cañon de Chelly and danced at the White House, these cigarettes go with those just described. Two of the four are painted black to symbolize males, and each is marked, near its eastern extremity, or tip end, on the right side, with a design representing the two eagle-plumes and the bunch of owl-feathers worn to this day in the dance of Naakqai by the male dancers. In figure 5a, I show this design; but when the kethawns are laid down on their faces to be sacrificed, the design comes only partly into view as shown in fig. 5. The two other small kethawns are merely painted blue to symbolize the yebaad or female characters in the dance. The black and the blue kethawns alternate just as the male and female characters alternate in the dance.

When the kethawns are completed, each is put in a separate corn-husk with twelve different articles which I will not now name and the husks are folded around their contents in a particular manner. The kethawns seen on this card, (Fig. 5) are arranged in the order of their proper precedence from north to south (from above downwards). This is the order in which they are made, painted, placed in the husks, folded in the husks, lifted, sacrificed and otherwise manipulated.

It takes about an hour to prepare these sacrifices. When they are done the patient sits in the west of the lodge facing the east, with lower extremities extended and with hands open resting on the knees. The shaman first puts the bundles containing the two long cigarettes into the patient's hands and says a long prayer (part of which I have repeated) which the patient recites after him, sentence by sentence. The shaman takes then the bundles and applies them to different parts of the patient's body, proceeding upwards from sole to crown. Pollen is then applied to the patient and the bundles are given to an assistant who carries them out of the lodge. The shaman lastly collects the bundles containing the smaller kethawns and repeats with them all the observances mentioned as belonging to the greater cigarettes.

The long kethawns are thus finally disposed of. The bearer carries them, running in an easterly direction from the lodge to the foot of a perpendicular rock that fronts the west, and such rocks are not hard to find in the Navajo land. This rock, some say, typifies the high-walled White House itself; others say, the towering cliff on whose face the White House is built. He makes a faint mark on the ground with the outer edge of his foot from east to west, near the base of the rock. He lays down in this mark a bunch of composite plant, *Gutierrezia euthamiæ*, usually collected *en route*. Taking the first kethawn from its husk, he places it on the *Gutierrezia*, at such a distance from the rock, that when the string is stretched eastward to its fullest extent its extremity will nearly touch the rock. He puts on the kethawn, in a certain established order, the twelve other articles contained in the husk and while crouching to do this he repeats in a low voice a short prayer. This finished he rises, measures off a foot's length to the southward of the first kethawn, makes at this distance, with his foot another mark, parallel with the first and places here the second kethawn with exactly the same forms which he observed in placing the first kethawn.

The smaller kethawns are also carried in an easterly direction from the lodge, until a piece of clean, level ground is found, representing the level surface on which is held the dance, wherein figure the characters symbolized by these kethawns. They are laid parallel, with their tips to the east a foot's length apart, in a row extending from north to south. In disposing of them, the observances connected with the longer kethawns are repeated. When the kethawns are all laid away the bearer returns to the lodge, observing the definite rules for return, and bearing back with him the empty corn-husks which are delivered up to the shaman to be later disposed of, according to established rules, the recital of which I shall now spare you.

I have referred to the outer or more obvious symbolism of these objects, but there is an inner and more recondite symbolism. The larger kethawns represent the White House where the devotee is supposed to stand in the centre of the world. The white cotton string is the *bike qajoni* or trail of happiness, mentioned so often in the prayers, which he hopes, with the help of the gods to travel. With all around me beautiful may I travel, says the prayer, and for this reason the string passes through beads which symbolize by their colors the four points of the compass. "With all above me beautiful may I travel. With all below me beautiful may I travel" are again the words of the prayer, so the string includes feathers of the turkey, the bird of the earth and lower world, and a feather of the eagle, the bird of the sky; "My voice restore thou for me," and "Make beautiful my voice" are expressions of the prayers, and to typify these sentiments the string includes feathers of warbling birds, whose voices "flow in gladness" as the Navajo songs say.

I shall next describe a set of sacrifices in which both cigarettes and hard-wood sticks are employed. They are shown on this card and partly represented in fig. 3. The sacrifices are 52 in number; four are cigarettes cut from cane and 48 are pieces of exogenous wood. Of the 48 sticks, 12 belonging to the east, are of mountain mahogany (*Cercocarpus parvifolius*); 12 belonging to the south, are made of a small shrub not found much beyond the borders of New Mexico and Arizona, the *Forestiera Neo-mexicana*, the maiça or coyote—corn of the Navajos; 12 belonging to the west are made of juniper (*Juniperus occidentalis*); and 12, belonging to the north are made of cherry. Mountain mahogany is probably selected for the east because its plumose fruit is white—the color of the east. Forestiera may be chosen for the south because its small olive-shaped fruit (it belongs to the Oleaceæ or olive family) is blue, the color of the south. Juniper is perhaps taken for the west because the leaves of its outer branches, have a tone of yellow, the color of the west. Cherry seems to be adopted for the north, because the fruit of *Prunus demissa*, the common wild cherry of New Mexico ripens black, and black is the color of the north.

The cigarettes are each three finger-widths, the sticks, four finger-widths in length. All the pieces are not measured with the fingers; but one piece having been thus measured it is used as a gauge for others.

The four cigarettes are cut from a single cane and prepared with the usual observances. The first is painted white for the east; the second, blue for the south; the third, yellow for the west; and the fourth, black for the north; no devices are painted on them.

The wooden kethawns are painted on the bark, thus : those of mountain mahogany, white; those of Forestiera, blue;

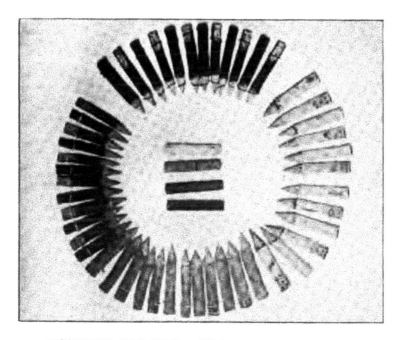

KETHAWNS (SACRIFICIAL STICKS AND CIGARETTES.)

those of juniper, yellow ; those of cherry, black. The outer or tip end of each male kethawn (every alternate one) is painted a contrasting color, i. e. the ends of the white sticks are painted black ; the ends of the blue sticks, yellow ; the ends of the yellow sticks, blue ; and the ends of the black sticks, white. The tip ends of the female kethawns are painted black for reasons which I explained when speaking of the incia or plumed wands. The wooden kethawns as I have before intimated are made to represent, alternately, males and females, by means which I have described in speaking of the plumed wands, with this difference that the males are not painted black nor the females blue to symbolize sex. Only the facets, which symbolize the female masks worn in the dance, are painted blue. The bark is removed from each stick only at the but end, where it is whittled to a point. This point should be one finger width in length, so should the facet which represents the mask.

The sacred basket, previously described is used to contain these sacrifices. A little pile of corn meal is put in the centre of the basket and on this the four cigarettes are laid, one after another, in order of their precedence, from north to south. The painted sticks are laid in the same basket in four groups : the twelve white sticks are laid in the eastern quarter ; the 12 blue sticks, in the southern quarter ; the 12 yellow sticks, in the western quarter and the 12 black sticks, in the northern quarter of the basket. They are laid in one by one. The most northern white stick, representing a male divinity, is laid down first ; the next white stick south of that, representing a female divinity, is laid down next. Thus male and female sacrifices are laid down alternately. When all the white sticks, sacred to the east, are put in place, the most easterly blue stick, sacred to the south, is placed in position and thus they proceed around the basket, in the direction of the course of the sun, until all the sticks are in the basket ; the most easterly black kethawn, a female, being laid down last.

These sacrifices are made to propitiate certain local divin- ities called Qastcéayuhi. The four central cigarettes are for the chiefs, the sticks are for their humbler followers. They are prepared in the afternoon and laid away in a safe part of the lodge until night.

Soon after dark, four men begin to dress themselves as divinities. When their toilet is finished they leave the lodge. The kethawns are then brought forth and the shaman and his assistants begin to sing that set of sequential songs known in the rites as aga'hoágisin or summit songs. These songs, some of which I have obtained on the phonograph, are sung unceasingly in their proper order until all the kethawns are taken out.

The four divinities are Qastcèyalsi Qastcegogan, the Home or Farm God, and two Qastcebaad or goddesses. There seem to be no bachelor gods among the Navajos and, although they are a people who practise polygamy, their gods seem to be monogamists. Each has his one accompanying goddess and no more. Each god, too, has his own peculiar cry, meaningless and often inarticulate; but the females, contrary to the custom among mankind, are silent.

Soon after the first song begins, the Talking God enters, runs towards the patient and applies his quadrangular talisman (method of application exhibited). This done he runs out of the lodge and returns instantly without his talisman. Again he approaches the patient at a run, and, being handed one of the kethawns, he applies it to certain parts of the body (soles, knees, palms, chest, back, shoulders, head) giving his characteristic whoop with each application. This done he runs with the kethawn out of the lodge. The moment he disappears his goddess (a man dressed as a goddess) rushes in, takes another kethawn from the hand of the shaman and repeats with it all the acts of the Talking God with his kethawn, uttering, however, no sound. As the goddess rushes out, the Home God enters and repeats with a kethawn all the performances already described. He is followed in turn by his goddess, who does exactly as the first goddess did. In this order they follow one another and repeat over and over again these acts, until all the kethawns are taken out. Then the Talking God returns once more and applies his folding quadrangular talisman as he did in the beginning. As there are 52 kethawns to be disposed of, each one of the gods makes 13 entries and besides these there are two visits of the Talking God to apply his quadrangle.

The kethawns are taken out in the exact order in which

they were placed in the basket, and the work is so arranged that the male divinities carry out male kethawns and the female divinities, female kethawns.

Each god, as he carries out his kethawn runs a short distance from the lodge (to the east when he bears a white kethawn, to the south when he bears a blue kethawn and so on) holds the kethawn in a peculiar manner, but end foremost and face up, supported on the back of his index finger, and throws it away from him into the darkness.

This ends my descriptions. I am aware that I have made them minute to a tedious degree ; but not otherwise could I have impressed on my auditors the character of these primitive observances, the thoughts and sentiments associated with these simple trifles which I have shown you. It may be some satisfaction for you, at the end of my discourse, to know that I have not told one half the particulars that I might appropriately have told you; but I trust I have said enough to show you how logical and elaborate is the symbolism of this crude people, and how, having once established for themselves a law of symbolism, they never lose sight of it, but follow it persistently and undeviatingly to the end.

DIURNAL BIRDS OF PREY AND MEXICAN SYMBOLISM.

BY COUNT H. DE CHARENCY.

IT is to the learned and lamented L'Angrand that we must attribute the discovery of the double current of civilization in ancient America. The first, that of the *Oriental Toltecs*, or Floridans, with flat heads, caused its influence to be felt especially among the *Yucatecans* and the Qquichuas of the Incaic period. As to the second—it was that of the *Occidental Toltecs*, or Californians with vertical heads to which belonged the civilization of the Pueblos of New Mexico, of the Guatemalans, of the Mexicans, properly so called and, without doubt, the mysterious builders of the Temple of Tiaguanaco in Bolivia.[1]

Beside, as the learned Americanist remarks, each of the currents in question shows certain special characteristics as concerns art, beliefs, and symbolism. One of the least important was certainly not the gynecocratic tendency of the Occidental Toltec religion, the predominance there attributed to the female principle over the male which is not found among the tribes of the Floridan stock.[2]

From this fact there seem to have developed various results, and, perhaps, among them the role assigned in the Occidental Mythology to birds of prey, either as the messengers of divinity, the beings destined to reveal to man the will of heaven, or as those beings who were far from being a good augury.

Without doubt the diurnal birds of prey, especially the different species of eagles, have always played an important role in mythology and symbolism among the races of the two continents, and we may give a very natural reason for this

---

[1] Th. Angrand, in a letter to Mr. Daly upon the Tiaguanaco Antiquities, in *Revue de l'Architecture des Travaux Publiques*.   [2] L'Angrand, manuscript notes.

fact. Is it not because these birds are in general those whose powers of flight are the greatest, elevating themselves further into space, so that they may even reach the abode of the gods ? Thence, doubtless, the opinion which was current among the ancients, that the eagle alone, of all living beings, enjoyed the power of placing the sun. It was also with this motif that this bird of powerful flight was considered among the Hellenes the minister of Jupiter, charged with executing his orders ; an irrefragable proof of it is the rape of Ganymede, transported into Olympus by the bird of the Lord of Thunder. We may, also, recall that in China the God of Lightning is figured with the beak and claws of an eagle.[1]

Now would not another motif, of more special character, have guided the Occidental Toltecs in the choice which they made of the diurnal species instead of the nocturnal, as sacred animals ? The matter seems hardly doubtful if we remember that among the birds of flight in question, the female is generally stronger and larger than the male : the difference in this respect is something considerable. The name of *Tiercelet*, given by woodmen of the middle ages to the males of various species of falcons, has been explained from this circumstance that it is but a third of the size of the female.[2]

Among the Pueblo Indians of New Mexico, and the neighboring regions whose civilization offers more than one point of contact with that of the ancient inhabitants of Tenochtitlan eagles are everywhere venerated as protectors of the tribe or of the village. They are enclosed in great wooden cages and nourished by rabbits, or other small animals taken alive whenever possible, in sacred hunts recalling somewhat that of the Tlascaltecs, in honor of the god Camaxtli, as also, the hunts of the Incas of Peru.

The party of hunters charged thus with providing for the alimentation of the sacred birds, is generally composed of the little children and old men of the nation. Not being able to pursue large game, they must, at least, consecrate their first, or their remaining strength and energy to a religious purpose.

[1] Lord Macartney. "Voyage dans L'Interieur de la Chine et en Tartare." See "Collection des planches et cartes " (Paris, 1804).

[2] A. Salacroux. "Nouveaux Elements d'Histoire Naturelle," p. 255 (Paris 1839).

The Pueblo of Zuni seems to be the one possessing the
most of these birds.   Thirteen of the enormous cages of
which we have spoken, serve as their asylum, or rather, as
their prison.   In a village of the Moqui Pueblos, some
American travellers have noted six cages full of eagles.

In exchange for the forced hospitality and nourishment
showered upon them by fortune, the birds must, several times
a year, yield up their plumage—to the women, a part of their
wings ; to the priests and medicine men, their soft feathers.
The operation which they are thus forced to undergo, does
not add to their beauty—nothing is plainer or has a more
miserable appearance than an eagle deprived of its plumage.
However, this may be, the feathers, once pulled out, are
treated with the greatest care.   Those of equal length are
placed together and carefully kept in boxes of cedar wood.
They serve especially to make plumes, sometimes of the most
artistic workmanship.   Captain J. G. Bourke would seem inclined to attribute to this source the beginning of the feather-
art so well developed among the Mexicans at the epoch of the
conquest.   To-day the living Indians to the North of the Rio
Grande have continued to be estimable artists in feather
mosaic.

They also plant eagle feathers, falcon plumes, and those of
other birds at the boundary of the fields, in order to preserve
the harvest from every unfortunate accident.   They take
good care not to mingle therewith feathers of the owl, owlet,
and analogous creatures, as they are considered in fact, a bad
augury.[1]

It is in the more northern regions of New Spain that we
see the eagle and the falcon play, in a very characteristic
manner, the rôle of envoys from the gods.   Thus, we see the
Tlotli, or hawk, charged by the goddess '' Citlallicuye '' (or
starry-skirted) to go and point out to the genii, or demi-gods,
born of the fragments of flint of which she had been delivered,
the manner in which they might proceed to create a new race
of men.[2]

Likewise, with the Quiché of Guatemala, the birds in ques-

[1] J. G. Bourke, " Sacred Hunts of the American Indians," p. 357, etc., from the
" Congres International des Americanistes."   8th session, (Paris, 1892).

[2] Mendieta, " Historia Ecclesiastica Indiana." Lib. 2, Cap. 1, p. 77. (Mexico, 1870).

tion are represented as instruments of the celestial vengeance against the human race, towards the end of the third cosmic period. Here are the terms in which the indigenous narrator expresses himself : " Then the *Xe'cotcovoh* (literally, face of the devouring eagle) tears out the orbits of their (guilty men's) eyes. The *Camatotz* (literally, who bites mortally) cuts off their heads. The *Cotzbalam* (literally, tiger-eagle) will devour their flesh. The *Tecumbalam* (literally, swallowing tiger-bird) will crush their bones and cartilages." [1]

The *Voc*, or *Vac*, also called *Xic* in Guatemala, which makes war against reptiles, seems to have filled a very varied rôle in Quiché legend. It cannot be doubted, in any case, that it was invested with a highly sacred character ; in fact, the sacred book sends it at the same time as the creating gods, *Xipiyacoc*, the grandmother of the sun, and *Xmucane*, the grandfather, or rather, the ancestor of light. [2]

In another passage of the same work we see the *Voc* hurried from Heaven to the earth by *Hurakan*, the God of Lightning, expressly to see the mythical hero of Guatemala playing raquet upon the route to *Xibalba;* that is to say, according to the symbolic language of the native writer, he prepared him for the revolt against the great empire of the Northeast. [3] It is known in fact that the game of raquet was par-excellence in Central America, that of princes and of the great. To devote one's self to it became in some way a sovereign prerogative, or at any rate, the proof of aspiring to supreme power.

Finally, the bird of flight in question appears once more as messenger of the Guatemalan hero.

Perhaps one will be astonished to see terrestrial princes simple mortals, thus employing a messenger ordinarily devoted to the service of the gods, but account must be taken of the real character of these personages. They were in fact, not men, although subject to death, but incarnate deities. Abbe Brasseur very incorrectly translates Hunahpu by "Sarbacane shooter" (tireur de sarbacane). [4] It is *pub* [5] and not *pu*, which means sarbacane. As l'Angrand has

[1] Popl Vuh.; the sacred book. Traduction de l'Abbe Brasseur du Bourbourg. 1st part, ch. 3, p. 27. (Paris, 1861). [2] *Ibid*, 3d part, ch. 3, p. 211.
[3] *Ibid*, 2d part, ch. 1, p. 71. [4] *Ibid*, 1st part, Introduction, p. 3.
[5] Abbe Brasseur de Bourbourg—"*Grammaire de la Langue Quiché*," p. 207. (Paris, 1862.)

shown, this word signifies the *down of pu, " vello de las partes secretas."* We should then recognize in him, so to say, the masculine principle.[1] On the contrary, *Exbalanque* "little tiger," "little ocelot," or "female tiger," will be established as the emblem of the female principle. Such is effectively the role usually assigned to this animal in Western Toltec symbolism. All this symbolism [2] seems to us, in very truth a little strange, but do we not say in French of a very vigorous fellow, or a man of energy, *" un homme à poil "* (a hairy fellow) ?

Finally, if *Hunahpu* and *Exbalanque* mount upon the pyre where they are to be immediately consumed,[3] it is to be reborn also soon after, under the form of the moon and of the sun, and to be avenged on their enemies. " Be henceforth invoked," says their descendant, to console their spirits. " You shall come thence (above the arch of the sky) the first. You shall, likewise, be the first adored by the cultivated people, and your name shall not be lost. Thus it was said to their fathers, to console their *manes*. We are the avengers of your death and of your ruin, of the suffering and the labors which they have caused you to undergo."

" Such were," adds the American author, " their orders in speaking to all the people of *Xibalba*, whom they had conquered. Then they mounted up there in the midst of the lights, and (their fathers) soon mounted up in these places. They dwelt in the sky, the sun falling by lot to the one, the moon, which lights the arch of the heavens, the surface of the heavens, to the other.

Afterwards the four hundred young men arose at the same time, who had been put to death by *Zipacna*. But they had been the companions (of the two heroes) and they became the stars of heaven."[4]

The recital of the death and the resurrection of our two heroes apparently constitutes nothing more than a repetition of the Mexican legend concerning *Nanahuatl* and *Meztli*, or " the moon."[5] The gods were assembled (it is said) at Teotihuacan (the ancient religious centre of the valley of Anahuac)

---

[1] L'Angrand, *Notes Manuscrites.*   [2] *Ibid,* Letter to Mr. Daly. (Loc cit).
[3] Popul Vuh. 3rd part, ch. 19, pp. 173, *et seq.*   [4] *Ibid,* ch 14, p. 199-3.
[5]—Sahagun, " Relacion de las cosas de Nueva Espana." Lib. vii., ch. 2, p. 246, *et seq.*

vainly awaiting the appearance of the orbs of the day and of the night. In order for these celestial bodies to be able to clear up the horizon, it was necessary that the two gods should consent to throw themselves upon a burning pyre. The horror of immolating himself first for the safety of all, was reserved to Meztli, but he could not bring himself to the performance of such a sacrifice. He therefore allowed Nanahuatl to precipitate himself before him into the midst of the flames, whence he immediately emerged transformed into the sun. Finally, Meztli took his turn, and imitated the generous example set before him, but the brazier had lost all of its vitality, and could not reduce this last person to ashes. He came out of the fire half consumed, under the form of an ocelot with spotted hide, symbol of the moon, assimilated by the Mexicans to the god Tecuzistecatl. Although the finer rôle is finally assigned to Nanahuatl, representative of the masculine and solar principle ; nevertheless, the primordial inferiority, essentially belonging to this personage clearly results from this circumstance, that the privilege of metamorphosing himself into the sun belonged at first to *Meztli,* and that his cowardice made him lose the chance.[1]

We cannot prevent ourselves from comparing this recital with that of the Japanese concerning their Adam, *Tsanaghino-mikoto,* literally, " the God who inundated all " ; and their Eve, *tsanami-no-mikoto* " the Goddess who creates all desires."

These two persons meeting each other in front of a pillar, doubtless the one which supports the celestial vault, after having made the tour of the universe, the Japanese Eve first commences to speak, but Tsanaghi, thinking that the woman ought not to speak before the man, demanded a second journey. The couple found themselves after this before the pillar in question, and this time it was the turn of the Japenese Adam to break the silence. Hardly any one will contradict the opinion that there is found here, as in the traditions of the people of New Spain, an allusion to an ancient form of religion impressed with gynecocratic features.

[1] D. L. Metchinkoff, " L'Archipel Japonais." 2d part. Chap. iv. p. 264 *et seq.* (Paris, 1882, L'orphee Americain, p. 13 of the " Centenaire de la decouverte du Nouveau Monde " (Caen 1892).

Let us not forget besides, that, according to a Buddhist school, of Thibetan origin, but disseminated to-day throughout Burmah, the creation of the world must be attributed to a woman, or rather to a female genius.[1]

In the four hundred young persons put to death by Zipacna, we recognize without difficulty, the centzon Vitznahuas, or four hundred southern Nahuas representing the population settled in the environs of Coatepec and of the famous city of Tulan, after the arrival of the emigrants from the Mexican nation. It is known that the god Huitzilopochtli, patron *par excellence* and emblem of the race of the Mexicans, would have exterminated the greater part of the Vitznahuas, according to the legend, and would have constrained the others to seek flight into the regions of the South,—they are given to us as brothers of the same god, Huitzilopochatli,—that is to say Tenochtitlan ; in other words, that they ought, as future inhabitants of Tenochtitlan, to attach themselves to the current of occidental Toltec civilization.[2] It may have been these who by chance established themselves after their defeat in Guatemala. This circumstance would explain why, in the recollection of Anahuac, they played at the same time the humiliating role of traitor and conquered people, while the Quiché tradition assigns them a much more honorable place, and shows them to us metamorphosed into stars. In any case, one can hardly doubt the identification of this *centzon Vitznahuas* with the *Tzentzonapan* sacrificed by *Huitzilopochtli* before Mount Coatepec.[3]

What we have just said suffices to demonstrate the nature of the symbolical role played by the diurnal birds of prey in the religion of the Occidental Toltecs. It cannot be better compared than with the sanctuary of the God Nebo in Chaldean Mythology, or with Mercury of the Greeks and Latins. Every time that the Olympians had anything to say to simple mortals, it was an eagle, a hawk, or a falcon, which they charged with the commission.

[1].—The Rev. Francis Mosson," Hints on the Introduction of Buddhism into Burmah," 2d. vol., p. 334 *et seq. Jour Am. Oriental Soc.* (New York and Lond. 1851).

[2].—Sahagun, Hist. gen. des choses de la Nlle. Espagne (trans. Jourdenet.) lib. 3d, p. 201 *et seq.*

[3].—Torquemada, Monarquia Indiana," vol. ii. lib. 6, p. 41, 42. "La Naissance miraculeuses d'apres la tradition Americaine," p. 291 *et seq, Revue des Religions.* (No. for July—Aug., 1892).

It was different with the Oriental Toltecs, and, according to them, the birds of brilliant plumage enjoyed the privilege of being chosen as emissaries by immortals.[1] We will limit ourselves to a single example.—"The Yucatecans personified fire which descended from heaven to consume the holocaust in a deity called, doubtless incorrectly, in Landa, *Kin-ich-kak-mo*. L'Angrand admits, and with reason in our opinion, that the real name of this personage ought to be *Kin-ik-kak-mo*, litaerlly "Ara of fire, breath of the Sun." In fact, the Ara was especially consecrated to him, and it was in the semblance of this creature that this god manifested himself as man. Let us add that that year of the lustrum (five-year period), whose dominical letter was *Muluc* and the presage *Canzicnal*, was consecrated to him. His statue was then carried upon a litter, called *Chocté* (literally red wood).[2]

This is not equivalent to saying that birds of prey may not have sometimes played a role in Oriental Toltec symbolism, but it was generally a sinister role and, besides, of secondary importance. So, in the year having as a dominical letter *Cauac*, and as a presage *hozanek*, and which besides was accounted as unfortunate, was made the image of the demon *Ek-u-uayeyab*, literally "Black Couch of the Year." When the road had been cleaned they had to carry this to the stone structures built to the west on a litter called *Tax-ek*, literally, "Green black," or "New black," this color constituting the livery of *Cauac*. On the shoulders of the idol was placed a dead man, a calabash, and a bird of the species called *Kuch*, apparently not the *Zopilote* of the Mexicans.[3]

---

[1].—Tezozomoc,'' Histoire de Mexique " (Trad. Ternaux Compans). vol i., ch. ii. p. 12.

[2].—Landa, " Descripcion des choses du Yucatan." (trad. de l' Abbe Brasseur de Bourbourg) § xxxvi. p. 216—218, Paris, 1864.

[3].—*Ibid*, xxxviii. p. 222.

DISCUSSION.

JOHN G. BOURKE, CAPTAIN 3D CAVALRY, U. S. A.

The views advanced by M. Charency in this paper and which, in my opinion, have been clearly established, are in line with those presented by him in a previous brochure upon "Colors considered as the Symbols of the Cardinal Points," and another link in the great chain of proof that mankind is one.

In his previous article, Charency showed that colors were sacred, each color being assigned to some cardinal point, or, as we might say, to the wind which proceeded from or controlled that point.

The reason of this belief which prevailed very generally over the uncivilized world, was that while in a nomadic state primitive man must at all times have felt the need of protection from his enemies, animal and human, and from being lost while on the war-path.

It was, in one word, necessary that he should at each moment of his life be able to take his bearings, to orient himself, to tell exactly where he was.

We who have the benefit of the compass cannot perhaps enter fully and appreciatively into this mental condition, but that it existed among all races is susceptible of proof.

Not to dilate too much upon this phase of our subject, I would like to say that I once saw an Apache Indian getting ready to go out upon the warpath who was painting upon his moccasins the crescent moon ; he had already decorated himself with the wind symbol or cross and was now, as he told me, putting on the crescent moon because he wanted to know where he was each night.

This same custom obtained among the ancient Romans and to such an extent that in the decadence of their power, when the meaning of the custom had been forgotten by themselves,

JOHN G BOURKE

the crescent moon marked on the sandal was the emblem of the nobility.

The Romans paid as much attention to the veneration of the winds and of the cross-roads or cross-trails as the savages of our own continent have done.

In regard to the present paper, it is well to remark that the functions ascribed to the various animal gods seem to have been identical among all peoples in the same grade of development.

Two general cases may be cited, as the limits allowed this discussion will not admit of more.

The eagle, a diurnal bird of prey, has been by all nations assigned to the function of serving or representing the principal deities ; he is at all times connected with the worship of the sun, and has been made by the American Indian, as by the Greek, Roman, Celt, Teuton or Slav, the symbol of reckless valor in war and of intelligence and daring under all circumstances.

On the contrary, the owl has been a bird of dire omen, its mournful cry has been pregnant with fateful meaning, death has visited the unfortunate cabin upon which it has perched.

To this opinion, there has never apparently, been an exception in any part of the world.   No less an authority than Albertus Magnus, the erudite Dominican, probably the greatest scholar of his century, asserted of the owl that if you placed its heart and right foot upon the breast of a man who was asleep, the sleeper would be compelled to reveal his inmost thoughts.   (Quoted from de Gubernatis, "Zoological Mythology," vol. 2, p. 249 ; "The Horned Owl," edition of New York, MacMillan, 1872).

I will not say more, at this moment, in regard to the reverence entertained for the little thunder bird which in the New World seems to occupy the post of honor held by the wren, or roitelet, or reyezuelo, in the old.   I might also, did time permit, have a little to say concerning the raven of the tribes of the northwestern coasts of America which proceeding farther south seems to have been superseded in Myths by the coyote.   Or, of the turkey, the symbol of the mountains, which of course has no companion in the myths of nations of the old world, although the parrot of the new

17

continent would seem to have been assigned functions closley resembling those played by the peacock.

The quail occupied a position of honor among the Aztecs, and to judge from what can be read in Sahagun and other early authorities, it must have been offered in sacrifice by hundreds on solemn occasions, I may say that in one of the old cliff dwellings on the Rio Verde, Arizona, in 1882, I came across several hundreds of the heads of the little quail of that region which would seem to have been wrenched from the bodies to which they had belonged and then to have been preserved, much as we may understand the Aztec priests did under the same circumstances.

The Romans used the quail for fights much after the style of those with game-cocks, but they were in great awe of this little bird; so much so that they regarded it as somewhat uncanny, saying that it was in the habit of eating the poison hellebore, and that it was subject to fits of epilepsy, the disease of which they stood in so much dread, esteeming it as sent direct from the gods and therefore calling it the "Morbus sacer," or Sacred Disease. (De Gubernatis, "Zoological Mythology," vol. 2, p. 277; "The Quail.")

The red-headed woodpecker, the yellowhammer, and the white-winged dove of Northern Mexico, with the cliff swallow of the same region occupied places of honor in the native theogony.

While treating of the sacred offices assigned to birds, either predatory or pacific, nocturnal or diurnal, we cannot ignore consideration of the medicinal values assigned or ascribed to their beaks, skins, feathers, down, excrement, and bones in primitive therapeutics which was part of primitive religion.

The use of the down of birds in religious sacrifices and offerings was at one time so widely diffused or disseminated that, in my own opinion, it gave rise to the ignominious punishment of tarring and feathering, on the well-established principle that each religion in the world seeks to make a burlesque or a punishment of practices which were held sacred by the religion which it supplanted.

The first mention of tarring and feathering, as a punishment, is to be found in a rule of discipline promulgated by Richard the Lion-Hearted on his way to the Crusades.

To the intelligent studies of scholars like Charencey we owe much ; unless we apply their method of comparative examination to Folk-Lore and Anthropology, these studies would forever remain on the plane of mere collections of literary bric-a-brac. It is less than a century since the suspicion first showed its feeble front that perhaps in the religions and customs of the East could be found the analogues of those of the rest of the world.

Anquetil du Perron, a French scholar, was the first who maintained this idea ; being without means, he enlisted as a private soldier in the French army for the purpose of getting to India, where he devoted himself to the work of securing some of the sacred books of the people. If I am not greatly in error, he was denounced as a fraud by no less a person than Sir William Jones, who became the first president of the Royal Asiatic Society.

Following out similar lines of thought was the Abbé Dubois who fled to India to escape the horrors of the French Revolution and devoted seventeen years of his life to missionary work among the people, of whose habits of life he wrote so instructively and wisely that his history was adopted and circulated by the East India company as a text-book.

Later on came the days of learned thinkers of the school of Max Müller and Grimm, and the editors of the edition of Oxford of the Sacred Books of the East. And in our own day we have seen the establishment of influential journals and magazines in Great Britain and Continental Europe, and in our own land, devoted to doing for the collection, preservation and comparison of the myths, folk-lore, and folk customs of the whole world what was formerly well done, but done for sections merely, by Brand, Hone, Ducagne, Thiers, Picart, Fosbroke, Montfaucon, Higgins, and many others.

PIGMENTS IN CEREMONIALS OF THE HOPI.

BY A. M. STEPHEN.

THE Hopi, that is the Wise people, as they call themselves, dwell in seven small village communities on the table-lands in North East Arizona, remote from the people of their own race; their desert region has preserved them from modern contact, and until quite recently no exotic innovation was apparent among them.

The villages lie upon the tips of three high, straggling capes, each about six miles apart, projecting from the upper table-land into the sandy valleys. They are clusters of stone houses, the flat roofs of the several stories forming a terraced front to the house groups, which are divided into numerous small compartments. The narrow limits of these refuge sites have compelled them to huddle their houses together with great irregularity, but in each village at least one open court is always preserved, and in these courts are the remarkable underground ceremonial chambers called Ki-va.

Their complex cycles of religious observances constantly engage the attention of the elders in the community, and as might be expected of a people in an arid region, their moisture deities are the chief objects of veneration, and supplications to them are expressed through two kinds of ceremonies, Katcina exhibitions and Society celebrations.

The Katcina are a host of beneficent intermediaries who no longer actually visit the haunts of men, but between the winter solstice and the July moon, devout men may assemble in the Kiva and arrange to personate them.

The priests prepare the prayer emblems called pá-ho, or plume sticks, to be deposited at the various rude shrines, and the sacred masks are renovated, and the pigments for personal decoration prepared. Each Katcina has its own characteristic display of paints and apparel, and the exhibi-

260

tion consists of processional dance and song-prayer in the village courts.

Quite distinct from these observances are those of the various religious societies, composed of regularly initiated members, who celebrate in the Kiva at prescribed periods of the other five months, and these celebrations also terminate with a public exhibition.

During the progress of a ceremony in the Kiva, all the fetich paraphernalia of the Society is introduced. Some have an altar of different colored sands, poured by the priest with his fingers into intricate symbolic designs upon the floor; others are structures of elaborately painted wooden slabs, surrounded with a multitude of fetiches, consisting of deity effigies, rods, laths, cones, crooks, and forms defying description; and at one of the ceremonies is a large screen of cotton cloth crowded with complex colored drawings.

There are five colors used in ceremonial decoration of the person and sacred objects, and are those which attach to the Cardinal directions, and of these it may be well to say a word. The Hopi orientation bears no relation to North and South, but to the points on his horizon which mark the places of sunrise and sunset at the summer and winter solstices. He invariably begins his ceremonial circuit by pointing (1) to the place of sunset at summer solstice, then to (2) the place of sunset at winter solstice, then to (3) the sunrise at winter solstice, and (4) the sunrise at summer solstice, next to (5) the above, and (6) the below.

The names of these directions and their emblematic colors are as follows :

1. Kwi-ni-wi ; yellow, because the anthropomorphic deity who sits there is yellow, wearing a yellow cloud as a mask which covers his head and rests upon his shoulders ; a multitude of yellow butterflies constantly flutter before the cloud, and yellow corn grows continually in that yellow land.

Similar phenomena are manifest at all the other directions, only of different colors, thus :

2. Té-vyüñ-a, Blue.
3. Tá-tyük-a, Red.
4. Hó-po-ko, White.
5. O-mi, Black.

6. At-kya-mi, all colors, and here sits the deity regarded as the maker of all life germs. He sits upon a flowery mound on which grows all vegetation ; he is speckled with all the colors, as also is his cloud mask, and before it flutter all the butterflies, and all the sacred birds.

Observing the above sequence of colors, I will briefly describe the methods by which they obtain their pigments.

The bright yellow is called Si-kya-pi-ki and is thus prepared by some old expert priest. A small fire is made at any convenient court nook, or on the roof of a house, and two or three flat stones set on edge around it support an earthen pot of about two gallons capacity, and about half a gallon of water is poured into it. The expert then puts in about two ounces of Si-ûña, an impure almogen, rubbing it to a powder between his fingers, and in the same way adds about the same quantity of tū-wák-ta, a very fine white calcareous sandstone. He stirs frequently with a gourd ladle, and as the mixture boils it foams violently, and having subsided, some more of the two substances are added, and then as much of the dried flowers of the *Bigelovia graveolens* as can be crowded into the vessel, and then enough water to fill it. The contents are allowed to boil for about half an hour, during which they are stirred as much as possible. A yucca sieve is placed over a large basin and the contents of the pot strained through it, the flowers being squeezed dry and thrown away, and there is thus obtained about two quarts of a dull yellow liquid. The process just described is repeated and the infusion is poured back into the pot, and as it again comes to a boil more of the earthy ingredients are added in small quantities from time to time.

The tint of the liquid is tested on the skin occasionally ; should it prove too pale, another vessel is put on the fire and another infusion obtained by the process first described, enough of which is added to the liquid in the first pot to bring it to the desired tint. Should the liquid be too dark, more of the mineral substances and water are added. The process occupies about four hours and the mixture has then boiled away to about a pint, of a bright yellow color and pasty consistency, which on drying forms a hard cake.

A dull yellow, also used for personal decoration, is called

Katcina Si-kyato-ka, it is an ochrey substance which they reduce to pulp and mix with water.

The blue pigment called Ca-kwa-pi-ki, is thus prepared. About ten ounces of piñon gum is put in an earthen pot and set on the fire, a very little water being poured in to keep it from burning and it is then allowed to roast. A large basin is set conveniently with about a gallon of water in it, and over this basin a yucca sieve is laid, and in the sieve a quantity of horse hair, or shredded yucca fibre. After the gum has melted and boiled for about ten minutes, it is poured upon the hair lying in the sieve and allowed to strain through into the water, where it accumulates in a white mass. The operator then puts about three ounces of fragments of blue and green copper carbonate into a small muller and rubs them into a pulp, then pours a little water in the muller and rubs the pulp into a liquid. He then turns to the gum, which is stiff but still pliable, and after kneading and stretching it back and forth, doubling and twisting and pulling, it becomes soft and of glistening whiteness. After manipulating the gum for about a quarter of an hour, he folds it up compactly, dips it lightly in the blue pulp liquid, and puts it back in the roasting pot, which has been filled with water, and sets it on the fire to boil. As the water heats, the gum melts, and just before it comes to a boil he pours in all the blue pulp liquid, then as the mixture boils he maintains a constant stirring with a long rod. He dips up some of the mass from time to time on the rod to examine its color, and the longer it boils the darker it grows, and after about twenty minutes he takes the jar off the fire, pours off the hot water and pours in some cold. He then takes the blue-green mass out, and works it around in his hands, forming a cake of about eight ounces.

Wi'-va-vi is another so-called blue, but which is really a dull green sandstone, probably colored with some salt of copper. It is quite soft and is readily pulverized, and when mixed with water is ready for use.

A red pigment called cŭp'-na-la is obtained by the following process : Three ears of dark purple corn are shelled and the kernels put in an earthen pot, in which are about three pints of water, and the pot is set on the fire to boil. About a quart of dried sumac berries are put in a basin, over which a yucca sieve is laid.   The corn having boiled about three-quarters of an hour, the pot is taken from the fire and its contents poured upon the sieve, through which the purple-stained boiling water is strained upon the sumac berries.   Some of the talc-like substance called potato-clay is then produced, and the operator puts a piece about the size of a walnut in his mouth, chewing it a little to soften it.   The berries and hot water having now cooled sufficiently, he spits out the clay into his hands which are dipped among the berries, and these and the clay he rubs thoroughly between his hands in the water.   He continues chewing bits of clay and spitting them among the berries, rubbing and squeezing them until by repeated tests upon the skin he obtains the desired tint, and which is usually a hue of lake.   The mixture is now ready for use, or it may be dried and used at a future time by again moistening with water.

Another red is an earthy ochre called pa-látc-ka, which needs merely to be mixed with water to be ready for use.

The most esteemed white is a sandy chalk rock called tü'-ma, crushed fine and moistened ; the other white is a clay called kü-tcatc'-ka.

Black is obtained from lignite coal, charcoal, soot, and corn smut ; these four substances, however, are never mixed to-gether, but are used separately for different occasions.

In addition to these pigments they use sands of correspond-ing colors in making the kiva altars, also for that purpose, the yellow pollen of corn, and the blue pollen of the lark-spur.

Besides the two reds I have mentioned there is a red ochre, called cü'-ta, in constant use, and to obtain this ochre they go about 120 miles west, to the Kohonini country, close to the Grand Cañon of the Colorado, and in that same region they also gather the fragments of copper ore for preparing their blue.

A typical display of all these colors is seen in the decoration of one of their Katcina', called the Ma'lo.   Si-kya'-pi-ki smeared upon the left shoulder ; Wi'-va-vi upon the right ; Cüp'-na-la upon the body ; and Tü'-ma around the loins, the opposite limbs in contrasting colors.

This pigmentary manifestation may be called chromatic prayer, as it is definitely regarded as a direct appeal to the clouds at the four directions to hasten with rain to the Hopi land.

The sacred mask is colored with ca-kwá-pi-ki, but no brush is used; some of that pigment having been rubbed down with water in a stone muller, the mask-wearer chews a few squash seeds and spits the saliva thus generated into the liquid, and dipping up enough of it, with a corn husk, to fill his mouth, he spurts it over the surface of the mask.

The pa'-ho, however, is always painted with a brush made by chewing the end of a strip of yucca, but ca-kwa'-pi-ki may not be used, it would be evil to use for this purpose any substance that has been boiled; for pa'-ho pigment, a fragment of copper ore is pulverized, a pinch of white bean meal is added and mixed with clear water direct from the spring.

All ordinary pá-ho are painted of this copper-ore pigment a blue-green, because, they say, that is the color of vegetation; on one occasion only, the Feast of the Departing Katcina, the chief priest, makes one set of yellow pa'-ho, and these are a supplication for flowers.

The pa'-ho of the Warrior Society are painted with cū'-ta ochre, because that is the warrior's color; he rubs cū'-ta over his body, blackens his face with charcoal, and sprinkles it with powdered specular iron, because this is the aspect of the twin war-gods.

The masks are bordered with black, and certain of the pa'-ho and other sacred objects are painted black, and for this purpose lignite coal is used; it is reduced to powder, but to liquefy it, instead of water, all the men of the kiva who are to use it, sit around the stone muller chewing musk-melon, or cotton seeds, and spitting upon the powdered coal.

The Hopi says, speaking secularly, that the saliva arising from seed-chewing causes the pigments mixed with it to adhere to the painted object, but they also say, this practice has the purport of a votive offering.

I have not designed to treat upon significances, but merely to invite attention to the curious pigments with which the Hopi ceremonial artist makes up his palette.

LEGENDARY LORE OF THE COAST TRIBES OF NORTHWESTERN AMERICA.

BY JAMES DEANS.

In this paper my field of research extends from the Columbia River, northwest, following the coast lines bordering the State of Washington, through British Columbia, north into Alaska as far as the Stickeen.

This division embraces the following nations, with their tribes. The Whull-e-mooch (Dwellers on Whull), Puget Sound, and their kindred. The Mis-tee-mooch (Island people) on Vancouver's Island, with their various tribes. Next them come the Guguals, with their various tribes and dialects, on Vancouver Island and mainland. Next to them, on the islands of British Columbia and Alaska, come the Haidas. Eastward, on the mainland of British Columbia, the Simshean, with their various tribes, on Naas and Skeena rivers and elsewhere. Next them, in Alaska, is the great Klingat nation, with its tribes. While speaking of the above mentioned, I shall chiefly treat of the Haidas and Alaskans, because they have a better and more copious legendary lore, if it may be so called, because it is entirely made up of tales bearing on the works of nature and of their family crests. Of the latter I shall first give a few.

Through many ages it has been customary, while seated around the evening fires, for the old people to tell stories for the amusement of the young folks, and in answer to questions on numerous natural subjects, such as the following, with regard to the beginning of the world, the old folks would be asked by whom, when and how was the world at first made. In answer to these, the following was always told.

At the beginning, where this world now is, nothing but darkness of the very densest existed. A darkness on which the god Ne-kilst-lass, in the form of a raven, brooded over through

JAMES DEANS.

eons of ages, until his wings beat it down to solid earth. After the earth became solid, the light shed upon it was so dim and hazy that nothing could be seen distinctly, so the god, whose design was to prepare the earth for the abode of sentient beings, was ever ready to take advantage of conditions. Seeing that before the new-made world could be worth anything it wanted light. Knowing that a chief whose name was Sathling-ki-juss had all the light in three boxes, he was determined to obtain them. Knowing that this chief had a daughter, he was determined to get into the family, and by these means obtain the boxes, so turning himself into the leaf of a spruce tree, he floated on the water she drank and he was swallowed by her; so in due season she bore a son, who was none other than Ne-kilst-lass. He soon grew up to be a sturdy boy, and became a favorite with the old man, who doted on his grandchild. One day he asked his grandfather for one of the boxes to play with; this he flatly refused to grant. Again, after a while he asked, with no better results. Being determined to have them, he made an uproar and gave the old man no peace until he finally granted his request. Happening to get hold of the one which held the sun, after playing with it a while, he broke it and let out the sun, which he placed in the heavens, giving light to the whole world as a consequence.

Having gained the sun, he set his plans to get the moon and stars. Knowing well he could not play the old game, he thought of another. Learning that the old chief had gone up the Naas to catch Oolachans (when he went fishing he usually took the moon with him, in order to fish by night) Ne-kilst-lass,—or as I shall call him, Yethel (the raven god), because, wherever he went over the face of the earth, he turned himself into a raven, consequently, he was better known by the name of Yethel or Yale,—in order to visit Sathling-ki-juss, took a canoe. Going along he saw a heron or crane feasting on Oolachans. In order to get the fish, he told the crane that his friend the shag was treacherous to him and he should not trust him. This the shag denied; a quarrel ensued which ended in a fight, during which the crane vomited up the fish. These he took, and after rubbing his canoe with them, went on to meet the old chief. When he met him, he asked him where he had been. "Catching fish," he replied, "like yourself," showing the scales on his canoe. Before going he made a false moon and hid it under his wings. "If you have been fishing," said the chief, "how did you see?" "Do not think," Yale replied, "you have all the moons. I have one of my own as good as yours, see," he said, showing a little of the moon under his wings. Believing he had the only moon and stars in the world, he became so disgusted that he would have no more to do with them. Seeing this, Yale took them, first putting the moon in the heavens, then the stars, where they have been ever since.

His next step was to form rivers as soon as he could get it from a chief Kanook, the wolf, who had all the fresh water in the world. This also he stole, and flew over the earth, letting a drop fall in various places, from which large rivers began to flow. His next step was to put fish in these rivers. These he stole from Sing the beaver, and put in the new-made rivers. And so with others through all his works of creation. He also stole fire from a chief and gave it to the world. This is how the Alaskans first got their fire. The people further south tell a different tale. Long ago, they say, all the fire in the world was owned by a little bird, who kept it on its tail. All the people ate their food raw, and kept themselves warm by living in holes in the rocks and ground.

One day the people were sitting round eating deer meat, raw as usual, when this bird came along. After flying around it drew near, and said: "Why do you eat your food raw?" "Because," they replied, "we know of no other way." "I am sorry for you all," replied the little bird. "To-morrow, if all of you meet me here, each one of you bringing a few sticks of Chumuch (pitch wood) I will give you all something which will be a great benefit to you and your children, forever. This will be Hieuc (fire); it is on my tail; all you have to do is to place your chumuch on it, after you catch me, but remember you can only have it conditionally. You must have got some good and noble action." Next morning all of the people were there, and so was the bird. When all was ready; "I go," said the little bird. So off it went, all following helter-skelter, onward over hills and dales, through bush and swamp, some falling over rocks and trees, some breaking their shins. Others turned back, saying anything so fraught with danger and trouble was not worth having. At last one man overtook it, saying: "Birdy, give me your fire." "No," it said, "you are too selfish. So long as you are right yourself, you care not for other people." So away it flew. Another man came up saying: "Birdy, give me your fire. I have been a good man and kind." "I believe you," said the bird, "no doubt you are kind enough, but you brought your friend to grief by stealing his wife. So you cannot have any fire from my tail." So on went the bird, few following, until it came to a woman nursing a poor old sick man. It flew directly to her, saying: "Good woman, bring your chumuch, and put it on my tail, you are welcome to the fire." "I cannot do it," said the woman, "I am not worthy of such a boon. I have done no good action that would make one deserving of it." "You have," said the bird. "You are always doing good, thinking it only your duty. Take the fire; it will, if you take care of it, serve you and your posterity forever. So she took the fire, and gave it to her neighbors. So that is how the Whull-e-mooch got, at first, their fire.

There is another remarkable legend amongst the above-mentioned people, which may be classed as a creation, myth, or legend, and as it has a remarkable bearing on the glacial period it is worthy of a place in this paper. It is as follows:

Long ago our fathers tell us the Whullemooch lived a long way further South than we, their children, do now. They did not like the country they lived in, and wished to emigrate, but did not know where to go. Southward lived a people stronger than they; northward the country was a mass of snow and ice; eastward, because of the high mountains, the country was little better.

One time they were met to consider what was best to do, whether to go to war with their neighbors or to remain where they were. While the subject was under discussion, Spaul the raven god came amongst them and listened to their conversation. After a while he spake, thus: "I have heard your complaints, and know your wants. To one and all of you, I say, 'Remain where you are, and I will give you a beautiful land to the North.'"

So saying he took all the snow and ice which he turned into Pe-kullkun (mountain sheep) so named from Pe (white) and kullkun (an animal). So in time the Whull-e-mooch moved northward.

That at one time their country was full of ice and snow is proved by the numerous ice grooves, which everywhere abound on the numerous rock outcrops.

That these people should connect the ice grooves with the mountain sheep, is not apparent. In all my dealings with these people I never once heard these grooves ascribed to the action of ice. In fact, if asked what made them, they either said, We do not know, or else they never saw them before. That means, the presence of the grooves never drew their attention.

One fact there is, that this legend has passed down from the dim and misty ages of the past, whatever might have been its origin.

The Haida tribes on Queen Charlotte's Islands, B. C., have a remarkable legend, bearing on a period of glacial action. Scannahgunnuncus (hero of the Scannah or Finback whale crest or class) they say took a canoe and went up Hunnah river on that island. Being tired he went ashore and lay down; he had not rested long until he heard a noise up stream; going to see what caused it, was surprised to see a body of stones coming down, going to see the cause, he was more surprised to find a body of ice coming down and pushing everything before it. Seeing this he ran into the bush for safety. In the bush he found the trees cracking and breaking. Everything seemed to say to him, Go away, go away. Hearing this he made for his canoe as fast as he could and never stayed till he reached the open sea. At that time, they say there was far more water than there is now. They say that they could sail miles up rivers into which at high water only a canoe can enter. A few years ago I made a survey of this valley and found everywhere traces of glacial action. In fact the valley had been formed by local glacial action at a comparatively late period. There is a rather interesting legend current amongst these people. It is called Tow es tassin (Tow and his brother). And is as follows :

Long ago a round hill stood far up Masset Inlet. Somehow tradition does not tell, probably through volcanic action, this hill got split in two. Afterward these two hills took the names of Tow and his brother.

From where the brother stands down to the sea is Masset Inlet. From the lower part of this inlet to the mouth of Hiellen river is a low tract more or less filled with salt water. This inlet and these hollows were scooped out by the action of ice. Not viewing it in this light, the Haidas have the following legend : Long ago, and after Tow (food) got separated from his brother, he became dissatisfied because he could get no dogfish to eat. Learning of his dissatisfaction, Yale asked him what he wanted. To this, Tow replied he wanted dogfish, and if he could not get some he would not stay there. "Go then to Hiellen, and stay there," Yethel replied. So off he went, stopping at Hiellen where he has remained ever since.

What is remarkable, both show unmistakable evidence of being at one time one round hill two hundred and fifty feet in height, and divided by some means. Tow, on the east, presenting a steep face, up which nothing could climb ; the brother presenting the same on the west.

LEGENDS OF A FLOOD.

Legends of this sort are purely local, each nation having a great flood of its own. A description of the floods of the Haidas of B. C. and the Klingat of Southern Alaska may be told in the account of a great flood given by a Haidah chief.

Long ago, he said, there was a great war between the Spirit of the Air and the Spirit of the Earth. The one of the air sent thunder and lightnings and rain. The one of the earth sent earthquakes and fire. The earth shook, heaved, and rent. Water rushed out of the cracks, the earth seemed to sink, and the sea rushed over the land. The people took to their canoes ; some were lost in the wild waste of waters, others were lost by their canoes being struck by floating timber. As the waters rose, trees were drawn up from the shattered earth, striking the canoes underneath. A few canoe-loads gained a high mountain and were saved. On the dry ground afforded by the mountain they lived until the waters left, when they returned to their former homes ; these they never found, owing to the change.

After wandering about a long while, they at length settled down on the best place they could find. Being few in number and downhearted for the loss of their relations, Yale came and said, "Don't be downhearted, you shall soon have plenty of company, pick up stones every one of you, and throw them backward over your heads." This they did, and as soon as they struck the ground they jumped up men and women ; consequently, they soon had plenty of companions. In this legend there is a remarkable resemblance to the story of Deucalion in Greek mythology.

The Indians of the Sunnich tribe near Victoria, B. C., have a legend of a flood different from all others, as follows :

Long ago a great flood covered the whole country, excepting one high mountain, whose top alone was dry. To this high mountain the people fled in their canoes. After a while their provisions ran short, and all of them were beginning to feel bad, when one of them remembered he had tied his canoe with a very long rope, near his house in which were plenty of provisions ; so this man and several others went to look for the canoe, which they found, floating at the end of the line. Having found the house, they sent down the sea otter to find the provisions and bring them up, which he did. By these means, they were able to live till the waters left.

I shall now briefly give a few stories of the crests, or clans.

CREST OR CLAN STORIES.

Among these peoples, society was divided into crests, first represented by two great divisions or phratries,—the raven and the eagle. In some villages the raven was highest ; in others, the eagle. The raven phratry had the wolf, bear, scannah, and a number of others ; while the eagle had the eagle, frog, beaver, shark, and several others.

If a person belonged to the raven phratry he was, or she was, allowed to have the birds or animals belonging to that phratry tatooed on his or her body, but not those belonging to the eagles. The same rule applied to the eagles with regard to the ravens. Each of these phratries and crests appears to have had a legend, a few of which I shall give, beginning with the hero of the scannahs above quoted. Scannah gun nuncas had nine or ten brothers who one after the other went to find the queen of the Cowgans (wood-mice) and never returned. It is as follows:

Scannahgunnuncus himself, having gone to find the queen of the Cowgans, saw while walking along the seashore what he took to be a man standing on the edge of the woods. Wondering who the stranger was he called to him, but got no answer. He then went up to it in order to see what it was, found it to be a stump with a man's head on it. While looking at it, a voice said, "Take me down," he did so, and it suddenly turned into a man, and gave the following account of himself: "I am a man, I went to find the queen or the Cowgans. I got along with her maids, they led me on until I commenced to take liberties with them, and then as a punishment they turned me into a stump, in which condition I was to remain until Scannahgunnuncus came to break the enchantment. You are the man, and I am again free. You are looking for the palace of the beautiful queen of the Cowgans. If you follow my advice, you will find her; if you do not, you will share the fate of your brothers. Over that hill on a log you will find a lame mouse, help it along. Do not run after it; your brothers did so, and were killed. I am once more free, thanks, go and do as I tell you."

When our hero got on to the hill he found a log on which a lame mouse was trying to walk; as often as it tried, it fell off, so he picked it up and placed it on again. At last the mouse, who was not at all lame, came to him and said: "You are Scannahgunnuncus, the hero of the Scannahs; you are not a hero by name, but one in deed. You wish to find the lovely queen of the Cowgans, I will show you. Your brothers wished the same, but ran after me and tried to kill me and so got killed themselves. Come along." So the mouse, who was one of the queen's guards, led the way to the palace. After passing through long grass and timber, they came to a beautiful country in the midst of which the palace stood. "Yonder

18

is her home," replied the guide. " I will show her to you."

When they got inside they found her sitting spinning. The mouse introduced him to her, saying, " I have brought you Scannahgunnuncus, great hero of the Scannahs. He has long tried to find you." To this she replied : " Welcome Scannahgunnuncus, great hero of the Scannahs ; I have often heard of you, thou friend of the Cowgans."

This is one of many legends of the Scannahs. The next I shall give is a story of the Simsheans of B. C., and is entitled the *Daughter of the Sun.*

Long ago two brothers took to themselves wives at the same time. In due season both of the wives were confined ; the one gave birth to a son, the other to a daughter. The former was very plain, even ugly, but with a kindly disposition. The latter was very beautiful, but of a proud and haughty disposition. These two cousins, growing up together, began to have a liking for each other, more so the boy. As they grew up to manhood and womanhood he asked her to become his wife ; this she refused, saying she did not want an ugly husband ; still, because he truly loved her, he undoubtedly pressed his suit. She asked him to do many things for her, thinking he would become tired of her ; but not so ; still he cheerfully did for her all she wished.

One day he so pressed her, that she said, One thing I will ask you to do for me and that will be the last. Say what it is and I will do it, he replied. Then go and cut your hair close. She knew very well if he did this he would be despised by the rest of the tribe and classed with the slaves. This last request he did not like, but after all went and did it. Then came and showed himself to her. When she saw him she said, You fool ! Do you think I would marry a slave ; besides, you are too ugly for me. Think no more of me. So with a heavy heart he went away, and wandered aimlessly about, not caring to see any one, or to do anything.

Wandering onward he came to a house. Not caring to be seen, he was hurrying past when he was seen by a woman who lived within. As soon as she saw him she asked him to come and rest himself. No, he replied, let me go ; I do not wish to live ; and he told her the story of his slighted love.

You have told me all your troubles, she replied. Come in and rest, and I will tell you what to do. So he came in. While resting, she said to him, You loved your pretty cousin. She is good-looking, but foolish and vain. You are plain in your looks, but a man at heart. You shall have a good wife, the daughter of the Sun, while your cousin shall make but a sorry match. When you are rested, and have had something to eat, I will show you the way. Which she did when he was ready to go. Do you, she said, see that pathway leading onward from this house? Follow it till you find a high and steep mountain. When you get to the top of it, you will see a road which will take you to the house of the Sun. When you get there, knock at the gate and one will come and ask what you want. Tell them you wish to see the daughter of the Sun; if they ask who sent you, tell them I did. With thanks and good-byes he left.

When he came to the mountain, it looked so high and so steep that he was afraid. While he looked at it he thought thus, It looks steep indeed, but for one to gain the daughter of the Sun for a wife it is well worth trying. Besides, the old woman told me never to look behind, but to go onward and upward. So he started and reached the top, very tired; in the distance he could see the palace of the Sun. After resting awhile he started, full of hope that he soon would be at his journey's end.

When he reached the palace, he was so awed with its splendor that he was afraid to knock. After awhile he mustered courage and knocked. A pleasing-faced man answered his call, and inquired what he wanted. The daughter of the Sun for my wife. Who sent you here? The old woman at the foot of the hill. Come in and welcome. After resting over night, he next morning asked to be shown the one he had come so far to see. In order to try him they first brought the daughter of the Stars—a pretty little girl with little, blinking eyes. This, said they to him, is the daughter of the Stars. What do you think of her? She is very well with her blinking eyes, but she is not good enough for me. Then they brought him the daughter of the Moon, majestic in her cold, radiant beauty. We have brought you, again they said, the daughter of the Moon. What do you think of her? She is all very well, he replied, in her cold beauty, but I want the daughter of the Sun only.

At last they brought him the one he cared for, the lovely daughter of the Sun. "This," said they, "is the one you cared for; take her, and welcome." So he took her and was happy. So, after all his troubles, he married a wife who made him great, while his old lover, with her beauty, came to nothing.

If I had time I could give a large number of these legends, but will have to be content with one. In bygone days, when anything unnatural or unusual was found which they could not explain, they generally appear to have made a story which would please, and at the same time have a moral effect on the people. For instance, up Stickeen River in Alaska, are a line of pillar-shaped rocks; two little ones on land, one little one at the edge of the river, and two or three bigger ones in the river. A mere casual glance at this freak of nature will show what it is. All the rocks are volcanic: at one time a large rent became filled with molten matter; this, after cooling, became harder than the older rocks. When the river commenced to flow through this valley a lake was formed above by this barrier, which was always becoming weaker by the falling water washing away the softer rock behind, until, finally, the weaker parts would give way, letting out the waters of the lake above and leaving a few harder places here and there standing like pillars in the river, as well as on the land, where once flowed the river. Of the above, the following legend has been told.

THE DOOM OF THE CATTIQUINS.

Long ago there lived amongst the Stickeens a very bad family called the Cattiquins. The whole family were notoriously wicked. The whole family were against everybody, and everybody was against them. At length they became so bad that nobody would have any dealings with them. When any of the people went a hunting, or a fishing, or gathering berries, all was kept secret from them.

One day all the people wished to go to the flat, where now stand these pillars. The Cattaquins, being a lazy lot as well, did not get up early. Knowing this, all the people got up and were off while the others were in bed. When the Cattiquins found the others had gone without them, they swore vengeance on the others. Thinking the others had gone up the river, they, too, went and found them. They pulled their canoes ashore and awaited the arrival of the others. After awhile the others arrived, bringing lots of nice berries with them. These the Cattiquins demanded, which the people refused to give, saying if they were not so lazy, they, too, might have plenty of fruit. Hearing this, the Cattiquins grew angry and trampled the berries under foot. Seeing this, the people armed themselves with clubs, bows, and spears, and were determined to kill the whole family. Seeing the turn of affairs, the Cattiquins made for their canoes and pushed into the river. The old folks were in such a hurry that some of the children were left behind. If they escaped the wrath of the people, they did not escape that of Yethal ; because, as a punishment for their wickedness, he turned them all into stone, there to remain forever as a warning to evil doers. And it was often said of a badly behaved person, "If he does not give up his evil way, the doom of the Cattiquins may befall him."

I could give many more very interesting tales, but believing my paper to be already too long, I must stop ; hoping all of you will be interested in these my humble translations, in which I have kept as near the original as possible.

THE ANTIQUITY OF THE FOLK-LORE OF THE AMERICAN INDIAN.

BY KATHERINE S. STANBERY.

(ABSTRACT.) ·

THE Aryan theorist is the modern iconoclast, who, like the Hindu theorist, makes his chosen people the veritable pioneers in intellectual development, and grants them the very first claim of ownership in the vast boundless plain of mental and social history. His theorem is that the American Indians never had any folk-lore of their own; that prior to 1492 they had no notion whatever of anything of the sort; that missionaries coming after Columbus, scattered at large a few seeds of sacred and secular tradition, which not only took root, but grew into wondrous trees.

One cannot but recognize certain ways and means by which all the American Märchen and some of the sagas might have been bodily imported, but I still insist that our aborigines had some preconceived notions of creation, of good and bad spirits, of fire, sun, moon, et cetera. Such ideas are innate in the human race. That these notions have become mixed with the stream of foreign tradition is a tenable conclusion, as an analysis of the American system can scarcely fail to show, whether made on the scheme of the English folk-lore society, of which Mr. Hartland has given us so admirable an illustration, or by that more radical method pursued by Andrew Lang.

A careful inquiry is fatal to that theory which may be called universal accidentalism, and opposed to it we have the theory which admits the importation of tradition, but places it at the earliest possible date. The new ideas brought to a people are dexterously interwoven into the fabric of their life. For example, the hero-story of Pa-bu ka-tawa told by Mr. Grinnell

KATHERINE S STANBERRY.

in his Pawnee Hero Stories bears such a striking resemblance to the life of Christ that we must look upon it as the modification of an early missionary account.

An analysis of the folk-lore of the American Indian leads to the conclusion that at least their legends and tales are recently borrowed from European sources.

THE EXPLOITS OF TAMARO-THE-TERRIBLE; A MYTH FROM MANIHIKI.

BY REV. WILLIAM WYATT GILL, LL. D.

INTRODUCTION.

ALMOST in the centre of the South Pacific, about 700 miles N. N. W. of Rarotonga, lie the twin atolls of Manihiki and Rakahauga. These islands, twenty-five miles apart, are inhabited by one race descended from a single pair, Toa and Tapairu, natives of Rarotonga.

The following myth was communicated to me by Ioane, a native minister of Manihiki. Ioane derived it from his aged father, one of the recognized repositaries of ancient wisdom, who was past middle age when Christianity was introduced to those atolls in 1849.

Three years and a half ago these atolls were, at the earnest request of the natives, annexed to Great Britain.

The food of these islanders consists merely of fish, cocoanut and a coarse kind of *caladium* (called by the natives puraka) grown on Rakahauga. Annual voyages are made by the natives of Manihiki to the sister-island in canoes, for the purpose of obtaining a supply of " puraka "; in these expeditions many lives are lost through sudden storms. The voyage should be accomplished between sunrise and sunset.

MYTH.

In Spiritland (Avaiki) the following wonderful feats were wrought :

Tamaro-the-Terrible [1] had two sons. In that land lived a cruel

---

[1] Ta-maro (Manihiki)-Te-maro (Rarotonga) *i. e.* The Girdle. The full name is Tamarohae (Manihiki)-Temaro-taae (rarotonga). Hae (M) Taae (R), means savage or terrible. I do not think that any stress should be laid upon the signification of the first part of the hero's name (Tamaro). It is extremely common.

man, Erekona (young cocoanut) by name. His method of slaying was on this wise ; if any one came near his dwelling, he would pleasantly call out, "Come in and get a drink of cocoanut water."[1] The unsuspecting victim enters, and when seated on the mat receives a young nut already husked.[2] Piercing "the monkey's eye," he drinks the refreshing beverage. To exhaust the contents, he necessarily holds the nut aloft and turns his eyes to the thatch.[3] In this unguarded moment the unpitying host snatches his wooden sword, and with one well-aimed blow severs the neck of his guest. In this way at various times many perished by the hand of Erekona.

One morning the sons of Tamaro passed the hut. Erekona, according to his wont, invited them to come in and refresh themselves. The lads accepted the invitation. To each Erekona gave a young cocoanut already husked and pierced for drinking. The sons of Tamaro were equal to the occasion. Being thirsty they gladly took the proffered nuts, but only one drank at a time. Erekona was greatly perplexed, for as soon as he extended his hand to grasp the wooden sword, finding his movements closely watched by the non-drinking lad, he hesitated to strike the fatal blow. And when that lad's turn came to drink, Erekona again felt about for his weapon. This did not escape the notice of the lad whose thirst had already been assuaged. Whispering to his brother, "Let us run !" they rushed through the doorway, but distinctly heard the muttering of Erekona, "Ha! you have narrowly escaped the oven and the cooking-leaves !"

The boys now went in search of their father to tell him what had happened. The father said to his sons, "Let us pay him a visit as if nothing had occurred." On seeing them, Erekona, as usual, invited them to enter, and gave to each a young

---

[1] In the Eastern Pacifics it is the correct thing for the owner of a dwelling to go outside and stand bareheaded shouting to the expected visitor to turn aside from the public path and enter the hut. The words used on such occasions at Mangaia are, Oi, na ko nee maira (Ho! come this way!) ! Amongst common people it is enough for the owner of the hut without altering his squatting posture, to throw his head back by way of salutation and then utter the words of invitation. Another courteous salutation is, Come! come (Aere mai! Aere mai!)!

[2] This is still customary. Nothing is more refreshing to the traveller on a hot day in the tropics. Those who have only tasted the so-called ' milk ' of an old cocoanut can form no idea of the refreshing qualities of a young cocoanut.

[3] Of course native dwellings are never ceiled. So if you ask a sick native how he passes the time the reply is sure to be " counting the rows of thatch! "

cocoanut to drink.   Tamaro drank first, taking about half the contents, and then gave the remainder to his host,[1] who of necessity turned up his mouth to exhaust "the milk."   At this Tamaro, unperceived by his host, grasped the wooden sword and smote his head clean off.   The headless body kept writhing awhile, and the severed head kept calling pitifully out :

O ! Tamaro purokua !	Alas ! Tamaro, how cruel you are !
O ! Tamaro purokua ! etc., etc.	Alas ! Tamaro, how cruel you are ! etc.

At sunset the voice ceased.

TAMARO'S VISIT TO THE HOME OF THE FISH-GOD.

Ocean fishing was the great delight of Tamaro and his sons.[2] One day they tried for bonito.   This fish is caught by a mother-o'-pearl hook with pendants of knotted string.   The glitter of the pearl attracts the bonito, whilst the knotted pendants seem to be the waving beard of the victim.

On this occasion hook after hook fouled and the line was severed by the sharp coral.   Only one hook remained—the most precious of them all.   With some misgiving Tamaro tied this highly-prized hook to the end of the line and again angled for bonito.   But alas ! this much-prized hook too was carried away.   Tamaro immediately dived to the bottom for his lost hook,[3] when to his astonishment he saw a dwelling there.   It was a beautiful house, but its peculiarity was this —one gable was ocean, the other land.   Only one man dwelt therein, Toroa-of-the-big-head.   A solitary cocoanut palm grew close by.   On that palm shot out one spathe only.   And there was but one nut inside that spathe.   If the Fish-god wished for a drink of cocoanut water, he would call out, "Let there be a young cocoanut !" and at once a young cocoanut appeared on the palm.   Forthwith he plucked the fruit, husked it, and took out the nut.   Then carefully closing .

---

[1] This is usual among equals and friends.   You dare not taste the cocoanut of your superior in rank ; the insult would be unpardonable.

[2] Fishing is the chief occupation of the natives of those atolls.   As the soil consists merely of sand, shells, and fragments of coral thrown up by the sea, the perpetual weeding and planting of the volcanic islands are out of the question.

[3] This is still customary.   A valued deacon, and eloquent preacher of mine in this way lost his life.

up the green husk, he hurled it back into its place in the spathe, and the fruit was restored on the palm as before.

If the Fish-god desired a half-grown nut, he merely shouted, " Let there be a half-grown cocoanut ! " and lo ! a half-grown nut was there. When he had plucked the fruit, husked it, and taken out the nut, he put together the green husk and hurled it back into its place in the spathe, and the fruit was restored as before. Toroa-of-the-big-head acted in exactly the same way when he wished for a fully-grown nut, or one with delicious soft pith in the cavity usually filled with " milk."

The greeting of the Fish-god to Tamaro was after this fashion : " Come, see my wives." The visitor asked, " Where are they ? " " Not far away," was the response. At this Tamaro entered the beautiful dwelling to inspect the interior. The sides of it were entirely covered with fish-hooks of all kinds and sizes, that had at different times been carried away by struggling fish. Amongst them he espied the hooks he had lost in that day's fishing ; hooks lost in the fishing of the day previous ; also the hooks lost during preceding days, months and years. Tamaro said, " Let me take away my fish hooks." The Fish-god replied, " Make a selection and take them only." Tamaro accordingly picked out all the best to carry back with him.

The mortal visitor now inquired of Toroa-of-the-big-head, " But who are your wives ? " " Fish," was the reply. " What sorts of fish ? " asked Tamaro-the-Terrible. " The Albacore, the Jew-fish, the King-fish," etc., etc. Tamaro now asked permission to carry one away. The Fish-god said, " Yes, if you can pluck out its eyes ; my fish are not to be just caught by the hand."

By this time the sun had set and the sons of Tamaro had gone home (without their father). It was about this time, too, that Tamaro was astonished to see all kinds of fish enter the Fish-god's dwelling to sleep. When it was quite dark the larger sorts arrived and came to the side of Toroa-of-the-big-head to rest ; some on his body, and others on his arms. And so the night was passed in sleep. At the first glimmer of morning light all the small fish, of many kinds, went on their travels. When the sun rose and it was daylight, the larger fish, of many kinds, went on their travels. But the largest fish of all waited on until the sun was high in the heavens ere they sallied forth.

By that time Tamaro was ready to depart. Round his waist was wound many times a fine sennit cord, from which the precious hooks were suspended. He now gripped one of the largest fish, plucking out both its eyes with his fingers. The great fish in agony raised its head, and putting forth all its strength, in a short time rose to the surface, carrying with it Tamaro, who held firmly on by the eye-sockets.

Close by where man and the blind fish rose, was the canoe with the boys in it; for the lads had come back in search of their father. Father and sons now slew the immense fish and drew it to the canoe. But when the tail was put on board, the frail craft was ready to sink. So they had to be content to paddle to shore, dragging the huge fish through the sea secured by a rope. All feasted grandly that day, and Tamaro was the first to give to his countrymen the strange news that at the bottom of the ocean is the capacious and beautiful dwelling of the Fish-god, whose name is Toroa-of-the-big-head.

TAMARO SLAYS AN IMMENSE WHITE SHARK.

Now the sea was infested by a fearful monster—an immense white shark. It was the terror of the land; for if any one went fishing the probability was that he would be devoured.[1] Bathers were picked off by it. Dry cocoanut fronds falling into the lagoon were swallowed by it. Even drift-wood came not amiss.

The brave Tamaro determined to put an end to this state of things. Suspending from his neck a large shark's tooth—the keenest of weapons—he went to the farther edge of the lagoon, swam to a flat block of coral, on which he stationed himself and awaited the arrival of his foe. Nor had he long to wait. On came the immense white shark, and when quite close turned itself on its back and opened its vast jaws, armed with several rows of movable teeth. Tamaro now leaped down the throat of the enemy. (Some assert that he changed

---

[1] It is almost impossible to exist on those atolls without frequent bathing; so great is the heat. The white shark attains the length of 37 feet.

his form into that of an octopus, in order to escape being bitten.)

As soon as Tamaro found himself inside the belly of the monster, he took firm hold of the shark's tooth with which he had provided himself and slashed the intestines of the foe. The helpless shark writhed in agony, and repeatedly leaped out of the sea, in the vain hope of getting relief. The inhabitants of that land crowded to the sandy beach to watch the strange behavior of the dreaded enemy. In a short time the shark died, and lo! Tamaro stood upon the shelving coral none the worse for his adventure and shouted in triumph, " The foe is no more ! " From thenceforth mankind fished and bathed in peace.

TAMARO DESTROYS THE DEMON EEL.

A woman kept a pet eel in a crevice of the reef, secured by strong sennit cord. She fed it regularly ; in the early morning, at mid-day, and in the evening. But one morning she had to go a distance and forgot to look after her pet. She got back in the afternoon and at once took up her basket of food to feed the eel. On arriving at the place where the eel was kept captive, to her astonishment the angry pet refused to eat, severed the sennit cord with its sharp teeth and sought to devour the woman. In its rage it came ashore and swallowed stones and sticks.

The poor woman now knew that it was a demon in the form of an eel that she had nurtured. In her terror she ran to Tamaro for help. As soon as she had told her story, Tamaro set fire to a heap of dry leaves and sticks close by. On the top of this heap he threw some blocks of coral. By the time the stones were thoroughly heated the demon eel had arrived in search of the woman. Tamaro instantly threw the hot stones to the foe, who swallowed them without hesitation. In a little while its belly burst, and so the woman was saved.

TAMARO KILLS A DEMON ROBBER CRAB.

A robber crab lived in a dense forest of Pandanus trees. So closely did these trees grow that no one could thread his way through. Intense darkness brooded over this fearsome place. The robber crab was of vast dimensions and was in reality a demon, Many a solitary traveller had this demon robber crab devoured.

At the edge of the forest there was a fountain of pure water, to which at dawn of day folks were wont to come, in order to fill their calabashes.[1] The demon crab, when hungry, adopted the following plan to secure its prey. When the water-carriers had filled their calabashes and were resting, it would get near the selected victim and softly say, "Sleep! sleep!" Such was its power that the doomed one would be at once overcome by drowsiness. The party would, after a time, one by one rise up and return to their respective homes, leaving the sleeper behind. When quite alone the demon robber crab would crawl to the head of the sleeper, pluck out the eyes, then drag the victim into the dark recesses of the Pandanus forest, and there eagerly devour the body.

One morning the children of Tamaro went to the fountain to fill their household calabashes. They were alone. The demon-crab uttered the charm and speedily put them into an enchanted sleep. The elder lad slept very soundly; the younger one but lightly. In a short time the younger lad was roused by the peculiar noise made by the crawling of the great crab over the sere Pandanus leaves. Guessing the deadly purpose of the crab he instantly shook his eldest brother and told him his fears. Then both ran for dear life.

And so the lads escaped and told their father their adventure. Tamaro now made three immense torches of dry cocoanut fronds—one for himself and one for each of his sons. The torches were then lighted and the attacking party soon made their way to three different points at the edge of the Pandanus forest. Tamaro first set on fire his side of the forest.[2] The demon-crab not liking the heat, soon made for the opposite side. But by the time it had arrived there, one of the lads had set that part in a fierce blaze. The demon-crab, in despair, then made for another part; but the other son of Tamaro had set that, too, burning. In fact the entire forest was on

[1] Of fully grown cocoanut shells.
[2] Any one familiar with thickets of Pandanus untouched by the hand of man will understand how readily the dry sword-like leaves ignite and how fiercely they blaze.

fire ; so that escape was out of the question.   Thus perished the demon robber crab.

When the fire had burned out, a careful inspection of the burned forest was made.   In the centre was an open space, strewn with the skulls and bones of the victims of the demon crab.

Such were the exploits of Tamaro-the-Terrible.

THE MYTHICAL STORY OF MAUI, THE PROMETHEUS OF POLYNESIA.

BY N. B. EMERSON, M. D.

IT would be impossible to compress into a paper of reasonable length an account of the whole story of the Polynesian hero and demi-god, Maui, which we find divided up into many branches, without putting it into such a dessicated condition as to make it unfit to be offered as literary pabulum. The mythical legend of Maui belonged to Southern, before it came into the possession of Northern, Polynesia, before it crossed the equator and rooted itself in Hawaiian soil. The chief centres for Maui-legends are New Zealand and the Hervey Islands. But there is hardly a group (in Southern Polynesia) that does not furnish its own variant, or commentary on this fruitful theme.[1]

No less than nine centres in South Pacific are mentioned as giving more or less important and different versions of this story. While in Northern Polynesia, the Hawaiian group turnishes not less than four versions which bear the stamp of originating independently of each other. The exploits of Maui concern affairs of vast human importance, the length of the day, the possession of fire, and the secret of its production, and they so often trench on the supernatural as to seem worthy of being classed as myths.

A Polynesian legend, as originally obtained, is generally so prolix, repetitious, and overladen, as to make a very dull story. The elements of human interest, however, are all there, and, for the sake of truth and science, must not be rudely or unwisely handled, lest something vital be lost, and the healthy aroma of mountain and ocean evaporate, leaving behind only a handful of mud.

[1] The Maori-Polynesian Comparative Dictionary, by Edward Tregear, Wellington, N. Z., 1891.

The abundant store of myths and legends of Southern Polynesia have been fortunate in falling into the hands of such men as Sir George Gray, Edward Tregear, S. Percy Smith, Wm. Wyatt Gill, and others who have dealt with them in wise and loving fashion.

The store of Hawaiian myth, legend, and tradition has also been skilfully touched by such writers as Sheldon Dibble, James Jackson Jarvis, Jules Remy, Abraham Fornander, W. D. Alexander, S. B. Dole, Rollin M. Daggett (with the late King Kalakaua) and others; but still the field does not begin to be exhausted.

In dealing with Hawaiian legends, it is necessary to bear in mind that many of them have a Southern origin, and valuable work is yet to be done in tracing some of them to still earlier and remoter sources, perhaps to Asia. The single version of the Maui story which I offer, is not by any means the most interesting, nor the most important of the four or five variants of this legend furnished by the Hawaiian Islands. It connects itself well, however, with Southern legends on the same theme, through the incident of Maui's voyage in pursuit of the Sun, in which he went as far as Kukulu-o-Kahiki, which was a general expression that included not only Tahiti but all the lands known to us as Southern Polynesia, until it came to mean any foreign country. I regret that I cannot present the version as given on Kauai, the westernmost island of the group, which has striking points of resemblance to the Southern legends, and is full of interest. But the Kauai variant I have, though rather long, is not entirely complete. The marks of this Southern origin are very evident. There is an Oahu-variant (Oahu is the southeastern neighbor of Kauai) which is of great interest, but as yet I have it only in a fragmentary form.

The Maui[1] version, places the scene of the hero's exploits in that vast caldera of Hale-a-ka-la (house-of-the-sun), which is famous as the greatest extinct crater in the world. The story of Maui's great exploit, of hooking up islands from the bottom of the ocean, is common property throughout Polynesia.

---

[1] This Maui is the name of the Island, and is to be pronounced, *Mow-ee.* (Mow as in the first part of mouth.)

For information embodied in this paper I am greatly indebted to my brother, Joseph S. Emerson.

A HAWAIIAN VERSION OF THE MAUI-LEGEND.

Hina was a famous maker of paper-cloth[1] (tapa), who lived with her four sons in the rainy district of Hilo. They were called Maui-first, Maui-second, Maui-third, but the youngest of them, the hero of this story, was *the* Maui par excellence.

The four brothers were fishermen, and resorted, with their canoes, nets, and tackle, to the little, rocky island in Hilo bay called Mokuola,[2] now popularly called "Cocoanut Island," whence they were wont to launch away on their frequent fishing excursions.

Often, while shivering at sea in damp and chilly weather, they would see the gleam of fires on their little island. They knew that these were lighted by the mud-hens (*alæ*), who alone possessed the secret of producing fire, and they longed to enjoy the comfort and luxury of this boon denied to mortals. But as often as they returned to shore the fires invariably disappeared.

Maui,[3] determined to get at the secret of producing fire, one day remained ashore hid in the shrubbery, while his brothers went on their fishing expedition. But the cunning birds observed this and said to each other, "There are only three in the canoe ; one has remained ashore ; we will make no fire to-day." So Maui was disappointed. The next day Maui went with his brothers in the canoe, and the fires gleamed as usual. Maui now resorted to stratagem. He rigged up a dummy-image, which he made to resemble himself by girding it with his own loin-cloth (*malo*), and placing

---

[1] *Tapa*, or *kapa*, was commonly made by beating out the macerated inner bark of the *wauki* (Broussonetia *papyrifera*, Morus *papyrifera* of Linnæus) into thin sheets. It was often decorated with patterns in different colors, applied by means of stamps made from plates of bamboo.

[2] *Moku-ola*—literally, "Island of life," so called because designated as one of the three cities or places of refuge on the island of Hawaii, to which resorted fugitives for safety.

[3] *Maui*—This proper name is to be pronounced *Mah-wee*, with accent on the penult, as is generally the case with Hawaiian words and proper names. The name of the island of the Hawaiian group, spelled in the same way, *Maui*, is to be pronounced *Mow-ee*.

on its head his own helmet, at the same time his paddle was put into its hands, as if in the act of rowing. Thus equipped, the three brothers sitting in their customary places, the canoe put to sea, while Maui himself laid low in the bushes.

Thinking that the four brothers were gone a-fishing, the birds built their fires and gathered to enjoy them in fancied security. Maui now made a rush, and having caught one of them, demanded to know the secret of how to produce fire. The *ala* [1] at first told Maui to rub the leaf of the taro [2] (kalo) with a stick and he would have fire; Maui did this, but no fire was produced. Repeating his demand, the bird bade him try the same operation on the banana leaf; still there was no fire. Then the lying bird said, " Try a sugar-cane leaf and you will have fire." Maui did this, and yet there was no fire. Then Maui was angry, and threatened to wring the bird's neck ; whereupon it said, " Rub two sticks together." This Maui did, but as the sticks were damp, he got no fire as yet. Maui, now in earnest, seized the bird by the neck to execute his threat, but the poor mud-hen begged him to desist, and it would tell the whole truth, plausibly arguing that if Maui took its life he would defeat his own purpose, as the secret would die with it.

Maui stayed his hand, and following the instructions of the bird, this time used dry sticks of hibiscus [3] wood (*hau*), and the result was fire. In spite of his success, Maui was so vexed that he rubbed the top of the bird's head and beak violently, saying, " Now let us see if we can't get fire out of your head."

As a result of this rough treatment, all the descendants of this mud-hen have red heads to this day; also the longitu-

---

[1] There are two species of the so-called mud-hen. The thick fleshy skin on the forehead of the one is white, on that of the other bright red. The other parts are blue-black, and in habits and appearance both birds resemble the loon.

[2] *Taro* or *kalo*, pronounced *tah-ro* or *kah-lo*, is the arum *esculentum* of Linnæus, or Colocasia *antiquorum* of Schott, the tuber of which, after cooking, was pounded into a dough-like mass, then mixed with water and eaten with the fingers as *poi*. It was the staff of life to the Hawaiians. There is no vegetable in the world equal to taro. It may be prepared in many ways. As *poi* it is, when fresh, especially adapted to invalids and those suffering from mal-nutrition, a wholesome food for all.

[3] *Hau*. Paritium *tiliaceum*—Hibiscus *tiliaceus* of Linnæus. Other woods are used in rubbing for fire ; but the *hau* or hibiscus is plentiful, and the one most commonly used.

dinal furrows found on the stem of the taro, banana, and sugar-cane leaf are pointed out as caused by Maui's rubbing them for fire.

This success, as may be imagined, won Maui not a little distinction. About this time Maui began to heed the complaints of Hina, that the Sun went through the heavens so fast, and the days were so short, that her sheets of tapa were not dried properly.

Maui was always good to his mother, and he resolved to take this matter in hand and see what he could do about it. So Maui go into his canoe and sailed far out, till he had reached the horizon, and found the place where the Sun came up from beneath the ocean. The moment the Sun rose, Maui seized him, and broke off some of the rays which stood out from his body, as do the sharp spines from the body of the sea-urchin. Blood poured from the wounds thus made, so that the Sun has looked red ever since. The Sun, also, was so weakened by Maui's rough handling, that he was obliged to slow down his pace, and as a result, the day has since then been considerably lengthened, to the great accommodation of the human race generally, and of Hina, the tapa-maker, in particular. These adventures made Maui unpopular with the gods; his continual successes also turned his head and made him haughty, so that he got to putting on airs, and swaggering about with a spear in his hand, hunting for adventures, after the fashion of a Knight-errant. At this time a certain chief of the district offered violence to Hina, and as the good woman resisted, he turned a portion of the Wailuku[1] stream into her cave to drown her out. The water rose higher and higher, until it had reached her chin and was about to cover her nose. At this moment Maui appeared, spear in hand, and thrusting it into the bottom of the cave succeeded in making a passage through which the water was drained away, thus saving his mother's life. The hole is still pointed out by which Maui discharged the water from Hina's cave. After this Maui became more than ever a braggart, and forsaking his honest calling as a fisherman, lived an aimless life, wandering about, ready to sponge on

---

[1] *Wai-luku*—Water of destruction, so-called because lives are often lost in this stream in times of high water.

anybody who would receive him. His wanderings at length brought him to the large, well-watered and fertile valley of Waipio, where he could easily sustain himself on the bananas that grew spontaneously in its wilds.

At this time the two great gods, Kane and Kanaloa, who are always represented as associated, were living together in Alakahi, one of the five tributary valleys that debouch into Waipio. Though surrounded by the countless lesser deities (Kini-a-ke-Akua, Mano-a-ke-Akua, Lehu-a-ke-Akua),[1] sprites and elves that peopled the wilderness, their bounden servants, whose duty it was to wait upon them, and fetch and carry at their bidding, Kane and Kanaloa lived in democratic simplicity, waiting upon themselves, plucking and roasting their own bananas.

One day, while these great gods were thus engaged preparing a frugal meal, Maui crept up, and by means of a long pole, such perhaps as the ancient bird-catchers were wont to use in snaring birds, reached across the narrow torrent that rushes through rocky Alakahi, and dexterously spearing the roasted fruit, secured them for himself. One of the gods noticed that the bananas were gone and said, " Who is this that has stolen our bananas ? " " It is that thievish Maui ; he is up to another of his tricks." But Kanaloa, Who was of violent temper, leaped across the stream, caught Maui, dragged him forth from his hiding-place, and dashed him against the cliff of Alakahi, staining the wall with his blood.

Thus ended the adventures of Maui. When the Alakahi stream is discolored by the red, ochrous, soil washed down from the cliffs, the natives say : " Look at the blood of Maui." Certain red-colored shrimp that abound in the waters of this romantic place are popularly said to be tinted with the blood of Maui. An old man relating the story of this mythological hero, ascribed the red color in the rainbow to his blood that had bespattered the heavens.

---

[1] In archaic Hawaiian, *Kini* meant 40,000, *i. e.*, an indefinitely large number ; *Mano*, 4,000 ; *Lehu*, 400,000, and was the highest in the Hawaiian series of numbers, representing a countless multitude. This multitude of minimal gods, which infested every Hawaiian wilderness, were capable of great mischief and must be propitiated with appropriate offerings before any important work was undertaken,

THE FOLK-LORE OF JAPAN.

BY REV. WM. ELLIOT GRIFFIS.

In the old days of Japan's seclusion, when the country was the Thorn Rose Castle of the Pacific Ocean, and herself the sleeping Princess, the wealth of Japanese folk-lore was scarcely dreamed of. The Europeans, both clerical and commercial, who resided or traded in Japan during the sixteenth and seventeenth centuries, have left in their writings little or no traces of this part of Japan's intellectual wealth. One may search the voluminous literature of the Jesuit and other missionaries, or the writings of travellers or traders in the various languages of Europe, and not find the heap worth the winnowing, if he be a seeker after folk-lore. Even the later investigators, Kaempfer, Von Siebold, and others, do not seem to have given much attention to this branch of inquiry, apparently, in their minds, so far apart from serious investigation. When, however, the country was thrown open to foreign trade and residence by the genius of American diplomacy, in the persons of Commodore Matthew Perry and Townsend Harris, the seekers after the fruits of the Japanese popular imagination were richly rewarded. The writer's first interest in Japan was excited by several pretty or amusing tales, like those of "The Monkey and the Crab," and "The Kioto and Osaka Frogs," told him by his classmate in college, now the Hon. R. C. Pruyn of Albany, N. Y., who had been with his father, the Hon. Robert H. Pruyn, the American minister in Yedo from 1861 to 1865. When, further, that genuine classic, Mitford's "Tales of Old Japan," was published, the whole English-speaking world was able to enjoy at least a few of the typical specimens of Japanese folk-lore. Now, there is at the disposal of the student the "Japanese Fairy Tale Series," published by the Kobunsha in Tokyo, numbering about two dozen booklets, and embodying excellent translations made from the originals by Professor Basil Hall Chamberlain, Mrs. T. H. James, Rev. E. Rothesay Miller, etc. There was also published at Yokohama, in 1874, a brochure entitled "Olden-Time Tales for Little People;" and, at Schenectady, New York, in 1880, with illustrations by Ozawa of Tokyo, a small duodecimo containing thirty-five stories from the wonder-lore of Japan entitled "Japanese Fairy World," by the writer of this paper. Most of the copies of this last publication, by the way, disposed of for cash were sold in England, but the large majority of the copies printed were distributed gratuitously among the libraries throughout the United States.

Yet apart from these well-known popular stories, which afford material for the study of the student, and which in Japan are usually published in the form of tiny booklets, very rough, cheap, and intended almost entirely for little children, there are thousands, possibly tens of thousands more, as yet uncommitted to script or print, found recorded in the local histories and gazetteers, or still floating on the lips of the people. The Japanese, living in an archipelago by themselves thousands of years, and on a soil which in itself is constantly active, owing to the interior forces of the earth, have been busy with imagination and fancy. The earthquake and the volcano are constantly ready to excite even the solid earth to undulation, explosion, or the manifestation of the phenomena that strike terror or pleasure to the senses. Surrounded on every hand by waters that are marvellously rich in many striking forms of animal life, and dwelling on a landscape that is beautiful, rugged and changeable, at times, even to fascination, they have in the forces and phenomena of nature abundant potency of reaction upon their imagination.

Further, they are a mixed people, whose congeners have come from the North, the South and the East. The Malay and Negrito blood from the sub-tropical South; the old Dravidian or Aryan elements, driven up northeastwardly through Asia, and entering Japan through Saghalien; the Highlanders of North Asia coming down through Corea and landing in Southern Japan, with a considerable amount of Chinese and, later, Corean elements blended, make up a remarkable ethnic composite. These various people bringing

their old hereditary traditions, the Tartar-Corean stock having the Shamanism and beast-idealizing and worship, together with all the repertoire of ideas and imaginings of
Chinese Asia; the Southern element carrying over to the
islands a wonderful mass of mythology that has close connection with the sea and the waters under the earth; the
Buddhists conveying fresh elements of myth and story from
both the cold and warm parts of the mainland, have all had
their share in making Japan's folk-lore.

Furthermore, the early prehistoric and indigenous tales
recited through centuries to admiring listeners, and forming
an integral part of the Kojiki or national Bible of the Japanese, have been mightily reacted upon by Buddhism. Professor Basil II. Chamberlain well says, that Buddhism has
shaped and colored the folk-lore of Japan.

Of that great mass of fairy and folk tales found in the
Kojiki, the chief literary basis of the Shintō religion, three
distinct strata or cycles may be distinguished. One group
of stories illustrates events or ideals from the extreme south,
the Riu Kiu islands and Kiushiu; another, from Idzumo and
the southwest; and the third from Yamato or central Japan.
Evidently, also, as has been proved by Professor Kumii of
the Historical Society in the Imperial University of Tokyo,
the early religion of the aboriginal inhabitants whom the conquerors from the mainland of Asia found on the soil when
they made conquest of the country and set up their tribe-
chief as Mikado, was something quite different from the
Kami-no-michi (that is, the Way, or Doctrine of the Gods,) or
Shintō religion. This Shintō *cultus*, in which the Mikado is
reckoned the descendant of the heavenly gods and their vicar
on the earth, and therefore the one to whom all allegiance
and obedience is due, is really a composite of two religions,
made by over-laying the ancient aboriginal cult by a usurpa-
tion of both politics and dogmatics. In a word, the conquerors from the mainland of Asia captured the indigenous
religion, which was probably the simple worship of Heaven,
with liturgy and bloodless sacrifices, and made it the engine
of their political power, giving it a head and front in the
person of the august Emperor, the Mikado. The superior
weapons, abilities, and higher culture of the conquerors,

together with their knowledge and resources of agriculture, could of themselves probably have made reasonably rapid conquest of the aboriginal tribes of fishermen and hunters; but they chose to secure quicker victory by what they believed to be superior dogmas.

Yet, even before the disciplined armies of the Mikado had brought all Japan obedient to his sway, Buddhism entered with her scriptures, codes, art and the paraphernalia of a sensuous cult, all backed by the superior zeal and abilities of the priests from the continent. It is reasonably certain that about seven or eight centuries, that is, from the fourth to the twelfth, were consumed in the political unification of Japan. It is demonstrable that Buddhism required nine centuries for the complete conversion of all the people in the Japanese empire to the faith of Shaka Muni.

While it is true that Buddhism has shaped and colored Japanese folk-lore, yet it is surprising to find on critical study how many of the oldest and most racy and interesting of Japanese folk-tales have escaped baptism into Buddhist ideas. It is comparatively rare, except in the stories of manifestly late origin, that we find Buddhist dogma made in any way prominent, or even integral and necessary parts of the narrative. On the other hand, it is true that within the radius of the shadow cast by every Buddhist temple and shrine in Japan, during the sun's daily career through the sky, there is a permanent crop of wonder tales,—how Buddha was manifested in stone or wood, gem, jewel or tree, washed ashore by the waves or found in bamboo or mushroom; how wonder and miracle-working bits of idols and images have literally "astonished the natives"; how love-lorn maidens have suffered and died, and have come to bedraggled resurrection; how lovers have been disappointed and come to a fiery "*resurgam*"; how the blood feud and vendetta have been carried out even beyond the grave; how the fox, badger, and cat have passed through manifold transformation; how the moon and sun, and all inanimate things in nature, have played various tricks and pranks; how the heavenly inhabitants and creatures from the planets have visited the earth;—all these are still precious local heirlooms. In the old days these stories were treasured up, and often made the means of theft,

swindle, and deceit, and occasionally of clan fight and neighborhood jealousy, and yet this Buddhistic jungle-growth of
fancy and imagination must not be confounded with that
national treasury of folk-lore which belongs to the nation at
large.

In entering upon the enchanted fairyland of Japan, we do
not meet with the same kind of creatures that inhabit the
worlds of Teutonic or European imagination. The gentle
fairies which we meet with on English soil are not here ; nor,
on the other hand, do the imps and demons in the Japanese
world seem to have as much power as those under the shadow
of the Scandinavian precipices or in the twilight of German
forests. There are mighty dragons, there are imps and
demons, to be sure ; but the *oni* that lurks everywhere in
Japan is rather a sly, mischievous fellow, than one armed
with supernatural powers.

Of course, the Japanese, Buddhist and Indian elements,
added to those which are indigenous, give us a range of forces
which is as wonderful as anything in the West. There are
transformations and metempsychoses of almost every imaginable sort. The elemental forces of nature are often at the
command of the creatures or personages ; time and space are
annihilated ; the potent wands and drugs and invisible coats
and earth-compassing wings are all here, and yet it cannot be
said that beauty is the predominating idea. Mystery is
everywhere present, and it may be said in general, that most
of the ideas illustrated in mid-Asiatic and Occidental lore are
set forth, though always in a way to suit the Japanese mind.

When we come to inquire in the light of, and with the
analytical spectroscope, so to speak, of history, we are able
to see that the folk-lore is often a distorted shadow of real
history, while also it is true that the events of prehistoric
times are brought before us by means of the folk-tales handed
down to us from ages older than writing in Japan. For example, the question of the existence of cannibalism in early
Japan, which has been settled by science through Professor
Edward S. Morse's brilliant discovery of the kitchen middens
or shell mounds at Omori, is conclusively proved also from
the folk-tale of the Shu-ten-doji. In the twenty-second story
in "Japanese Fairy World," we have the picture of a great

human monster, dwelling in the mountains of Tango, who feasted upon the Japanese, preferring, of course, beautiful virgins. This great red-faced creature, of lusty youth and almost invincible power, lives with his fellow-demons in a great cave palace ; their wine-cups are made of empty human skulls; their teeth are tusks and fangs; their heads have short horns, and they subsist chiefly on human flesh, while near by their habitations are heaps of human bones. Raiko, the hero, brings some famous wine to their palace and drinks with them. Having mingled a sleeping potion with the draught, he slays the demon and restores the captive virgins to their people. This story, it seems to me, is in itself clear evidence that cannibalism was practised in early Japan.

The stories of Yorimasa, the brave archer, who shot the night-beast that disturbed the Mikado's sleep, and Watanabé who cut off the oni's arm, belong to a cycle which illustrates the old Imperial life in early Kioto. These are but examples of a score of folk-lore tales, or cycles of such stories, which in their general features, and especially in their details, throw much light on the history of the people of Dai Nippon. Indeed, what passes for history with the Japanese at the present time, and is supposed to be the story of facts before the fifth century, is probably hardly much better than what could be pieced together from folk-lore itself. The field of early Japanese history invites the investigator and literary constructor. The true history of both the nation and the state cannot be restored, even in its main features, except after a thorough sifting and comparison of the legends in the Kojiki, the poems in the Manyōshiu or Myriad Leaves, the liturgies of the Shintō religion, and all that mass of early fragmentary literature which thus far has been considered beyond the notice of the serious historian.

Very noticeable is the cycle of legends about the underworld. In the Kojiki we have, almost as a matter of course, almost as a necessity in human nature, the descent into the Japanese Hades or invisible world, as they call it "The Land of Roots." Izanagi, the first of the male gods who came to the earth, goes down to find his beloved consort, Izanami, and coming back from the filth and pollution of the lower world and washing himself in the sea, many gods of various

grades are born from the rinsings of his august person. It
is rare, however, that descents like this, that is, into the solid
land or within the bowels of the earth are noted, while the
most casual student will not fail to remark the frequency of
the pilgrimages which are made by favored heroes, warriors
and gentle youth, into the realms beneath the water. Usually
the region visited is Riugu or the Realm of the Dragons.
Over this same realm reigns Kai-Riu-ō, (Sea Dragon King)
who is the mighty monarch with a living dragon for his
casque and helmet, and lord of the scaly hosts. The queen
of the realm under the sea is also a mighty, but still more a
gracious personage, while the daughter of Kai-Riu-ō showers
her favors on elect lovers from the earth. She is surrounded
by a vast train of attendants, maidens like herself. All these
are dressed in garments made of the nacre of the gems of the
deep and with edgings having serrated points, and further
adorned with all nature's devices of beauty which she lavishes
so freely upon the shells of the shore or the creatures of the
deep. The Queen and her attendant maidens have for their
headdresses not only their own beautiful flowing hair, but
some precious sea-gem or shell, or living creature, or flashing
crystal as frontlet. Down in Riugu there are, guarded by
mighty dragons, the jewels of the ebbing and the flowing
Tide. In one case, Isora, summoned from the depths,
comes, at the command of Kai-Riu-ō, with the scintillating
spheres which command the ebbing and the flowing tide.
With these he equips Ojin the god of war, who, though unborn, is, through his mother, to conquer Corea. In another
case, these jewels of the ebbing and flowing tide are lent to a
young man who has been badly treated by his brother, and
who by making a flood which—if the Noahic flood must be
matched all over the world—was probably large enough in
volume. At any rate, the rising waters compelled his brother,
after being nearly drowned, to come to terms. We do not
here interpose any rationalistic explanation to hint that possibly these jewels may be the mythological representation of
the sun and moon, but simply remark in passing that down
in Riugu there is no note made of the flight of time. In
Japanese poetry it is said that "there are three things which
wait not for man ; they are running rivers, fading flowers, and

passing time." But in Riugu there is no sun to mark the day, nor moon the month, but there, one day is as a thousand years and a thousand years as one day.

Hence we have one of the forms of the ubiquitous Rip Van Winkle myth which concerns itself with Riugu. Urashima the fisher boy, who treats kindly all animal life, and allows the tortoise to go free, is transported at the invitation of the daughter of Kai-Riu-ō to Riu-Gu. As favored lover, he spends what he supposes to be several happy days down amid the treasures of the realms of the deep. When, finally, moved by filial affection, he secures permission to visit his old home, he is given a casket and warned on no account to open it. Returning to his native village, where the dogs bark at him, and the children laugh at the antique figure, he finds that no one knows him. But an old man in the last stages of senility and decrepitude answers his anxious questions by telling him that, seven or eight centuries ago, a family of his name lived in the village. The house had fallen to ruins long ago, but among the mossy and lichened stones of the Temple graveyard he finds, nearly obliterated, "the names he loved to hear." Overcome with loneliness, and possessed with curiosity, he opens the casket, only to find a purple vapor issuing. In a moment he becomes stiffened in senile decrepitude, a long white beard sweeps his bosom, and he discovers himself an old man and soon dies of grief.

In one case a hero descends into a submarine paradise, which, strange to say, is in fresh water and in central Japan. A great dragon-centipede which has ravaged the neighborhood of a mountain near Lake Biwa is overcome by the arrow of the invincible archer, who succeeds in killing the monster, after several arrows have bounded back harmlessly, by moistening the point of one shaft with his saliva. Here, we have an illustration of the human saliva-charm, once so common in our own country. Among the presents which he receives in the world beneath the waters are a large bronze bowl, a sword, a suit of armor, a roll of silk, which is always the same length, no matter how much is cut from it, and a bag of rice, which, though he feeds his whole concourse of retainers from it, is never exhausted while he lives.

Time and space would fail to tell the details of the set of

symbols and the catalogue of forces and personages which take part in the world of Japanese folk-lore. Of the mythology of the Japanese, the writer has already treated in one chapter of his work entitled: "The Mikado's Empire." The papers of the Asiatic Society also afford the student good aid in enjoying and interpreting the wonders of the Japanese imagination. Our paper is meant to be merely suggestive, and, therefore, we conclude our hasty survey by calling attention to the fact, that this branch of folk-lore finds its richest illustration in Japanese decorative art. Told first without a thought of ink or pen, and handed down from lip to ear, and from mouth to mouth during many generations, these stories were first committed to manuscript, and in some cases to print. At first the literary artist reproduced and elaborated these myths, setting them as jewels of the national literature. In Japan, where the skins of sheep or goats were never used as material for the author's page, the tattooer pricked in gay colors the nation's folk-lore on the human cuticle. To this day the backs of the *betto* contain the best illustrations of the favorites of the Japanese people. Yet they are also embodied in lacquer, ivory, crystal, carved wood, silk and paper. The artists have added, modified, and freshly and wittily interpreted the details. Usually loyal to the main outlines of the story, they allow their lambent wit to play over the surface, and here and there add bits of fancy, of color, of light, of mirth, which make Japanese art so rich in suggestion.

As the Centennial Exposition at Philadelphia, in 1876, delighted so many thousands of visitors by showing, as it were, the photographs of the Japanese fancy and imagination in their art products, so it is possible that the World's Columbian Exposition in this city will surpass the former encyclopædia of fancy and yield richer delight. Besides enjoying the sight of the Japanese works of art and use, admiring the technical perfection, and learning something of their processes, the visitor to the Exposition will wish to have insight into their art ideas, symbolism, mythology, and history. Almost every article of Japanese production, from the colossal vase and urn to the fan and the opening water-flower, *

* Shreds of pith which, dropped upon water, unfold into various designs, symbols, and suggestions of stories.

is full of allusion and suggestion to one who reads the thought in its symbol. Bronzes, porcelain, ivory, crystal, embroidery, bristle with poetic or mythic allusion. The artist of Japan pours upon his work a prodigality of symbolism, which to the average Occidental mind is dumb or enigmatic. With some knowledge of the groundwork of their mythology, history and the aspects of nature, much of their art and symbolism may be understood. Like all the sets of symbols peculiar to particular nations or civilizations, the art-radicals or basic stock of ideas are few, yet these are expressed in numberless forms and combinations. To that phase of the illustrations and interpretation of the folk-lore of Japan, as well as to its increasing literature, we invite all those who enjoy the study of the Japanese mind as it blossomed out in days long distant from ours. In general, it may be said, that the forms which folk-lore take are the witnesses of processes of thought which are outlived, and which have emerged into higher and nobler methods of illustration and reasoning; but in the progress of the race these steps in advancement are not to be ignored. Apart from the utility and value of folk-lore study, is the enjoyment which comes to the student; and to that enjoyment, as especially furnished in this World's Columbian Exposition, we invite you all.

GRÆCO-ROMAN AND JAPANESE FOLK-LORE AND MYTHOLOGY.

BY ERNEST W. CLEMENT.

DR. GRIFFIS's paper on "The Folk-Lore of Japan" is modestly called by the author "merely suggestive." It is richly suggestive, and, *therefore,* of the highest value. It is a very careful and thorough analysis of the sources and elements, and an admirable presentation of the philosophy, of Japanese folk-lore. It has suggested to me two lines of thought for the few remarks which I have been asked to make.

I might carry into practical operation Dr. Griffis's suggestion, that Japanese folk-lore is richly illustrated in her decorative art at the World's Fair, and might guide you to several points of view ; but the lack of time to make the necessary investigations among the numberless exhibits of Japan compels a postponement of this plan. The other line of thought several times suggested by the paper of Dr. Griffis is, "Græco-Roman and Japanese Mythology and Folk-Lore." But, in the few minutes allotted to me, I shall be able only to give a mere mention of some dozen or so cases of similarity or even identity.

To go back to the very beginning, the Japanese story of the creation sounds very much like a translation from Book I of Ovid's Metamorphoses. At first all is chaos, confusion, conglomeration ; in this mass is the breath of life, "self-produced, including the germs of all things." Then the pure and perfect (ether) ascends and forms the heaven ; the dense and impure coagulates, is precipitated, and produces the earth. Gradually the other elements (fire, water, wood, metal) are separated ; then plants, animals, and beings, or gods (*Kami*), are evolved ; and from the gods, by union with earthly elements, mankind in time is born.

It is also very early in Japanese Mythology that we find, as among the Greeks and Romans, the deification of natural

ERNEST W. CLEMENT.

elements, phenomena and forces, such as the sun, the moon, the wind, the thunder, the lightning, etc.

In Japanese Mythology the first manifestations of the male and the female principle are Izanagi and Izanami. In one tradition (related in Dr. Griffis's paper), that many gods of various grades sprang from the rinsings of Izanagi's august person, we are reminded that blood from the wounded genitals of Uranus produced giants, fairies and nymphs. And as Venus sprang from the foam produced when the mutilated parts of Uranus fell into the sea; so her Japanese (but Buddhist) counterpart, Benten, goddess of beauty, is fabled to have sprung from the sea. In another tradition Izanagi corresponds to Saturn, each of whom assigns to his three children the kingdoms, respectively, of the heaven, the night (Hades), and the sea. Still a third legend to which Dr. Griffis alludes is the Japanese version of Orpheus and Eurydice. Izanami had died in bringing forth her last born, the god of fire, who was then slain by his father. The latter descends to the lower world in search of his wife, who, however, speaks to him, warning him not to try to enter, but to wait patiently, as she hopes to be able to persuade the Japanese Pluto, named Emma, to allow her to return. Izanagi, however, impatiently rushes in, only to find "her corpse a mass of putrefaction."

The Græco-Roman explanation of an eclipse of the sun by a story of Phaeton's unsuccessful attempt to drive his father's chariot of the sun has a counterpart, though somewhat different, in Japanese lore. Amaterasu, the first-born of Izanagi and Izanami, is the sun-goddess, who, being provoked by her boisterous brother, Susanro, retires to a cavern, and leaves the world in darkness. After long effort, a shrewd appeal to feminine curiosity and jealousy succeeds in enticing her out once more to shine again on the world.

In Græco-Roman tradition, Philemon and Baucis, an aged and poor couple, living in a mean hut, nevertheless, do not hesitate to be hospitable to Jupiter and Mercury in disguise. The neighbors, who had been rude to the strangers, were overwhelmed in destruction; but the poor couple, who had entertained angels unawares, were bountifully rewarded. So in Japanese tradition, that unruly Susanro, on account of his misdeeds having been expelled from heaven, "on his way to

20

the nether regions," was overtaken by a storm, and could find shelter nowhere except in the hut of a poor man named Somin.   The next day the other villagers died from a plague; but Somin and his family, wearing each a belt of twisted grass, were saved.   This is said to have been also the origin of the practice of fastening a straw rope across the entrance of a house at New Year's time, to keep out the plague-god; for thus Susanro had instructed his hospitable Somin to do.

The uncanny fox of the witch of Mount Vesuvius is dupli-cated probably a thousand-fold in Japanese folk-lore.   And, as under Mount Ætna was supposed to lie a giant (Enceladus) who, by the movements of his body, "made all Trinacria to tremble," so under the Japanese islands is said to be a huge cat-fish (or "trout," or "backbone fish of the world," among the Ainos), which is similarly responsible for the frequent earth-quakes in Japan.   The dragon-centipede, mentioned by Dr. Griffis, is an easy reminder of the hydra slain by Hercules, and the story of Raiko and the flesh-eating demon, Shuten-doji, naturally seems an Oriental version of the tale of Theseus and the Minotaur.   Again, as Neptune, assisted by Æolus, the Tritons, the Nereids and the very fish ("cete") themselves, propelled the fleet of Æneas; so, when the Empress Jingu made her expedition against Korea, "the Wind-god sent a breeze; the Sea-god raised the billows; all the great fishes of the ocean rose to the surface and encompassed the ships;" so that "without the labor of the oar" they reached Sylla.

A story of a Japanese hamadryad, living in a willow tree, is related by Lafcadio Hearn, in the *Atlantic Monthly*, for July, 1892.

The deification of emperors and heroes is not only Roman but also Japanese: and the worship of the lares and the penates is duplicated in Japan in the worship of family ancestors.

To such an extent, moreover, had all the superstitious wor-ship become a mere form among both the Occidentals and the Orientals, that they soon learned to practise deceit: in Rome, by offering not human, but garlic heads, not a living, but a dough or wax animal, to the gods; and in Japan, by appeasing the spirit of a deceased prince, not with the enforced death of animals or servants, but by images of horses, men, etc.

In many other rites and ceremonies also are found similarities between the Græco-Roman and the Japánese methods; but the limit of time forbids more than the mention of weddings, infant consecration, and night funerals.

This is but a bare outline of a few points of similarity, and only the opening of a subject which it is our hope more thoroughly to exploit. It may prove nothing more than that many minds run in the same channels; or it may possibly be one link in the chain of evidence, that the old and pure Japanese civilization had reached just about the same stage of development as the Græco-Roman civilization about the time of Christ.

KOREAN FOLK-LORE.

BY HOMER B. HULBERT.

In order to give an intelligent idea of Korean folk-lore, it will be necessary for me to premise it with a rapid sketch of the most probable theory as to the origin of the Korean people. This will give us a background against which to group the more salient facts of Korean lore. How or when the ancestors of the Chinese race migrated from the Iranian plateau, and found their way across the vast mountain ranges into China, is the merest matter of conjecture. Sure it is, at least, that it occurred in the very remotest antiquity, before the first idea of a true alphabet had been evolved. Subsequently, another race swept eastward until it reached the apex of the Himalayas and the Altaic ranges. These were the progenitors of the great Turanian family. This horde did not cross the mountains but split into two great streams; one of which flowed toward the south and peopled the peninsula of India, and the other swept northward toward Siberia, where, splitting again, one part went westward toward the Urals and beyond, while the other went eastward into Mongolia, Manchouria, and finally to the shores of the Pacific. It was by some branch of this family that northern Korea was thinly settled. But let us now turn to that other branch of the same family, which peopled India. In the course of time the Sanscrit-speaking people arose somewhere to the north and east of India, and moving eastward impinged upon the earlier settlers of that great peninsula. The result was inevitable. The superior civilization of the Sanscrit-speaking race rapidly drove out or subjugated the Turanian element. Then began a grand flight. The Turanian peoples fled eastward across the Bramapootra and Irrawady into Burmah or else southward into the Deccan, where some found refuge in the hill country, where they live to-day. Others went over into Cey-

HOMER B. HULBERT.

lon, and from there across to the Malay peninsula and the adjacent islands.

But they did not stop there. They swarmed along the coast of what is now Siam and Annam, into the Philippine islands, into Formosa, into the island of Quelpaert, and finally to the shores of southern Korea.

It is not the province of this paper to go into the discussion of the merits of this theory. It has been my privilege to collect and translate the first rare Korean manuscript histories of Korea, and they show, as plainly as words can show, that Korea was colonized from the south. The northern settlers from Manchouria crept southward and the southern colonists crept northward, until the two met at the Han river.

This is the grand fact which divides Korean legendary lore into two distinct branches, the northern and the southern. But in the course of the centuries there has come a blending of the two, so that it is impossible at present to make a clear line of demarkation between them. It is the province of comparative folk-lore to decide which of them show a southern origin, and which show a northern origin.

In Korean folk-lore, there are thirteen principal types, and I desire to illustrate each of them by a characteristic tale ; for it is only in this way that we can gain a bird's-eye view of the whole subject. The thirteen types deal with :

1. The miraculous origin of the ancient heroes.
2. Communications between the inhabitants of dry land and mermen.
3. Divine beings walking upon the earth.
4. The changing of men into beasts and of beasts into men.
5. Simple myths.
6. Omens of evil.
7. Aid given by the dead to the living.
8. Fabulous animals.
9. Virtue's reward.
10. Aid given by animals to men.
11. Prophecies fulfilled.
12. Stratagems.
13. Miscellaneous.

Korean tradition mentions three kinds of origin for the

ancient heroes. The first is by Divine Incarnation as illustrated in the legend of the Tangun.

In primeval times, when Korea was a vast wilderness, a
wonder was seen.

On the slopes of Pak Tou San, the hoary-headed, a bear
and a tiger met and held a colloquy.

"Would that we might become men," they said.

Even as they spoke, they heard the voice of the Supreme
Ruler, who said: "Here are twenty bunches of garlic for
each of you. Eat them, and keep yourselves from the light
of the sun for twenty days, and you shall become men."

They ate, and retired into the recesses of the cave to spend
the allotted time in darkness; but the tiger, by reason of the
fierceness of his nature, could not endure the long restraint
and wandered forth too soon, whereby his nature was rendered fiercer than before.

The bear, with greater faith and patience, waited the
allotted time and then stepped forth into the sunlight, a perfect woman.

Meanwhile, another wonder was seen in Heaven. The son
of the Supreme Ruler, tiring of the delights of Heaven, asked
his father to allow him to go to earth and become ruler of an
earthly kingdom. Permission was given, and earthward he
fared to seek an earthly form.

As the woman sat beside the stream under an ancient cedar,
the only thought in her heart was that of maternity.

"Would that I had a son," she said.

At that moment there passed her on the wind, the spirit of
the Supreme Ruler's son seeking earthly form. It beheld
her there, lone—sitting by the stream. It circled round her,
breathed upon her, won her, and her cry was answered. She
cradled her babe in moss beneath that same ancient cedar,
and when in after years the wild people found him sitting
there in holy contemplation, they made him their king. He
ruled two thousand years and then went back to his Father.

The second form of origin of ancient heroes is from the
egg. This is by far the commonest and most characteristic
mode, and is common to both the northern and southern
branches of Korean lore.

This is well illustrated in the legend of the origin of the

first king of Silla, the southern kingdom that arose about 200 B. C.

The chiefs of five of the scattered tribes of southern Korea met and decided to form a central government which should cement the tribes into a closer union. But the greatest obstacle was the fact that they could decide upon no one to put upon the throne. They were all too modest. As this question was being anxiously discussed, the attention of the company was drawn toward a neighboring mountain, on whose wooded slope was seen a gleaming object like a star. With one accord they drew near to the mountain, and beheld a white horse seated upon a round, gleaming object. As they approached, the horse with a loud cry, rose into the air and disappeared. There lay the gleaming egg, for egg it was. They reverently picked it up and carried it to the town. As it did not open of itself, they tried to break it with sledges, but it withstood their blows. They desisted, when suddenly of its own accord, the egg split open, disclosing a handsome child. A regency was proclaimed until he should come of age, when he ascended the throne as the first king of Silla.

The third form of hero origin is not so common, but it is one of the most cherished traditions of the people.

In the island of Chay Ju (the modern Quelpaert), when as yet it was only a tangled forest, the ground split open, revealing a fathomless abyss piercing to the very centre of the earth. From this abyss there arose, in slow succession, three sages of venerable appearance. Without a word they struck off through the forest, until they reached the slopes of the lofty Hal La San. Entering a grotto there, they beheld three stone chests. Each man approached his chest and lifted the heavy cover, and to the eyes of each were revealed, a colt, a calf, a kid, a dog, and a woman, besides sundry kinds of seed grain. Each sage took his colt, his calf, his kid, his dog, and his woman, and went forth and made a home for himself.

This tale not only gives the origin of the people of Quelpaert, but it is a commentary on the status of woman in early Korean times.

ED. NOTE.—The following stories, read by Mr. Hulbert as illustrations of the other types of tales, have since been returned to him in Seoul, for publication in a book on Korean folk-lore :

A Submarine Romance.

Put Yourself in Her Place.

The Priest's Translation.

A Glimpse of Hell.

The Haroun Al Raschid of Korea.

How the Siege of Pyeng Yang was Raised.

The Wonderful Pear.

MARY ALICIA OWEN.

VOODOOISM.

BY MARY ALICIA OWEN.

I SHALL not begin this paper as the little boy does his greeting on the morning of April 1st, with "look behind you !"—for my eerie acquaintance, the Voodoo "conjurer," is not behind you, a shadowy figure of your Southern neighbor's past. In substantial flesh and almost superhuman power for mischief, he stands, a verity of the present, shoulder to shoulder with you and me, instantly ready, at the instance of his own hate or another's hire, to jostle us from our place and despoil us of our goods and health. Here he is, grinning at conscience, mocking at law, jeering at all virtues but self-control. Utterly heartless, abnormally conceited, trained by self-torture to the highest pitch of endurance, he might be a menace to civilization were there not one talisman that sends him cowering as did the seal of Solomon the genii. The one talisman that wards him from his dupes is the star of our nineteenth century magician—the policeman—the star, not he who wears it ; *he* is but as other men when he takes it off. Why the star has become a talisman, no Voodoo will, or possibly *can*, tell. If any one in this city knows, it is your Police-Detective Wooldridge, who has already given to the world through the agency of the press reporter an interesting account of Chicago's famous Voodoo, "Old man" Allen, and his troublesome followers, the Polk Street footpads, a band of negresses "rendered absolutely fearless by their belief in Voodooism."

Who is the founder of Voodooism ?

Old Grandfather Rattlesnake.

"In the old, old times, the oldest times of all,"—I am quoting Alexander, the highest Voodoo I ever knew—"Old Sun took a notion to make some live things. He squatted down on the bank of a great river and began to make all sorts of birds, creatures, and folks from clay. He stopped a moment and tore a fragment from his body and flung it into the weeds. It came hissing forth after a while, a great rattle-snake, and watched him at his work. When Old Sun's work was done—that is, all except the making of people, for his first attempt of that sort was a failure—he breathed life into his creatures 'without going to the trouble of stepping in circles or saying words.' When each began to move with its own peculiar motions, and cry out in its own peculiar voice, the delighted creator bent over his work, breathing flames of joy, and all caught fire. At this juncture, the watching snake bored a hole in the moist earth and saved himself from harm. After Old Sun had put out the conflagration, Grand-father came out to console his parent and thereby obtain a hold on his affections, but Turtle, erstwhile the despised one, was before him. Turtle's hair was singed off, his eyelids were shrivelled, his eyes were weakened by the smoke and heat, but he was unmistakably alive, and stronger from his baptism of flame.

"'Hello, my child! do you still live?' cried Old Sun.

"'Oh, yes! my big fine daddy, oh, yes! oh, yes! but my back is dried hard as a gourd in the fall, and my innards is all swivelled up like the grass. Can't you spit on my back, my daddy so fine; can't you spit on my back and cool me off?'

"'Oh, yes, child, yes! I can cool you off; oh, yes, child, yes! I can cool you off; but if I spit on your back to cool you off, you will live so long you'll forget your own name.'

"'Oh! I won't mind that, my old daddy so fine; oh! I won't mind that, my old daddy so fine. If you can make out, oh! why shouldn't I? oh! if you can make out, oh! why shouldn't I? So just spit on my back and cool me off.'

"So then Old Sun spat and cooled him off, and the sacred spittle gave poor homely Turtle a great increase of vitality, a gift his irritated creator had no thought of bestowing upon him before the great fire, for you must know that Turtle was Old Sun's first experiment at forming man. Old Sun 'was not any too well pleased' with Turtle's appearance when first moulded, but when the clay image became instinct with life, and the large-bodied, small-limbed, hairy, awkward creature weakly ' wabbled around ' (I am quoting) on his hind legs, the august creator flew into a passion and slapped the work of his hands over on all fours, saying (I am again quoting the exact language of my informant), ' There! you fool, CRAWL! you ain't fitten to walk.'"

Well! to abridge a long story in unimportant particulars, Old Sun, having "swallowed his spite" at Turtle, and being, like some other high-tempered individuals, exceedingly kind and obliging when not in a rage, asked what gift this blinking "last of creation" desired.

Turtle meekly replied that he wished a fine plumy tail such as the burned-up creatures had had. Old Sun was about to make it when Grandfather Rattlesnake stepped up and suggested that a plumy tail would get all torn and draggled. Old Sun resented the interference but accepted the suggestion and gave Turtle a *plain* appendage suited to his method of locomotion.

When Turtle, with the double purpose of again cooling his back and avoiding participation in a mighty "fuss," had jumped into the water and disappeared, Rattlesnake endeavored to "claim kin" and "act smart" with the great Sun. Old Sun attempted to annihilate this unwelcome addition to his family, but Grandfather was a part of him and could not be destroyed. He therefore had to content himself with driving the uncreated one into the hole from which he had emerged, there to remain until creation should be finished. Grandfather obeyed perforce, but he "hilt his head up and peeked." The knowledge he gained surreptitiously he employed to good advantage after Old Sun had re-created all things but Turtle, and climbed up into the sky to keep from causing another conflagration.

At the second creation, Old Sun made mates for everything but Grandfather Rattlesnake, so Grandfather married an ash-tree. Growing discontented with this union, when other pairs had young and he and Ash-Tree had none, he retired to a cave and "worked his mind" for a long time. When he came forth he had perfected Voodoo, as he proved by making a wife like himself from the dead branch of a tree. After he had plenty of children, the Grandfather was satisfied, and did nothing to show his might as a conjuror for

a long time. Then he "got hoppin' mad" and began to
" work his mind," and get power again. The cause of this was
that the jealous Ash-Tree poisoned many of his children, and
the other creatures refused to allow their families to associate
with the survivors. When he felt himself full of strength
and poison, he called his enemies about him, he organized
from them a Voodoo circle, taught them dances, taught them
the healing properties of fire, taught them the fascination
and cunning of the snake, told them his origin and the rites
necessary in consequence, taught them the use of poisons
and medicines. This he did to mock them, for at the end of
his discourse he "*thought* death to them all."

After the death of the enemies, another circle was organized.

Long, long after, as my chroniclers state, Old Grandfather
Rattlesnake saw in his trances that he must go away. Before he went, he made a solemn promise to "fling hisself
outen his hide," as any high Voodoo can, and return at intervals to strengthen his adherents. This promise, I am
solemnly assured, has been kept. Whenever a bride to his
liking has been made ready—a terrified little "goat without
horns " who is thrown into convulsions from fright and over-
doses of whiskey and wormwood, and declared to be in an
ecstacy—he has manifested his presence by emitting odors
like boiled gooseberries. An ordinary rattler, as we know,
has the odor of grasshoppers.

The little virgin above mentioned and the white kid
slaughtered in her presence are both spoken of as "the goat
without horns," and are both said to "seem to be something
they stand for." What does this mean ? There is a great,
shadowy "boogger " in the form of a hornless goat, which is
said to appear sometimes for the purpose of receiving a passing soul, but this surely cannot be the thing which the bride
of the snake represents, and as for the white kid, it is merely
the girl's ransom. As she lies twisting and shivering on the
ground, the kid is killed and eaten as she would have been
killed and eaten in " the old time."

Another puzzler in the Pantheon over which Old Sun and
Grandfather Rattlesnake preside is the Old Boy, as he is
familiarly called, an old devil whom we would consider an

estray from the theology of the camp-meeting, did he not have along with him his handsome, jealous wife, the queen of the wuller-wups or will-o'-wisps, the patroness and friend of Old Rabbit. The Old Boy, in spite of his many adventures and blunders, might be overlooked were he not the husband of his beautiful, terrible, vengeful wife who makes it her business to serve out venom to the snakes. One year, we are told, all the snakes were harmless in consequence of her irate spouse, who is powerful enough when he rouses himself, taking possession of the "cunjer-bag" containing her "tricks" and poisons. The ownership of this bag goes to prove, if all other testimony were wanting, that she is a veritable Voodoo, as does Old Rabbit's incantation, accompanied by the strewing of red clover, in the tale of the "Silver Luck-Ball." Like all other conjurors, she seems not always able to bring good fortune to herself—witness, the weather proverb, "When rain falls from a sunny sky, the Old Boy is beating his wife." That she sometimes "hits back" we have proof in the story of :

THE JOKE FISH-HAWK PLAYED ON THE OLD BOY.

I really must give it in dialect ; it loses its character in grammar-school English :

"One time in de old time, de Ole Boy, he ez so *on* common wid some *mo'* common folks, he hed er fuss with he ole ooman, an' dat time she comed out ahead, *pintedly*. Dey fussed an' dey cussed, an' dey fit an dey clawed, an' den huh strenk kinder gun out, an' she runned out de do' an' riz up on de rocks, an' he loped arter huh wid de noshin ter smack 'er jaws w'en 'e ketched 'er, but, lan' she des tuhn right roun' in 'er tracks, an' up wid er rock an' hit 'im fa'r an' squar' on de shin, wid er ker-*bim!* dat mos' bustid de bone. Truf tell, dat laig am a-pesterin' de ole mon yit, kase 'e kyarnt cunjer off de huht an' de misery dat he own ole ooman mek. No suh! No! kase she de bigges' man o' de two pun 'casion, e'en ef he hev got dat sneakin', tattlin' Blue-Jay a-spyin' an' a-kyarin' news an' debbilmint foh 'im. No, suh! he kyarn't cunjer um off. Howsomeddevveh, hit am er heap betteh now dough 'e hitch yit in 'e walk w'en

dey's fallin' weddeh a-comin',' an' dat's mighty bad, ez dis
hyeah niggeh know by de twis' in de marrer ob he own bone
wut smell de rain w'en he nose kyarn't.   W'y, des las' week
sez I ter Mandy sez I, ' Mandy, borry de loan ob my ole
yoller ombrell, my chile, kase hit's gwinter rain.'   I knowed
hit, dough de sky wuz cl'ar, kase my cunjered laig buhn lak
er red-hot trace-chain wuz run thu hit—dat laig dat wuz'
cunjered 'fo' I larnt how by er lil niggeh dat up an' died
'thout tellin' wut de trick wuz so's I c'd tek hit off."

" I thought, uncle, this was to be a fish-hawk story.

" So 'tis ! so' tis ! ef e'er I gits de charnce ter tell de tale,
but how dat gwine be, ef yo' grabs de wuhd right outen my
mouf, arnser me dat, now ? Shuh ! Shucks ! ez I wuz des a-
sayin' w'en yo' flustrate me so, one day w'en de win' wuz in
de east an' de rain wuz drap sorter drizzle-drozzle an' den
quit, dat shin huht so mighty bad dat de Ole Boy' low dat
'e kyarn't ten, ter bizniz nohow.'   E riz up, 'e did an' den 'e
grunt an' set down 'gin, an' throw hisse'f back an' look
'cross de lake de w'ich 'e wuz asettin' on de aige ob.   Den
'e lif up de laig sorter easy an' 'e rub hit some sorter sorf
an' den 'e e—e—ease hit down offen de well one, an' ' e pro-
jec' how 'e gwine ter cross dat lake.   Troof tell, dey wuz er
m-ighty likely witch-gyurl on turr side de watteh an' he got er
wuhd dat 'e hone ter say in huh yeah.   In co'se, 'e could
a-cunjered huh 'cross de watteh unter 'im, but dat won't do
tall, kase 'e ole ooman am mighty onreasonable 'bout de
gyurls.

" Well den ! 'e set an' study an' study, an' 'e rub 'e laig some
mo' an' cuss, but dat don' he'p out none.   'E hone mighty
hahd foh de sight o' dat gurl, but 'e ain't hone hahd 'nuff ter
hanker arter kickin' out dat lame shin twell 'e swim 'cross
dat ice-cole watteh.

" Den 'e see er big fish-hawk a-sailin' eroun' an' a-peekin' in
de watteh, an' 'e ax 'im howdy.

" ' Howdy yo'se'f,' say Fish-Hawk, mighty s'prise.

" ' Po'ly, my fr'en', po'ly.   Ise hed er tech o' de rheumatiz
all dis winteh an' spring.'

" ' I spoge hit sech er light tech dat yo' ain't tuck de trouble
ter cunjer hit off.'

" ' Nuh,' say de Ole Boy, a-rollin' er blade o' grass in he

fingehs an' a-chawin' hit up an' a-spittin' hit out ergin soster look sorter kinder keerless, " 'tain't skusely wuth w'iles ter cunjer hit off ur dose hit, an', sidesen dat, Ise a-studyin' de kimplaint, but hit pester me des now, kase why I wanter git 'cross dis hyeah pond, an' I don't feel lak a-wettin' ob my laig.'

" ' Ef yo' ain't too proud,' sez Fish-Hawk, a-bowin' an' a-scrapin' twell de breeze ketched 'im in he tail-feddehs an' mighty nigh flung 'im inter de lake, " shuh !—ow !—drat de win' !—Scuse me, Misteh Ole Boy, de win' pesteh me so dat I plum fegit whahbouts I is. Ef so be dat you ain't too proud, I feel mighty sot up ef yo' lemme tote yo' 'cross.'

" ' 'Deed, my fr'en', dat's er mighty kine offeh, but Ise sholy 'fraid Ise too heaby.'

" ' No, no, Misteh Ole Boy, no, no, suh ! Ise sho yo' ain't."

" ' Ise 'fraid I spile yo' fishin'-pahty, pun 'count ob makin' yo' too late.'

" ' Dat ain't nuttin' 'tall. Ise er ole han' at de fishin' an' ef I lose one day 'tain't nuttin' ter de pledger o' sarvin' yo', Misteh Ole Boy.'

" Well suhs ! dey kep' a-drorin' off an' a-comin' on dataway twell mos' sundown. Den de Ole Boy see hit time ter close in, kase dat gal's mammy mek 'er come in de house 'fo' dahk, so 'e git on do back o' Fish-Hawk and staht 'cross.

" Ole Fish-Hawk, he fly low, an' dey go smoove an' slow twell dey git 'way out o'er de lake at de place whah de lil ilun uster wuz. De ilun wuz all out a' sight at dat time, 'cept des one big, holler stump ob er oak dat wuz a-stannin' up ez tall ez de Co'te House. Fish-Hawk, he bat de eye an' grit de bill w'en 'e see dat. 'E fly low an' 'e fly slow, twell 'e wuz right 'bove de stump an' den 'e stop an' ballunce hissef pun 'e wing.

" ' Wut yo' stop foh, my son ?' ax de Ole Boy.

" ' Pear lak I see er fish-nes' in de bottom ob dat stump,' say Fish-Hawk.

" ' Nemmine um now, my son. Des git me 'cross ter de lan' fust, an' den come back foh fish-nestes.'

" ' Des ez yo' say," arnser back Fish-Hawk, turrble p'lie. ' Hyeah we go !'—an' dey do go sho 'nuff, kase Fish-Hawk duck 'e haid an' hunch 'e wing, an' dat land Ole Boy haid-fust in de stump wid nuttin' a-stickin' out but 'e two footses.

"Den Ole Fish-Hawk, he skaddle off des ez hahd ez e'er 'e could clip, an' 'e packed up all 'e plundeh an' 'e moved clean outen de kyentry."

"And the Old Boy?"

"Him? Oh! 'e des kicked eroun' twell 'e turr shin wuz lame too, an' den 'e bust thu de bottom ob de stump an' spit out de mud an' de splintehs so's 'e could cuss free, an' den 'e swum back home. 'E wuz dat mad an' flustehed dat 'e ain't wunst thunk twell de nex day dat 'e could a-cunjered hisse'f out right off."

"And Fish-Hawk?"

"Fish-Hawk? Oh! he's a-runnin' yit. Dey wuz er heap mo' run den fun in dat joke ob hissen."

This Old Boy, sometimes spoken of as Old Master, the husband of Old Mistis who carries the snake venom, evidently is not the Old Master, the snake-king, the Grandfather whose aid is invoked in such incantations as this:

Hear, Old Master! hear! hear!
By the fire at night,
By the dead black hen,
By the bloody throat,
By the goat in the pot,
By the bleeding hand,
By the whiskey on the ground,
By the bitten tongue,
By the bloody mouth,
By the black dog with his tongue pulled out,
By the black cat with her bleeding haunch skinned,
We call, we whoop, we beg and scream
To get strength, to get power
To put the trick on this man
Known by name of Richard Roe,
So that he can get no peace in his bed,
Or at his victuals,
Or at his work,
Or with his wife,
Or with his friends or kin,
Or trying to take pleasure,
Or any place he can go or hide.
Slit him
And burn him
And waste him
And cut him
And wear him
And tear him
As these creatures
Were slit
And burned
And wasted
And cut
And worn
And torn.

To this is sometimes added, send him sickly girl-children, double-jointed and knock-kneed; and let him not die, but live and mourn.

This invocation is said over fire and snake.

Here is another, which may be to the Old Boy. It is mumbled as a pin or honey-locust thorn is driven into a little wax figure, or rude likeness to the human form, made of mud from the mouth of a crayfish's hole :

"Old Master, now is the time to keep the promise you made. Curse him as I curse him, spoil him as I spoil him. I ask it in the name of the god."

In this case there is strength in numbers. The words must be repeated four times four times four (4 x 4 x 4), the "great," or invincible number.

One Voodoo told me that he believed that the Old Boy's wife was the sister to Old Grandfather Rattlesnake, a relative whom he "cunjered" into being, but my informant could not or would not adduce any proof of this.

A more important female deity is the moon.

In the old, old times, we are told, when Old Grandfather Rattlesnake was still visible to his followers, it was the custom of the Voodoos to build great fires, as much for illuminating purposes as to develop strength of body. Now Old Sun hated Grandfather, and dreaded the power of his sorcery ; so he took all the fire and pent it up in a rock and set a very terrible woman boogger, with a knife in her hand, to guard the rock. The darkness of the night was so very dense that it was necessary to have some sort of luminary for the hours when Old Grandfather and his circle worked and Old Sun slept. The Frog offered herself as the light of the night, and was accordingly skinned and set in the sky. For illumination she answered very well, and in addition exhibited her power as a witch by controlling the growth of plants and animals and the movements of waters. This was well, but it was ill that her silvery light was cold and did not strengthen the body like fire. Fire must be obtained, but how? Again a frog volunteered : this time, a male. Thereupon, Old Grandfather raised by the power of his magic a very terrible storm, with rushing winds and great waters pouring, and awful thunderbolts striking, and while the attention of the boogger who guarded the rock where Fire hid was taken up with the rage of the elements, Grandfather, by the power of a cunjerstone which he spat from his royal jaws, split the rock. A great spark flew out. Frog at once seized it in his jaws and started, "with leaps as long as the leap of flame to dry grass," to a place outside the storm, where heaped leaves, and twigs,

21

and branches covered with gum, were made ready to receive the fire. The flash of light was perceived by the boogger. She turned and saw the fire flaming in the rift and the fire dancing as Frog leaped. She closed the rift, she pressed the sides of it shut with her hands, then, she ran after Frog. She almost caught him. He jumped into a river. She lifted her knife as he swallowed the fire to save it from the river, and brought it down with great force to split him in halves and allow the spark to be quenched by the water ; but only his tail was cut away, his beautiful bushy tail, finer than Fox's. He spat the fire into the fuel made ready, and all the Voodoos danced with joy.

Here the story very improperly ends, with no mention of a reward bestowed on this humble Prometheus.

Let us recapitulate :—The great gods of Voodoo are Old Grandfather Rattlesnake, who in America takes the place of the Green Serpent of African tradition, though according to Mr. Leland the sacred snakes of Dahomey are brown or yellowish-white ; Old Sun ; the Old Boy ; the Old Boy's wife, who has no name, but is sometimes spoken of as Old Mistress ; and the Moon,—if a god and his wife are one, four deities, the sacred number.

Below these are innumerable hosts of "hants," "booggers," "rubber-devils," "free-jacks," and the immortal sorcerers, Old Woodpecker, Old Rabbit, Old Blue Jay, Old Wolf, Old Perarer-Chicken, Old King Catfish, etc.

Voodooism is of these, but what is its inner nature ? It is hypnotism, it is telepathy, it is clairvoyance—in a word, it is WILL. Its motto is, "Control yourself perfectly and you can control the rest of the world—organic and inorganic," or as Alexander expressed it, "Make up your will strong against yourself, and you will soon have it strong enough to put down everything and everybody else." He added that no conjurer needed tricks, balls, or luckstones for himself if he had a strong head and good learning. He ought to be able to *look* a man dead, or make him see things that were not before him, or do what his heart despised. "I'm the snake man," he boasted, "and my enemies are flapping, squeaking birds." This has an imposing sound, but it is a matter of fact that Alexander wore a luck-ball for thirty years. The time was, he said, when he needed it, and after he had gone through all the degrees and ordeals of Voodoo he wore it for "old times' sake." The degrees he referred to are four. The primary instruction in the use of poisons, remedies, in the significance of dreams and in the names of the various materials of the charms into which the "power" of the sorcerer is most easily attracted, is but preparatory. "Any fool," said Alexander, "can know the way to mix sulphur, salt, alum, mayapple, clover, feathers, needles, blood, or rags the color of blood—four things together—and he may say the great number, four times four times four, over them with strong words, but he can't throw his own spirit made up strong from Old Grandfather into them."

On another occasion, he told me that some tolerably successful conjurers had their power from others and not from within, but they were very "low down." He illustrated his meaning by a tale of a young woman whom he had known in Arkansas. She had a great wolfskin-bag full of rabbits'-feet, luckstones, snakes' fangs, jaws of lizards and squirrels, toads' bones, frogs' ashes, black hens' feathers and bones, black lambswool saturated with the sweat from the back of an angry toad, bats' hearts, doves' hearts, mole-skins, wax and clay images, candy made of brown sugar mixed with putrid liver, mud from the edge of a swamp, obeah poison and a half-dozen each of the little bags, bottles, and balls known as "tricks." From this collection, which must have resembled a famous one kept by Old Rabbit inside three wooden boxes, she gained some strength, and, having a good deal of natural cunning, she made up some "tricks" of alum, snakeweed, river sand, and hair, and sold them at a profit which should have gone to the pockets of the true professionals. She was a Voodoo believer though not a priestess, so instead of "plum ruin-atin," her without warning, Alexander remonstrated. She replied with "some sass," but afterwards invited him to her cabin. He went, willed her to sleep, made her tell in her sleep where the bag was hidden, took it out and burned it. From that moment she was helpless, and he was so indignant at the remembrance of her former insolence that he refused to make a real witcher-woman of her.

If he had granted her petition how would he have proceeded?

He would have commanded her to hide herself and fast for many days, at the same time keeping her thoughts, not on her deprivation, but on the great glories that would be hers when she attained high rank ; he would have commanded her at other times to fast and go cheerfully among people as if she fasted not ; he would have commanded her yet again to eat to satiety of pleasant food and then to eat of offal, of filth, of live catfish, of any substance loathsome to the eye or palate ; he would have commanded her to go sleepless, to go cold and weary, to burn and cut and bruise and lash herself and think not at all that she suffered, to drink awful potations of whisky or blood, or that which may not be named, and to swallow tobacco smoke ; he would have commanded her to walk in cemeteries, in dense woods, beside bean-hills, through lonely streets, at night when the moon was on the wane and ghosts were strongest and most threatening ;—in short, he would have commanded her to try her courage by every test that precedent or imagination could supply, and he would have had her dance till her feet were bleeding and her brain frenzied, at the dances of the Snake, the Fire, the Moon.

If she had faithfully and successfully executed these commands for weeks or months or even years, until she had stifled every womanish, or, if you please, every human qualm, then he or one of a score of his under-teachers would have said to her that now she was ready to conquer others as she had conquered herself, and the final advice would have been, "Never obey any one, never know any will but your own except when you are helping another Voodoo against a common enemy, make every one give in to you. Never change your purpose once it is fixed ; if you do, you will form a habit of scattering power, and will bring against yourself Old Grandfather Rattlesnake, who never changes, never forgets."

From that time she would have met the Circle, not as a pupil, but either as an assistant or a rival, as circumstances demanded.

The "Circle"?

The Circle is a society for the dissemination of knowledge, and the trial of strength. The knowledge is principally biographical, with a fine flavor of autobiographical boastfulness. The members meet when the moon is dark, or when her light is hidden by clouds, and talk of their own and one another's exploits, and give and receive news of the Voodoos scattered from New York to Florida. These wise men and women wander widely, and convey from town to town, and state to state, a vast amount of curious history, not only of their affairs but of their clients, *white* as well as colored, and prominent people with and without closet-skeletons. The rapidity with which news is carried from one end of the country to the other is amazing. I am at a loss to understand how it can be done. The iron horse travels swiftly for them, as he does for us, on his beaten track; but not all their tracks, by any means, are beaten. The water snake and the swallow are fit emblems of the Voodoo traveller going his secret way and leaving no more trace than the snake does on the pool, or the bird on the air. The man of mystery has a swift foot, but he cannot outspeed the locomotive and the telegraph, and yet, sometimes his messages anticipate steam and electricity. Telepathy is one of their agents, but that, I am assured, is never quite reliable for more than one vivid impression.

Clairvoyance is another agent, as I have before stated.

Hypnotism is the Voodoo's pastime, as well as his power. In the Circle he and his brethren make a game of it by willing one another from where they would be to where they would not. A—.M—. related to me an experience he had, which made the trial of strength more than an amusement. In the latter part of May, 1891, the members of the Circle were in a church loaned them by the sexton, as it was a nice, quiet place where police would not be likely to seek them. They were entertaining themselves by "willing." One man would stand in the front of the building and will one from the group at the back to come to him. By turns, every one except Alexander was willed from his place. Suddenly, a strange black man rose up from a dim corner, willed them all to him, put them to sleep, and went off with the contents of their pockets. In 1892, when they were assembled in the same place to choose a successor to Alexander, who, died in January of that year, the same man appeared and subjected them to the same treatment. He was entirely unknown to all of them. When I asked my informant if he were sure that a man and not a ghost appeared, he naively replied that one never felt like sleeping in the presence of a ghost. He continued that this was undoubtedly a travelling Voodoo king, that the Circle would soon hear from him again.

Alexander boasted of many such exhibitions of his "strength" in Circles scattered about the country. It was reported that he was very sore over his defeat by the unknown, and sourly declared that the visitor was "some low-down Arkansas nigger who sneaked in and prevailed by surprising the folks and scattering their will."

I pitied the old conjurer, though I considered his mortification uncalled for. To cause sleep is not the test of the trained scholar. Though the humblest of students I have done this myself even when I desired exceedingly that my discourse should be heard. On the contrary, my one claim to power consists in my ability to rouse an audience with this brief line from an incantation :

"I have finished."

ANNAH ROBINSON WATSON.

COMPARATIVE AFRO-AMERICAN FOLK-LORE.

BY ANNAH ROBINSON WATSON.

To adjust with scrupulous nicety the scale of values in any line of investigation one must train his eye, his heart, and his brain in the work of faithful comparisons. If this be true in the general literary, scientific or sociological departments of research, it is doubly so in the comparatively new field of thought presented by Folk-lore. One may unearth from lower strata of soil curios of unique and wonderful workmanship. What are they more than objects for pleasant speculation and admiration unless, by comparison with objects found elsewhere, and in many far separated localities, they go to support or establish certain theories of value in the general summing up of human knowledge?

It is to the unearthing of Folk-lore curios we must look for facts found in no so-called chronicles, for truths that have eluded the most faithful historians, for secrets that have escaped the scrutiny of closest observers along the usual lines of investigation. Through the researches of Folk-lore will be presented to us the everyday lives of a people, and at the same time there will be presented, as by the power of a spirit lens, a psychological picture, a representation of the thoughts and inner existence, the intellectual, moral, and social conditions of those to whom the research relates. It has been said in this connection that, " out of the ignorance of a people may be built their only monument of lasting fame." Posterity may have received from them no legacy save a testimony to certain truths borne by their customs and beliefs; but when these, through the typical legends of all primitive peoples are secured, brought together, and compared, we will have received the most valuable and incontestable evidence as to the origin and first principles of the species.

Whether the literal statements contained in the Mosaic account of creation be accepted, or the theory advanced by some that from separate divisions of the ape family the various races of man descend—this latter idea seeming to presuppose that the progenitor ape for the Caucasian will some day be discovered, a fossil—the fact remains that the wonderful analogies existing between such legends of different nations as are compared up to date, seem to affirm very strongly the original oneness of the human family, the original oneness of all sources of knowledge.

It is outside the limits of this paper to enter upon the discussion of comparative Folk-lore in its entirety. Comparative study as it bears upon the Afro-American demands our consideration. The Folk-lore of our Southern negro— what is it ? to what forces does it owe its individualism ? and what relationships does it discover ?

*   *   -   *   *   -   *

" How shall a man escape from his ancestors, or draw off from his veins the black drop which he drew from his father's or mother's veins ? " This query was put by one of our giant intellects : the answer may be discerned in the outcome of the truth declared by Lemarck, " All that has been acquired, impressed, or altered in the organization of individuals during the course of their life is preserved by generation, and transmitted to the new individuals which spring from those who have experienced these changes." The query bears witness to the Nemesis we call heredity ; the answer, to its antidote, the force of environment. The consideration involved is, in the language of Herbert Spencer, " The question which demands, beyond all others whatsoever, the attention of scientific men."

The American negro is many generations nearer the savage existence than any race—excepting the Indian—whose proximity invites practical study from our home student. His nearness to this primitive state accounts for his rich possession of legends, his dower of heredity accounts for the character of these legends.

The Southern negroes of the past were, under the most favorable conditions, in a large sense, children. When our ancestors found them, a century or more ago, safely ensconced in our homes, the traits manifested for consideration were in certain families, docility, affection, and loyalty, associated with a certain measure of intelligence, in other families, brutality, dishonesty, indolence, and general worthlessness. A slave was spoken of as belonging to a good or bad family, reference being made to the traits of his blood. There were among them many instances of unusual shrewdness and discretion, and in many cases there were ties of warm affection binding the families of masters and slaves together.

In a condition of slavery which is accompanied by physical comfort there is present a certain phase of mental freedom. That is, freedom from care and responsibility,—the freedom "which taketh no thought for the morrow." This was the condition of the negro, and a condition it was which contained the most favorable elements for stimulating his imagination and encouraging the more romantic side of his nature.

Our negroes of the past were, above everything else, superstitious; they were governed in a most surprising degree by their faith in charms, spells, witches, and conjuring in general. This superstition they unquestionably brought with them from the older country, and as the outgrowth of this superstition we have their legends.

To those who have not crossed seas and challenged for themselves the secrets of the Dark Continent, the superstitions of that region must be sought in the reports made by reliable travellers. From these it would appear that the superstitions transplanted from that country to this have only taken on the unavoidable coloring of new environment.

To the native African, " trees, stones, herbs, all contain imprisoned spirits, which if released may rend and destroy."

The Afro-American holds these same beliefs in a diluted form. The serpent worship does or did prevail in certain portions of Africa. To it may doubtless be traced the many curious beliefs of the Afro-American relating to the serpent and its supernatural powers. The superstitions in the mother country connected with birds and fowls, sprinkling meal or seed on the ground to propitiate deity, with the manner in which animals deport themselves, with the beliefs relating to witches and disembodied spirits, show a marked similarity to beliefs connected with the same by our Southern negroes. Among the latter, if one man has an enmity against another and wishes to accomplish his death, he takes a charmed nail and drives it, every day a little, into a tree. When it touches the heart of the tree the doomed individual falls dead.

This would seem to be a remnant of the ancient faith in the supernatural attributes of trees, or of tree worship.—The African chief is said to trace a line of ashes round his hut to protect it against evil spirits. The Afro-American sprinkles mustard seed before his stable door to keep out the witch, claiming that she cannot enter until every seed has been picked up, and so the dawn will come before her work is accomplished. To the African the hooting of an owl means that the Angel of Death is stealing silently through the cluster of huts to select a victim, our Africans consider it always the forerunner of death or some other great evil.

As a charm against an enemy's spear, the Africans tie around the waist a thin fibre, cover it with a cloth, put a nut in the mouth and knife in the left hand. This is quite suggestive of the directions given a little later for using the Devil's shoe-string. This Devil's shoestring also recalls a medicine used by the Africans to render themselves invincible. Our Negroes and the Africans have almost identical beliefs regarding the passing of the souls of the dead into the bodies of lower animals.

Old Uncle Simon Hollowfield told me very gravely of several different rabbits into whose bodies had passed "de sperits" of certain individuals who were dead, one of these rabbits contained the spirit of his old mistress and guarded her grave. It has been proven that the same legends and superstitions obtain all over the South ; though the stories may have many variants, the divergencies are unimportant and do not detract from their weight as testimony establishing the fact that they all came over in the slave ships from the old to the new country.

Mr. Joel Chandler Harris found a legend current among Georgia negroes to be identical with one told by a descendant of a Guinea negro living in South America, and it is probable that many such instances exist. Our Africans are a race of prolific proverb makers, and doubtless much of their homely wisdom and many of their legends yet await the writer who shall secure and give them permanent form.

It will easily be seen that specimens of Folk-ore, to be of value, must be given in dialect. The speech of the people is inseparable from their thought. So long as they think in dialect and talk in dialect, the form of speech will remain an important factor in all representations of them which are in any sense faithful.

*　　*　　*　　*　　.　　*　　*

Under the head of Curative Lore, or, as the old negroes would say, "Cunger means," may be classed many of their curious remedies for various ills and the charms used to accomplish special ends. One of my colored friends, old Uncle Willis, who seems greatly to enjoy coming to talk to me "a spell," as he terms it, was speaking of tricks, medicines, and "cunger means," he said; "Now dars supp'n w'uts oncom'n pow'rfu' fer ter rub wid w'en yet got de mizries. You mus' git some butter en put 't in er jar. Den git er toad frog en put dat in de jar 'long wid de butter. Nex' you mus' shet up de jar tight en clost so no ar' won' git in no ways. Arf'er dis you jes set 't up er w'ile by 't se'f. Bimeby dat frog 'll tuhn ter butter he-se'f en mek de berry bes' sort o' lin'men' fer ter rub wid w'en yer been tuk wid de pains."

"Now hyears er rem'dy fer er nudder trouble. Ef any time yers in er house en kyarnt pay de ren' yer mus' sweep de flo' en git up eb'ry bit er dus', den wrop 't in er piece er red flan'l en put 't in de stove. W'en 't comes ter ashes jes tek 't en sprinkle 't bout de house w'en de ownder's gwine cum fer ter git de ren'. He won' say er dis'gree'ble word en he won' bother yer neider, not ef yer stays in dat house forty year. You see mum, w'en yer sprinkle dese means wid er wush hit refrecs on de pusson w'ut come in. Now dis look like fool'shness, but so 'tis.

"In de woods dars er vey'y impo't'nt root w'ut yer kin git. Hits w'ut goes by de name o' de Devil's shoestrin'. Now yer

know y'rse'f dars fo' co'nders ter de yearf, Eas', Wes', No'f
en den de Sou'f. Yer mus' be pertic'ler in hunt'n ter git de
tap root, de one w'ut don tuhn in none dem d'rections but jes
goes right straight down inter de yearf. We'n yer fine 't pull
't up 'dout axin' no questions, yer kyarnt break't no ways.
Now dis yer mus' steep in er point er fine bran'y. Dis is fer
er man's biz'ess en yer mus' wauk 't in dis way. Arf'rn 't
steep er w'ile jes tek de root 'n wrop't roun' de muscle uv
bofe er man's a'ms en he k'n by dis means jum' right inter de
street w'uts full uv men on he k'n whup ev'ry one uv 'm, he
kin, er fight'n right 'n lef'. He kin overcome es many es
he's mine t'r cep'n dey hes weepins ter fight wid, dis means
'll overcome any 'mount er muscle. Ef er man puts dis
bran'y on he face he k'n go any w'eres en wid any peoples en
meet 'm all in peace, hit deman's peace en dar won' nobody
say nothin ter 'm but w'ut's peac'ble."

" Den dars er mon'sus cu'ous sump'in but hits ter do wid
de ways uv ebilniss en I' se fear'd ter vencher sich, hits heap
too barb'rous fer me, I ain' meddle long sich es dat do I
knows 't ter be de troof.

" You teks er black cat w'ut ain' got er single w'ite har on
'im en' puts 'im inter er kittle w'uts full o' bilin' water,
mindin' dat he mus' go in erlive. Yer better put er powerfu'
heavy led on 'cause he's gwine rar' mightily. Well yer cooks
'm twell he's done so de meat'l drap off'n de bones, den yer
gits er lookin' glass en yer stan's er look'n right inter 't dout
mov'n ner bat 'n yer eye, yer jes' stan's er lookin' in de glass
er pick'n er de bones out'n de pot en er pass'n em all froo
yer mouf. Yer goes on er pick'n en er pick'n en er th'ow'n
uv de bones and de meat 'way twell yer comes 't er little
roun' bone bout de size uv er buckshot. Well suz, w'en yer
comes ter dat pertic'ler bone, eb'ry thin' roun' yer'l be jes es
black en dark es midnight en yer kyarnt see nothin' tall, hit'l
be plum dark, but dat bone's w'ut yer bin er wukin' fer. De
nex thin' arf'er yer fine 't yer mus' wush in de name o' de
Laud en put dat bone in one jaw wid er little loadstone in
de udder. Well, mum, now yer's got er gret mixtry, bout yer,
yer kin go any w'ars en wid any peoples, ter be sho, dey kin
hyear yer, dey'll hyear er ve'y peculy noise, sorter like er rat
mebbe, but dey kyarnt see yer no ways.

" Black cats mighty impo'tan' fer pussons w'uts got de hea't ter wuk wid 'm—ain' yer never hyear dat ?

"Now I'se er fool ter 'r wise man, but I kin do anythin' I wan's ter im wid sich means, en I tell yer ef deys been wuk'd on y'r self, don' ch'r tek no physical rem'dies fer dey'l kill yer sho, jes git er cunger doct'r quick, he's got mixtries w'ut'l git yer all right, sho en sartin, hit teks pizin ter tuhn pizin."

When the old man imparted this last information regarding the cat, his voice sank to a hoarse whisper and he constantly glanced about on all sides in an anxious furtive manner to see if any eavesdroppers were near. He stands in great fear of what his fellows might do or say should they know that he had spoken with me upon such a subject as the black cat mystery.

There can be no doubt that in their Curative Lore there are some germs of valuable knowledge. Their teacher has been Nature ; her laboratory, their place for experiments. The most notable instance bearing upon this point in my own personal experience is so remarkable that it borders almost upon the miraculous.

A young mother bent above her baby, her only one, who was desperately, hopelessly ill. For weeks she had watched the little sufferer ; now, broken in heart and spirit, she watched for the end. A negro woman, a stranger, came upon some errand, she entered the room, gazed upon the mother, then turned her eyes upon the child—in a moment she was gone. A short while and she returned, entered the room softly, and touching the mother who still bent above the little form where only a slight uncertain breathing told that the spark of life was not quite extinguished, she said in a husky voice, " Put dis round de baby's neck, it done save two o' my chilluns."

A necklace of tiny roots it was she placed in the mother's hand, tiny roots of irregular shape, strung on a thread and emitting a strong aromatic odor. The dark face was full of sympathy, from the eyes shone the compassion of a mother's heart ; there was a common language which the souls of the two women, the African and the Caucasian understood.

Tremblingly the white fingers clasped the strange object, influenced by the idea, It can do neither good nor harm, the one who brought it shall not be wounded by the thought that its efficacy was not even tested. So the necklace was placed about the baby's throat and its donor immediately disappeared.

Another hour the mother bent hopeless above the little one—another—and suddenly, as she watched, there seemed a faint quiver about the eyelids—then there was a little sigh and next a slow, half-perceptible motion of the hands; a few movements more, and the weak little arms were lifted. A wild hope throbbed through the mother's heart, there had not been for many hours such signs of life.

Just at this moment the old family physician came to inquire for the little patient he had pronounced beyond earthly aid, and immediately directed certain measures of restoration. The mother told him of the necklace—he replied very gravely that its power could not be doubted, that there were many potent natural agents of which as yet we were ignorant.

The baby wore the necklace until quite well, and it was then placed in the mother's jewelry case, but one day it was gone—no one could tell where nor how.

Among their legends none are more curious than those which treat of witches. The one following was told me by old Uncle Simon Hollowfield :

"Witches ! ye's s'm—I know's cunsid'ble 'bou' dem. Dey's humins, witchesis, dey's people w'ut sheds dey skins 'er night same's you sheds yer close. I'se sted'd 'bou' witchcraf' myse'f. Yer see, dey puts yer in er ku'ous cundition dat yer don' know nothin' 'n kyarnt hep yerse'f no ways, den dey jes ties yer up. Arf'er dis dey easy 'nouf puts er bridle on yer by witch means. I know'd er cull'd man way long time 'go down in Gawgy w'ut said he mistis wuz er witch uhman. Well, dis man he gin ter fall off so en ter git so po', dat he marster ax 'im w'ut wuz de matter. Den de man he up en tole 'im de sho 'nough troof, dat is, dat de mistis were er witch en dat she rid 'im ebbry night same's he wuz er hoss. De marster he uv cose mighty suspris'd, en he ain' say nothin' tall jes' at fust, den he spon' dat he'd fix 'er. Well, he sot off, he did, en he got 'im er bridle wid er silvuh bit. Silvuh! hit's got mo' pow'r den mose any udder thin' whar witches is cunsarned, hit's got strenf w'ut witches kyarnt withstan' frum.

So de marster he give dis bridle ter his sarvan'. Dat night de witch put de bolster by de side her ole man same's she bin er doin' ebbry night en she slips out widout he know'n hit.

"W'en she got ter whar de sarvan' wuz she walk in en hang her close on he wall, nex' she shed huh skin en wuz in 'pearence jes er skinn'd humin. She hed de bridle in huh han' en she tried en she tried ter bridle dat man, but he wuz wuk'n de same time fer ter put de silvuh bit in huh mouf, en case she could'n complush noth'n 'ginst hit. So he kyard his pint en bridl'd huh arfer so long er time en den he jes tuk huh right ter de stable en hitch her ter de rack same's she wuz er hoss, en in de mo'nin' dar she wuz.

"W'en de marster wake up dar wuz de bolster by he side en no wife, he w'en ter de stable en she wuz dar wid de silvuh bit in huh mouf en he jes sont fer de neighbers en dey come en hab er big confab 'bout hit. De cons'quince wuz dey jes up en bun huh 'live.

"She had been er ridin' dat man fer de longis' ebbry night ter de place whar de witches met. Dey me't ter heve er frolic same's folkes, dey hed sumpin' like er trainin' school ter teach de young uns. W'en dey meet dey sings en frolics en don' know w'ut else dey mout er done, but hit's been provin' dat dey rides hosses en men—yes ma'am—

"Ef er witch ever come 'bout you, you jis git er needle wid er extra big eye en break hit inter two pieces, den tek der pint uv hit en stick't in de eye. Nex' yer mus' prepar supp'r en sot 't on de hyarf er layin' de needle down by 't. De witch'l sho come ter git some dat supper en de mo'nin', yer'll fine'r wid huh big toe er stickin' in'r eye. Dat needle done mek'r do't, she done fas'n huh own se'f. No doubt dat de eend er dat witch."

At this juncture the old man rocked himself back and forth laughing in the most delightful and infectious manner. I asked once, "Uncle Simon, have you ever seen a spirit?" "No 'm, I ain't seed 'm, but I'se hyeard 'm many er time. I'd er be gwine 'long er moonlight night thro' de woods en 'ud hyear er stick break, er whack! en den hyear one on 'em say, "Ain' I done tole yer so? Ain' I done tole yer so?"

He could not explain the meaning of the words or give the reason for the remark, but a few months since I was in the far South on the Louisiana line and talking with an old servant by the name of Cuffy. In response to a similar question, he said : " Dar's sperits w'ut ain' sat'sfied, w'ut's res'less, en dey wan'ers 'bout de yearf all de time. W'en yer goes long, not thinkin' bout nothin' en hes er warm winter strike yer face, en smells hit sort er tainty en dis'gree'ble, dats ghosties er passin' by. Dey kin see you, but you kyarnt see dem. At night dey goes roun' er many er time en dey will be er disputin' 'bout who 'tis er walkin by. One uv 'm w'ut knows me'll say, ' Dars goes Cuffy er passin by.' Den de udder'll 'spon' ' No tain' Cuffy t'all.' ' Dey 'll spute bout 't en den de one w'ut know'd me 'l break er stick ter mek er noise so's I'l tuhn 'roun' en dey kin see my face en know me. ' Right den, if yer lissens hard, you'll *hyear* one uv 'm say, ' Didn' I tole yer so, didn' I tole yer so ? ' ' "

This old man Cuffy introduced to me a character in folk lore which I have neither heard of nor seen elsewhere. It is " *Soo-loo.*" He said,—

" Now Soolo, he wuz er witch en de rabbit he's haf witch hese'f. Sooloo had natch'l har sames de rabbit en he 'n de rabbit dey wuz parnders. Onct pun er time dey buy some butter tergedder en dey put 't erway in de house en wen' on ter wuk in de patch. Bimeby de rabbit he wan' some dat butter mighty bad en he up en say, 'Hello,' same's ef he hyear somebody er callin'. Sooloo say, ' Wu'ts dat yer hollin' bout.' Rabbit 'spon,' ' Somebody er callin' me 't house.' Sooloo say, ' You better go see w'ut's de matter.'

" Den de rabbit he bre'k en run, he did, ter 't house en he hep hese'f ter de butter den wen' lopin back ter de patch ter wuk. W'en he got dar Sooloo, he say, ' W'ut wuz de matter ?' De rabbit he say, ' My wife got er little one,' en Sooloo say, ' W'ut he name ?' rabbit say, ' Skim Top.' 'Twan long fo de rabbit holler gin, ' Hello !' en Sooloo say, ' W'ut de matter ?' rabbit 'spon,' ' Don' yer hyear somebody er callin' me 't house ?' Sooloo say, ' Yer better go see who 'tis.' De rabbit he go, stay little w'ile, den come back en Sooloo say, ' W'ut de matter ?' De rabbit say, ' My wife got little one.' ' W'uts he name ?' say Sooloo. ' Midways,' say de rabbit.

" 'Twan but nudder little w'ile fo de rabbit say 'gin, ' Hel-

lo !' en Sooloo say 'gin, ' W'uts de matter ? ' Somebody er
callin' me 't house,' de rabbit spon' ' You better go see w'ut
de matter.' W'en de rabbit come back dis time dar wan no
mo' butter in de pail 't all but cose ' Sooloo didn' know
de rabbit don clean de bottom. Dis time Sooloo say 'gin,
' W'ut wuz de matter,' en de rabbit he say, ' My wife got er
little one,' w'en Sooloo ax,' W'ut he name ? ' de rabbit say,
' Cleanbottom.'

"Dat night w'en he en Sooloo come home dey fine dar ain'
no butter 't all in de pail en dey wuz bofe dat sus-spr-i' -s' -d.
Den dey cunsult'd tergedder es ter who could er bin dar ter
do sech er outdacious ac'. De rabbit he up and say, ' Sholy
't wan' you, Sooloo, en I know 't wan' me, but dars er way
ter prove hit, sez ee. We'll buil' er big fire en lay down clost
ter 't en it 'll skew de grease out'n de one w'ut done tek dat
butter.'

"So dey collect'd some light wood en mek er fire en bofe
uv'm stretched dey se'fs out befo't. Now Sooloo he wuz er
fambly man en he wuk hard all de day long, but de rabbit he
ain' sted'n bout wuk 't 'all, Sooloo wuz ti'de but rabbit wan'
so Sooloo wen' sleep but de rabbit did'n. He jes lay dar
think'n twell de fire done draw all de grease out'n 'im sho
nough den he got up 'n rub hit all over Sooloo who wuz sleep
en not spicionin' nothin'.

"Now all uv er sud'n he call Sooloo en dar he wuz all
kiver'd wid de grease. Sooloo, cose he know'd he ain' eat dat
butter so he up en run de rabbit twell he hop in er holler
tree en dar Sooloo cotch 'm by de hine laig. Den de rabbit
he holler, ' Oh, please Brer, Sooloo, doan kill me in de bri'r
patch, do anythin' 't all but cep'n tho me in de bri'r patch.'
Den dat de berry thin' dat Sooloo done, he heave 'm right in
de bri'r patch sho nough. Wel-l-suz, dat rabbit he jes holler
en laf-f ' Oh brer Sooloo, dis de berry place I wuz bon'd in,
dis de berry place I wuz bon'd in.' Uv cose Sooloo couldn'
ketch 'm no ways, de rabbit he's heap smart'r nor w'ut de
udder beastis is."—Here old Cuffy laughed until the tears
came into his eyes thinking of the rabbit's "butter scrape'
as he called it.

This legend, as a whole, is unlike any of those I have seen.
It has several features peculiarly its own, but the allusion to

22

the briar patch is identical with the close of the famous Tar
Baby story, and several other points will be found in other legends.   This mixture seems to be a strong argument for one
original source of them all.

       ●   ◦   ◦   ▬   ▬   ▬   ▬

As a natural consequence of the present environment of the
Afro-American, his legendary gifts are fast leaving him; with
the present generation they will be quite lost to the world,
and if any effort is to be made to secure them it must be
done quickly and skilfully, for the generation of to-day scorns
the old time legends and superstitions.   Only the old-timers
prize and cherish them, and these are not only rapidly passing
away, but it is difficult to find the key to their hidden treasures.   When they have vanished, the curio-hunter in the
realm of Afro-American folk-lore will realize that the mines
he sought to open have disappeared like submerged lands, and
that the generation most closely allied to the primitive state
of man, and which yet was near enough to him for scientific
investigation, has disappeared forever.

Having briefly compared some of the distinctive superstitions of the Afro-American and African proper,—having
realized that the negroes in different parts of the South hold the
same superstitions just as they do national other peculiarities,
attention must be directed to another division on the subject.
Before turning to this reference, must be made to the very
remarkable book recently published by Miss Owen ; but
since it deals with a separate and distinct class of folk-lore,
that in which the Negroes and Indians unite as collaborators
and equally share the percentage of the legends, it will not
be discussed here.

The other division, and one which sustains an important
relation to the subject of this paper, is to be discovered in the
legends of the Indians of the Northwest which are yet to be
unearthed by the student of ethnology.   I have found among
legends secured from the Indians themselves, and such as
were located in distant portions of the country where it is
not possible that Afro-American influence could have penetrated, some which contain identical incidents with those in
legends current among our Southern negroes.   How shall we

account for this fact ? It seems to confront us with a problem quite different from any other in connection with the study of folk-lore on this continent.

Besides these close resemblances in the legends of the two races, there are ideas held by both which discover remarkable likenesses to the best authenticated folk-tales of the old world. In the Kalevala, the great Finnic epic, perhaps the richest find of folk-lore in the last fifty years, are embalmed the thoughts of men as they probably were thousands of years ago. We find here marvellous resemblances to the Chaldean invocations preserved on clay tablets, to the beliefs of the ancient Babylonians, and stranger still, to those of the American Indian—yet the Kalevala is self-dependent and original, and the idea of its being a copy or imitation is positively denied by scientific authorities.

We find in it a rune which deals in a serio-comic manner with Otso, the bear, in much the same way as our negroes do in their legends. We find another in which the hare is given the place of honor above the bear, the wolf, and the fox, for its superior sagacity and adroitness. If the Kalevala, together with the results of philological research should prove, as seems quite possible, that the American Indian is related to the Finns; and if identical legends, ideas, and linguistic peculiarities demonstrate that two of the most primitive races on this continent, the Afro-American and Indian, are distant cousins,—a new and very attractive thought will be presented to the patriotic American.

According to the general idea, at the time of the dispersion of the human family from its home in Central Asia, some of the tribes journeyed eastward and crossed, probably on dry ground, the present Behring Straits. When others went southward from Asia to the Dark Continent, and others again went westward to the country of the Lapps and the Finns and the Saxons and at last to our own shores, they must, have carried, stored away with their Lares and Penates, a chain of primitive legends. Is it chimerical to suggest that the two ends of this wondrous chain, with its curiously wrought links, are destined to meet in the land discovered by Columbus ? Is it chimerical to suggest that we may realize that a chain of legends has at last girdled the globe with its romance as well as its testimony to great scientific facts ?   If this suggested theory, this idea that east and west, during all the past ages, has the chain stretched, until now and here it has met, if this prove to be true ;—then upon America, our native land, will be conferred the distinction of being the meeting-place of the two branches of the human family that started out from their common home centuries ago in opposite directions ;— then to America, the land latest known, but best beloved of the gods, will belong the honor of gathering together the magicians, who with the ever-potent fire of knowledge, will weld together the long-sundered ends of that chain now circling our glorious sphere.

VENEZUELAN FOLK-LORE.[1]

BY DR. TEOFILO RODRIGUEZ.

Members of the International Folk-Lore Congress:

DEEPLY grateful for the distinction with which I have spontaneously been the object, on the part of the honorable associates who have planned and organized this wise assembly, I have not hesitated to attempt to respond, as well as the brief time and my lack of skill permit, to the honor which has been bestowed upon me. But far be it from me, Gentlemen, to wish to offer in this work, whose execution requires conciseness and brevity, a complete collection of those beliefs which, now original in the land, now imported from others in remote or recent epochs, constitute Venezuelan Folk-Lore. This vast undertaking would require, as you so well comprehend, greater efforts and still greater time. I must limit myself, then, to citing the principal works which have been published in Venezuela upon this branch of literature, so much cultivated and so far advanced now in the old Continent; and keeping in mind the motto of this Congress, "Men, not things," to enumerate the writers who, now moved by especial inclination, now incited by the stimulus of their erudition, have contributed to give an idea of the legendary tales, superstitions, and traditions which prevail among our people, which, according to the technology of modern science, constitutes Folk-lore.

"The "Tradiciones Populares-coleccion de cronicas y legendas narrandas por varios escritorios nacionales" was published in Carácas in the year 1885, by Dr. Teofilo Rodriguez, a member of the National Academy of History and of various foreign scientific bodies. The said collection forms a large volume of 352 pages, in royal 8vo, and is divided into two parts, of which the first consists of the Introduction,

---

[1] Translated from the Spanish by Lieut. F. S. Bassett.

written by the compiler, thirty-six legends and Venezuela
traditions, of which eight were written by the said Dr. Teofilo
Rodriguez ; two by D. Juan Vicente Camacho ; one by Dr.
Nugel M. Alamo ; one by Dr. Ramon Diaz ; one by the Li-
cenciado Juan Vicente Gonzalez ; one by Dr. Ramon Isidro
Montez ; one by D. Julio Calcano ; one by D. Andres A.
Level ; one by General Jose Antonio Paez, in his *Autobiogra-
phie ;* by D. Pedro Ezequil Royas ; one by Dr. Cristóbal L.
Mendoza ; one by Dr. F. C. Vetancout Nigas ; one by Dr.
Jose Gil Fortoul ; one by Dr. Simon Camacho ; four by Don
Miguel I Romero ; one by the Presbyter, Dr. I. A. Ramos
Martinez ; three by D. Aristides Royas ; one by Nicanor
Bolet Peraza ; two by D. Andres A. Silva ; and the second
part consists of the " Visions of the Night " and " The Ter-
rors and the Treasures," by Dr. Teofilo Rodriguez.

" Reminiscences Historicas " is the title of another work,
published in 1886, in the city of Valencia, capital of the
state of Carabobo, by Dr. Francisco Gonzales Guinan, member of the National Academy of History of Carácas, and which
consists of a volume in 8vo of 250 pages. It contains twenty-
seven legends, of which some are simple tales and the others
philosophical-political studies, as the author says in his pre-
face, and with these he uses a special kind of literary workmanship. But, as the same asserts, and as it is in reality for
these studies, not only has he drawn materials from the pages
of history, but also from the fund of popular tradition, said
work has a place in this enumeration. Besides, the work
was well received by the public for its literary merit.

" Cuentos y Tradiciones," a small volume in 18mo of 48
pages (edition of Carácas in 1888), by Dr. Andres A. Silva,
member of the National Academy of History of Carácas, and
of the Society of Popular Traditions of Paris, is a work comprising seven stories and four fables in verse, and which has
merited the eulogium of his countrymen and of strangers.

" Révue Des Traditions Populaires," says : " These relations, properly speaking, are not popular in the scientific sense
of the word. By the form and grace of diction they recall some
of the " Provençal tales " of Romaille ; one of the most divert-
ing is the one entitled : " Cadanus, etc." " Each one has his
own way of killing lice." In another, St. Peter denies entrance

into Paradise to a man who has married three times. On page 43 are found other curious details concerning the procession of Good Friday. It is to be hoped that Senor Andres A. Silva, who has demonstrated in this little book veritable qualities as a narrator, shall apply them to writing the really popular tales of Venezuela, his natal country ; the harvest will be rich and interesting." (*Sébillot.*)

"Legendas Historicas " and "Estudios Historicos " are the titles of two other works, constituting the first of two volumes, and the second of one volume in grand 8vo, and of more than 300 pages each, published in 1890 and 1891, by Dr. Aristides Rojas, an individual member of various scientific and literary associations of both hemispheres, and one of the most prolific modern writers of Venezuela. In the two small volumes (1st and 2d series) of the legends, Dr. Rojas has abridged some of those published before by him and many others unedited up to that date ; all of which he offers to his country as his contingent to its history. A more valuable contribution towards the same history, although larger than that offered by the first named work, is found in the *Estudios*, and from this point of view we may not add here anything further ; but so great materials of value for folk-lore are found in both of these works, and they have a place among those referred to under this head.

A very excellent contribution to national folk lore is a work upon the " Cancionero Populee de Venezuela," published in *El Cojo Ilusdrads*, a literary periodical of Carácas (No. 27, February 1st, 1893), by Dr. A. Ernst, a distinguished naturalist and lecturer at the Central University. In this Dr. Ernst compiles fifty-nine ballads, which he offers to Dr. Rojas as materials for the work of folk-lore, which he proposes to write. This work is worthy of every encomium, and in it are found twenty ballads pertaining to the " National Song Book," corresponding, the greater part of them, to those of the " Spanish Song Book," as Dr. Rojas observes with such accuracy in the feuilleton (8th page, Caravus, February, 1893) which he wrote upon the occasion of this work, dedicating it to him as its author. " Leyendas de la Conquista—Honanaye a Colon (volume of 300 pages, in royal 8vo., Carácas, 1893) by General Francisco Josta Garcia, a writer of fecundity, is

another work which we ought to cite here.   Besides the *pro-
logue*, which contains twenty-two legends, in many of which
are found materials for Venezuelan folk-lore—the author is an
amateur elevated for some time to this part, to this branch of
literature devoted in the work which he has just published,
and in which he seems to follow the kind of literary work
begun by Dr. Francisco Gonzalez Gumian, he recurs with
frequency to popular tradition, imparting animation and
graec to the relation.

"Tradiciones Barcelonesas," is the title of the manuscript
of an unedited work of Senor Miguel I. Tomero (of Barcelona, Venezuela) whom death prevented from publishing just
as he was preparing to do it.   It comprehends an assemblage
of legends, of which four are found inserted in the "Tradiciones Populares" of Dr. Teofilo Rodriguez, having also in
some of these no small amount of materials for national folk
lore.   It is to be hoped that the sons of S. R. Romero shall
soon publish this work, which has been approved by the National Academy of History at Carácas, to whose consideration
the government submitted it as being worthy of being
known.

"Miscelanea Pretica Lu Venezoliada" (a small volume of 366
pages, Carácas, 1892) is a most curious work, and in one of
its sections or chapters are indicated in verse, free and full
of grace, a multitude of traditions; just as if the author,
who possesses vast erudition and a prodigious memory, should
have proposed to pass in review the beliefs, superstitions,
and fables current among the vulgar, and also among many
people of distinction, serving as an index of the great number of our popular traditions.   This work occupies, then, a
place here, and it will serve us to close with it this enumeration and we will also now cite some productions of the same
literary class, such as "La Bayada de Los Rejers," in El
Vallo (a suburban village of Carácas), by General Nicanor
Botet Peraza ; "El Caraco," by Bienvenedo (a pseudonym);
"La Mula de Guijada," by Dr. Doroteo De Armas, and some
other articles published in Carácas or in the other cities of
the republic.   The haste with which this work has been
accomplished has prevented us from obtaining them, so as
to speak of them with exactness and propriety.   We can

really say that all of them provide materials, nevertheless, for the great work of Venezuelan folk lore.

To conclude, we may be permitted to say, that the field of popular science has commenced, so as to say, to be explored among us and that as soon as it may be cultivated, with the interest and solicitude which it merits, it will produce abundant and seasonable fruit. This short memoir is a short example of that already done, which is, in truth, little. It will serve for the object proposed by the wise assembly to whom I have the honor of addressing it, and my satisfaction will be complete.

SOME SUPERSTITIONS OF SOUTH AMERICAN INDIANS.

BY ROGER WELLES, LIEUTENANT, U. S. NAVY.

In the winter of 1891 and '92 it was my good fortune to make quite an extended trip up the Orinoco, from its mouth to San Fernando de Atobapo, thence up one of its large branches the Guaviare for a few miles, thence up the Inisida several hundred miles until I arrived at a small branch called the Caño Chucuto or Cholmoa—the Indian name—which I ascended for about sixty miles to a small settlement of Indians.

During this extended trip of twelve or fifteen hundred miles I passed through the lands of many tribes of Indians, as the Caribes, Rio Meta, Piasva, Guaivos, Puinabos and Piapocos ; but I was thrown more intimately with the Guaivos living on the banks of the Rio Vichada, and the Puinabos, living on the banks of the Inisida, and of the folk-lore of these two tribes I shall speak to-day. I shall speak only of what I observed when in the company of these Indians.

Although the Guaivos have their permanent villages on the Rio Vichada, and, I understand, on the banks of the Rio Meta near its source, still they come in families down to the Orinoco to exchange their hammocks, tonqua beans, and rubber with the traders, for calicoes, knives, tobacco, fish-hooks, and articles which Indians usually make use of. It was among such families of this tribe that I was able to gather what l am about to say.

In going from Maiperres to San Fernando de Atobapo, the crew of the canoe was composed of three Guaivos Indians. I noticed, one Indian never ate with the other two, but always alone, and rarely ate the same food. If the two had fish, he would wander off and find an iguana, which he would prepare and cook himself, and eat quite alone ; if the others had wild turkey, he would catch himself a fish. And so it always happened that he was found during meal hours off by himself, and eating a different kind of food than the others. It took me some time to find the exact cause, but at last I found he was a married man and his wife was *enceinte,* and should he eat with the others, and the same food as the others, she would be made sick, although she was many miles away.

I noticed another curious custom which I saw nearly every day. In that country, although it was supposed to be the dry season, small clouds would rise and develop in short but very heavy rain squalls. If the course of one of these squalls seemed to be such that it would pass over our heads and wet us, the Indian would stand up in the canoe or on the ground, face the cloud and try to blow or puff and wave the cloud to one side, so that it would pass clear of us. Some of these Indians—the richer ones—wore around the neck an amulet to assist him in this work. This was a sort of a pear-shaped nut of some kind, usually carved a little, with a hole through one side, and a small stone of some kind stuck in the other. Holding this up in front of his eye, with the stone to the cloud, he would puff and wave the clouds to one side, as before described.

Another amulet consisted of a tooth of an alligator, the hollow end being filled with the gum of some tree in which was stuck a stone from the river ; when the owner desires to go into or near the river, he first waves this tooth over the river, which drives away all the alligators which may be loitering about, and then he goes into the river without fear.

A tiger's tooth similarly arranged and waved will, they believe, drive away tigers.

They carry in a small basket or bag hanging at their side many articles believed to possess great power to accomplish different things. I found in one basket a small lock of hair which the Indian assured me was taken from the head of his dead wife, and was now used to keep away bad men. This they waved toward the man, muttering some words, probably a curse, when the man would leave never to return again and they believe that he goes away somewhere to die.

In one of these bags I found a small gourd filled with a mealy, cork-like material, which is given to women to make them love the giver more passionately.

IRISH LEGENDARY LORE.

BY VERY REV. JOHN CANON O'HANLON.

POPULAR superstitions derive their origin from remote periods and various motive causes. They usually result from disordered intelligence, imperfect knowledge, and neglected education. However widely extended absurd and irreligious notions may have been, and notwithstanding the distinction prevailing in the habits, customs, and usages among different races, classes, and creeds, inhabiting our globe, almost universal belief in irrational supernatural illusions prevail, and can be assigned to obvious natural causes. Sacred Scripture and even profane history are frequently interspersed with accounts of ancient errors and idolatry, the fruitful parents of popular delusion and impiety reaching even to our own times.

The legends of Ireland, and tales illustrating many superstitious notions of our peasantry, are usually full of lively fancy, imagery, harmless humor, and playful imagination. Popular superstitions are not confined to the Irish, as can easily be proved, by comparing our fairy lore with that of other nations. The English, Welsh, and Scotch are much more superstitious than the Irish. Nor are superstitions restricted to the less educated classes, in those various countries where they prevail. Even in cases where education might be supposed to exclude vulgar errors, early prepossessions or associations leave their impress on minds of superior intelligence. Vague and undefined fears, the observations of lucky and unlucky days, or omens, or predestined anticipations of future success or misfortune as a consequence, characterize the habits or feelings, and influence the conduct of persons, moving in the very highest circles of society.

It is rather remarkable, and it serves probably to account in a great measure, for the natural good-humor, gentleness, and generous disposition of the Irish, that our popular myth-

ology has few revolting superstitions or horrible creations
of fancy connected with it. Even those fictions of fearful
import and of gross conception, linked to the indigenous,
sportive and light, airy fabrications of our legend-mongers,
would seem to have been incorporated with brain illusions,
derived from foreign sources. The blood-stained spectres
and fleshless skeletons of German legends; the terror-inspir-
ing night howls of demons, and the monstrous shapes of ogres,
giants, or perturbed warriors recurring in the Scandinavian
Eddas and Sagas; the fearful *dénouements* of revenge and dis-
aster following such apparitions, and freezing the very soul
of sensibility with horror; these and kindred subjects rarely
intrude on our imagination, or if introduced, they seem toned
to a degree more in unison with ancient and modern instincts
of civilization. As forming a deeply seated theory among the
superstitions of our sister island, with those monstrous re-
pressive enactments of no very remote legislation and of ex-
ecutive severity, witchcraft does not appear to have prevailed
extensively in Ireland, previous to the twelfth century. The
practice of threatening to place changelings or weaklings on
a red-hot shovel, to expel the fairy spirit, or of throwing suspected wizards or witches into water to discover whether they
would sink or swim, or of terrifying suddenly preternatural beings with a heated poker or some such instrument, was deriv-
able probably from that class of judicial trials which caused
accused persons to walk bare-footed over the glowing plough-
share, or which kindled the fires of persecution for victims of
popular delusion. Well-authenticated cases of racking torture and of gross cruelty, inflicted on innocent and suffering
human beings within these realms, while traceable to gross ignorance and revolting superstition, but resulting in the death
of such unfortunate persons, have in too many instances
stained criminal jurisprudence and outraged all the finer feelings of humanity. Happily for the fair fame of our island,
those barbarous incidents rarely occurred within it, nor can
decided traces of such humiliating enactments and monstrous
usages be discovered among our law records.

The vast treasure-store of legends contained in our Irish
manuscript literature has hardly yet been touched, nor, except in very few publications, has it been presented to the

public. In various forms, both in prose and verse, it abounds
in the shape of historic romance, inventive tales, and bardic
verses. Hundreds of such volumes are still preserved in our
Dublin libraries, and especially in those of the Royal Irish
Academy and of Trinity College. Numbers of such Irish
manuscripts are to be found, not alone in Great Britain, but
scattered through all the great public libraries on the Continent of Europe. Not only do those romances contain original
sources and materials for the information of folk-lore societies and students; but they are essential for the understanding and elucidation of Ireland's ancient mythology during
the Pagan period, and for the future historian's use in clear-
ing difficult problems and obscurities of tradition, conveyed
to us through our brief and imperfect annals—the oldest and
most authentic in the world for the great and varied quantity
of facts they contain. Besides a more perfect knowledge of
such manuscripts must be acquired, before the earliest Celtic
migrations in Europe and the social conditions of Great
Britain herself can be known, in ages long previous to the
introduction of Christianity. This should prove too exhaustive a subject here to be treated, by the present writer, even
were he fairly competent to undertake the task. However,
owing to the patriotic and zealous efforts of literary men and
scholars, the Council of the Royal Irish Academy have published in a magnificent style, and at reasonable cost, the most
valuable *fac-similes* or correct Irish texts of the Leabhar nah-
Uidhrs of the Leabhar Breac, of the Book of Leinster, and
of the Book of Ballymote. As all profane history draws its
origin from fables, so must these be carefully examined and
sifted with discrimination, before the true historian can
emerge from the labyrinth of error to the ways of light.

It seems rather strange, that so few of our native writers
have sought subjects for thought and expression, in English
prose and verse, from the legend lore of Erin. Assuredly
this is capable of arresting and captivating imagination and
fancy to the highest degree. However, our earlier poets and
romancists, who wrote in the English language, generally
selected other themes than such as might be derived from
popular superstitions and national legends. Although so far
back as the reign of Elizabeth, Edmund Spenser has some

fanciful images and ideas characterizing a romantic period or
locality, and scattered through his magic lines, "of spring of
elves and faryes ; " yet do we look in vain through the poems
of Sir John Denham,[1] or those of the vigorous writer Dr.
Jonathan Swift,[2] or of his friend Parnell[3] for corresponding
fantasies. Still among the poems of this latter graceful
writer we find a fairy-tale in the ancient English style, as the
poet informs us. However its scenes and names may be
Anglicized, Parnell acknowledges, in one of its concluding
stanzas, he had learned the subject matter from an Irish nurse.
Nevertheless Edwin, Edith, and Sir Topaz are transferred to

"Britain's Isle and Arthur's days
When midnight fairies danced the maze."[4]

Nor do we discover anything legendary in the poems of Samuel
Boyse,[5] of the gifted Oliver Goldsmith,[6] of John Cunning-
ham[7] or of Mathew West,[8] all of whom belonged to the
eighteenth century.

In a whimsical and pedantic collection of poems,[9] published
by Samuel Whyte, only one of the lucubrations intituled,
"The Hone, a Piece of Irish Mythology," has any affinity
with our legendary literature. In this particular instance,
too, the inventive power, taste or delicacy of the author does
not appear to advantage. A beautiful English metrical translation of an Irish *Caoine*, or a Lament for Miss Mary Bourke,
by Morian Shehone, will be found in Barry's "Songs of Ireland." It is replete with feeling we have no doubt, in the
original, which probably belongs to the last century, as in
the translation, which appears to have been versified in the
present ; and it illustrates a national custom, now nearly
obsolete. In Rev. William Hamilton's "Letters Concerning
the Northern Coast of the County Antrim,"[10] we have few

---

[1] Born in Dublin, A. D. 1615.   [2] Born in Hoey's Court, Dublin, A. D. 1667.
[3] Born in Dublin, A. D. 1679.
[4] This tale is almost identical with the "Lusmore," of Crofton Croker.
[5] Born in Dublin, A. D. 1708.
[6] Born in Pallas, Parish of Forgney, County of Longford, A. D. 1728.
[7] Born in Dublin, A. D. 1729.
[8] Poems. etc., on several occasions, by Mathew West, A.M., Curate Assistant of
St. Mary's, Donnybrook, and Chaplain to Right Rev. Isaac, Lord Bishop of Cork,
Dublin ; John Exshaw, 86 Dame Street. 4to.
[9] The "Shamrock or Hibernian Cresses." Dublin, 1772 ; 4to.
[10] Published in Dublin, 1790, 8vo.

legends.   However one of these relating to the Scotch M'Don-
alds and to the Irish M'Quillans, must be noted.[1]   In another,
we learn that Finn McCool built the Giant's Causeway to
connect the shores of Ireland and Scotland.[2]   Some of the
magazines, conducted in Dublin during the last century, have
a few references to Irish legend lore ; but the information
conveyed has little to recommend it of a novel, an authentic,
or an interesting character.

It must ever be regretted, that our illustrious poet, Thomas
Moore, had not directed the play of his lively and varied
genius towards that inexhaustible mine of wealth, which our
Irish traditions must have afforded his bright imaginings.
In the " Irish melodies," it is true, he has left us a legacy
that must be greatly prized by his countrymen ; and perhaps
all the greater, because his national legendary allusions are
so rarely detected.   If, instead of seeking so many themes
for immortal song in Eastern climes, he had confined the
muse to subjects culled from our Island's history and romance,
we cannot doubt, his fame as a poet should not suffer decrease,
while his patriotic services to Ireland must have extended her
renown, and have rendered his own name even more a household word by Irish firesides.

We have now briefly to deal with the romantic literature of
the present age, so far as it is concerned with Irish song and
story.   The " Life of Thomas Dermody," edited by James
Grant Raymond,[3] is found interpersed with various pieces of
original poetry and private correspondence.   These serve to
exhibit the unexampled precociousness of his genius, before
the early death of that intemperate and unfortunate young
poet.   Rarely, however, does he " The native legends of his
land rehearse."

In the early part of this century, his young friend, Miss
Owenson—afterwards the brilliant and accomplished Lady
Morgan—sent forth in rapid succession her " Lay of an Irish
Harp," with her " Wild Irish Girl," " O'Donnell," " Florence
McCarthy," " The O'Briens and O'Flaherties," etc.   Al-
though this admired authoress produced highly effective
tales of national life and manners, spiced with sarcastic and

---

[1] See Part i., letter vii.   [2] Part ii., letter i.
[3] Published in two volumes.   London, 1806, 8vo.

merited attacks on the disorganization, ascendancy, and covert popular discontent, arising from a wretched state of society and oppression, prevalent at that period; she has casually alluded—but in a few instances only—to the legendary lore of her native land. The amiable and erudite authoress, Mrs. Henry Tighe of Rosanna, produced one of the most charming classical and moralistic allegories in our language, in the Spenserian stanza, and she has left rather beautiful fragments of verse.[1] Here, indeed, we find allusions to Irish scenes, persons, and subjects. Yet, we detect a total absence of any additions to our popular legendary literature, which the elegant fancy and imagination of that gifted authoress could have invested with peculiar graces of conception and composition.

It may not be generally known that John D'Alton wrote a metrical romance, in twelve cantos, intituled "Dermid,"[2] which procured him the acquaintance and correspondence of Lord Byron and of Sir Walter Scott. This juvenile, yet highly creditable poem, contains allusions to many curious customs, usages, and superstitions of the Irish and Danes. In the text and notes such information is found gracefully and pleasingly distributed. We exempt altogether from this brief account all reference to the valuable volumes which our dear, deceased old friend published, and which so well serve to illustrate Irish local and family history.

In the "Fairy Legends and Traditions of the South of Ireland,"[3] T. Crofton Croker evinces a brilliant, sportive, and poetic fancy in his mode of treatment, while he combines singular erudition in tracing the connection between our Irish fairy traditions and those current among people living in other countries. To his charming pages we are indebted for a rich vein of invention and of illustration. To him may well be applied the exquisite lines of his own provincial bard,

---

[1] See "Psyche, with other poems," By the late Mrs. Henry Tighe, London. 1811. 4to.

[2] Published at London, in 1814, by Longman & Co. 4to.

[3] This highly popular work appeared anonymously for the first time, in 1825, and was published in London, by Murray. A second edition, illustrated by Maclise, rapidly followed to supply the exhaustive demand for the first. Thomas Wright, Esq., a friend of the author, has edited a beautiful and portable octavo edition, published by William Tegg, London, in 1869. It is preceded by a brief memoir of Crofton Croker.

23

J. J. Callanan, in those inimitable stanzas descriptive of
Gougane Barra.   By tireless industry, enthusiasm, and aptitude for the task, it was T. Crofton Croker, who

> " Gleaned each gray legend that darkly was sleeping,
>   When the mist and the rain o'er their beauty were creeping."

In the poetic vein, also, Croker has rendered the fairy
romances of "Cormac and Mary," and "The Lord of Dun-
kerron" into rhythmical lines, which evidence his taste and
genius.   He had likewise previously described many curious
customs and usages of the Irish, in connection with fairies
and supernatural agency, keens and death ceremonies, in the
fifth and ninth chapters of an interesting illustrated work,
intituled, "Researches in the South of Ireland."[1]
Excepting the "Songs of Deardra," versified from an old
Irish manuscript, and recounting the tragic adventures of
this heroine, and the death of the sons of Usna, in his volume
of poems,[2] Thomas Stott has left us nothing which serves to
illustrate Irish legendary story.   In Thomas Furlong's post-
humous national poem, "The Doom of Derenzie,"[3] much
curious information on Irish fairy mythology and popular
customs will be found scattered throughout the text and
notes.   One of the principal characters in this poem is an
Irish Fairyman or wizard.   The original, from whom he was
drawn, is regarded as having been a native of Wexford
County.   He was named Shane Wrue, or John Roe.   The
remains of the Rev. Charles Wolfe, A. B., as edited by the
Rev. John A. Russel, M. A.,[4] present us with nothing
fanciful referring to "Faerieland."   In that most interesting
work, "Irish Minstrelsy," edited by James Hardiman, we
find many bardic remains of the native tongue.   These are
elegantly rendered into English verse, by such writers as
Thomas Furlong, John D'Alton, Edward Lawson, Henry
Grattan Curran, and Rev. William Hamilton Drummond.
In this scarce and valuable work, we have many of Carolan's
remains and other ancient relics included.   They have been
introduced with a richness of illustration most creditable to

---

[1] Published in London, by Murray, 1824.   4to.
[2] Published in London, 1825.   8vo.
   Published by Robins of London.
[4] See Ninth Edition, London, 1847.   12mo.

the taste and erudition of Mr. Hardiman.[1] About this time, likewise, our Irish novelists and poets, John Banim and Gerald Griffin, were achieving fame for themselves and their country, by those admirable productions, which issued from the press in London, and which must still continue to instruct and amuse unborn generations. The Rev. Caesar Otway's "Tour in Connaught,"[2] and "Sketches in Ireland,"[3] with other narratives, contain many a droll legend and story, related in a rollicking and humorous vein, but with improbable circumstances often infused, and tending to throw unworthy aspersion on the old religious creed of our countrymen.

The "Dublin Penny Journal" of 1832 to 1836, the "Irish Penny Magazine" of 1833-34, and the "Irish Penny Journal" of 1840-41, contain many racy tales and legends of Ireland, by accomplished native penmen. Some of the foregoing writers, with others unknown, were facile contributors to the columns of these illustrated miscellanies, the prized *feuilletons* of our school-boy days. Then, poor Edward Walsh placed on record some of Munster's traditional folk-lore. Carlton, likewise, penned that awe-inspiring romaunt, "Sir Turlough, or the Churchyard Bride." Many another talented contributor obtained insertion for various Irish tales and legends.

From our early reminiscences to the present date, occasional acquaintance with numbers of the "Dublin University Magazine"[4] had introduced to us the now familiar names of several national writers, in connection with Irish legendary lore. Here have we met with the racy "Kishoge Papers"—the metrical version of Dame Alice Kettle's trial for sorcery, and intituled "The Witch of Kilkenny"—the inimitable "Golden Legend and Voyage of St. Brendan," with other metrical contributions, by one foremost among our modern poets, Denis Florence McCarthy. The "Songs of the Superstitions of Ireland," with several legendary ballads,[5]

---

[1] His work was published in two volumes by Joseph Robins, London, 1831. 8vo.

[2] Dublin, Wm. Curry, Jun., & Co., 1839. 12mo.

[3] Dublin, Wm. Curry, Jun., & Co., 1839. 12mo. Second edition.

[4] First issued, January, 1833, and continued for many years subsequent.

[5] These have been since published in a collective form by Chapman and Hall, London.

issuing from the pen of the facetious Samuel Lover ; those beautifully picturesque and historic narratives, "Hibernian Nights' Entertainments," by the late Sir Samuel Ferguson ; the anonymous "Legends and Tales of the Queen's County Peasantry," true to life and redolent of genius, which are now known as the contributions of an humble country school-master, John Keegan ; many beautiful and anonymous metrical productions of the gifted James Clarence Mangan, and all of which have not been as yet published in book shape ; those spirit-stirring Orange slogans of Lieutenant-Colonel Blacker, [1] and those equally intensified true blue lines of Miss E. M. Hamilton ; William Carleton's exaggerated "Traits and Stories of the Irish Peasantry," with a visible improvement in etching and coloring national life and character, as he advanced in novel writing ; various graceful and descriptive papers on "Irish Rivers," by J. Roderick O'Flanagan ; these and various other contributions, gave a permanent interest and popularity to our stock of island legends. Editorial and frenzied attacks on Daniel O'Connell, deprecating his claims to be considered a distinguished Irishman, because of his advocating Reform, Abolition of Tithes, and Repeal of the Union ; lashing Thomas Moore for his Judges in England ; abusing Samuel Lover for his Rory O'More, as being dangerously national ; ungallantly denouncing Miss Harriet Martineau for being a liberal ; dealing unmeasured strokes on the Whig Archbishop Whately, Lord Mulgrave, and the Rev. Sydney Smyth ; while proclaiming the mountebank Rev. Mortimer O'Sullivan and Rev. Robert McGee, political and religious Solomons ; we may now indulge some pleasantry over reversed judgments, and the less intellectual pages of that fine serial. Such distinguished litterateurs or *femmes savantes* as Mrs. Hemans, Rev. Cæsar Otway, William Allingham, Anna Maria Hall, Rev. James Wills,[2] John Anster, LL. D., Charles Lever, Maxwell, William R. Wilde, with "Speranza," Aubrey de Vere, Jonathan Freke Slingsby (John Francis Waller, LL. D.), T. Irwin, John Fraser, and John Fisher Murray, are found pleasantly caricaturing or truth-

---

[1] Some elegant and dramatic sketches and other poems of this writer were published in Dublin, A. D., 1847, in 8vo. The Disembodied and other poems were issued in 12mo. by the same author.

[2] He often writes under the signature of Fitz-Stewart, Bannside.

fully illustrating some peculiar features of Irish life, character, and scenery. These writers, with a kindly elasticity of spirit, rose above the billows of party feeling which then seethed and effervesced. They lent to Irish national literature those strokes of wit and genius which must ever serve to perpetuate their memories in popular estimation.

It must suffice to state, that about the year 1842, Mr. and Mrs. Hall's beautifully illustrated work, "Ireland; its Scenery, Character," etc., first appeared. It is richly studded with legends and highly dramatic sketches of graphic national delineation. Indeed, it must almost prove an impossible task to enumerate the various short-lived Irish periodicals published in this country, with the names and productions of writers who have merited honorable mention, connected with this peculiar subject. Although Davis certainly composed many noble, historic and soul-stirring ballads, he has not at all turned his powers of versification to the less exciting subject of mere legendary romance. However, we need only refer to the "Ballads of Ireland," collected and edited by Edward Hayes, for confirmation of the fact, that our legendary literature has been cultivated with great taste and genius by native writers. Among our modern poets and publicists, Richard D. Joyce, Patrick Kennedy, Hercules Ellis, T. D. Sullivan, J. F. O'Donnell, and that modest son of genius, the anonymous author of the "Monks of Kilcrea," deserve highly honorable record. These frequently recurred for inspiration to the clear fount of Irish legendary lore. That the subjects it presents can ever be exhausted is simply impossible, while the sooner what remains is gleaned and garnered, whether in verse or prose, the better chance must exist for the preservation of many interesting popular traditions.

An attempt at instructing the humbler orders of people through the medium of their superstitions has been advocated as one among the most attractive and successful methods for imparting information, while combining knowledge with amusement. It is certain, that many foolish and even barbarous superstitions, habits, or customs, have often been eradicated by means of delicate sarcasm and effective publicity. Rooted prejudices and relics of bygone absurd usages or superstitions, gradually give place to the force of enlightened public opinion and of advancing civilization.

Among the earliest impressions made on youthful minds, the wanderings of our imaginative faculties are sure to leave their impress before judgment can assert the exercise of her corrective powers. To visit the light-hearted peasant's cabin, or to form one of its social circle during long winter evenings, is popularly known by the Irish term *courdheaghing,* which means "assembling." It was the privilege of the present writer, and frequently availed of during his school-boy days. How agreeable to our youthful fancies, the harmless and pleasant jokes of young and old, at these humble and cheerful reunions? How many weird tales of goblin and fairy were told, and to auditors predisposed for receiving most wonderful descriptions and adventures with reverential assent? How many romantic and long-drawn narratives were spun out through the night by some professional story-teller, and which were only varied by the rustic ballad, containing an almost interminable quantity of verses? How often has not the Irish peasant's child fallen asleep, through downright tension of eager desire to follow the story-teller to his *dénouement* of a giant's mishap, and a successful exit of adventure to the youngest son of some imaginary Irish king and queen? The subject matter for such tales beguiled the hours of evening rest, and often of field labor, among our humbler classes. Similar narratives, in prose and verse, once engaged the attention of "high-born ladye" and belted chieftain in the time-honored keep or baronial hall, many ages past, nor can we doubt that such practice of story-telling descended from the old castle and bard, or *shanachie,* to the modern cabin and wandering *bocagh* or *shuler,* who received a bed, bit, and sup, "for God's sake," from the humble but generous peasant, and whose arrival was welcomed all the more, by parent and child, when naturally though rudely gifted with "sweet wit and good invention," like the Irish bards of whom the English poet Spenser writes. Those tales, however, were only intended to while away time agreeably, without making any great demand on the cottier's credulity. Is it therefore wonderful, that early associations and training should accustom the Irish peasant, from his very childhood, to receive romantic impressions, and to cultivate ideality, thinking or talking, asleep or waking?   Hence, likewise, we can scarcely feel surprised that the number of Irish tales and legends is so varied, agreeable, and inexhaustible.

Under the *nom de plume* of Lageniensis, the writer of this paper has already published "Legend Lays of Ireland," and "Irish Folk-Lore: Traditions and Superstitious of the Country, with Humorous Tales." These were designed to preserve some old traditions, popular notions, historic facts, scenic delineations, and local legends. However, they comprise very few selections from a number of similar subjects, gleaned by the writer, yet hitherto unknown to the reading public.

HISTORY OF THE SWASTIKA.

BY MICHEL dE ZMIGRODZKI.

LADIES AND GENTLEMEN : I have prepared a diagram, destined for the Columbian Exposition. On this diagram I have gathered 1360 objects, all bearing a certain symbolic sign belonging to the oldest form of worship.

What was that worship? and according to what rules have I made choice of the objects represented on the diagram ?

The first teacher of mankind was death and the grave. The first and greatest impressions that man was forced to feel were caused by death and by the sudden destruction of beings which live or increase. What must he have remarked in such cases ? He perceived that by death the warmth of the body vanishes, and also that plants grow better in warmth and in the light of the sun, than without it, or in the cold. The present conclusion was that all life on earth depends on warmth and light. He also perceived that warmth, and subsequently fire and flame with light—let us say artificial light in opposition to the natural light of the sun—can everywhere be produced by friction.

On the other hand, I am of the conviction that at first existed the conception of simply Deity, of the one and highest Being, which afterwards degenerated into polytheism. Let us put together all of those primitive conceptions and we shall conclude by the synthesis : that God-Creator of the world, maintains all of his creatures by warmth and light. It is, I think, a simple religious philosophy which was comprehensible to the most primitive human mind.

The most natural necessity of all religious thought is everywhere to form a corresponding symbolism. What thought could be nearer to those men, than to take as a symbol of their supreme Being—of their Creator—the two instruments of fire : the heavenly instrument in the hand of God—the sun ; and

MICHAEL DE ZMIGRODZKI.

the instrument for churn-fire in the hand and for the use of men—the swastika. But the chief characteristic of the sun is its *round* form and *rotation* conformably to the belief of all half-civilized peoples ; consequently, the symbol of the sun should have the same characteristic. Fig. 1.

By rubbing one object on another, the latter must be fixed, because its symbol must also express the fixedness. Figs. 2, 3, 4. It must also be acknowledged that the warmth and fire of the sun are the same as those on earth, because there can be formed a synthetic symbol, in which both these characteristics are expressed together. Fig. 5.

The symbols as for life and increase, as for death and decline have presented themselves in the nature surrounding us, and also our great-grandfathers. The leaves and branches growing upwards, and forming between themselves the angles, apex down, were taken as symbols of the divine life-giving principle. It is the symbol of the Hindu god Vishnu. Fig. 6. The faded leaves hanging down and forming the angles, apex up, became the symbols of destruction, and that is the symbol of the god Shiva. Fig. 7. But both together make one, the almighty God, because there may be made a synthetic symbol by joining both the angles. Fig. 8.

A symbol much expressive of light was presented in the moon, the crescent moon being the symbol of life, decrescent of death, and both together the symbol of God's All-might—the synthesis. Figs. 9, 10, 11, 12.

In the graphic development of every symbol there are always two opposite directions—one, by adding one part to the other towards the formation of an ornament—and the other by taking off one part from another, forming an unclear sign, which, when it loses its intermediate forms, only with risk can be taken for a symbol. Figs. 13, 14, 15, 16, 17.

If we retain all that is preserved above, and consequently make the review of our chart, we will see that this symbol, although in appearance very multiform, may be reduced to some half-dozen original forms. Fig. 18 Swastika, and San-vastika Fig. 19. It is very difficult to enumerate on r.y chart all of the objects marked with this symbol—the contrary would be easier. The same is the case with all representations of the sun. Figs. 20, 21, 22.

Of different cross forms—it is of two trees crosswise posed and spiked with four nails for expressing the fixedness—we have almost an hundred. Figs. 23, 24.

In the ornamentative direction of our symbol occurs for the most part, the doubling or the trebling of the same form. Figs. 25, 26, 27.

If we apply the doubling to other principal forms, and put a swastika on a sanvastika we will receive a form very well-known and named Maltese cross. Fig. 28.

The same doubling of primitive form is presented by the form of a cross that is named Jerusalem cross. Fig. 29.

It is possible that this doubling is not only for ornamental purpose (letter of Max Müller in Schlieman's "Ilios"); that the swastika represents the sun of spring, and the sanvastika, the sun of autumn, because Fig. 30 and Fig. 31 would be the symbols of synthetic signification, as we have seen it above.

The symbols of life and growing, apex downwards, and the contrary symbol, the angle apex upwards, placed together form the Fig. 32, a little ornamented form the Fig. 33 or 34, and redoubled give the form Fig. 35.

If we take it, one up, another down, we have Fig. 36, which, symmetrically re-joined make the well known Fig. 37. It may be re-joined otherwise, Fig. 38. All of these forms are the same symbols synthetic of God's All-might. I may be permitted to prove that the doubtful triçula of India is only a combination of the same two symbols, but it is altered in such degree with ornamentation that it is very easy to be mistaken. Its origin is shown in Fig. 39.

If we would make the combination in this manner, Fig. 40, and afterwards to ornament the single lines and to round the angles, we will have the Fig. 41. If we make this figure otherwise, Fig. 42, and afterwards divide it through the middle, we have Fig. 43. Take the half of this figure and we have a symbol named *lily-flower*, and known in Middle Ages as a symbol of the king's power. Such a symbol we observe on altars in the Greek-Roman epoch. If we would round off the lines and angles in opposite directions, we receive Fig. 44.

Let us take one-half of this figure and we have the hilts of

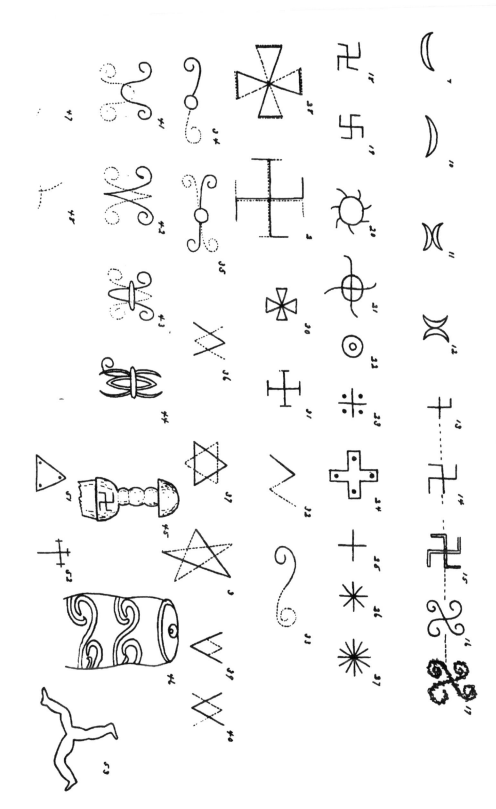

our ancient swords, and the swords of another form are made with the ornamental swastika, as Figs. 45–46. The first quarter of the moon is the symbol of life, the last quarter, or the waning moon, the symbol of death, together it is a synthesis.

It may be of other forms, Fig. 47. If we join the corners we have Fig. 48, a symbol well known in the Middle Ages. It may be also formed otherwise, Fig. 49. The sun in its course of the day ascends, reaches its zenith, and descends. It was symbolized with three points, forming a triangle, apex upwards, Figs. 50–51.

These three points were sometimes designed with three objects forming with their extreme ends the triangles, and such a figure was named *trignetrum*.

The one most used was formed of three human legs. Fig. 53.

Consequently it is to be noted that the triangle, apex upwards, symbolizes the principle of destruction only when it is placed in opposition with another, apex downwards.

The three branches that we usually see on the tops of trees mark also the angle of the sun. If we would make these branches upright we would have the cross named Patriarchal. Fig. 52. Very similar to the cross of Jerusalem, but solely different in their origin. If we exclude from our chart all of the objects that have been mentioned to the present moment, we have only some dozens that are designed also because they are a transition from one form to another—or they present a distinguishable specialty. If we will review our chart in the chronological direction it is necessary to note, that the objects from India, Persia and Asia Minor are most important, because they date back to the highest antiquity; especially those from the excavations of Schliemann.

The objects that are found in the buried city, reaching from twenty-one feet to thirty in depth, date at least 1,500 to 2,000 years B.C. The symbols that we find on those objects prove to us that the population of this city has believed in a Supreme Being, good, humane, giving life to all on the earth and immortality to the human soul. The same is true of Asia Minor. I wish to call your attention to the figures on two vases of lamiros, where you can see very clearly the symbolic signification of angles, apex upwards or downwards. The warrior who is mortally wounded, or is about to

be so, has for his symbol the angle apex upwards, while his
adversary is symbolized with the angle apex downward. The
same symbolism we find in the prehistoric epoch of Europe.
We have the vases of graves signed with this symbol, proving
that the people of those times believed also in immortality of
the soul. The north of Europe gives the richest material
for our symbolism, and especially for the combination of
angles, apex upwards and downward, also for two moons
posed together, and for the thunder, clearly the angles,
apex down and apex up. We have a very important custom
in Ukraine—the day of Palm Sunday—that is named by us
the Sunday of Willow. This tree is the first to be green.
When the people go out of the church, friends meeting together strike one another with a willow branch and repeat a
religious formula.

"Not I, that strike thou, but the willow—in a week went
the great day—the red egg is not far." The red egg mentioned here is the Easter egg. They are painted in many
colors and ornamented with different symbols. Swastikas
and suns symbols prevailing. The same Easter egg we find
in Moravia and in France, but painted only in red. Those
eggs habitually are given as a mark of distinction to the
parents or to the older relatives or distinguished persons in
the village.

When giving this present they say, "Christ is resurrected,"
and the one accepting answers, "In truth He is resurrected."
Afterwards they divide and eat the eggs. In more civilized
society the host and hostess prepare a plate of sliced eggs,
with which they meet each guest at the door, and as they exchange greetings they each eat of the egg. Easter with us is
a day for renewing acquaintance and friendship. The Sunday
after Easter the widow brings the painted eggs to place on the
grave of her husband and bemoans her misfortune. We
have also many other sun festivals. In the country of Cracow
we see the village boys run with flaming torches along the
limits of their fields to protect it from calamity. In Ukraine
the girls and boys dance round a great fire, sometimes jumping over the flame. In Servia the boys stay around the burning
wheel and repeat a religious formula. On the shore of the river
Rhine a wheel is tied round with straw, set on fire and rolled

into the river. It comes on the 24th of June in summer equinoxes — in winter equinoxes we have in Poland the boys carrying round a star formed of paper, singing religious songs. We have in Germany and Poland many houses decorated with swastikas and other sun symbols. But the most remarkable fact is the common ceremony in the country of Cracow where we find all the symbols that we have seen in the form of the letter Z. The two moons placed back to back and forming a synthetic symbol, are nowhere to be found outside of India, France and Scotland.

We begin the historic epoch with numismatic of Asia Minor, where we found a great many of our symbols. Later on the Greek vases we see some very interesting examples. We see there a cross very regular in form, worn by the Goddesses Diana, Athené, and other deities. It is not possible to be mistaken in the symbolic meaning of this sign.

If we will place together all the figurations belonging to the altar and to the column of the Ionic style we will be forced to the conclusion that the chapter of Ionic style is the same as the angle of Vishnu : it is apex downward applied to architecture flattened with the might of architraves. I regard the group labelled Christianity as of very great significance, because here can be seen clearly that in the symbolism of the swastika, there is no meaning of fetichism. They had adored the sun and the fire, not as the Deity, but as the implement in the hand of God, single and omnipotent. Against the phallic interpretation witness can be given by the idol of Venus found in Hissarlik in juxtaposition with Hermaphrodite of Dr. Berthaud's collection in St. Germain. They assume that in early centuries of Christianity swastika was much in use because it is very similar to the cross, and has represented a heathen cross. But I pray every one to analyze the inscription that I have placed under No. 1.[1] We see there the well-known Christian symbols. I do question what could the swastika mean to the heathen here. Now this inscription must be read otherwise—namely, the man, the martyr, who rests here is martyrized for Jesus Christ's sake, whose monogram we see here ; but he regards his death as the victory (the palm) which merits eternity. Then Christ is

---

[1] On Chart in Collection of International Folk-Lore Association.

Alpha and Omega (*Ä-Ω*) is the same God, whom we have
adored from the earliest times under the symbol of swastika,
so we place the monogram of Jesus Christ—our new religious
symbol, in the same rank with the swastika, our old symbol.
I have gathered also a great iconographic series that proves
evidently the application of suns to God and Trinity—and
nobody, even God's Mother, who was, according to Church-
fathers, *Dei para,* has not the right to bear this symbol.
Since the supremacy of the Christian religion over the old
religions of the classic epoch : the swastika and the other
sun's symbols commence to disappear, or rather to become
Christian symbols.

On my chart, I have tried to show, century by century,
in what manner the numismatic of Byram was already
in the VIII century overfilled with swastikas and suns
symbols.

The same process we mark also in the development of
numismatics of Charles the Great and his successors. When
Pope Gregory the Great sent missionaries into England he
gave them the following injunction : "Don't destroy the
heathen temples, but only the idols, and the temples take
for divine service of God. The people accustomed to come
in, will come also afterward to adore a veritable God." This
was the same idea largely practised in the Catacombs. This
idea afterwards became the prescription for the Church and
its ministers. We can see it in the numismatics of the IX
century. Ludwig's pious coins present us the application of
this rule. We see there the perfect heathen temple on Roman
coins, but the idol on the door is destroyed and replaced by
the Maltese cross, which, though a heathen symbol, was easy
to transform into a Christian symbol. On the top of the
temple was placed the cross, and the inscription surrounding
the coin proclaimed the Christian religion ; on the reverse
was : *Ludovicus Rex.* It was by his order that the temples
became the Christian churches. It was a king's medal-
diploma which was going into each of the humblest homes,
proclaiming the order of Regent. When the temples had
disappeared there still remained the heathen symbols that
it was necessary to christianize.

We see in the X. and XI. centuries, in the German numismatic, that the cross well known to us since the earliest time is surrounded with inscription, *Crux Christi*.

What would this inscription signify if there was not any other *Crux* that was not *Christi*, though it was adored by the people. The same process we see in Polish numismatics till the end of the XII century, and in Scandinavia it existed still in the XIII century. Then this symbol vanished, but only officially, while by common people in many countries it remains still in the present century.

I cannot omit a very curious point. The earliest Anglo-Saxon coinage is in many types identical with the Gallic coinage that had not at that time existed for many centuries. Lelevel Joachim, our celebrated numismatist, named it the reappearance of the Gallic type. I cannot agree with him in this expression—reappearance. I think that the numismatic is due to the fact that the Anglo-Saxon even as Gallic people had had the same symbolism. I have said that this symbolism had disappeared in numismatic since the XIII century, but it remains among the common people as a superstition or custom of a religious character until the present time. In the embroideries of the Ukraine people we find very distinctly the different forms of swastika. We find similar embroideries in Brittany, also in the excavations of Schliemann Hissarlick.

We are at the end of our study, and we see that 2000 before Christ, and almost 2000 years after Christ, existed the same religion certified to by the same symbolism. So, for conclusion, this chart informs us that back, of all the worship that we name, or have named, heathen, the principle of every religion is and was the belief in a Supreme Being, Creator and Preserver of the world, but from time to time this primitive religion was observed with more or less rough superstition.

Finally, I ask the question: Is this religion the especial property of the Aryan race? Now, we have swastikas and suns wheel in China and in America also, and the primitive religion of fire gives a very large ethnologic and geographic perspection. I conclude with the hope that some one will make a study of the swastika in America.

TAMING OF THE SHREW, IN THE FOLK-LORE OF THE UKRAINE.

BY PROFESSOR M. DRAGOMANOV.

THE commentators upon Shakespeare have already demonstrated that the illustrious dramatist had taken the subject of his comedy, The Taming of the Shrew, from an Italian novel of Streparola, adding to it details found in analogous novels among Germanic peoples, and which the English writer might well have found in oral tales in existence during his time in England.

A short note upon the people of the Ukraine will not, we believe, be useless. The name Ukraine, or Little Russia, is given to the northern provinces of European Russia, from the river Kouban, at the foot of the Canege, as far as the left bank of the western Boug.

All these provinces are peopled, for the most part, by a Slavic race, belonging to the Russian branch, as the Muscovites or Great Russians, or the White Russians, but having its ethnographic peculiarities and its own original history. There may be as many as nineteen or twenty million Ukrainians. To this race belong also nearly three and one half millions of the population of Galicia, of the Bukovine and of Eastern Hungary, in the Austro-Hungarian Empire.

Notes upon this same theme are found in old texts and in the folk-lore of various European countries; in Spain, Italy, Denmark, France, Germany, as also in Slavic countries, in Russia and in Bulgaria. A German journal of 1829 published a translation of a Persian story with the same plot. It will be readily admitted, from numerous analogies, that the plot of the European stories on this theme has really penetrated into our country from Asia, which should be considered as the country of adages and misogynic tales. But

it must be observed that very often the European imitators
of Asiatic stories surpass the oriental originals in their mis-
ogyny, impelled by a coarse vivacity on the subject, which
the grave humor of the oriental restrains within certain
limits. This is the case with the tales upon the "Taming
of the Shrew." The Ukraine stories upon this theme are interesting, first, because, with the other Slav variants, they
can complete the geographical chain of the traditions of the
subject between Europe and Asia, and also because they show
how an Asiatic tale whose subject has been suggested by the
life of the harems, transported into the middle of our
country, where life is much more simple, adapts itself with
difficulty to the new and different entourage. The details
are shuffled about, less their coherence and sometimes their
common ideas, up to the point where the European story-
teller loses patience, as it were, and does not seize upon the
details or even the plot of the foreign story, unless it is to
create a new tale with an argument different, if not entirely
opposite. The tales having as a theme the Taming of the
Shrew may have penetrated into the Ukraine from Western
Europe as well as from Asia. The state of folk-lore study
in the countries adjacent to the Ukraine does not as yet permit us to pronounce definitely upon that point. We will do
no more here than to sum up the tales on this theme which
have been found in our country, and to indicate their analogies with foreign tales, and we may end with an Ukrainian
variant which may be considered as an original creation ;
made under the impression of these tales and as a foil
against them.

We may recall that in the greater part of the variants of
the story in question the husband commences by chastisement,
inflicted upon animals which will not obey him ; cat, dog,
horse, etc., and that in several of the variants, the correction,
after having borne good results with the young spouse, is then
applied to her mother, who serves as an example to her, and
who even counsels her to acts of disobedience. The episode
of the punishment of the cat, to which the wise young husband first gives his commands, is the principal base of the
Persian variant. This episode is strangely transformed in
the Ukrainian variants. Two of these variants recount to us

24

that the father of the obstinate wife had forewarned the
fiancé that the daughter would do no housework, but that
he had responded, " We have at the house a cat which will do
all the work." The young bride herself ordered the cat to
prepare the dinner ; the cat did not obey ; then the husband
beat it, putting it in a sack which he gave his wife to hold
on her back ; or, in another version, he ordered the woman
to hold the cat by the paws. In the first case, the woman
received the blows upon her back, in the second, the cat
scratched her hands, and when the woman ended by letting
it go, her husband beat her,—a detail which disfigures the
idea of the Persian variant, which is to frighten the lady
without touching her body. After this experience the woman
sets to work herself without trusting to the cat.

In the novel of Streparola, the young husband proposes to
his wife to fight with flails in order to decide which of them
should rule, and which obey. The wife, frightened, promises
obedience, and keeps her promise better when she sees her
husband kill his unruly horse. This punishment of the cat is
changed in another story, where the husband punishes his
wife for infidelity by giving her blows with a cat, which is
cruel as well as wanting in sense. In the Danish tale, the
husband kills the horse during the trip to the house, and the
wife is obliged to finish the journey on foot. In a Gascon
tale, the lady is obliged to carry the saddle of the horse which
her husband has killed as a punishment. In an old German
rhyme the husband, after having killed the horse, saddles
the woman and compels her to carry him thus a mile on the
way, after which the woman promises obedience. A third
Ukrainian variant commences with the question of the husband to the wife." Which of us ought to obey the other ?"
The woman chooses the command. The husband obeys during three years, but after the delay he claims his turn of pre-
eminence, and proposes to the wife to go together to visit some
relatives. Having received the order to hitch up the horse,
the woman puts it head-first in the shafts, and when the horse
pushes the cart backward instead of going ahead, the husband kills it and hitches the woman in its place. It is in
this manner that he arrives at his father-in-law's home,
where he has the complete approval of the old man, who

had suffered all his life from the obstinacy of his wife. The correction of the latter by the wise son-in-law follows.

In Streparola there are two brothers who espouse two sisters, and one spoils his wife by indulgence, while the better advised one corrects his, who would willingly follow the example of her sister. Having learned from his brother the key to the secret, the elder wishes also to employ his means of correction, but his wife derides him, saying that he commenced his work too late. In the Spanish tale there is no mention of two sisters, but of the daughter and mother; the results are the same. A German rhyme shows us also a mother and daughter, the latter of whom wishes to follow the example of the former, but who is corrected, as we have just related, after which comes also the correction of the old woman by her son-in-law.

The Ukraine variants have seized upon the theme of the correction of the mother-in-law, while repeating the episode of hitching up the woman. The father of the young woman who is corrected, enchanted with the result obtained by his son-in-law, sends his own mate to visit him. The son-in-law harnesses his mother-in-law to the plough, and gives her strokes of the whip while he tills the fields. In another variant, the young man forces his wife also to inflict blows upon her mother, and to repeat "Mother, you should not give your daughter lessons in disobedience toward her husband. Besides these tales, the Ukrainian folk-lore offers some satirical poems, which the popular rhapsodists recite with the accompaniment of the kobze or of the lyre, and in which the wicked woman is corrected by hitching her to the cart.

Although oral literature is often described as the mirror of the life and of the soul of the people, it is not to be concluded from the notes which we have just summed up that the customs of the peasants of the Ukraine are coarse, or that the treatment of woman is severe. In reality, the position of woman is relatively rather high in the Ukrainian family. Marriages are usually contracted freely by choice, the share in the agricultural and domestic work between the husband and wife is proportioned to the strength of each, and gives to the woman complete independence within her sphere.

In reading the Ukrainian variants of the tales upon the

Taming of the Shrew, it is seen that we have to deal with a foreign theme upon which the people have seized because it lends itself to pleasantry—doubtless rather coarse,—but whose details even are not familiar to them, from which comes often the confusion in the tales which cannot be explained except by the aid of comparative study. The imagination of the people of Ukraine ended by the creation of a new tale which had arranged quite freely the details of the strange story, and at the same time had changed its dominant idea. This new recital commences by transforming the episode of the refractory animal in the following manner :

There was once upon a time a poor widow with her son. Both were very industrious. The mother had saved money, but it only sufficed to buy a single ox, and not two, which they ordinarily harness together in their country, in order to work the fields with a plough. In spite of this, the son hitched up this ox, and was doing his work in the fields. One day there passed a rich man who lived in the village near by, who saw his difficulty and promised to give him the second ox as a present. But this ox had not been well trained, and had acquired some bad habits, being very obstinate. Nevertheless, by means of patience, the young man succeeded in correcting this ox. Having learned this, the rich man invited the young man to marry his own daughter, who was very greatly spoiled.

The marriage being celebrated, the young couple go to the poor hut of the husband, and only carry as *dot* a very small chest.

The next day, the young wife refuses to work, and will not even carry water and wood to use in cooking. After some hours, the husband and his mother, who had prepared the dinner, commenced to eat, but did not invite the wife, who remained in the corner behind the stove. The dinner ended, the mother and son went out to their tasks. The wife found only a little bread in the house, which she eagerly devoured in her place of refuge. The same thing was repeated at supper. The next day, the wife, who was very hungry, rose early, ran to the fountain and brought water, but hid herself, as before, in her corner. The mother-in-law prepared the dinner and said to her daughter-in-law ; "Come, my daughter, eat the soup, it is made of the water that you brought." But she gave her no meat after the gruel. The third day, the daughter-in-law sees that in that house they do not play with work, arises at dawn, brings water and then wood, but goes back again behind the stove. The mother prepares the dinner again, invites the younger woman to eat, saying "Seest thou, my daughter, this dinner is cooked with the wood and with the water thou hast brought ; thy husband has gathered some millet, and I have made the broth, and I have done the work at the stove. All of us have worked, and all of us may eat of this dinner." The daughter-in-law had learned that in this house they only nourished those who had worked, and set to work herself to perform her domestic tasks conscientiously, becoming gay and gentle. After a time, her father wished to see her. The daughter received him with pleasure, did the honors of the home for him, but did not forget the work, and finally, seeing her mother-in-law approaching, gave to her father a small piece of fur, and invited him to rub it (this is done to make the skin softer). " Look, father," said she, " rub this, because it is the custom in this house only to give those who work something to eat." The father was very much pleased with the transformation of his daughter, and invited her husband to his house, and gave them all sorts of riches, clothing, cattle, ploughs, bees, etc. The couple became rich, but continued good workers.

The same history forms the plot of the tale of the Ukrainian story-teller, Storoyenko. " One should teach an idle person to work by hunger, but not with a hammer."

We see that the popular reciters of this tale agree with St. Paul in the idea that " he who labors not, may not eat," an idea much more humane than that which the " Taming of the Shrew " would teach.

But one cannot have misogynic adages without results, and the histories in which woman is hitched up like a horse are no more. It is not long since we read in a journal of Southern Russia a different fact—the history of a peasant, who, as a punishment for infidelity, had hitched his wife to a cart beside the horse and came thus to market. It is evident that the goodman was inspired by the satiric poetry which he had heard recited, perhaps in the same market-place.

A STUDY ON THE LIGOTNES, POPULAR LATAVIAN SONGS OF ST. JOHN'S EVE.[1]

BY ANDRÉ JURJAN.

A. W. AMBROS, one of the most learned musical investigators of the present century, is the first, so far as I know, who has given out the hypothetical idea of an Aryan Music. In the first volume of his history of music, having found, after comparison, many traits of resemblance between some ancient melodies and some modern European melodies, he says : "That has some importance, if we remember our Aryan origin."[2] For five years since this, this hypothesis has tended more and more to become a verity, so much so that at this time one can really speak of a comparative musical ethnography of all the Aryan races.

In order to be convinced of this, it is sufficient to cite the very learned studies upon the popular songs of different countries of L. A. Bourgault-Ducoudray, Professor of the general history of Music at the Conservatory of Paris ; of P. P. Sokalsky and of A. S. Famitzine, Russian musical investigators and composers. L. A. Bourgault-Ducoudray, in the introduction to the "Thirty Popular Melodies of Lower Brittany," after having shown the striking analogies which exist between ancient music, and the Popular Melodies of different European countries, says as follows:[3] "It appears to be proven to-day that identical characteristics are found in the familiar music of all the people composing the Indo-European group, that is to say, of the Aryan race."

If this is so, is not one led to conclude that a fund of musical knowledge already existed in the cradle common to all

---

[1] Translated from the French by Lieut. F. S. Bassett.

[2] A. W. Ambros, " Geschichte der Musik " B. 1. p. 52.

[3] L. A. Bourgault-Ducoudray, Trente Melodies Populaires de Basse-Bretagne, Paris, Lemonte et Fils, Editeurs, 1885.

the branches of this race, and that it was transmitted to them before their dispersion ?   The hypothesis of an Aryan Music comes also to confirm the conclusions of modern science in all that touches upon the common origin of all the Aryan people. The study of popular songs brings to the knowledge of Aryan unity, a new argument—" the musical argument."

This opinion is confirmed a little later by P. P. Sokalsky,[1] in a work, "Popular Russian Music," and by A. S. Famitzine in his musical and ethnographic study, "The Ancient Indo-Chinese Gamut in Asia and in Europe."[2]

It is to be regretted that the popular Latavian songs should not have entered into the study of comparative popular songs.   But little is found there concerning the popular Lithuanian songs.   Nevertheless, it is known what importance the Lithuano-Latavian nation has under the mythological and linguistic aspects for the ethnography of the Aryan race.[3] Would it not be the same in the musical domain ?

Here is why I have ventured to hope that the observations which I have made upon a part of the popular Latavian songs may not be without interest for Ethnographists.   For all time, the Latavian people has passed for a singing people. And this is with reason.   During a dozen years, I have gathered about two thousand popular songs, which demonstrates that the life of the Latavian is inseparable from song.   There is no event in life, no phenomena of nature, which has not its songs.

The Latavian people comprehend under the name of popular song, " *Daina* " or "*trantas dziesma,*" the intimate union of poetry and of music.   Also in Latavia do we find that which Bourgault-Ducoudray has found in Lower Brittany ; " the *notion* of a poetry repeated or recited does not exist; all verse is sung, if not to a very striking melody, at least with a musical intonation which may be written down."[4]

According to the general character of the melodies, the Latavian songs may be divided into two groups.   In the first, one may class the melodies in which are sung the various

---

[1] P. P. Sokalsky, "Musique Populaire Russe," Kharkoff A. Darri, 1888.

[2] A. S. Famitzine, "L'ancienne Gamme Indo-Chinoise," St. Petersburg, 1888.

[3] Henri Wissendorff, "Legendes Mythologiques Lataviennes," Extrait de la *Revue des Traditions Populaires* T, iii. May '92.

[4] L. A. Bourgault-Ducoudray, op. cit. p. 9.

couplets of four verses, which have not between them any close connection as to sense. These are the songs of the seasons, of the shepherd, cradle songs, songs of different ceremonies and of work in general, always added to festival, accompanied with "disputes" sung. They have a rudimental character, like a declamation set to music. The most of these songs are executed by a solo with a chorus, divided into two parts. The chief of the chorus " teiceja " intones the first verse of the couplet ; after the second verse, the chorus joins in the song ; a part of the chorus " vilceji " (the holders,) maintain a deep note like an organ stop, while the other part "locitaji " (the balancers) repeat in a sharp tone a phrase of several notes, like a swinging of the sounds. To the second group belong the melodies in which are executed songs of many couplets of four verses, united by a common sentiment ; therefore, in the romance, complaints, ballads, etc., their character is more melodious, more tender. They are executed either as a solo, or in chorus, in union, or in octaves. From the first of these groups, I have chosen at first the " ligotnes," or songs of the fine season, and here is the extent of my observation after the examination.

Those of the popular Latavian songs in which such verse is accompanied by a refrain, " ligo," are called " Ligotnes," " songs of Ligo " or of St. John.

What is Ligo or Liga ? This question has particularly occupied the modern explorers of Latavian mythology. Up to the last dozen years it was never doubted that it was the divinity of joy, of concord, of love, of the ancient Latavians divinity honored by a feast at the summer solstice, with special songs, called " Ligotnes," or *Ligo-dziesmas.* During these later years this notion has encountered some contradictions. A. Bielenstein, in his article, " Feast of the St. John of the Latavians,"[1] after having observed the ceremonies and the songs executed on St. John's Eve, says that he has found many mythological traits ; but he doubts the existence of gods, and above all of this god "Ligo." After having compared some verses of the " ligotnes " with those of the song of the " Uhsin," finds that " Ligo," as " Uhsin," is a solar divinity,

---

[1] *Ballische Monatschrift*, B. 23, 1874, 1, 46.

and that Liga is not, then, any other than the beautiful "soule," the sun.

Besides, Mr. A. Famintzine, one of the most remarkable explorers of the day of Slav mythology, expresses himself in favor of the existence of a Latavian divinity "Ligo."[1] In his exploration "Divinities of the Ancient Slavs," in demonstrating the existence of the Slav divinity "Lago," he compares her with the divinities of the Lithuano-Latavian people, "Lado," "Lido," or "Ligo" and finds that all these, divinities of the same nature, of concord, of spring, of joy, of love, correspond, according to the sense of their names, entirely to the "Corcordia" of the ancient Italians, and by this approach the divinities "Bona Dea," "Maius" and "Maia," "Faunus" and "Fauna," to whom were rendered the honors upon the approach of springtime, up to St. John's or St. Peter's day, that is to say, during the summer solstice. But if the existence of the Slav divinity "Lado," was really shown by M. Famintzine, it would be the same with the Latavian Divinity, "Ligo" or "Liga." . . .

Whatever may be the belief about the name "Liga" or "Ligo," no one will deny that the refrains "Ligo," which are closely bound to a Latavian solar cult, which had its origin in a remote antiquity, that their origin must be sought at the epoch when the Latavians, as all ancient people, adored the sun as a beautiful divinity, and honored her at all of its phases, by songs and by feasts. The Latavian poetry is a proof of this. The Latavians honored the summer sun by the Ligotnes, during the fine season, that is to say, in the month of June, season which they still terminate now by a great feast on St. John's eve.

If this solar cult, inseparable from various ceremonies and songs, has been preserved up to this time among the Latavian people, is not one led to conclude that melody, which exists inseparably from poetry and ceremony, may also have been preserved up to the present? May one suppose that the melodies of the Ligotnes, in being transmitted from mouth to mouth, may not have been exposed to some changes among people who, during several centuries, have been exposed to

[1] "Divinités des Anciens Slavs," par A. Famintzine, t.i.-253-277. St. Petersburg, 1884.

the powerful influence of the Catholic chant, of the Lutheran choral, and entirely, during the last half century, to the popular German songs in the schools ?

Before deciding this question, let us see the conclusions of the most noted investigators in the studies upon the popular music of various countries.

Mr. R. Westphal, in his studies upon Greek music, says :— " The most ancient music is from its origin as old as poetry, for the most ancient poetry was everywhere sung."

P. P. Sokalsky, in his studies upon Russian popular song, demonstrates that the most ancient popular melodies are those which are connected with the ceremonies of a pagan cult and that their origin dates back to an epoch when the music of the church of the middle ages was not known, and that they are based more or less upon the tetra-chord system of the Greeks.

M. Bourgault-Ducoudray, in the introduction of his collection, "Trente Melodies populaires de Basse Bretagne" says : " I have formed the conviction that the facts which are pointed out to us as characteristic of the music of the ancient people are found to-day, existing and flourishing in popular songs. And why is it thus ? It is because for five thousand years, it is very probable that popular melodies have changed very little. There is among men of the same race, a common fund of sentiments which is transmitted and perpetuated without modification. If their sentiments have never varied in their essence, one cannot see why popular melody, which is the spontaneous and instinctive expression of them, should have changed. To recover in antiquity certain musical modes of Lower Brittany at the present day, we must go back to an epoch anterior to Homer." " In ancient Greece," says M. Gevaert," soon after Homer, the intimate tie which binds music and poetry together commenced to yield. It is not so in Brittany, where the notion of a poetry dictated or recited does not exist."

I have already remarked above that it is not the same also in Latavia.

Finally, A. S. Famintzine, in his ethnographic and musical study " The Indo-Chinese gamut in Asia and Europe," in trying to show that the above-named gamut was already known

in the cradle of all people of the Indo-European race, says,
that it is the ceremonial chant, which was preserved by the
people as a sacred mystery, that formed within the limits of
popular life the domain which is the least accessible to influence from without ; that in that chant, we must seek for
the remains of the ancient days, and that it is capable as well
from its verbal as from its musical side, of revealing to the explorer some distinct phases, and to light up the profound
shades of centuries gone by.[1]

As it is averred that the Solar Latavian cult, accompanied
by the " Ligotnes " is one of the ancient traditions which has
been preserved from centuries past up to our days, among the
people ; then, from all that precedes, one may suppose with
good reason, that if there be anything of ancient Latavian
music preserved up to our days, it ought in every reason to be
the melodies of the " Ligotnes."

This is the reason for making a detailed examination of them.

We know, by the history of the different people, that the
more the condition of the people is primitive, the simpler, the
poorer is the scale of the intervals occurring in the chants,
the more simple and more monotonous are the melodic con-
tours of the airs (A. Famintzine). That is to say, that the
scales used in popular song are only developed little by little.

In relying upon the idea of a progressive development of
the scale used in popular song, I have, in a study upon
popular Latavian music published thirteen years ago, in the
weekly Latavian journal " Balos " (The Voice), classed according to their age, in three epochs, the popular Latavian
melodies.

To the first epoch, a prehistoric one, I have referred the
melodies whose range does not pass beyond the interval of a
fourth ; to the second epoch, or pre-christian, or middle age
section, I have assigned the melodies whose ambition extends
from a fifth to an octave in interval, and in which are recognized the gamuts used in antiquity ; to the third epoch, the
modern, the melodies based upon the modern major and minor
gamut, in which traces are already found of the influence of
harmony with sensible effect.

That this classification is not without reason is confirmed

---

[1] .A. S. Famintzine, " L'Anciene gamme Indo-Chinoise."

later by P. P. Sokalsky,[1] who, without knowing of any article in his study upon Russian song, classes the Russian melodies in three epochs, also according to their antiquity, designating them by the names : 1st, Epoch of the fourths ; 2d, Epoch of the fifths, and 3d, Epoch of the thirds.   Except the first, to which he refers, the melodies represent an incomplete phase of the gamut, called Chinese, without limiting its scope ; this classification corresponds exactly to mine.   This accidental coincidence makes me believe the more in the correctness of such a classification.

According to this classification, nearly all the melodies of the " Ligotnes " belong to the first and the second of these epochs.   There are two hundred of them, counting all the variations.

The half of all these melodies whose range extends to fourths, belong to the first epoch.   According to the order of the intervals which form the fourths, the groups may be arranged in three categories ; the melodies—1st, of the Dorian fourths ; 2d, of the Phrygian ; 3d, of the Lydian fourths.[2] The most primitive, and consequently the oldest of this epoch, are the melodies (if one may so call them) composed of two sounds extending to major seconds.   In comparing the variants, one sees that the melodies of two sounds take their origin in those of two degrees.   The scale of two degrees, by adding the third degree—1st, by a half tone below ; 2d, by a half tone above ; and 3d, by a tone above or below, is transformed into thirds from a major second, Dorian, Phrygian, and Lydian thirds.

In the same way the melodies of three degrees, constructed upon their three species of thirds, by associating with them the fourth degree, are transformed into fourths, Dorian, Phrygian, and Lydian.   One sees by this that in many melodies, having an extent of fourths, this fourth degree is very seldom found, and only plays the role of appoggiatura.

The melodies of the second epoch, whose range extends from the fifths to the octave, and even as far as the ninth, come in their turn, from the melodies of the second epoch. In order to be convinced of this, it is only necessary to com-

[1] P. P. Sokalsky—" Musique Populaire Russe. "
[2] Greek nomenclature.

pare the variants, which show that in several examples the 5th and 6th degrees, added to the flat or sharp, only play the role of appoggiatura. The Dorian and Phrygian fourth, in progressively joining to themselves the 5th, 6th, 7th and 8th degrees from the Dorian and Hypodorian octave, the Lydian fourth forms, in the same way, the Lydian octave with the 7th degree, sometimes natural, sometimes changed.

In designating the melodies by the names : Dorian, Phrygian and Lydian. I had at first only their range in view. As to their modality (pitch) it is another thing. While the song only extends over fourths, the determination of the mode is very difficult, because the scales of four degrees may be referred to several modes. Nevertheless, following the rests and the final note of the melodies, the mode may be discovered, although approximately.

After having observed from this point of view, the melodies of the first epoch, it is seen that those of the Dorian thirds and fourths end, for the most part, on the first degree, that is, the final tone of the Dorian or Mixolydian mode ; when they end on the third, they should be referred to the Hypophrygian, or as it is wished, to the Phrygian mode.

The melodies of the thirds, and of the Phrygian fourths, when they end on the 2d degree, this is the final cadence of the Dorian mode ; in ending on the 1st degree, they are in the Phrygian mode.

The melodies which are based on the tierce and on the Phrygian fourth, end partly on the 1st degree—this is the Lydian mode ; part of the 2d degree, then they belong to the Phrygian mode.

If the determination of the modes to which the melodies of the first class belong is so doubtful, the melodies of the second epoch is now easier.

Among the melodies of this epoch there are no examples of melodies constructed upon Dorian fifths. In one example, having a Dorian sixth as its extent, the fifth degree is absent ; while, as it ends on the second degree, it belongs to the Hypolydian mode. Two melodies built upon the complete Phrygian octave, and on the third degree. This is the Hypophrygian mode, or rather the mode of the major gamut reversed.

The melodies of the Phrygian (or Hypodorian) fifth, may be referred to the Phrygian mode, if they end on the first degree, having the fourth degree as a tonic; they belong to the Hypophrygian mode; if they terminate on the first degree having the fifth as dominant, ending on the second and third degrees, they belong to the Dorian and Lydian mode. When the melodies of the Phrygian fifth unite into the sixth and seventh, degrees in the melodies of this class, are the minor sixth and seventh, and as the most of them end on the first degree, having as dominant the fifth degree—this is the true Hypodorian mode (the minor mode without an *apparent* note). Some melodies of this kind end on the second degree. This would be the final cadence of the Mixolydian. There is also a representative melody of the Dorian mode of Westphal.

The melodies having the Lydian fifth and sixth for their range, for the most part, and on the first degree, and belong, according to the *role,* to the first degrees they play; to Lydian or Hypophrygian modes; when they end on the second degree, having sometimes for twice the fifth degree, sometimes for dominant the sixth, they are Phrygian and Hypodorian. The melodies based on the Lydian octave, with the seventh degree altered by cutting out the octave, and by the final note on the first degree, belong partly to the Lydian mode, with the changed seventh degree, or to the reversed major gamut, partly to the Hypophrygian mode. Ending on the fourth degree, they represent the major mode or the Hypophrygian with a changed fourth degree. Those of the melodies which have for a range the Lydian octave with a natural seventh degree, by cutting out the fifth degree of the octave, and with final note on the first degree, belong to the Hypophrygian mode with the fourth degree changed or to the major mode; if they end on the second degree they represent the Phrygian mode.

There are almost no melodies of the third modern epoch; if, however, modes of this epoch are found in some of them, there are only melodies of the preceding epochs, completed because of the accompaniment of the harmonica, an instrument now very much used in Latavia.

Three-fourths of all the melodies do not pass beyond the

exact fifths; then come, progressively *diminishing*, the melodies of six, seven, eight degrees, and a few of nine degrees.

According to their modality, the greater part of them belong to the Hypodorian mode, and then to the Hypophrygian (or mode of the major gamut) *reversed* because of the instability of the *roles* of the fourth and fifth degrees. These two modes, says Bourgault-Ducoudry, "are exactly those which, in antiquity, characterize the cult of the worship of the inspiring gods of music, Apollo and Bacchus."

The Hypodorian, by its character of serenity, of virility and of nobility, belongs eminently to the cult of Apollo, god of light and of harmony, which symbolize the idea of order, of justice, of moral law, the superior and immaterial spirit which does not change, and which does not perish. The Hypophrygian mode, on the contrary, a mode of enthusiasm and of Bacchic delirium, was consecrated to the dithyrhamb, and reserved for the cult of Bacchus, father of joy and inventor of the vine, who symbolized physiological life, temperament, passions, the principle of the material and exterior phenomena, which undergo in nature continual variations and incessant transformations.[1]

The striking analogies which exist between the qualities attributed to the gods Apollo and Bacchus, and those attributed to " Ligo " or " Liga," divinity of joy, of concord, of spring, of light, of song, of love, as well as the co-incidence of the modalities consecrated to their cult, do they not bear testimony eloquently in favor of the existence of the Latavian divinity, " Ligo " or " Liga " ?

The expressive character of the other modes used in the melodies of the " Ligotnes," excepting the exact intervals, do not correspond precisely to the modern well-arranged system. The other intervals are often executed, sometimes a little higher, sometimes a little lower. The distance of the minor third is sometimes divided into two equal parts; that is to say, in intervals of three-quarters of a tone.

Chromatism is wanting in the Ligotnes. If one encounters it in some melodies in the same degree, sometimes natural, sometimes altered, it is because of the application

---

[1] Bourgault-Ducoudray, Trente Melod., pop. De Basse Bretagne, p. 12.

·of the system to which the ancients gave the name of *im-movable system*. There are found in these melodies an example of the scale of nine notes, used among the ancients under the name of the perfect little system or of the united system, as well as specimens, representing the incomplete diatonism of the scale called "Indo-Chinese." There are three melodies having as a range the correct fourths, where the third degree does not figure. There is one of these of the extent of the exact fifth, where only the first, fourth and fifth degrees are used (this is the scale designated by P. P. Sokalsky as the most primitive); besides this, all the melodies constructed upon the Lydian octave have the character of the Indo-Chinese gamut. In many examples the third and the seventh degree do not appear at all, while among the others they are seldom found, and only as accidentals.

As to the rhythmic point of view, the melodies of the " Ligotnes " are somewhat uniform. As the greater part of the " Ligotnes " are formed of short verses, the melodies of these are constructed in a system equal to double time, broken by rests in the middle and at the end of the song ; the people change, according to circumstances, the same airs from a measure of two beats to one of three. This is seen in several variants.

The periodical construction of the melodies is not always submitted to a pattern ; on the contrary, there are sufficient examples in which the musical phrases are freely composed of two, three, of four or five, of six, and of seven measures, so much so, that according to the number of measures, and repeats comprised therein, there are melodies of four, six, seven, eight, nine, ten, eleven, twelve, fourteen, sixteen, eighteen measures.

Although we are permitted to believe that popular music knows no harmony, nevertheless, the " Ligotnes " show some trace of it ; being executed by solo with chorus, they form harmonies, although simple and rudimentary.

It results from all that precedes, that the melodies of the " Ligotnes " offer much of interest for the ethnographic explorer. Here are found all the things which are signalized as belonging to the music of the ancients, and in this they entirely confirm the conclusions of preceding investigators, which I have mentioned above. Besides, in giving a picture of the progressive development of the musical scale they testify that before the epoch of the fourths (tetra-cord) there was an anterior epoch, when the primitive people only used the scale of three and even of two degrees in their songs. This is, also, confirmed by many other categories of ceremonial songs of the Latavian people, and, without any doubt, of many other people.[1]

The simultaneous presence of melodies of the "Ligotnes" constructed on the primitive scales of 3, 4 and 5 degrees, and of many other categories of Latavian songs, constructed upon modern major and minor modes, whose extent surpasses the octave, among a cultivated people who are acquainted with the plain chant of the Catholic church for six centuries, the Lutheran choral for two, and all the knowers of modern music since a half century, induces us to believe that the "Ligotnes" take their origin at a prehistoric epoch.

The detailed study of all which precedes, which is supported by original songs, is found in my work : "Materials for Popular Latavian Music," vol. 1, "Ligotnes," which will shortly be edited by the Latavian Musical Society of Riga.

---

1 I have at hand a Russian melody of the ceremony of the expulsion of death, set to music, by the government of Kowake in Russia, where only three degrees of Dorian thirds figure at all.

25

GENERAL SKETCH OF THE LATAVIAN PEOPLE.

BY HENRY WISSENDORFF.

IT is for the first time, that the Latavian people presents itself in a congress of the learned world. It has been living hitherto in a quiet undisturbed mood, and has rarely been taken notice of. Yet it deserves a greater consideration, to which it is entitled not only by its present geographical situation and importance as the "Russian Holland," but still more particularly by its venerable old age, the consideration it enjoyed in times past, its language, traditions, and the position it has a right to as a member of the noble Aryan race.

Before entering upon the proper subject I intend to treat here, I must observe for a better intelligence, that I understand under "Latavian" people the same people which nowadays the west-European tongues have generally indicated by the erroneous denomination of "Lettonian" or "Lettish" people. I propose the designation "Latavian" as the more correct.

The ancient name of "Latovici" is still to be found involved in that analogical of "Latwieshi," as the Lettonians or Latavians call themselves. As to their country, they call it "Latwija" and the portion of the government of Witebsk (Inflantia), inhabited by this people, bore of late the denomination of Lothavia australis. According to these facts, we have the root *Lat* (= Lot), but none "Let." It is more correct, therefore, to name the people the *Latavians* and the country *Latavia*.

When the German conquerors had landed on the banks of the Düna (Daugawa), they at first came in contact with the Lives. The latter called the neighboring Latavians in their tongue "Lettli," their country "Lettma."[1] That denomination was heard by the Germans, who adopted and spread it.

[1] J. A. Sjoegren—Livonian-German Dictionary. St. Petersburg, 1861.

LATAVIAN NATIONAL COSTUME.

If we are to throw a glance upon the past of the Latavian people, we find them, so far as the oldest informations reach, as the aborigines of the much praised amber-coast.

The bulk of the people resided between the Duna (Daugawa) and the Vistula (Visla), comprehending the Latgalians, Letonians, Zemgalians, Lithuanians, Yatwingians, Russians (that Lithuano-Latavian branch, which was comprised under the name of Russians *before* the year 862.[1]), Porussians (Prussians), Zemians (Sembi), etc.

We may accept it for sure, that the trading Phœnicians did know the Baltic amber-coast, and it is a well-stated fact, that the Greeks were already able at Homer's time (about 1,000 years B. C.), to appreciate the electron coming from the Baltic coast. Herodotus, Tytheas, Plinius, *Tacitus,* Ptolemæus, Cassiodorus, *Wulfstan,* etc., give us more or less valuable enlightenment on the amber-coast, the situation of which the Phœnician merchant describes to the Greek as, "lying at the world's end," far beyond the pillars of Hercules.

We encounter here the Lithuano-Latavian peoples under different names, sometimes general, sometimes partial : Guttians, Aistians (not to be confounded with the actual Finnish Ehsts), Ostians, Wendes, Guddians, Sudenians, Galindians, etc., till at historical times the whole dissolves itself in the name of Prusso-Lithuano-Latavians.

It is only with the appearance of the German knights of the cross, that we obtain more precise information of the country and the people from the different chronicles which have been hitherto preserved. With the arrival of the Germans, however, ends the happy, independent period of the Latavian peoples, who, under the guidance of their Krives (Krihwi— the Latavian pontiffs), had attained a considerable wealth. This circumstance hastened their ruin. Their riches in amber, gold and silver, fine horses and well cultivated-acres (the renown of which is still celebrated in the old Latavian and Lithuanian *daïnas* or national songs), were too tempting for the covetous and rapacious German knight-robbers. Thunderclouds, pregnant with mischief, gathered over the heads of

[1] Cf. N. Krostomaroff, " Natchalo Russi." (The commencement of Russia). St Petersburg.

the inoffensive and kind-hearted race. Hard times began for the once so happy population of the Baltic country.

The knights of the Teutonic order raged in a frightful manner from the Duna to the Vistula, destroying the bloom of the Prusso-lithuano-latavian race, and plunging the population into mischief and slavery.

At the present day we stand before the remainders of that once so great and important nation : these are the Lithuanians and Latavians (Lettonians), counting altogether 4¼ millions souls, of which 3¼ millions fall upon the first and 1¼ million upon the latter dialect. My present communications shall refer exclusively to the latter portion of the population, inhabiting the governments of Sud-Livonia, Coorland and a portion of the government of Witebsk.

The Latavian population amounts :

In the government of Coorland (Kurzeme) on 27,285 square kilometers........ .	555,000 souls.
In the government of Livonia (Widzeme) on 22,800 square kilometers........	490,000 "
In the government of Witebsk (Inflantija) on 14,000 square kilometers..........	255,000 "
In the other governments of Russia and in foreign countries ca................	70,000 "
	Total 1,370,000 "

The increase of the population amounts to 1–1½ per cent. which yields an annual accretion of 13,000 to 15,000 souls. As a certain percentage denationalize themselves by mixing up with the Germans, Poles and Russians, we accept the least cipher of accretion, and thus obtain for the space of ten years an increase of 130,000 souls ; in addition to this the above said number, 1,370,000 souls, gives a total of 1,500,000 souls.

The number would be far more considerable if the people had not been obliged to undergo such hard times.

When the German robber-knights had invaded the Latavian country under the pretext of religion, which, however, they took very little care of, a time of hardship began for the Latavian nation, who had been deserving a better fate. Their nobility was crushed and annihilated by fire and sword, the people robbed of their native property and reduced to servitude. For full 600 years the Germans have been feeding on the sweat of the Latavian peasantry, suppressing mercilessly that most important civil community.

At last dawned the nineteenth century. Garlieb Merkel ([1]) (1769–1850), although himself a German, undertook the defence of the scoffed human rights with fiery eloquence and was the first to induce the abolition of the bondage, which then was proclaimed in 1820. Since then the Latavian people enjoy personal freedom, but the country their ancestors were robbed of has not been returned to them—they are obliged to buy it with their hard-earned money from their ancient oppressors.

Let us now consider the Latavian in reference to his creed, mode of life, activity and business.

By far the greatest part of the Latavian people belong to the Lutheran confession ; the 255,000 souls in the government of Witebsk and about 30,000 in Coorland are Catholics. Since the year 1845 there are in Latavia about 70,000 Greek-orthodox. Of the Protestant sects the Baptists are the most numerous.

Actually all Latavians know how to read printed books (in their tongue, with Gothic characters) and half of them might be able to write (with Latin characters). Of late years there is a considerable movement for printing books also with Latin characters.

The following table gives an approximative idea of the state of popular instruction in the Latavian-Baltic provinces in comparison with the whole of the Russian Empire.

In Livonia are about 1850 popular schools with............................	82,000 children
In Coorland are about 608 popular schools with........................ ...	39,000 children
In Latavia there is one school to about...	425 inhabitants
In Russia " " " "	2,500 "

([1]) Cf. Garlieb Merkel (a) Die Vorzeit Lieflands, Berlin, 1798, 2 vols. This work is very important for studies of the Latavian nationality, customs, situation, etc. (b) Die Letten in Liefland, Leipzig, 1800. (c) Wannem Ymanta, a Latavian tale, Leipzig, 1802. Cf. Imanta und Kaupo by Linde, Moscow, 1891. (d) Sitten Lieflands aus der ersten Haelfte des XVI Yahrh, (in Wieland's Mercur XI, page 293). (e) Dichtergeist und Dichtung unter den Letten, (Mercur V, page 29), etc.

In Latavia upon 1,000 inhabitants...... 115 scholars
     among these, girls 52
In Russia upon 1,000 inhabitants....... 26 scholars
     among these, girls $6\frac{1}{2}$

These ciphers speak an eloquent language and raise the Latavian people on a level with the most learned nations on earth. Besides this, the Latavian is an excellent pedagogue and therefore the popular schools may boast of very satisfactory results; and indeed they are proceeding with so much success, that their scholars are not seldom admitted to the middle classes of gymnasiums.

It is quite different in Russia, where the popular schools still are on a very low degree of development, the success being far from satisfactory, and the pedagogical forces very weak. Besides, we must take in consideration the proportionately small number of popular schools, of which there are in European Russia, excluding Finland, the Baltic provinces, Poland and the Caucasus, about 18,027. Considering the wide extension of the Empire, there is consequently one school upon 231 square werst, respectively upon 14 villages. It is therefore no wonder, that of 1,000 boys only 29 get instruction. As a natural consequence, a great many Russian recruits are not able to read and to write, while in the Latavian provinces such a case does not occur at all, or at least very rarely.

In European Russia $5\frac{1}{2}$ million roubles are spent on popular instruction, of which sum the Government allows only about $12\frac{1}{2}$ per cent, the rest being afforded by communities, territories, churches, and private persons. It is easily to be conceived, that with so insufficient a provision the popular schools can but poorly prosper. The sum appointed for popular instruction ought to be twenty-fold larger if the popular schools are to attain a level worthy of the beautiful wide Empire.

In the Latavian provinces, Livonia and Coorland, the communities entertain their schools by themselves, not even being granted any subvention in behalf of the popular schools, on which they spend considerable sums.

The desire of knowledge of the Latavians is to be admired;

the frequentation of schools by the youth very zealous ; the esteem Latavian pedagogues enjoy in the whole Russian Empire is equally remarkable.

Latavian professors, lecturers, teachers, are employed at nearly every Russian University and Gymnasium, to say nothing of elementary schools. In art and science there are those who belong to the first celebrities and authorities (I cite only the eminent bacteriologist on the Imperial Institute for Experimental Medicine at St. Petersburg, his Excellence Professor emer. E. Zemmer, and the famous painter, Professor Fedders.[1]

In consequence the Latavian nation not only yields the Russian Empire the best renowned soldiers, but besides a considerable number of learned men, who contribute to enlighten the immense Russian Empire in the interior, and to carry its fame over its boundaries.

Concerning the Latavian popular schools, it is very much to be feared, that in future the popular instruction will keep decreasing as the Russian Government, misled by the erroneous desire for Russification, has given orders to introduce as school language the Russian instead of the Latavian.

The peasants' children going to school for no more than three winters, it is easy to understand that they will leave it in nearly the same condition as they entered it, instruction being given them in a language they will not be able to understand. It is to be hoped that the Russian Government will soon become aware of its error and retract a prescription, which is a sin unto God and mankind.

Diligence, perseverance and a strong sense of morality, under the shelter of the mighty Russian eagle, visibly increases the prosperity of the Latavian nation. Whilst in the first moiety of the present century they were not entitled to call their own a single parcel of land, they have now appropriated by sale about three-fourths of all the peasants' land.

The principal occupation of the Latavian has been and still is husbandry, which they have brought to an important degree of development.

In spite of the soil not being particularly fertile, nay, in a

---

[1] Dr. Berg, Director of the Argentinian National Museum, Buenos Ayres, etc.

great many places quite the contrary, yet by way of a more rational economy the Latavian obtains considerably better results than the Russian husbandman from his more productive soil,—the black-earth regions not being excepted.

Latavian agriculturists are therefore searched for by Russian proprietors as well on account of their sobriety and sureness, as for their skill.

Trade and industry are equally developing at the present time, especially the mill and spinning trade most certainly going to prosper by virtue of the wealthy and skilled miller corporation. In Livonia and Coorland the more considerable mills, for the most part moved by hydraulic force, have been transformed into manufacturing establishments, where they not only fabricate different sorts of meal, peeled grain and barley, but where they also spin, and at times weave and full. If the progress would be the same in all branches, the result might be called brilliant.

It is with a particular zeal that the little Latavian nation has taken to navigation, they had already been successful navigators before the arrival of the Germans in the 12th century, sometimes in alliance with the Normans, whom, the Zemgalians, Coors, Warego-Russians and Zemlanders, had supplied with rather a considerable number of auxiliaries, sometimes warring them, whereat they often conquered and devastated Swedish and Danish cities and provinces. It seemed as if the following 600 years of servitude, the so-called bondage to the Germans, had suffocated all nautical inclinations, but this supposition, however, proves false. Now-a-days Latavian mariners are as well known in the Russian sea-service as throughout the world. Next the Finlanders, they rule the cabotage-navigation in the Baltic Sea; but they also possess proportionally a great many vessels for transatlantic navigation. At the end of December, last year, there were registered in the different Baltic harbors about 200 large Latavian vessels, together of about 50,000 registered tons.[1] Of this number six vessels belong to the Latavian navigation company, "Austra." The said company was founded in 1882 at the suggestion of the late Christian Waldemar, an expert in naval affairs. He was also the founder of the excellent Russian

---

[1] Cf. List of sailing vessels by A. Bandrewitch. Riga, 1896.

naval schools, and one of the most active promotors of the Russian commercial navigation. It is to him that the "Imperial Company for promotion of the Russian commercial navigation" is indebted for its origin. Owing to the naval-schools, founded according to a system of Waldemar's invention, Russian navigation and ship-building have been developing during the last decennary in unexpected dimensions. Those schools will become an immense benefit to the Russian empire, provided that the Russian Government by means of erroneous designs of Russification will not be hitting the root of the mighty oak, causing it to dry up, if not to fall.

The mode of life of the Latavians is mostly solid and regular, in conformity to their serious, trusty character. Hospitality is an ancient legacy of their ancestors. It will give you an approximate idea of the sociable life of this people and his busy mind, if I shall tell you, that his various forms of activity utter themselves in more than half a thousand different, officially-sanctioned, companies and societies. Of these about 317 fall upon Livonia, and 200 upon Coorland. The above, mentioned reports depend on the following, however, low-ciphered historical dates :

	In Livonia.	In Coorland.
Charity Societies	42	28
Mutual Assistance Societies...........	17	30
Societies for Agriculture and Cultivation of Bees.	10	20
Consumption Societies.....................	2	12
Saving and Pawn-banks ⎫ Industry Companies ⎭	22	43
Mutual Insurance Companies.....................	184	31
Singing and Music Societies.......................	33	24
Temperance Societies.............................	3	5
Social Societies.................................	4	7
Total...................... 517	317	200

Besides the nearly daily occurring foundation of new companies some associations, as for instance, the numerous funds for survivors, have not been mentioned, nor have I noticed the several Latavian associations in all the other parts of Russia.

In America there are also Latavian societies, of which the Philadelphia Latavian (Lethonian) Society is known to me. As to the music and singing companies, I must observe, that the above-mentioned number of officially-sanctioned societies does not nearly give an exact idea of the real state of things. In Livonia and Coorland, not counting the Witebsk territory, there are more than 1000 communities, and with regard to the great predilection the people have for singing and music, we might accept at least one singing-choir upon every three communities. Thus we have the considerable number of about 330 singing choirs, a cipher rather too small than too high, as may already be concluded from the sole fact that about 150 choirs composed of 3000 songsters and songstresses were partaking in the third Latavian singing feast at Riga in the year 1888.

To get an approximate idea of the sphere of activity of a social Latavian society, let us briefly remember the progress of the Riga Latavian Society (Rigas Latwieshu Biedriba). Founded in 1868, this society may be considered the mother of all the Latavian societies. Arisen from a modest origin, this exemplary association has become one of the most remarkable institutions under the careful guidance of most capable men. It counted 931 members at the end of the last year. The successful development of the society proves itself by no less than nine different commissions :

1. Scientific commission (Zinibu Kommisya).
2. Commission for the publishing of useful books.
3. Musical commission.
4. Theatrical commission.
5. Orderly commission.
6. School commission.
7. House administration commission.
8. Examination (inquiry) commission.
9. Gymnastic commission.

The three first-mentioned are of eminent use. The duties incumbent on the Scientific commission do not only comprise scientific and literary works, but also collecting of national traditions, administration of the national museum and assistance of needy students, in whose behalf it has already spent the sum of 15,349 roubles.

The Literary section of the Mitau Latavian Society (Yelgawas Latwieshu Biedriba) is likewise displaying a praiseworthy activity, especially as to the department of national traditions.

The Riga Scientific Commission, as well as the Mitau Literary Section (Rakstniecibas Nuodala) publish once every year its memoirs " Rakstu Krájums," very precious for folklorists, and equally for linguists by their specimens of Latavian dialects.

Literature in all its branches has been enormously raised in the last decennum.

A very busy activity is displayed in the department of the folk-lore. Innumerable pens are employed in writing down the inexhaustible treasures of Latavian national poetry, comprising *dainas* or *tautas dziesmas* (national songs), *Aeikas* (legends), *pasakas* (fairy tales), etc. The most considerable among the published collections are :

1. *G. L. Buettner.*—2854 Latavian national songs, published in the " Magazine" of the Latavian Literary Society, t. VIII, 1844.

2. *Y. Sprogis.*—Pamiatniki latishskavo narodnavo tvortchestva. Wilna, 1868. Latavian national songs with Latavian and Russian texts.

3. *F. Treuland-Briwzemnieks.*—(*a*)—Trudi po archeologii i ethnographii, ed. by Dashkoff, Moscow, 1873. 1118 dainas with Latavian and Russian texts.

(*b*)—Materiali po ethnographii latishskavo plemeni, Moscow 1881. Ed. by the Society of Lovers of Science of Nature, Archeology and Etnography, with Latavian and Russian texts. 1707 proverbs, 1682 enigmas, 717 magic formulas, etc. This collection is very important ; we find in the magic formulas many names of Latavian pagan divinities, among others. *Trimpus* (or Potrimp), pag. 173, the third of the Prusso-Lithuano-Latavian Divine Trinity : *Potrimp, Pèrkun* and *Pìkol.*

(*c*)—Sbornik materialov po ethnographii, ed. by the Dashkoff Museum. Moscow, 1887. 148 tales and legends ; Russian text.

4. *K. R.—Auning.*(*a*)—Wer ist Uhssing. Magazine, 1881.

(b)—Puhkis (of the Latavian dragon myth) Mita·u,2981 Both in German language.

5. *Dr. A. Bielenstein.*—(a)—4793 national songs. 2 vol. 1875.

(b)—1000 Latavian enigmas, interpreted and translated in German. Mitau, 1881.

(c)—The limits of the Latavian people (Die Grenzen des lettischen Volks stammes). St. Petersburg, 1892. This work, however, containing no folk-lorist's materials, is to be mentioned in respect to its importance to the Latavian nation.

6. *E. Wolter.*—Materiali dla ethnographii Latishskavo plemeni Witebskoi gubernii (Materials for the ethnography of the Latavian tribe in the government of Witebsk). St. Petersburg, 1890. Latavian and Russian texts.

7. *Lautenbach-Fùsmin.*—(a)—Salksha lihgawa (Bride of the serpent), Latavian legend in epic form. Felgawa (Mitau) 1880. Latavian text.

(b)—Diews un Welns (God and Devil), epic fragment from the Latavian mythology. Latavian text.

(c)—Niedrishu Widewuts, the great Latavian national heroic poem. Editor, H. T. Drawin-Drawniek. Felgawa (Mitau) 1891. Latavian text.

8. *Pumpurs.*—Lótchplésis, a Latavian heroic poem (B. Dihrik & Co. Riga, 1888. Latavian text.

9. *A. Lerchis-Pushkaïtis.*—(a)—Kurbads, a Latavian hero. Felgawa, 1891.

(b)—Latwieshu tautas pasakas (Latavian national tales). I, II, III, Editor H. Allunan. Felgawa. IV, Editor H. T. Drawin-Drawniek. Felgawa, 1893. Latavian texts.

10. *Krehslinu Fahnis.*—Latwju teïkas iz Malienas (Latavian tales from the boundary-country). I, Riga, 1888, contains the Wissukuok legend. II and III, Riga, 1891.

11. *Rakstu Krájums*, the annual publications of the Scientific Commission of the Riga Latavian Society [Rigas Latwieshu Biedribas Zinibu Kommisÿa] and the Literary Section of the Mitau Latavian Society (Felgawas Latwieshu Biedribas Rakstniecibas Nuodala). At last the Ethnographic News from the Latavians (Etnografiskas zinas par Latwieshiem), edited by the editors of the journal Dienos Lapa.

12. *H. Wissendorff de Wissukuok.*—(a)—" Légendes lata-

viennes," and "Notes sur la Mythologie des Lataviens," in
the Paris Revue des Traditions populaires, t. II, III, VII,
VIII.

(*b*)—Notes sur la mythologie des Lataviens. Vannes, Lafolye, 1892.

(*c*)—Matériaux pour l'ethnologie latavo-lithuanienne.
Vannes, Lafolye, 1892, etc.

The most voluminous work on folklore as yet published
in Latavian language will be the great collection of daïnas or
tautas dziesmas (national songs), Christian Baron has been
classifying for these last twenty years, and the edition of
which I am undertaking in common with him in the beginning of the next year, The materials as yet gathered contain no less than 60,000 daïnas, but fresh supply being
incessantly provided to Mr. Baron, as well as to me, the
thesaurus may finally contain about 100,000 songs, a collection never yet reached by any other nation.

From what I have said, it appears, that great treasures are
still hidden in the Latavian people. This may also apply to
the Lithuanian-dialect-speaking part of the nation. The
greater part of the traditions in Latavia and in Lithuania is
identical.

The quality of the Latavian traditions are by no means
inferior to their quantity. With the Latavians and Lithuanians are still nowadays to be found songs and myths, by far
surpassing in age the sagas of Scandinavia and Iceland.

As to linguistic, the Lithuano-Latavian nation, which we
must consider as the primitive Aryan race in Europe,
equally deserves the greatest regard. The Lithuano-Latavian
language is the one displaying the greatest analogy with
Sanscrit ; the Latavian dialect is more interesting in regard
to its etymology ; the Lithuanian in relation to its forms, the
etymological part appearing somewhat altered by their
contact with the Slavic Poles.

According to the investigations performed by Bergmann,
no less than 500 out of 1,000 Latavian words belongs to the
Sanscrit, a result which the other Aryan languages cannot
show.

The study of the Latavian and Lithuanian languages is
therefore an absolute necessity for linguists and phil-

ologists. It is of no less value for historians, especially for those who choose the northwest of Europe as department of their researches. Many an absurdity, that is now luxuriantly flourishing, might not have been written or printed, if people had applied themselves to the study of the Lithuano-Latavian language.

Let this suffice. I flatter myself with the hope that the learned world, certainly far from every narrow-mindedness, will take in future a greater interest in the Latavian people and proceed to the examination of its story and popular traditions with a more fervent zeal than has been hitherto the case.

In finishing I beg to present my best thanks to the Congress Committee for the hospitality it has obligingly accorded to the Latavian nation in the Columbian World's Congress.

THE LATAVIAN EPOPEE, "NIEDRISHU WIDE-WUTS."

BY HENRY WISSENDORFF.

THE great cycles of traditions of the Latavian people having come to its complete conclusion, I think it worth while to recommend it to the attention of the honorable Congress, so much more I am convinced that this work will serve in future as a point of departure and of union for every investigation about the Latavian tradition, as well with regard to its commonalty with the other nations as its undeniable influence over the Finnish-Esthonian neighbors.

It is this the Latavian heroic poem, Niedrishu Widewuts, exposed to our view in twenty-four songs with 11,491 four-footed dactyl verses altogether, published by J. Lantanbach Jusman, lecturer of the Latavian language at the University of Dorpat, so well known in all circles, far and near, by his poetical works.

The rich and productive collections of famous Latavian folk-lorists as Brivzemnieks, Barons, Dr. Bielenstein, and others, had no little influence in regard to the purpose of the author. He already found in those collections several dispersed parts of the Latavian Epopee. The thought ripened in him to unite in one epic poem the still yet living songs and traditions among the people. Ten years of toilsome, indefatigable labor and investigation were required to sift and join together the immense material, partly borrowed from some collections already published, partly personally or annotated by capable fellow-laborers to be relied on.

Lantenbach, descending himself from the Latavian people, more familiarized than any other with the intellectual life of his fellow-countrymen, had the right comprehension for the various sounds of the ancient dainas (songs) and teikas

(legends).   Therefore he met with success in translating in a
pootical form,—answering to the genius of the Latavian
poetry—the material of prosaic composition on hand.   Without exhausting the whole epic richness of the Latavian people,
he has dedicated him a capital work, which is worthy to be
put in a row with the epic traditions of the great Arian
nations.

The daytimes, seasons and mythos of eternity, which are
here pointed out, are sufficient for the severest exigency. If,
however, slight defects may be proved now and then, the
whole work will always offer, nevertheless, to Latavian mankind, new comfort and hopes, to him with all his sufferings
and joys, with his longings and strivings.

A world vanished long ago is unrolled before his eyes,
abounding with gods and heroes, daughters of the sun (Sau-
lesmeitas) and sons of god (Dieva Deli), with wise kings and
noble aristocracy, with valiant warriors and proud women,
with embittered battles and heroic deeds, with deep sorrow
and sublime enjoyment. He feels therein flesh from his
flesh, blood from his blood. His nobility from immemorial
times, but destroyed now-a-days, is testified by the legend of
Wissukuok ; he has before his eyes the theatre of valiant
deeds of his heroes, by the appellation of castles, seas and
rivers, as : Wissukuoki, Sehlpils, Pehrknone, Saka, Dangawa,
Melnupe, Memele, Muhse, Lielupe, Wisla, etc., existing until to-day and being connected with the legend, while those
heroes continue to live till this day under various names, as
Kurbads, Eglons (Gelons), Lacis (Alcis), etc.; nay, even as
the tradition mentions, the recollection of the campaign to
Italy, "the warm country," (Uzsiltuo Zemi), as it is related
by the legend has been sustained up to this day, and im-
printed in the memory of the people, although it surpasses
their comprehension and in spite of centuries which have
passed and roared away.

The Latavian Epopee of Widewuts has an entirely culture-
like meaning, through which is opened a new source of investigations of the Arian Mythologie (mythos).   Among the
Lithuanian-Latavian people has been kept up much community with the Arian people, even from times far off as never
has been found elsewhere with other yet living people.   The

manner and the way of the old Latavian people in worshipping their gods, the whole sphere of activity and labor of this important old primitive people is evident before our eyes. We learn how the Latavian has worshipped his gods, how he has brought his offerings to Pehrkuns, how he has believed in Puhkis (dragon) and in different bugbears, how he had fought with Sumpurni [1] how he had represented himself hell and the continuance after death in eternity; how he had wedded his Lihgawa (bride), how he had held his wedding for three days long, how he had been adorned for the war by his bride and loving sister—in one word, his whole life with its sunny side and its reverse.

In the meantime the booty for the archæologist will be in no wise of little value, for we get acquainted with his armures and clothings, as well as with the implements of his working room and household of his own, as with his food and beverages. It appears only too evident that the primitive Latavian people had possessed in times of yore (in the remote antiquity) their Runic letters, carved into tallies or embroidered in fans, girdles, etc.

Ruma means speech, in the Latavian language; run at, talk; the very letters were, then and to-day, called burti, (Lithuan burtai), whence derives burtinieks (Lithuan burtininkas)—priests or Waidelots having the knowledge of reading, designation, which later on included the definition of the magician, still in use to-day.

Let us have a look in the interior of those boundaries where is displayed the epos. They will embrace Old-Prussia, Lithuania, Courland, Livonia, and one part of the government of Witebsk, in including the chief branches of the Latavian nation.

The great motive power of the whole is the high and superior personality of Widewuts, before whom his mates in arms step into the background. He performs his heroic exploits by dashing all in pieces through his bravery with his

[1] Sumpurnis, plural Sumpurni, signifies literally, men with dogs' heads. Some have presumed in them the German knights, having made an invasion into the Latavian countries in the twelfth century; others assert to see in them the Finnish neighbors. These two hypotheses appear to me not exact. One can find rather in the Sumpurni some accounts of old relating to the invasion of the Huns, the time of the migration of nations; whence one can have a notion of the ancientness of the traditions in question.

26

powerful arm, where Pehrkun's sword plays a great part, and moreover, through his own cleverness; by means of a magic spell of the sorcerers and witches, especially in combating the nether world, cowardly, perfidious creatures try to harm him, but he destroys all their machinations. He never makes use of his moral and physical superiority to vile designs, on the contrary he is benevolent and charitable and eternally remains the protector and benefactor of his people.

Having reached the age of 116 years, he divides his great kingdom between his twelve sons; steps, voluntarily and of his own accord, upon the funeral-pile in the face of his assembled people and thus sets a sublime example to his people by his perishing by flames, by self-denial, love and sacrifice. Also, he does not die.

When the black and white birds one day will cease to flutter around his tomb, then Widewuts will resuscitate (rise from the dead) and again reign over his people and lead it to a new and glorious life.

This short notice may suffice; yet may it be allowed to me to express the wish to see Lautenbach's work translated in one of the most spoken living tongues, and if possible with the shortest delay.

LITHUANO–LATAVIAN MYTHOLOGY.

BY E. W. WOLTER.

THERE is hardly another subject of scientific pursuit which appears to be more confused and puzzling than the Lithuanian-Latavian mythology. Notwithstanding all progress made in modern times—a renewed examination of the discoveries made hitherto—the following points are to be observed :

The indisputable merit of Mannhardt consists in his having examined thoroughly in historical and folk-loristic manner the Latavian solar mythos, in having found out " that (the Latavian solar myths [mythos–os, the sun] is, upon the whole, in accordance with the primitive Arian in the Veda, and likewise with the primitive Grecian mythos, and that he who might have kept in his mind a true conserved copy of the pro-ethnical Indo-European solar mythology, will hardly encounter with contradictions.") Mannhardt treats the material in eight chapters, about : 1, God (dievas, dievs) ; 2, sun (saule) ; 3, daughters of the sun (saules meita, dievo dukte) ; 4, sons of God (diewa deli, diewo sunelei) ; 5, moon (menesis, menulis); 6, Perkun (Perkons, Perkuns, Perkunas) ; 7, forger of heaven (debess kalis, kalvelis) ; 8, nocturnal heaven, as sojourn of the souls. Here is to be observed that till to-day, in the district of Oschmiany, government of Wilna and the moon is called deveicis, that is devaitis—little god.

1. [1] Among those gods of nature there is one in particular who occupies the centre of all others, and has received, in the course of time, a special national ethical accomplishment :

Perkons, Perkuns, Perkunas, the god of thunder and lightning, who has been compared with the Slavonian Perun and

---

[1] Compare G. Buhler, for the Mythology of the Rig-Veda, I. Parjanya Orientu Occident. Gottingen 1862, vol. i. p. 214. 229.

with the Indian Pardzanya. According to the mythological conception of the Lithuanian and Latavian people, conceptions which in general exist until to-day, Perkun appears to us as a high grown man, who helps the hunter (men) to kill, by means of silver or metal bullets, the Velns or Velnias, the devil of the Latavian and Lithuanian people. This scene frequently takes place in or around about an often hollow and a hundred-years-old, oak tree, whereat the devil changes in different forms, either in that of a bleating goat mocking at the dark thunder-cloud, or that of a black cat, black dog, black bird, or some animal of an undefined figure or name. If the devil in some way appears as man he freezes at bright and broad summer daylight, enveloped in a sheepskin, and tries to escape from Perkuns, whom it is permitted to strike him to death but once in the interval of seven or nine years, under a stone where there is a hidden treasure. Or the man wants to rescue his son from death by thunder-stroke, which has been foretold him at his birth, and builds iron vaults, in order, if need be, to conceal his son, but the son takes to flight, and in worshipping Perkun, he remains alive ; but all vaults were now destroyed—dashed down in nothingness.[1]

2. A second characteristic Lithuano-Latavian mythical point of view is the worshipping of the mother of the earth : Lith., Zeminele ; Latav., Zemes mate (of Tacitus Aists, the Mater Deorum). Crassa erat ignorantia, ut porcam immolarent, deæ telluri. Pigs' heads and hogs' roast were offering foods ; hogs' pictures, amulets. The tilled ground was adorned in dirvolyte or laukopatis (zempatis), laukosargos (soil-commander, guardian of the fields).

3. To the demon of the plants was offered the he-goat ; the primitive Yatwinguians, or the so named Sudinians, being known for their goat-worshipping. They used to celebrate, even until to-day, in different remote corners of Lithuania and Latavia, after the autumn harvest, the demon of the plants. This feast is called by the Latavian people Redungi. They also worship the demon of the plants, and vegetation

---

[1] H. Wissendorff de Wissukuok. Revue des Traditions Populaires, tome III., Paris, 1888. Legends similar to those have been written down from me, in the Lithuanian language, at different posts of Lithuania. Cf. Legends, traditions, about Perkun, in a report of mine relating to an ethnographical journey for Lithuania and Zemaitia, in the year 1887, St. Petersburg.

and growth, under the figure of the double-ear, Zumis, called in the diminutive, jumulen (twins).

4. The thunder-oak, which in Perkun's legends (the Latavians say, "Perkons Juodus gaina") plays the aforesaid part, also the primitive wood has its special ghosts. The wood nymph is called Medeins Medzojuna, Ragana. Even to this day the east Latavians of the Government of Witebsk are called Poddubniki, which means people worshipping their god under the oak trees.

5. Especially the Christian missionaries and clergy felt uneasy about the usage, spread far and near, concerning the treat for the souls and the worshipping of the souls of the dead, in the Latavian language called "veli" or "gari"; in the Lithuanian language "veles, velionai, welukai or gari." The custom of this superstition has been kept up till this day.

6. The goddess, called "Dieves (in the singular Dieva, deive)," Laime[1] and Laume," decide and direct the destiny of the Latavian and Lithuanian people, and at the time of the introduction of the Christianism from West Europe the belief in Laimes (in Greek, raua) was allied to the worshipping of the Virgin Maria, the mother of God, the Holy Virgin Mahre (holy Mary), plays in the mythical songs of the Latavian people a high poetical part and appears as goddess of birth and protectress, likewise as patroness of weddings and orphans. To her, as well as to Laime, are offered and consecrated cows and sheep, according to primitive mythical views.[2]

7. At length, in regard to the idols and divine images, the testimonials of the Middle Ages speak of divine stones (deivnu-stones) and images of God, which in some respects were looking forth from the oak trees.

8. In reference to the Lithuano-Latavian nation, relative to the ethnical, anthropological, allied or not allied people, is to be remarked the non-conformity of some important denominations:

(a) The inequality for the expression of the name of God in general: the Slavonians use Bog (Bhaga), the Latavians

---

[1] Cf. "Zhivaja Stauna," Petersburg, 1891, part iii., page 262.
[2] Materials for the Ethnography of the Latavians of the Government of Witebsk, page 128.

and Lithuanians ' Dievs, Dievas, Dievaitis (good God, son of God, divine image); the Germans use ' Gott.'

(b) The thunder and rain god, Perkons, Perkuns, Perkunas, concording, however, with the mythical apprehensions of nature, does not exactly harmonize in the etymology, the national etymological interpretations of the mythical fictions, having had influence over the phonetic form.

Perkun reminds us of the idea of striking, "dashing to the ground" (pr-ti), while the Indian Parjanya is less leaning upon spurj (crack) than upon pry, prish ; thence, parjanya, rain. However, hut. in the Indo-Germanic investigations would prove lately the equivalency of Parkana-quercus, thunder-oak, used in pro-ethnical times.

(c) Mannhardt, too, having several times pointed out a near contact of the Latavian and Finnish traditions (in his Latavian solar mythos, 1, c. 329). Further examples offer the worshipping of trees (the veneration for old oak trees and fir trees) from the Latavians, Lithuanians and Esthonians ; likewise reports which we have about the priesthood, the most ancient called papæ (Latinized popus) papus, papas, used to exercise.

(d) Universal ethnological parallels offer themselves beyond measure in relation to creation. Legends,[1] the maiden of destiny or Laimes ; the souls of the dead (Weli, in Slavonian viles, cf. Walkyren). The designation of the constellations, the rainbow and the aurora-borealis. It should be most desirable to receive further intelligence from the American folklorists, for more ample anthropological and folk-loristic comparing studies of the Latavian and Finnish peoples in Russia, about the following questions :

1. How is called the aurora borealis (northern light) ? and how is it explained as to popular superstition ?

2. Which forms of the aurora borealis are distinguished in the popular language, with particular definitions ?

3. Which legends and traditions are connected with the aurora borealis ?

4. In which sense has the aurora borealis any relation with dead warriors and the souls of the ancestors ?

---

[1] Cf. "Latavian Creation, Legends of." H. Wissendorff, in the *Revue des Traditions Populaires.* "Mythological Latavian Legends," 1887, Paris.

(In the Latavian language they say : "Kawi kaujas," the warriors are fighting.)

The Latavian-Lithuanian language is also rich in expressions for rainbow.

MARRIAGE AMONG THE ROUMANIANS.[1]

BY ARTHUR GOROVEI.

Young girls, in order to know if they are going to be married in the course of the year, consult the presages on New Year's Eve. So, at midnight, they enter into the stable and they strike the foot of the first ox they come across, saying, "This year; next year, etc." If the ox gets up at the first stroke, the girl will marry soon, this same year; if the ox gets up at the second stroke the girl will marry the next year —The same thing is done in a sheepfold, or with the pigs, etc.

In order to learn the qualities of her future husband, the young girl partially disrobes, looses her hair, bandages her eyes, and braving the cold, goes out in the courtyard, and commences to count the stakes in the hedge. She binds the ninth stake with a ribbon, or with some threads of hair, and re-enters the house. The next day, she examines the stake; if it is upright and sound, her husband will be young, strong and handsome; if the stake is bent, her husband will be ugly and old.

In order to know whom she shall marry, a cake made with salt only is eaten, and during the slumber *he* will give her water to drink.

The young girl has not wedded; the gallant who has courted her for some time does not propose to her, or, rather, no one courts her. Time passes, and with it the freshness of youth. She threatens to become an "old maid." All these evils may be remedied by sorcery :

Here is one method.—

At daybreak, the young girl who wishes to get married introduces her hands into the water of a brook, and repeats thrice the following charm :—

"Good-day, Jordan water, with the drops of Abraham; Good-day, water of skim, with the drops of wine. Since I arose on Tuesday, I have not washed my cheeks. I have prayed before the Images, I have travelled on the path, upon the path not frequented, upon the dew not shed, upon the love not aroused, and with one stroke I found my feet tied, my hands bound, with hate reflected in my countenance, deaf, mute, blind, weeping, sighing, worn out with fatigue. No one has seen me, no one has heard me, except the Virgin Mother, she only saw me, she only heard me, from the Empire of the Heavens, from the gate of Paradise. And as soon as she saw me, as soon as she heard me, she came to me with rum and with wine ; and she asked me : 'Why dost thou weep ? Why sighest thou ? Why art thou so wearied ?'

"Virgin Mother : how should I not weep tears of blood ? How should I not be wearied ? for Tuesday morning I arose, my cheeks I have not washed, before the Images I have not prayed. I have travelled upon the path, upon the path not frequented, upon the dew not shed, upon the love not aroused, and with one stroke I found my feet tied, my hands bound, with hate reflected in my countenance ; deaf, mute, blind, crying, sobbing, and worn out with fatigue."

"'Be silent ; weep no longer with tears of blood, for I am going to unbind thy feet and thy hands : thou canst hear, speak, and see. Be silent, do not weep with tears of blood for I am going to deliver thee from hatred, I am going to sprinkle thee with rum and with wine. I will make the sun rise over thy head : I am going to clothe thee with the moon for stockings, with the stars I am going to embellish thee ; I will put the roses of the sun in thy cheeks ; the rays of light (lucifer) on thy shoulders ; I will make for thee a beautiful toilet ; I will cover thee with love ; a trumpet of silver will I put between thy lips ; cuckoo's bill will I place in thy right hand ; silver lance will I put in thy left hand ; I will cause thee to mount the horse of holy Sunday ; I will make thee set out for the church. When thou comest into the street, the boys and the men will leave their table, over the hedges, watch thee, and ask each other, "What Empress ? What

Princess ? What great lady ? what Priest's wife ? What
Choir-master's (chantre) wife ? What major's lady ? " "I am
not major's lady, not Choir-master's wife, not Priest's wife, not
great lady, not Princess, not Empress, but I am N. chosen
and beautiful. When I enter into the church, the saints rejoice, the Priest forgets himself, book in hand, and watches
me. All the men who are in the church look at me and ask
each other : What Empress ? What Princess ? What great
lady, what Priest's wife ? What Choir-master's wife ? What
major's lady ?'

"I am not major's lady, not Choir-master's wife, not Priest's
wife, not great lady, not Princess, not Empress, but I am
chosen and beautiful. When I sing with the cuckoo's bill I
will touch the lance. As every one desires to hear the cuckoo,
and as the cuckoo is cherished ; may I also be cherished by the
gallants and by all the world. And as the sound of the trumpet is agreeable, and the sounds from afar, and the men hear
it, may all the gallants hear me also, and may they understand my words."

After repeating these verses three times, the young girl
takes some water in the hollow of her hands, and casts it over
her head, while repeating three times these lines,—

"As many drops as pour over me, may so many men say
good things of me."

By these means, the gallant who formerly courted her is
wrought to ask her hand in marriage.

THE PROPOSAL OF MARRIAGE.

The young man who wishes to marry, after having obtained
the consent of his parents, sends two friends to demand the
hand of the young girl. These two friends are called PET-
TITORI or STAROSTI, the pettitori take a bottle of wine or of
brandy, which the young man gives them, and goes to the
parents of the young girl.

They speak together ; and when the conversation turns
upon marriage, she leaves the room. Then one of the
STAROSTI proposes to the parents to marry their daughter
to one of their friends. The parents ask his name. The
STAROSTE says these lines :—

"Our young Emperor N. he who is praised by all the world, has chosen us as two faithful servants of little stature, but good counsellors and good talkers, and has charged us to bring him chariots of hay, and casks of wine, fat calves and good bread. Our young Emperor has learned that in your fine and large garden there is a tree which grows and flourishes always, but never bears fruit ; he has also learned that the young branches of this tree grow and flourish but never bear fruit ; and our young Emperor begs you to give him this branch so that it may grow, that it flourish, and that it may bear fruit."

If the parents are not pleased with the young man, they reply that their daughter is not to marry yet, that she is still too young ; if, on the contrary, this marriage suits them, they permit the young man to come himself to ask the hand of their daughter.

On Thursday or Saturday evening, the gallant, accompanied by his parents, by his Starosti, by some members of his family and by some musicians (Cantari) comes to the house of his chosen bride. There, one of the Starosti says in verse :

" Good-day, great lords and princely counsellors ; let the master within come to speak with us."

The father of the girl asks :

" Who are you, and what do you seek at our Court ? and what is it that you wish ? "

The Staroste says that their "young emperor in leaving for the hunt, found the imprints of a ferocious beast and as he did not know to what species of beast these footprints belonged he held a council of philosophers and of great men. Some said that these were the traces of a great, ferocious beast, destined to be attached to the emperor for life ; others said that it was a flower of the garden devoted to the same destiny. The young emperor chose then two men to seek the flower for him. They have sought everywhere without finding it. Suddenly a star fell on this court, and it was in this way they perceived in the garden of this court the flower sought which they ask of the great lords in order to give it to their emperor."

The father replies that he has not seen in their house such beasts, and he calls out the grandmother of his daughter :

" Is it she whom you seek ? "
" No, not she."

He causes the mother of the girl to come :

" Is it she ? "
" No, not at all."

An old and ugly servant-girl is then called, clothed in rags, and they say :

" Ah ! now you have found her ; here she is."
" Ah, no, no. We do not seek this one. Ours has golden hair, eyes as black as aloes, teeth like pearls, lips like roses, the countenance of the sun ; she is as beautiful as a sprite."

After these ceremonies, the young girl is brought forth, the musicians play as if to break their strings, wine is poured out into the glasses. They drink and enjoy themselves for several hours.

THE BETROTHAL.

Formerly, among all the Roumanians, and to-day still, among those dwelling under foreign domination, the engagement is made with a religious ceremony. The rings are put into a plate filled with wheat or rice. The parents call the young people, saying to them that they are gleaners and that the wheat is to be harvested. The young people seek the rings, take them to the priest, who blesses them and returns them.

To-day, among free Roumanians, this custom has almost disappeared. The young people and their parents cross hands, another person wishes them a good and long life, and they congratulate each other.

Sometimes they dance, they dine, each one amuses himself in the best way.

Before celebrating the marriage, the *fiancées* carry presents to their mothers-in-law. The present of the swain is composed of a pair of boots, and that of the girl of a chemise, wrought by herself. These presents are called " Mother-in-law boots and shirt."

THE CEREMONY OF MARRIAGE.

A Roumanian proverb says : "So many cabries, so many customs." The marriage customs are varied among the Roumanians, as among all people. We will describe the customs observed in several villages of the department of Succava.

Habitually, the young man about to be married takes his fiancée from her parents' home to conduct her to his own home. After having sent the invitations to the wedding by two or three of his friends, named "Vornicei," who carry a handkerchief in their canes, the swain takes leave of his parents. His father takes him by the hand and they make the tour of the table two or three times, while the musicians play something saddening. Suddenly, the melody changes ; all those present dance, and leave the room dancing to go to the fiancée's house. Some pistol-shots announce their arrival. There, in the middle of the court, the fiancée is bound with a cord, and several people, her cavaliers of honor, ask the newcomers what they seek.

One of the young men who accompanies the swain responds in verse that they are the army of an emperor who has sent them to bring him the flower which is found in this garden. After a long Oratzie, everybody enters into the court, then into the house, and they always dance until the foster-father stops at the head of the table. The musicians play no longer, and everybody sits around the table. The father of the girl proposes the health of the foster-father, and says :

> " Foster-father, you are welcome."
> " You are well pleased, father-in-law."

The father-in-law gives all the guests something to drink : the mother of the girl puts at the head of the table a fine loaf covered with a handkerchief, and the meal commences.

After having eaten, the foster-father asks that the cook be called. She takes a child in her arms, shows it to the guests and says that it is this one that prepared the dishes. A present is given to the child, but the cook is not believed. Then the father of the fiancée leads her to the swain, who is at the head of the table, near the foster-father ; the swain gives her his hand, he makes her sit at his right hand and kisses the hand of his father-in-law.

The foster-mother asks that they bring the clothes of the swain, one of his parents brings a sieve in which there is a shirt, a pair of knee-breeches and a cravat, all covered with a shawl and presenting the sieve to the swain says : "Good-day, guests, and above all, good-day, sir affianced : madame the fiancée, presents to you her homage, and also begs that you will have the kindness to accept a present on her part." The swain extends his hand towards the sieve, but the bearer of the present withdraws it and says to him, "Do not hasten to take the presents, as you have hastened to get married." Finally, the swain takes the presents.

The same thing is done with the present brought by the swain to the fiancée. These are : shoes, a shawl, figs, apples, and two citrons.

After the repast the dance commences, and they go out dancing into the court. A circle is formed, the parents are seated in the centre on chairs, and the fiancée kneels before them to ask forgiveness.

The swain and his friends re-enter into the house, in order to take the dot of his future bride. The dot is put upon a chariot, and when the fiancée mounts upon it, the swain strikes her with his staff. She makes the sign of the cross, prays God to come to her aid, and, breaking a loaf over the top of her head, casts the pieces towards the four cardinal points.

They go towards the house of the swain. While on the road, all cry out and pistol-shots are fired.

The mother of the swain awaits her daughter-in-law and introduces her into the house. They place themselves again at battle, then they dance until the next day.

The people gone, the young girls array the fiancée in the garments given by the swain, and he dresses in those presented to him by the fiancée.

Then they go to the church to celebrate the marriage.

These ridiculous formalities terminated, they dance to the exit from the church. The fiancée with her foster-mother and the demoiselles of honor (bridesmaids) in the chariot or on the sledge—if this proves in winter—and the swain with his friends goes on foot. At the swain's house, an old woman receives everybody with a vase filled with water in the hand

and with bread. The vase is put on a chair ; a " vornicel " cavalier of honor—carries the loaf on a staff, whose ends are held by two " vornicei." The affianced couple pass three times under it ; the third time he seizes the loaf and tears it in several pieces.

Everybody sits at table.

When the dish of rice (pilof) is served, the foster-father asks that they bring two apple-sprouts over which the " vornicei " place a veil with which the fiancée is covered.

Upon the table before the swain there is, in a covered dish, a roasted fowl. When he uncovers the plate they say :

" Let us see if the swain is strong enough to break this chicken into."

If he do not succeed, all laugh at him ; the swain is too feeble to be able to manage the household.

The foster-father gives the legs of the fowl to the musicians, who thank the swain, saying to him :

" For these two chicken legs, affianced sir, we give you two little feet of a young girl."

The foster-father serves everybody with the roast, then the young girl's fiancé asks of the " cavaliers " that they bring their sticks to her : she changes the handkerchiefs suspended on their extremities and they give her some pieces of money.

The foster-father gives the signal for dancing ; They make three times the tour of the table, and at the moment of coming out of the room, one of the " vornicei " says, " have luck and God will aid you." And at the same time he makes with his staff the sign of the cross over the door, and emerging thence he fires his pistol.

In the court, the dance continues until evening. Towards sunset, the foster-father sends " vornicei " into the village to invite the friends to a " grand repast."

THE REPAST.

THIS same evening, Sunday, the father-in-law of the fiancée prepares the repast. The " vornicei " with the swain come to lead to the feast the foster-father, who withdraws to his own home with the elders of the village, who are amusing themselves with the songs of the (cantari) musicians. A pistol-shot announces to the foster-father that they come to bring him to the repast. They go out. The affianced couple meet the foster-parents with the wedding candle lighted, and kiss their hands.

Everybody enters into the house, where they place themselves at table. The affianced couple present water to the foster-father, who washes his hands; and they pour water at the root of a tree, or in another appropriate place. The foster-father leaves a piece of money in the vase where he washes himself. This is a present for the affianced couple.

They eat, and drink. The foster-father asks that they bring him "the sweet verses" (the wine) One of the guests named Echanson (cup-bearer) brings the wine, and serves it to every one, pronouncing a discourse in verse. After the foster-father has drunk the wine, the cup-bearer wipes his mouth with the swain's handkerchief.

The mother-in-law and several friends of the house conduct the swain into a little room, and veil her; then they lead her into the dance hall where a special table is set for the affianced couple, who from this moment call themselves *young married people.*

The women present cloth to the mother-in-law in the shirt given to her by her son-in-law.

The dance commences, and at day-break everybody leaves for the inn where they pass the day dancing and drinking.

BRIDAL COSTUME, SOFIA PROVINCE, BULGARIA.

MARRIAGE CUSTOMS IN BULGARIA.

BY DR. VULKO I. SHOPOFF.

IN a country where the maxim is " to every house its own
law, to every village its own custom," and where transporta-
tion is so primitive that the great majority never go out of
their own community, and where the ideas of space and
distance are very limited, it will be very difficult to undertake to describe the prevailing customs even of such a
universal ceremony as that which unites man and woman
together for life, for better or for worse. Costumes and
customs are so vastly different in the various districts that I
am not at all astonished at the almost incredulous look in
the eyes of our visitors at the Fair as they ask the question,
looking at the most typical costumes of the country exhibited there, " Do all these represent Bulgarian peasants ? "

Steering clear of possible criticism, and simplifying my subject the best I may, I shall relate in the simplest possible way
the ceremony as it takes place in the village where I was born.

To begin with, there is no such thing as " courting " the
girl you are going to marry in Bulgaria. Of course young
people meet and pass happy times together in their way, as,
for instance, at the frequent spinning bees that take place
during the long winter evenings, when the boys come in to
keep the girls company with shepherd's pipe and song and
joke, ending often with a pretty village dance, while the old
dame works in the corner by the hearth. And yet, when the
important question comes to be answered it is not the young
man or the young woman, in the majority of cases, that are
consulted.

The parents of the young man, as soon as " the hope of
their life and the staff of their old age " reaches the age of
eighteen, begin to cast about as to who would be the most

suitable daughter-in-law that they could hit upon. Now the dominant sentiment at such a juncture is "what girl in the village, or within their circle of acquaintances, would be the best help for the mother, the best worker at the loom, and the quickest in field work. When the idea has ripened in the minds of the old people they begin to prepare their son in the same direction.

A story is told of an old father who made the introduction to the solemn speech that he was going to make to his son by saying that "as their donkey was getting too old and the work was too hard, they thought"—and here most provokingly the old man was interrupted and did not finish his remarks. But the son, as if by intuition guessing which way lay the drift of the talk, took the first chance he had to talk with his father alone to ask, "What's that, father, about the donkey getting too old?" "Well," said the old man, "don't you see, we shall have to be looking about and find some woman who would be bringing your breakfast to you when you are working away out in the fields." This story has made it almost an adage among the peasant-folk when they wish to introduce the subject of marriage simply to ask "what, is the donkey getting old?" By this I do not mean to imply that there are no genuine love-stories and romances in Bulgaria. Our national songs are full of the deepest pathos in expressing the simple but true love of the shepherd and the ploughboy for the fair ones whom they had to win through many a bloody contest and rivalry.

It may seem strange to American ears that the begging gypsy that goes from house to house should be a match-maker. But where there is no writing and no knowledge of the usefulness of the post-service for the conveyance of Cupid's messages the artful gypsy plays a very important part, having very often concocted the whole affair, either by her star-gazing or card-drawing, for the gypsies I refer to always know who is going to be the maiden's future husband, and vice versa, and they are so positive in their assertions that the simple peasant folk are greatly influenced by their prophecies.

However, once the old donkey question arises, a solution is sought in the following way. After the mother has found all the excellent qualities, or thinks she has, in a certain girl, and has talked it over with the old man, of course the boy is asked whether he cares for such and such a girl, in which case he answers generally, he "doesn't know, but he may get to like her." The next thing is to see and to prepare from fifteen to thirty flat gold coins which are to be the token (called nishan, which means the centre of the target) of the offer the young man makes to the girl through his envoyées. These are three of the married friends of the family, who take a special wooden vessel of wine and the coins, and after some preliminary feeling of the way through gypsies, etc., has been done, they go to the home of the girl. The family is found assembled, with the girl in question looking on from some corner of the room. The guests are seated, and invite the father and mother to drink with them. The parley is then something like this :

"Where is the rest of the family ? We have heard that you have a grown daughter, where is she, why is she not here ?"

"Oh no, what are you saying ? Why, she is only a baby, just a child yet," says the mother.

"Oh, a baby indeed, don't the neighbors complain of the noise she makes with the loom, and we have not seen you for a long time now going to fetch water from the well. But of course if you like to treat her as a baby and keep her tied to the strings of your apron, she is yours, and you can do as you like with her." The father then interferes and says, "Why what nonsense are you talking, wife ? Don't you see that our Evanka is as tall as you are, milks the cows, and makes better bread than your old hands can knead ? In fact, neighbors, you are right. I have a grown daughter, and I am proud of her."

By this time the daughter has stepped out of her seclusion, holding tight the distaff and giving extra twists to her spindle, which sings under the stress of her muscular arm as if to disprove what her mother has said about her minority.

"Well," say the guests, "we are here with our wine and propose to drink the health of this daughter of yours, asking her to accept this bundle sent to her by one of the best young men that our village ever produced, handsome, active, and in a good social position."

The girl gives a good jerk to her spindle and retires blushing, and the mother takes up the discussion, which as it lasts
pretty nearly the whole evening I must refrain from detail-
ing. Suffice it to say, that if the match is considered good
the token is accepted by the girl, and the next day or so her
parents are expected to send word to the young man's family
when they can have the engagement proper. On the evening fixed, after the necessary preparations on both sides have
been made, the young man and his parents with a few friends
and two or three musicians betake themselves to the young
woman's house. The priest also comes to perform the short
ceremony of betrothal, almost as binding as marriage.

When all are assembled the young man's father asks the
girl's father what dowry he is going to give his daughter.
" Oh, I will give her a rug."

"What size will it be ?   How much will it weigh ? "

" Oh, so many pounds, it shall be an allishte" (the usual
heavy bedcovering of the villagers).

" And what else will you give her ? "

" Well a piece of felting for a mattress."

" And how about her clothes ? "

" Oh, she will have plenty of them, she is a very industrious
girl, and she has prepared a good outfit.   But how much will
you give us for her ? "

" How much do you want ? "

" She is such a fine girl, and so useful to us, and her
mother will miss her so much, you must give us twenty-five
dollars."

" Oh, what a price ! Why you think that our pockets are
full then ? This is only an excuse. You want to dismiss us
you mean to send us away, eh ? " So after more talk in the
same style a compromise is finally made for ten or fifteen
dollars. When this is settled the priest comes forward and
sings two or three hymns, after which he declares the couple
formally engaged to be married as soon as convenient for
both parties. During the short interval before the wedding,
more freedom is allowed the girl, who is considered as already
belonging to the young man, and he is permitted to accompany
her to the village well, and so forth.

The day before the wedding, which is always on Sunday, a

week or so after the betrothal, the young friends of the groom assemble to see him shaved and trimmed by the village barber, which ceremony takes place out of doors in front of the house, amid much joking and quizzing and to the accompaniment of the gay tunes of the fiddlers engaged for that and the three following days. After that they go to the bride's home to see that all is ready there.

When Sunday morning arrives the young man is dressed in his gayest holiday suit, and the wedding procession starts led by the fiddlers. It sets out about ten o'clock, the fiddlers in front, then a cart drawn by bullocks, decorated with green boughs, and covered with a gay blanket, and behind it the groom and his friends.

When they reach the bride's house they are all led to the bride's room, and the groom knocks three times, and is admitted by the bride. Her face is covered by a thick veil and she is guided by her two bridesmaids. The groom and best man go up to a small table in the middle of the room on which is placed a large pie. In the centre of it has been placed a new horse-shoe or other trinket, and it is considered very unlucky if the groom fails to get it when he cuts out the centre of the pie. With morsels from the pie he then feeds the bride, lifting her veil as far as her mouth. After this they proceed to the cart, into which her father lifts her amid much laughing and joking, and her mother stands crying and sobbing as the procession moves off, the groom walking behind the cart as before with his best man who is adorned with two small red and white banners. When they reach the church a bargaining ensues, just as they enter it, between the priest, who insists on prepayment of the wedding fee, and the godfather who has to pay it. As all parties have been drinking the wedding-wine this sometimes causes high words to pass before it is all settled. Then the bride and groom are led to a little table set before the altar, on which is the bread and wine. The godfather or godmother, as the case may be, then holds two metal crowns joined with a little chain over their heads, and the best man follows with a large lighted wax candle, and the priest leads them thus three times around the table, singing a hymn called "Rejoice, Isaiah." Rings are exchanged, and the sacred elements are given then; in doing this the groom breaks the bread and offers it to the bride, noticing carefully in which direction the bread breaks, for if the larger piece be toward the bride he must make up his mind to lead a henpecked existence for the rest of his life. Then the priest leads them out of the church and the bride is lifted into the cart with the bridesmaids beside her where they stand until they reach the house of the groom. Meanwhile some of the young men run a race to carry the news that the couple are married and approaching. The winner receives an embroidered kerchief, the others something apiece of less value. When the party reaches the groom's home, before the bride is lifted from the cart, the groom's father and mother and friends are asked for gifts to set the young couple up with. The gifts promised are registered with an axe on some tree near by or on the door-post, and then the party enters the house. The bride is conducted to a room by herself and the groom to another. The groom in fact does not see his bride at any time during the day, and thus it may happen, as it sometimes does, that the story of Leah and Jacob is repeated, only in such a case all hope of Rachel is lost, as polygamy is never permitted and divorce is rare and difficult.

The guests begin to arrive as soon as the couple have been received, and the feasting begins with a free distribution of wheat porridge cooked in large cauldrons and the serving of wine. Later in the day a table is spread on the threshing-floor and the guests are seated about, having brought each a bag of corn as a contribution to the host and a small vessel of wine to begin the drinking with. The godfather presides over the feast, and during its progress the chief musician, beginning with him, passes around behind the guests, singing for each some ballad of love or adventure, sometimes improvised for the occasion, and rewarded by coins dropped into his fiddle. After the feast the guests depart and the festivities are over for that day. Early on Monday morning a fiddler climbs on the roof of the house and plays until he is paid to come down, after a vain effort to dislodge him with pebbles has been made, "lest the devil should come to listen to his music." His song there freely translated runs something as follows :—

Yesterday our spry young man got himself a wife. The

very first thing she did was to quarrel with her mother-in-law and thrash her. To-day she chased her father-in-law, who to save himself bounds across the fence and hides among the nettles, while to calm her wrath she waves the stick and screams, "Oh, you old ass, if only I could lay my hands on you!" etc., etc.

Brandy is sent around to the groom's friends to announce that the couple are happily married, and the bride appears, her hands covered with handkerchiefs and face unveiled, to perform the ceremony of washing the godfather's hands, in which she is helped by the bridesmaids. Later in the day a formal visit is made by the parents of the bride to her in her own home, and their visit is returned by the groom's family on the next day, after which comes a great dance led by the bridesmaids and best man.

On Wednesday the godfather is escorted to his home by a party of the groom's family and friends, and the wedding festivities are at an end.

There still remains, however, the private ceremony of giving the bride permission to speak, which is done by each member of the groom's family separately, and is made the occasion of an exchange of gifts. Until this has been done, and it is at the option of each one to delay it as long as he or she likes, the bride is not expected to speak to any of the family but the groom.

From this description of the marriage customs in one village you can see how easily its many details can be varied, producing other customs in other localities.

But since Bulgaria became independent some eighteen years ago, and education has become compulsory, a great many of the older customs and ceremonies are looked upon as obsolete and the young generation, even in the villages, are drifting into freer customs that look very much like the rest of the civilized world.

FOLK-MUSIC.

BY FREDERIC W. ROOT.

FROM the brute creation to man in his highest development, there is almost an infinite scale of vocal sounds and combinations, which symbolize all phases of emotional excitement from the rudimentary affections of the animal to the subtle and complex feelings of highly developed man. We have learned these various sounds as a sort of a language, and they express to our minds something of the inner life of the being that utters them. The higher development of this emotion-language, that which comes when intellect gives symmetry and a pleasing relationship to emotional sounds gives us music. The music of a people is an interesting and accurate means of studying the inner life of that people ; and, during our studies of the products and peculiarities of the different nations of the globe during the World's Fair, the happy thought occurred to the Folk-Lore Society of Chicago of putting alongside of costumes, languages, manners, religions and industries of the remarkable aggregation of nationalities represented here, the music of these peoples. No such opportunity had ever before presented itself of bringing together upon one program characteristic selections performed by nations of every part of the globe, and exhibiting as it were a panoramic view of musical development, from the formless and untutored sounds of savage people to the refined utterances of our highest civilization. It was impossible to represent upon a single program all the material that was within reach, for nearly or quite all those in charge of national exhibits, either in the Midway Plaisance or the rest of the fair, seemed inclined to put their resources at the disposal of the Folk-Lore Society for this purpose. Therefore, excepting some selections representative of the music of our North

424

FREDERICK W. ROOT

American Indians, the utterances of the savage peoples were omitted, these being hardly developed to the point at which they might be called music; but it was decided to include a good showing from the Orient and semi-civilized nations. Selections of this sort coming more nearly into modern musical classifications. These selections, together with the contributions from those nations which excel in the fine arts, gave those interested in the performance a comprehensive view of people's music from its more elementary and formless stage up to the final developments of our own time. In arranging the program no attempt was made to put the numbers composing it in logical order. It would have been interesting to show how at the present day there exist contemporaneously most of the forms of musical utterance which would be found in the history of musical evolution during many thousands of years of man's history, but there was not time, in view of the multitude of attractions claiming one's attention during the fair, to go into the subject with so much attempt at scholarship. It is thought, however, that the collected numbers that appear on the following program were such as to give scholars considerable data of an interesting and valuable character.

THE FOLK-LORE CONGRESS

AT THE ART PALACE (LAKE FRONT)

Friday Evening, July 14, 1893, at 8 o'clock,

UNDER THE DIRECTION OF

FREDERIC W. ROOT,

ASSISTED AT THE PIANO BY MRS. A. H. BURR, AND IN CONDUCTING
BY MR. D. A. CLIPPINGER.

This Concert is given as one of the Sessions of the Folk-Lore Congress,
and is Free to the Public.

PROGRAM.

---

1. **GERMANY. CHORALE.** "Nun ruhen alle Wälder."

Sung by a select semi-chorus under the direction of Mr. Frederic W. Root.

The secular folk-melodies of Germany are more widely known than those of any other country. But the phase of German folk-music here given is not as well known.

The chorale "Nun ruhen alle Wälder" is a German folk-song of the 15th century put to devotional uses in the 16th.

The plan of adapting sacred words to secular melodies of the people was prevalent at that time. Especially during the Reformation did Luther endeavor to reach the masses by associating devotional sentiments with their familiar songs. Many of the most impressive chorales in use to-day originated in this way.

Among these may be cited "O Haupt, voll Blut und Wunden," which Bach has used in his "Passion Music."

426

2. BOHEMIA. FOLK-SONGS.

a. Husitská (A Hussite song).

This is a war song of the 15th century. Its melody has been utilized by Balfe in his "Bohemian Girl," which should have more properly been styled "Gypsy Girl." There is nothing Bohemian (Slavonic) in the heroine.

b. Byvali Cechové (An old Bohemian chorale).

c. Zamítnuté Pozvání (an invitation declined), harmonised by Laub, sung by a male chorus from the Lyra and Lada societies of Chicago, under the direction of

MR. ADOLPH ERST.

These translations from the Bohemian are by Mr. Joseph George Král.

HUSITSKÁ.

I. Let us cherish the blissful hope,
That the golden times will come again,
That our Chekh swords shall flame
And our Chekh voices shall resound.
Let us wear our own Chekh dress,
Let us defend our ancient rights,
And above all, that true Chekh rule:
Let us love, let us drink, and then let us fight !
Amen ! May the Lord grant it !
Pray thou for us, Saint Wenzeslaus,
Prince of the Chekh land !

II. We have regained Freedom,
Let us defend it as a precious jewel,
So that we may not lose it again,
Let us live in harmony, let us be vigilant !
Let the Chekh nation rise,
Let the Chekhs rejoice;

Our grandsons may sing as we do ·
Let us love, etc.

[" Chekh" is the Slavonic term for " Bohemian." A white lion is the national emblem of Bohemia.]

BYVALI CECHOVE.

I. Once the Chekhs were brave men,
They were heroes, men like flowers,
They used to fight, they used to sing,
Thus the world knew them.

ZAMITNUTÉ POZVÁNI.

I. A mountain, lo, a mountain,
A green mountain,
Some one is calling me
From beyond the mountain.

II. 'Tis my sweet love,
 She calls my name :
" Come to me, my darling,
 I am lone in the house."

  * * * *

V. " I will not go to thy house,
 It is too early, dear,
 Maiden, fair, thou wilt not,
 Thou wilt not be mine.

VI. Thou wilt not be mine,
 Thou must not be mine,
 In vain, in vain,
 Dost thou think of me ! "

3. ITALY. VENETIAN GONDOLIER'S SONG.

 Guarda che notte splendida. Sung by

SIGNORINA AMALIA PEROTTI and SIGNOR CARLO ZEMELLO.

(By courtesy of the Venetian Gondola Company, World's Fair.)

See ! this glorious night has come,
The Giudeca is aflame ;
All things breathe their happiness,
Nina, I can do no more.

The most propitious night of our Saviour,
Nina, its presence persuades you,
It was surely made for love.

4. NORWAY. FOLK SONGS.
 a. Aagots Fjeldsang (Aagot's mountain song).
 b. Eg ser deg ut för gluggjin (I see your shadow yonder).

 Sung by MRS. RAGNA LINNE STROBLE.

Norway is one of the countries that is most rich in genuine folk-music. As Mr. Auber Forestier says of these songs : " Who made them ? "

The people themselves.

Of each one it may be said in the words of the old folk-songs :

" It made itself as it sped along ;
 A floating log brought to me my song."

(These translations from the Norwegian are by Auber Forestier.)

AAGOT'S MOUNTAIN SONG.

I.

O'er the ridge the sun now glides,
 Shadows make long paces ;
Night comes on with strides,
 Gently me embraces ;
Cattle seek the fold once more,
 I the pasture dairy door.

I SEE YOUR SHADOW YONDER.

I.

I see your shadow yonder,
O dearest, sweetest friend;
But longer you must wander,
Till word to you I send,
For I have forgotten to put out the token,
You need not go mad, tho' my word thus be broken;
Remember that father is home and is watching.
O dearest, sweetest friend!
Hush a-baby, hush a-baby-by.

II.

I'll rock my little brother
Until he falls asleep;
But me there is no other
Who him can quiet keep.
And if you are freezing, pray go in the stable,
I'll send for you there just as soon as I'm able
For father is going out soon, pray be careful.
O dearest, sweetest friend!
Hush a-baby, hush a-baby-by.

5. POLAND. FOLK-SONGS.

   a. Ukraina (A song of exiled Ukrainians).

   b. Mazur (A song of peasants merry making).

   c. Kosciusko Polonaise (An old folk-song to which are adapted modern patriotic words.)

Sung by a semi-chorus from the United Polish Singers of America, under the direction of MR. ANTHONY MALLEK.

(Translation from the Polish by Mr. Anthony Mallek.)

UKRAINA.

It is sad, brethren, sad, beyond the Danube's tide.
It is the land of graves and tombs (han);
The wind bows the grass upon the steppes, and among the steppes the insolent
   usurpers live:
Ukraina! Ukraina! the glorious land of the Kossacks.

MAZUR.

Hej! Mazurs! hej, ha! While the spring of life lasts and the heart beats warmly, let us enjoy life and be happy. So, husbandmen, servants, dance when music calls to you. Now, in a rushing torrent, the instruments strike up the tune. Go, brethren, respond with alacrity, and let the tapping of the shoe heels show how you can hop!

Forward! forward! in the spirited mazurka dance, while our comrades pour in on all sides. Our land is a garden of Eden!

KOSCIUSKO POLONAISE.

Kosciusko, look on us! See how we fight Poland's enemies! We need thy sword to free our fatherland. Raise we our song to Liberty; for Liberty we'll shed our blood. White-robed Liberty flies aloft on golden wings. Look, brethren, in the front, how our Liberty star shines! [This refers to Kosciusko in the white dress of a peasant.] Our enemies must flee before us, for Kosciusko, the friend of Washington, is our leader.

6. SPANISH AMERICA. Popular Love Song of Ecuador. "La Cervatilla."

Sung by SEÑOR J. GUALBERTO PÉREZ, Secretary of the Ecuador Commission at the World's Fair.

She is as the fawn-hued doe, who stretches her neck from her mossy bed; and at sight of the dog, lies couched with timid, fearing eyes.

7. CEYLON. A Cingalese Folk Song.

Sung by CADIRIWAIL, (a Tamil of Ceylon). The accompaniment is by the singer and by THAMIN HAMIT (a Malay of Ceylon) and JOHN PERERA (a Sinhalese), who make use of a Fiddle (so called by them), a Tambour (tambourine) and a Dole (a drum, played with the fingers).

These performers are present by courtesy of Hon. J. J. Grinlinton, Commissioner from Ceylon.

The song recounts a conversation between a prince and a demon. The prince, tired of the pleasures of his royal life, is on his way to a desert to live the life of a recluse, when he is confronted by a demon in the form of a lovely woman. She seeks to entice him back to his pleasures and so frustrate his good intentions. He moralizes, and she continues her blandishments, till finally the prince gains his end by his firmness of purpose and strength of will, and is left by the demon to carry out his object.

8. INDIA. A Sacred Solo.

a. Last Padi in Bhopali (In praise of God).

> Oh God, Ramchund, hear my entreaties,
> I, a poor, obedient servant, who am miserable.

* * * * * * * * * * *

Gotum, a monk, turned his wife into stone as he saw her sleeping in the moonbeams. But Ramchund, who was the seventh incarnation of God, coming and seeing that she was stone, brought her to life and bestowed upon her wealth. So the man said, "Do for me as you have done for her. You care for all; do for me, too, and I will be your own servant."

(The Sitar used in this selection is one of the stringed instruments of India.)

b. Love Song.

Nobody brings any news of my friend. My breath is on my lip, and it will go out. You are with others and I am bewailing your absence. Oh! show me some mercy and cease this cruelty. You are lightly giving the wine cup to another. I am drinking my blood.

c. SONG OF LOYALTY.

Praise to Her Majesty the Empress Queen Victoria ; every one trembles in the fear of your Majesty. Her Majesty made laws for our comfort, to succor the poor and to punish the thief, the cruel and bad man. Her Majesty established dispensaries for the sick, and schools where we might acquire knowledge. From her comes the light of Justice. God bless our Empress the Queen Victoria and save her Majesty.

Performed by PUNDIT GOBINDPURSHAD Shukul (Head Priest, Hindu), Delhi.

(By permission of Messrs. S. J. Telleryand & Co., East India Pavilion, World's Fair.)

9; JAPAN. No; a ceremonial dance, with song.

Performed by MR. and MRS. K. S. MORIMOTO, artists, of Tokio.

In Japan, certain dances are practised and regarded with sentiments similar to those which Europeans associate with popular melodies, music not occupying the place in their social life which it does with us. "No" originated in the 16th century, but is founded upon incidents which occurred five hundred years earlier.

Yuya was the wife of Munemori of the great Hei-ke clan. She was the most beautiful woman of her age, and much beloved by her husband. She wished to go and visit her mother who was quite aged, and was living in the distant province of Azuma, where now is the city of Tokio. She was her only child and loved her very much, but her husband would not permit her to go.

One day she went with her husband to see the cherry flowers at Kiomizu, in Kyoto, then the capital. While walking through the vast cherry gardens she was constantly depressed, thinking of her aged mother, and she composed a poem to her husband, of which the meaning was something like this : "Since even the blossoms of young and strong cherry trees fall to the ground, how can I expect that my mother's life will be prolonged, and that I shall ever see her again unless I set out immediately."

(Translated from the Japanese by Rev. D. A. Murray.)

10. TURKEY. LOVE SONG.

Performed by SIT MELEKY SROOR, SIT LATIFY KHASKEY and KOWAJA KHALEEL ZAKARIA, of Beyreut. The accompaniment is upon the Kanoon (a stringed instrument), the Ood (a sort of mandolin) and the Dayrie (tambourine).

The performers appear by kind permission of Pierre Antonious & Co., concessionaires of the Turkish Theatre, World's Fair.

O day so dear to me, thou hast brought me prosperity and pleasure ! By Heaven ! do not pass so quickly away.

I call to thee, O kind and beautiful night, for my lover hath made peace with me ;

A light shone in his o'erflowing cup when I drank the wine from it.
May the covenant of our love never fade.
O God, sanctify our Apostle with a sanctification that shall never fail.

(Translated from the Turkish by Mr. Naaum Moghabghab.)

11. ABORIGINAL AMERICA. INDIAN SONGS.

   a. Song of approach (processional in the sacred calumet ceremony).
   b. Raising the pipes (same ceremony).
   c. Resting song (Hae-thu-ska).
   d. Love song.
   e. Song of dismissal (Hae-thu-ska society).

These songs are from the Omaha tribe of Indians, and will be sung by MR. FRANCIS LA FLESCHE, an Omaha Indian, now a trusted employé of the Indian Bureau, Washington, D. C.

These numbers are furnished by Mr. J. C. Fillmore of Milwaukee.

12. CANADA. FRENCH CANADIAN FOLK-SONGS.

   a. En passant près d'un moulin.
   b. C'etait un vieux sauvage.
   c. Mariann' s'en va-t-au moulin.

Sung by MR. L. GASTON GOTTSCHALK.

"En passant près d'un moulin" might be called a song of remorse; for some one with a burdened conscience in passing a mill hears the wheel go ke-ti-ke-ti-ke-tac, and imagines it to say "attrappe, attrappe, attrappe" (catch him! catch him!); and again in passing a church the "Allelujah-lu-jah" is changed by his imagination into "Ah! le voilà, voilà!" (There he is! there he is!) and he rushes on and on, panic-stricken, his imagination transforming all sounds into accusations or threats. "C'etait un vieux sauvage" evidently had its origin where Indians and their language were somewhat familiar.

The words "Tena-ouich', tena-ga, ouich'ka" are in imitation of the ejaculations of the Indians.

"Mariann' s'en va-t-au moulin" is a French folk song imported with little change to Canada. Marianne is described as going to mill mounted on the donkey Catin. At the miller's invitation she leaves Catin tethered behind the mill and enters. The wolves eat poor Catin, and Marianne returns home explaining that St. Michael on that day changed the skins of donkeys, and

       J'vous ramèn' le même âne Catin
       Qui m' porta au moulin.

13. RUSSIA. FOLK SONGS.

   a. Lootchina.
   b. Ya vetcho'r moloda.

Sung by MADAME EUGNIE LINEFF.

Madame Lineff furnishes these selections from her remarkable collection of Russian folk-songs, and gives the following explanation of their significance.

"LOOTCHINA"—Birch light—is a women's song of Great Russia, and belongs to the cycle of songs called "Possidelotchnia." *Posisdelki* are social gatherings in villages, and usually begin late in the fall, when the weather becomes inclement, and the evenings dark and unsociable outdoors. These gatherings are usually arranged in the house (izba) of a widow, and a contribution is made at holiday times for the use of the room. From time immemorial the Russian *izba* was lighted by burning a birch or pine lath (*lootchina*), stuck in an iron fork, standing over a wooden trough filled with water to prevent live coals burning the floor. This device is usually put in the corner of the room, and the people sit round it. At best it gives a very flickering light and plenty of smoke, but when the *lootchina* happens to be damp, the discomfort and dreariness in the *izba* is great indeed.

Each Russian song is a reflection of some characteristic traits of peasant life. In the *lootchina* is depicted the unhappy lot of a young married woman, "given out" (as they say in Russian for married) into a strange, unlovable family. The mother-in-law hates her and does everything in her power to make her life wretched. Being ordered to toil late into the night, the young woman is sitting in the *izba* and lamenting in her song the poor light of birch splinter she has to work with. She thinks the light is so poor because the mother-in-law threw some water in the oven while the wood was drying. . . .

The words are simplicity itself, and so is the melody, yet it is difficult to find a more pathetic song in the whole range of musical folklore. The family tyranny, which swayed for so many generations the women's lot after their marriage, must have been hard indeed to be reflected in such pathetic complaint.

The next song, "YA VETCHO'R MOLODA," is as complete a contrast to the first one as it is possible to imagine—both melody and words.

A young woman is on a spree. . . .

> She was at a feast last night,
> She was at a neighbor's,
> She "tested" not only beer
> But sweet brandy;
> She drank it not in tiny glasses,
> Not in tumblers either,—
> She drank it in large bowls.
> But she went home steady,
> Only when near the house she felt giddy.
> She took hold of the gate:—
> My dear, old gate, do support me,
> Do help a poor, weak woman.

The song goes on describing in humorous terms what she found at home, how her husband got tipsy on drinking water, what mess she made with the cakes, and how she made the rooms tidy before going to bed.

14. SWEDEN.

a. FOLK-SONG, Necken's Polska (Necken's Song).

b. CHARACTERISTIC SONG. Scene from a Swedish peasant wedding, composed by Söderman. Sung by the Swedish Glee Club of Chicago, under the direction of

MR. JOHN R. ORTENGREN.

"Necken" is the god of the lakes and the rivers, living at the bottom of the sea in a palace of diamonds and crystals. He once, so the "saga" tells us, loved "Freja," the goddess of beauty, who, for an offence, was doomed by allfader (all beings' father) "Odin," to shine from "Gimle" (heaven) as a beautiful star ("Venus") to the end of the world. Every night, when the star rises above the horizon, Necken comes up to the surface of the water, surrounded by his nymphs and najads, and playing his golden harp greets his mistress and sings to lighten his heavy heart, always continuing to love her, although without hope. The song is one of the most characteristic of Swedish sentiment in folk-lore.

The wedding song describes a dance, and contains the following sentiments :

We will dance in the cottage of the peasant ; and the musician on the barrel will play enough for two. The girls trip lightly about on the light fantastic toe, and look wistfully at the bridal wreath. O musician, put your violin under your chin and strike up. Play so that no one can keep his feet still. Hey, hey, so shall the dance go on with spirit and with joy.

The old men are drinking, the old dames are nodding ; so now, boys, keep the time with your feet.

15. GREAT BRITAIN AND IRELAND.

a. IRISH FOLK-SONG, "The Moreen," to modern words, by Moore, The Minstrel Boy.

b. ENGLISH POPULAR SONG (17th century), The Leather Bottel. Sung by

MR. GEORGE ELLSWORTH HOLMES.

WELSH FOLK SONGS.

a. Llwyn Onn (The Ash Grove). An exquisite melody of the 14th century.

b. Hob y Derry Danno (Away to the Oaken Grove). A quaint melody of the 10th century. The title refers to the Druidic custom of assembling under the oaks for song, oratory and love making.

Sung by a delegation of the Chicago Cambrian Choir of the World's Fair Eisteddfod, under the direction of

MR. W. APMADOC.

THE ASH GROVE.

Down yonder green valley where streamlets meander,
   When twilight is fading, I pensively rove;
Or at the bright noontide, in solitude wander,
   Amid the dark shades of the lonely Ash Grove.
'Twas there, while the blackbird was cheerfully singing,
   I first met that dear one, the joy of my heart;
Around us for gladness the bluebells were ringing,
   Ah! then little thought I how soon we should part.

HOB Y DERRY DANNO.

Joy upon thy bright cheek dances,
   Hob y derry danno,
   Jane, sweet Jane;
From thine eye love's arrow glances,
   Jane, sweet Jane.
In the greenwood I am waiting,
   All alone, sweet Jane,
To the tuneful birds relating,
   How I love thee, Jane;
Come unto the trysting tree,
   Jane, sweet Jane.

SCOTCH FOLK SONGS.

   a. Wae's me for Prince Charlie.
   b. When the Kye come hame.

Sung by MR. MACKENZIE GORDON.

WAE'S ME FOR PRINCE CHARLIE.

A wee bird cam' to our ha' door,
   He warbled sweet and clearly,
An' aye the o'er-come o' his song was
   'Wae's me for Prince Charlie!'

Oh! when I heard the bonnie, bonnie bird,
   The tears cam' drappin' rarely,
I took my bonnet off my head,
   For weel I lo'ed Prince Charlie.

WHEN THE KYE COME HAME.

Come a' ye jolly shepherds that whistle thro' the glen,
I'll tell ye o' a secret that courtiers dinna ken;
What is the greatest bliss that the tongue o' man can name?
'Tis to woo a bonnie lassie when the kye come hame.

16. UNITED STATES—CREOLE FOLK SONGS.
   a. Belle Layotte.

    b. Caroline.

    c. Musieu Bainjo.

Sung by MISS EVE EMMETT WYCOFF.

(These numbers, and much valuable assistance, have been furnished by Mr. H. E. Krehbiel, of New York.)

NEGRO SPIRITUAL SONGS.

    a. Keep movin'.

    b. Waters chilly an' cool.

Sung by the STANDARD QUARTET (colored), Wm. Cottrill, 1st tenor ; Edward DeMoss, 2d tenor ; Henry Archer, 1st bass ; R. L. Scott, 2d bass.

These songs, that originated among the negroes in the South, are considered by some to be the genuine folk-music of the United States. They are very interesting from any standpoint. But it is not probable that they will have the same relationship to our musical development which the folk-songs of European countries have had to the musical attainments of those countries, because these negro melodies are associated with discreditable political conditions, which neither whites nor negroes recall with pleasure.

PATRIOTIC SONGS.

    a. CHESTER.

For a century and a half after the settlement of New England the only music used in the colonies was English, mostly the church tunes by Ravenscroft and others.

In 1770 Wm. Billings, a native of Boston, published a book containing mostly original compositions. Billings was the first American composer of music, at least the first whose name and fame became known. His compositions were entirely church tunes and anthems, modelled upon the English. When the Revolution came and patriotic songs were needed, Billings adapted the words of Dr. Geo. F. Root, to one of his church tunes called Chester.

    b. BEFORE ALL LANDS. Among the first compositions of Lowell Mason, who gave the first distinctively American touch to musical composition in this country, is this song, printed in 1837 in a collection of tunes for schools and classes. This is among the first secular music produced in this country.

Sung by a select chorus under the direction of

MR. FREDERIC W. ROOT.

    c. THE BATTLE CRY OF FREEDOM. (Revised by the author.) The most enduring songs of a people are usually produced under some great stress of popular feeling. During our Civil War several songs appeared having the characteristic of national songs, songs calculated to endure and to arouse patriotic sentiment among the people. Two of these are pre-eminent—"Marching Through Georgia," and the "Battle Cry of Freedom." Both were strongly sectional when written, and one must always remain so. But the other, with but slight changes in the words, can now represent the entire country and be sung as heartily in the South as in the North.

CHESTER AND THE BATTLE CRY OF FREEDOM.

Sung by the author, DR. GEO. F. ROOT.

INTRODUCTION TO THE GERMAN PAPERS.

THE papers contributed to the Folk-Lore Congress by folk-lorists of Germany and Austria all bear the stamp of German workmanship, in that they show patient labor, exhaustive research, and exquisite care of detail,—qualities which no anthropologist will deny are esssential in that science above all others, for the reason that the material now at the disposal of this "modern science of man," owing to the extreme youth of the science, is distressingly meagre, often exposing enthusiastic folk-lorists to the reproach of wasting their time in what appears to others a bootless pursuit. Collection and classification of material are the first important steps in building up a science, especially where that science is still contending for a place among her elder sisters, and is so little recognized as belonging to them that many splendid investigators in other fields of knowledge are incapable of realizing the aims or the methods of anthropology. I have found reports of journeys taken by naturalists of note for scientific purposes at public expense, which contained a great deal of matter that might have been of an anthropological character, observed by the way, but clearly exhibiting an utter incapacity on the part of the travellers to observe primitive races in such a way as to yield reliable material of value to anthropology. If that is true of minds trained to scientific observation, what can be expected of ordinary travellers ?

The peculiar aptitude of the German mind for patient, plodding research has been abundantly exemplified in many departments of knowledge where the student who looks for original information is sure to be led to German sources. It receives fresh illustration from the papers that were contributed to the Folk-Lore Congress.

The study of primitive beliefs, usages, and customs among the peoples of Europe still remains a matter of great importance and value. It was such study that produced the

HENRY E. O. HEINEMAN.

works of Grimm and his disciples, down to the recent books of Rydberg, and has done more than any other single cause to upset the ancient traditional notions that all good came from the Latin race ; to vindicate the tremendous historical importance of the Teutonic spirit of individuality and customary popular law and government, as against the oppressive absolutism that has characterized Latin influence at all times and in all places. We in America cannot set too high store by researches along such lines, since we are, above all others, the immediate heirs and beneficiaries of that spirit of what Professor Fiske calls "fierce individualism."

We should bear in mind that the European folk-lorist works under enormous handicaps. It is indeed difficult to trace genuinely primitive beliefs and usages among peoples which have been for two thousand years under foreign influences, political, social, and religious. If he is able, with a great deal of winnowing, to separate a grain of valuable knowledge from a vast amount of foreign matter, it is an achievement of note. In the United States we are apt not to value such labor properly. While the difficulties here, also, are great, it is, nevertheless, true that we have a comparatively virgin field to work in, since we are dealing with races that still remain in a primitive state and are so widely separated in culture from the whites that assimilation is impossible, and even the absorption of small amounts of foreign matter by them remains very imperfect and the segregation of such matter from the indigenous stock offers no such intricate problems as is the case in Europe. We owe a great duty to anthropology and science in general, since no people has had such opportunities for the observation of primitive humanity under so favorable conditions.

We should not, therefore, in these German papers, look for such rich mines of novel and valuable information as are presented to us quite frequently in the reports of those who study the American Indian.

If we approach the papers contributed by the German folk-lorists in the light of the above considerations, we shall be rather pleasantly disappointed than otherwise, and shall read them with satisfaction and profit. What has been said of research in Europe is equally true of other fields which archæology, language, and mythology have been exploring most assiduously for decades past, and if it was possible for a German folk-lorist to extract something new and interesting from ancient Egyptian religion and publish it at the Folk-Lore Congress in Chicago, we have reason to congratulate ourselves. No apologies are offered for publishing the paper here referred to in full and attempting no circumlocution in its terms. There is much that is valuable, also, in the reflections of a general character in the paper on comparative jurisprudence as connected with ethnology, defining the aims of research in that direction and explaining the importance of anthropological study.

As to his own work in the preparation of these papers for publication, the translator and editor would apologize to those contributors whose papers were not printed in full, and offer only this excuse, that the limitations of this report of the proceedings of the Folk-Lore Congress did not permit the insertion of all the papers in full, and that those were condensed which lent themselves most readily to such treatment, there being no desire, by such discrimination, to express any judgment of the relative merits of the contributions. In the case of the little Slavic epic, a faithful metrical translation was the only alternative of total omission, as a mere narrative in prose, or an abstract, would have destroyed entirely that peculiar individuality which is the reason of its contribution. Ignorance of the Slavonic tongue in which the original stands compelled the adoption of Dr. Krauss's German translation, which was followed in spirit, words, and verse as closely as lay in the power of the translator, so as to preserve the original character of the poem without doing much violence to the common forms of expression and the idioms of the English language.

HENRY E. O. HEINEMANN.

Chicago, 1897.

COMPARATIVE JURISPRUDENCE ON AN ETH-NOLOGICAL BASIS.

BY DR. THOMAS ACHELIS.

SINCE, in recent years, the principles and methods of the comparative science of language have found application in other branches of philological-historical disciplines, there has been opened to the mind's eye a boundless world of new and grand discoveries. True, as in every crisis of scientific development, sometimes an hypothesis of more or less uncertain character is called into requisition, or, which is a great disappointment to the scholar, he must at times refrain altogether from forming any definite opinion, owing to the actual condition of the material at hand. This methodological defect, however, in nowise detracts from the vast importance of the principle. As comparative linguistic science for the first time gave us an insight into our own primitive Aryan history, beyond time and space and historical or monumental tradition ; as by this means for the first time our mental horizon expanded from the narrow area of Græco-Roman culture into the conception of a comprehensive history of our own tribe, with all its creations, religion, mythology, law, customs, art, etc.,—even so were we prepared for grasping an idea of a history of the world, expanding almost infinitely the development of human civilization beyond those narrow limits within which our fathers attempted to confine it. To this were added the brilliant discoveries in physical anthropology and the life of prehistoric ages, throwing a startling light upon the early stages of human development which previously appeared lost in impenetrable darkness ; furthermore, the results of modern ethnography, making us acquainted with great civilizations in distant continents where there could have been no connection, either in place or time, with the culture of the occident ; finally, the most significant fact that outside of any ethnographical relationship or historical contrast, certain conceptions and institutions were found at the most remote points of the world, necessitating the assumption of certain great universal laws of the social evolution of mankind.

Upon such principles is based the modern science of a universal jurisprudence working with the wealth of material of modern ethnology, and it cannot, therefore, any longer observe the topographical limits of the old schools of historical jurisprudence—like that of Savigny, for instance—or yield to the seductive inspirations of metaphysical speculation. . . .

Comparative jurisprudence on an ethnological basis is the organic connecting link between the physical sciences and philosophy, the two old-time enemies. For while in its entire method and structure purely empirical and inductive, its final aims are of a philosophical nature; i. e., they give us an insight into the development of the human mind. . . .

The student of comparative jurisprudence entirely ignores the traditional guidance of chronology. . . . for ethnology is not confined to any one race, but by means of analogy extends its work to all mankind. The identical characteristic legal custom or view may be found among peoples of altogether different races, at the most distant periods where there can be no transmission; and, on the other hand, the most divergent institutions and forms of thought are found within the same decade. The object of ethnology is to exhibit certain phenomena which appear uniformly, everywhere on the basis of a uniform human nature.

It may be of interest to illustrate by some examples the psychogenetic procedure of ethnology, which show conclusively the utter insufficiency of a simply historical consideration. When such problems appeared embarrassment found expression in such terms as "caprices, anomalies, curiosities," etc.; the real psychological nature of them remaining unelucidated. Such was the case with the so-called men's childbed, or the curious custom of marrying boys under age to full-grown girls who live with other men until their boy husbands arrive at maturity; or that institution which appears so strange to our sensibilities, viz., the family based on connection by the mother as it prevails among the Nairs of the Indian Malabar coast, where the father is connected with the children of his body by no legal or even moral tie, whereas he is at liberty to sell or kill the sons and daughters of his sister. What purpose would a careful historical and chronological investigation serve in such a case? It is utterly incapable of giving us the key of such social conditions, and the problem can be only solved by a comparative treatment of the subject, going beyond the narrow historical and ethnographic bounds and investigating the peculiar organization of the tribes in question. This method alone can produce a truly pragmatical understanding of the conditions and, as Tyler observes, put in the place of an unscientific accident and arbitrariness, a development according to a strict law and necessity.

On the other hand the objection is made that comparative ethnology does not, like comparative philology, keep within topographical and ethnographical limits, there being an erroneous impression that the kind of comparison in the two disciplines is the same. It cannot be stated too emphatically or frequently that similar legal conceptions are not bounded by the same limits as are the corresponding parallels in cognate languages. . . . Conceptions of right and law, and the corresponding institutions, are determined so little by ethnographic standards, that comparative jurisprudence has succeeded in our days in showing similar conceptions and customs among peoples of altogether different blood; so that originally it was thought that there had been a process of borrowing and transmission, which, of course, did occur at times and within certain limits. . . . Ethnology finds at any given time all kinds of legal customs, from the most primitive to the most highly developed, side by side among the various peoples of the earth. The material on which it bases its conclusions consists of similar facts, which, among the different peoples, lie decades and whole centuries, even thousands of years apart. . . . The chronology of ethnological jurisprudence is not the counting of years from some arbitrary point, but rather the gradual development of some characteristic legal conception or custom among certain tribes.

As to the method of ethnological jurisprudence, the author says, in brief, that the first step is the collection of reliable inductive material, which is easily prepared where there are at hand judicial decisions, customs, and written laws. Among the great mass of primitive peoples the relevant facts must be gathered from officials or travellers, proceeding always with due care against error or deception, for which purpose constant comparison with the material already sifted is very useful. In order to amplify the material for our science it is important to gather and perpetuate authentic reports regarding the primitive peoples which are destined to disappear rapidly before our levelling civilization. After the material has been gathered the real work of the science begins, which consists of a methodical sifting of the raw material according to certain principle. The basis for this sifting process is given by the comparison of analogous legal institutions and forms, the collecting of parallels.

Certain legal or customary institutions are repeated so regularly among all the peoples of the earth that they may be looked upon as the common property of humanity. Others are found all over the world but sporadically, others are confined to certain groups of peoples, others to certain individual tribes or still smaller ethnic divisions. Accordingly, some display universal features of the race, while others show more or less marked deviations from certain basic principles. In the final form of established law the various layers often appear curiously intermingled, and even in modern codifications there are fragments of ancient, prehistoric descent, which have survived from an altogether different period. It is insufficient to explain any phenomenon of jurisprudence from individual psychological causes, it is always necessary to look for social causes.

The far-reaching results of comparative jurisprudence can be touched upon only in faint outlines. The first place is due to the peculiar gentile community which is scattered over the whole world and is so radically different from our social forms of to-day. In this system, which was discovered by Post, the characteristic element is the typical communism of this organization which depends upon the mother of the tribe or family, who represents the unity of blood. The consciousness of the unity appears drastically at times in the duty of blood revenge, which is surrounded with a certain religious nimbus. The closer the union within, the stricter is seclusion from without. There is no individuality; everything is held in common; the actions of one are the actions of all, his guilt is to be visited upon the tribe; even women and children are common property. This appears to have been the original condition of the human race the world over, the patriarchal stage being very much later, and our present monogamous marriage only a comparatively recent development. Among the universal customs are the marriage by the violent carrying off or purchase of the bride. Next to these rudimentary social formations of nature are the communities growing out of the joint occupation of a limited territory. A third stage of social differentiation is that of government based upon the difference between the free and the unfree caused by birth, warlike enterprise, or slavery for debt, leading to the rise of chieftains and finally of kings. Still later is the separation of the human mass according to occupations and classes, influenced largely by age, rank and race.

The history of civilization depends entirely upon comparative jurisprudence in connection with ethnology for its information concerning the earliest stages of human culture. But the science also serves to throw light upon the elucidation of the great questions of philosophy, including the greatest problems that ever engaged the human mind. It gives a solid foundation to psychology by showing the gradual unfolding of the mind in its collective capacity, as against the Ego which stands in the front of the boldly constructed realm of reason, whereas in reality it plays but a subordinate part in the life of the race. The important idea of an universal spirit, which is gaining ground in philosophy, could find an inductive foundation for the first time in modern ethnology. Still greater is the influence of our science upon ethics. In contradistinction to the old idea where, in a deductive method, everything was derived from some arbitrary ideal, ethnology proves that ethics is purely relative, that there is no universal idea of good and evil. All changes in ethical conceptions and standards are but the result of social differentiation.

Finally, in regard to the most difficult part of philosophical thought, the theory of cognition, ethnology points from the inventions of metaphysical imagination to the possibility of a strictly empirical solution.

WHY NATIONAL EPICS ARE COMPOSED.

SOME REFLECTIONS ILLUSTRATED BY A SONG OF GUSLARS OF BOSNIA AND HERZEGOVINA.

BY DR. FRIEDRICH S. KRAUSS.

THE *guslar* of the southern Slavs is not controlled by the Muse. And the ancient Greek? Neither is he. Our writers of artistic literature who live by their pens, generally look for compensation, which is determined, generally, by the quality of the work, as is well-known, or by the prospective sales of the publisher.

If the writer possesses great ability and is fully informed in his line and very industrious, he has an advantage over competitors. The same applies to the composer of folk-songs : it is always more or less a matter of compensation. A distinction should be made, however, especially among the southern Slavs, between the original poet-fiddler (*pijevo guslar*) and the mere performer, the *guslar*, who is satisfied with repeating the productions of others which he has committed to memory in order to entertain his audience and win their "appreciation." The mode of expressing this appreciation depends upon the composition of the audience.

The desire of men to gain the good report of others,—i. e., to be praised, appreciated, and honored,—is universal. Vanity, a desire for glory, power, wealth, and strength feel the need of glorification. The publishers of our sporting journals really do no other service for their patrons than did the poet-*guslars* for their "heroes," who at that time, just as at the present, were or are obliged to provide the cost of being made famous.

It does not matter that the "star" desires other advantages than glory. His actions at times most urgently demand poetical glorification, and this is sometimes the last thing he will relinquish.

The deeds of the knights and other champions of the southern Slavs had all the characteristics of an ennobled sport. We often flatter ourselves that daring sport is one of the acquirements of our enlightened civilization. Thus Halil the Falcon, the brother of the border chieftain Mujo the Harelip, was a sportsman of that type. In sheer bravado he releases the nine captive Panjevic brothers and their standard-bearer Komneu, in order to kill each of them in single combat instead of having them killed in prison. Knight Tale of Orasje, the fierce jester, is both delighted with the valor of Halil and envious of his glory, in which he would fain have a share. He says to Mujo :

Halil's name will in song be celebrated
From now to everlasting, Brother Mujo.
But suddenly cried out in loud voice Tale :
Leave him to me, the standard-bearer Komneu;
Myself would grip him by his mighty shoulders.
I am a hero greater than Halil.

Curious sacrifices were made by the heroes to gratify the desire for fame in song. *Vixere fortes ante Agamemnona*, of whom the world knows nothing, as is properly said by Horace. The curse of oblivion on one occasion appalled the hoary Cejvanaga of Udbina and the above-mentioned Halil of Old-Kladusa in the Lilka, the Karst land. This was enhanced by envy of the glory, largely undeserved, according to their view, of their leader, the border and robber chieftain, Mujo. Our song tells how their envy led them into great harm and obloquy until they returned penitent and confessed that in all justice, glory and honor were due to the only Mujo above all the heroes, and that he alone deserved the unstinted praise of the guslars.

The epic poetry of Servia and Bulgaria—one cannot speak of national Croatian or Slavonic epics—has but few really important epic centres. Most important are the songs treating of the fall of the Bulgarian and Servian empire, and commemorating the fortunes of the court and nobility of King Lazar, or the deeds of the Bulgarian pretender, Prince Marko. A more recent centre of epic poetry originated about two hundred and fifty years ago, when the Moslem-Slavic feudal lords of Bosnia and Herzegovina formed the principal protection of the border lands against the German and Italian west. Along the entire border, more particularly towards Dalmatia and Croatia, castles of robber knights were built, the masters of which, with their own soldiers and at their own risk, visited the adjacent border lands at every favorable opportunity, for the purpose of gaining booty of all kinds, killing and burning. To curb these fierce land filibusterers even the viziers at Stamboul were powerless. Those viziers who were sent to Bosnia as governors were satisfied, and were compelled to be satisfied, with filling their own pockets during their short terms. Among themselves the noble families were often united by blood or marriage, and invariably by alliances or as blood-brothers according to ancient Slavic custom. Those who did not belong to the great family alliances, and were under no one's protection or ownership, stood without the law. Certain privileges granted by the state were without doubt enjoyed by the Moslem, and in return he alone was obliged to pay blood-money at his own cost. The Christians of either denomination might live undisturbed on Turkish soil, provided they faithfully delivered to their lords the tithes or thirds according to agreement. On the whole, the Christians lived according to their own habits, in ignorance and without ambition, entirely dependent upon the clergy, who wasted their time in dull intellectual idleness at the expense of a credulous people living in un-Christian superstition.

However rotten and hopeless social conditions were at that time in Bosnia and Herzegovina, they were by no means so horrible and desperate as in the German countries from the twelfth to the end of the sixteenth century. They were also free from the Inquisition, with the horrible trials of witches and persecutions of the Jews. The torture chamber was unknown among those Slavs. The Slavic Moslems were remarkably tolerant in matters of faith. Whether and by what means an individual prepared himself for paradise or Gehenna was looked upon as a private matter for which each one would some time have to answer before the throne of God. Hospitality was boundless, even towards visitors from the neighboring states. Another feature is characteristic of our heroes, in spite of their boastfulness; viz., honesty and truthfulness in everyday—or as we could say—civic life and

29

conduct. Their armor, weapons, clothes, and horses, and also women, they were wont to carry away from their enemies in a fight, or to buy honestly for cash.

Among the Moslem Slavs there was no real hereditary nobility. The knights and feudal lords were peasants in armor. The security of their possessions depended chiefly upon the personal bravery of the holders. The consciousness of having, as it were, only another person's property for use may have had great influence in inducing the knights to found numerous sacred institutions for the care of widows and orphans, and caravansaries for the free entertainment of wanderers; also to construct many wells for the sake of bringing the drinking water within the reach of everybody, and to leave a good name by similar public-spirited works.

Among the heroes of this kind were Mujo, Halil, Cejvan, and Susa, of whom our song tells.

I wrote down the text on January 24, 1885, at Bjelina in Bosnia, from the recitation of the *guslar* Avdija Salijevic, who had learned it some forty years before from a *guslar* from Visegrad in Bosnia. Subsequently, I wrote down three variants in other parts. The same subject forms the theme of a *guslar* song in the collection of Simon Milutinovic which appeared at Leipsic in 1836 in the Servian language. According to the language, that form seems to have been fixed on the borders of Montenegro.

THE DEATH OF CHIEF SIMON.

Be full of cheer, O patriarch of this house !
So may God give us joy and happiness
And keep us safe from plague and accident,
From every plague and fierce assault of robbers !
5   Then let me sing to you a song of deeds
Of olden times, of happenings long ago.
· That flock is lost which goes without the shepherd,
Without the shepherd it will not forth to pasture.

*   *   *   *   *   *

Early at morn rose Mujo from his couch,
10   Before the dusk and dawn of early morning,
And from his sleep awaked Halil, his brother :
"Awake, Halil, arouse thee ! Up my brother !
(The younger never must gainsay their elders)."
Halil sprang from the floor upon his legs.
15   "Now listen well to me, Halil, my brother !
The wine has disappeared from all our vessels,
Pocket and purse alike of ducats empty !
Nor have I wherewithal wine might be purchased.

Now I have heard, and common is the saying,
20 In Sibinj, in the radiant, white-walled castle—
Twelve years have passed until the present day
Since that the Turk no more descended on it,
Descended on the level town of Sibinj—
There might we find and carry off rich booty.
25 Then go, and take with thee two signal pistols,
Load each with full a pint of powder grits
And weigh down each one with a quart of dry lead ;
Take the war pennant with our coat-of-arms
Forth on the dewy meadow by the castle,
30 And plant the flagstaff in the yielding turf ;
Then fire off both the heavy signal pistols,
Call forth my men all through my borderland.
Gather for me, Halil, a company ;
Take only warriors of approved valor.
35 Six hundred heroes gather me about,—
Six hundred without house and without home,
Who know not fond embrace of faithful wife,
Accustomed to eye death indifferently,
To whom a cloak is house and home and hearth,
40 Their sword their father, and their musket, mother ;
Collect me such a band of warriors."
The younger never must gainsay his elders.
He went, and took with him two signal pistols,
And took the war pennant into his hands ;
45 Swiftly he steps across the dewy meadow
And fires off both the heavy signal pistols.
Through all the borderland sounds the report,
Four mountain ranges echo back and forth,
Bukovica and Orahovica,
50 The Beaverwood, and Kunar's lofty peaks,
Thus went the call through all the borderland.
The warriors speedily begin to gather,
Halil writes all their names upon the roll.
While Mujo arms himself within the castle,—
55 Arms both his body and his snow-white steed ;
Six hundred men Halil has mustered in.

    *   *   *   *   *   *   *

From thence the company rode boldly forth,
On his white steed Chief Mujo led the column.
The hoary Cejvanaga follows him ;
60 White is his head and also his long beard,
His last tooth has been lost these many years,
And empty rattle now his shrivelled jaws ;
One hundred years and thirty has he seen.
On Cejvan follows close Halil the Falcon,
65 And on Halil the other company.
They ride together through the spreading fields,
Have left the fields behind them, unassailed ;
Ascend the steep heights of the Kunar mountains,
On Kunar peak up to the cooling fountain,
70 Where once Knight Ramo dug a well of water.
The warriors all drew near the mountain spring,
When Mujo spoke to them from his tall horse :
"Dismount, my brothers, from your weary steeds ;
Let rest and sleep here follow on our labors,
75 To banish weariness from heroes' limbs."

So spoke he and the counsel was obeyed.
They mounted from their noble chargers all,
They lay and rested under graceful pines,
They drew well-filled canteens from bags and pockets
80 And drank refreshment in the purple wine.
Ere long, when with the wine they were refreshed,
The color mounted in their sunburnt cheeks,
And loosened were the tongues of all the heroes.
This wanton word spoke young Halil the Falcon :
85 " Had we but each a buxom, blushing maiden
To share beneath these pines our soft green couch."
Ho, what observed the hoary Cejvanaga ?
" Albeit my beard has grown so long and white,
Still would I find delight in maiden's love ;
90 What can be sweeter than the rosebud's sugar ?
What can be swifter than a noble charger ?
What can be broader than the azure ocean ?
What can be dearer than a pretty damsel ?
My love is sweeter than the rosebud's sugar,
95 The eyes are swifter than a noble charger,
The heavens broader than the azure ocean,
But naught is dearer than a pretty damsel."
    Approval laughed the merry company,
But scorn broke from the lips of Mujo thus:
100 " What would the graybeard with the prettiest damsel ?
Woe to the musket in a coward hand,
And woe the damsel on the graybeard's arm,
Too late the children, orphans from their birth."
Swiftly sprang up the hoary Cejvanaga,
105 Swiftly he sprang, as though stung by an adder,
And these words spoke the hoary Cejvanaga :
" Up, Mujo, up !   We will divide the party.
I rode with thee till now upon adventure,
From this day ride I with thee nevermore.
110 Whenever warriors charge for the assault,
Thou, Mujo, send'st another leader forward
That he may draw the living fire on him,
Whilst thou art hiding, Mujo, in the rear.
And yet thy praise alone the songs proclaim.
115 None will remember me and my exploits,
The song of my deeds never yet was sung ;
Hence will I not ride with thee on adventure."
Then spoke to him the border chieftain Mujo:
" Betake thee hence, O hoary Cejvanaga !
120 Do not divide my company in arms,
The band of warriors which I have gathered.
If thou didst think to part my company,
Why didst not thou tell me at Udbina,
While we were tarrying near the white-walled castle ? "
125 To him replied the hoary Cejvanaga :
" Should I ask thy permission, Harelip Mujo ? "
Up sprang he from the ground upon his legs,
Selected from the band two hundred heroes,
The best among the best selected he.
130 When Cejvan had picked out his company
He leaped upon his stout and powerful charger ;
Sir Cejvan parted and rode through the mountains—
Sir Cejvan parted, leading off his band.

Halil remained, gazed after him in sorrow ;

135 And when Halil saw this with his own eyes,
Hot anger in his heart began to rise
And he addressed his brother Mujo thus :
" By my own mother brother, Harelip Mujo,
Arise now and divide our company.

140 I rode with thee till now upon adventure ;
But henceforth nevermore, my brother Mujo.
Whenever warriors charge the foe, O Mujo,
Thou always bidd'st me lead the men to fight,
That I may draw the living fire on me,

145 Whilst thou art biding, Mujo, in the rear.
And yet thy praise alone the songs proclaim ;
The song of my deeds never yet was sung.
Hence ride I no more with thee on adventure.
Arise then, Mujo, and divide the party !

150 Two hundred well-armed men I claim for me,
And if thou dost deny my prayer, Mujo,
Alone I ride among the Christians, Mujo,
Though I should lose my head upon the venture ! "
And lightly sprang he on his nimble legs

155 And ran to where his little jennet stood
And shouting " Allah ! " leaped into the saddle.
Halil spurred fast him through the mountain range.
When Chieftain Mujo saw Halil alone
Ride forth to go into the Christian country,

160 Then Mujo felt compassion in his heart,
He feared Halil alone might lose his head.
With raised voice shouted Mujo after him :
" Halil, my brother, come back to the camp !
The adder bite thee ! Back into the camp !

165 And here select thy company in arms,
Select the men according to desire."
No sooner did Halil the Falcon hear
Than did Halil return into the camp,
Halil went in, selected his companions,

170 Two hundred valiant men selected he,
Selected all the best among the best.
When thus Halil had picked out all his party,
To him spoke thus the border-chieftain Mujo :
" Halil the Falcon, look at this, thou fool,

175 Look at this leather-bottle full of wine.
I hang it to the limb of this tall pine.
Shouldst thou return before me from the forage
Homeward to ride into our borderland,
Throw down this leather bottle from the pine tree,

180 That I may know that thou hast safe returned
And tarry not to wait for thee, Halil."
Off rode Halil and took with him the men.
Among the lofty mountain peaks stayed Mujo.
When Mujo Harelip there reviewed his band,

185 Saw but two hundred men of small renown,
Sorrow and anguish of his heart took hold.
Then Mujo, lost in thought, revolved the question.
" What cause have I, unfortunate, to love
This life ? I still desire to persevere,

190 Despite luck, to descend on level Sibinj,
In Sibinj should I find much valued booty,

Could easily supply a hero's needs.
Now has my company been quite divided,
I have not wherewith to descend on Sibinj."

195 Think as he might he could think one thought only,
And thus spoke Chieftain Mujo to his band :
"O listen to me, my two hundred fellows,
Arise with speed and arm yourselves for battle ;
For we will still descend on level Sibinj."

200 Scarce heard two hundred men this bold command,
They all began to weep and cry with fear,
And thus protested to their Chieftain Mujo :
"Give up the plan, oh, lead us not to Sibinj !
We all shall surely lose our lives, O Mujo !

205 Never before did we ride on adventure,
Are inexperienced in adventurous exploits,
We know not even how to handle muskets."
To them spoke thus the chief, paunch-bellied Mujo :
"Listen to me, two hundred worthless fellows !

210 You must for sure descend upon Sibinj,
Though all were killed like dogs in the exploit."
The Harelip's glances of a sudden strayed
Towards the straight trunk of the slender pine-tree,
And there behind the pine-tree noticed Mujo

215 His war-companion Susa of Posusje.
Sir Susa hid himself behind the pine-tree,
Hid from the sharp gaze of Halil, the small,
So that Halil might not lead him away.
When his form met the sight of Chieftain Mujo

220 A gleam of sunshine spread through his sad spirit.
This word he spoke to Susa of Posusje ;
"O dearest brother, Susa of Posusje,
Come forth from thy concealment by the pine-tree.
Behind the pine why dost thou hide thyself ?"

225 Forth stepped to him Sir Susa of Posusje
And spoke this word to border-chieftain Mujo :
"I hide myself, O border-chieftain Mujo,
From thine own brother, from Halil, the Falcon.
With him I do not wish to travel further.

230 Share rather adverse fortune with a hero
Than at the festive board sit with the unworthy."
What said thereon the border-chieftain Mujo ?
"Well said, dear brother, Susa of Posusje !
Forward, dear brother, and equip thy charger !

235 Take in thy right the tightly braided kantscha,
To which twelve rods are cunningly attached.
Drive after me two hundred worthless fellows,
That we may now descend on level Sibinj
And then take that which God and fortune give.

240 There can be gained much valued spoils and booty."
When Susa of Posusje heard these words,
Went Susa forth his saddle horse to harness.
Down to the valley rode they through the forest,
Came straight and whole to the white town of Sibinj,

245 Arriving in the broad fields within sight
Of the watch-tower of the Chieftain Simon.

*　　*　　*　　*　　*　　*

When they had reached the midst of the broad plain
Chief Simon's wedded wife descried the band—

But recently had Simon wedded her,
250 In truth, not quite a year had since gone by—
From out a window in her white watch-tower.
And when she saw the martial band approach,
Horror and fear upon the young wife seized;
For she saw the frontiersmen were the guests.
255 Chief Simon was not tarrying at home,
Had led from Sibinj all his fighting men—
Led them into the level border lands,
To bring aid to his neighbor and heart-brother,—
To his heart-brother Smiljanic Elijah!
260 For him the Turks had suddenly assailed,
The Turks of the frontierland had assailed him.
The first charge from the hoary Cejvanaga,
Two hundred men marched with him to the charge.
From one side Cejvan had assailed the Christians;
265 Halil the Falcon, from the other side,
Two hundred men marched with him to the charge.
So was he gone to help his dear heart-brother.
When Simon's wife the bordermen descried
She called within her faithful messenger:
270 " Come hither quick, my faithful messenger,
Lead forth the fleetest-footed Arab courser
Lead forth him on the courtyard's marble floor.
Delay not then to buckle on the saddle,
There lacks the time to harness well the mare,
275 Ride rather bare the mare without the saddle,
And fly into the level border land,
To the tall tower of mighty Smiljanic.
Haste quickly to seek our Chieftain Simon,
Report to him straightforward and in full,
280 How that the Turks have here surprised the castle,
The Turks of the frontierland have surprised us;
They carry hence me to their borderland."
No sooner had the servant heard the words
Than he led forth the mare out of the stable,
285 He sprang upon the back of the stout mare.
Hence flew the little Christian through the fields,
Bareheaded, on the mare without a saddle;
Descended whole into the borderland.
Soon found among the men the chieftain Simon,
290 And whispered hurriedly to Chieftain Simon:
" O my dear lord and master, Chieftain Simon!
Ill sitt'st thou still, my dearest lord and master,
Ill sitt'st thou still refreshing thee with wine!
The Turks have made assault on our town Sibinj!"
295 When Chieftain Simon heard this evil message:
" Betake thee hence, my faithful messenger,
Betake thee hence, that story is not true;
'Tis only now that we dispelled the Turks,
And only now sat down to take our rest.
300 Whence came into your parts the border Turks?
Of what description were the men who led them?"
The little capless Christian said to him:
" The Turk who led the band against Sibinj
Was seated on a white and mighty charger.
305 A black mustachio covered half his face,
Fain would I say, and almost swear to it,

That by his teeth a black lamb is suspended.
The buttons shine from underneath his beard
As the bright moonbeams though the pine-tree's branches
810 Two hundred strong may be the troop that follows.
The Turk who rode the last of all the train
Rode proudly on a plump bay-colored steed ;
He carried in his hand a braided kantscha,
The ends hang downward from his red mustache."
815 When Captain Simon heard the man's description,
He spoke thus to the faithful messenger :
My son, I know him—so may ill betide him—
The Turk who proudly his white charger rides,
None other than the border-chieftain Mujo.
820 The Turk who rode the last of all the train,
My servant, it is Susa of Posusje."
And hurriedly he sprang up from the ground
And ran to where his swift brown courser stood,
He leaped into the saddle of his charger.
825 Downward to Sibinj travelled Captain Simon ;
He rode away, descended down to Sibinj.
Ha, couldst thou see the border-chieftain Mujo !
Before he came had Mujo robbed the castle,
Despoiled it of all valuable goods,
830 Despoiled completely Simon's tall watch tower
And carried off his faithful wedded wife,
Set fire to all the buildings, reared of stone,
And heaped up hay around about the castle.
When Mujo thus had fired the stately castle,
835 He rode away into the Kunar mountains,
And took with him the gathered spoils of Sibinj,
Ha, couldst thou then behold the Captain Simon !
Sir Simon came before his towering castle
And galloped on his bay into the courtyard :
840 " Behold, the whore, the border chieftain Mujo !
He heaped up hay around about the castle
And threw into it brands of living fire.
But then the Harelip would no longer tarry
Until the heaps of hay had caught the fire ;
845 He swiftly bore his plunder to the mountains,
It happened that the hay was somewhat damp,
And did not readily take up the fire."
  When Mujo reached the lofty mountain ridge
It suddenly came into Mujo's mind
850 That he had left behind him his wild musket,
In Simon's blooming garden in the valley,
Leaning against a yellow orange tree.
Against this tree Sir Mujo placed the gun,
While he was laying fire about the castle.
855 He soundly struck his palm upon his knees.
"See my ill luck, O Susa of Posusje !
My musket left behind me down in Sibinj,
In Simon's blooming garden in the valley !
I must, my brother, go and fetch the gun.
860 Guard well our plunder on the mountain range."
This speech was heard by Simon's wedded wife,
And thus spoke she to Aga Mustaphaga :
" Let rest the musket, Aga Mustaphaga !
Enough have I of shining golden ducats,

865 A better one will I have made for thee,
And have it cast in pure gold if thou wishest."
What said to her the border-chieftain Mujo ?
"Take thee away, thou filthy Christian beast !
I know that thou hast many golden ducats,

870 And that a better one thou couldst have made,
But never the good luck of my own musket."
He turned about and leaped upon his horse,
So rode Sir Mujo down to Sibinj castle.
At Simon's tower Mujo soon arrived

875 And on his white horse galloped to the courtyard.
But when Chief Mujo nearer drew and saw
That fire did not destroy the castle wholly,
Anew he put the firebrands to the buildings,
At four opposing corners set the fire,

880 Then leisurely into the garden went,
And in the garden safely found his musket.
Here Mujo sat himself upon the greensward,
And Mujo tarried in the verdant garden
Until the hay should well have caught the fire,

885 And wildly roared the blaze throughout the castle.
At last the castle all about took fire ;
Upon his well-fed white horse leaped Sir Mujo
And galloped off across the spreading fields.
　Ha, could'st thou then behold the Captain Simon !
He flies across the level meadows swiftly,

890 To reach the Harelip flies Sir Simon forward.
When he had reached the middle of the field,
His fleet bay courser caught the scent of fire
Time and again the bay horse turned his head

895 And each time patted on his head Sir Simon :
"Make haste, my brown horse, haste my dearest treasure,
Why dost thou turn thy head back in thy footsteps ? "
Ha, could'st thou then behold the Captain Simon !
He cannot keep his bay horse looking forward,

400 So that his bay horse will not turn his head.
At last did Captain Simon turn about,
He fiercely looks about with his black eyes ;
The stone-constructed castle is in flames !
At once he turned the head of his brown courser.

405 "See then, behold the whore, paunch-bellied Mujo !
Did not the whore my dwelling set ablaze ?
While I, the warrior, was about the castle
The desolate building had not taken fire,
Since in the stone walls was the fire extinguished.

410 Where lay the crafty Harelip in concealment,
That I could fail to be aware of him ?
After the whore accompanied me forth
He set the blaze around about my castle ! "
About this time the Harelip also came,

415 Came forth into the spreading smiling valley.
From one side Mujo ; from the other, Simon,
So met they one another in the field.
And on the spot went to attack each other ;
Each one discharged a musket on the other,

420 But neither one received a wound thereby.
And so they closed and grasped their sharpened irons,
Down to the hilts they broke the sword-blades off ;

They dropped themselves down from their horses' backs,
And from the ground they sprang upon their legs,
425   Their powerful bones against each other braced.
And wrestled there for three, four hours together.
Ha, couldst thou see the border-chieftain Mujo!
A white foam stood on Mujo's mouth and face,
But red and bloody was the foam on Simon,
430   For weightier was Mujo than was Simon.
Both champions had gotten sick and weary
In desperate struggle wrestling in the field.
But Captain Mujo firmly set his teeth,
He set them hard and lifted Simon up.
435   And hurled the Captain Simon on the ground,
Hurled headlong him into the yielding meadow.
He bit off with his teeth the enemy's head,
And threw the head into his saddle-bag;
Took Simon's bay horse by the hanging reins.—
440   Thus Mujo rode straight up into the mountains,
He rode and rode and mounted higher up.
When Mujo reached the lofty mountain crest,
Found his heart-brother Susa of Posusje,
He found the brother covered all with foam,
445   Guarding the plunder on the lofty mountains;
For homeward did the slaves all want to fly;
Two hundred worthless fellows lay asleep,
And Susa of Posusje could not wake them.
Then went to awaken them the Harelip Mujo.
450   He kicked them with his feet hard in the back,
One after other Mujo roused them up.
"Arouse yourselves, two hundred good-for-nothings!
Arise—the dogs may carry off your mothers——
How do you come to be so very sleepy,
455   Since you with no one fought in deadly struggle?"
Dismounting from his horse, Mujo sat down
And seated his heart-brother next to him:
"Let us have rest, my brother, here sit down,
And take refreshment from heroic labors."
460   They sit and rest beneath the slender pine-tree
And here refresh themselves in ease and comfort,
Here did they stay and comfortably rest.
Ha, couldst thou see the border-chieftain Mujo!
He took the head of Simon from the bag,
465   And in these words to his heart-brother spoke:
"Here, my heart-brother, is the head of Simon."
When Susa of the head had taken note,
Then softly Susa spoke to Mujo, thus:
"Where didst thou find him, speak, so help thee God!"
470   And Mujo told according to the truth
Of the encounter in the spreading fields.
Just then the glance of Aga Mustaphaga
Went up among the branches of the pine-tree;
There still hung undisturbed the leather bottle.
475   None of the others, then, had passed the place.
Hence Mujo spoke these words to his heart-brother:
"O my heart-brother, Susa of Posusje,
Has neither of those whores returned this way?
How now! Shall we here tarry their return?
480   Or shall we up and journey to Kladusa?"

While thus in conversation they sat still,
A cry of pain came sounding through the forest.
The caller's voice was recognized by Mujo,
He recognized the hoary Cejvanaga,

485 And this word spoke he to his dear heart-brother:
" O my heart-brother, Susa of Posusje,
There comes the whore, the graybeard Cejvanaga.
Go, brother, and descend the mountain side,
Lend your strong arm to hoary Cejvanaga,

490 Lead him to me here on the mountain crest."
Sir Susa went and found the hoary Cejvan,
He carried Cejvan up the mountain-side;
But when he led him into Mujo's presence,
The border-chieftain Mujo eyed him closely.

495 In shreds the garment hung on Cejvan's body,
Wild was his long gray beard and all dishevelled
—Lost from his jaw the last remaining tooth.
Ha, couldst thou see the border-chieftain Mujo !
He questioned thus the hoary Cejvanaga :

500 "Thou worthless blackguard, graybeard Cejvanaga,
How is thy beard so wild ? May it remain so !
How is thy garment torn in shreds and tatters ?
Where didst thou, ninny, lose thy company ? "
To him replied the hoary Cejvanaga :

505 "What dost thou ask of me, O Chieftain Mujo ?
I did attack the Christians' borderland
From one side I myself led the attack,
Halil, thy brother, from the other side.
Almost had we achieved the victory,

510 When to the rescue came the Captain Simon
He came to aid the mighty Smiljanic,
Hadst thou beheld him, Border-Chieftain Mujo,
Beheld him with thine own affrighted eyes,
Thy throbbing heart had burst within thy breast ;

515 Where hadst thou found the heart to fight him, Mujo ?
All our companions, Simon cut them down.
Myself, the hero, barely could escape,
And fled until I reached the mountain range.
When I found safety here among the mountains.

520 Had I escaped and kept my strong brown horse,
Had I in that wise sought the mountain-sides,
Simon would surely have o'ertaken me.
There did I separate from my fleet courser,
I let the bay horse run among the mountains.

525 Myself, O Mujo, climbed the mountain peaks,
Kept hidden ever in the darkest thicket,
Until I reached thee on the lofty mountain.
The woods have torn my garments into tatters,
Have combed out clean my wild, dishevelled beard

530 While I was dragging myself through the mountains."
Ha, couldst thou see the border-chieftain Mujo.
He took the head of Simon from the bag
And threw it at the feet of hoary Cejvan :
"Is this, thou whore, the head of Captain Simon ? "

535 Scarce did old Cejvanaga see the head
When he sprang up all horrified and trembling.
There fell upon him a three-summers' fever.
To Mujo flew the hoary Cejvanaga

And with hot kisses covered Harelip's forehead.
540 "Incomparable !   Falcon Mustaphaga !
Once did I break apart thy company,
But from this day, O Aga Mustaphaga,
Though we should live a hundred years together,
I'll nevermore part company with thee.
545 The song of thy deeds shall be sung, O Mujo,
It will be sung, for such is but thy due."
    Meanwhile, who comes ?   It is Halil the Falcon.
His lamentations wake the Kunar mountains.
The voice was recognized by Chieftain Mujo,
550 He spoke in these words to his dear heart-brother,—
His dear heart-brother, Susa of Posusje ;
There, my heart-brother, comes Halil, my brother !
Most like, the whore is suffering with wounds.
Go, my heart-brother, seek and help Halil
555 And bring him to me on this mountain top."
Susa descended from the mountain top,
And in the forest met Halil the Falcon.
When Susa of Posusje there beheld him,
Upon his body not a thread of clothing,
560 He led Halil before his Aga Mujo.
When Border-Chieftain Mujo thus beheld him
He eyed him with the most profound amazement
How that Halil was come thus bare and naked.
He, therefore questioned thus Halil, his brother :
565 "Where is thy company, Halil the Falcon ?
Where is thy company ?   Is it all lost ?
How was thy garment thus completely torn ? "
Halil replied to him in low, soft tones :
" What dost thou ask of me, paunch-bellied Mujo ?
570 I did attack the Christians' borderland
From one side I myself led the attack,
The hoary Cejvanaga from the other.
Almost had we achieved the victory—
All of a sudden, lo, the Captain Simon !
575 To aid his dear heart-brother, Simon came,
All our companions, Simon cut them down.
Hadst thou with thine own eyes beheld him then,
Thy throbbing heart had burst within thy breast,
Where hadst thou found the heart to fight him, Mujo ?
580 Myself, the hero, barely could escape,
I must from my fleet courser separate
And climb up through the dark green mountain forests.
The thickets tore completely off my garments,
That not a thread of cloth on me remained ;
585 All that the savage forest tore to shreds,
While I was crawling up among the mountains,
Through vines and gloomy thickets climbing, Mujo."
When border-chieftain Mujo heard the tale
He took the head of Simon from the bag
590 And threw it down before Halil the Falcon.
" Is this the fearful head, Halil the Falcon ?
Is this the fearful head of Captain Simon ? "
Scarce did Halil behold the bloody head
When he sprang up all horrified and trembling ;
595 There fell upon him a three-summers' fever,
So did the head of Simon rouse his fear.

Now he spoke to his brother Mujo thus,
And pressed hot kisses on his brother's forehead :
" Incomparable, brother by my mother !
600 Once did I break apart thy company,
But nevermore from now to everlasting.
The song of thy deeds shall be sung, O Mujo,
It will be sung, for such is but thy due ! "
Here did they put an end to weariness,
605 To weariness here in the lofty mountains,
Then from the ground arose upon their legs
And rode down through the dark green mountain forest,—
Rode to their own home, to Old-Kladusa,
The powerful, white-walled castle built of stone.
610 They parted company at the castle walls
And every man went thence on his own way,
But in the white-walled castle stayed Sir Mujo,
To dally there with Simon's wedded wife.
In dalliance sweet, stayed Mujo in the castle.
615 But I came hither to relate the story,
To tell you all according to the truth.
This song is mine, and may God grant you health !

EXPLANATIONS.

Every *guslar* knows a number of blessings and greetings,
with which he accompanies the introduction or conclusion of
a song.   Although I never allowed my guslars to recite to me
in any considerable company, as the presence of a large number of people would have distracted the attention of the
singer from me, I never neglected to require of each his customary introductory address, which he usually employs.   Of
that character are lines 1—9 and 621—623 in our song.   I discussed this kind of verses at length in my Servian book,
"Smailagic Meho.   Pjesannasih muhamedovacá."   (Ragusa,
1886,)pp. 69–78 and 153–162.

V. 8, 9, and 14 are adages.   V. 14 emphasizes the right of
the master of the house, against whom no member of the
household must rebel.   As to the domestic relations of the
Southern Slavs see Krauss, "Customs and Usages of the
Southern Slavs " (Vienna, 1885), ch. v.   "The Governors and
Managers of a Domestic Community."

V. 15. This line is of established form to designate the
greatest haste.   People sit with crossed legs on the floor,
which is usually covered with rugs or carpets.

V. 17. The Slavic Moslems did not despise the use of wine
even in principle.   Wine is the beverage (pivo) par excellence.

To be able to drink large quantities of wine without becoming intoxicated is one of the standard qualities of the Slavic-Moslem champions as well as the Christian. See Krauss: "Orlovic, the Burggrave of Rab." (Freiberg i. B. 1889, pp. 110—111.) In extenuation it may be urged that the wines of the Southern Slavic countries are scarcely inferior in quality to those of Hungary.

V. 21. Sibinj is really the name for Hermanstadt in Siebenbuergen. The *guslar* has no idea where in the world the real Sibinj is situated. The name is a mere makeshift, the real name of the castle in the coast land having been forgotten and being incapable of discovery.

V. 26. The mercenaries were engaged in front of the castle gate. The small number of the garrison were not sufficient for an extensive adventure, and the castle could not be left without protection. Simon suffered for his carelessness in this regard, as our song teaches The mercenaries "worked" for a share of the spoils, the lion's share, of course, going to the "hero."

V. 50—51. Four mountain ranges, between Zengg and Spalato. Here is an exaggeration. There were plenty of robbers, and a number sufficient for the enterprise could be speedily collected.

V. 60. Compare the description of the appearance of Cejvan in my "Orlovic," cited elsewhere, verse 67, etc., also commentary p. 80, etc. Such characterizations are stereotyped and in general the *guslar* songs, like the epics of the other tribes, are, as to language and style, largely made up of fixed formulæ, which the singer groups according to the requirements of his subject.

V. 65. The *guslar* songs know Cejvan only as a very old man having a son and two marriageable daughters.

V. 71. Ramo was a blacksmith by trade and a good knight as well.

V. 85, etc. The warriors speak freely and candidly about love and are fond of its pleasures. Pure, true love is not unknown to them, but they were spared the chivalrous service of love which flourished in the middle ages. To the Moslem his wife is his sweetheart for life, his truest comrade and friend. His domestic life in many ways is similar to the comfort and heartiness of the Jewish family. The Moslem-Slav was very largely monogamous. The women who were carried off in war, or the concubines, were not much more than servants and friends of the first one who possessed all the rights of a wife.

V. 98. Adage. V. 91—104 may have been borrowed from Turkish poetry, although the Moslems remember them elsewhere as coming from Cejvan.

V. 104. Mujo, a true peasant, sees no purpose in idle love-making, hence his coarse, scornful laugh. He who takes a wife must beget children, and if he brings forth children must care for them. So think the common people, and Mujo, so declares.

V. 117. The complaint of Cejvan and the subsequent one of Halil were unfounded, for both are remembered amply by *guslar* songs.

V. 127. Mujo's upper lip was split, hence his epithet of Harelip, which the angry Cejvan repeats to him. Mujo also was a great eater and allowed a paunch to grow on him which was not fitting for a hero, and provoked ridicule.

V. 140. "Brother by my mother." We should say, my own brother; but the Slavic form contains a survival of a very old family relation by which the common mother forms the connection for the family in the narrow sense. The father is of secondary importance. As Telemachus on his voyage, so a Servian champion in a *guslar* song once said : "I know the mother ; but that such a man is my father I must take upon faith from her." He does not mean to cast suspicion on his mother's honor, but only implies that the question about the father is unimportant and idle, since it all depended on the mother.

V. 213. Dogs ran about without masters. If they increased too much, they were killed unmercifully. The Moslem as well as the Christian, esteemed only the shepherd-dogs, watch-dogs, and hounds. Lap-dogs and dogs as domestic companions were unknown. It was known, however, that degenerate women practised sodomy with dogs and it was believed that new creatures could spring from such a union.

V. 217. *Pabratim—*Chosen Brother, I translate, after mature deliberation, by "heart-brother," not by "ally and

brother " as has been done.   Either of these terms conveys a
false idea of the relations of such friends.   See " Cust. and
Us. South. Slavs," ch. xxvi.   Posusje is the name of a lovely,
fertile valley in the Herzegovina.   Susa is rarely mentioned in
the *guslar* songs.

V. 232. *Kukovati* — to sing mourning songs over the dead.
Pilav — Rice meat ; *pirovati* — to enjoy a wedding feast.

V. 273. The whip as the insignia of the master, to chastise
insubordinate servants if necessary.

V. 248. In the variants of this song, Simon is called *Bre-
vulja, Brehulja,* or *Breulja.*   Possibly it is a corrupted Italian
name.   This Christian knight is otherwise unknown.

V. 261. Smiljanic Elijah, whose castle stood at or near
Zengg.

V. 273. *Bedevija* — a Bedouin horse, of Arab descent.

V. 278. The districts are level, inasmuch as they have good,
smooth roads.

V. 353. *Cresa,* a gun from Brescia, Italy, where the finest
weapons were made.

V. 365. The sudden change in the sentiments of the
woman who is anxious for the life of Mujo may be explained
from the consideration that she looks upon him as her lord
who will afford her protection, whereas her first husband is
forever lost to her after she once becomes a Turkish prisoner.
The ducats are worn, according to custom, for ornament
around the neck and on the dress.

V. 373. This passage was discussed at length in my monograph "Sneca, Fortune and Fate in Popular Belief among
the Southern Slavs " (Vienna, 1886), pp. 16–18.

V. 370. This reproach is to be explained by the fact that
Christian women do not wash their bodies regularly, whereas
the Moslem women are obliged by their ritual to take great
care of their bodies.   The difference between a Christian and
a Moslem peasant woman may be literally smelled.   The one
stinks more with the exhalations of the body ; the other, with
loathsome ointments, oils, and perfumes of roses ; both smell
ad nauseam of basilicum, which they always carry in their
bosoms.

V. 399. Simon pats his horse on the nostrils with the palm
of his hand.   The Southern Slavonian knight generally treats

his horse as his dear, close friend. He never uses a whip or cane. In racing only he will, in extreme cases, employ a whip and spurs or stirrups in order to incite the horse to the greatest exertions.

V. 409. In a society based on family ties there is no place for the prostitute. A venal person separates herself from society as a depraved creature. Hence, in former times the word " whore " contained the worst offence among the Southern Slavs. ⌐ ⌐37 ?

V. 449. An exaggeration ; for to the Moslem, as to the Jew, human blood is the most repulsive thing imaginable.

V. 500. The *guslar* thoughtlessly repeats verse 62, which is entirely superfluous here and positively improper.

V. 519. The heart is called "living" because it beats. The heart is the seat of courage. The meaning is simply : you would lose courage completely.

537 V. 542. A fever which torments for three years.

V. 544. A kiss on the forehead is a mark of special esteem and reverence.

617 V. 623. Only the original composer could say the song was his own. The words were retained by the recitators without any intention, however, of passing the song for their own production. The last three verses are a survival, since only the eye and ear witness—which the original poet must have been—could properly employ such language. But this little feature serves to increase confidence in the faithfulness and genuineness of the tradition, and it also shows why the *guslar* composed the poem ; he desires only to communicate the deeds which he witnessed to more extensive circles in order to preserve the memory of them. It is but rarely that the poet-*guslar* speaks of himself in the first person while reporting his own share in an adventure ; but regularly, in the third person, mentioning his own name like that of any other. To tell a story in the first person is contrary to the epic form of narration, as it almost excludes the further spread of the song by other persons.

30

AN ANCIENT EGYPTIAN CREATION MYTH.[1]

BY PROF. A. WIEDEMANN.

IN ancient Egypt the closest connection existed between religious sentiment and the entire mode of thought and feeling of the people. The ancient Egyptian was distinguished —as was observed by the nations of classical antiquity—by great piety. In all his actions, even the most commonplace, some part was played by gods or demons. Awake and asleep, from birth to death, and far beyond that limit, he was surrounded by spirits; some good, who gave him existence, some evil, who studied to ruin his fortune. He must become and remain master of them, if he would attain any object, if his health and life were not to be endangered, or unless he was ready to abandon hope of a blessed life beyond the grave.

This intimate bond between faith and life was still more closely tied by the fact that religion did not form a distinct circle in the civilization of the inhabitants of the Nile valley and never lost its most intimate connection with the development of the same. Religion, there, never became a self-contained dogma, its fountains always continued to flow. There were no sacred scriptures, from which every doctrine must take its foundation and justification, and to the contents of which every Egyptian was obliged to hold fast or appear as an apostate from the faith of his fathers. There were no poets whose mythological elaborations could control and systematize religious thought. The latter path was found by the Greeks in order to arrive at a consistent faith without binding it in the fetters of a system. Homer and Hesiod created their mythological ideas, as is reported by Herodotus, II. 53, Xenophanes, and others. They did not freely invent their doctrines, but smoothed over inconsistencies in the existing myths, connected the various legends, and thus estab-

---

[1] A number of footnotes are omitted.

lished histories and genealogies of the gods to which posterity
continually referred. . . .

Egypt never had a system of religion that could have been
formulated in the shape of a collection of dogmas or a cate-
chism as THE religion of Egypt. But once in the history,
covering thousands of years, of the realm of the Pharaohs,
was the attempt made to force a uniform, consistent faith
upon the people. It was when Amenophis II. in the 15th
century B. C. sought to compel the worship of his henotheistic
deity, Aten, the solar orb. All gods were to recede before
him, even the one who for some centuries had begun in fact,
though not in name, to permeate the entire pantheon, the
solar deity Ra, who, in contradistinction from the purely
material deity Aten, represented an intelligent, anthropomorphic power controlling the sun.

This attempt of the king who went so far as to lay aside
his name, Amenophis, "the gift of Amon," because it contained the name of one of the old gods, and adopted the
name Chu-en-aten, " radiance of the sun-orb," was bound to
fail. After his death the cult of Aten was suppressed by the
efforts of the priest, and the Ra faith resumed its career of
conquest. One after another the gods were amalgamated with
him, Amon was changed to Amon-Ra, Chnum to Chnum-Ra,
etc., and those gods who did not take the name, assumed the
properties of Ra. When the Greeks entered Egypt nearly all
deities had become representatives of the sun and its properties, the sun itself, the morning, noon, and evening sun,
the burning heat of the sun, the fructifying and nourishing
warmth of the sun, and similar conceptions. This process
was a free one that went on in the people as with the necessity of a law of nature. An Egyptian, even of the hellenistic
period, would have been much surprised had he been told
that his religion was a cult of the sun. While his gods had
become identical in their utterances of life and power he did
not go so far as to make them equal dogmatically. Each one
continued a separate existence, ... there was no national,
uniform religion, there were no recognized and unrecognized,
or heretical, doctrines. In this lack of system the Egyptian
went so far that he suffered the most glaring contradictions
to stand side by side, that each circle of conceptions may be

represented in different views and variations. Such contradictions and variants of doctrine and myth must naturally arise, for thousands of years passed over that which to-day is called Egyptian religion, and men in all classes of the population, from the king and scholar down to the artisan and husbandman contributed their share and left in the mirror of faith a reflection of their thought and sentiment. . . .

This origin impressed a peculiar stamp upon the religious ideas of the people. Close to the loftiest ideas are found the crudest and most primitive forms of thought ; in one and the same text we meet with the intellectual attainments of centuries lying far apart, regardless of whether they fit together or not. As a result, the religious traditions of Egypt present themselves to the student to-day in a chaotic condition, and it requires some courage to enter the maze of this labyrinth. But having once taken this step and having laid aside the *à priori* desire to find a united, consistent system of Egyptian religion such as never existed, one follows the different individual thoughts and thus the texts gain new interest every day.

From these religious writings there arises a picture of the thoughts and the inner life of the people on the banks of the Nile from the time of the pyramids, that is, not less than 4,000 years B. C., down to the time of the Greeks and Romans, —a picture of such variety and wealth of color as is shown by no other ancient people. Every newly disclosed text adds new lights to the picture, and fresh life blossoms from every fragment of Egyptian tradition.

The following pages are devoted to one of these fragments, a most peculiar creation myth of the highest antiquity which, up to the present time, has not found coherent treatment or proper appreciation.

The number of Egyptian creation myths, some of which are known only in fragments, is very large. A large number of deities are occasionally credited with the act of creation : Ra, Osiris, Chnum, Ptah, and others claim the honor. Sometimes a certain god completed the work alone, again he had the assistance of other powers, which either worked as his servants or continued on their own responsibility the work begun by the first god. The modes of bringing forth new beings, also, are of various character. Here we have merely material forces which are ordered by the gods, the universe is rent asunder by sheer force, separating heaven and earth; again, the world is fashioned on a potter's wheel; again, a world-egg is formed from which everything springs. Other authors have the world created, not by physical force, but by the word. The god pronounced the name of an object, and the object was. Others held this too laborious a process and unworthy of a deity. According to them the god merely uttered inarticulate sounds, lacking all connection with the object which came into existence at their utterance, which idea was subsequently elaborated in detail by the Greco-Egyptian gnostics. But even here we find variety. Sometimes the sounds uttered are certain letters, generally vowels, again their place is taken by certain natural sounds, as laughing, smacking the lips, etc. To this circle of ideas appears to belong the peculiar report that the Pelusians worshipped the act of breaking wind. If sounds emanating from the mouth could possess creative power, it could be ascribed finally to any natural sound. The weeping of gods is frequently mentioned in such connection, and to the tears flowing from the eye of Horus especially did humanity owe many objects, particularly incense and similar articles. That a myth has even men originate from tears will appear below.

The most common and simple mode in which the texts describe the origin of gods is the natural one of being begotten by a father and borne by a mother. To make this possible it was necessary to presuppose the existence of two deities, a male and a female, which actually occurs in many Egyptian myths. Occasionally, however, the number of pre-existent beings has been reduced still further, leaving but one primary god who performed the act of creation alone. The manner in which the Egyptian conceived the process in such a case is described most minutely in the comprehensive hieratic papyrus dated from the year 306–5 B. C., No. 10,188 of the British Museum. It was found in 1860 at Thebes, came into the Rhind collection and thence to the Museum. The contents are variegated, consisting of festival songs to the goddesses Iris and Nephthys, litanies of the god Sokaris, the book of the overthrow of the serpent Apepi.

The myth which is the subject of this paper occurs twice in it (p. 26, l. 27 a. f., and p. 28, l. 20 a. f.).

A duplicate in such an Egyptian religious papyrus is not a remarkable thing. These texts do not contain continuous works, although it might be sometimes expected from their titles, but compilations of widely different religious writings from which the copyist or his employer selected this or that chapter. It was not a rare thing if the same text occurred twice in the originals, that the copyist thoughtlessly copied it twice regardless of the repetition. He was all the safer in doing so as his work, upon being finished, was at once consigned to the grave with a dead body, and there was little probability of mortal eye ever discovering his carelessness. For the same reason, i. e., the security from control, the copyists were generally careless in their work in all respects. The texts designed for the dead are usually full of gross errors, wrong letters, omissions of letters or whole words or sentences. Thus the Musée Gimnet at Paris has an hieratic papyrus from the Theban time, supposed to be a fragment of a book for a dead person, but which is really no more than a conglomerate of disconnected fragments of sentences with letters. The unreliability even of those texts, which at first glance appear to be written carefully and show artistic vignettes, is so great that it is often impossible to translate them or discover their meaning without comparing several copies.

So, in the case of our creation myth, there is cause for especial congratulation that a fortunate accident caused the writer of the papyrus to be careless enough to copy the report twice, and thus make it possible, or at least easier, to understand the thoughts. The form in which he clothed his report the first time is as follows, the translation being as faithful as possible.

The book of the Knowing the creations of Ra, the overthrow of Apepi.

The word χεπερ, which has been translated by create, creation, etc., means : to enter into existence, to be, to exist, to call into being, etc. It is, therefore, to be understood both in the transitive and the intransitive sense. From it is derived, among others, the name of the god Chepera, strictly the nascent one, afterwards the rising sun.

In contradistinction to Chepera, sometimes Tum is considered as the god of the setting sun, but generally means the sun-god in general, who was especially worshipped at Heliopolis by the name of Tum.

Apepi is a great serpent looked upon as the principal enemy of the sun and as the power of darkness and evil. It must be overthrown each day unless the sun is to perish. The texts are full of spells for conjuring and overthrowing the Apepi. It was not possible to destroy it. Scarcely vanquished it reared its head anew. As the alternation of light and darkness never ends, so the struggle between Ra and Apepi continues through eternity, the more so as Egyptian mythology does not seem to have known an end of the world.

Words of the Lord of the Universe

"Lord of the Universe" is a frequent attribute of various deities. It is generally employed in texts referring to the hereafter, in designating Osiris, the lord of the nether world. But, as in the present text, it is also a designation of Ra, who being the creator of the world must also have the first claim to dominion over it.

which he spoke after he entered being: I am the nascent one as Chepera. When I took being, then was creation, all creations were after I took being. Numerous were the formations that proceeded from my mouth. There was not heaven, nor was the earth, nor had been created the good and the evil serpents in this place (i. e., on earth).

A similar description of the condition of creation is found in the burial pyramid of King Pepi I. of the 6th dynasty, about 3000 B. C., on l. 663–4 : "Pepi was borne by his father Tum. There was not yet the heavens, nor was the earth, nor were the men, nor were born the gods, nor was death."

The sentence which is rendered by "the good and the evil serpents," reads in Egyptian, *sa-ta-u t'etfet-u*. *Sa-ta* is provided with the determinative, so that strictly it should be translated by "things of the ground of the earth." The connection with *t-etfet*-reptiles, however, shows that there is an error and that the determinative must be the serpent. The word *sa-ta* also signifies the serpent, more especially the good serpent, the agathodemon of the temples. The serpents are here mentioned above all other creatures because that animal plays an extremely prominent part in Egyptian

thought ; it occurs persistently in the texts ; spells to con-
jure the reptiles make up the greater part of Egyptian magic
formulæ ; in the descriptions of the hereafter, it occurs constantly.   Manifestly, in ancient times the animals were even
more common than to-day, and therefore so dangerous that
popular fancy was continually engaged by them.

I raised them (i. e., heaven, earth, reptiles) from the primodial waters Nu, from
the state of rest. I found no place on which I could stand. I issued radiance
from my heart, I planned Shu, I made noble figures. I was alone. Nor had I
caused to emanate (*ashesh*) Shu, nor had I caused to trickle out (*tef*) Tefnut.

The god Shu and his sister Tefnut play a considerable part
in the Egyptian texts.   In the dynasty of the gods at Memphis, they stand after Ptah and Ra ; in that of Thebes, after
Amon-Ra and Tum.   They are pictured sometimes in the
form of two lions, or a double lion, and in later times represent the sign of Gemini.   They are spoken of especially at
Heliopolis.   Together with Tum, they form his great lords
("Book of the Dead," 18, 4) ; with Ra, his spirits (Ib. 115, 7).
They carried fresh breath to the dead, particularly the breath
of the north wind.   Mythologically they are generally looked
upon as solar deities.   In the myth of the destruction of the
human race, for instance, Ra when abdicating government
makes Shu the new sun for mankind (Wiedemann, "Rel. d.
Alt. Aeg.," p. 36).   The god is therefore often shown with
the sun-disk on his head.   His form of incorporation, the
lion, also shows his connection with the great light of day.
The "Book of the Dead" mentions his creative activity : he
raised the sun (17, 50), the pillars of heaven (109, 3), etc.
In worship, Shu and Tefnut possess but little importance ;
they always appear in second or third place after the local
deities, who are superior in influence.

There was no other who worked with me. I planned in my heart
that there might be plenty of creations in creations of them that
were born, in creations of them that were born to them. I begot
with my fist, I practised lewdness with my shadow, I caused fluid
to emanate (*cher*) from my orifice (*re*), I myself.

For shadow, which is a part of the soul of the Egyptian,
see the data collected by Birch, *Transact. Soc. Bibl. Arch.*
8, p. 386 a. f.   For the parts of the soul in general, see Wiede-

mann, in the *Jahrb. d. Ver. v. Alterthumsfr. i. Rheinlande*
86, p. 46 a. f.

Re usually refers to the mouth, but also at times to other
orifices, for instance the mouth of the stomach and here, according to the context, of the phallus. *Cher*, carries the ex-
planatory mark of the flowing wound, and hence must be
rendered by "flowing," not "speaking."

I flowed out as Shu, I trickled out as Tefnut. My father Nu
spoke: "They tremble."

We have here a thoroughly Egyptian inconsistency. Just
now Ra was the god who created everything, but immediately
afterwards his father is mentioned, i. e., the personified
primordial waters, chaos conceived as a liquid, from which
other legends make the world and the gods came forth. Our
legend generally conceives Nu only as pre-existent matter,
beside which the one deity pre-exists.

My eye was behind them for centuries. They separated from me
after I became from one god three gods with reference to myself. I
took being in this land. Glad were at this Shu and Tefnut in the
tranquil waters in which they were. They brought me my eye in
their following.

The meaning of this somewhat obscure sentence is:
When I had created Shu and Tefnut, they trembled—not
with reverence, probably, but to show their vitality as Batan
in "Pap. d'Orbiney" 14, 7, trembled when life returned to
him. My eye, the sun, was behind them for centuries and gave
them light. Then they became independent so that there
were three individual gods. When this had happened I
went into this land, on the newly created earth, and when
Shu and Tefnut who had remained in the primordial waters
saw this, they were glad and came to me and brought with
them, in their following, my eye, the sun, which I had left
with them at first.

I gathered my members, I wept over them, and man came from
the tears which emanated from my eye.

The idea that men came from the eyes of the sun-god appears repeatedly in the texts. In the representation of the
four races of men in the grave of Seti I., the god, who is here

called Horus, says of the Egyptians : " You are a tear (*remit*) of my radiant person in your name as men (*ret-u*) (" Leps. Denkm." III. 136, 10–12).   The sun-god also is called the weeping one (*remi*) (Naville, "Litanie du Soleil," m. 27, p. 40). In the grave of Rameses II. (ib.), the weeping god (*reminti*), is implored to give life to the king ; it is said that he formed himself by his tears, etc.   Other things also come from the tears of the sun ; thus the magical papyrus (Salt M. 825, London), from the time of the 21–26 dynasty, says, p. 2, l. 5 : " When the sun weeps for the second time and drops waters from its eyes this is changed into working bees ; they work in flowers of all kinds, and produce honey and wax instead of water."

This creative power of tears is based upon the belief that in them, as in every part of the body and in every secretion, is contained some part of the ego secreting it.   For that reason the ancient Egyptian magician, like the conjurers of other lands, employed something coming from the person or article, which was the object of his spells, in order to obtain or increase the necessary power.   Thus, according to an Egyptian myth (Wiedemann, " Re., l. d. alt. Aeg," p. 29) Isis kneads from earth, and the saliva flowing from the mouth of the sun-god, a serpent whose bite is so destructive that it threatens death even to Ra himself.   Only by a counter spell, which he purchased dearly from Isis, could the sun-god save himself. If it was impossible to obtain any part of the person, a picture of him was drawn and the magic spells exercised over it, for to the Egyptian the picture embodies part of the being represented.   He who injures the picture, injures the original ; destruction of the picture may involve the destruction of the original.   Instead of the picture, the name of the god or man may be used, which also is an integral part of that which it designates.   Knowledge and, therefore, possession of it may also give power over the bearer of the name.

Then it (my eye) became furious against me when it came and found that I had made another in its place giving it radiance. I put it in its place in my head. Afterward, it ruled this whole earth."

When he left his eye in the primordial waters Ra created a new one, a second sun.   When the first sun was brought

back to him and saw this, it became angry, but Ra pacified it
by restoring it to its old place in his head.

Their (the eyes') fury fell on their plants, I ordered once more
what it (fury) took away in it (earth). I issued forth from the plants,
I created all reptiles, all the growing power in them (plants).

The double sun at first burned too hot upon the newly created
plants, and Ra was forced to restore and revive the withered
plants which had been thereby removed from earth. Then
he issued from these plants and created the serpents, which
are here mentioned for the same reasons as in the early part
of the legend.

Shu and Tefnut bore Seb and Nut. Seb and Nut bore Osiris, Hor-
chent-neu-ma, Set, Isis, and Nephthys from their bodies one after
the other among them. Their children multiplied upon this earth.

Hor-chent-neu-ma is a form of the older Horus or Harneris,
who was thought to be blind and was worshipped especially
at Setopolis. It symbolizes the eclipse of the sun. The
shrew-mouse was sacred to it which, according to Plutarch, enjoyed divine worship in Egypt because it was believed to be
blind, and darkness was held to be older than light.

The sequence of creation, according to this myth, was as follows : Pre-existence of the sun-god and of matter, Nu. The
former creates Shu and Tefnut, then earth with its sun ; the
latter creates man. Shu and Tefnut emerge from the primordial waters, the nether and the upper suns are united ;
creation and protection of plants from the heat of the sun,
creation of the reptiles, birth of the gods of the Osiris circle.
Accordingly, the latter are younger than man, which is contrary to other legends that praise Orisis as the creator of the
world. Thus a hymn to Osiris (on a stela from the 18th
dynasty in the Paris library) : " He (Osiris) made with his
hand the earth, the water thereon, the air, the plants, all
its domestic animals, all its birds, all its fowl, all its reptiles,
all its quadrupeds (literally goats)."

The second version of the myth appears in the papyrus, at
first glance, almost twice as long as the first. Upon closer
examination, however, it is seen that this is only apparent.
The copyist here worked very carelessly and took long pieces
twice. These are found once at the proper place where they

are contained in the first text, and the second time either before or after at some other place, where the copyist was induced by some word in the text to copy the sentence again
regardless of the context.   In that way great confusion was
caused which, however, may be corrected in places by comparison with the first text.   Moreover—which is of greater
importance to us—the author endeavored to introduce into
the composition a new fundamental mythological thought,
viz., numerous references to the names of the gods and their
magic power, in order to promote the practice of incantations
and magic more than was done by the writer of the first
sober text.

The beginning of the second version, of which a translation
follows for the purpose of comparison, affords an example of
this prominence of the mystical tendency prevalent in it :

" When I took being, then was creation ; I took being in the creations (i. e., I assumed his formations) of Chepera, and took being for
the first time.   I took being in the creations of Chepera.   When I
took being then happened the creations of my being (?) to the circles
of gods which I made.   I took the form of the circles of gods in my
name of Ausars, the nine-in-one of the divine nine-in-one.'

Ausars is an otherwise unknown name of a god.   Budge
suggests a possible connection with Osiris, but this name is
in later years written Usar, Usiri and in similar forms, but a
final *s* is always absent.   I would prefer to divide the word
into a verb-form *an s–ar–s* " it (the circle of gods) is made,"
but this interpretation also is uncertain.

I make all that I wish in this land, I make it broad, I order with
my hand.   I was alone, nor had they been born, nor had I caused
Shu to emanate, nor had I caused Tefnut to trickle out.   I made
myself, that is, my magic name.

The creation of Shu and Tefnut is twice reported alike :

" I begot with my fist.   I brought my innermost (literally, my
heart) forth from the phallus (literally, from the hand of the phallus), it fell from my orifice (*re*).   I flowed out as Shu, I trickled out
as Tefnut ; I became, with reference to myself, from one god three
gods, who took being in this land.   Then were Shu and Tefnut glad
in the tranquil primordial waters, in which they were."

The word for phallus here is *āaā*.   It is derived from the
root äa—to be big ; the determination as the male member

shows the implied meaning which otherwise appears but
rarely. It is found, though, as the designation of an ithyphallic
form of the sun-god. Moreover, *āa* with the same determinative serves to designate the donkey, which was considered
lascivious above all animals. The donkey is in the first place
an evil animal, an embodiment of the companions of Set, the
adversary of Osiris; but some notes also point to a connection
of the animal with the sun-god (for instance, "Book of the
Dead," ch. 40, p. 125, l. 40). In the medical papyrus at
Leipsic, the word *āa* signifies a disease, which has not yet
been explained. . . . . .

The point of this creation myth on which interest in it
principally rests is the peculiar origin of Shu and Tefnut.
The oldest reference to a creation of this nature by masturba-
tion is found in the inscriptions of the pyramids of the 6th
dynasty, i. e. about 3,000 B. C. :

"Tum became an onanist at Heliopolis. He enlarged his
phallus with his hand, he gave himself pleasure with it.
There were born the twins Shu and Tefnut." In the "Book
of the Dead," there is a passage which is frequently quoted in
the Theban texts, referring to Ra indulging in self-pollution.
In the ritual books of Osiris, Amon-ra, Tum, Ptah, and Isis
from the time of Seti I. it is said of Tum : "thou flowest out
as Shu, thou tricklest out as Tefnut." A pantheistic hymn
of Hibis from the time of King Darius says : "The gods emanated from thee, O Amon. Thou flowest out as Shu, thou
tricklest out as Tefnut, to form for thyself the nine gods in
the beginning of creation; thou art the twins of the two
lions" i. e. Shu and Tefnut. Somewhat later is a text from
Edfu, written down in the time of the Ptolemys, in which the
god Amon-Ra of Choïs is addressed in this way : "Thou
art the one god who became two gods, the creator of the egg,
who begot his twins," i. e. again Shu and Tefnut.

Among all these references to our myth, the first one
quoted is the most important, not only on account of its high
antiquity, but because it speaks only of the birth of Shu and
Tefnut, and does not yet connect the emanation of Shu with
the verb *ashesh*, or that of Tefnut with *tef, tefen*, both signifying "to emanate, to flow out." It thus appears that the
development of the myth was not ætiological for the pur-

pose of explaining the names of the gods by an etymological play, but that this play upon words was introduced at a later period into the myth, the fundamental thought of which was much older than this embellishment.

The conception, which appears strange to people who have grown up under the influence of modern thought, viz., that the male semen alone is sufficient for the creation of the gods, loses every remarkable feature in the light of the ancient and mediæval ideas concerning the physiological processes of propagation.   As late as 1677, after Ludwig von Ham discovered the spermatozoa in the male semen, the basis of generation and development was sought in them alone, the female organs being looked upon as breeding-places only.   That such opinions were held at that time was partly due to the influence of a semi-religious conception upon the explanation of a purely physiological process.   According to the theory of evolution or preformation which prevailed in the 17th century, there occurred no new formation in the development of an organism, but only a growth or unfolding of parts which had been preformed and were complete from eternity but of minute size.   To the adherents of this theory the only question could be whether these preformed beings were present in the egg and received the impulse for development by impregnation, as was asserted by the ovulists, or if, according to the animalculists, they were contained in the semen and found suitable soil for development in the female body. Such mystical thoughts were remote from the ideas of antiquity, but on the basis of the then prevailing knowledge, or rather ignorance, of nature, the notion was readily reached that the male semen could develop not only in the female, but also on some other nutritive soil, which conception is presumed in our myth.

In its fundamental features, our creation myth has all the marks of a very ancient origin.   It appears much older than those Egyptian legends on the same subject which have been hitherto known.   This appears mainly from the simple narrative form, which is free from the syncretism which the other creation myths usually contain when, starting from pantheistic conceptions, they make all the gods equal to the Creator, and make them emanations of him, instead of independent beings. We generally become acquainted with these myths by hymns to the creator, who is represented as henotheistic. For purposes of comparison, it may be interesting to subjoin the beginning of a characteristic text of that nature contained in a papyrus dated from the time of Rameses IX, about 12, B. C.:

"Waking one, resting one, thou wakest in rest, waking one that begetteth himself. Nothing is created on earth save by the plans of his heart. He gives being to his creations, he is the form which gives birth to all that is, the procreator who creates all beings. Glory be to thee, Ptah-Tatunen, great god that conceals his form, that opens his soul. Thou growest in peace, father of fathers of all the gods. The sun-disk (*aten*) of heaven (is the radiance) of his eye lighting the lands with his rays in peace. Glory be to Nut, the beginning of all that is on earth in peace. Chnum, mother, that gave birth to the gods, bearer of all men, that lets them live in peace. Great Nu (primordial waters) that gives gifts (to men), that makes green the fields in peace. Crocodiles, bitter seas, Red Sea, floods in the mountains . . . in peace. Thou who makest green the lands, the mountains, the islands, the mountain lands, that givest bloom by the waters which come from heaven, in peace. He makes the sweet wind (which tempers) the heat by its breath, which comes (from the north). Waking one, resting one, thou wakest in resting. Waking one, that paces through eternity; lord of nourishment, that gives abundance by his love, in peace. He hears if one implores him; before him tremble all; him worship the spirits in all lands, in peace. He comes to thee, Pharaoh, to thee, Ptah, he comes to thee, creator of forms. Glory be to thee before the circle of thy gods, which thou didst make after thou didst take being, a god of members, that himself builds his members. There was not heaven, nor was the earth, nor was the flood. Thou didst order the earth, thou didst unite thy members, thou didst order thy members. What thou didst find alone, for it thou didst make a place, god, creator of the lands. Thou didst have no father that begot thee when thou didst take being; thou didst have no mother that bore thee when thou didst renew thyself. Order, that came forth as order. Thou art sublime above the earth in its beings which it united to itself after thou didst take being in thy form of Tatunen, in thy taking being for the union of the lands, in thy begetting thyself.   That which thy hands created thou did separate from the primordial waters, etc."

From this myth, also, a creation myth can be extracted, in which the hero is Ptah-Tatunen, a form of the god Ptah worshipped, among other places, at Memphis, whom the Greeks, for reasons that are not quite intelligible, compared to Hephaistos.   But it is far removed from the clearness of the legend first treated in this paper.   Above all, the identification of Ptah with many other forms, the sun-disk, the androgynous Chnum, with Nu, with the seas, etc., show that this form of it comes from a time when the priests could no longer confine themselves to the worship of their local divinities, but were obliged to extend their worship to the gods of other cities and districts.   True, the thoughts of this hymn are more poetical and lofty than in the first legend, but the very materiality of conception in the latter, which corresponds thoroughly to the mode of thought of the Egyptians that was unfavorable to all abstraction, testifies its great antiquity.

The time of its origin will probably never be determined with certainty, as the beginnings of Egyptian religion, like those of the entire civilization of the people, are lost in the mists of antiquity.   At the time of the pyramids, at which Egypt enters history, at the moment at which the oldest preserved texts of greater religious works were written down, it already formed part of the religious conceptions of the inhabitants of the Nile valley.   From that time on it remained with them down to the time of the Ptolemys, when ancient Egyptianism began to die out.   For nearly three thousand years it had then been believed in, and a myth of such vitality, so closely interwoven with popular life that all the storms of life did not suffice to efface it, deserves better than other features of civilization that appear only at intervals, to be consulted when an attempt is made to make a sketch of the mode of thought and feeling of the ancient Egyptians, of the ethnography of the ancient tribe on the banks of the Nile.

CHRISTMAS USAGES AND BELIEFS IN SCHLESWIG-HOLSTEIN.

BY DR. HEINRICH CARSTENS.

THE personage presiding over the Christmas festival in Schleswig-Holstein is generally called *Kienjees, Kindjees,* or *Klingeest,* these being corruptions of the expression *Kind Jesus* (Child Jesus). He brings the presents to the children and occasionally punishes the naughty ones. They give him various residences, according to the locality, either in the nearest mountains, or on the church steeple, or even in the loft of the house.

I.—*General Usages.*—At Friedrichstadt, the preliminary celebration of Christmas begins as early as the sixth day of December with what is known as the *Sünner-Klaas.* It was customary, in former years, to bake big cakes weighing from one to twelve pounds, and play for them, the cakes representing St. Nicholas. An essential part of the feast was a boar or hog made of rye bread six or seven inches high, with a gilt snout and tail and having golden rings around its knees. Business men put the goods they have exhibited for sale on a revolving disk and raffle them off. There are a number of rhymes remaining in popular use containing the name *Sünner-Klaas* which are supposed to be remnants from the time of the Reformation. One of them runs as follows :

Sünner Klaas Áb'nd
Dunn gât wi nâ bâb'n,
Dâr klingelt de Klokk'n
Dâr danst de Popp'n.
Inn'n Grötvâder's hûs
Dâr pip'n de Mûs
Lütje Mûs de wern de Hakk'n verfrôr'n
Dârawer hârr'n se de Ring verlâr'n.

481

TRANSLATION.

Santa Claus eve
Then go we above,
There ring the bells,
There dance the dolls.
In grandfather's house
There pipe the mice.
Little mouse had frozen its heels,
Thereover they have lost the ring.

It is indispensable to kill a pig shortly before Christmas, as roast pork and sausage must not be wanting at the festal board. At Hennstedt, in Ditmarsh, a special swine market is held December 6.

In every house, special bread and cake are baked the week before Christmas. The productions of the bakers are more elaborate. They make what is called *Kienjeestüg*, that is, human or animal shapes painted in loud colors or covered with gold leaf.

The custom of giving presents to the poor is quite common. The threshers in Ditmarsh get a loaf of bread, and the letter-carriers often carry loads of them home.

It is customary to eat but little during the day preceding Christmas eve in order 'to have a big appetite for the great feast in the evening. On this occasion the cattle in the barn even receive an extra allowance of fodder, and cats and dogs get better meals. At times, the cattle are admitted to the higher joys to the extent that a candle is placed above the trough from which they feed, just as each member of the family used to have his own candle, which he made himself, when tallow was universally used. These candles must be made heavy and big, for he whose candle goes out first will die first.

After the great dinner the dishes must not be washed at once in the usual fashion. They are left until about ten minutes before midnight, when the young folks take them out to a well and wash them there, for in the water they can, at midnight, see the faces of their future lovers and sweethearts.

Every one must eat heartily, for he whose appetite gives out first will die first. As a consequence of this hearty dinner people find it difficult to sleep. In the straightforward peasant language they therefore call Christmas eve and New Year's eve, *Vull-Bûks-Abend,* or Full-Belly Night.

II.—*Processions and Begging Songs.*—Begging customs and songs are universal at Christmas and New Year. Grown people and children go begging freely, and gifts must be given, for it will not do to refuse on those sacred nights. Occasions have been known when thirty or forty people at once would enter a house and sing their song, after which they had to be entertained or receive presents. They go around, frequently, carrying a huge star, showing King Herod at a window. The songs are of a traditional character mixing biblical and profane elements, but their meaning has been lost.

A peculiar custom is what is known as *Rummeltopf.* They take a pot of earthenware, fasten a bladder skin over it tight, and pass through the bladder a piece of cane. Moistening the thumb and index finger and rubbing them along the cane, a peculiar muffled roar is produced, which serves as an accompaniment to the songs. In Ditmarsh the so-called *Kaland* singing obtained. The school teachers would pick out six to a dozen of their best singers and make the rounds with them, singing some Christmas carol, followed immediately by a begging song containing rather broad hints as to what would be acceptable in the way of presents, mostly sausages, bread, etc.

In Ditmarsh the new year is "shot in," and the shooters are entertained with cake and *schnaps.* Others will "throw in" the New Year, throwing bottles, plates, dishes, etc., against houses and doors. The owners of the houses do not enjoy this particular form of celebrating, and fights often follow. It used to be so common, however, that wheelbarrows were required in the morning to "remove the débris." Boys will knock at the walls of houses with hammers, or shoot pease at the windows. In the morning you will find your door barricaded, your gates tied up or carried half a mile away. It has been known to happen that a shed was carried up to the roof of the main building.

III. *The Twelve Nights.*—The real festival begins Christmas eve, and lasts twelve days. During this time it is unlawful to wash, spin, thresh, etc. Those who disregarded these prohibitions have been known to have disagreeable encounters with demons. The twelve days determine the weather for the year. People take a dozen onions, cut them them into halves, hollow them out, and fill them with salt. Those in which the salt is completely dissolved indicate the wet months of the coming year.

Between twelve and one o'clock Christmas night, the dead hold divine service. A woman who heard the church bell ring, and went to church at that time, did not leave soon enough, for as she went out it struck one, her shawl was caught in the door which shut itself, and the next morning pieces of her shawl were found scattered on all the graves in the churchyard.

During Christmas and New Year's nights the horses have the power of speech and prophecy, their sayings referring to members of the family. Just at midnight the water in all the wells is turned to wine. A woman who went to the well at that time was met by a demon, who said : "All water is wine, and what stands by is mine" and carried her off.

During the twelve nights the Wild Hunt rides through the air, seeking the souls of children that died without baptism. The furious company are heard in the wind, and if you mimic their call you will receive a visit from the Wild Huntsman. There are stories of men who never could hit the game they aimed at, and were met by an old man who advised them to abstract the wafer which the priest would give them at communion, nail it on a tree and shoot at it. In each case when they raised their gun, they saw instead of the wafer the body of the Saviour, but they shot, nevertheless, and thereafter never missed, but they were unhappy all their lives, and one was condemned to hunt through all eternity.

In Holstein, on New Year's eve, or Sylvester night, chairs were placed around the table, one for each member of the household, and towards midnight each person stood on a chair. On the last stroke of twelve they jumped down and into the New Year.

IV. *Superstitions concerning the Twelve Nights.*—In addition to the beliefs mentioned incidentally in the course of this paper, a few more may be enumerated :

If a girl that wants to marry will, on Christmas eve at twelve o'clock, take two candles and look into a mirror she will see her future lover standing behind her.

If you want to know if a sick person in the house is going to die, sit down to a meal with him, leave him at the table, go to a neighbor's house with a bed sheet wrapped about your head, and look into a window. If you see the sick person with a grass sod on his head he will die; otherwise, he will recover.

If you look through the window into the sitting-room, you will see those who are going to die within the year without their heads.

If the horses hang their heads, some one will die in the house. If they hold up their heads, they will draw a bridal couple to church within a year. ·

Girls can see their future lovers by looking into the baking oven. In some places they have to crawl through the oven.

The slippers of the party are thrown into the hall. The owners of those pointing to the door, will be carried out dead in the course of the year.

If a photograph falls from the wall during the feast, the one whom it represents will die within a year.

If a person dies during the twelve nights, twelve deaths will occur in the village during the year.

REMARKS BY HENRY E. O. HEINEMANN.

Most of the usages and beliefs enumerated and described by Mr. Carstens are not peculiar to the region in which he found them, but seem in most cases to be of common Pan-Teutonic origin. The *Sünner-Klaas* is a similar corruption of St. Nicholas, as our *Santa Claus* or the *Claesvaer* of the Netherlands. The general character of the celebration is much the same as elsewhere.

The *Kinjeestüg,* or peculiar bakery goods used at Christmas, is common in many other parts of Germany. I remember seeing them not only in the city of Hamburg, which is close to Schleswig-Holstein, but also in the old city of Brunswick, in the heart of Germany and near the Hartz mountains. The processions and begging customs, also, are similar to those in vogue elsewhere. Let me mention only the custom in connection with the *wassail bowl* in England.   There, the festival of Christmas extended sometimes as long as twenty days.   It was customary in some places in England that the poor of a village would go around to their wealthier neighbors carrying with them a wassail bowl decked with ribbons, and a golden apple, singing a Christmas carol.   At Chippenham, in Wiltshire, on Christmas Eve, five or six strong men carrying a gayly-decorated bowl, make the rounds of the village singing a rhyme :

> Wassail ! Wassail ! All over the town,
> Our toast is white and our ale is brown.
> Our bowl is made of a mapling tree ;
> We be good fellows.   I drink to thee !

There are more " verses " to the song.

We are struck at once with the custom of making boars of cake and making pork the principal dish of the Christmas feast.   The gilded boar is especially interesting.   Boars' heads in England are still used at Christmas dinners.   In Sweden a log covered with a boar's skin is brought in on Christmas Eve and on it the household perform their vows for the ensuing year.

The gilded boar makes more striking than the other customs the reference which we see in them all to the boar *Gullinbursti,* him of the golden bristles, of our common Teutonic mythology, the animal owned by Freyr, the god of fruitfulness, who presided over the yule feast and over marriage.   To this reminiscence are due the various forms—some of which we find in Mr. Carstens' paper—of consulting the occult powers during the Twelve Nights regarding future lovers and sweethearts.   The special importance of the night before the festival is also a Teutonic feature.

It is interesting to note the belief that at midnight on those sacred nights the water in the wells is turned to wine, and that it possesses magic powers in that it shows the likenesses of future lovers or sweethearts.   According to ancient Teutonic belief, the gods travelled over the earth on those nights blessing the wells, and at midnight men would go out and get the holy water.   This belief appears here to have been mixed with Christian ideas, the turning into wine being probably derived from the miracle performed by Christ and the use of wine at the Lord's Supper.

The Wild Hunt also is a belief universally held by the Teutonic nations. The Wild Huntsman is the degraded remnant of the figure of Woden, as the Anglo-Saxons called him, the Odin of the Norse records, who, during the Twelve Nights, travelled over the earth and sang the mighty song heard in the storm at that time, which marked the victory of the powers of light and warmth over the giants of frost, when plant life recovered and prepared for the coming of Spring. He was, even in ancient times, a psychopomp and as such was likened to Mercury by the Romans.

We cannot fail to remark the similarity of the customs described by Mr. Carstens to those prevalent in the United States at Hallowe'en. Probably most of us have been annoyed at finding our garden gates off their hinges the morning after, and seeing everything about the house that was not nailed down scattered within a radius of half a mile about the place, even if we did not see a shed climb the roof of the house. The "tick-tacks" of our boys are not so very different, in their effects upon our nerves from the custom of throwing pease at the windows.

I call attention to these few resemblances for the purpose of emphasizing once more what Americans, unfortunately, are so apt to lose sight of, namely, that they are of Teutonic origin, the same as the inhabitants of Schleswig-Holstein whence came part of the tribes that settled in England with the Saxons ; that is, from that part which is still called Angeln, the home of the Angles who gave their name to England.

ANCIENT SHROVE-TIDE CUSTOMS, WITH SPECIAL REFERENCE TO ROMAN GERMANIA.

BY C. RADEMACHER.

THE customs prevailing in the Germanic countries around Shrove-tide are remnants of ancient spring festivals, the long period of feasting having been, according to the author, divided by the Christian Church into two sections by inserting in the midst of the heathen celebrations the period of Lent, with its fasting and meditation; while the spring festival of Easter was used for the purposes of the Church as a celebration of the Resurrection, and the Roman carnival found ready adoption prior to Lent.

The feasts of our rude ancestors were probably held on what the Anglo-Saxons called the *Dhing-stead*; the Germans, *Malstätte*. To this meeting-place the individuals brought contributions of food and drink. In most cases this custom survives in the usage of children of marching around through the villages, singing begging-songs and collecting eatables with which to have a feast at the village inn. Many of these begging songs are quoted by the author in the dialects of different regions.

Curious instruments are used by the children in making a noise and attracting attention, as the *Rommelspott*, a pot over which an animal skin has been stretched. By rubbing with a stick, a peculiar low growl is produced. Often, too, full-grown young men perform the office of the children, and, in the Eiffel, the poor of the community take advantage of the custom and gather in unusually liberal gifts. The name *Zimbert*, which occurs in connection with this feast in Rhenish Prussia, is traced to St. Bertha or Hertha, the goddess of spring. Some of the songs clearly preserve references

488

to ancient spring festivals and the expulsion of winter from his domain.

There is a remarkable degree of similarity in all the songs used in widely separated regions and by people of different tribes, showing how universal these customs were in ancient times.

Another general and ancient Germanic feature of these festivals is the lighting of fires, especially on hills and mountain sides. The manner of burning, the drift of the smoke, and other incidents form material for divinations by the old women, the smoke is believed to benefit trees or houses to which it is carried by the wind, remnants of the fire-wood possess healing power. In some cases, a basket containing a live cat or a bound fox or rooster is placed on the top of three poles erected tent fashion, the fire being started under these poles. The people dance around, carrying torches, and often run through the ashes after the fire is out (cf. need-fires). Neighboring villages start their fires all at once, illuminating the heavens for many miles around. Often the merriment changes to solemn prayer. Yarn spun by the light of the holy fires by the girls possesses magic virtues. The kindling wood, straw, etc., is often collected in a similar manner as the material for the banquet. Wheels are wrapped in straw and rolled burning down the hillside. The author is of opinion that in ancient times these fires were accompanied by sacrifices, perhaps even human sacrifices, and that the cat, rooster, or fox, or in some places, a straw man or a cross called "the witch" which is placed on the poles, is a survival of those primeval rites.

Many things done during the holy eve of Shrove-Tuesday bring good luck, as pruning trees, hanging wreaths of straw on them as a protection from vermin, etc. If milk is drunk it protects from sunstroke. A peculiar belief is that if the moon shines those persons whose bodies cast no shadow will soon die. There are numerous superstitions of a similar kind.

Some villagers prepare dainty food and leave it on the window sills over night, for the spirits of their departed friends are supposed to come down during the night.

The author describes a number of games and pastimes

practised in different regions and at different times, tracing them several centuries back. The costuming and manners show many an ancient heathen trait.

In conclusion, the author gave the words of a song used near Cologne in the night after Whitsunday, together with the air of this song as he caught it in his native town recently.

CONTRIBUTION TO THE STUDY OF WELL-SERVICE ON THE LOWER RHINE.

BY O. SCHELL.

THE author points out the universal custom of well-worship among primitive races, and gives reasons to show that it was an essential part of divine service among the ancient Teutons. Reference is had to the prominent place occupied in Germanic mythology by the great fountains from which the waters of the world flow, more particularly the fountain of Urd, the greatest of the three Norns (fates), who sat at the roots of the world-tree Yggdrasil, and took part in the daily moots of the gods at that place. This spring survives in folk-lore, as in the tale of the well which a youth watched who found that whatever dropped into the water turned to gold.

The worship of wells continued after the conversion of the race to Christianity, being in many cases utilized in the familiar way by the priests of the new faith, and the wells consecrated to saints of the church in place of the old gods. The character of the worship of these wells appears from various ordinances by sovereigns during the middle ages, limiting or prohibiting it, and clearly shows its ancient heathen nature, down to the year 1669. It consisted in divinations, vows, sacrifices, prayers, etc.

The author enumerates several springs in Bergen and Hesse which although not known to possess any real healing powers are still held sacred by the common people, and surrounded by circles of myths and traditions.

Summing up his results, the author says :

" A thousand years of Christian culture were not sufficient to suppress the heathen remnants entirely, but the ancient heathendom of our forefathers reaches down into the present time. Most of the features which were mentioned as connected with the popular beliefs and customs regarding these wells are the remains, or Christian modifications, of a primeval heathen well-worship.   That this worship concerned the wells themselves directly appears from the names among which the word " holy " occurs more frequently than any other.   The waters of the wells were supposed to possess miraculous virtues to cure physical ailments, diseases, and epidemics.   At certain times the water turns to wine.   Excursions and pilgrimages are commonly made to these wells, and festivities held around them.   Myths and legends cling to them, the children are believed to come from their depths, the waters are consulted about future events.   Some fountains are credited with a miraculous origin.   The imagination of the country folk peoples them with nixies and elves of either sex ; but there are few stories of them, as they do not like to mingle with men, and generally do so to the disadvantage of the mortals.   Next to the trees of the sacred forests, the wells springing from the mysterious depths of the earth enjoyed the highest worship among the ancient Teutons.   The sacred fountain of Duisburg is the most prominent and best known of the holy waters of the lower Rhine region."

DEATH AND BURIAL.

Superstitious Beliefs and Customs in Pomerania.

BY DR. A. HAAS.

MANY persons possess the gift of foreseeing an approaching death. As a rule the gift is confined to persons born on a Sunday, or only those born between 12 and 1 P. M. on that day, or during the sermon or the communion. But persons born on a Thursday, during the hour before noon or midnight, possess the gift, as well as that of seeing spirits.

The gifted ones perceive an approaching death in the following manner : They see a funeral procession at a distance and know each of the mourners following the hearse, and can tell who is in the casket. Sometimes they are engaged at work when the apparition comes. In that case they must drop their work, step in front of the door leading to the garden or the road and see a funeral procession which is invisible to others. They must allow the procession to pass and look after it until it dissolves in mist or otherwise becomes invisible. If a seeing one walking with an unseeing one on the highway meets such a spectral procession he must step aside while the other walks on seeing nothing out of the ordinary and may walk through the procession ; at most he will feel as though he were stumbling over a stone or some other obstruction.

On the island of Ruegen it is related that these "Sunday-children" show great unrest when the coming death of a person is to be shown them ; they cannot remain in the room, but must go out, no matter whether night or day, good weather or bad, and without, they are compelled to look in the direction where the dying person is. This happened to a woman of Trent (Ruegen) who worked on the farm of Granskevitz.

On one occasion she suddenly rose from the noonday meal, went into the garden and gazed towards a neighboring farm where a sister of her employer was married. The latter noticed and accosted her, but she made no reply and continued to gaze in the same direction. The owner of the farm had heard of her peculiar gift and left her alone, until she turned around, and said : "Sir, Mr. —— (mentioning the name of the neighbor)."—"Never mind," said the man, "keep still. I know." At the same hour and minute his sister died.

Another woman in the same neighborhood was wont to predict deaths a week in advance. She said that on such occasions she saw something lying at her feet like a molehill.

Some persons can tell, on the occasion of a funeral, who will die next, as they see his ghost following the hearse.

It is believed that one can always see this by looking through the left eye ring of the left hand horse drawing the hearse.

Some persons other than "Sunday-children" can foretell death. An orchestra at Trent consisting of a shoemaker and a weaver and their journeymen were playing at a wedding when suddenly the shoemaker turned pale and without saying a word rose and went out. On arriving at home he said that in the middle of the merrymaking he saw a funeral possession pass by and in the casket lay his comrade, the weaver. Two days later the weaver took sick and died shortly after.

Whoever sees an apparition of himself will die soon. Likewise whoever draws his own picture, or at least he will fall seriously ill.

It is a general belief that freemasons know exactly the day and hour when they must die, and that they generally die a sudden death.

There are numerous oracles by which to foretell the death of oneself or of friends, especially those oracles which are consulted during New Year's Eve. If a casket or a funeral train is seen at midnight of New Year's Eve over one's roof there will be a death in the house during the year ; otherwise all will remain well. In some places it is customary to look at all the neighbors' roofs as well. In the neighborhood of Stettin it is believed that if one will during New Year's night walk three times around a house and each time look through the same window and then see a funeral procession, some one will die in that house within three days. A tailor of Wartenberg would go to the cemetery every New Year's Eve and claimed to see there the people who were to die during the year. But he never told the names until after the persons were dead, when he pretended to have foreknown that they would die.

Another way, on Sylvester night, to see if one will live through the year, is to look quickly at one's shadow when the lamp is lighted. If the shadow has a head, the person will live ; if not, the person will die in the course of the year. At other places some little heaps of moist sand formed in a thimble are placed on the table, one for each person present. The one whose heap collapses before morning will die before the new year is out. At Polzin salt is used instead of sand. In the vicinity of Pasewalk three plates are filled with sand, water and fresh green follage, respectively. Some one reaches for one of the plates and thus learns if the next year will bring a death, a christening, or a wedding into the family. In Alt-Bewersdorf, district of Schlawe, a heap of sand, a key, a wreath, and a doll are placed upon the table and each covered with a plate. Some one who did not observe the arrangement picks up a plate. If he uncovers the sand it means death during the year ; the key means that he will get a house, the wreath that the person will be a party to a wedding, the doll means christenings. At the same place it is customary to bake as many cakes as there are persons in the house. Each one gets a cake and presses a dent into the dough with his finger. If the hole closes up in baking, the owner of the cake will die that year.

Another oracle at New Year's Eve is the throwing of the slipper. One sits down on the floor, the back turned to the door and with a foot throws one slipper backwards over the head. If the slipper falls on the uppers, the questioner will die during the year ; if it points to the door, he will leave the house ; otherwise, remain at home. At Stettin, if the slipper points outside, there will be a death ; if inside, a birth.

The entire time of the Twelve Nights is favorable for oracular use. If a person dies during that time, it means that twelve more will die in the village that year; likewise twelve children if a child dies. There must be no washing of clothes during that period; or at least the clothes must not be hung to dry in the open air or the attic, or a clothes line left strung. Violation of any of these rules means that a member of the family will die during the year. Nor should any leguminous fruits be eaten during the same time.

Children singing while going along the street are fore-runners of a funeral procession. Little children at play sing-ing hymns foretell a death in the village.

On the way to the church bride or groom must not turn their heads. If either does, it means that he or she is looking for another companion and the present one will die soon. A bridal couple returning from church after the ceremony must pass the threshold at the same time. else the one passing in first will pass out first, i. e., will die.

A dream that one has lost a tooth means the death of a friend or relative. A dream of a black dog means the death of an acquaintance. If one hears the bells toll in a dream, a member of the family will die. If one dreams of a dead per-son one should not tell about it for twenty-four hours, other-wise a member of the family will die.

Horses and cows are gifted with speech and prescience New Year's Eve. Other animals of prophetic vision with respect to the impending death of their master or his rela-tions are the dog, mole, hen, raven, cuckoo, owl, horse-beetle, cricket, and the beetles known as the "death-watch." The howling of a dog presages death, especially where there is a sick person; likewise a molehill thrown up in the house: the crowing of a hen, but in this last case death can be pre-vented by killing the hen. Peacock feathers must not be placed in the room. Ravens flying over a house in which a sick person lies mean death.

On hearing the cuckoo for the first time in the spring one should ask him how many years one has to live, and the cuckoo will repeat his call the right number of times.

The call of the screech-owl means the death of a closely related person; the appearance of an owl, the death of a per-son near by in point of space. The cry of owls and bats means the death of some one in the house.

The bite of the common adder makes nine holes, one healing each year. After the last one is healed the person bitten dies. A horse-beetle flying into the room indicates a death in the family. Likewise, the chirping of a cricket in the house or the gnawing of the "death-watch."

Inanimate nature also may serve to forewarn men. If one brings home white water lilies, some one in the family will die, The anemone should not be taken home, otherwise there will be a death within a year. If one has a wild pansy given him there will be a death in the family within a year. In order to learn whether a sick person will recover or die, put nettles in water. If the water turns black the patient will die, if it remains green he will recover, Bread of which a sick person has eaten is placed where neither sun nor moon shines. If the disease becomes worse the bread gets darker and six hours before the death of the patient it turns perfectly black. Rub the forehead of a sick person with bread or the soles of his feet with bacon and throw it to a dog. If he eats it, the sick person will live, if the dog leaves it, the patient will die.

Dust should not be swept from under a sickbed. A figure like a piece of shaving formed by the tallow flowing from a candle points to a death in the house. Candles lighted at a baptism must be allowed to burn out. If extinguished before, the life-light of the one baptized is extinguished. The sudden stopping of a clock in the house means the death of a near relative. Every man must before his death have eaten a bushel of sand.

Leaving the signs and premonitions of death, and turning to the dying and dead persons themselves, many curious superstitions are found.

People cannot die on beds made of chicken feathers, and such beds must be removed before the time of death comes, for death should be made easy. But there must be no complaints or expressions of compassion which make the struggle of death more difficult. The name of the dying person must not be called out aloud, otherwise the soul will linger or return temporarily and undergo more pain. Promises given to dying people must be kept to insure their resting peacefully.

32

Dying persons sometimes visit relatives or friends at their death, particularly their parents, whose attention they attract by loud noises or upsetting furniture.   They announce themselves sometimes to other persons, as joiners who make caskets.   As many grains of salt as one has wasted during one's life, so many hours (or minutes) the dead one must wait at the gate of heaven.

The death of the owner of a farm is at once communicated to the live stock, including the bees, in order to prevent their dying or leaving the place.   When the body is removed, the hired hands are sent into the barns and stepping between every two head of cattle say to them: "They are carrying your master off."   If the weather is good, the cattle are marched out to see the body carried away.   Even the fruit trees in the orchard are notified.   If the straw on which the body lay before burial is put in the barns where the cattle lie, the animals will get stiff in the joints.

All the tools and clothes used in cleaning and dressing a dead body must be destroyed or put in the grave except the razor and scissors, but these must be freshly sharpened.   If used before newly ground, the person's hair will drop out, or he will cut himself and the wounds will heal badly.   Nothing belonging to a living person must be placed in the grave, else the person will soon be drawn after the deceased.   This applies also to clothes moistened with perspiration or tears of the living.   There must be no knots in the threads used in sewing the shrouds, for the dead would not have done untying the knot when the day of judgment comes.

The mouth of the dead body must not touch any of the clothing, else it will draw all the relatives after him.   To this end a sheet of white paper is placed under the chin.   A hymn book is put in the same place to close the mouth and prevent the dead calling others after him.   If the eyes of the body cannot be closed, another member of the family, or the person on whom the eyes are directed, will soon die, for which reason the face is covered in such cases.

Wreaths of myrtle are given to bodies of girls, bunches of the same to youths.

A woman dying in childbed receives a hymn-book and two

groschen (small coins), in order to enable her to sacrifice in heaven as she used to do on earth at church.

If a member of a family dies, the father lays a hatchet on the breast of the body.

The stockings of dead persons are always provided with garters, candles are placed in their hands, and sometimes they are given a stick of buckthorn to defend themselves against the devil.

Among the Kassubes in eastern Pomerania every relative, from the oldest to the youngest, must give to the deceased something belonging to him, some hairs from his head, a piece of his coat, or shirt, or necktie or something of the sort, which is put in the casket. Topers sometimes receive a bottle of brandy. The Kassubes give their dead many other objects which is connected with their old belief in the "Greedy One." This curious and horrible superstition is as follows :

It happens sometimes that a child is born with a delicate covering on the head, similar to a cap, perhaps a part of the amnion. These so-called capuce-children become very dangerous after death unless they are deprived of their evil properties shortly after they are born. The cap must be taken off, dried and carefully preserved. Six weeks after, before the mother goes to church and sacrifice, she must burn the cap so that it can be ground to a powder, which is fed to the child with the milk. This may also be done earlier, that is, very soon after the birth of the child. Sometimes the midwife takes the cap, burns it without saying a word to anybody, grinds it to a powder and feeds it to the child. Above all, care must be taken that the child may not die before it has swallowed its own little cap, for otherwise it will become a "Greedy One," or "*Unhier, Unhuer*" (contracted from Ungeheuer-monster), i. e., after its death it draws every member of the family into the grave, one after another. The Greedy One, although apparently dead and buried, is not really under the control of death but continues to live. He raises himself in the casket and gnaws the flesh of his body where he can reach it with his teeth ; i. e., chiefly on the hands, arms, legs, and breast ; he also eats the shroud. Red stripes form along his face, on his head is formed a "nest" ;

i. e., the hairs curl up to a knot, as is often seen on hogs. At night the Greedy One comes forth from the casket and the earth, and walks abroad to visit his relatives and satisfy his voracity. He draws his relatives into the grave one after another, one each year or oftener, first the nearest and then the more remote relatives of the insatiate dead one die. After they are all dead, he goes to the church bells. The Greedy One tolls the bells and as far as their sound can be heard everybody, old and young, is carried away. Some think that the last one of the family who is fetched by the Greedy One climbs the church steeple at night and tolls the bells.

Fortunately, however, there are many means to make the Greedy One harmless. The best remedy is to exhume the apparently dead body and cut off the head if possible with a graveyard spade. The head is then placed between the legs of the body which is buried again. The theory is that the Greedy One still retains life and should be killed entirely. If any blood splashes on any one in cutting off the head, he will die soon. A cloth which the Greedy One possessed in life is often immersed in his blood and extracted in brandy. Whoever drinks of this brandy is safe from the Greedy One. Three drops of his blood in whiskey will answer the same purpose.

At Gnewin, district of Lauenburg, and vicinity, so many Greedy Ones were found among the dead in the last few years that a special custom developed there of which the object is, in case the deceased should be a Greedy One, to give him occupation in the grave and thus keep him from doing mischief on earth. Thus they give the deceased an old stocking which is partly unravelled. The dead one, who is allowed to unravel but one mesh in a year, is thus occupied for many years and the survivors are safe from being carried away should the deceased really be a Greedy One. Some put a sieve or an old net into the casket, of which the Greedy One can undo but one mesh in a year. Others, again, give the dead one a book, in which the pages are blotted over with ink or smeared with charcoal, making the print illegible. The dead one will endeavor continually to decipher the letters, but never accomplishes it.

Others place a coin, best of all a copper piece, between the *Unhier's* teeth and if it has been forgotten the body must be exhumed and the omission made good. The custom of putting a penny in the casket may be connected with this belief.

Finally, at times, when a capuce-child is carried from the village to the cemetery, they scatter cabbage seed or pease on the way. Each year the deceased comes forth and picks up one seed grain. Only after he has done with this can he attack his relatives, who will all be dead by that time. But if it is forgotten to take such precautions, it is necessary to cut off the head at midnight and place it between the legs.

The *Unhiers* do not decompose in the grave until all their relatives have died.

A variation of the Greedy Ones are the *Naegedere* or Nine-killers, i. e., children born with teeth. They do not grow old. When they are dead their heads must be cut off, otherwise they carry off nine of their nearest relatives. A short time ago a child with a tooth was born at Windish-Plassow, district of Stolp, and died soon after. The parents and relatives of the child who expected soon to be called away were in great fear. When they could not obtain permission to cut off the child's head they begged permission at least to pull out the tooth.

As a general thing, the Kassubes keep their superstitions and customs relative to the Greedy One very secret and speak of them but little. But in secret all these old customs are observed strictly and conscientiously.

Leaving the special superstitions of the Kassubes and taking up again beliefs and customs in other parts of, or general all through, Pomerania, it is found that the hands of the dead are often believed to possess healing powers. At Wartenberg toothache, rash, and eruptions of the skin are cured by passing the hand of a dead body over the afflicted parts. Likewise warts and moles. Pricking the udder of a cow with a pin taken from a body lying in the casket, stops the production of milk.

The soul remains near the body until burial. Hence one must not speak ill of the dead while the body is above the ground ; otherwise, the deceased will take revenge. In the funeral procession room must be left for the ghost of the departed, and mourners must not step too close behind the hearse.

If an article that was dropped by a thief is thrown into the grave at the next funeral, the thief will soon die a slow and painful death.

The ghosts of the dead are invoked to help discover thieves. Some wise persons can raise the ghosts and charge them with the punishment of thieves which they carry out by bringing about the death of the thieves within four weeks of the time or of each other.

Sailors must not keep a dead body on board more than twenty-four hours; otherwise, the voyage will last three times as long.

The dead can re-appear on earth, especially on Christmas and New Year's Eve. They even hold divine service on such nights. A woman of Stralsund happened to be present at the services of the dead between twelve and one o'clock. A year later she was dead. Children who die unchristened appear after death as will-o'-the-wisps. A certain woman was laid in the grave by miserly relatives in a shirt with but one sleeve. She appeared at the window the following night, rapped and complained. They put a new shirt outside and it disappeared. After that time the ghost remained still. Mothers appear after death to care for their children, wives appear at the wedding of their husbands to a second wife.

A certain girl at Neuenkirchen undertook to pluck a rose from a grave at night when a dead hand reached forth and held her. She was found dead in the morning. Persons not regularly buried, or having died a violent death, or dying while under a curse often re-appear on earth. (Several examples are given which do not offer anything peculiarly characteristic).

A suicide is followed by a strong wind. A piece of clothing of a suicide burned to ashes and put in a snuff-box can be used to recover stolen property by strewing it on the grave of a relative, whereupon the thief dies and the property is recovered. A piece of the rope by which some one hanged himself brings good luck. Suicides go about as ghosts until the time comes which was appointed by God for their death. Suicides are not buried in holy ground, and their graves should be noticed by all passers-by, who will put some object on them. Failing in this they will be pursued by the suicide at night. Perjurers find no rest in the grave, but go about in the shapes of black dogs.

Executed criminals never find rest in the grave. Objects coming from them possess great power to bring good fortune. A murderer's blood increases a merchant's business. If a consumptive drinks it and then is carried in very quick motion, for instance between a couple of horsemen, he may be cured.

Fingers of dead men touched to pastry and bread cause a rapid sale. Merchants who keep a criminal's finger in the whiskey barrel do a very large business.

WHAT SHALL WE HAVE FOR DINNER?

BY A. TREICHEL.

THIS paper contains a collection of names of curious and impossible dishes, together with questions, answers, and general terms and phrases employed to tease or rebuke children or others inquiring about what they are going to have to eat, etc. The phrases are all thoroughly idiomatic in German and German-Polish.

HOUSE SPRITES (FAMILIARS) IN POMERANIA.

THIS is a collection of stories, myths, traditions, customs, and beliefs concerning house-sprites in the Pomeranian country, where such stories are unusually common. Most of those here brought together have never been published.

Mr. Knoop has gathered no less than fifty, from all parts of the province. Many of them are very similar, in some cases almost identical. The following are selected as typical.

The house-sprites, sometimes identified with the devil, bear the names of *Alf, Drak, Pük* and *Rook* or *Rak*.

1. At Petznick, in the district of Pynitz, it is believed that misers or economical persons who thrive in farming or in business receive their wealth at night from the *Rook* who enters through the chimney. The *Rook* appears in the form of a fiery mass which enters the chimney at night, and there are many persons in the village who claim to have seen the *Rook*.

3. At Meddersin, district of Bütow, the devil appeared as the *Alf*, and in a great wind lifted a big lot of linen from the grass and tried to escape with it. The woman to whom the linen belonged saw him in time and shouted after him: "Fie, Swinedirt." By this call she caused him to drop his booty.

4. He who sees the flying dragon must call out to him: "*Schwiedrecks-brauder, schmiet nerre, wat du lade hest*" (Swinedirt brother, drop down your load), and must quickly step under a roof else the spirit will drop on him a load of dirt, the stench of which will never leave him. If he finds shelter in time, he will find large amounts of gold and money in the place where the load dropped.

13. Sometimes the spirit has the form of a boy in a red jacket or with a red cap ; again, that of a hunter. He also

appears in animal form, as a tom-cat, a three-legged hare, or a cock. On one occasion a girl found him in the highway in a bundle which she took home and put in a drawer. But she became restless during the night, rose repeatedly, became more nervous and frightened, and the next morning was dead. When the bundle was opened, it was found to contain a *Pûk* who brought great wealth to the owner.

14. At Cörlin it is told that if one puts a perfectly black tom-cat into a bag, tying it well, and at midnight carries it around the church three times, at the third time the Evil One will appear in person, taking the bag with the cat, and giving the person a coin which no matter how often it is spent always returns to the first owner, who is thus enabled to live high for the rest of his life. But woe to the unfortunate one if the devil should succeed in untying the sealed bag and seeing the cat. In that case he will hasten after the fleeing mortal, and if the latter has not reached his home, will throw him down and take from him the coin (*Glücksthaler, Heckthaler*) and his guilty soul. Many persons in the vicinity of Cörlin are said to have lost their lives in that way.

18. In Altenschlawe there lived a woman who went to church every Sunday, but when she came home the dinner always was ready and on the table. A servant who wondered at this fact one day during church time peeped through the chimney and saw the goblin cooking. When at dinner he would not eat. The woman asked him why he did not eat, and he said he could not eat what a goblin had cooked. From that time on the goblin never returned.

19 to 25 show goblins and devils employed in menial services, running a mill, cleaning out a barn, watching the farm hands at work, feeding horses, driving game to the hunter, and frightening away thieves.

26. Many traditions state that food must be set for the goblin at a certain place in the house. At Sassnitz it is held that baking must be done on New Year's Eve, otherwise the subterranean spirits will take a share of the food of the family during the whole year. In place of the subterranean spirits, generally, the Pûk is named ; and in many places it was or still is customary to bake a pancake for the Pûk, to keep

him from eating with the family during the coming year. In former times it was the custom to take the cake to church and have it blessed, after which each member of the family ate of it; some of it was given to the live stock, even to the bees, by putting it into the inlet holes of the hives. Unless these things were done, the hearth would be bewitched for the whole year or all the flour would turn to ashes. Once, a woman at Putgarten related, it was forgotten, whereupon there came a call from the kitchen: "Bake, bake, and if you have nothing but ashes, bake from ashes."

According to ancient Teutonic belief, the spirits travel abroad during the Twelve Nights, and it is a common practice to set out food for them, light candles, and have everything ready to receive them. For this reason, W. Schwartz considers these usages as the survival of an ancient sacrificial action, the neglect of which entailed the revenge of the lower world, or the Pûk.

A laborer's wife of Bergen had a Pûk dwelling in the attic. Every New-Year's Eve she baked potato pancakes for her children, but the first cake that was done she sent to the attic for the Pûk who always ate it before the next morning.

27. Housewives make three crosses over every loaf of bread before cutting it, to prevent the bread being bewitched and the Pûk from eating of it.

29. A boy of Wusseken, district of Buetow, who insulted the Alf, was covered with lice half an inch long, which could not be removed until nine of them, counted backwards, were put in a goosequill with some mercury and hung in the chimney. They disappeared over night, together with those on the boy's body.

30. Another scoffer was carried off through the air and dropped in the millpond. He walked home sadly and died three days after.

31. The devil sitting behind the stove in a minister's study charged the latter with having stolen some rolls. The minister confessed to having done so when a boy, but added he had done penitence, whereupon the devil disappeared.

32. A minister at Glovitz, who tried to exorcise a devil who possessed a peasant, was charged with his own sins by the evil one, but finally succeeded in driving him away.

39. A fishmonger saw a heavily laden drak enter a peasant's house. He jumped from his wagon, took off a wheel and put it on again wrong side out. The house at once was ablaze. The peasant woman sat surprised and cried and cried, but there came no tears. She was burned with the house, and the devil carried off her soul to hell.

34. A wealthy couple lived in a certain village. Their wealth was brought by a spirit who served them. When his term of service expired, the people of the village one day heard a terrific noise in the house where the couple were alone. After quiet was restored, they found the peasant and his wife lying dead and terribly mutilated. The devil had carried off their souls.

36 and 37 tell of freemasons who had made compacts with the devil.

42. An innkeeper in the country had given himself to the devil, for whom he would set down a mug of beer every evening, which the devil always drank. One day a showman with a bear came to the village and stopped at the inn. Accidentally he went to the room where the beer stood for the devil, and being thirsty he drank it. The devil arriving and finding the mug empty, asked the showman if he drank it, and when the latter admitted it, the devil said : "Then you belong to me." The man begged the devil to allow him to go out to attend to some business before killing him, which the devil granted. The showman went out and got the bear and carefully pushed it into the room where the devil was waiting. The bear at once caught hold of the devil and then began a terrific struggle, chairs and tables were broken, till finally the devil was worsted and flew away through the chimney. Next day the innkeeper, whose name was Kretschmann, was riding over the heath, when he saw the devil on a tree. The devil called to him : " Kretschmann, is Möhlmu (meaning the bear) there yet?" The innkeeper replied : " Yes, and it has nine cubs." The devil at once fled. He never returned to the inn, so great was his fear of the terrible Möhlmu.

46. A peasant who was annoyed by a devil whom he had found in the road in the form of a rooster with his legs tied together, wished to be rid of the tormentor that never ceased

demanding work. A wise old man advised him to tie the devil to a door-post and thrash him with a stout cane, saying : " One, two,—strike the devil dead." But he cautioned the peasant never to count more than two. The peasant did accordingly. The devil kept saying : "Why don't you count three ?" But the peasant kept on until the devil could bear it no longer and flew away. But in parting he filled the house with a horrible stench which never left it, and the peasant was obliged to build a new one, which he was able to do with the money that the devil had brought together while in his service.

50. A girl from Capelle, near Gingst, hired out to Patzig. On her way to that place, she found under a signpost a little naked boy. She picked him up, and took him in the wagon, intending to leave him with some kind people. She found a house in Woorke, left the boy, and went on to Patzig. Hardly had she arrived there when the boy appeared, and he could not be removed from her. He was very troublesome. When she worked, he pushed her aside ; when she wanted to eat, he interfered ; and when she went to sleep, he would not let her rest. Being unable to work, she was discharged from her position and went home. The boy accompanied her, and gave her no rest. She became seriously ill, and no physician knew how to help her ; but the boy continued his tricks, and rolled the patient in her bed from one side to the other. Finally, the terrified parents consulted a smith at Ummanz, who was experienced in such matters. He advised them to take a black hen, cut it open before killing and plucking it, and to stick a lot of pins in its inside ; at ten o'clock at night he came himself to complete the work. At midnight, he put the chicken into a pot on the fire. Instantly there began outside a howling and yelling ; the people in the house were frightened, and their hair stood on end. The smith kept on cooking the chicken until one o'clock, when he took the pot to the garden to bury it. A hole was made under a pear tree. Just as the pot was to be buried two horrible monsters appeared, which tried to hinder the smith and the girl's father in their work. But the smith had guarded against this by drawing a circle around the tree, so that the monsters could not reach them. While the father buried the

pot, the smith kept reading from the Bible. When the hole was filled up, the monsters vanished, the girl soon recovered, and the boy never returned. She married subsequently, and lived long and happily.

GERMAN LEGENDS AND CUSTOMS IN LONGFELLOW'S "GOLDEN LEGEND."

BY DR. ROBERT SPRENGER.

SUMMARY.—One of Longfellow's favorite books was the *Wonder-Horn*. His poems contain many translations therefrom. The legend of the *Sultan's Daughter* is a free version of the ballad *The Sultan's Daughter and the Master of the Flowers*. (Longfellow's version and the German original are here given side by side.) The author deems it possible that Longfellow himself heard the story told among the people without having reference to any published form of it. The poem was probably written during the time of Longfellow's sojourn at Heidelberg, being at a later date woven into the *Golden Legend*.

The material of the tale of "King Robert of Sicily" in the *Tales of a Wayside Inn*, was probably taken from the third volume of T. H. von der Hagen's *Gesammtabenteuer*. This material is also found in other sources quoted by the author.

The reference in Longfellow to "the rascal who drank wine out of a boot," is traced to a poem by Gustav Pfarrius, of Kreuznach, which poem the author quotes in full.

The rhymes of the monk Claus:

> At Bacharach on the Rhine,
> At Hochheim on the Main,
> And at Wuerzburg on the Stein
> Grow the three best kinds of wine,

with slight variations, form the beginning of a drinking song by Erasmus Wittmann, published at Nuremberg in 1623, (*Musikalische Kurzweil*) which is contained in the *Wonder-Horn*.

Many references in the *Golden Legend* can be traced to Scheible's *Kloster*, which is frequently mentioned by Longfellow himself.

The words of Prince Henry in regard to Elsie,—

> O pure in heart ! from thy sweet dust shall grow
> Lilies, upon whose petals will be written
> " Ave Maria " in characters of gold.

may have reference to the *Kloster* where the following words are found for the 29th day of March :

"The golden legend, a book which was read by every one instead of the New Testament, but of late has been much less used, tells of a saint who is worshipped on this day, the knight Eustachius, who although of noble birth was very ignorant. In order to lead a godly life he went into an abbey. Being unable to read, he could recite nothing but 'Ave Maria.' These words he repeated wherever he walked or stood. After his death he was buried in the graveyard of the abbey. A short time after, a lily—which is Mary's flower —grew from his grave, and on each leaf of the flower stood the words 'Ave Maria,' in golden letters. The monks, being much surprised by the oracle, opened the grave, and found the root of the flowers in the mouth of the deceased. They then became aware that his devotion to the Blessed Virgin, by the constant recitation of the ' Ave Maria,' secured this distinction for him."

Another reference to a German legend is what Prince Henry says of Elsie :

> Thy words fall from thy lips
> Like roses from the lips of Angelo,
> and angels
> Might stoop to pick them up !

The author repeats a legend in which a certain monk who had been in the habit of decorating the pictures of the Virgin with flowers, was protected by her from robbers. She accompanied him through a dark forest and took fifty red roses from his mouth. Afterwards the monk converted the robbers, who went to the monastery with him and spent the remainder of their days in religious devotion. Kirchhof tells of a monk from whose mouth roses dropped during prayer.

The stories of the *Devil's Bridge* were probably picked up by Longfellow himself among the people. A number of them are found in various parts of Germany, several of which the author repeats. In most cases the devil is outwitted, having stipulated that he shall have the soul of the first living being that passes over the bridge he builds, whereupon some animal is driven across the bridge as soon as it is finished.   A passage is quoted from Edmund Spencer's *Sketches of Germany and the Germans in 1834, 1835, and 1836*, where a cock on an old crucifix at Frankfort is described, and the explanation given that the monument was erected in memory of the erection of a bridge by the devil, who was outwitted in the manner indicated by a cock being driven over the bridge in place of a human being.

Some instances are cited where Longfellow mentions superstitions which are peculiar to Germany, as that " death never takes one alone, but two," etc.

In the description of the festivities at Easter, *Golden Legend,* III. 2, where it is said :

> The churches are all decked with flowers,
> The salutations among men
> Are but the angels' words divine :
> "Christ is arisen," and the bells
> Catch the glad murmur as it swells
> And chant together in their towers.

it appears that the poet referred Russian customs to German medieval times.   The custom continues in Russia even at this day, that when friends meet in the street on Easter-day, after divine service, they kiss one another with the greeting : "Christ is risen."

Lightning Source UK Ltd.
Milton Keynes UK
UKHW011958180119
335819UK00009B/597/P